Garde Manger

Garde Manger

THE ART AND CRAFT OF THE COLD KITCHEN, second edition

The Culinary Institute of America

JOHN WILEY & SONS, INC.

This book is printed on acid-free paper.

Published by John Wiley & Sons, Inc., Hoboken, New Jersey
Published simultaneously in Canada

JOHN WILEY & SONS, INC.
Robert Garber, *Vice President and Group Executive Publisher*
Natalie Chapman, *Vice President and Publisher*
Pamela Chirls, *Senior Editor*
Diana Cisek, *Production Director*
Monique Calello, *Senior Production Editor*
Kevin Watt, *Manufacturing Manager*
Tom Hyland, *Manufacturing Manager*

COVER AND INTERIOR DESIGN BY Vertigo Design, NYC

COVER PHOTOGRAPHY BY Ben Fink

For general information on our other products and services or for technical support, please contact our Customer Care Department within the United States at (800) 762-2974, outside the United States at (317) 572-3993 or fax (317) 572-4002.

Wiley also publishes its books in a variety of electronic formats. Some content that appears in print may not be available in electronic books. For more information about Wiley products, visit our web site at www.wiley.com.

Library of Congress Cataloging-in-Publication Data

Garde manger : the art and craft of the cold kitchen / by the Culinary Institute of America.—2nd ed.
    p. cm.
  Includes bibliographical references and index.
  ISBN 0-471-46849-5 (cloth)—ISBN 0-7645-7663-1 (cloth: custom)

    1. Cookery (Cold dishes) 2. Quantity cookery. I. Culinary Institute of America.
  TX830.G37 2004
  641.7'9—dc22
                              2004007051

Printed in the United States of America

10 9 8 7 6 5 4 3 2 1

EDITORIAL

Tim Ryan, *President*

Victor Gielisse, *Vice President and Dean of Culinary and Baking and Pastry Arts Studies*

Susan Cussen, *Marketing Director*

Lisa Lahey, *Editorial Project Manager*

Mary Donovan, *Editorial Project Manager*

Margaret Otterstrom, *Editorial Assistant*

Rachel Toomey, *Editorial Assistant*

PHOTOGRAPHY

Ben Fink, *Photographer*

Lorna Smith, *Photographer for the Food and Beverage Institute*

CONTENT LEADER

Victor Gielisse

FACULTY TEAM

Chef Olivier Andreini

Chef Pierre Leblanc

Chef Daniel Turgeon

Chef Jim Heywood

Chef Russell Scott

Chef Mark Ainsworth

Chef Ryan Baxter

Chef Ronald DeSantis

Chef John DeShetler

Chef Eve Felder

Chef Mike Garnero

Chef Thomas Gumpel

Chef Tom Kief

Chef Tom Griffiths

Chef John Kowalski

Chef Bruce Mattel

Chef Corky Clark

Chef Anthony Liqouri

Chef Hubert Martini

Chef Mike Pardus

Chef Thomas Peer

Chef Henry Rapp

Chef John Reilly

Chef Kathy Polenz

Chef Greg Zifchak

Chef Jonathan Zearfoss

Finally, we wish to especially thank a few members of the team particularly— Chef Olivier Andreini, Chef Tom Griffiths, Chef Pierre Leblanc, Chef John Kowalski, Chef Daniel Turgeon, Chef Bruce Mattel, Chef Jim Heywood, Chef Corky Clark, Chef Russel Scott, Chef Hubert Martini—for their dedication to this edition.

contents

Preface   viii

one: The Professional Garde Manger   1

two: Cold Sauces and Cold Soups   15

three: Salads   75

four: Sandwiches   137

five: Cured and Smoked Foods   179

six: Sausage   227

seven: Terrines, Pâtés, Galantines, and Roulades   271

eight: Cheese   333

nine: Appetizers and Hors d'Oeuvre   361

ten: Condiments, Crackers, and Pickles   467

eleven: The Modern Buffet   495

twelve: Basic Recipes   521

Glossary   551

Bibliography and Recommended Reading   561

Recipe Index   564

Subject Index   579

Preface

In writing *Garde Manger: The Art and Craft of the Cold Kitchen*, we have drawn widely from within the contemporary practice of garde manger, putting those skills and techniques into words, pictures, and recipes and gathering them into a single volume. This book is geared to meet the needs of students and seasoned practitioners alike, giving not only the basics of technique but also the sound principles that result in the highest quality foods.

The book begins with a basic overview of the history of the garde manger and the charcutière. An understanding of how garde manger has moved from its origins to become the vibrant and exciting work it is today is especially relevant when you intend to make this work your career. Today's garde manger has a wide range of career options, some harking directly back to the traditional methods for preparing sausages, pâtés, and cheeses. Others look to more contemporary ways and may find their ultimate expression in banquets, catering, or event management. Throughout this book, the work of the garde manger is explored with an eye toward basic methods, safe food handling techniques, and cutting-edge approaches to combining flavors, colors, and textures in the foods prepared on the cold side of kitchens in restaurants, hotels, banquet halls, and specialty food producers.

Beginning with cold sauces and soups, both traditional and newer adaptations of cold emulsion sauces (vinaigrettes and mayonnaise) are explained and illustrated. The recipes were selected not only to give a practical means of putting those techniques to use but also to provide recipes for a cross section of cold sauces and soups found on menus worldwide.

Cold sauces and soups are followed by salads. The salad chapter discusses the proper selection of ingredients and their care, as well as fundamental rules for preparing and presenting salads. Often, the care and handling of salad greens, herbs, and other salad components is the first assignment given to novice kitchen workers, regardless of whether they have their eyes set on the goal of becoming a line cook on the hot side or pursuing a career dedicated to all that the cold side encompasses.

Sandwiches were not always the popular menu item they are today. However, an increasing interest in healthful, satisfying, and unusual fare has prompted the garde manger to look beyond deli and diner specialties to embrace a variety of breads, fillings, and garnishes that make sandwich making more intriguing and challenging. Methods and practical advice for preparing sandwiches for an à la carte menu as well as for teas and receptions are provided. Recipes from classics to less widely known sandwiches drawn from the global scene are also included.

Sausages, pâtés, terrines, and cured and smoked foods were once the province of professionals known as *charcutières*. The foods produced by the charcutières of days gone by are still familiar to us—from classic andouille sausage and sugar-cured bacon to gravlax and duck confit. These foods are appreciated today for their satisfying flavors and textures. Chefs are finding that a thorough understanding of the hows and whys of curing and preserving meats, fish, and poultry is indispensable in the quest for healthier, lighter, and more contemporary approaches to these ancient practices. It is in these foods and their safe, wholesome preparation that the cold kitchen most clearly retains its original intent and purpose.

Cheeses have always had a place in the cold kitchen. Like other cured and preserved foods, cheeses are a time-honored, practical solution to the problem of keeping a constant supply of wholesome, nutritious foods on hand throughout the year. They are also the showcase for the talents and originality of their producers. Local and artisan cheeses are once more in the limelight, and the garde manger is faced with the challenge of learning to select, maintain, and present these complex and fascinating foods to an increasingly sophisticated audience. This chapter reviews the basics of cheese making, defines and describes various cheese families, and provides guidelines for putting together a cheese selection. In addition, the basics of preparing fresh cheeses as well as special preparations featuring those cheeses are included.

Hors d'oeuvre and appetizers represent an opportunity for the garde manger to pull together all the various skills and preparations of the entire discipline in a high-impact way. Just as hors d'oeuvre set the tone for a reception or banquet, so can a well-executed appetizer selection on a menu set the tone for the entire dining experience. There are a few classic standards to guide you in preparing and presenting appetizers and hors d'oeuvre. Many of the elements of these composed dishes are typically drawn from the chapters that precede this one. A perfect cold sauce provides the counterpoint to a silken pâté. A flourish of baby greens offers texture and color contrast to a luxurious slice of smoked salmon, and so forth.

Relishes, compotes, pickles, chutneys, mustards, ketchups, and crackers provide the little something that takes a presentation from run-of-the-mill to memorable. These finishing touches, offered as condiments and garnishes to bring out all the flavors and textures of a dish, are gathered together in a chapter that explores another time-honored realm of the cold kitchen: garnishing.

A new addition to the second edition of this book is a chapter devoted to the modern buffet. You will find information about developing the concept or theme for a buffet, establishing prices and controlling costs, using basic design principles for platter layout, and contemporary solutions to setting up a buffet to maximize flow, interactivity, international flavors and themes, and management concerns for buffets.

The book concludes with a chapter containing a variety of basic preparations, from stocks and aspics to marinades and spice rubs. The glossary provides thumbnail descriptions of a wide range of cooking terms and tools.

The instructions, photographs, and recipes in this book are meant to help you, whatever your current challenge may be. Perhaps you will choose to use them as a resource and a teaching tool. You may want to use them as a foundation that you can modify to your particular needs by adjusting seasonings and garnishes to create signature dishes, or scaling recipes up or down to match your production standards. One thing is certain: the continued appreciation on the part of diners and chefs everywhere for the foods that are prepared by today's garde manger makes this one of the most fascinating and exciting areas of the professional culinary arts.

THE PROFESSIONAL GARDE MANGER

The term *garde manger* was used originally to identify a storage area. Preserved foods such as hams, sausages, and cheeses were held in this area. Cold foods were prepared and arranged for banquets there as well. Over time, the term has evolved to mean more than just a storage area or larder. It also may indicate the station in a professional kitchen responsible for preparing cold foods, the cooks and chefs who prepare these cold foods, and/or an area of specialization in professional culinary arts. Members of today's garde manger share in a long culinary and social tradition, one that stretches back to well before the dawn of recorded history.

one

The European Garde Manger Tradition

As our ancestors became herdsmen and farmers, they developed the practical skills necessary to ensure a relatively steady food supply. This meant learning not only to domesticate animals and raise crops but also to preserve those foods. Fish were brined in seawater and left to dry on the shore, where they either fermented or dried. Meats were hung off the ground and near the fire. This kept them out of the reach of scavenging animals and insects. The smoky bath surrounding them darkened, flavored, dried, and preserved the meats and kept them from spoiling.

Records of various curing methods have been tracked back as far as 3000 B.C.E., when it is believed the Sumerians salted meats as a way to preserve this valuable but perishable food. Historical evidence shows that the Chinese and the Greeks had been producing and consuming salted fish for many years before passing their knowledge on to the Romans. In 63 B.C.E., the Greek writer Strabo detailed the importance of fish-salting centers in Spain and the existence of salt producers in the Crimea. Salt cod, made in the same basic way Strabo described, is still an important food in cuisines around the world.

Food-preservation skills and the necessary ingredients, including salt, sugar, and spices, were greatly valued. Cities such as modern-day Rome and Salzburg were founded near a ready source of salt. As the Romans extended their empire, they conquered lands rich in a variety of resources, including foodstuffs. They brought with them to new territory their own recipes and formulas for a variety of preserved meats, fish, cheeses, wines, and cordials. But the culinary exchange was never in one direction. The conquering forces also learned to appreciate the local specialties. The Gauls, in what became France, were credited as highly successful hog domesticators and became renowned for their preserved hams and bacon. These products were regularly sent from Gaul to Rome and served at the Romans' legendary banquets. After the fall of the Roman Empire, the great houses of the Church and the nobility throughout Europe kept alive both local food traditions and those learned from the invaders.

Into the twelfth century, approximately 80 to 90 percent of the world's population still fell into a category known as *rural peasants*. These peasants worked the nobles' lands to raise crops and farm animals. One of the most important activities of the year occurred at the end of the growing season. Vegetables, fruits, and grains were harvested and preserved by drying or placing into cold storage, along with pickles, jellies, and cheeses. Cows, sheep, and other animals were butchered and the meat preserved by a variety of means: pickling, salting, brining, curing, drying, packing in fat, or smoking. Once the foods had been prepared, they could be held in storage.

The right to collect and keep these foods, as well as to trade and tax them, was a visible symbol of power, wealth, and rank. During the Middle Ages, this privilege belonged to the kings, lords, dukes, and other nobility, as well as the monasteries and convents of the Catholic church. The castles and manor houses of the nobility each had an area devoted to food storage. This was typically located in an area below ground level to keep the foods cool. Garde manger (literally, "keeping to eat") was the term used to identify this storage area. It is still used to indicate a larder or pantry—a place for cold food storage. The member of the household staff known as the *officier de bouche,* or steward, was responsible for managing this storeroom, dispensing foods as necessary.

garde manger kitchens **A.** Historical garde manger kitchen. **B.** Contemporary garde manger kitchen.

The Growth of the Guilds

Some of these special stored items, such as hams and cheeses, became part of the commerce and trade between towns and states. They were included as dowries and tributes, along with livestock, buildings, servants, and jewels, and served as a kind of currency to acquire other goods. Eventually, rules were established governing how merchants prepared and sold these goods and services, the goal being to prevent monopolies and pricing abuses. The work itself was clearly defined and assigned to various groups known as *guilds*. The guilds developed training systems for their members, taking them from an apprenticeship to the journeyman stage and, finally, conferring the status of master. Each individual guild was granted a charter that gave its members specific rights.

By the end of the sixteenth century, approximately two dozen guilds were dedicated specifically to food. These fell into two groups—those that provided raw materials and those that provided prepared foods. The guild that prepared and sold cooked items made from the pig was referred to as *charcuterie*, derived from French root words meaning "cooked flesh." This guild kept the practical work of preserving meats alive and thriving, making bacons, hams, sausages, and pâtés.

Numerous strategies were devised to get around restrictions imposed on any given guild, and the charcutières (members of the charcuterie guild) were no exception. One of their tactics led to the development of terrines: Charcutières were not permitted to sell foods baked in pastries. Making and selling forcemeat loaves baked in pastry—pâté en croûte—would not have been allowed, according to a strict reading of the charcutière's charter. Rather than stop making pâté en croûte, the charcutières baked the forcemeat in an earthenware mold instead of pastry—and so pâtés en terrine were created.

Restaurants and the Role of the Garde Manger

The more essential the food, the more closely it was regulated. The more lucrative a guild's activities, the more likely it was that another guild might be tempted to infringe on it. Each guild fought to protect its individual rights. Several cases were brought before judges to determine if one guild's activities had crossed the line into the work of another's.

One such case had a profound impact on the work of today's garde manger. In 1765, Monsieur Boulanger, a tavernkeeper, was brought to court for selling a hot dish, which he referred to as a *restorante* ("restorative"). Traditionally, the right to sell hot prepared foods such as this restorative had been the exclusive privilege of another guild. The judge ruled that M. Boulanger had not broken any law, and so the first restaurant was born. Others quickly followed this new type of venture.

When the French Revolution began in 1789, the upheavals in noble house-holds were enormous. Noblemen left France to escape the guillotine, leaving their household staffs to care for themselves. The garde manger (or steward), as well as chefs and cooks, were household employees and as such did not have a formal guild of their own. These workers found their way into restaurants in increasing num-bers throughout Europe and the British Isles.

At first, there was no widely recognized structure for kitchen workers. There were no established duties or areas of specialization. It took several years before a serious attempt was made to organize the kitchen workers. Eventually, the brigade system, as recorded by Auguste Escoffier, detailed a logical chain of command that brought order to the unruly working arrangements of his day. We still use the brigade system and refer to the various stations in the kitchen with the names assigned by Escoffier: saucier, rôtisseur, pâtissier, and garde manger.

When the guild system was abolished in 1791, some members of the charcu-tières' guild also joined the ranks of restaurant and hotel kitchen garde manger staffs. Others continued to operate their businesses as before. The work of the charcutière and that of the garde manger have always been closely linked, since both are founded on cold preserved foods. When the term *garde manger* is used today, it is often understood to include the work of the charcutière as well.

Today's Garde Manger

The garde manger, recast in a restaurant setting, has retained its tradition of preparing a variety of preserved and cold foods. It has also expanded its scope to include hors d'ouevre, appetizers, salads, sandwiches, and the accompanying cold sauces and condiments. Garde manger is involved in à la carte service as well as receptions, buffets, and banquets.

The techniques required to prepare pâtés, terrines, sausages, and fresh cheeses are the particular domain of the garde manger. To support the techniques and production in the cold kitchen, a wide variety of hot food-preparation techniques that are essential to the foundation of any culinary discipline must be mastered: roasting, poaching, simmering, and sautéing meats, fish, poultry, vegetables, grains, and legumes.

It is precisely because the skills and responsibilities are so broad that many of today's most highly regarded chefs began their careers in the garde manger department as an apprentice or commis. In addition, recent years have seen a rebirth of the more traditional practices of charcuterie and cheese making by purveyors with retail shops and wholesale businesses. Handcrafted foods such as country-style hams, sausages, pâtés, and fresh and aged cheeses are increasingly available to both the restaurant chef and the home cook.

Establishments

Hotels, full-service restaurants, and private clubs may have one or more people working exclusively in the area of garde manger, though its specific name varies from place to place. Some operations refer to it as the pantry, others may call it the salad station, still others the cold side, and so on. The specific foods for which this station is responsible can include cold sauces and soups, salads, hors d'oeuvre, and canapés.

This station may, in some kitchens, supply other stations with particular items. The garde manger, in some operations, also shapes and portions meats, poultry, and fish, adding marinades or stuffings as appropriate.

During service, the garde manger typically plates salads and cold appetizers and may also be responsible for plating desserts. The breakfast, lunch, and brunch menus often rely heavily on the garde manger as well.

Cooks and chefs working in banquet and catering operations practice all the same basic cooking skills as the garde manger in an à la carte restaurant. The approach to work is slightly different. This work is so stimulating and challenging that many professionals choose it as their lifelong career path. Here, where the goal is to produce and serve flavorful, attractive food to large numbers of individuals simultaneously, you learn to use the special equipment and cooking techniques of volume production. The chef not only develops a menu but also does all the planning necessary to come up with scaled recipes, accurate and timely orders for food and other items, and food costs. Presentation is often a significant component of banquets and receptions. Décor, appropriate and effective garnishes for plates, platters, and other food displays, and concerns for food quality and customer safety are considered. The nature of large events often involves a certain level of risk and always calls for the ability to think under pressure and come up with a creative solution to a crisis. To read more about the development and management of a buffet, read Chapter 11.

Delicatessens, charcuteries, and shops selling prepared foods of all types offer yet more options for the professional garde manger. Some operations feature handcrafted foods such as cheeses and sausages. Their goods may be sold through a retail shop or exclusively to those in the restaurant trade. Large companies, including hotel and restaurant chains and food manufacturers, look to those with strong skills in garde manger to undertake projects such as the development of a new line of sauces or condiments, spice rubs, or salad blends.

Types of work

Both employers and schools recognize that formal education on its own is not enough to assure excellence. Garde manger is a practical art. To succeed, you must work hard to develop precise skills. Whether you work for yourself or for someone else, you must make choices about your work carefully. It is tempting to make a decision based on salary, location, or similar immediately tangible reward.

However, if you consider each job as an investment in your future, it is far easier to evaluate its long-lasting rewards.

Making wise career choices is complicated, so take the time to evaluate any career move. Develop your own plan for the future as specifically as you can so you can determine the type of establishment and the type of work that will set you up to secure the next level in your career.

Look for work environments where every person has a stake in getting things done correctly. When every person has the opportunity to help make decisions and has the tools he or she needs to perform well, everyone succeeds. If you want to do a job well, you need to know the quality standards. Objective evaluations, constructive criticism, and additional training are part of every good working situation.

Entry level

Work at the entry level includes cleaning and cutting produce, making vinaigrettes and composed platters, and following simple standard recipes under supervision. It is important to ask questions and follow advice, watch carefully what goes on around you, and supplement what you see and hear by reading. Learn the skills necessary for handling special equipment safely and efficiently. Slicers, mixers, grinders, blenders, food processors, thermometers, smokers, sausage stuffers, and salometers are just a few of the specialized pieces of equipment used in the garde manger and smokehouse.

Advanced level

As your skills improve, you move from entry-level positions into positions of more responsibility. You take on more advanced and challenging work, and you may advance to lead or executive chef. At this level, you have more responsibility for conceiving new menu items, including recipe development, recording standard recipes, and costing and developing and maintaining a budget. You train kitchen and dining room staff in the proper presentation of the new and standard menu items.

Banquet and buffet chefs develop menus—both standard and custom—and go through the process of scaling and costing each menu item. Staffing and scheduling responsibilities for the banquet chef include maintaining and training a relatively large pool of talent, often in conjunction with the dining room manager. Some special aspects of this work include coordinating with other service providers such as florists, musicians, and photographers.

Entrepreneurs develop handcrafted specialty items that are produced on both small and large scale. Their work focuses more on the development of a product or product line that is for sale in the retail or wholesale market. They must be concerned with a variety of regulations, certifications, and inspections in order to be sure that foods prepared for sale meet all the necessary legal requirements. Food quality and cost remain as important as ever, and additional business concerns accrue.

The Practice of a Profession

Any profession has a great many sides; the culinary vocation is no different. A culinary professional is an artist, a businessperson, a scientist, and a cultural explorer, among other occupations. Acquiring the skills and knowledge necessary to succeed in this profession is a lifelong journey.

Education and training

Employers today look for both experience and education when they hire at virtually all levels higher than entry level. At the most prestigious shops, even entry-level positions may require a degree or some sort of formal training. Employees look for jobs that offer the opportunity to use the skills and education they already possess and, at the same time, to learn new skills.

Formal education

The increasing emphasis on a formal education goes hand in hand with the emergence of a number of programs dedicated exclusively to the culinary arts. Employers rely on the general and specific skills of the craft taught by schools to establish a common ground of ability. This saves them hours of on-the-job training. The demand for graduates continues to grow each year, and so has the number of programs specializing in the culinary arts. The best education couples as much hands-on practice as course work devoted to product and equipment knowledge. In addition, a well-rounded program provides study in important aspects of culinary arts as a business: customer service, math, food and menu costing, and team skills.

Programs that are recognized in the industry attract high-quality instructors and offer opportunities for students to network, join clubs and organizations, compete, and do advanced studies in an area of specialization. Their graduates receive plenty of hands-on experience and develop confidence and control in all areas of culinary arts. Industry leaders look to graduates of those programs to staff their companies because they bring with them a solid foundation.

Even garde manger chefs who already have achieved significant success in their careers take advantage of the many opportunities offered through continuing education. Classes custom-fit to a specific topic give professionals exposure to new techniques and methods and new equipment and ingredients.

Food knowledge

The ingredients the garde manger uses every day run the gamut from the mundane and utilitarian, such as calves' heads and pigs' feet, to the priceless and exotic—saffron, foie gras, caviar, and truffles.

When you know how an ingredient looks, tastes, and reacts with other ingredients, you can use that knowledge to be more creative, more adaptable, and more efficient. At first, you may rely solely on recipes or formulas. As long as everything required by the recipe is on hand, things should work out. Take an extra minute or two to examine each ingredient closely and make note of what it looks likes, how it smells and feels, its shape, and its color.

Classes, workshops, and demonstrations that offer an opportunity to do comparison tastings are excellent learning opportunities. This experience is invaluable, whether your responsibility is to use ingredients appropriately or to buy them in a way that maintains quality and profit.

Beyond knowing the color, taste, and cost of an ingredient, today's garde manger typically faces an increasing number of special concerns about the manner in which foods are grown, harvested, and processed. A safe and wholesome food supply is a growing concern of both the public and the profession. Topics such as sustainable agriculture, bio-engineering, genetically modified organisms (GMOs), organics, and the support of local and regional growers all factor into the decisions you and your business must make.

Equipment knowledge

It is true that the foods made by the garde manger and charcutiére are not beyond the technical skill of any good cook, and many individuals enjoy making their own sausages, bacon, and smoked trout. You need not only the correct equipment and ingredients but also the appropriate storage space, one you can keep at the correct temperature and humidity, to produce some items. In addition to being knowledgeable about knives, pots, and pans, the garde manger must be well versed in the use of equipment such as meat slicers and grinders, food processors, smokehouses, brining tubs and salometers, and, for some practitioners, ice-carving tools.

Learn to use important business tools: Computers, the Internet, budgets, accounting systems, and inventory control systems all play a role. Many organizations, from the largest chains to the smallest one-person catering company, rely on software systems that allow them to administer a number of areas efficiently: inventory, purchases, losses, sales, profits, food costs, customer complaints, reservations, payroll, schedules, and budgets. If you are not using a system capable of tracking all this information and more, you cannot be as effective as you need to be.

Communication skills

A well-written résumé can sell you to a potential employer. Your own mission statement, if properly worded, keeps you on track and helps you make the best possible career moves. A precise and specific plan for an event can keep it on track and on budget. A thorough and fair interview can unearth the perfect employee or business partner. Each of these activities demands good communication skills. Today's garde manger must communicate using a wider variety of media than ever before, from written memos and letters to e-mails and reports to videoconferencing and interactive learning. A good education program addresses the general and specific communications needs of students and offers courses, workshops, and tutoring or labs in a wide range of communication skills.

Continuing education

Your education and your experience combine to be the most important source for your professional development. Every career choice or move you make is part of your lifelong education. If you have a long-term plan, you can choose jobs that give you the opportunity to learn new skills and take on greater responsibility as you advance toward your goals.

Keeping current with basic skills and new trends is a lifelong task. Once initial training is completed, continuing education is equally important, as the industry is constantly evolving.

Evaluate your career, both as it is right now and as you would like it to be in the future, and then take the appropriate steps to keep on top of the latest information in the areas about which you are most concerned. Attend classes and workshops, hone your skills in specialized areas, keep up with new ingredients and equipment, learn new management strategies, and strengthen your skills in team building, writing and communication, and marketing and promotion.

Some of the courses or seminars you attend can earn you credits (continuing education units, or CEUs). These may be necessary to achieve certain certifications or advancements. Continuing education and professional development programs are available through many colleges and universities, both in traditional and long-distance learning environments.

Not all continuing education occurs in a classroom or over an Internet hookup. Magazines, television programming, newsletters, Web sites, government publications, and books are all excellent sources. Directed travel programs can open up a completely new way of seeing the profession by exposing you to a new cuisine, a new part of the world, a new ingredient, or a new contact.

Networking

The old saying that "it's who you know" has a great deal of truth. The group of professionals you know is known as a *network*. A solid network is an indispensable tool for the professional and should include members of your profession from as many areas as possible. Knowing someone in a niche not obviously related to your own can turn up unexpected opportunities.

Creating a professional network is a task that should be taken seriously. Working with other professionals to share information and knowledge is an important avenue of growth, both professional and personal. Networks can be formal or informal. The way to begin is simply to introduce yourself to others in your field. Have business cards with you when you go to restaurants or trade shows. Write letters to individuals whose work you have seen and admired.

Join professional organizations to expand your network. Well-run groups typically have a variety of meetings and forums to allow members to come in contact with each other. Take advantage of local and national meetings and conventions to learn more about your profession.

When you make a good contact, follow up with a phone call or a note. The communication you develop with your peers will keep your own work fresh and contemporary, and an established network makes it much easier for you to find a new job or an employee.

Competition

Contests and competitions offer you a chance to stretch yourself. Professional magazines, journals, newsletters, and Web sites have information about contests on the local, national, and international level. Whenever you submit your work to the scrutiny of a panel of judges, you learn. Critical review provides you a means to keep improving in a way that daily production work never can. Practice, research, and the stress of competition exercises your professional muscles, the same way competing in sporting events strengthens an athlete. Even if you are not entered in the competition, attend the judging if possible so you can benefit from the experience.

The Garde Manger as
Businessperson

Managing physical assets

Physical assets are the equipment and supplies needed to do business. In the case of a restaurant, these might include food and beverage inventory, tables, chairs, linens, china, flatware, glassware, computers and point-of-sale systems, cash registers, kitchen equipment, cleaning supplies, and ware-washing machines. When we talk about managing physical assets, we are considering how anything you must purchase affects your ability to do business well.

The first step in bringing the expenses associated with your physical assets under control is to know what your expenses actually are. Then you can begin the process of making the adjustments and instituting the control systems that will keep your organization operating at maximum efficiency.

One of the biggest expenses for any restaurant is food and beverage costs. You or your purchasing agent will have to work hard to develop and sustain a good purchasing system. Because each operation has different needs, there are no hard-and-fast rules, just principles that you will apply to your own situation.

Managing time

It may seem that no matter how hard you work or how much planning you do, the days aren't long enough. Learning new skills, so you can make the best possible use of the time you have, certainly ought to be an ongoing part of your career development. If you look over your operation, you will see where time is wasted. In most operations, the top five time-wasters are (1) no clear priorities for tasks, (2) poor staff training, (3) poor communication, (4) poor organization, and (5) missing or inadequate tools for accomplishing tasks. To combat these time-wasters, use the following strategies.

INVEST TIME IN REVIEWING DAILY OPERATIONS Consider the way you, your coworkers, and your staff spend the day. Does everyone have a basic understanding of which tasks are most important? Does everyone know when to begin a particular task in order to bring it to completion on time? It can be an eye-opening experience to take a hard look at where the workday goes. Once you see that you and your staff need to walk too far to gather basic items or that the person who washes the dishes is sitting idle for the first two hours of the shift, you can take steps to rectify the problem. You can try to reorganize storage space. You may decide to train the dishwasher to do some prep work, or you can rewrite the schedule so the shift begins two hours later. Until you are objective about what needs to be done, and in what order, you can't begin the process of saving time.

INVEST TIME IN TRAINING OTHERS If you expect someone to do a job properly, take enough time to explain the task carefully. Walk yourself and your staff through the jobs that must be done, and be sure everyone understands how to do the work, where to find necessary items, how far each person's responsibility extends, and what to do in case a question or emergency comes up. Give your staff the yardsticks they need to evaluate the job and determine if they have done what was requested, in the appropriate fashion, and on time. If you don't invest this time up front, you may find yourself squandering precious time following your workers around, picking up the slack, and handling work that shouldn't be taking up your day.

LEARN TO COMMUNICATE CLEARLY Whether you are training a new employee, introducing a new menu item, or ordering a piece of equipment, clear communication is important. Be specific, use the most concise language you can, and be as brief as possible without leaving out necessary information. If a task is handled by a number of people, be sure to write it out, from the first step to the last. Encourage people to ask questions if they don't understand you. If you need help learning communication skills, consider taking a workshop or seminar to strengthen your weak areas.

TAKE STEPS TO CREATE AN ORDERLY WORK ENVIRONMENT If you have to dig through five shelves to find the lid to the storage container you just put the stock in, you aren't using your time wisely. Planning work areas carefully, thinking about all the tools, ingredients, and equipment you need for preparation and throughout service, and grouping like activities are all techniques that can help you organize your work better. Poor placement of large and small tools is a great time-waster. Use adequate, easy-to-access storage space for common items such as whips, spoons, ladles, and tongs. Electrical outlets for small equipment ought to be within reach of everyone. While you may be forced to work within the limits of your existing floor plan, be on the lookout for products and storage strategies that can turn a bad arrangement into one that works smoothly.

PURCHASE, REPLACE, AND MAINTAIN ALL NECESSARY TOOLS A well-equipped kitchen has enough of all the tools necessary to prepare every item on the menu. If you can't purchase new equipment, then think about restructuring the menu to even out the workload. If you can't remove a menu item, then invest in the tools you need to prevent a slowdown during service.

Managing information

The garde manger is part of the much larger culinary world. Read about all areas that might affect your career and your industry: business and economics, arts and entertainment, society and politics. Popular culture has a curious way of influencing your work. Your customers and clients do not live in a vacuum, and neither should you.

There are numerous print and online sources devoted to the specifics of new or unusual ingredients, unfamiliar dishes or equipment, and more. Information gathering can become a full-time task on its own. To make use of available information, you must be able to analyze and evaluate carefully to sift out the important material from useless data and use all sorts of media and all sorts of technology effectively.

Learn more about the profession's history, not just because it is interesting, but because it gives relevance and ballast to the decisions you make.

Managing people

Restaurant operations rely directly on the work and dedication of a number of people, from executives and administrators to line cooks, wait staff, and maintenance and cleaning staff. No matter how large or small your staff is, your ability to engage all your workers in a team effort is one of the major factors in determining whether you will succeed or not.

Most people prefer to work in an environment where everyone can make a distinct and measurable contribution. The first task in creating such an environment is a properly written job description. Training is another key component. To do a job well, the employee needs to know the quality standards and have those standards consistently reinforced with clear, objective evaluations, feedback, constructive criticism, and, when necessary, additional training or disciplinary measures.

Everyone has the right to work in an environment that is free of physical hazards. This means that, as an employer, you must provide a workspace that is well lit, properly ventilated, and free of obvious dangers, such as improperly maintained equipment. Employees must have access to potable water and bathroom facilities. Beyond this bare minimum, you may offer a locker room, a laundry facility that provides clean uniforms and aprons, or other such amenities.

Workers' compensation, unemployment insurance, and disability insurance are also your responsibility. You are required to make all legal deductions from an employee's paycheck and to report all earnings properly to state and federal agencies. Liability insurance (to cover any harm to your facility, employees, or guests) must be kept up to date and at an adequate level.

Employers may choose to offer additional forms of assistance as part of an employee benefits package. Life insurance, medical and dental insurance, assistance with dependent care, adult literacy training, and enrollment in and support for those enrolled in substance abuse programs are examples of the support an employer can provide employees.

Summary

Every member of a profession is responsible for the profession's image. Those who have made the greatest impact in their fields know that the cardinal virtues of the culinary profession are an open and inquiring mind, an appreciation of and dedication to quality wherever it is found, and a sense of responsibility. Success also depends on several character traits, some of which are inherent, and some of which are diligently cultivated throughout a career. These include:

A COMMITMENT TO SERVICE The food-service industry is predicated on service; therefore, a culinary professional should never lose sight of what that word implies. Good service includes (but is not limited to) providing quality food that is properly and safely cooked, appropriately seasoned, and attractively presented in a pleasant environment—in short, making the customer happy. The degree to which an operation can offer satisfaction in these areas is the degree to which it will succeed in providing good (and, ideally, excellent) service. The customer must always come first.

A SENSE OF RESPONSIBILITY A culinary professional's responsibility is fourfold: to him- or herself, to coworkers, to the restaurant, and to the guest. This should include respecting not just each customer and his or her needs but also staff, food, equipment, and the facility itself. Waste, recklessness, disregard for others, and misuse or abuse of any commodity are unacceptable. Abusive language, harassment, ethnic slurs, and profanity do not have a place in the professional kitchen. When employees feel that their needs are given due consideration, their self-esteem will increase and their attitude toward the establishment will improve; both will increase productivity and reduce absenteeism.

JUDGMENT Although it is not easy to learn, good judgment is a prerequisite for becoming a professional. An ability to judge what is right and appropriate is developed throughout a lifetime of experience. Good judgment is never completely mastered; rather, it is a goal toward which one should continually strive.

COLD SAUCES AND COLD SOUPS

Sauces and soups are among the first true tests of a chef's skill. For the garde manger, the ability to produce perfectly balanced vinaigrettes, subtly flavored and creamy mayonnaise sauces, and cold soups of all varieties requires skills that should be honed constantly throughout a career.

two

Cold Sauces

The successful pairing of sauce and food demonstrates an understanding of the food and an ability to judge and evaluate a dish's flavors, textures, and colors. Evaluating why some combinations work well while others are less successful offers valuable lessons in composing a dish. What does the sauce bring to the dish? How does it function in the total composition? How does it taste? Sauces are not just an afterthought. They add flavor, color, texture, sheen, and moisture to a dish. In the cold kitchen, the chef's sauce repertoire includes:

- **COLD EMULSION SAUCES**: vinaigrettes and mayonnaise

- **DAIRY-BASED SAUCES**

- **SALSAS**

- **COULIS AND PURÉES**

- **COATING SAUCES**

- **MISCELLANEOUS COLD SAUCES** such as Cumberland, horseradish, and mignonette

Cold emulsion sauces

Vinaigrettes and mayonnaise are made by combining two ingredients that would not otherwise blend into a homogeneous mixture. In order to demonstrate how these sauces are prepared, we first discuss what an emulsion is and how it is formed.

An emulsion consists of two phases, the dispersed phase and the continuous phase (see Figure 2-1). When making vinaigrette, for example, the dispersed phase is the oil, meaning that the oil is handled in such a way that it is broken up into very small droplets. Each oil droplet is suspended throughout the continuous phase—in this case, the vinegar.

Temporary emulsions, such as vinaigrettes, form quickly and require only the mechanical action of whipping, shaking, or stirring (see Figure 2-2). To make an emulsion stable enough to keep the oil in suspension, additional ingredients known as *emulsifiers* are necessary. The emulsifiers used to make cold sauces include egg yolks, mustard, and glace de viande. Starches such as those in garlic or modified

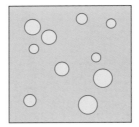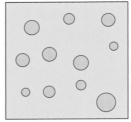

2-1. **Phases of an emulsion.** An oil-in-water emulsion (left) consists of oil in water. A water-in-oil emulsion (right) consists of water droplets in oil.

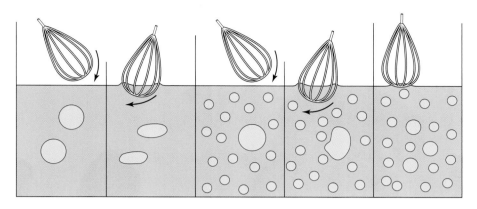
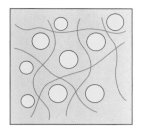

2-2. Temporary emulsions (top left). When oil droplets are sparse (left), they easily evade the whisk and are hard to divide. When, after much work, they are smaller and more numerous (right), the droplets themselves become obstacles to new drops of oil, and help break them up.

2-3. Emulsifiers are able to attract and hold (top right). Long molecules like starches and proteins stabilize emulsions by getting between droplets and interfering with coalescence.

starches such as cornstarch and arrowroot are also used. These emulsifiers are able to attract and hold both the oil and liquid (see Figure 2-3).

Stable emulsions, such as mayonnaise, are made by carefully controlling the rate at which the oil is added to the egg yolks. Egg yolks provide both the liquid that holds the oil droplets in suspension and a special emulsifier, known as *lecithin*. The oil is added very gradually at first so the droplets can be made extremely fine. The more oil added to the yolks, the thicker the sauce becomes. If the oil is added too rapidly, the emulsion cannot start to form properly—and if the emulsion becomes too thick early in the mixing process, the full amount of oil cannot be added, unless the sauce is thinned with a little water or an acid, such as vinegar or lemon juice.

Vinaigrettes

Vinaigrettes are closely associated with green salads, but they are used in other applications: as a marinade for grilled or broiled foods; to dress salads made from pastas, grains, vegetables, and beans; as a dip; as a sauce served with hot or cold entrées and appetizers; as a component of some sandwiches.

It is interesting to note that while oil is the largest component by volume and weight of a vinaigrette, the sauce is most often named for the acid—red wine vinaigrette, balsamic vinaigrette, lemon vinaigrette, tomato vinaigrette. The flavor of the acid dominates that of the oil. When an oil has a distinctive enough flavor, however, the vinaigrette may be called by the oil's name.

MAKING A BASIC VINAIGRETTE The challenge of making a good vinaigrette lies in achieving what chefs refer to as *balance,* a point at which the acidity of the vinegar or juice is tempered but not dominated by the richness of the oil.

Many chefs use the standard vinaigrette ratio of 3 parts oil to 1 part acid. This works well as a starting point, but it is important to taste and evaluate the vinaigrette whenever a change is made in the type of oil, acid, or specific flavoring ingredients. Some vinaigrette formulas call for either a quantity of water to dilute

2-4. Emulsified vinaigrette.   **A.** Making emulsified vinaigrette with mustard.   **B.** Adding the vinegar to the mustard.   **C.** Slowly whisking in the oil to create the emulsion.

very acidic vinegars, or a bit of sugar to soften the acidity, instead of calling for additional oil.

A basic vinaigrette is a temporary emulsion made by blending measured ingredients until they form a homogeneous sauce. The sauce remains an emulsion for only a short time, quickly separating back into oil and vinegar. To keep the sauce well balanced each time it is used, stir or whisk the vinaigrette each time it is served.

The best way to check for flavor and balance in a vinaigrette is to dip a piece of lettuce into it, shake off the excess, and then evaluate the taste of the sauce on the lettuce.

MAKING AN EMULSIFIED VINAIGRETTE The ratio for an emulsified vinaigrette is the same as for a basic vinaigrette. To make these sauces, egg yolks, mustard, garlic, fruit or vegetable purées, or glace de viande are included in the formula, both to add flavor and to help stabilize the sauce.

1. COMBINE THE VINEGAR AND ALL OF THE SEASONING INGREDIENTS. Add the vinegar to the salt, pepper, herbs, mustard, or other ingredients (see Figures 2-4A and 2-4B) to be sure they are evenly dispersed throughout the sauce.

   NOTE: Fresh herbs give vinaigrettes a wonderful flavor and color. However, if they are added too far in advance, the vinegar can start to discolor their fresh green color and start to break down their lively flavors. When preparing a large batch of vinaigrette intended to last through several service periods, it may be preferable to add the fresh herbs to the sauce just before service begins.

2. ADD THE OIL GRADUALLY. Slowly add a few droplets of oil at a time into the bowl, whisking constantly. Once the emulsion starts to form, pour or ladle the oil in a fine stream while whisking the sauce (see Figure 2-4C). Another way to create a stable vinaigrette is to use a blender, immersion blender, standing mixer with a whip, or food processor. Vinaigrettes made this way can hold their emulsion longer than those that are simply whipped together by hand.

3. ADD ANY GARNISH AND CHECK THE SEASONINGS AT THIS POINT. Fresh or dried fruits and vegetables, crumbled cheese, or other garnishes can be added, if desired. Review the previous section for information about how to check the seasoning and serve this sauce.

REDUCED-FAT VINAIGRETTES The total amount of oil in a vinaigrette can be greatly reduced by replacing up to two-thirds of the oil normally used with a lightly thickened stock or juice. Add enough diluted arrowroot or other modified starch to simmering stock or juice so it will mimic the consistency of a salad oil once cooled.

Purées of fruits and vegetables can also be used in place of part of a vinaigrette's oil. Naturally thick purées such as those made of tomato or red pepper may not need to be thickened further. Tomato Vinaigrette (page 33) is one such vinaigrette.

Store reduced-fat vinaigrettes as you would basic or emulsified vinaigrettes and follow the appropriate steps for recombining and adjusting seasoning before service.

Mayonnaise

Mayonnaise and dressings made with mayonnaise as a base can be used to dress salads, as a dip or spread, and to produce a coating sauce, such as Mayonnaise Collée (page 534). This sauce is made by combining egg yolks with oil so a stable emulsion forms. Unlike vinaigrettes, this cold sauce should not break as it sits. Mayonnaise is a sauce that requires skill and finesse to prepare correctly. It also requires careful handling to avoid contamination.

1. SELECT AND PREPARE THE INGREDIENTS FOR THE MAYONNAISE. Classic recipes for mayonnaise-style dressing call for 6 to 8 fl oz/180 to 240 mL of oil for each egg yolk. To avoid any possible food-borne illness (such as salmonella), professional chefs should use pasteurized egg yolks. Since mayonnaise is often intended as a base sauce that can be used for a variety of purposes, it is usually best to choose an oil that does not have a pronounced flavor of its

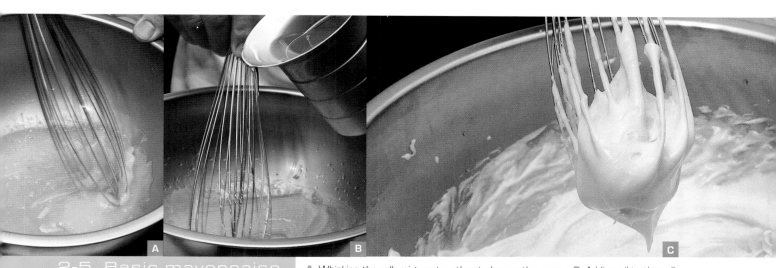

2-5. Basic mayonnaise. A. Whisking the yolk mixture together to loosen the eggs. B. Adding oil to the yolk mixture. C. The proper consistency for mayonnaise.

own. There are exceptions to this general rule. For example, a mayonnaise made with extra-virgin olive oil or a nut oil would be appropriate to serve as a dip with a platter of grilled vegetables or crudités. Various acids may be used to prepare a mayonnaise, including lemon juice, wine, and cider vinegars. The acid is used both to give the sauce flavor, and, along with water, to adjust its consistency.

2. **BLEND THE YOLKS WITH A BIT OF WATER.** Whisk the yolks and water together to loosen the eggs and get them ready to absorb the oil (see Figure 2-5A). You may also wish to include lemon juice or vinegar and mustard at this point, if your formula calls for those ingredients.

3. **ADD THE OIL A LITTLE AT A TIME,** whisking it in completely. It is important to proceed cautiously when the oil is first being added. The oil must be whipped into the egg yolks so it is broken up into very fine droplets. This stage is where the emulsion first starts to form. If the oil is added too quickly, the droplets will be too large to blend into the yolks, and the sauce will appear broken. Adding the oil slowly allows the eggs to absorb it properly, and the sauce will start to thicken. Once about one-fourth to one-third of the oil is properly blended into the egg mixture, you may start to increase the amount you add (see Figure 2-5B). When preparing a mayonnaise in a mixer, add the oil in a thin stream as the machine runs. It is still true that the oil should be added more slowly at the beginning than at the end.

4. **ADJUST THE THICKNESS AND FLAVOR OF THE SAUCE** by adding a bit more acid or water as you incorporate the oil. Additional lemon juice, vinegar, or a little water is added once the eggs absorb enough of the oil to become very thick. If this step is neglected, the sauce will become too thick to absorb any more oil. Continue adding oil until the amount specified in the recipe is added. A finished mayonnaise is thick enough to hold soft peaks (see Figure

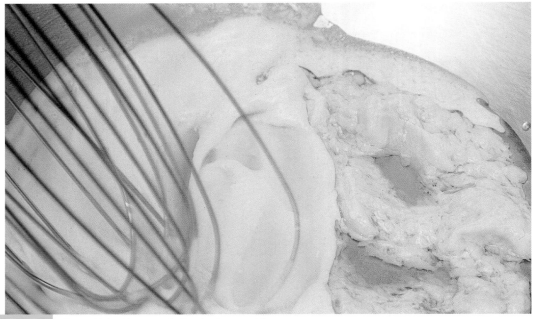

2-6.   Recombining the sauce to fix a broken emulsion.

2-5C). However, depending on your intended use, you may wish to thin the sauce with water to make it more pourable.

5. **ADD ANY FLAVORING OR GARNISH INGREDIENTS** at the point indicated in the recipe. Aïoli (page 36), a garlic-flavored mayonnaise, calls for a good quantity of garlic to be included from the earliest stages of mixing. Other ingredients, such as vegetable purées or pastes, fresh herbs, chopped pickles, and so forth, may be blended into the sauce once the oil is fully incorporated. Green Mayonnaise (Sauce Verte) (page 35) and Rémoulade Sauce (page 36) are two such variations.

WHEN MAYONNAISE BREAKS Mayonnaise and similarly prepared dressings may break for a number of reasons:

- The oil was added too rapidly for the egg yolk to absorb it.
- The sauce was allowed to become too thick.
- The sauce became either too cold or too warm as it was being prepared.

A broken mayonnaise can be corrected as follows (see Figure 2-6):

1. Beat a pasteurized egg yolk until foamy.
2. Gradually incorporate the broken mayonnaise, whisking constantly.

The mayonnaise should recombine into a homogeneous sauce.

STORING MAYONNAISE Mayonnaise should be kept refrigerated at all times once it is prepared. Transfer it to a storage container, cover it carefully, and label it with a date. Before using mayonnaise that has been stored, stir it gently and check the seasoning carefully. If the sauce needs to be thinned, add a bit of water.

Dairy-based sauces

Dairy-based sauces are used as salad dressings or dips. They are made from soft cheeses such as fraîche, quark, mascarpone, and cream cheese; cultured milks such as sour cream, crème fraîche, and buttermilk; cream; or low- or reduced-fat versions of ricotta, sour cream, and cottage cheese. These dressings are generally white or ivory, so they can take on the color of purées or coulis of herbs, fruits, or vegetables.

Typical additions to dairy-based dressings are cheeses (especially blue cheese, Parmesan, and feta), fresh lemon, black pepper, and minced or puréed herbs. Diced, minced, or grated vegetables, pickles, capers, and olives add texture as well as flavor.

Creamy sauces can be prepared in a range of textures, from a relatively stiff sauce to serve as a dip or spread to a pourable sauce that easily dresses a green salad. For a light, almost mousselike texture, whipped cream can be folded into the sauce at the last moment.

Salsas

Salsas are typically made from uncooked fruits or vegetables. They often include an acid, such as citrus juice, vinegar, or wine, to add a sharp flavor. Spices, chiles, and herbs are sometimes added to these sauces to give them a potent flavor and a higher-than-average level of "heat."

Sauces made from vegetables and fruits are becoming increasingly popular. Both fresh (or raw) and cooked versions of salsas, chutneys, relishes, and compotes are found in cuisines from Mexico to India. While aficionados will always make distinctions about when the term *salsa* is correctly used—versus *chutney, relish,* and even *compote*—in practical terms, the differences among these sauces have more to do with their country or cuisine of origin than a difference in preparation method. (Recipes for a variety of chutneys, relishes, and compotes can be found in Chapter 10.)

Coulis and purées

The classic definition of a coulis, written by Escoffier in *Le Guide Culinaire,* is the "well reduced, highly concentrated essential flavours of a food, in either purée or liquid form."

In the modern cold kitchen, coulis are made by puréeing raw or cooked fruits or vegetables to a saucelike consistency. The term *purée* is frequently used interchangeably with *coulis.* The texture of these sauces can range from very light and smooth to coarse. They may be served as is, or they may be adjusted by adding stocks, wines, infusions, oils, or cream.

Coulis and purées may begin to weep a clear liquid as they sit. To prevent this, bring the sauce to a simmer and add a small amount of diluted arrowroot or cornstarch. This is a helpful practice whenever advance plating is required, as might be the case for a banquet or reception.

2-7. Working with gelatin.   **A.** Sprinkle gelatin evenly over the liquid.   **B.** Fully bloomed gelatin.

Coating sauces: chaud-froid and aspic gelée

Although these sauces are not as popular as they once were, they still have several applications for the garde manger. They can be used to coat canapés and other hors d'oeuvre, to prepare platters for display and service, and to coat timbales and other appetizers.

Chaud-froids are made by adding gelatin to a warm sauce, such as demi-glace, béchamel, or velouté. Clear coating sauces, known as *aspic gelée* or simply aspics, are made by clarifying stocks, juices, or essences and adding enough gelatin to achieve the desired strength. Techniques for working with gelatin are illustrated below.

WORKING WITH GELATIN In order to achieve the correct results when preparing aspic or any other item containing gelatin, you must be able to handle gelatin properly and incorporate it correctly. Ratios for producing aspic gelée in a variety of strengths can be found in Table 2-1.

1. WEIGH THE GELATIN CAREFULLY. Granulated or powdered gelatin, gelatin sheets, and instant gelatin can be used interchangeably.

2. ADD THE GELATIN TO A COOL LIQUID. Sprinkle the gelatin powder evenly over a cool liquid (see Figure 2-7A). If the liquid is warm or hot, the gelatin cannot soften properly. Scattering the gelatin over the liquid's surface prevents the formation of clumps.

3. BLOOM THE GELATIN. As the gelatin absorbs the liquid, each granule becomes enlarged; this is known as *blooming* (see Figure 2-7B).

4. MELT THE GELATIN ENOUGH TO DISSOLVE THE GRANULES. Bloomed gelatin (or gelatin solution) can be dissolved in one of two ways: add it directly to a warm liquid (at 100° to 110°F/38° to 43°C), or warm the mixture over a hot water bath. As the softened gelatin warms, the mixture will clear and become liquid enough to pour easily. Combine the gelatin thoroughly with the base liquid to be sure it gels evenly.

TABLE 2-1 | **Ratios for Aspic Gelée**

RATIO PER GALLON	RATIO PER PINT	GEL STRENGTH	POSSIBLE USES
2 oz/57 g	¼ oz/7 g	Delicate gel	When slicing is not required. Individual portions of meat, vegetable, or fish bound by gelatin. Jellied consommés.
4 oz/113 g	½ oz/14 g	Coating gel	Edible chaud-froid. Coating individual items.
6 to 8 oz/170 to 227 g	1 oz/28 g	Sliceable gel	When product is to be sliced. Filling pâté en croûte, head cheese.
10 to 12 oz/283 to 340 g	1¼ to 1½ oz/35 to 43 g	Firm gel	Coating platters with underlayment for food show or competition.
16 oz/454 g	2 oz/57 g	Mousse-strength gel	When product must retain shape after unmolding. Production of a mousse.

NOTE: In some kitchens, chefs prefer to have bloomed, softened gelatin on hand at all times, and refer to it as a *gelatin solution*. This mixture can be held for several weeks and used as required to prepare aspics and other jellied sauces and soups.

5. **TEST THE GELATIN STRENGTH.** To test the strength of both aspics and reduced stocks, chill a plate in the freezer. Ladle a small amount of the aspic or reduced stock onto the plate and chill under refrigeration until it gels. Adjust the strength by rewarming the aspic and then adding more gelatin or more base liquid as necessary.

The term *chaud-froid* means "hot and cold," a name that reflects the way in which the sauce is prepared for use. It is warmed over a hot water bath to the point at which it flows easily. Next, it is cooled over an ice water bath (see Figure 2-8A) to the point at which the gelatin thickens and the sauce starts to cling to the sides of the bowl. Chaud-froid is being used to prepare a platter in Figures 2-8B and 2-8C. In Figures 2-9A and 2-9B, port wine aspic gelée is being applied to an appetizer plate and garnished with grape slices. It can also be used to coat individual slices of pâté en croûte (see Figure 2-9C).

A quickly prepared substitute for chaud-froid, known as a *mayonnaise collée*, is made by thickening mayonnaise and/or sour cream with an appropriate amount of gelatin to produce a coating consistency.

2-8. Working with chaud-froid. **A.** Tempering the gelatin over an ice water bath. **B.** Carefully laying down pluches of dill as decoration. **C.** Sealing the chaud-froid with a layer of heavy-strength gelatin.

2-9. Working with aspic gelée. **A.** Pouring port-flavored aspic onto an appetizer plate. **B.** Placing a grape slice onto the aspic before it congeals. **C.** Aspic gelée coating slices of pâté en croûte.

Miscellaneous sauces

In addition to the sauces discussed above, the garde manger may be called on to prepare special sauces that do not fit into a single category. Cocktail, Cumberland, Oxford, mint, and horseradish sauces are in the basic repertoire of the cold kitchen. Dipping sauces, such as those served with saté and tempura, are also considered cold sauces. Consult specific recipes for information about preparing and serving these sauces.

Cold Soups

Traditionally, soups prepared by the garde manger are served chilled. They are found as first-course offerings, as appetizer courses, and as desserts. They may be presented in a variety of ways—in chilled stemware, in traditional soup plates or cups, and in tiny tasting portions served at stand-up receptions. Cold soups refresh the palate, regardless of the point in the meal at which they are served. They can be rich and suave, as in the case of cream-based soups, or bold and robust. Whenever you intend to serve chilled food, be sure to taste it carefully at the correct service temperature. Remember to allow soups sufficient time to develop their flavor; some soups are at their best and ready to serve as soon as they are prepared, but others develop a more complex and satisfying flavor if they are allowed to mellow (under refrigeration) for several hours or overnight.

Cold soups may be prepared in one of three ways, depending on their type. Vegetable and fruit soups are made by puréeing or chopping fruits and vegetables finely enough to form a souplike consistency; cream soups are made from a thickened base such as a velouté, béchamel, or potato purée; and clear soups are made by clarifying and fortifying a rich broth and, if desired, thickening the base with a little gelatin.

Vegetable and fruit soups

Cold vegetable and fruit soups are popular hot-weather offerings around the world. Many cuisines have special cold soups that feature a seasonal food—for example, cherries, melons, tomatoes, peppers, or cucumbers. You will find an interesting range of soups in the following pages, as well as distinctive garnishing and presentation ideas.

Cream-style soups

Cold cream soups should have the same velvet-smooth texture as hot cream soups. Taste and evaluate the flavor carefully, and give equal attention to texture and consistency. Cold soups may thicken as they cool, so be certain you have adjusted the consistency to make a soup that is creamy but not stiff. Good cold soups should not leave your mouth feeling coated with fat, so keep the amount of cream in good proportion to the other ingredients.

Vegetable and fruit soups range in texture from the appealingly coarse texture of gazpacho to the velvet smoothness of chilled melon soup. A broth or juice is often added to the fruits or vegetables to loosen the purée enough to create a good soup consistency. Other ingredients, such as cream, milk, buttermilk, garnish items, and granités, may be added to the soup for additional interest.

Vichyssoise is a classic example of a cold cream-style soup. It is made by preparing a purée of potato and leek. Other cold soups are made by preparing a cream-style or velouté soup. They are typically finished by adding chilled cream, yogurt, or crème fraîche. The cold pea soup on page 68 is a good example.

Clear cold soups

Clear soups must have a deep and satisfying flavor in order to be successful. The body of the soup can be adjusted by adding gelatin, if you prefer to serve it jellied. (To review the information about working with gelatin, read pages 22–24 earlier in this chapter.) Not all clear soups are jellied, however, and some of the recipes included here are based on a delicious broth, garnished or left plain according to your intended presentation.

Clear cold soups require a rich, full-bodied, clarified broth or juice. Infusions, essences, or well-strained purées are often used to create the special character of the soup. Traditional clear cold soups such as jellied consommés are made by adding enough bloomed and dissolved gelatin to the soup to make it gel. Jellied clear soups should barely hold their shape and should melt in the mouth instantly.

Basic Red Wine Vinaigrette

YIELD: 32 FL OZ/960 ML

8 fl oz/240 mL red wine vinegar

2 tsp/10 g mustard (optional)

2 shallots, minced

24 fl oz/720 mL mild olive oil or canola oil

2 tsp/10 g sugar (optional)

2 tsp/10 g salt, or to taste

½ tsp/1 g ground black pepper, or to taste

3 tbsp/9 g minced herbs, such as chives, parsley, tarragon (optional)

1. Combine the vinegar, mustard, if desired, and shallots.

2. Whisk in the oil gradually.

3. Season with sugar, salt, and pepper. Add the fresh herbs, if desired.

Balsamic Vinaigrette

YIELD: 32 FL OZ/960 ML

4 fl oz/120 mL red wine vinegar

4 fl oz/120 mL balsamic vinegar

2 tsp/10 g mustard (optional)

24 fl oz/720 mL mild olive oil or canola oil

2 tsp/10 g salt, or to taste

½ tsp/1 g ground black pepper, or to taste

3 tbsp/9 g minced herbs, such as chives, parsley, tarragon (optional)

1. Combine the vinegars and mustard.

2. Whisk in the oil gradually.

3. Season with salt and pepper. Add the fresh herbs, if desired.

Grapefruit Emulsion

YIELD: 32 FL OZ/960 ML

30 fl oz/900 mL grapefruit juice

6 fl oz/180 mL olive oil

½ oz/14 g grapefruit zest, finely grated with no pith, blanched and shocked 2 or 3 times

1. Combine the grapefruit juice, olive oil, and zest in a blender. Blend on high speed until emulsified, about 2 minutes. Strain the emulsion through cheesecloth into a clean container.

2. Store under refrigeration for later use. Blend briefly to reemulsify before service if necessary.

Truffle Vinaigrette

YIELD: 32 FL OZ/960 ML

When fresh truffles are available, you can offer this dressing on Spring Herb Salad (page 87) topped with shaved truffles, prepared at tableside.

12 fl oz/360 mL red wine vinegar

4 fl oz/120 mL balsamic vinegar

2 fl oz/60 mL water

2 tsp/10 g Dijon mustard

2 shallots, minced

14 fl oz/420 mL mild olive oil

1½ fl oz/45 mL truffle oil

2 tsp/10 g sugar

2 tsp/10 g salt, or to taste

½ tsp/1 g ground black pepper, or to taste

1 black or white truffle, chopped (optional)

1. Mix together the vinegars, water, mustard, and shallots.

2. Whisk in the oils gradually.

3. Season with sugar, salt, and pepper. Add the truffle just before serving, if desired.

Tangerine-Pineapple Vinaigrette

YIELD: 32 FL OZ/960 ML

10 fl oz/300 mL tangerine juice

5⅓ fl oz/160 mL pineapple juice

1 fl oz/30 mL lemon juice

2 tsp/10 mL white wine vinegar

2 tsp/10 g prepared Creole mustard

10 fl oz/300 mL vegetable oil

5⅓ fl oz/160 mL olive oil

2 tsp/10 g salt, or to taste

½ tsp/1 g ground black pepper, or to taste

1. Combine the juices, vinegar, and mustard.

2. Whisk in the oils gradually.

3. Season with salt and pepper.

ORANGE (OR BLOOD ORANGE) VINAIGRETTE: Substitute 16 fl oz/480 mL orange (or blood orange) juice for the tangerine and pineapple juice. Reduce lemon juice to ½ fl oz/15 mL.

LEMON VINAIGRETTE: Substitute 12 fl oz/360 mL lemon juice and 4 fl oz/120 mL water for the tangerine and pineapple juice. Eliminate the garlic and mustard.

Vinaigrette Gourmande

YIELD: 32 FL OZ/960 ML

4 fl oz/120 mL sherry vinegar

3 fl oz/90 mL lemon juice

2 tsp/10 g salt, or to taste

½ tsp/1 g ground black pepper, or to taste

16 fl oz/480 mL olive oil

10 fl oz/300 mL vegetable oil

1 oz/28 g Fines Herbes (page 526)

1. Combine the vinegar, lemon juice, salt, and pepper.

2. Whisk in the oils gradually.

3. Add the herbs; adjust seasoning with salt and pepper.

WALNUT AND RED WINE VINAIGRETTE: Substitute walnut oil for the vegetable oil and red wine vinegar for the sherry vinegar. Substitute parsley and chives for chervil and tarragon in the fines herbes.

Lemon-Parsley Vinaigrette

YIELD: 32 FL OZ/960 ML

6 fl oz/180 mL lemon juice

2 fl oz/60 mL Champagne vinegar

1 oz/28 g Dijon mustard

½ oz/14 g garlic, minced

1¼ oz/35 g shallots, minced

Salt, to taste

Ground black pepper, to taste

1 tbsp/6 g fennel seeds, crushed

1½ tsp/3 g red pepper flakes

12 fl oz/360 mL olive oil

1 oz/28 g chopped parsley

½ oz/14 g chopped oregano

1. Combine the juice, vinegar, mustard, garlic, shallots, salt, pepper, fennel seeds, and red pepper flakes.

2. Whisk in the oil and reserve.

3. Whisk in the parsley and oregano just before service. Adjust seasoning if necessary.

Apple Cider Vinaigrette

YIELD: 32 FL OZ/960 ML

Use hard cider to replace the apple cider for a deeper, more complex flavor in the finished dressing.

16 fl oz/480 mL apple cider

6 fl oz/180 mL cider vinegar

1 Granny Smith apple, cut into brunoise

24 fl oz/720 mL vegetable oil

2 tbsp/6 g chopped tarragon leaves

2 tsp/10 g salt, or to taste

¼ tsp/0.50 g ground white pepper, or to taste

½ tsp/2.50 g sugar, as needed

1. Reduce the cider to 6 fl oz/180 mL. Combine the cider reduction, the vinegar, and the brunoise apple.

2. Whisk in the oil gradually.

3. Add the tarragon and season with salt, pepper, and sugar.

CHEF'S NOTES: Six oz/170 g apple juice concentrate may be substituted if apple cider is not available. This dressing can be puréed in a blender for a smooth, creamier vinaigrette.

Curry Vinaigrette

YIELD: 32 FL OZ/960 ML

6 fl oz/180 mL cider vinegar

4 fl oz/120 mL orange juice

Juice of 1 lemon

1½ oz/43 g honey

1 oz/28 g minced ginger

1 oz/28 g minced lemongrass, tender inside leaves

18 fl oz/540 mL Curry-Infused Olive Oil (page 491)

2 tsp/10 g salt, or to taste

2 tsp/4 g coarse-ground black pepper, or to taste

1. Combine the vinegar, juices, honey, ginger, and lemongrass.

2. Whisk in the curry oil gradually.

3. Season with salt and pepper.

Mustard-Walnut Vinaigrette

YIELD: 32 FL OZ/960 ML

8 fl oz/240 mL Champagne vinegar

2 oz/57 g spicy brown mustard

½ oz/14 g sugar

4 shallots, minced

20 fl oz/600 mL mild olive oil

4 fl oz/120 mL walnut oil

½ oz/14 g chopped dill

½ oz/14 g chopped flat-leaf parsley leaves

2 tbsp/6 g minced chives

Salt, to taste

Coarse-ground black pepper, to taste

1. Combine the vinegar, mustard, sugar, and shallots.

2. Whisk in the oils gradually.

3. Add the herbs and season with salt and pepper.

HAZELNUT-OREGANO VINAIGRETTE: Substitute hazelnut oil for the walnut oil. Replace the dill and parsley with 1 oz/28 g chopped oregano. Eliminate the chives, if desired.

Chipotle-Sherry Vinaigrette

YIELD: 32 FL OZ/960 ML

7 fl oz/210 mL sherry vinegar

1 fl oz/30 mL lime juice

4 chipotles in adobo sauce, minced

2 shallots, minced

2 garlic cloves, minced

24 fl oz/720 mL olive oil

1 oz/28 g chopped Fines Herbes (page 526)

1 fl oz/30 mL maple syrup

1 tsp/5 g salt, or to taste

½ tsp/1 g coarse-ground black pepper, or to taste

1. Combine the vinegar, lime juice, chipotles, shallots, and garlic.

2. Whisk in the oil gradually.

3. Add the fines herbes just before service and season with maple syrup, salt, and pepper.

Roasted Shallot Vinaigrette

YIELD: 32 FL OZ/960 ML

20 shallots, peeled

20 fl oz/600 mL olive oil

8 fl oz/240 mL sherry vinegar

2 tsp/2 g chopped rosemary

2 tsp/2 g chopped thyme

2 fl oz/60 mL honey

2 tsp/10 g salt, or to taste

1 tsp/2 g cracked black pepper, or to taste

1. Rub the shallots with a little of the oil and roast in a warm oven (300°F/149°C) until very tender, well browned, and sweet-smelling. When cool enough to handle, cut into quarters.

2. Combine the shallots with the vinegar.

3. Whisk in the remaining oil gradually.

4. Add the herbs and season with honey, salt, and pepper.

Tomato Vinaigrette

YIELD: 32 FL OZ/960 ML

This nontraditional juice-based vinaigrette may be served with vegetable terrines or the Poached Salmon and Lemon Terrine on page 314.

1 lb/454 g ripe tomatoes, seeded

1 oz/28 g minced shallots

4 fl oz/120 mL red wine vinegar

1 oz/28 g pasteurized egg yolks

8 fl oz/240 mL mild olive oil

2 fl oz/60 mL lemon juice

2 fl oz/60 mL lime juice

2 tbsp/6 g chopped basil

1 tbsp/3 g chopped tarragon leaves

2 tsp/10 g salt, or to taste

1 tsp/2 g ground white pepper, or to taste

1. Purée the tomatoes, shallots, vinegar, and egg yolks in a blender or food processor. Add the olive oil slowly with the motor running to form a thick sauce.

2. Add the juices and herbs, and season with salt and pepper.

Beet Vinaigrette

YIELD: 32 FL OZ/960 ML

2 lb/907 g beets

12 fl oz/360 mL cider vinegar

6 fl oz/180 mL extra-virgin olive oil

1¾ oz/50 g chopped dill

2 tsp/10 g salt, or to taste

1 tsp/2 g ground black pepper, or to taste

1. Simmer the beets in acidulated water until tender. When the beets are cool enough to handle, peel and chop.

2. Place the beets and vinegar in a blender and purée until smooth. Whisk in the oil and season with the dill, salt, and pepper.

CHEF'S NOTES: For a more intense color and flavor, use a juicer to juice the raw beets. Combine the juice and vinegar, whisk in the oil, and season with dill, salt, and pepper.

Acidulated water is made by combining 1 gal/3.84 L water with 1 fl oz/30 mL lemon juice or vinegar.

Port Vinaigrette

YIELD: 32 FL OZ/960 ML

6 fl oz/180 mL ruby port wine

6 fl oz/180 mL Ficklin Port

8 fl oz/240 mL red wine vinegar

½ oz/14 g minced shallots

2 tsp/6 g minced garlic

1 tsp/5 g salt, or to taste

¼ tsp/0.50 g ground black pepper, or to taste

12 fl oz/360 mL walnut oil

12 fl oz/360 mL vegetable oil

1. Combine the ports in a heavy-gauge saucepan and reduce by half over medium heat, about 10 minutes. Remove from heat and cool to room temperature.

2. Combine the reduced port, vinegar, shallots, garlic, salt, and pepper.

3. Whisk in the oils gradually, or use an immersion blender to emulsify the sauce. Taste the vinaigrette and adjust seasoning as needed.

Basic Mayonnaise

YIELD: 1 GAL/3.84 L

Sometimes referred to as the *mother sauce of the cold kitchen,* mayonnaise can be seasoned to fit many needs. Variations can be made by adding purées of herbs, peppers, or tomatoes. Saffron can be infused in some of the oil to lend brilliant color; diced or chopped pickles, capers, or olives may be added to increase flavor and texture.

12 oz/340 g pasteurized egg yolks	1¾ oz/50 g kosher salt
4 fl oz/120 mL white vinegar	96 fl oz/2.88 L vegetable oil
4 fl oz/120 mL water	2 tsp/4 g ground white pepper, or to taste
½ oz/14 g dry mustard	4 fl oz/120 mL lemon juice, or to taste

1. Whisk together the yolks, vinegar, water, mustard, and salt until slightly foamy.

2. Add the oil gradually in a thin stream, whipping constantly, until all the oil is incorporated and the mayonnaise is thick.

3. Season with salt, pepper, and lemon juice, as needed. Refrigerate immediately.

GREEN MAYONNAISE (SAUCE VERTE): Finely chop 4 oz/113 g cooked spinach. Squeeze it in a cheesecloth to extract the juice. Add the juice to the mayonnaise. Add chopped herbs, such as parsley, basil, chives, and dill, to taste.

Aïoli (Garlic Mayonnaise)

YIELD: 32 FL OZ/960 ML

6 oz/170 g pasteurized egg yolks

1 tbsp/10 g garlic paste

24 fl oz/720 mL vegetable oil

8 fl oz/240 mL olive oil

1½ tsp/7.50 mL red wine vinegar

2 tsp/10 mL lemon juice

Salt, to taste

Cayenne pepper, to taste

Prepare as for Basic Mayonnaise (page 35), adding the garlic to the egg yolk mixture. Refrigerate immediately.

ROUILLE: Reduce 6 oz/170 g Red Pepper Coulis (page 54) to about 4 oz/113 g. Add crushed cayenne to taste. This sauce should have noticeable heat.

SAFFRON AÏOLI: Infuse ½ tsp/1 g lightly crushed saffron threads in 1 fl oz/30 mL boiling water. Add this infusion to the egg yolks along with the garlic paste.

Rémoulade Sauce

YIELD: 32 FL OZ/960 ML

24 fl oz/720 mL Basic Mayonnaise (page 35)

2 oz/57 g capers, drained, rinsed, and chopped

2 oz/57 g cornichons, chopped

3 tbsp/9 g chopped chives

3 tbsp/9 g chopped chervil

3 tbsp/9 g chopped tarragon leaves

½ oz/14 g Dijon mustard

1 tsp/5 g anchovy paste

Worcestershire sauce, to taste

2 to 3 dashes Tabasco sauce

Combine all ingredients thoroughly. Refrigerate immediately.

Clockwise from top:
Aïoli, Tapenade, and Hummus

Russian Dressing

YIELD: 32 FL OZ/960 ML

In spite of its name, this dressing is all American. It is believed that its name was inspired by its resemblance to dressings first seen in Russia.

20 fl oz/600 mL Basic Mayonnaise (page 35)

7 fl oz/210 mL prepared chili sauce

2 oz/57 g prepared horseradish

½ fl oz/15 mL Worcestershire sauce

Salt, to taste

1 tsp/2 g ground black pepper

Combine all ingredients thoroughly. Adjust seasoning to taste. Refrigerate immediately.

THOUSAND ISLAND DRESSING: Add 4 oz/113 g pickle relish and 2 oz/57 g chopped hard-cooked egg to Russian Dressing.

Green Goddess Dressing

YIELD: 32 FL OZ/960 ML

24 fl oz/720 mL Basic Mayonnaise (page 35)

2 fl oz/60 mL tarragon vinegar

1 oz/28 g chopped flat-leaf parsley leaves

4 tsp/4 g chopped chives

3 tbsp/9 g chopped tarragon leaves

1 tsp/5 g anchovy paste (1 to 2 fillets)

1 tsp/2 g coarse-cracked black pepper

Salt, to taste

Combine all ingredients thoroughly. Adjust seasoning to taste. This dressing may be puréed in a food processor, if desired. Refrigerate immediately.

CHEF'S NOTE: If tarragon vinegar is unavailable, substitute white wine vinegar and add 2 tbsp/6 g additional chopped tarragon.

Creole Honey-Mustard Sauce

YIELD: 32 FL OZ/960 ML

1 oz/28 g minced shallots

¾ oz/21 g crushed green peppercorns (brine-packed)

½ fl oz/15 mL vegetable oil

6 fl oz/180 mL dry white wine

1 tbsp/6 g coarse-cracked black pepper

2 oz/57 g Dijon mustard

6 oz/170 g Creole mustard

8 fl oz/240 mL Basic Mayonnaise (page 35)

8½ oz/241 g sour cream

1½ oz/43 g honey

Kosher salt, to taste

1. Sweat the shallots and peppercorns in the oil; do not brown.

2. Add the white wine and reduce until the wine is almost completely evaporated. Cool.

3. Add the remaining ingredient, mix well and check seasoning. Refrigerate immediately.

Creamy Black Pepper Dressing

YIELD: 32 FL OZ/960 ML

2 fl oz/60 mL lemon juice

3 oz/85 g pasteurized egg yolks

1 oz/28 g Dijon mustard

½ oz/14 g anchovy paste (3 to 4 fillets)

2 tsp/6 g minced garlic

1 tsp/15 g salt

12 oz/360 mL olive oil

fl oz/360 mL vegetable oil

2 oz/71 g grated Parmesan cheese

tbsp/6 g coarse-ground black pepper

1. Whisk together the lemon juice, eggs, mustard, anchovy paste, garlic, and salt.

2. Add the oils gradually, whisking constantly.

3. Add the remaining ingredients and mix well. Refrigerate immediately.

Roquefort Dressing

YIELD: 32 FL OZ/960 ML

This dressing can be made with other blue-veined cheeses such as Maytag, Danish Blue, or Gorgonzola.

6 oz/170 g crumbled Roquefort cheese

1 lb/454 g Basic Mayonnaise (page 35)

4½ oz/128 g sour cream

6 fl oz/180 mL buttermilk

½ fl oz/15 mL lemon juice

2 tsp/10 mL Worcestershire sauce

1 tsp/2 g ground black pepper

1 tbsp/3 g chopped flat-leaf parsley

Salt, to taste

1. Mix the Roquefort, mayonnaise, sour cream, and buttermilk well.

2. Season with lemon juice, Worcestershire sauce, salt, pepper, and parsley. To thin, add more buttermilk. Adjust seasoning to taste. Refrigerate immmediately.

CHEF'S NOTE: For a thicker sauce to use as a dip, add half of the Roquefort and purée the dressing until smooth. Fold in the remaining cheese.

Ranch Dressing (Reduced-Fat)

YIELD: 32 FL OZ/960 ML

12 oz/340 g part-skim ricotta cheese

8 oz/227 g nonfat yogurt

12 fl oz/360 mL buttermilk

1 fl oz/30 mL lemon juice

1 fl oz/30 mL red wine vinegar

1 tsp/3 g minced garlic

1 oz/28 g minced shallots

½ oz/14 g Dijon mustard

½ tsp/1 g celery seed

1 tbsp/15 g kosher salt

1 tsp/2 g ground black pepper

1 fl oz/30 mL Worcestershire sauce

2 tsp/2 g chopped flat-leaf parsley leaves

1 tsp/1 g chopped chives

1. Combine the cheese, yogurt, buttermilk, lemon juice, vinegar, garlic, shallots, mustard, celery seed, salt, pepper, and Worcestershire sauce. Purée in a food processor until smooth.

2. Mix in the parsley and chives and adjust seasoning. Refrigerate immediately.

Maytag Blue Cheese Dressing (Reduced-Fat)

YIELD: 32 FL OZ/960 ML

The Maytag Company of Iowa has been producing world-class blue cheese since World War II. This reduced-fat dressing is based on a purée of ricotta cheese and buttermilk flavored with a moderate amount of this fully flavored blue cheese.

3½ oz/99 g Maytag blue cheese

12 oz/340 g part-skim ricotta cheese

12 fl oz/360 mL buttermilk

2 fl oz/60 mL cider vinegar

½ fl oz/15 mL Worcestershire sauce

½ tsp/2 g Roasted Garlic (page 543)

2 tbsp/6 g chopped chives

1½ tsp/3 g cracked black pepper

Salt, to taste

1. Combine the cheeses, buttermilk, vinegar, Worcestershire sauce, and garlic and purée in a food processor until smooth.

2. Stir in the chives and pepper. Adjust seasoning to taste. Refrigerate immediately.

Yogurt Cucumber Sauce

YIELD: 32 FL OZ/960 ML

32 fl oz/960 mL yogurt

1 fl oz/30 mL lemon juice

2 tsp/10 g salt

1 garlic clove, crushed

8 oz/227 g cucumber, peeled, seeded, and cut into small dice

1. Combine the yogurt, lemon juice, and salt until smooth and well blended. Place the mixture in a bowl and add the garlic. Fold in the diced cucumber.

2. Cover and refrigerate for at least 1 hour and up to 24 hours before use. Remove the garlic clove before serving. Adjust seasoning with salt and additional lemon juice, as desired.

Tahini Sauce

YIELD: 32 FL OZ/960 ML

32 fl oz/960 mL yogurt

4 oz/113 g tahini

3 fl oz/90 mL lemon juice

2 tsp/10 g salt

Place all ingredients in the bowl of a food processor fitted with a blade attachment. Pulse until the mixture is smooth and homogeneous. Adjust seasoning with salt. Refrigerate immediately.

Salsa Verde

YIELD: 32 FL OZ/960 ML

2 shallots, finely diced

2 fl oz/60 mL red wine vinegar

Salt, to taste

4 salt-packed anchovy fillets

3½ oz/99 g chopped flat-leaf parsley

1 oz/28 g chopped chives

½ oz/14 g chopped chervil

½ oz/14 g chopped thyme

1 oz/28 g chopped capers

1 tbsp/9 g finely chopped lemon zest

8 fl oz/240 mL pure olive oil

2 fl oz/60 mL olive oil

1. Cover the shallots with the vinegar in a small bowl and season with salt. Let them macerate for about 20 minutes.

2. Rinse the anchovies well. Chop fine.

3. Combine the chopped herbs, capers, lemon zest, anchovies, and oils to make a saucelike consistency. Add the shallots and vinegar. Adjust seasoning.

4. Transfer to a clean storage container. Refrigerate immediately.

Salsa Fresca

YIELD: 32 FL OZ/960 ML

1 lb 1½ oz/496 g seeded and diced tomatoes

3¼ oz/92 g minced onion (1 each)

2⅔ oz/75 g diced green pepper (1 each)

2 garlic cloves, minced

1 tbsp/3 g chopped cilantro

1 tsp/1 g chopped oregano

Juice of 2 limes

1 jalapeño, minced

1 fl oz/30 mL olive oil

¼ tsp/0.50 g ground white pepper

2 tsp/10 g salt

Combine all ingredients and adjust seasoning. Refrigerate immediately.

Mango-Lime Salsa

YIELD: 32 FL OZ/960 ML

1 lb/454 g small-dice mango

3 oz/85 g small-dice red onion

2 tsp/10 g minced jalapeños

2 fl oz/60 mL lime juice

2 fl oz/60 mL extra-virgin olive oil

3 tbsp/9 g chopped basil

2 tsp/6 g finely chopped lime zest

Salt, to taste

Pepper, to taste

1. Combine all ingredients.

2. Allow to sit 1 hour before service. Adjust seasoning.

Papaya and Black Bean Salsa

YIELD: 32 FL OZ/960 ML

6½ oz/184 g cooked black beans

1 ripe papaya, cut into small dice

5⅓ oz/151 g red pepper, cut into small dice

3¼ oz/92 g red onion, cut into small dice

2 jalapeños, minced

3 tbsp/9 g chopped cilantro

2 tsp/4 g dried Mexican oregano

1 oz/28 g minced ginger

2 fl oz/60 mL olive oil

Juice of 2 limes

1 tsp/2 g ground black pepper

2 tsp/10 g kosher salt

Combine all ingredients and adjust seasoning. Refrigerate immediately.

Chipotle Pico de Gallo

YIELD: 32 FL OZ/960 ML

1 lb 2 oz/510 g plum tomatoes, seeded and chopped

3 oz/85 g red onion, chopped

2 fl oz/60 mL lime juice

1½ tsp/4.50 g minced garlic

2 tsp/7 g chipotle in adobo sauce, mashed to a paste

Salt, to taste

Pepper, to taste

1 oz/28 g chopped cilantro

1. Combine the tomatoes, onion, lime juice, garlic, and chipotle. Taste and season with salt and pepper. Refrigerate at least 4 and up to 24 hours before serving.

2. Mix the cilantro into the pico de gallo just before serving.

Tomatillo Salsa

YIELD: 32 FL OZ/960 ML

1 lb 4 oz/567 g tomatillos

5 oz/142 g jalapeño, trimmed, seeded, deribbed, and coarsely chopped

4 large garlic cloves, bruised

8 fl oz/240 mL water

Salt, to taste

Ground black pepper, to taste

1 bunch cilantro, cleaned and stemmed

1. Cut the tomatillos into wedges and place in a saucepan with the jalapeño, garlic, and water.

2. Cover and bring to a boil, reduce to a simmer, and cook for about 20 minutes, or until the tomatillos are olive green in color.

3. Put the tomatillo mixture into a food processor and process until fully blended. Taste the mixture to check the heat and adjust the seasoning with salt. Cool slightly.

4. After the mixture is cool, add the cilantro to the processor and pulse to chop and combine. Add salt and pepper to taste.

Pesto

YIELD: 32 FL OZ/960 ML

5 oz/142 g pine nuts, toasted

1 oz/28 g minced garlic

12 oz/340 g basil leaves

7 oz/198 g Parmesan cheese, grated

12 fl oz/360 mL olive oil

1 oz/28 g salt

2 tsp/4 g ground black pepper

1. Combine the pine nuts, garlic, basil, and Parmesan in a food processor fitted with a metal chopping blade. Process to blend.

2. Add the olive oil with the processor running and process until smooth. Season with the salt and pepper.

Mint Pesto Sauce

YIELD: 32 FL OZ/960 ML

2½ oz/71 g mint leaves

1¾ oz/50 g parsley, chopped

3 oz/85 g Parmesan cheese, grated

3¾ fl oz/113 mL olive oil

2¼ oz/64 g pine nuts or walnuts

1 fl oz/30 mL lemon juice

4 garlic cloves, chopped

½ tsp/2.50 g salt, and as needed

¼ tsp/0.50 g ground black pepper

4¼ oz/120 g sour cream

1. In a food processor or blender, combine the mint, parsley, Parmesan, oil, nuts, lemon juice, garlic, salt, and pepper.

2. Process until a coarse paste forms. Add the sour cream and blend until fully incorporated.

3. Use at once, or cover and refrigerate up to 3 days.

Sun-Dried Tomato Pesto

YIELD: 32 FL OZ/960 ML

1 oz/28 g basil leaves

6 oz/170 g sun-dried tomatoes in oil, drained and chopped

6 garlic cloves

2 oz/57 g Parmesan cheese, grated

2 oz/57 g pine nuts, toasted

12 fl oz/360 mL olive oil

Salt, to taste

Ground black pepper, to taste

1. Combine the basil, tomatoes, garlic, Parmesan, and pine nuts in a food processor and pulse until the ingredients are evenly chopped.

2. With the processor running, add the olive oil and purée to an even-textured paste. Season to taste with salt and pepper.

Cocktail Sauce

YIELD: 32 FL OZ/960 ML

1 lb ¾ oz/475 g chili sauce

1 lb ¾ oz/475 g ketchup

Juice of 1 lemon

1 oz/28 g sugar

2 tsp/10 mL Tabasco sauce

2 tsp/10 mL Worcestershire sauce

2¼ oz/64 g horseradish

1. Combine all ingredients thoroughly.

2. Use the sauce immediately, or cover and refrigerate. After storage, stir the sauce and adjust seasoning if necessary before serving.

Cumberland Sauce

YIELD: 32 FL OZ/960 ML

2 oranges

2 lemons

1 oz/28 g minced shallots

1 lb 10¾ oz/758 g currant jelly

1 tbsp/6 g dry mustard

12 fl oz/360 mL ruby port wine

1 tsp/5 g salt

Small pinch cayenne

Small pinch ground ginger

1. Remove the zest from the oranges and lemons and cut into julienne. Juice the oranges and lemons.

2. Blanch the shallots and zest in boiling water; allow the water to return to a boil and strain immediately.

3. Combine all ingredients. Simmer for 15 to 20 minutes, until reduced by one-third. Refrigerate immediately.

Asian-Style Dipping Sauce

YIELD: 32 FL OZ/960 ML

16 fl oz/480 mL soy sauce

8 fl oz/240 mL white vinegar

8 fl oz/240 mL water

4 garlic cloves, minced

4 green onions, minced

1 oz/28 g minced ginger

2 tsp/4 g dry mustard

1 tsp/5 mL hot bean paste

3 oz/85 g honey

1. Combine all ingredients thoroughly.

2. Use the sauce immediately, or cover and refrigerate. After storage, stir the sauce and adjust seasoning if necessary before serving.

Orange-Jalapeño Sauce

YIELD: 32 FL OZ/960 ML

1 lb 12 oz/794 g orange marmalade

8 fl oz/240 mL ruby port wine

4 fl oz/120 mL lemon juice

2 jalapeños, minced

2 tbsp/12 g chili powder

1 oz/28 g minced shallots

2 tsp/10 mL soy sauce

1 tsp/2 g ground cumin

2 garlic cloves, minced

1. Simmer all ingredients for 10 to 15 minutes.

2. Cool to room temperature. Use the sauce immediately, or cover and refrigerate.

Tempura Dipping Sauce

YIELD: 32 FL OZ/960 ML

20 fl oz/600 mL water

10 fl oz/300 mL soy sauce

½ oz/14 g minced ginger

3 fl oz/90 mL mirin (sweet rice wine)

3 tbsp/9 g bonito flakes

Combine all ingredients. Let the flavors blend for at least 1 hour before serving.

Peanut Sauce

YIELD: 32 FL OZ/960 ML

1 lb/454 g peanut butter

1½ oz/43 g minced jalapeño

2 oz/57 g garlic, minced

1 oz/28 g sugar

¼ tsp/0.50 g cayenne

8 fl oz/240 mL lime juice

8 fl oz/240 mL soy sauce

8 fl oz/240 mL peanut oil

8 fl oz/240 mL water

1 oz/28 g chopped cilantro

GARNISH

Chopped, toasted peanuts

1. Combine the peanut butter, jalapeño, garlic, sugar, cayenne, lime juice, soy sauce, oil, and water in a small saucepan. Heat over medium heat, stirring frequently, until the sauce comes to a boil.

2. Reduce the heat to low and simmer for 2 to 3 minutes. Adjust the consistency with water. Remove from heat and stir in the cilantro.

3. Garnish with chopped, toasted peanuts and serve warm with saté.

Guacamole

YIELD: 32 FL OZ/960 ML

The original Aztec name for the avocado, the primary ingredient in guacamole, was *ahuacatl*.

10 avocados, halved, pitted, and peeled

Juice of 2 limes

7 oz/198 g diced tomato (optional)

1 jalapeño, seeded and minced (optional)

1 bunch green onions, sliced

3 tbsp/9 g chopped cilantro

1 tsp/5 mL Tabasco sauce

Salt, to taste

Ground black pepper, to taste

1. Push the avocados through a medium-coarse screen.

2. Combine all ingredients thoroughly. Taste for seasoning and adjust with lime juice and salt and pepper.

3. Refrigerate the guacamole in a tightly covered storage container. It is best to make guacamole the same day it is to be served.

Roasted Eggplant Dip with Mint (Baba Ghanoush)

YIELD: 32 FL OZ/960 ML

4 lb/1.81 kg eggplants, cut in half length-wise

Salt, to taste

Ground black pepper, to taste

2 fl oz/60 mL olive oil

3 shallots, minced

3 fl oz/90 mL lemon juice

4 oz/113 g tahini

1 oz/28 g chopped flat-leaf parsley leaves

½ oz/14 g chopped mint

2 garlic cloves, minced

Harissa (page 473), as needed

1. Season the eggplant with salt and pepper and lightly coat the cut faces with some of the olive oil. Roast cut side down on a sheet pan in a preheated 375°F/191°C oven until soft, 30 to 40 minutes. Cool to room temperature; scoop out the flesh and discard the seeds.

2. While the eggplant is roasting, macerate the shallots in the lemon juice with ¼ tsp/1.25 g salt.

3. Combine the roasted eggplant and macerated shallots with the remaining olive oil, the tahini, and parsley.

4. Season with mint, garlic, salt, pepper, and harissa. Chop the dip coarsely by hand or purée smooth.

Hummus

YIELD: 32 FL OZ/960 ML

1 lb 8 oz/680 g cooked chickpeas, drained

4 oz/113 g tahini (sesame paste)

1½ fl oz/45 mL lemon juice, or to taste

2 fl oz/60 mL extra-virgin olive oil

4 garlic cloves, minced, or to taste

1 tbsp/15 g salt

Ground black pepper, to taste

Combine all ingredients. Purée in a food processor (in batches, if necessary), adding water to thin if needed. Adjust seasoning with lemon juice and garlic (see photo on page 37).

CHEF'S NOTE: Hummus can be passed through a drum sieve for a very smooth texture.

Tapenade

YIELD: 32 FL OZ/960 ML

12 oz/340 g Niçoise olives, pitted

8 oz/227 g black olives, pitted

4 oz/113 g salt-packed anchovy fillets, rinsed and dried

3 oz/85 g capers, rinsed

2 oz/57 g garlic, minced

Ground black pepper, to taste

Lemon juice, to taste

Olive oil, to taste

Chopped herbs, such as oregano or basil, to taste

1. In a food processor, combine the olives, anchovies, capers, garlic, and pepper. Incorporate the lemon juice and oil slowly. Blend until chunky and easily spread. Do not overmix; the tapenade should have texture and identifiable bits of olive.

2. Adjust seasoning and finish with the herbs (see photo on page 37).

Muhammara

YIELD: 32 FL OZ/960 ML

This spicy-hot sauce made with peppers, walnuts, and pomegranate molasses, originated in Aleppo in Syria. Pomegranate molasses is produced by cooking ripe pomegranates and sugar to a thick, jamlike consistency. Muhammara is best when made four or five days in advance and held chilled to allow the flavor to develop fully.

1 lb 8 oz/680 g red peppers

1½ oz/43 g coarsely ground walnuts

½ oz/14 g fresh white bread crumbs

Juice of 1 lemon, or to taste

1 oz/28 g pomegranate molasses

¼ tsp/1 g prepared red chili paste

Salt, to taste

½ fl oz/15 mL olive oil

¼ tsp/0.50 g ground cumin

1. Roast the peppers. Peel, seed, and set them aside to drain in a colander.

2. Process the walnuts and bread crumbs in a food processor until finely ground. Add the peppers, lemon juice, and pomegranate molasses; purée until smooth and creamy. Add the chili paste and salt to taste. Chill at least overnight before serving.

3. When ready to serve, decorate with a drizzle of olive oil and a light dusting of cumin.

Hazelnut Romesco Sauce

YIELD: 32 FL OZ/960 ML

This is a rich and flavorful sauce for use with a variety of foods, including fish, lamb chops, and such vegetables as beets, potatoes, asparagus, green beans, grilled baby leeks, and green onions.

4 dried anchos	¾ oz/21 g Spanish paprika
4 Marinated Roasted Peppers (page 94)	½ tsp/1 g cayenne
10 fl oz/300 mL olive oil	4 oz/113 g tomato paste
6 garlic cloves, minced	1 lb/454 g ground, roasted hazelnuts
2 fl oz/60 mL red wine vinegar	Salt, to taste

1. Place the anchos in a small saucepan and cover with water. Bring to a boil, then turn off the heat and let steep for 20 minutes.

2. Combine the reconstituted anchos, roasted peppers, olive oil, garlic, vinegar, paprika, cayenne, tomato paste, and hazelnuts in a food processor. Purée to a smooth consistency. Allow the sauce to rest overnight to develop full flavor. Season with salt before serving.

CHEF'S NOTE: Hazelnut Romesco Sauce should be made the day before it is to be served.

Garlic and Parsley Compound Butter

YIELD: 1 LB/454 G

1 oz/28 g garlic, coarsely chopped	1 tsp/5 g salt
1½ bunches parsley, without stems	1 lb/454 g butter, cold, cut into small dice

1. Place the garlic, parsley, and salt in a food processor fitted with a blade attachment and pulse until the ingredients are evenly minced and the mixture is well blended.

2. Place the butter and the garlic-parsley mixture in a mixer fitted with a paddle attachment. Blend on medium speed until the butter is softened and the mixture is well blended and light green in color.

3. Press the compound butter into a ramekin or shape it into a log. Cover with plastic wrap and refrigerate or freeze until needed.

Red Pepper Coulis

YIELD: 32 FL OZ/960 ML

4 lb to 4 lb 8 oz/1.81 to 2.04 kg red peppers, diced	12 fl oz/360 mL dry white wine
2 oz/57 g minced shallots	12 fl oz/360 mL Chicken Stock (page 529)
4 fl oz/120 mL olive oil	Salt, to taste

1. Sweat the peppers and shallots in the olive oil until they are tender.

2. Deglaze with white wine.

3. Add the stock and reduce the liquid to approximately half its original volume.

4. Place the mixture in a food processor and purée until smooth. Season with salt.

ROASTED RED PEPPER COULIS: Roast, peel, and seed the peppers before preparing the coulis.

Chaud-Froid Sauce

YIELD: 32 FL OZ/960 ML

16 fl oz/480 mL Velouté (page 532)

12 fl oz/360 mL Aspic Gelée (page 57), warmed to 110°F/43°C

4 fl oz/120 mL heavy cream

2 tsp/10 g kosher salt

¼ tsp/0.50 g ground white pepper

1. Bring the velouté to a simmer and combine with the aspic.

2. Add the cream, salt, and pepper. Strain into a bowl set over an ice bath.

3. Cool to coating consistency and use as needed.

CHEF'S NOTE: Béchamel may be substituted for the Velouté.

Apricot-Ancho Barbecue Sauce

YIELD: 32 FL OZ/960 ML

6 oz/170 g bacon, diced

6 oz/170 g onion, diced

1 garlic clove, minced

4 oz/113 g dried apricots

7 oz/198 g ketchup

2 fl oz/60 mL malt vinegar

2 fl oz/60 mL orange juice

6 oz/170 g dark brown sugar

2 anchos, diced

1 tsp/2 g paprika

1 tsp/2 g dry mustard

1 tsp/5 mL Tabasco sauce

1 tsp/2 g cayenne

Salt, to taste

Ground black pepper, to taste

1. Sauté the bacon until almost crisp. Add the onion and sauté until browned. Add the garlic and sauté another minute.

2. Add the remaining ingredients. Simmer until the apricots are soft. Purée in a blender. Reheat and adjust seasoning with salt and pepper.

3. The sauce can be used cold or warm and can be stored, covered, up to 1 week.

Barbecue Sauce for Lamb Tamales

YIELD: 32 FL OZ/960 ML

2 fl oz/60 mL vegetable oil

4 oz/113 g onion, finely diced

1 tbsp/9 g minced garlic

1 tbsp/6 g dry mustard

1 oz/28 g dark chili powder

2 tbsp/12 g ground cumin

2 tbsp/12 g ground coriander

1 tbsp/6 g dried Mexican oregano

2 chipotles in adobo sauce

32 fl oz/960 mL plum tomatoes, seeded and coarsely chopped

1 fl oz/30 mL sherry vinegar

1 oz/28 g molasses

10 oz/283 g ketchup

1 fl oz/30 mL Worcestershire sauce

4 fl oz/120 mL Chicken Stock (page 529)

1. Heat the oil in a saucepan over medium-high heat. Add the onion and sauté, stirring from time to time, until lightly caramelized and tender, 5 to 6 minutes. Add the garlic and sauté until aromatic, about 1 minute.

2. Add the mustard, chili powder, cumin, coriander, and oregano and sauté briefly.

3. Add the chipotles, tomatoes, vinegar, molasses, ketchup, Worcestershire sauce, and stock. Bring to a simmer over medium heat. Adjust the heat as necessary and simmer until flavorful, about 1 hour. Stir and skim the sauce as it simmers. Strain.

4. The sauce is ready to use at this point, or it may be properly cooled and stored under refrigeration for up to 1 week.

Aspic Gelée

YIELD: 1 GAL/3.84 L

The classic method for preparing an aspic gelée calls for a very strong and extremely gelatinous stock made by adding veal shank and calves' feet to a standard stock as it simmers. Today we use powdered gelatin or gelatin sheets, which act in the same way as the high percentage of cartilage in the shank and feet.

CLARIFICATION

1 lb/454 g Mirepoix (page 522)

3 lb/1.36 kg ground beef

10 egg whites, beaten

12 oz/340 g tomato concassé

1 gal/3.84 L stock (see Chef's Note)

1 Standard Sachet d'Épices (page 523)

1 tsp/5 g kosher salt

Ground white pepper, as needed

Gelatin powder (see Table 2-1, page 23), as needed

1. Mix the ingredients for the clarification and blend with the stock. Mix well.

2. Bring the mixture to a slow simmer, stirring frequently until a raft forms.

3. Add the sachet d'épices and simmer for 45 minutes, or until the appropriate flavor and clarity are achieved. Baste the raft occasionally.

4. Strain the consommé; season with salt and pepper to taste.

5. Soften the gelatin in cold water, then melt over simmering water. Add to the cooled clarified stock. Refrigerate until needed. Warm as necessary for use.

CHEF'S NOTE: Choose an appropriate stock, depending on the intended use. For example, if the aspic is to be used to coat a seafood item, prepare a lobster stock and use ground fish for the clarification.

PORT WINE GELÉE: Replace half of the stock with ruby port wine.

Cucumber Granité

YIELD: 32 FL OZ/960 ML, OR 8 SERVINGS [2 OZ/57 G EACH]

1 lb 8 oz/680 g cucumbers, peeled and seeded

1½ fl oz/45 mL white wine vinegar

⅔ oz/19 g sugar

¾ oz/21 g pasteurized egg white, lightly beaten

1. Purée the cucumbers in a blender until very smooth.

2. Place the cucumber purée in a bowl with the vinegar, sugar, and egg white and stir until combined.

3. Pour the mixture into a hotel pan and allow it to freeze for at least 3 hours. To serve, scrape a kitchen spoon over the surface and shape into quenelles or balls. Serve at once.

Celery Granité

YIELD: 32 FL OZ/960 ML, OR 8 SERVINGS [2 OZ/57 G EACH]

2 lb/907 g celery

1½ fl oz/45 mL white wine vinegar

⅔ oz/19 g sugar

¾ oz/21 g pasteurized egg white, lightly beaten

1. Trim the celery, cut into dice, and juice or purée in a blender until liquid. Strain through a fine sieve to remove fibers.

2. Place the celery purée in a bowl with the vinegar, sugar, and egg white and stir until combined.

3. Pour the mixture into a hotel pan and allow it to freeze for at least 3 hours. To serve, scrape a kitchen spoon over the surface and shape into quenelles or balls. Serve at once.

Lime Granité

YIELD: 32 FL OZ/960 ML

32 fl oz/960 mL water

1 lb/454 g sugar

Zest of 4 limes, finely minced

4 fl oz/120 mL lime juice

Combine all ingredients in a shallow pan. Freeze the mixture for 3 hours or until firm, stirring every 25 minutes.

Gazpacho Andalusia

YIELD: 1 GAL/3.84 L, OR 20 SERVINGS (6 FL OZ/180 ML EACH)

1 lb 8 oz/680 g tomatoes, cored and diced

1 lb 4 oz/567 g cucumbers, peeled and diced

10 oz/283 g green peppers, seeded and diced

10 oz/283 g red peppers, seeded and diced

1 lb/454 g onions, sliced

1 lb 4 oz/567 g crustless white bread, diced

24 fl oz/720 mL tomato juice

¼ cup/60 mL tomato purée

4 garlic cloves, mashed

½ tsp/2.50 g minced jalapeño

2½ fl oz/75 mL olive oil

3 fl oz/90 mL white wine vinegar

2 tsp/10 g salt

1 tsp/2 g ground black pepper

4 oz/113 g Garlic-Flavored Croutons (page 549)

1. Reserve about 1 oz/28 g each of the tomatoes, cucumbers, peppers, and onions for garnish.

2. Soak the bread cubes in the tomato juice.

3. Place the mixture in a food processor. Purée the soaked bread with the diced vegetables, tomato purée, garlic, jalapeño, olive oil, and vinegar.

4. Season with salt and pepper; chill.

5. Serve with a garnish of the reserved diced vegetables and croutons on the side.

Gazpacho Southwest Style

YIELD: 1 GAL/3.84 L, OR 20 SERVINGS (6 FL OZ/180 ML EACH)

1 lb/454 g Vidalia onions, sliced thick, grilled

1 lb/454 g green peppers, grilled, peeled, and seeded

1 lb/454 g red peppers, grilled, peeled, and seeded

1 jalapeño, grilled, peeled, and seeded

1 lb/454 g eggplant, peeled, sliced, and grilled

3 lb/1.36 kg tomatoes, halved and grilled

1 lb/454 g tomatillos, peeled, halved, and grilled

1 lb/454 g seedless cucumbers, peeled

1 head roasted garlic, flesh only (page 543)

2 tsp/2 g chopped marjoram

½ oz/14 g chopped cilantro

4 fl oz/120 mL lime juice

12 fl oz/360 mL olive oil

8 fl oz/240 mL red wine vinegar

32 fl oz/960 mL tomato juice

1 oz/28 g salt

2 tsp/10 mL Tabasco sauce

1. Press the grilled vegetables, cucumbers, garlic, and herbs through the fine plate of a grinder.

2. Whisk together the remaining ingredients and add to the ground vegetables to taste.

3. Stir well; refrigerate. Adjust seasoning before serving if necessary.

PRESENTATION IDEAS: Garnish with julienned corn or flour tortillas that have been baked or fried and dusted with chili powder or ground toasted cumin seeds.

Chilled Cucumber Soup with Dill, Leeks, and Shrimp

YIELD: 1 GAL/3.84 L, OR 20 SERVINGS (6 FL OZ/180 ML EACH)

1 lb 4 oz/567 g shrimp (26/30 count)

64 fl oz/1.92 L Shellfish Stock (page 530)

SOUP BASE

1 lb/454 g yellow onions, diced

1 lb/454 g celery, diced

2 oz/57 g butter

6 lb/2.72 kg cucumbers, peeled, seeded, and diced

1 oz/28 g arrowroot

1 lb 9½ oz/723 g sour cream

8 fl oz/240 mL heavy cream

1 bunch dill, chopped

¾ oz/21 g salt

1 tsp/2 g ground white pepper

Tabasco sauce, to taste

Juice of 3 lemons, or to taste

GARNISH

2 cucumbers, peeled, seeded, and finely diced

4 oz/113 g leeks, cut into julienne and fried until crisp

¼ bunch dill sprigs

1. Poach the shrimp in the stock. Cut in half lengthwise and reserve for garnish. Reserve the stock.

2. Sauté the onions and celery in the butter until translucent.

3. Add the cucumbers and reserved stock and simmer for 30 minutes.

4. Purée in a blender and strain through a sieve. Thicken with arrowroot. Return to a boil. Remove from the heat and cool to 40°F/4°C.

5. To finish the soup, blend 16 fl oz/480 mL of the soup base mixture with the sour cream, heavy cream, and dill. Add this to the remaining soup base mixture. Season with salt, pepper, Tabasco, and lemon juice.

6. Garnish individual servings of the soup with the reserved shrimp, the diced cucumbers,, fried leeks, and dill sprigs.

Cantaloupe Soup with Lime Granité

YIELD: 1 GAL/3.84 L, OR 20 SERVINGS (6 FL OZ/180 ML EACH)

3 lb/1.36 kg diced cantaloupe

Juice of 4 oranges

Juice of 3 lemons

48 fl oz/1.44 L sparkling water

½ oz/14 g grated orange zest

½ oz/14 g grated lemon zest

1¼ oz/35 g cornstarch

5 oz/142 g sugar, or as needed

GARNISH

12 oz/340 g small melon balls

32 fl oz/960 mL Lime Granité (page 59)

1. Purée the cantaloupe and orange juice in a blender and reserve under refrigeration.

2. Bring the lemon juice, water, and zests to a boil. Thicken with cornstarch and chill.

3. Add the melon purée to the chilled lemon juice mixture and season with sugar to taste.

4. Add the melon garnish to the soup, and serve with approximately 1½ fl oz/45 mL lime granité per serving.

Cold Roasted Tomato and Basil Soup

YIELD: 1 GAL/3.84 L, OR 20 SERVINGS (6 FL OZ/180 ML EACH)

4 oz/113 g garlic, minced

1 fl oz/30 mL olive oil

1 lb/454 g celery, chopped

1 lb 8 oz/680 g onions, chopped

4¾ oz/135 g leeks, white part only, chopped

3 lb/1.36 kg Roasted Plum Tomatoes (page 544)

64 fl oz/1.92 L Vegetable Stock (page 530) or tomato water (Step 1, page 71)

4 oz/113 g basil

2 bay leaves

1 tsp/5 g salt

¼ tsp/0.50 g ground black pepper

GARNISH

1 lb/454 g yellow tomatoes, diced

1 oz/28 g basil chiffonade

1. Lightly sauté the garlic in the oil.

2. Add the celery, onions, and leeks and continue to sauté until fragrant.

3. Add the tomatoes, stock, basil, and bay leaves. Simmer 40 minutes, or until the vegetables are tender.

4. Remove the bay leaves and purée the soup in a blender; season with salt and pepper. Chill.

5. Adjust seasoning before service, if necessary. Garnish with yellow tomatoes and basil.

Vichyssoise

Chef Loise Diat of the Ritz Carlton is credited with creating Vichyssoise. This recipe is adapted from one featured in Chef Diat's book, *Cooking à la Ritz* (Lippincott, 1941).

1 lb 4 oz/567 g leeks, white part only, chopped fine

1 onion, minced

1½ fl oz/45 mL vegetable oil

1 sachet containing 4 cloves, 4 parsley stems, 3 peppercorns, and 1 bay leaf

2 lb 8 oz/1.13 kg diced potatoes

80 fl oz/2.40 L Chicken Stock (page 529)

24 fl oz/720 mL half-and-half, chilled

1 bunch chives, snipped

2 tsp/10 g salt

¼ tsp/0.50 g ground white pepper

1. Sweat the leeks and onion in the oil until tender and translucent.

2. Add the sachet, potatoes, and stock. Bring to a full boil, then reduce heat and simmer until the potatoes begin to fall apart.

3. Remove and discard the sachet. Place the mixture in a food processor and purée. Cool rapidly.

4. To finish the soup for service, add the half-and-half, fold in the chives, and season to taste with salt and pepper.

Cold Carrot Soup

YIELD: 1 GAL/3.84 L, OR 20 SERVINGS (6 FL OZ/180 ML EACH)

This brilliantly colored bisque calls for carrot juice. You can purchase carrot juice or make your own using a juice extractor. The soup should have a strong fresh carrot flavor, enhanced but not overpowered by the orange juice.

1 oz/28 g minced shallots	2 fl oz/60 mL white wine
2 garlic cloves, minced	½ tsp/1 g ground cardamom
¾ oz/21 g minced ginger, or to taste	32 fl oz/960 mL orange juice
4 oz/113 g minced onion	7 oz/198 g yogurt
1½ oz/43 g butter	16 fl oz/480 mL carrot juice
3 lb 8 oz/1.59 kg carrots, sliced thinly	1 oz/28 g salt
80 fl oz/2.40 L Vegetable Stock (page 530)	

1. Sauté the shallots, garlic, ginger, and onion in the butter.

2. Add the carrots, stock, wine, cardamom, and orange juice; simmer for 30 minutes or until the carrots are tender.

3. Place the mixture in a food processor and purée to a smooth texture; chill.

4. Finish with yogurt. Thin with carrot juice. Season with salt just before service.

CHEF'S NOTES: Soup servings can be garnished with a dollop of whipped cream, chives, and carrot chips. Fried ginger chips make a spicy garnish.

Chilled Potato Herb Soup with Lobster

YIELD: 1 GAL/3.84 L, OR 20 SERVINGS (6 FL OZ/180 ML EACH)

Like the recipe for Vichyssoise, which inspired this elegant reinterpretation, a delicate purée of potatoes and leeks is the foundation of this soup. The lobster garnish could easily be omitted, or replaced by a scattering of finely julienned and fried leeks.

4 oz/113 g medium diced leeks, light green and white parts

2 oz/57 g butter

1 lb 4 oz/567 g thinly sliced potatoes

96 fl oz/2.88 L Shellfish Stock (page 530)

8 fl oz/240 mL heavy cream

1 tsp/5 mL Worcestershire sauce

1 fl oz/30 mL dry sherry

1½ tsp/7.50 g salt

GARNISH

1 lb/454 g cooked lobster meat, cut into medium dice

½ oz/14 g chopped chives

½ oz/14 g chopped tarragon leaves

½ oz/14 g chopped chervil

½ oz/14 g chopped flat-leaf parsley leaves

1. Sauté the leeks in the butter until soft, about 5 minutes. Add the potatoes and stock; simmer over low heat until tender, about 20 minutes. Purée through a food mill or in a blender.

2. Finish with the heavy cream. Season to taste with the Worcestershire, sherry, and salt.

3. Garnish with the diced lobster and chopped herbs just before service.

Fresh Spring Pea Purée with Mint

YIELD: 1 GAL/3.84 L, OR 20 SERVINGS (6 FL OZ/180 ML EACH)

This soup has a delicate texture and flavor, making it suitable for elegant menus in the spring and early summer. Cook the soup just until the peas are tender for the freshest green color in the finished soup.

8 oz/227 g leeks, minced

8 oz/227 g onions, minced

1 fl oz/30 mL vegetable oil

14 oz/397 g shredded green leaf lettuce

2 lb 12 oz/1.25 kg fresh peas

80 fl oz/2.40 L Vegetable Stock
(page 530)

1 sachet containing 6 chervil stems, 6 parsley stems, and 6 white peppercorns

10 to 12 fl oz/300 to 360 mL light cream or half-and-half

½ oz/14 g salt

¼ tsp/0.50 g ground white pepper

GARNISH

2 tbsp/6 g fine chiffonade mint
(or 20 chervil pluches)

1. Sauté the leeks and onions in the oil.

2. Add the lettuce and peas and smother briefly.

3. Add the stock and the sachet; bring to a boil.

4. Reduce the heat and simmer until the vegetables are very tender.

5. Remove and discard the sachet. Purée the mixture in a blender until smooth. Chill thoroughly.

6. To finish for service, add the chilled cream to the cold soup. Season to taste with the salt and pepper. Fold in the mint, or garnish each portion with a chervil pluche.

Chilled Cauliflower Soup with Sevruga Caviar

YIELD: 1 GAL/3.84 L, OR 20 SERVINGS (6 FL OZ/180 ML EACH)

In this presentation, cauliflower reveals its delicious nutty side, offering a perfect contrast to the slight bite of the crème fraîche and the briny savor of fine caviar. The caviar garnish can easily be omitted to make a more modest, but still delicious, soup.

6 lb/2.72 kg cauliflower, chopped coarsely (5 heads)

32 fl oz/960 mL half-and-half

32 fl oz/960 mL milk

Pinch ground nutmeg

1 tbsp /15 mL lemon juice

2 tsp/6 g minced lemon zest

¾ oz/21 g kosher salt

½ tsp/1 g ground white pepper

GARNISH

4 oz/113 g Crème Fraîche (page 351), whipped

1 oz/28 g Sevruga caviar

2 tbsp/6 g minced chives

1. Place the cauliflower in enough salted water to cover completely; simmer until tender, about 15 minutes.

2. Purée the cauliflower in a blender, adding cooking liquid as needed to assist in forming a thick purée.

3. Add the half-and-half, milk, nutmeg, lemon juice, and lemon zest. Blend well and chill.

4. Season with salt and pepper after the soup is cold. Garnish each serving with a dollop of crème fraîche, a bit of caviar, and a sprinkle of chives.

Caribbean Coconut and Pineapple Soup

YIELD: 1 GAL/3.84 L, OR 20 SERVINGS (6 FL OZ/180 ML EACH)

48 fl oz/1.44 L coconut milk

32 fl oz/960 mL milk

16 fl oz/480 mL heavy cream or half-and-half

LIAISON

16 fl oz/480 mL half-and-half

6 egg yolks

¾ oz/21 g arrowroot

48 fl oz/1.44 L pineapple juice

4 fl oz/120 mL Simple Syrup (page 540), or to taste

1 fl oz/30 mL lime juice, or to taste

GARNISH

13 oz/369 g diced pineapple

2 fl oz/60 mL light rum

1. Bring the coconut milk, milk, and half-and-half to a simmer.

2. Combine the liaison ingredients and temper. Add to the simmering mixture and continue to cook over low heat until thickened, 4 to 5 minutes. Chill thoroughly.

3. Add the pineapple juice, then adjust flavor with the simple syrup and lime juice.

4. Macerate the pineapple in the rum and garnish the soup at service.

PRESENTATION IDEAS: Garnish with Plantain Chips (page 486) that have been fried or baked. Serve in a glass dish on shaved ice with a skewer of pineapple chunks alternating with sliced bananas rolled in toasted coconuts.

CHEF'S NOTE: Rum may be reduced or omitted as desired.

Chilled Tomato Saffron Soup
with Shellfish

YIELD: 1 GAL/3.84 L, OR 20 SERVINGS (6 FL OZ/180 ML EACH)

9 lb/4.08 kg tomatoes

96 fl oz/2.88 L Shellfish Stock (page 530)

¾ tsp/0.50 g saffron, crushed

Zest and juice of 3 oranges

¾ tsp/3.75 g salt

¼ tsp/0.50 g ground black pepper

GARNISH

8 oz/227 g cooked lobster meat, diced

8 oz/227 g cooked scallops, diced

2 oz/57 g cantaloupe, scooped into pea-sized balls

2 oz/57 g honeydew, scooped into pea-sized balls

4 fl oz/120 mL diced yellow tomato

4 fl oz/120 mL diced red tomato

3 tbsp/9 g fine chiffonade basil

½ oz/14 g fine chiffonade mint

1. Chop the tomatoes, salt well, and hang in cheesecloth overnight. Reserve the collected tomato water.

2. Combine the stock with the saffron, orange juice, and zest; bring to a simmer. Season with salt and pepper and strain through several layers of cheesecloth. Add the reserved tomato water and chill thoroughly.

3. Garnish with the lobster, scallops, melon balls, tomatoes, basil, and mint at service.

CHEF'S NOTES: Prepare the Shellfish Stock on page 530 using lobster shells. Be sure the stock is very clear.

Add 1 oz/28 g gelatin solution (see page 23) along with the tomato water in Step 2 for a lightly jellied version of this soup.

Chilled Clear Borscht

YIELD: 1 GAL/3.84 L, OR 20 SERVINGS (6 FL OZ/180 ML EACH)

8 lb/3.63 kg raw beets, peeled and grated or chopped

1 gal 32 oz/4.8 L White Duck Stock (page 529)

2½ fl oz/75 mL red wine vinegar

½ oz/14 g sugar

32 fl oz/960 mL sweet white wine, such as Riesling

1¼ oz/35 g kosher salt

1 tsp/2 g ground white pepper

GARNISH

8 oz/227 g cooked beets, cut into julienne

4 oz/113 g Smoked Duck (page 203), breast only, cut into julienne

4 oz/113 g radishes, cut into julienne

1. Simmer the beets gently in the stock and vinegar for 1 hour.

2. Strain through doubled cheesecloth or a paper coffee filter; add the sugar, wine, salt, and pepper to taste. Chill.

3. Garnish with julienned beets, duck, and radishes at service.

CHEF'S NOTE: Smoked Ham (page 214) can be substituted for the smoked duck.

Infusion of Vegetables

YIELD: 1 GAL/3.84 L, OR 20 SERVINGS (6 FL OZ/180 ML EACH)

Traditional French country cooking boasts a wealth of soups and stews that feature tender and succulent vegetables straight from the garden. Here, baby carrots, petits pois, fresh fava beans, and asparagus tips are presented in a subtly flavored and satisfying vegetable infusion based on leeks and celeriac.

3 lb/1.36 kg red tomatoes, quartered

INFUSION

2 lb/907 g leeks, white and light green parts, sliced

10 oz/283 g sliced celeriac

5 oz/142 g minced shallots

3 oz/85 g minced parsley

1 oz/28 g minced chives

1 gal/3.84 L water, or as needed

3 garlic cloves, minced

2 thyme sprigs

1 bay leaf

1 oz/28 g salt

1½ tsp/3 g ground black pepper

GARNISH

4 oz/113 g baby carrots, sliced on bias

4 oz/113 g petits pois, blanched

4 oz/113 g fresh fava beans, shelled and cooked

4 oz/113 g asparagus tips, parcooked

4 oz/113 g tomatoes, peeled, seeded, and cut into diamond shapes

20 chervil pluches

1. Make a tomato broth by combining the tomatoes with 24 fl oz/720 mL water. Simmer gently for 30 minutes, then strain through a fine sieve or cheesecloth. Chill thoroughly.

2. Make the vegetable infusion by gently simmering the ingredients in 96 fl oz/2.88 L water, covered, for 1 hour. Add a little water to bring the liquid back to its original level, return briefly to a boil, remove from heat, and allow to cool. Strain through a fine sieve or cheesecloth. Chill thoroughly.

3. Mix the tomato broth and the vegetable infusion; adjust seasoning.

4. Toss the garnish vegetables together. At service, garnish each portion with 1 oz/28 g of the mixed vegetables and a chervil pluche.

SALADS

Salads appear on the menu in so many guises and are embraced by today's garde manger with such enthusiasm that one might imagine salads were invented by this generation of chefs. In fact, salads have played a key role throughout culinary history. Fresh concoctions of seasoned herbs and lettuces, known as *herba salata*, were enjoyed by the ancient Greeks and Romans alike. According to legend, the Greek philosopher Aristoxenus was so obsessed with freshness that while the lettuce was still growing he would sprinkle it with vinegar and honey the night before he planned to prepare a salad. We are indebted to the Romans for our very word *salad*, deriving as it does from their word for *salt*.

three

The early European settlers of America also valued salad greens. Thomas Jefferson recorded that the markets of his day supplied the cook with a variety of lettuces, endive, sorrel, corn salad (mâche), and cress. After a long absence from the market, the greens Jefferson favored are again appearing in salads served as appetizers, entrées, accompaniments to other items, and intermezzi. This chapter discusses three major salad categories:

- **GREEN SALADS**

- **SIDE SALADS** made from vegetables, potatoes, grains, pastas, legumes, and fruits

- **COMPOSED SALADS**

Green Salads

By selecting the appropriate greens and pairing them with properly chosen dressings, the chef can create a wide range of salads suitable to several menu needs, from a delicate salad of butterhead with a light lemon vinaigrette served as a first course to an appetizer salad of bitter greens, walnuts, and blue cheese with a sherry vinaigrette.

Salad greens

Commercially prepared salad blends are now available, but chefs can also create their own by combining lettuces from within one category or by selecting from among two or more categories. The greens that are selected determine the character of the salad. Today's garde manger can choose from:

- **MILD GREENS**

- **SPICY GREENS**

- **BITTER GREENS OR CHICORIES**

- **PREPARED MIXES OF GREENS**

- **HERBS AND FLOWERS**

MILD GREENS Mild lettuces can be grouped into four categories (see Figure 3-1):

- **ICEBERG/HEADING:** Crisp heads have closely packed leaves and very mild flavor.

- **BUTTERHEAD:** Loose rosette of soft, thick leaves have a soft, delicate texture and mild flavor; includes Boston, Kentucky Limestone, and Bibb varieties.

- **LOOSE-LEAF:** Open, deeply indented, loose leaves have a delicate flavor and a moderately soft texture; includes red and green leaf lettuce, oak leaf, and lola rosa. Baby varieties are often included in special salad blends.

3-1. Mild greens.   **A.** Boston lettuce.   **B.** Green leaf lettuce.   **C.** Green and red leaf lettuce heads.
D. Romaine lettuce.   **E.** Baby spinach.

- **ROMAINE/COS:** This lettuce grows as a long cylindrical head, with the leaves joined to a core at its base. The outer leaves are heavily ribbed and sometimes savoyed (crinkled). Leaves closer to the center have a milder, sweeter flavor than the outer leaves. The inner leaves, sometimes known as the *heart*, may be used exclusively in some salads. Baby romaine is also featured in mixed greens or specialty blends. The name *Cos* derives from the Greek island of the same name, where some believe this lettuce to have originated.

In addition to the lettuces described above, the mild greens also include mâche (also called *corn salad* and *lamb's lettuce*), some of the spicy greens when they are still young or immature, and baby varieties of various cooking greens and cabbages.

SPICY GREENS Spicy greens have a distinct pepperiness or assertive flavor but are still delicate enough to eat in salads. The younger they are, the less spicy they taste (see Figure 3-2).

The spicy greens include but are not limited to:

- **AMARANTH:** Spinachlike in flavor, amaranth varies in color from green to purple to red.

3-2. Spicy greens. **A.** Arugula. **B.** Baby tat-soi. **C.** Mizuna. **D.** Watercress.

- **ARUGULA (ALSO CALLED *ROCKET* AND *ROQUETTE*):** Taste ranges from mild and nutty to peppery and pungent; best used when leaves are small and narrow.

- **WATERCRESS:** With peppery, small leaves on tender branches, watercress is dark green.

- **MIZUNA:** A Japanese mustard, mizuna has a mild flavor.

- **TAT-SOI:** A flat, black cabbage whose round leaves form an open rosette, with a faint but pleasant cabbagelike taste; used in its very young stages.

BITTER GREENS AND CHICORIES Chicories are heading or loose-leaf greens characterized by a distinctive bittersweet flavor (see Figure 3-3). When young, they may be used in salads. More mature chicories are considered cooking greens. This group includes:

- **BELGIAN ENDIVE:** As endive grows, soil is mounded over the heads to prevent them from turning green; this is known as *blanching* the endive. Belgian endive has white, tight heads with spearlike leaves and a succulent, very crisp texture. Red Belgian endive is a type of radicchio known as *treviso*.

- **DANDELION, MUSTARD, BEET, SWISS CHARD, AND COLLARD GREENS:** These distinctly bitter varieties have dark green, long, narrow leaves, some with white or red ribs. If they are overmature, they may give salads an unpleasant flavor. Beet greens have a tendency to bleed when combined with a dressing.

- **ESCAROLE:** Large heads of greenish-yellow, slightly crumpled leaves are succulent and slightly nutty.

- **CURLY ENDIVE (ALSO CALLED *CHICORY*):** This green has narrow leaves with deeply ridged edges, and an assertive flavor and texture. When very young, it may be sold as *frisée*.

- **FRISÉE:** With fine white to pale green curly leaves, frisée is similar to chicory but with finer, smaller leaves. The flavor is slightly bitter, though generally less intense than curly endive.

3-3. Bitter greens.

A. Belgian endive. **B.** Curly endive. **C.** Frisée.

3-4. Mesclun mix.

- **RADICCHIO:** Sturdy purple-red leaves form a tight head. The flavor is bitter.

- **TREVISO RADICCHIO:** Resembling an elongated loose Belgian endive, this has red streaks or tips and a succulent texture, with a flavor similar to heading radicchio.

PREPARED MIXES OF GREENS The market provides a number of specialty items for salad making. Among the most popular of these are convenient, prewashed, and trimmed mixes of greens. Their ready availability and ease of use have made them popular, even to the point of indiscriminate use. The three most commonly available mixes are:

- **MESCLUN:** This mix of small salad leaves is often found in combination with herbs or flowers (see Figure 3-4). Throughout Provence, where this mix is believed to have originated, seasonal greens of all sorts are paired with herbs and flowers. Today, commercially available mesclun mixes contain blends of various mild, sweet, and peppery greens, with or without a flower or herb component. Different suppliers offer different blends, so it is well worth the time to conduct a taste test.

- **ORIENTAL MIX (OMX):** This mix typically includes a combination of some or all of the following: tat-soi, lola rosa, red oak, arugula, beet greens, Swiss chard, sorrel, amaranth, dill, purslane, mizuna, red mustard, bok choy, red shiso, red fire, sierra, and shungi ku.

- **BABY MIX (BMX):** A generic term for mixes of very young leaves of several varieties, colors, and textures, this is sold both in heads and as prewashed leaves. A typical combination includes lola rosa, tango, baby red oak, baby romaine, and baby green oak.

3-5. Herbs. **A.** Dill. **B.** Parsley. **C.** Basil. **D.** Cilantro.

HERBS AND FLOWERS Some varieties of herbs and flowers are used in salads. Herbs can range from pungent to lightly fragrant, and they can add a wonderful accent to a special dish. Herbs that have a naturally tender texture or soft leaves—young basil, chives, small mint leaves, pluches of chervil or flat-leaf parsley (see Figure 3-5)—are the ones to choose for salads. Flowers and herbs can turn an ordinary salad into something distinctive and beautiful, as long as they are not overdone.

Edible flowers are normally divided into two groups:

- **GARDEN FLOWERS:** Bachelor's buttons, borage, calendula, carnations, fuchsia, geraniums, johnny jump-ups, marigolds, nasturtiums, pansies, primroses, roses, sunflowers, and violets (see Figure 3-6).

- **HERB FLOWERS:** Anise hyssop, arugula, borage, chive, lavender, mustard, oregano, rosemary, sage, and thyme.

3-6. Edible Flowers. **A.** Nasturtium. **B.** Pansies. **C.** Calendula.

Dressing the salad

Place the greens (about 2 oz/57 g, or ¾ cup/180 mL, per serving) in a bowl and ladle a portion of salad dressing over them (1 to 1½ fl oz/30 to 45 mL per serving).
Use a lifting motion to toss the greens and dressing. Tongs, spoons, or, where appropriate, gloved hands can all be used to toss the salad. Each piece of lettuce
should be coated completely but lightly with the dressing. There should be just
enough dressing for the greens; if the dressing pools on the plate, there is too much.

Vinaigrette recipes are in Chapter 2 and include the following options: Basic
Red Wine Vinaigrette, Balsamic Vinaigrette, Vinaigrette Gourmand, Truffle
Vinaigrette, Apple Cider Vinaigrette, Curry Vinaigrette, Chipotle-Sherry
Vinaigrette, Roasted Shallot Vinaigrette, and Mustard-Walnut Vinaigrette. Two
reduced-fat vinaigrettes are Tomato Vinaigrette and Beet Vinaigrette.

Creamy-style salad dressings can be used successfully with green salads.
Recipes for these dressings include Russian Dressing, Green Goddess Dressing,
Creamy Black Pepper Dressing, and Rouquefort Dressing. Two reduced-fat dress-
ings, Maytag Blue Cheese Dressing and Ranch Dressing can also be used.

Caring for salad greens

Nothing is worse than a gritty salad. Salad greens should be kept properly chilled
from the time they arrive until they are ready to be plated. The following guidelines should also be observed when handling salad greens.

3-7. Storing lettuce.

1. RINSE GREENS THOROUGHLY IN PLENTY OF COOL WATER
TO REMOVE ALL TRACES OF DIRT AND SAND. Sturdy greens
may be able to hold up to a spray, but delicate greens, herbs,
and flowers should be gently plunged into and lifted out of the
water repeatedly to remove dirt or sand. The water should be
changed as often as necessary until there are absolutely no
traces of dirt, grit, or sand visible in the rinsing water.

2. DRY GREENS COMPLETELY. Salad dressings cling best to
well-dried greens. In addition, greens that are carefully dried
before they are stored will last longer. Spinners are the most
effective tools to use, either large-scale electric spinners for
volume salad making, or hand baskets. Spinners should be
cleaned and sanitized carefully after each use.

3. STORE CLEANED GREENS IN TUBS OR OTHER CONTAINERS. They should not
be stacked too deep, since their own weight could bruise the leaves. They
should be loosely wrapped or covered with dampened toweling o prevent them
from silting rapidly (see Figure 3-7). Once greens have been cleaned they
should be used within a day or two.

4. CUT OR TEAR THE LETTUCE INTO BITE-SIZED PIECES. Traditional salad-mak-
ing manuals have always called for lettuces to be torn to avoid discoloring,
bruising, or crushing the leaf. Today's knives are not likely to discolor the
leaves, and there is no reason to believe that properly sharpened knives could
bruise the lettuce more than tearing. This is still a matter of personal style and
preference, of course.

Choose from a variety of vegetable garnishes according to the season and your desired presentation: slices or wedges of tomatoes, cucumbers, carrots, radishes, jícama, mushrooms (raw or marinated), olives, peppers, and so forth. In addition to these vegetable garnishes, the chef may also opt to use more unusual ganishes: raw or very lightly blanched asparagus, green peas or beans, pea shoots, sprouts of all sorts. These ingredients may be tossed along with the greens as they are being dressed or marinated separately in a little vinaigrette and used to top the salad.

Adding a crisp component to the salad gives another level of interest, in terms of both flavor and texture. Consider several recipes included in the book, such as the following: Assorted Vegetable Chips (page 486); Pepper Jack and Oregano Crackers (page 487); Cheddar and Walnut Crisps (page 488); Potato Crisps and Parsnip Crisps (page 488); toasted nuts (page 546); and Parmesan Crisps (page 547).

Breads and breadsticks can be served with simple green salads to make them more interesting and satisfying as well: see Focaccia or Grissini (page 540). Sliced peasant-style breads can be served along with the salad, spread with a bit of Tapenade (page 52); or drizzled with one of the flavored oils found in Chapter 2.

Savory granités are another interesting way to garnish some salads. The granité may be based on a variety of fruit or vegetable juices. Cucumber and celery granités (page 58) are good examples.

Side Salads

Vegetable salads

Vegetables for vegetable salads are prepared as required by the specific recipes. Some are simply rinsed and trimmed; others may need to be peeled, seeded, and cut to the appropriate shape. Some vegetables may require an initial blanching to set colors and textures, while others must be fully cooked.

If the salad is to be served raw, the prepared vegetables are simply combined with a vinaigrette or other dressing and allowed to rest long enough for the flavors to marry. When the vegetables are partially or fully cooked, there are two options for applying the dressing. In the first option, the vegetables are drained and combined with the dressing while they are still warm for faster flavor absorption. This works well for root vegetables such as carrots, beets, and parsnips as well as leeks, onions, and potatoes. Some vegetables (especially green vegetables like broccoli or green beans) may discolor if they are combined with an acid in advance; these vegetables should be refreshed and chilled before being added to the dressing. In either case, the vegetables should be thoroughly drained and blotted dry to avoid watering down the dressing.

Potato salads

Potatoes should be cooked until fork tender. Waxy potatoes (Yukon golds or Finnish) hold their shape better after cooking than starchy potatoes (russets or baking potatoes).

The classic American potato salad is a creamy salad, typically dressed with mayonnaise. Other potato salads enjoyed around the world are often dressed with a vinaigrette. In some traditional European-style recipes, the dressing is based on bacon fat, olive oil, stock, or a combination of these ingredients. The key to success with this style of potato salad is to combine the potatoes and dressing while the potatoes are still warm. The dressing is typically brought to a simmer before the potatoes are added for the best finished flavor.

Pasta and grain salads

Grains and pastas for salads should be cooked until tender to the bite, but care should be taken to avoid overcooking. Cooked grains and pasta can still absorb some of the liquid in the dressing and can quickly become soggy.

If a pasta or grain salad is held for later service, be especially careful to check it for seasoning before it is served, because these salads have a tendency to go flat as they sit. Salt and pepper are important seasonings, of course, but others, such as vinegars, herbs, or citrus juices, can give a brighter flavor.

Legume salads

Dried beans should be cooked until they are tender to the bite and allowed to cool in their own cooking liquid. The center should be soft and creamy, and it is even possible that the skins may break open slightly. If a salad is made from a variety of dried beans, it is important that beans with different cooking times be cooked separately to the correct doneness.

Unlike grains and pastas, which might become too soft as they sit in a dressing, beans will not soften any further. In fact, the acid in salad dressings will make the beans tougher, even if they are fully cooked. Bean salads, therefore, should not be dressed and allowed to rest for extended periods. If the salad is used within four hours of preparation, however, there is little significant texture change.

Fruit salads

Different fruits have different characteristics, making some fruit salads fairly sturdy, while others lose quality very rapidly. Fruits that turn brown (apples, pears, and bananas) can be treated with fruit juice to keep them from oxidizing, as long as the flavor of the juice doesn't compete with the other ingredients in the salad. Dilute acidic juices, such as lime, with water.

Mixed fruit salads that include highly perishable fruits can be produced for volume operations by preparing the base from the least perishable fruits. More perishable items, such as raspberries, strawberries, and bananas, can then be combined with smaller batches or individual servings at the last moment, or they can be added as a garnish.

Fresh herbs such as mint, tarragon, basil, and lemon thyme may be added to fruit salads as a garnish. Experiment to determine which herbs work best with the fruits selected for the salad.

Composed Salads

Composed salads are made by carefully arranging items on a plate rather than tossing them together. A main item, such as grilled chicken or shrimp, a portion of cheese or grilled vegetables, and so forth, is often set on a bed of greens. The salad

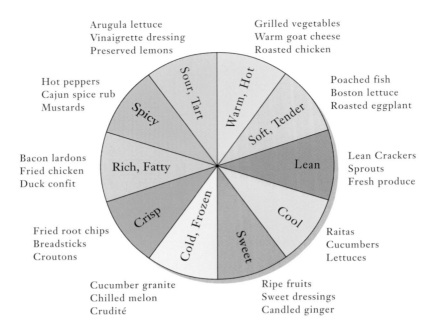

Arugula lettuce
Vinaigrette dressing
Preserved lemons

Grilled vegetables
Warm goat cheese
Roasted chicken

Hot peppers
Cajun spice rub
Mustards

Poached fish
Boston lettuce
Roasted eggplant

Bacon lardons
Fried chicken
Duck confit

Lean Crackers
Sprouts
Fresh produce

Fried root chips
Breadsticks
Croutons

Raitas
Cucumbers
Lettuces

Cucumber granite
Chilled melon
Crudité

Ripe fruits
Sweet dressings
Candled ginger

3-8. Balancing Favors and Textures of Composed Salads.

is garnished and dressed. Some composed salads feature foods that have contrasting colors, flavors, texture, heights, and temperatures. Others are based on a single motif that holds the plate's elements together.

Although no specific rules govern the requirements for a composed salad, the following principles should be kept in mind:

- Consider how well the elements combine. Contrasting flavors are intriguing; conflicting flavors are a disaster.

- Repetition of a color or flavor can be successful if it contributes to the overall dish, but generally, too much of a good thing is simply too much.

- All of the components on the plate should be capable of standing alone. However, the composition should be such that each part is enhanced by being in combination with the others. This produces a more intriguing eating experience than is possible when the components are eaten separately.

- Components should be arranged in such a way that the textures and colors of the foods are most attractive to the eye. The appearance of the plate should be given careful thought.

Warm Salads

Warm salads, known in French as *salades tièdes*, are made by tossing the salad ingredients in a warm dressing, working over medium to low heat. The salad should be just warmed through. Another approach is to use a chilled crisp salad as the bed for hot main items, such as grilled meat or fish.

Spinach Salad with Tangerines and Pomegranate

YIELD: 10 SIDE SALAD SERVINGS

1 lb 4 oz/567 g young, tender spinach leaves, stems removed

10 fl oz/300 mL Tangerine-Pineapple Vinaigrette (page 29)

1 red onion, sliced into paper-thin rings (see Chef's Note)

5 tangerines, segments only

1 pomegranate, seeds only

1. Clean and thoroughly dry the spinach. Portion as necessary for single servings or a larger batch.

2. **Salad Assembly:** Just before serving, whisk the vinaigrette vigorously and reseason. For each portion, toss 2 oz/57 g spinach with 1 fl oz/30 mL vinaigrette. Arrange on chilled plates. Top with onion rings, tangerine segments, and pomegranate seeds. Serve immediately.

CHEF'S NOTE: Place the sliced onion rings in a container of ice water for up to 24 hours to crisp them. This will also mellow the harsh bite of the raw onions, which some people find offensive.

Parson's Garden Salad

YIELD: 10 APPETIZER SERVINGS

This recipe is adapted from one featured on the menu of Michel Guerard, a famous French chef considered one of the great innovators in contemporary cuisine. This dish has been pleasing diners for more than twenty years.

5 oz/142 g mâche

5 oz/142 g frisée lettuce

5 oz/142 g red treviso radicchio

5 oz/142 g watercress leaves

6½ oz/184 g soybean sprouts, blanched and chilled

6 oz/170 g shelled peas, blanched and chilled

2 tbsp/6 g chopped chives

2 tbsp/6 g chopped parsley

GARNISH

16 fl oz/480 mL olive oil

2 garlic cloves, crushed

8 black peppercorns

8½ oz/241 g julienne carrots

6 oz/170 g julienne celeriac

Salt, as needed

10 fl oz/300 mL Vinaigrette Gourmande (page 30)

5 oz/142 g slab bacon, cut into medium dice, cooked crisp

30 quail eggs, poached in red wine and water (see Chef's Note)

1. Clean and thoroughly dry all the lettuces. Combine all mixed greens. Portion as necessary for single servings or larger batch salads. Refrigerate until ready to serve.

2. Up to 2 hours before service, heat the oil, garlic, and peppercorns to 325°F/163°C. Add the carrots and celeriac and fry slowly until very crisp. Drain on absorbent toweling and keep warm. Salt to taste, if desired.

3. **Salad Assembly:** Just before serving, whisk the vinaigrette vigorously and reseason. For each portion, toss 2 oz/57 g mixed greens with 1 fl oz/30 mL vinaigrette. Arrange on chilled plates. Top with fried vegetables and bacon. Add 3 warm, poached quail eggs. Serve immediately.

CHEF'S NOTE: To poach quail eggs, combine 32 fl oz/960 mL red table wine, 32 fl oz/960 mL water, and a pinch of salt. Bring to 200°F/93°C. Carefully crack the eggs into cups and add to poaching liquid. Reduce heat to 170°F/77°C and cook until the eggs are set, 2 to 3 minutes. Remove with a perforated spoon and blot dry before adding to salads. Refrigerate until ready to serve.

Spring Herb Salad

MIXED GREENS

10 oz/283 g baby arugula

5 oz/142 g mizuna

5 oz/142 g baby tat-soi

½ head radicchio, cut into chiffonade

1 bunch flat-leaf parsley, leaves only

2 bunches chervil, separated into pluches

1 bunch chives, sliced ½ in/1 cm long

10 fl oz/300 mL Truffle Vinaigrette (page 28)

Shaved truffle, as needed (optional)

Salt, as needed

Coarse-ground black pepper, as needed

1. Clean and thoroughly dry the mixed greens. Portion as necessary for single servings or larger batch salads. Refrigerate until ready to serve.

2. **Salad Assembly:** Just before serving, whisk the vinaigrette vigorously and reseason. For each portion, toss 2 oz/57 g mixed greens with 1 fl oz/30 mL vinaigrette. Arrange on chilled plates, top with shaved truffles, if desired, and season with salt and pepper. Serve immediately.

CHEF'S NOTE: Other herbs, such as dill, fennel, and tarragon, may be used in place of or in addition to the herbs listed.

Frisée with Walnuts, Apples, Grapes, and Blue Cheese

1 lb 4 oz/567 g frisée lettuce

2 tart apples

10 fl oz/300 mL Apple Cider Vinaigrette (page 31)

5 oz/142 g green grapes, peeled and cut in half lengthwise

2¼ oz/64 g toasted and coarsely chopped walnuts

5 oz/142 g blue cheese, crumbled

1. Clean and thoroughly dry the frisée. Portion as necessary for single servings or larger batch salads. Refrigerate until ready to serve.

2. Just before serving, slice the apples. If necessary, hold the apple slices in acidulated water.

3. **Salad Assembly:** Just before serving, whisk the vinaigrette vigorously and reseason. For each portion, toss 2 oz/57 g frisée with 1 fl oz/30 mL vinaigrette. Arrange on chilled plates. Top with apple slices, grapes, walnuts, and blue cheese. Serve immediately.

Georgia Peanut Salad

YIELD: 10 SERVINGS

DRESSING

3 garlic cloves, minced

1 tbsp/3 g tarragon, finely chopped

1 tbsp/3 g chives, finely chopped

1 tbsp/3 g parsley, finely chopped

½ tsp/1 g ground black pepper

1 oz/28 g brown sugar

3 oz/85 g malt vinegar

6 fl oz/180 mL peanut oil

2 fl oz/60 mL salad oil

1 oz/28 g peanut butter

½ tsp/2.50 g salt

3 splashes Tabasco sauce

SALAD

5 oz/142 g multigrain bread (about 3 cups/720 mL)

1½ oz/43 g olive oil

½ tsp/1.50 g garlic, finely minced (about ½ medium clove)

½ tsp/2.50 g salt

¼ tsp/0.50 g ground black pepper

12½ oz/354 g baby greens

10 oz/283 g peanuts, roasted

10 oz/283 g red seedless grapes, peeled and halved

1. Combine the dressing ingredients thoroughly and adjust seasoning if necessary. Reserve separately.

2. Cut the multigrain bread into ½-in/1-cm cubes.

3. Toss the bread with the olive oil, garlic, salt, and pepper.

4. Toast in a 325°F/163°C oven for 10 to 15 minutes, turning the croutons once, or until golden brown.

5. **Salad Assembly:** For each serving, toss 1¼ oz/35 g greens with about 1 fl oz/30 mL dressing. Arrange the mixed greens on a salad plate. Garnish with croutons, roasted peanuts, and grapes.

Watermelon and Red Onion Salad with Watercress

YIELD: 10 SERVINGS

4 bunches watercress

2 red onions, sliced paper thin

2 fl oz/60 mL white wine vinegar

Salt, as needed

Cracked black pepper, as needed

4 fl oz/120 mL vegetable oil

1 lb 10½ oz/751 g seeded and cubed watermelon

½ oz/14 g roasted pine nuts (optional)

1. Trim the stems of the watercress. Rinse the watercress and dry thoroughly. Keep chilled until ready to assemble the salad.

2. Place the sliced onions in ice water and allow them to soak for at least 2 hours and up to 24 hours in advance.

3. Combine the vinegar, salt, and pepper. Gradually whisk in the oil. Adjust the seasoning with additional salt and pepper if necessary.

4. **Salad Assembly:** For each portion, toss 1½ oz/43 g watercress with ½ fl oz/15 mL dressing. Lift the watercress from the bowl, allowing the dressing to drain back into the bowl. Arrange on a chilled salad plate. Add the watermelon to the bowl and toss or roll until coated with the remaining dressing. Place the watermelon on top of the watercress. Garnish with a few slices of drained red onion and ½ tsp/2 g pine nuts, if desired. Top with a few turns of freshly ground pepper.

Greek Salad with Feta Cheese and Whole Wheat Pita

YIELD: 10 SERVINGS

10 oz/283 g Kalamata olives

16 fl oz/480 mL Lemon-Parsley Vinaigrette (page 30)

2 lb 4 oz/1.02 kg romaine lettuce

10 whole wheat pitas, cut into 8 wedges each

1 lb 4 oz/567 g European cucumbers, peeled, sliced ⅛ in/3 mm thick

1 lb 4 oz/567 g cherry tomatoes, halved

10 oz/283 g yellow peppers, cut into julienne

10 oz/283 g red onions, peeled, sliced ⅛ in/3 mm thick

15 oz/425 g feta cheese, crumbled

1. Drain the olives, mix with 4 fl oz/120 mL vinaigrette, and allow to marinate overnight.

2. Clean the romaine lettuce and partially remove about a third of the stem. Wash and spin dry.

3. Just before serving, whisk the vinaigrette vigorously. Toss 3½ oz/99 g romaine lettuce with 1 fl oz/30 mL vinaigrette for each serving.

4. **Salad Assembly:** Arrange the wedges of one pita around the rim of a chilled plate. For each serving, place the dressed romaine lettuce in the center of the plate and top with 2 oz/57 g sliced cucumbers, 2 oz/57 g tomatoes, 1 oz/28 g each of the peppers, onions, and olives, and 1½ oz/43 g feta cheese.

Caesar Salad

According to culinary lore, this salad was created by Caesar Cardini in 1924 at his restaurant in Tijuana, Mexico. Today, Caesar salads may be served as a salad buffet item, a plated first course, or a main course salad garnished with smoked seafood, sliced grilled chicken, or duck breast.

1 lb 4 oz/567 g romaine lettuce

DRESSING

1 tbsp/9 g minced garlic

5 anchovy fillets

¾ tsp/3.75 g salt, or to taste

½ tsp/1 g ground black pepper, or to taste

2 oz/57 g pasteurized egg (whole or yolk only)

2 fl oz/60 mL lemon juice, or to taste

10 fl oz/300 mL extra-virgin olive oil

6 oz/170 g finely grated Parmesan cheese, or to taste

12 oz/340 g Garlic-Flavored or Plain Croutons (page 549)

1. Separate the romaine leaves. Clean and thoroughly dry. Tear or cut into pieces if necessary. Refrigerate until ready to serve.

2. To prepare the dressing, mash together the garlic, anchovies, salt, and pepper in a bowl to form a relatively smooth paste. Add the egg and the lemon juice and blend well. Gradually add the olive oil, whisking as it is added to form a thick emulsion. Stir in the Parmesan. Adjust seasoning with salt and pepper, if necessary.

3. **Salad Assembly:** For each serving, combine 2 oz/57 g greens with 1 fl oz/30 mL dressing, tossing gently until evenly coated. Garnish with a few croutons.

Marinated Tomatoes

5 lb 8 oz/2.50 kg tomatoes (plum, beef-steak, yellow, pear, currant, or cherry)

DRESSING

8 fl oz/240 mL extra-virgin olive oil

4 fl oz/120 mL red wine vinegar

4 tbsp/12 g basil chiffonade

5 tbsp/15 g chopped marjoram

½ oz/14 g salt

1½ tsp/3 g coarse-ground black pepper

1. Peel the tomatoes and cut into halves, quarters, or wedges, if necessary.

2. Combine the dressing ingredients.

3. Add the tomatoes to the dressing and let rest 2 hours before serving.

CHEF'S NOTES: Use a single type of tomato or a combination of tomato varieties in this salad. If the tomato skins are thin and tender, peeling is optional.

Roasted Beet Salad

Use red or golden beets for this salad. The beets are roasted in this recipe, but they could also be boiled or steamed. For a special presentation, alternate the sliced beets with orange slices.

8 beets, greens trimmed to 1 in/3 cm

Kosher salt, as needed

DRESSING

2½ fl oz/75 mL extra-virgin olive oil

1 fl oz/30 mL red wine vinegar

1 fl oz/30 mL lemon juice

Pinch cayenne

1. Preheat the oven to 375°F/191°C. Arrange the beets in a 2-in/5-cm hotel pan. Add water just to cover the bottom of the pan. Season with salt. Cover with foil and roast until fork tender, about 1 hour, depending on size.

2. While the beets are roasting, combine the dressing ingredients.

3. Trim the beets, slip off the skin, and slice into rounds. Add to the dressing while still warm.

4. Let rest at room temperature for at least 30 minutes before serving or cooling for storage.

Marinated Roasted Pepper Salad

YIELD: 15 SERVINGS

This dish can be served as a salad or as a healthful alternative to traditional high-fat sauces with grilled meats, fish, and poultry.

12 oz/340 g roasted red peppers, peeled and seeded (4 each)

12 oz/340 g roasted green peppers, peeled and seeded (4 each)

12 oz/340 g roasted yellow peppers, peeled and seeded (4 each)

7 oz/198 g tomatoes, peeled and seeded

1⅓ oz/38 g golden raisins

2 fl oz/60 mL dry sherry

DRESSING

10 fl oz/300 mL Balsamic Vinaigrette (page 27)

6 oz/170 g red onions, cut into julienne

3½ oz/99 g black olives, cut in strips (20 each)

¾ oz/21 g chopped cilantro leaves

1 jalapeño, minced

2 garlic cloves, minced

GARNISH

1 oz/28 g Parmesan cheese

1 oz/28 g toasted pine nuts

1. Cut the roasted peppers into ½-in/1-cm strips. Cut the tomatoes into strips. Plump the raisins in the sherry.

2. Combine the dressing ingredients and pour over the peppers, tomatoes, and raisins.

3. Toss to combine. Let the salad rest at room temperature for 30 to 45 minutes before serving at room temperature, or cool and store properly for later service.

4. **Salad Assembly:** Just before serving, shave Parmesan curls over each serving and top with toasted pine nuts.

MARINATED ROASTED PEPPERS: Omit the tomatoes and plumped raisins. Dress with a plain balsamic vinaigrette, omitting the olives, onions, cilantro, jalapeño, and garlic. Use as required in other recipes (see Grilled Chicken Sandwich, page 154).

MARINATED PEPPERS AND MUSHROOMS: Prepare marinated peppers, adding 12 oz/340 g julienned shiitake or white mushrooms.

Hearts of Artichoke Salad

YIELD: 10 SERVINGS

10 artichokes or 30 baby artichokes

2 lemons

DRESSING

9 fl oz/270 mL olive oil

3 fl oz/90 mL balsamic vinegar

Salt, as needed

Ground white pepper, as needed

½ bunch flat-leaf parsley, leaves only

6½ oz/184 g Kalamata olives, pitted (about 30)

1 red onion, sliced into thin rings or julienne

4 lb/1.81 kg plum tomatoes, peeled, seeded, and quartered

1. Cut the ends off the artichokes and trim off the outer leaves. Scoop out the chokes, quarter each heart, and rub with the juice of the lemons. Hold in acidulated water.

2. Simmer the artichoke hearts in a cuisson (see Chef's Note) until tender, 8 to 12 minutes. Drain and let dry on absorbent toweling while preparing the dressing.

3. Whisk together the dressing ingredients. Add the artichoke hearts, olives, onion, and tomatoes.

4. Let rest at room temperature for at least 30 minutes before serving or cooling for storage.

CHEF'S NOTE: To prepare a cuisson, combine 1 gal/3.84 L water with 2 fl oz/60 mL lemon juice, 4 cloves, 1 bouquet garni (see page 522), and 2 tsp/10 g salt. Bring all ingredients to a simmer.

Preparing an artichoke.   A. Cutting off the top leaves.   B. Trimming the choke.   C. Scooping out the choke.

Poached Leek Salad

YIELD: 10 SERVINGS

When ramps are available, they can be poached and served in this manner for a special springtime dish. If your leeks are large, they may be halved or quartered. Small leeks can be trimmed but left whole. Use the white and light green parts only; reserve the trimmings for use in stocks.

10 leeks (about 3 bunches or 4 lb 4 oz/1.93 kg)	8 fl oz/240 mL Vinaigrette Gourmande (page 30)
5 each plum tomatoes, halved (1 lb 4 oz/567 g)	Salt, as needed

1. Rinse the leeks completely and cut as necessary. Cook in simmering salted water until almost tender, about 15 minutes. Drain the leeks and dry well on absorbent toweling. Reserve 2 fl oz/60 mL cooking liquid for the dressing.

2. Roast the tomatoes in a 375°F/191°C oven until dried and lightly browned, 25 to 30 minutes. Cut into strips.

3. Add the reserved cooking liquid from the leeks to the vinaigrette and mix well. Adjust seasoning with salt, as needed.

4. Pour the dressing over the warm or room-temperature leeks and tomatoes. Let the salad rest at room temperature 30 minutes before serving or storing.

CHEF'S NOTE: For a special occasion, other vinaigrettes may be substituted, such as Mustard-Walnut Vinaigrette (page 32) or Truffle Vinaigrette (page 28).

TO WORK WITH LEEKS: First rinse away the dirt that clings to the roots and the exterior leaves. Next, trim away the root ends and the dark green outer leaves. Leave enough of the root end intact to prevent the layers of the leek from falling apart. If your leeks are large, split them into halves or quarters. Very small baby leeks may not need to be split.

Thoroughly rinse the leeks once they have been trimmed and halved or quartered. Be sure to rinse them long enough to remove all traces of dirt. If baby leeks are left whole, it is especially important to check that no dirt is left trapped in the layers. Spread the leek layers out gently to permit the water to run through easily and flush out the sand or dirt.

Haricots Verts with Prosciutto and Gruyère

YIELD: 10 SERVINGS

This salad could be featured as a side salad for a pâté, terrine, or galantine. Or it could be served on its own or as part of a salad sampler appetizer plate. If haricots verts are unavailable, this salad is equally good prepared with regular green beans, asparagus, or leeks.

1 lb 4 oz/567 g haricots verts

5 oz/142 g prosciutto

5 oz/142 g Gruyère cheese

DRESSING

1 fl oz/30 mL lemon juice, or to taste

½ fl oz/15 mL white wine vinegar

½ tsp/2.50 g salt

¼ tsp/0.50 g ground white pepper

½ oz/14 g minced shallots

2⅔ fl oz/80 mL vegetable oil

1. Trim the haricots verts and rinse. Cut the prosciutto and Gruyère into fine julienne.

2. Combine the lemon juice, vinegar, salt, pepper, and shallots. Gradually whisk in the oil to make a dressing.

3. Blanch the haricots verts in boiling salted water until barely tender to the bite. Refresh in cold water. Drain and blot dry.

4. Add the haricots verts, prosciutto, and Gruyère to the dressing. Toss to combine and let rest at room temperature for at least 30 minutes before serving or storing.

HARICOTS VERTS WITH WALNUT AND RED WINE VINAIGRETTE [PAGE 30]: Paul Bocuse, the famous chef of Lyons, France, combines 12 oz/340 g haricots verts, 8 oz/227 g sliced white mushrooms, a few slivers of truffles, and a dressing made with walnut oil and Beaujolais wine vinegar for a simple but elegant salad.

Shaved Fennel and Parmesan Salad

YIELD: 10 SERVINGS

Slices of very fresh raw cèpes (porcini or *Boletus edulis*) are superb in this salad.

1 lb 4 oz/567 g fennel bulbs (about 2 large bulbs)

4 to 6 fl oz/120 to 180 mL extra-virgin olive oil

2 fl oz/60 mL lemon juice

Salt, as needed

Pepper, as needed

½ oz/14 g chopped flat-leaf parsley leaves

10 oz/283 g raw cèpes, sliced thin (optional)

GARNISH

3 oz/85 g Parmesan cheese

½ to 1 fl oz/15 to 30 mL white truffle oil or hazelnut oil

1. Trim, core, and shave the fennel very thin using a knife or mandoline.

2. Combine the olive oil, lemon juice, salt, and pepper thoroughly. Add the fennel, parsley, and sliced cèpes, if desired; toss to coat evenly.

3. Serve immediately, or cover and refrigerate for later service.

4. **Salad Assembly:** For each serving, arrange 2½ oz/71 g salad on a chilled plate. Shave some Parmesan over the salad and drizzle with a little truffle or hazelnut oil.

FENNEL AND PERSIMMON SALAD: Prepare the salad through Step 3. Garnish with shaved fuyu persimmon and finish with a few drops of balsamic vinegar.

ARTICHOKE AND FENNEL SALAD: Replace half the fennel with cooked artichoke hearts. Dress and finish as above.

GRILLED FENNEL SALAD: Slice the fennel ¼ in/6 mm thick, brush with a little of the dressing, and grill until tender. Cool the fennel before combining with the remaining dressing in Step 2.

Coleslaw

YIELD: 30 SERVINGS

A mixture of cabbages, peppers, carrots, and onions makes a colorful variation on the classic coleslaw.

For a more traditional slaw, omit the peppers and onions.

3 lb 8 oz/1.59 kg green cabbage, cut into chiffonade

1 lb/454 g red cabbage, cut into chiffonade

5 oz/142 g carrots, cut into julienne

5 oz/142 g red and yellow peppers, cut into julienne

5 oz/142 g red onions, cut into julienne

DRESSING

4 oz/113 g sugar

2 tbsp/6 g dry mustard

1 tbsp/6 g celery seed

10 fl oz/300 mL Basic Mayonnaise (page 35)

10 oz/283 g sour cream

3 fl oz/90 mL cider vinegar

1 oz/28 g prepared horseradish

½ oz/14 g mild brown mustard

Salt, as needed

Ground white pepper, as needed

Tabasco sauce, as needed

1. Combine the cabbages, carrots, peppers, and onions. Reserve.

2. Stir together the sugar, mustard, and celery seed to work out lumps. Add the remaining dressing ingredients and stir to combine.

3. Fold the cabbages, carrots, peppers, and onions into the dressing. Serve immediately, or cover and refrigerate.

Roasted Corn and Tomato Salad

YIELD: 30 SERVINGS

DRESSING

16 fl oz/480 mL olive oil

12 fl oz/360 mL white wine vinegar

½ oz/14 g roasted garlic paste

½ oz/14 g salt

1 tsp/2 g coarse-ground black pepper

3 lb 11¼ oz/1.68 kg roasted corn kernels (11 ears)

3 lb 3 oz/1.44 kg tomato concassé (15 plum tomatoes)

2 oz/57 g sliced green onions (about 8)

3 tbsp/9 g chopped cilantro

3 tbsp/9 g chopped flat-leaf parsley

1. Blend the oil, vinegar, and garlic paste. Season with salt and pepper.

2. Add the corn, tomatoes, green onions, and herbs. Toss to coat evenly. Adjust seasoning. Serve immediately, or cover and refrigerate.

Asian Vegetable Slaw

YIELD: 10 SIDE SALAD SERVINGS

1 lb 4 oz/567 g savoy cabbage, cut into fine chiffonade

10 oz/283 g carrots, cut into julienne

1 oz/28 g coarsely chopped cilantro

5 green onions, thinly sliced on the bias

DRESSING

8 fl oz/240 mL vegetable oil

2 fl oz/60 mL olive oil

2 fl oz/60 mL peanut oil

1 tsp/5 mL sesame oil

4 fl oz/120 mL Japanese rice wine vinegar

½ fl oz/15 mL soy sauce

½ fl oz/15 mL fish sauce

¼ tsp/0.50 g ground white pepper

Pinch cayenne

GARNISH

2½ oz/71 g chopped toasted peanuts

¾ oz/21 g toasted sesame seeds

1. Toss together the cabbage, carrots, cilantro, and green onions.

2. Blend the dressing ingredients and pour over the cabbage mixture. Adjust seasoning as necessary with pepper and cayenne. Garnish each portion with peanuts and sesame seeds.

Celeriac and Tart Apple Salad

YIELD: 10 SERVINGS

Both celeriac and apples oxidize when exposed to air. This turns their creamy white flesh an unappetizing brown color. Although acidulated water containing lemon juice is often used to keep apples from browning, it might give the apples a strong lemon taste. We prefer to use apple juice combined with a few drops of apple cider vinegar. The acid in the juice and the vinegar keep the apples from browning, and they add another apple flavor dimension.

2 lb/907 g celeriac

DRESSING

3 oz/85 g Crème Fraîche (page 351)

3 oz/85 g Basic Mayonnaise (page 35)

1 oz/28 g Dijon mustard

1 fl oz/30 mL apple cider vinegar

½ oz/14 g sugar

Salt, as needed

Ground black pepper, as needed

3 Granny Smith apples

1. Cut away the outer rind of the celeriac and cut the root into allumettes, about 1½ in/4 cm long. Hold in a blanc (see Chef's Note) to prevent discoloring.

2. Combine the dressing ingredients.

3. Rinse the celeriac, boil until tender in acidulated water (add ½ fl oz/15 mL lemon juice to each 32 fl oz/960 mL water). Refresh in cold water; drain on absorbent toweling.

4. Peel and dice the apples. Fold the apples and the celeriac into the dressing. Adjust seasoning with salt and pepper, if necessary.

5. Serve immediately, or cover and refrigerate.

CHEF'S NOTE: To prepare the blanc, whisk together 32 fl oz/960 mL water with 1⅛ oz/32 g all-purpose flour and 1 fl oz/30 mL lemon juice.

Mushroom Salad with Celery and Tuscan Pecorino

YIELD: 10 SERVINGS

3 fl oz/90 mL lemon juice

1 tsp/3 g lemon zest

6 fl oz/180 mL olive oil

2 tsp/10 g kosher salt, and as needed

¼ tsp/0.50 g ground black pepper, and as needed

7½ oz/213 g celery

10 oz/283 g white mushrooms, cleaned

10 oz/283 g cremini mushrooms, cleaned

1¼ oz/35 g celery leaves

2½ oz/71 g arugula

1½ oz/43 g green onion, sliced thin

2 tbsp/6 g flat-leaf parsley chiffonade

2 tbsp/6 g mint leaves chiffonade

5 oz/142 g Tuscan pecorino, shaved

1. Whisk together the lemon juice and zest. Slowly drizzle in the olive oil, whisking constantly. Season to taste with salt and pepper. Set aside.

2. Slice the celery ribs on the bias, about ⅛ in/3 mm thick. Slice the mushrooms ⅛ in/3 mm thick.

3. Combine the mushrooms, celery, celery leaves, arugula, green onion, parsley, and mint in a bowl.

4. Whisk the lemon vinaigrette from Step 1 to recombine. Add 8 fl oz/240 mL vinaigrette to the salad. Toss well to combine and season to taste with salt and pepper.

5. Place 8 oz/227 g salad in the center of a ring mold in the center of a plate.

6. Remove the ring mold and garnish with ½ oz/14 g cheese. Drizzle some of the remaining vinaigrette around the salad on the plate.

7. Repeat Steps 5 and 6 for each serving. Grind a bit of fresh pepper over the salad before serving.

Mushroom Salad

4 fl oz/120 mL olive oil

1 lb/454 g cremini mushrooms, quartered

1 lb/454 g white mushrooms, quartered

2 lb/907 g assorted wild mushrooms, sliced

1 tbsp/9 g minced garlic

2 oz/57 g shallots, minced

2 tbsp/6 g minced marjoram

2 tbsp/6 g minced parsley

2 tbsp/6 g minced mint

1 fl oz/30 mL truffle oil

1½ fl oz/45 mL sherry vinegar

3 fl oz/90 mL lemon juice

2 tsp/10 g salt

¼ tsp/0.50 g ground black pepper

1. Heat ½ fl oz/15 mL of the olive oil in a large sauté pan over high heat. Add half the cremini, white, and wild mushrooms and sauté 5 to 7 minutes, or until lightly browned and cooked through. Transfer to a mixing bowl. Cook the remaining mushrooms in the same manner, adding more oil as needed. Allow the mushrooms to cool.

2. Mix the garlic, shallots, marjoram, parsley, mint, truffle oil, vinegar, lemon juice, salt, pepper, and the remaining olive oil in a bowl.

3. Combine the mushrooms and vinaigrette. Cover and refrigerate for at least 2 hours and up to 24 hours.

Mediterranean Potato Salad

YIELD: 10 SERVINGS

2 lb 8 oz/1.13 kg waxy potatoes (such as Yellow Finn or Yukon gold)

DRESSING

7 fl oz/210 mL extra-virgin olive oil

3 fl oz/90 mL red wine vinegar

1 fl oz/30 mL balsamic vinegar

1 oz/28 g coarsely chopped flat-leaf parsley

1½ oz/43 g chopped capers

½ oz/14 g chopped anchovies

1 tsp/3 g minced garlic

1 tsp/5 g salt

¼ tsp/0.50 g ground white pepper

1. Steam the potatoes until just cooked through.

2. While the potatoes are cooking, mix the dressing ingredients.

3. Drain the potatoes and dry briefly to remove excess moisture. Peel and dice the potatoes while still very hot and place in a bowl.

4. Whip the dressing to recombine and pour over the potatoes. Let rest at room temperature for at least 30 minutes before serving or cooling for storage.

CHEF'S NOTES: This salad can be served either warm or cold. If the salad is to be served warm or at room temperature, it should be made just prior to service and held no longer than 3 hours. If the salad is to be held or served cold, cool it to room temperature once assembled.

MEDITERRANEAN POTATO SALAD WITH MUSSELS: This salad makes an interesting addition to a seafood buffet or antipasti and is a creative way to feature mussels. Steam or poach mussels or other shellfish until just cooked through. If the salad is being served warm, poach the seafood just before serving and fold into the salad while still warm. For a cold presentation, steam or poach the mussels, chill well, and add to the cooled salad. Store as described above.

German Potato Salad

YIELD: 10 SERVINGS

2 lb 4 oz/1.02 kg waxy potatoes (such as Yellow Finn or Yukon gold)

DRESSING

2 oz/57 g diced bacon

20 fl oz/600 mL Chicken Stock (page 529)

2 fl oz/60 mL white wine vinegar

4 oz/113 g diced onions

1 tsp/5 g salt, or to taste

1 tsp/5 g sugar, or to taste

Ground white pepper, as needed

2 fl oz/60 mL vegetable oil

1 oz/28 g mild brown mustard

½ bunch chives, snipped

1. Steam the whole potatoes until just tender. Drain and dry. While the potatoes are still hot, remove the peels and slice the potatoes ⅓ in/8 mm thick.

2. While the potatoes are cooking, prepare the dressing: Render the bacon, remove it with a slotted spoon, and keep it warm.

3. Bring the stock, vinegar, onions, salt, sugar, and pepper to a boil.

4. Combine the oil, rendered bacon fat, and mustard with the warm potatoes. Add the boiling stock-vinegar mixture, the rendered bacon, and chives; toss the salad gently.

5. Cover the salad and allow it to set overnight, under refrigeration before serving.

Tabbouleh Salad

YIELD: 10 SERVINGS

This recipe offers a faithful rendition of a salad that, according to many authorities, is more a parsley salad with some bulgur than a bulgur salad with a little parsley.

1 lb/454 g bulgur wheat

2½ oz/71 g coarse chopped flat-leaf parsley

14 oz/397 g diced tomatoes

1 oz/14 g finely sliced green onions, white part only

1 oz/28 g chopped mint

DRESSING

8 fl oz/240 mL extra-virgin olive oil

4 fl oz/120 mL lemon juice

Salt, as needed

Ground black pepper, as needed

1. Place the bulgur in a bowl and cover with warm water. Soak for 30 minutes and drain well.

2. In a large mixing bowl, combine the bulgur with the parsley, tomatoes, green onions, and mint.

3. Whisk together the dressing ingredients, pour over the salad, and toss to coat evenly. Allow to set 1 hour before serving, or cover and refrigerate.

Israeli Couscous and Heirloom Grains

YIELD: 10 SERVINGS

2 oz/57 g kamut-rice blend

3¾ oz/106 g green lentils

5½ oz/156 g Israeli couscous, cooked

9½ oz/269 g European cucumber, peeled and cut into small dice

3½ oz/99 g savoy cabbage, cut into medium dice

1½ oz/43 g green onion, thinly sliced on the bias

8 fl oz/240 mL Lemon-Parsley Vinaigrette (page 30)

1. Cook the kamut-rice blend and green lentils separately and allow them to cool to room temperature.

2. Reconstitute the couscous and allow it to cool to room temperature.

3. Mix the cooled grains and lentils together in a large bowl. Add the cucumber, cabbage, and green onion to the grains and mix to combine.

4. Fold in the vinaigrette.

5. Serve about 4½ oz/128 g per serving, or cover and refrigerate until needed.

Lentil and Walnut Salad

YIELD: 35 SERVINGS

Legumes will toughen if they are left in contact with an acid, such as this vinaigrette, for extended periods. As with all bean salads, this salad is best when prepared and consumed on the same day.

2 lb/907 g French lentils

3 carrots, cut into brunoise and blanched

2 stalks celery, peeled, cut into brunoise, and blanched

1 leek, white part only, cut into small dice and blanched

1 lb/454 g toasted walnuts, toasted skins removed

10 fl oz/300 mL Mustard-Walnut Vinaigrette (page 32)

1. Simmer the lentils in water until they are tender. Refresh in cold water and drain well. Drain, rinse until cold, and drain well again.

2. Combine the lentils, carrots, celery, leek, and walnuts. Reserve until ready to serve.

3. **Salad Assembly:** Up to 4 hours before serving, combine the lentil mixture with the vinaigrette. Adjust seasoning. Serve at room temperature or chilled.

Mixed Bean and Grain Salad

YIELD: 30 SERVINGS

1 lb/454 g chickpeas (garbanzos), sorted, rinsed, and soaked for 12 to 24 hours

1 lb/454 g green lentils

8 oz/227 g acini de pepe pasta

1 lb/454 g bulgur wheat

16 fl oz/480 mL Lemon-Parsley Vinaigrette (page 30)

10 sun-dried tomatoes, minced

Salt, as needed

Coarse-ground black pepper, as needed

1. Cook the chickpeas and lentils separately in water. Cook the pasta in salted water. Refresh in cold water and drain well. Combine.

2. Place the bulgur in a bowl and cover with cold water. Soak for 30 minutes and drain well. Combine with the chickpea mixture.

3. Whisk the vinaigrette together with the sun-dried tomatoes, salt, and pepper. Pour over the salad and toss to coat evenly. Serve immediately, or cover and refrigerate.

Fattoush (Eastern Mediterranean Bread Salad)

YIELD: 10 TO 12 SERVINGS

Sumac is a favored seasoning in Syrian, Lebanese, and other Middle Eastern cuisines. It is made from the berries of the sumac tree and has a tart, slightly bitter flavor.

6 pitas

1½ fl oz/45 mL olive oil

Salt, as needed

Ground black pepper, as needed

DRESSING

2 fl oz/60 mL lemon juice

½ fl oz/15 mL white wine vinegar

1 tbsp/6 g ground sumac

2 garlic cloves, minced

4 fl oz/120 mL olive oil

Salt, as needed

Ground black pepper, as needed

2 tbsp/6 g chopped thyme

½ tsp/1 g cayenne

2 tsp/10 g sugar

VEGETABLES

1 bunch green onions, chopped

1 oz/28 g chopped flat-leaf parsley

6 plum tomatoes, seeded and cut into medium dice

1 European cucumber, peeled, seeded, and cut into medium dice

8 oz/227 g radishes, cut into brunoise or sliced thin

1 yellow pepper, cut into small dice

1. Cut the pitas into small wedges. Toss with the oil, salt, and pepper. Bake on a sheet pan at 300°F/149°C for about 15 minutes, turning halfway through the baking. The pita wedges should be crisp but not crumbly.

2. Combine the dressing ingredients thoroughly and adjust seasoning, if necessary. Reserve separately.

3. **Salad Assembly:** Combine the vegetables with the dressing and toss until coated. Fold in the pita wedges. Adjust the salt and pepper. If the salad is too dry, sprinkle with a little water to moisten.

Panzanella (Bread Salad Tuscan Style)

YIELD: 30 SERVINGS

Panzanella evolved as a thrifty way to use bread that had become too dry for slicing and eating. Combined with ripe tomatoes and fresh herbs, the stale bread was transformed into a luscious summer salad.

1 lb/454 g country-style bread

3 lb/1.36 kg plum tomatoes, cut into medium dice

8 oz/227 g European cucumbers, cut into medium dice

4 oz/113 g celery hearts, cut into medium dice

4 oz/113 g thinly sliced red onions

1½ oz/43 g basil chiffonade

DRESSING

1 fl oz/30 mL red wine vinegar

3 garlic cloves, minced

Salt, as needed

Ground black pepper, as needed

4 fl oz/120 mL olive oil

1. Cut the bread into medium dice. Let dry for 8 to 12 hours.

2. Combine the bread with the tomatoes, cucumbers, celery, onions, and basil.

3. Combine the vinegar, garlic, salt, and pepper. Whisk in the olive oil. Let rest for 30 minutes at room temperature. Adjust seasoning before serving.

4. Toss the dressing with the salad ingredients.

CHEF'S NOTE: To prepare this salad à la minute, keep the vegetables and bread separate. For each serving, toss together a spoonful of each, plus 1 fl oz/30 mL dressing.

VARIATION: Green olives or sweet peppers are sometimes added to this salad. For this recipe, use 6⅓ oz/180 g pitted green olives or diced peppers.

This salad can be garnished with shaved Parmesan and drizzled with extra-virgin olive oil.

Tubettini Pasta Salad

1 lb/454 g tubettini pasta

DRESSING

1½ fl oz/45 mL white wine vinegar

1 tsp/5 g salt

4 fl oz/120 mL olive oil

½ oz/14 g shallots, minced

¼ tsp/0.50 g ground white pepper, and as needed

½ oz/14 g minced chives

2 oz/57 g red, green, or yellow pepper, or a combination, cut into brunoise

Salt, as needed

Ground black pepper, as needed

1. Cook pasta in boiling salted water until al dente. Refresh in cold water; drain and dry.

2. To prepare the dressing, stir together the vinegar and salt. Whisk in the oil and the remaining dressing ingredients.

3. Pour the dressing over the pasta and adjust seasoning with salt and ground black pepper. Serve immediately, or cover and refrigerate.

ASIAN-STYLE BUCKWHEAT NOODLES: Prepare buckwheat noodles (sold as *soba*) according to the package directions. Drain well and dress sparingly with a little vinaigrette made by combining 1 fl oz/30 mL safflower oil, ½ fl oz/15 mL dark sesame oil, ½ fl oz/15 mL rice wine, and very finely minced garlic and ginger to taste.

Couscous Salad with Curried Vegetables

YIELD: 10 SERVINGS

1 lb 8 oz/680 g asparagus, trimmed and cut on the bias 2 in/5 cm long

12 oz/340 g cauliflower florets

12 oz/340 g fennel, cut into julienne

6 oz/170 g cooked chickpeas, drained and rinsed

8 fl oz/240 mL Curry Vinaigrette (page 113)

Salt, as needed

Ground black pepper, as needed

1 lb 8 oz/680 g dry couscous

1 cinnamon stick

1 oz/28 g flat-leaf parsley leaves, whole or cut into chiffonade

3 oz/85 g slivered almonds, toasted

2 oz/57 g dried currants, plumped in warm water

1 lb/454 g grape or cherry tomatoes

1 oz/28 g Harissa (page 473)

1. Steam or boil the vegetables separately until tender; drain well. Combine the vegetables and the chickpeas with the vinaigrette while the vegetables are still hot. Season with salt and pepper. Cover and marinate under refrigeration for at least 2 hours and up to 12 hours.

2. Steam the couscous with the cinnamon stick until hot, fluffy, and tender. Remove the cinnamon stick and fluff the couscous to break up lumps and fold in the parsley, almonds, and currants. Adjust seasoning with salt and pepper. Top with the marinated vegetables and tomatoes. Drizzle a few drops of harissa sauce on the salad.

NOTE: Artichoke bottoms or hearts, quartered, can be included with the vegetables as they marinate.

Soba Noodle Salad

YIELD: 10 SERVINGS

1 lb 4 oz/567 g soba noodles

1 fl oz/30 mL rice vinegar

4 fl oz/120 mL tamari

2 tsp/7 g light miso

4 fl oz/120 mL sesame oil

¾ oz/21 g sesame seeds, unhulled

½ tsp/1 g red pepper flakes

6 oz/170 g carrots, cut into fine julienne

4 oz/113 g green onions, thinly sliced on the bias

Salt, as needed

Ground black pepper, as needed

1. Cook the noodles in boiling salted water until al dente. Rinse with cold water and drain.

2. To prepare the dressing, stir together the rice vinegar, tamari, and miso. Whisk in the sesame oil, sesame seeds, and red pepper flakes.

3. Toss the carrots and green onions in the dressing.

4. Pour the dressing over the pasta and season with salt and pepper.

5. Serve immediately, or cover and refrigerate.

Orzo Salad

YIELD: 10 SERVINGS

12 oz/340 g orzo

1½ fl oz/45 mL olive oil

3 oz/85 g ham, cooked, cut into small dice

3 oz/85 g black olives, small whole or larger, quartered

3 oz/85 g broccoli florets, cooked, cut into medium dice

3 oz/85 g white Cheddar, cut into small dice

5 large hard-cooked eggs, sliced

1 fl oz/30 mL lemon juice, or to taste

½ tsp/2.50 g salt, or to taste

½ tsp/1 g ground black pepper, or to taste

1. Cook the orzo in boiling, salted water for about 9 minutes or until still slightly firm. Rinse quickly with cold water and drain.

2. Toss the orzo in the olive oil, then gently combine all of the ingredients. Adjust seasoning with additional lemon juice, salt, and pepper to taste.

3. Serve immediately, or cover and refrigerate.

Black Bean Salad

YIELD: 10 SERVINGS

8 oz/227 g dried black beans, sorted, rinsed, and soaked for 12 to 24 hours

7 oz/198 g white rice

4 oz/113 g red peppers, cleaned, trimmed, and diced

5 oz/142 g onions, diced

1 tbsp/9 g minced garlic

2 fl oz/60 mL olive oil

2 tsp/10 g salt, or to taste

Juice of 1 lime

3 tbsp/9 g cilantro, chopped

8 oz/227 g queso blanco, crumbled

1. Soak the black beans overnight. Discard soaking water.

2. Place the soaked beans in a medium saucepan and cover with fresh cold water. Bring to a boil, cover, and simmer gently until tender, about 2½ hours. As the beans are cooking, watch the liquid level and add water to prevent scorching. When fully cooked, drain well and cool slightly.

3. Cook the rice in abundant rapidly boiling salted water just until tender, about 20 minutes for white medium-grain rice, then drain well and cool slightly.

4. Sauté the red peppers, onions, and garlic in 1 fl oz/30 mL of the olive oil. Season lightly with salt and cool slightly.

5. Fold the red pepper mixture into the cooked beans.

6. Just before service, make a vinaigrette using the remaining olive oil, the lime juice, cilantro, and the 2 tsp/10 g of salt. Pour over the bean mixture and gently fold, coating the salad.

7. Gently fold in the rice.

8. Gently fold the queso blanco into the salad. Adjust seasoning with salt.

Corona Bean Salad with Basil

1 lb/454 g corona beans, sorted, rinsed, and soaked for 12 to 24 hours

2 fl oz/60 mL olive oil

3 oz/85 g celery, halved

3 oz/85 g carrot, peeled and left whole

3 garlic cloves, crushed

1½ rosemary sprigs

1½ thyme sprigs

½ bay leaf

2 oz/57 g pancetta (optional)

Salt, as needed

3½ oz/99 g red onion, cut into fine julienne or small dice

2½ oz/71 g celery hearts (including leaves), chopped

½ oz/14 g lemon zest chiffonade, blanched

2 tbsp/6 g flat-leaf parsley leaves

2 tbsp/6 g basil chiffonade

1 tbsp/7 g garlic, thinly sliced

2 fl oz/60 mL extra-virgin olive oil

½ fl oz/15 mL white balsamic vinegar

1 tsp/5 g salt

¼ tsp/0.50 g ground black pepper

1. Combine the beans, oil, celery halves, carrot, crushed garlic, rosemary, thyme, bay leaf, and pancetta, if desired, in a saucepot. Add enough fresh cold water to cover the mixture by 4 in/10 cm and bring to a full boil. Reduce the heat to establish a simmer and cook until the beans are tender, 1 to 1½ hours. Stir occasionally to prevent scorching. Add water as necessary to keep the beans covered by about 2 in/5 cm.

2. Add salt to season the beans. Remove and discard the celery, carrot, garlic, and herbs. Cool directly in the cooking liquid. Cover and keep refrigerated until ready to prepare the salad.

3. Drain the beans. Combine the red onion, celery hearts, lemon zest, parsley, basil, and garlic slices. Drizzle with the extra-virgin olive oil and vinegar, season with the salt and pepper, toss to combine, and set aside. Add the drained beans and toss to combine. Adjust seasoning with salt and pepper. Cover the salad and let rest for at least 30 minutes and up to 3 hours before serving.

RED BORLOTTI BEAN SALAD WITH ROSEMARY: Substitute red borlotti beans for the corona beans, adjusting the cooking time as necessary. Replace the basil chiffonade with 2 tsp/2 g minced rosemary leaves.

Waldorf Salad

YIELD: 30 SERVINGS

This classic fruit salad combining apples, celery, and walnuts in a mayonnaise-based dressing is credited to Oscar Tschirky, maître d' of the Waldorf-Astoria Hotel in New York City. Since the early 1890s a few modifications have been made, but the essential salad has the same fresh taste and texture as the original.

5 Red Delicious apples, peeled and cored

5 Golden Delicious apples, peeled and cored

5 Granny Smith apples, peeled and cored

DRESSING

8 oz/227 g Basic Mayonnaise (page 35)

8½ oz/241 g sour cream

1 tsp/5 g salt

½ tsp/1 g ground black pepper

Lemon juice, as needed

1 stalk celery, peeled, cut into medium dice

4⅓ oz/123 g coarsely chopped walnuts, toasted

1. Cut the apples into medium dice.

2. Mix together all the dressing ingredients. Adjust seasoning to taste. Fold in the apples, celery, and walnuts.

3. Serve immediately or cover and refrigerate for up to 8 hours. This salad should be made the same day it is to be served.

CHEF'S NOTES: Peeling the celery removes the tough fibers and gives this salad additional refinement. Choose the tender celery from the heart whenever possible. If your celery is large and bitter, simply omit it from the salad.

Ambrosia Salad

YIELD: 30 SERVINGS

In Greek mythology, ambrosia was the food of the gods and was thought to confer immortality. Today, the word also refers to two distinct Southern specialties. The first is a cocktail created at the famed New Orleans restaurant Arnaud's. The second, and perhaps better-known, ambrosia is a chilled concoction of fruits (usually oranges and bananas) and flaked coconut. Originally served as a layered fruit dessert, this Southern classic also works quite well as a salad.

8 fl oz/240 mL whipping cream	2 lb/907 g bananas, peeled and sliced
2 oz/57 g sugar, or to taste	1 lb/454 g green grapes, halved
12 oranges, cut into suprêmes	8 oz/227 g unsweetened coconut flakes, toasted
1 pineapple, cubed	

1. Whip the cream to soft peaks and add sugar to taste.

2. Fold the oranges, pineapple, bananas, and grapes into the whipped cream.

3. Let the salad rest under refrigeration at least 30 minutes before serving.

4. **Salad Assembly:** Garnish each serving with toasted coconut.

PRESENTATION IDEAS: Serve this salad with turkey or chicken sandwiches, grilled or smoked shrimp or scallops, or to accompany hearty game or pork pâtés. It offers a refreshing counterpoint of sweetness and texture.

CHEF'S NOTES: Make this and other fruit salads only when fruits are ripe and full-flavored. This salad should be made just prior to service and should not be held overnight.

Grilled Pineapple, Jícama, Red Onion, and Grapefruit Salad

YIELD: 10 SERVINGS

1 pineapple, peeled and cored

8 oz/227 g red onion, sliced

8 oz/227 g jícama, cut into julienne

1 fl oz/30 mL vegetable oil

¾ oz/21 g white wine vinegar

1 tbsp/9 g minced shallot

Pinch ground cumin

GARNISH

1¼ oz/35 g cilantro chiffonade

2 red grapefruit, cut into suprêmes

1. Slice the pineapple into rounds ¼ in/6 mm thick and grill each side for 1 to 2 minutes, or until the slices have grill marks and the pineapple begins to become translucent. Quarter the grilled pineapple slices and reserve.

2. Toss together the red onion and jícama.

3. Whisk together the oil, vinegar, shallot, and cumin. Pour the dressing over the onion-jícama mixture and toss to coat evenly.

4. **Salad Assembly:** For each serving, place about 1¼ oz/35 g (about 10 pieces) pineapple on a salad plate and arrange 2½ oz/71 g onion-jícama mixture on top. Garnish with the cilantro and suprêmes of grapefruit.

Salad of Crab and Avocado

YIELD: 10 SERVINGS

1 lb/454 g red peppers

1 lb/454 g yellow peppers

2 fl oz/60 mL olive oil

1 tsp/5 g salt

½ tsp/1 g ground black pepper

10 oz/283 g tomato concassé

1½ oz/43 g red onion, finely chopped

1 tbsp/9 g minced garlic

1 tbsp/3 g chopped cilantro

1 jalepeño, seeds removed, finely diced

10 oz/283 g ripe avocado, cut into ¼-in/6-mm dice

1 fl oz/30 mL lime juice

1 lb 4 oz/567 g crabmeat, picked over

4 oz/113 g crème fraîche

Paprika, as needed

10 cilantro leaves

1. Rub each pepper with about 1 fl oz/30 mL olive oil.

2. Roast the peppers on a rack in a 375° to 400°F/191° to 204°C oven until the skins become loose, 35 to 45 minutes. Do not allow the peppers to gain color. Remove the skin and the seeds from the peppers.

3. Cool the peppers, purée the colors separately in a food processor, and pass each color purée through a fine-mesh strainer. Season each with about ½ tsp/2.50 g of the salt and a pinch of the pepper and place into squeeze bottles.

4. One hour before molding, mix the tomatoes, onion, garlic, cilantro, and jalepeño to form a salsa.

5. Combine the avocado, lime juice, and the remaining ½ tsp/2.50 g salt and pinch of pepper.

6. For each serving, in a ring mold measuring 2 in/5 cm in diameter and 1¼ in/3 cm in height, layer 1½ oz/43 g avocado mixture, 1½ oz/43 g tomato salsa, and 3 oz/85 g crabmeat. Press each layer into the mold gently. Make sure that the last layer is pressed firmly into the ring mold.

7. Spoon about 1 oz/28 g crème fraîche on top of the crab and smooth it even with the rim of the ring mold, using a small offset spatula.

8. Lightly dust the crème fraîche with paprika.

9. Transfer the filled ring to the center of an 8-in/20-cm plate and carefully lift off the ring mold. Place a cilantro leaf on top of the crème fraîche.

10. Use the squeeze bottles to create two concentric circles of sauce around the crab salad.

Baked Goat's Milk Cheese with Garden Lettuces, Roasted Figs, Pears, and Toasted Almonds

YIELD: 10 APPETIZER SERVINGS

This recipe blends flavors and textures in an intriguing way. The cheese's texture is rich and creamy, in contrast to its crust. Figs and almonds add deep, rich flavors to the dish. The pungent backdrop of the mesclun lettuce mix pulls all the elements together.

1 lb 4 oz/567 g Marinated Goat's Milk Cheese (page 354)	15 fl oz/450 mL Balsamic Vinaigrette (page 27)
8 oz/227 g dry bread crumbs	Salt, as needed
10 roasted figs (see Chef's Note), halved	Ground black pepper, as needed
1 lb 4 oz/567 g mesclun lettuce mix	2½ oz/71 g Toasted Almonds (page 546)
2 pears, sliced into thin wedges	

1. Drain the goat's milk cheese of excess oil. Gently dip the cheese into the bread crumbs and place on sheet pans. Chill at least 2 hours or overnight.

2. **Salad Assembly:** For each serving, bake 2 rounds of cheese in a 450°F/232°C oven until lightly browned, about 10 minutes. Let the cheese cool while roasting the figs. Lightly grill the figs to heat. Toss 3 oz/85 g mesclun and 3 to 4 pear slices with 1 fl oz/30 mL vinaigrette; season with salt and pepper. Mound on a chilled plate. Top with goat's milk cheese rounds, figs, and a few almonds.

CHEF'S NOTE: To roast figs for this salad, remove the top portion of the stem. Season with salt and pepper and place the figs in a hotel pan 2 in/5 cm deep. Add enough chicken stock to cover the figs halfway. Add a bay leaf and a thyme sprig. Cover and roast at 350°F/177°C until tender and plump, about 20 minutes. Warm skin side down on a grill just before service, if desired.

Avocado, Tomato, and Corn Salad with Aged Cheddar and Chipotle-Sherry Vinaigrette

YIELD: 10 ENTRÉE SERVINGS

This salad highlights one of Vermont's famous culinary resources, aged Cheddar cheese, along with a variety of ripe tomatoes. It makes an excellent appetizer salad or a meatless main course for lunch menus.

3 red beefsteak tomatoes, sliced thin

3 yellow beefsteak tomatoes, sliced thin

5¼ oz/149 g cherry tomatoes, halved lengthwise

5 oz/142 g pear tomatoes, halved lengthwise

5 oz/142 g currant tomatoes

5 ears corn on the cob

1 lb 4 oz/567 g mesclun lettuce mix, rinsed and dried

15 fl oz/450 mL Chipotle-Sherry Vinaigrette (page 32)

5 ripe avocados

10 oz/283 g aged Vermont cheddar, crumbled

1 red onion, sliced thin, separated into rings

Coarse-ground black pepper, as needed

1. Portion the tomatoes for each salad as follows: 2 slices each red and yellow tomatoes and 2⅔ oz/75 g combined cherry, pear, and currant tomatoes.

2. Roast the corn and cut the kernels away; you will use about ½ ear per salad.

3. **Salad Assembly:** For each serving, toss 2 oz/57 g mesclun with 1 fl oz/30 mL vinaigrette. Mound on a chilled plate. Peel and slice or dice half an avocado and scatter over the salad. Top with tomatoes, corn, cheese, and red onion. Drizzle with an additional ½ fl oz/15 mL vinaigrette. Grind black pepper over the salad. Serve at once.

Buffalo Chicken Salad

YIELD: 10 ENTRÉE SERVINGS

This salad is a variation on the popular appetizer Buffalo Chicken Wings, created at the Anchor Bar in Buffalo, New York, in 1964 by owner Teressa Bellissimo.

2 lb 8 oz/1.13 kg chicken wings, tips removed, disjointed

8 oz/227 g flour (seasoned with salt and pepper), as needed for dredging

HOT SAUCE

8 fl oz/240 mL Frank's Hot Sauce

1 oz/28 g butter

Tabasco sauce, as needed

Cayenne, as needed

Lemon juice, as needed

1 lb 4 oz/567 g mixed greens, washed, dried, and chilled

10 fl oz/300 mL Basic Red Wine Vinaigrette (page 27)

½ bunch celery, cut into 4-in/10-cm allumette strips

¾ lb/340 g carrots, cut into 4-in/10-cm allumette strips

1 seedless cucumber, peeled and sliced

20 Celeriac Chips (page 488) (optional)

15 fl oz/450 mL Roquefort Dressing (page 40)

1. Dredge the chicken wings in the flour and deep-fry in 350°F/177°C oil until golden brown and crisp, about 12 minutes. Drain well.

2. Simmer the ingredients for the hot sauce. Pour over the warm chicken wings; hold in the sauce.

3. **Salad Assembly:** For each serving, warm 4 oz/113 g chicken wings, if necessary. Toss 2 oz/57 g mixed greens with 1 fl oz/30 mL vinaigrette. Arrange the mixed greens in a soup bowl or salad plate and top with the wings. Garnish with the celery, carrots, cucumbers, and celery chips. Serve with 1½ fl oz/45 mL dressing.

Cobb Salad

Cobb salad was created at the Brown Derby Restaurant in Hollywood, California. Various interpretations call for either chicken or turkey. The garnish suggestions here are typical, but some versions also include watercress, celery, Cheddar cheese, hard-boiled eggs, black olives, or alfalfa sprouts.

5 chicken breasts, on the bone

Salt, as needed

Ground black pepper, as needed

20 bacon slices

1 lb 4 oz/567 g romaine lettuce, washed, dried, and torn into pieces

10 fl oz/300 mL Basic Red Wine Vinaigrette (page 27)

10 oz/283 g tomatoes, skin on, cut into medium dice

10 oz/283 g crumbled blue cheese

3 avocados, cut into medium dice

5 green onions, thinly sliced on the bias

1. Season (see Chef's Note) the chicken breasts with salt and pepper and roast to an internal temperature of 165°F/74°C. Cool and remove from the bone. Cut the meat into ⅓-in/8-mm dice.

2. Bake, broil, or fry the bacon until crisp. Drain on absorbent paper and keep warm.

3. **Salad Assembly:** For each serving, toss 2 oz/57 g romaine with 1 fl oz/30 mL vinaigrette. Mound on a plate, top with 4 oz/113 g chicken, 2 oz/57 g tomato, 1 oz/28 g blue cheese, 2⅔ oz/75 g avocado, 1 oz/28 g green onions, and 2 bacon strips, crumbled.

CHEF'S NOTES: If you use a spice rub on the chicken before roasting, you may opt to leave the skin on for additional flavor in the salad.

Shrimp and Bean Salad

YIELD: 10 SERVINGS

2 lb 8 oz/1.13 kg shrimp, peeled and deveined

1 tsp/5 g sea salt

Ground black pepper, as needed

4 fl oz/120 mL olive oil

2 oz/57 g garlic, minced to a paste

3 tbsp/9 g minced oregano leaves

3 tbsp/9 g minced mint leaves

Pinch red pepper flakes

1 lb 4 oz/567 g Corona Bean Salad with Basil (page 117)

8 oz/227 g Oreganata Crumb Mixture (below)

10 lemons wedges, for squeezing as needed

1. Slightly butterfly the shrimp. Place in a hotel pan, laid out flat. Season with the salt and a little pepper.

2. Combine the olive oil, garlic, oregano, mint, and red pepper flakes. Spoon over the shrimp, coating them lightly. Marinate at least 30 minutes and up to 2 hours before broiling.

3. **Salad Assembly:** For each serving, mound 3 oz/85 g bean salad on a plate. Remove 3 oz/85 g shrimp from the marinade, draining well. Place on a sizzler platter, top with ¾ oz/21 g oreganata crumb mixture. Broil until the shrimp are fully cooked and the crumbs are golden brown, about 3 minutes. Arrange the shrimp on the salad and season with a squeeze of fresh lemon juice. Serve immediately.

Oreganata Crumb Mixture

YIELD: 10 OZ/283 G

7 oz/198 g dry bread crumbs

3 oz/85 g Parmesan cheese, grated

3 tbsp/9 g minced oregano leaves

3 tbsp/9 g minced flat-leaf parsley leaves

1 tbsp/3 g minced mint leaves

1 tbsp/9 g finely grated lemon zest

⅛ tsp/0.25 g red pepper flakes

Salt, as needed

Ground black pepper, as needed

2 fl oz/60 mL olive oil, or as needed to moisten

1. Blend the bread crumbs, Parmesan, oregano, parsley, mint, lemon zest, red pepper flakes, salt, and pepper.

2. Use a fork or wooden spoon to work in enough olive oil to moisten the mixture; the mixture should look like coarse grains of sand.

Corona Bean Salad with Grilled Baby Octopus

YIELD: 10 SERVINGS

½ oz/15 mL olive oil

2 oz/57 g onion, cut into medium dice

2 oz/57 g carrot, cut into medium dice

1 oz/28 g celery, cut into medium dice

3 garlic cloves, crushed

2 lb/907 g baby octopus, cleaned and cut into portions

4 fl oz/120 mL dry white wine

12 fl oz/360 mL water

8 fl oz/240 mL tomato juice

4 thyme sprigs

2 rosemary sprigs

2 bay leaves

½ tsp/2.50 g salt

¼ tsp/0.50 g ground black pepper

MARINADE

4 fl oz/120 mL olive oil

½ oz/14 g thyme leaves

½ oz/14 g rosemary leaves

¾ oz/21 g garlic cloves, crushed

Salt, as needed

Ground black pepper, as needed

PLATE COMPONENTS

2 lb/907 g Corona Bean Salad with Basil (page 117)

20 lemon wedges

2½ oz/71 g flat-leaf parsley, leaves only

1 oz/28 g fennel fronds

5 oz/142 g frisée, white heart only

2 oz/57 g celery heart leaves

Basil Oil (page 490), as needed

Olive oil, as needed

Sea salt, as needed

Ground black pepper, as needed

1. Prepare the octopus: Heat the olive oil in a saucepot over medium heat. Add the onion, carrot, and celery; sweat, stirring occasionally, until tender and translucent, 5 minutes. Add the garlic and sweat until aromatic. Add the octopus and continue to cook, turning the octopus until it is stiff on all sides, 2 to 3 minutes.

2. Add the white wine, stirring to deglaze the pan, and continue to simmer until the wine is reduced to one-third its original volume. Add the water, tomato juice, thyme, rosemary, bay leaf, salt, and pepper, or to taste. Braise the octopus over very low heat, uncovered, until tender, about 1 hour. Remove and discard the bay leaf and herb sprigs. Cool and reserve the octopus in the braising liquid until ready to grill.

3. Prepare the marinade: Combine the oil, thyme, rosemary, and garlic. Add salt and pepper to taste and reserve.

4. **Salad Assembly:** Mound 3 oz/85 g bean salad on a plate. Remove 3 oz/85 g octopus from the braising liquid, draining well. Brush or roll the octopus in the marinade and grill over a hot fire until marked and very hot, 1 to 2 minutes per side. Arrange the grilled octopus on the salad and season with a squeeze of fresh lemon juice. Garnish the plate with a lemon wedge, parsley, fennel fronds, frisée, and celery hearts. Drizzle with a little basil oil and extra-virgin olive oil. Scatter with sea salt and freshly ground pepper. Serve.

Mediterranean Salad with Tuna Confit

This salad was composed by the late Chef Catherine Brandel to celebrate the grand opening of the Culinary Institute's California campus at Greystone in St. Helena. It combines a rich tuna confit with the fresh produce grown on campus.

VEGETABLE GARNISH

10 red potatoes

10 plum tomatoes, peeled and quartered

10 radishes, sliced thin

5 celery stalks, sliced

2 green peppers, cut into strips

1 Spanish onion, sliced

4 oz/113 g Niçoise olives (3 per serving)

3 tbsp/9 g chopped basil

15 fl oz/450 mL Lemon-Parsley Vinaigrette (page 30)

1 lb 4 oz/567 g mixed lettuces, washed and dried

1 lb 14 oz/850 g Tuna Confit (page 220)

20 anchovy fillets

5 hard-boiled eggs, quartered

Ground black pepper, as needed

1. Steam the potatoes in their skins until tender. Dry and slice thin while still warm. Combine the potatoes with the remaining vegetable garnish ingredients and pour 5 fl oz/150 mL vinaigrette over the mixture. Toss gently until evenly coated. Let rest at room temperature 30 minutes before serving.

2. **Salad Assembly:** For each serving, toss 2 oz/57 g mixed greens with 1 fl oz/30 mL vinaigrette. Mound on a chilled plate. Top with 4 tomato quarters and about 4 oz/113 g of the other vegetables. Top with 3 oz/85 g drained tuna confit, 2 anchovy fillets, and 2 hard-boiled egg quarters. Grind fresh black pepper over the salad just before serving.

Smoked Duck and Malfatti Salad with Roasted Shallot Vinaigrette

YIELD: 10 ENTRÉE SERVINGS

Malfatti means something that is poorly made or irregularly shaped, so when making the pasta for this salad, exact dimensions are not important. This warm salad combines several flavors and textures that may appear to be unusual, but when this salad is executed properly, it is hard to find a more pleasing dish.

8 oz/227 g Malfatti Pasta (page 539)

1 lb 4 oz/567 g mixed bitter greens (such as arugula, frisée, and radicchio), washed and dried

10 oz/283 g chanterelles, halved or quartered if necessary

2 to 3 fl oz/60 to 90 mL olive oil for sautéing, or as needed

1 lb/454 g Smoked Duck (page 203), breast only, cut into strips across the grain

15 fl oz/450 mL Roasted Shallot Vinaigrette (page 33)

Salt, as needed

Ground black pepper, as needed

3 oz/85 g Parmesan cheese

1. Cook the pasta in boiling salted water until al dente. Refresh in cold water; drain and dry. Toss with a small amount of olive oil if cooked in advance.

2. Tear or cut the greens into bite-sized pieces. Refrigerate until needed.

3. **Salad Assembly:** For each serving, sauté 1 oz/28 g mushrooms in 2 tsp/10 mL oil until tender. Add about 2 oz/57 g cooked pasta and 1½ oz/43 g duck. Toss over high heat until hot. Add 2 oz/57 g mixed greens and 1 fl oz/30 mL vinaigrette to the pan. Toss briskly and mound on a warm plate once the ingredients are just warmed through. Drizzle with an additional ½ fl oz/15 mL dressing. Season with salt and pepper and garnish with shaved Parmesan and some of the shallots from the dressing. Serve while still warm.

CHEF'S NOTES: This salad is best made in a nonstick pan in small batches done at the very last minute before being served. Be certain to distribute the shallots evenly over the salad.

Southern Fried Chicken Salad

YIELD: 10 ENTRÉE SERVINGS

2 lb/907 g chicken breasts, boneless and skinless (about 7)

8 fl oz/240 mL buttermilk

5 butterhead lettuce (such as Boston, Bibb, or Kentucky Limestone)

30 cherry tomatoes

2 Vidalia onions

4 oz/113 g flour (seasoned with black pepper and salt)

12 fl oz/360 mL peanut oil

3¾ oz/106 g white mushrooms, sliced

1½ oz/43 g capers

⅔ oz/19 g minced shallots

2½ fl oz/75 mL white wine vinegar

2⅔ oz/75 g Dijon mustard

1¼ oz/35 g chopped tarragon

1. Trim the chicken breasts and cut into ½-oz/14-g strips. Pour the buttermilk over the chicken and marinate under refrigeration for no more than 1 hour.

2. Separate the lettuce into leaves; wash and dry. Core and quarter the tomatoes. Slice the onions thinly and separate into rings. Refrigerate all separately.

3. **Salad Assembly:** For each serving, remove 6 pieces of chicken from the buttermilk and dredge in the seasoned flour. Pan-fry in 1½ fl oz/45 mL peanut oil. Remove and drain on absorbent toweling while finishing the dressing.

4. Add 2½ oz/71 g sliced mushrooms to the peanut oil along with 1 tsp/5 g capers and ½ tsp/2 g shallots; sauté until the mushrooms are tender. Add ½ fl oz/15 mL vinegar and 1½ tsp/8 g mustard. Heat through, remove from the heat, and stir in 1 tbsp/3 g tarragon.

5. Arrange 2 oz/57 g lettuce on a chilled plate. Top with the chicken, tomato, and onion. Pour the warm sauce over the salad and serve immediately.

Arugula Salad with Hot Italian Sausage, Cannellini Beans, and Roasted Peppers

YIELD: 10 SERVINGS

SALAD GREENS

1 lb/454 g arugula (about 4 bunches)

1 head frisée lettuce

20 leaves red endive

2 lb 8 oz/1.13 kg hot Italian sausage

1 red onion, peeled

16 fl oz/480 mL Balsamic Vinaigrette (page 27)

2 roasted red peppers, cut into batonnet

2 roasted yellow peppers, cut into batonnet

15 oz/425 g cooked cannellini beans

1 oz/28 g capers, rinsed and drained

5 oz/142 g Parmesan cheese

Salt, as needed

Coarse-ground black pepper, as needed

1. Rinse the salad greens, dry thoroughly, and tear or cut into pieces if necessary. Refrigerate until needed, keeping endive separate.

2. Grill the sausage to an internal temperature of 155°F/68°C. Let the sausages rest for 15 minutes before slicing into 4 or 5 pieces, cutting on the bias. Keep warm.

3. Thinly slice the onion across the grain and break into rings. Refrigerate until needed.

4. **Salad Assembly:** For each serving, toss 2 oz/57 g combined arugula and frisée with 1 fl oz/30 mL vinaigrette. Mound on a chilled plate. Add 3 spears of endive. Top with a sliced sausage, about ½ oz/14 g each of the red and yellow peppers, 1½ oz/43 g beans, and a few onion rings and capers. Drizzle with another ½ fl oz/15 mL vinaigrette. Shave Parmesan over the salad; season with salt and pepper. Serve immediately.

SANDWICHES

Sandwiches have been part of virtually all cuisines since well before any written records were kept, though they have not always been called *sandwiches*. The honor of naming this favorite luncheon item goes to the infamous gambler John Montague, the fourth Earl of Sandwich. According to legend, this gentleman refused to leave the gaming tables because he didn't want to break his winning streak. He asked that some bread filled with meat be brought to him, and the rage for sandwiches was born.

four

Louis P. De Gouy published *Sandwich Manual for Professionals* in 1940. His approach to the assembly of sandwiches, based on his work as the chef at New York's famous Waldorf-Astoria Hotel, detailed hundreds of sandwiches organized into specific categories. This classic work has stood the test of time and is still a valuable resource of practical information and inspiration.

Sandwiches can range from delicate finger and tea sandwiches served on doilies to pan bagnat, traditionally served wrapped in plain paper from stalls in open markets in southern France. The term may be used for an elegant bite-sized morsel of foie gras served on toasted brioche as an amuse-gueule or a grilled Reuben on rye served with potato salad and a pickle. We can select from diverse culinary traditions, from Scandinavian smørrebrød to American regional favorites like the po'boy to Italian bruschetta and panini to Mexican tacos and burritos. What unifies the concept of the sandwich in all instances is a tasty filling served on or in bread or a similar wrapper.

In this chapter you will learn about handling and preparing ingredients to make the following styles:

- Cold sandwiches

- Hot sandwiches, including grilled sandwiches

- Finger and tea sandwiches

Cold sandwiches include standard deli-style versions made from sliced meats or mayonnaise-dressed salads. Club sandwiches, also known as *triple-decker sandwiches,* are included in this category as well.

Hot sandwiches may feature a hot filling, such as hamburgers or pastrami. Others are grilled, such as a Reuben sandwich. In some cases, a hot filling is mounded on the bread and the sandwich is topped with a hot sauce.

Finger and tea sandwiches are delicate items made on fine-grained bread, trimmed of their crusts and precisely cut into shapes and sizes that can be eaten in about two average bites.

Sandwich Elements

The garde manger may be called on to prepare sandwiches for receptions and teas, for lunch and bistro menus, for special appetizers, and for picnics. In order to produce high-quality sandwiches, it is important to understand how basic filling, cutting, and holding techniques contribute to the overall quality of sandwiches.

Breads

Breads for making sandwiches constitue a fairly wide range, including many ethnic specialties. Sliced white and wheat Pullman loaves are used to make many cold sandwiches. The tight crumb of a good Pullman makes it a good choice for delicate tea and finger sandwiches, which must be sliced thinly without crumbling. Whole-grain and peasant-style breads are not always as easy to slice thinly.

Specific breads, buns, rolls, and wrappers are used to make specific sandwiches. The characteristics of the bread and how they fit with the filling should be considered. Bread should be firm enough and thick enough to hold the filling, but not so thick that the sandwich is too dry to enjoy.

Most bread can be sliced in advance of sandwich preparation as long as the slices are carefully covered to prevent drying. Some sandwich recipes call for toasted bread; the toasting should be done immediately before assembling the sandwich.

Bread choices include:

- PULLMAN LOAVES (white, wheat, or rye)

- PEASANT-STYLE BREADS such as sourdough

- FLATBREADS, including focaccia, pita, ciabatta, and lavash

- ROLLS, including hard and soft

- WRAPPERS such as crêpes, tortillas, egg roll wrappers, and phyllo

Spreads

Many sandwich recipes call for a spread that is applied directly to the bread. This element acts as a barrier to keep the bread from getting soggy. Spreads also add moisture to the sandwich and help it to hold together as it is held and eaten. When the sandwich filling includes a "spread" directly in the filling mixture (for example, a mayonnaise-dressed tuna salad), there is no need to add a separate one when assembling the sandwich.

Spreads can be very simple and subtly flavored, or they may themselves bring a special flavor and texture to the sandwich. The following list of spread options includes classic choices as well as some that may not immediately spring to mind as sandwich spreads.

- CREAMY SALAD DRESSINGS

- MAYONNAISE (plain or flavored, such as aïoli or rouille)

- PLAIN AND COMPOUND BUTTERS

- MUSTARD AND KETCHUP

- SPREADABLE CHEESES such as ricotta, cream cheese, and mascarpone

- TAHINI, OLIVE, AND HERB SPREADS
  (hummus, tapenade, and pesto, for example)

- NUT BUTTERS

- JELLY, JAM, COMPOTES, AND CHUTNEYS

- AVOCADO PULP AND GUACAMOLE

- OILS AND VINAIGRETTES

Fillings

Sandwich fillings may be cold or hot, substantial or minimal. In all cases, they are the focus of the sandwich. It is as important to properly roast and slice turkey for club sandwiches as it is to be certain that the watercress for tea sandwiches is perfectly fresh and completely rinsed and dried.

The filling determines how all the other elements of the sandwich are selected and prepared. Choices for fillings include:

- SLICED ROASTED AND SIMMERED MEATS
  (beef, corned beef, pastrami, turkey, ham, pâtés, and sausages)

- SLICED CHEESES

- GRILLED, ROASTED, AND FRESH VEGETABLES

- GRILLED, PAN-FRIED, AND BROILED BURGERS, SAUSAGES, FISH,
  AND POULTRY

- SALADS OF MEATS, POULTRY, EGGS, FISH, AND/OR VEGETABLES

Garnishes

Lettuce, slices of tomato and cheese, onion slices, and sprouts can be used to garnish many sandwiches. These garnishes become part of the sandwich's overall structure.

When sandwiches are plated, a variety of side garnishes may also be included:

- GREEN OR SIDE SALADS

- LETTUCES AND SPROUTS

- SLICED FRESH VEGETABLES

- PICKLE SPEARS AND OLIVES

- DIPS, SPREADS, AND RELISHES

- SLICED FRUITS

Presentation Styles

A sandwich constructed with a top and a bottom slice of bread is known as a *closed sandwich*. Some closed sandwiches have a third slice of bread, making a *club sandwich*. Still other sandwiches have only one slice of bread, which acts as a base; these are *open-faced sandwiches*.

Finger and tea sandwiches (as well as canapé bases; see page 364) are cut into special shapes (see Figure 4-1). To prepare them, the bread is sliced lengthwise so the greatest possible surface area is available. The bread is coated with a spread, filled, garnished if desired, then closed if desired, cut to shape, and served at once.

Straight-edged shapes give the best yield with the lowest food cost. These shapes are created by cutting with a sandwich knife or bread knife into squares, rectangles, diamonds, or triangles. Cutters in various shapes are used to cut rounds, ovals, and other special shapes. The yield is generally lower when preparing these shapes, making them slightly more expensive to produce.

Time should be taken to cut shapes in an exact and uniform fashion so they will look their best when set in straight rows on platters or arranged on plates. It is best to cut tea sandwiches as close to service as possible. If these sandwiches must be prepared ahead of time, they can be held for a few hours, covered with damp cloths or in airtight containers.

4-1. Sandwich styles. **A.** Making specially shaped sandwiches. **B.** Workflow for making open-faced sandwiches.

Spicy Catfish Sandwich

YIELD: 10 SANDWICHES

2 lb 12 oz/1.25 kg catfish fillets

Oil for deep-frying, as needed

2 eggs, beaten

1 fl oz/30 mL milk or water

1 tbsp/3 g Cajun Spice Blend (page 525), as needed

4 oz/113 g flour, or as needed for breading

5⅓ oz/151 g cornmeal, or as needed for breading

9 fl oz/270 mL Rémoulade Sauce (page 36)

10 soft sandwich rolls, split

3 to 4 tomatoes, cut into 20 thin slices

2 red onions, cut into 10 thin slices

10 romaine lettuce leaves (1 head)

1. Trim the catfish and cut into 4-oz/113-g portions. Preheat a deep fryer to 350°F/177°C.

2. Beat the eggs with the milk or water to make an egg wash.

3. Season the fillets with the Cajun spice blend. Dip the catfish into the flour, then the beaten eggs, and then the cornmeal.

4. Deep-fry the catfish until golden brown and cooked through, 2 to 3 minutes. Drain on absorbent towels. Keep warm.

5. **Sandwich Assembly:** For each sandwich, spread 1 fl oz/30 mL rémoulade sauce on a roll. Layer the tomatoes, onions, lettuce, and catfish on the bottom half. Close the sandwich and serve immediately.

PRESENTATION IDEA: Accompany the sandwich with Coleslaw (page 99).

Chicken Burger

YIELD: 10 SANDWICHES

This alternative to beef hamburgers is very popular with guests looking for lower-fat, healthier fare.

1 oz/28 g minced shallot (1 large)	2 tsp/2 g chopped herbs (such as chives, oregano, and basil)
1 fl oz/30 mL vegetable oil	½ tsp/0.50 g chopped rosemary
1 lb 8 oz/680 g white mushrooms, minced	Salt, as needed
3 fl oz/90 mL dry white wine	Ground black pepper, as needed
½ tsp/2.50 g salt, or to taste	½ tsp/0.50 g poultry seasoning, or to taste
¼ tsp/0.50 g ground black pepper, or to taste	5 oz/142 g provolone cheese (10 slices)
2 lb 8 oz/1.13 kg ground chicken	10 soft sandwich rolls, split and toasted
4 oz/113 g dry bread crumbs	10 oz/283 g Tomato Ketchup (page 476)

1. Sauté the minced shallot in the oil over medium heat. Increase the heat, add the mushrooms, and sauté until all the moisture has cooked off. Add the wine and continue to sauté until dry, as for duxelles.

2. Season with salt and pepper. Remove from the heat and chill thoroughly.

3. Combine the chicken with the bread crumbs, mushroom mixture, herbs, salt and pepper, and poultry seasoning.

4. Make a test as for forcemeat (see page 275). Adjust seasoning as necessary.

5. Form the chicken mixture into patties, about 4½ oz/128 g each.

6. Sauté or griddle the patties until browned on both sides.

7. Transfer to a sheet pan or sizzler platter. Top each patty with a slice of provolone. Finish cooking the patties in a medium oven (350°F/177°C to 375°F/191°C) to an internal temperature of 165°F/74°C.

8. **Sandwich Assembly:** For each sandwich, place a patty on a roll, top with 1 oz/28 g tomato ketchup, and serve at once.

Croque Monsieur

YIELD: 10 SANDWICHES

Croque Monsieur is a classic French sandwich available almost everywhere in France, from the beach to the train to sidewalk cafés. Muenster cheese is not a traditional ingredient, but it makes a nice addition. *Croque* implies crisp or crunchy.

20 slices Pullman bread	1 lb 4 oz/567 g boiled ham (10 slices)
10 oz/283 g Dijon mustard	8 oz/227 g Muenster cheese (10 thin slices)
8 oz/227 g Gruyère cheese (10 thin slices)	4 oz/113 g soft butter

1. To assemble the sandwiches for grilling, spread the bread slices with mustard.

2. On 10 of the bread slices, layer 1 slice each of Gruyère, ham, and Muenster over the mustard.

3. Top the sandwiches with the remaining bread slices.

4. Griddle both sides of the sandwiches on a lightly buttered 325°F/163°C griddle until the bread is golden, the cheese is melted, and the sandwich is heated through.

5. Cut the sandwiches on the diagonal and serve immediately.

CROQUE MADAME: Some recipes simply add a fried egg to the Croque Monsieur. In the United States and England, the ham is usually replaced with sliced chicken breast. Use Emmenthaler instead of Gruyère. Grill as directed.

MONTE CRISTO: Dip any of the variations in beaten egg and grill as you would French toast.

Oyster and Shrimp Po'boy

YIELD: 10 SANDWICHES

The po'boy is a specialty of New Orleans. Like heroes, submarines, hoagies, and grinders, the po'boy can contain almost any ingredient, although seafood seems to be one of the most popular fillings.

Oil for deep-frying, as needed

2 eggs

1 fl oz/30 mL milk or water

20 shrimp (16/20 count), peeled and deveined

30 oysters, shucked and drained

1 tsp/5 g salt

¼ tsp/0.50 g ground white pepper

Pinch cayenne

4 oz/113 g all-purpose flour, or as needed for breading

5⅓ oz/151 g cornmeal, or as needed for breading

10 baguettes or hero rolls, split lengthwise

12 fl oz/360 mL Rémoulade Sauce (page 36)

1 head green leaf lettuce, shredded

3 tomatoes, sliced into 20 slices

2 red onions, sliced into 20 slices

3 lemons, cut into wedges (optional)

1. Preheat the oil for deep-frying to 350°F/177°C.

2. Beat the eggs with the milk or water to make an egg wash.

3. Season the seafood with the spices. Dip the shrimp and oysters into the flour, then the egg wash, and then the cornmeal.

4. Deep-fry the breaded shrimp and oysters in batches until golden and cooked through. Drain on paper towels and keep warm.

5. **Sandwich Assembly:** For each sandwich, spread each side of a baguette with ½ fl oz/15 mL rémoulade sauce. Fill the baguette with lettuce, tomato, and onion. Top with 2 shrimp and 3 oysters. Top the seafood with another 1 tsp/5 mL rémoulade sauce, or serve with a serving of sauce on the side. Close the sandwich and serve at once with either sauce or lemon wedges, if desired, on the side.

Barbecued Pulled Pork Sandwich

YIELD: 10 SANDWICHES

2 lb 8 oz/1.13 kg Carolina Barbecued Pork Butt (page 218)

12 oz/340 g Barbecue Sauce (recipe follows)

10 Kaiser rolls

1. Pull the meat off the pork butt and shred it. Remove and discard excess fat.

2. Simmer the shredded pork meat with the barbecue sauce about 15 minutes.

3. Split the Kaiser rolls and grill or toast.

4. **Sandwich Assembly:** For each sandwich, mound approximately 4 to 5 oz/113 to 142 g barbecued pork on the roll and serve immediately.

PRESENTATION IDEA: Accompany the sandwich with Coleslaw (page 99) and Assorted Vegetable Chips (page 486).

Barbecue Sauce

YIELD: 1 GAL/3.84 L

2 fl oz/60 mL vegetable oil

2 lb/907 g minced onions

7 garlic cloves, chopped

10 dried anchos, stems and seeds removed, chopped

3 dried chipotles, coarsely chopped

3 ripe mangos, peeled, seeded, and chopped

64 fl oz/1.92 L ketchup

16 fl oz/480 mL hoisin sauce

32 fl oz/960 mL Chicken Stock (page 529)

8 fl oz/240 mL bourbon

8 fl oz/240 mL cider vinegar

4 oz/113 g brown sugar

4 fl oz/120 mL Worcestershire sauce

4 fl oz/120 mL lemon juice

2 tsp/4 g ground black pepper

1. Heat the vegetable oil in a large saucepan; add the onions and caramelize. Add the garlic and cook until the raw aroma is gone.

2. Add the remaining ingredients and simmer for 1 hour.

3. Purée in a blender until smooth. Reserve until needed. Adjust consistency with water as necessary.

Reuben Sandwich

YIELD: 10 SANDWICHES

6 oz/170 g soft butter

20 slices rye bread

15 oz/425 g Swiss cheese, sliced thin

3 lb 8 oz/1.59 kg corned beef brisket, sliced thin

1 lb 8 oz/680 g Braised Sauerkraut (recipe follows)

4½ fl oz/135 mL Russian Dressing (page 38) (optional)

1. Butter each slice of bread. Lay the slices butter side down on a sheet pan and top with a slice of Swiss cheese.

2. Place 2 oz/57 g beef on each bread slice. Top 10 sandwich halves with 2 oz/57 g sauerkraut, adding ½ fl oz/15 mL Russian dressing if desired.

3. Preheat a sandwich griddle or frying pan to medium heat.

4. For each sandwich, transfer two sandwich halves (one with, one without sauerkraut) and griddle, butter side down, until golden brown, and hot enough to melt the cheese.

5. Invert the sandwich half without sauerkraut on top of the half with sauerkraut.

6. The sandwich may be placed in a 350°F/177°C oven to heat through if needed. Cut the sandwich diagonally in half and serve.

Braised Sauerkraut

YIELD: 1 LB 8 OZ/680 G

6 oz/170 g minced onions

1 fl oz/30 mL bacon fat

1 lb 8 oz/680 g prepared sauerkraut, rinsed and drained

1 oz/28 g sugar

8 fl oz/240 mL Chicken Stock (page 529)

Salt, as needed

Ground white pepper, as needed

1. Sauté the onions in the bacon fat over low heat until tender and translucent. Add the sauerkraut, sugar, stock, salt, and pepper.

2. Simmer for 30 to 40 minutes, or until most of the liquid is absorbed by the sauerkraut.

3. Check seasoning and adjust if necessary. Serve immediately or refrigerate until needed.

Pan Bagnat

YIELD: 10 SANDWICHES

This tasty sandwich is built on excellent fresh, crusty bread. Without that key element, this recipe will produce only an ordinary sandwich.

DRESSING

3 fl oz/90 mL red wine vinegar

½ oz/14 g chopped basil

1½ oz/43 g coarsely chopped Italian parsley (¾ bunch)

4 anchovy fillets

1 jalapeño, roasted, peeled, seeded, and chopped fine

8 fl oz/240 mL extra-virgin olive oil

10 hard rolls

1 lb/454 g Tuna Confit (page 220) or drained oil-packed tuna, flaked

10 oz/283 g tomato concassé

15 oz/425 g Marinated Roasted Peppers (page 94)

3 oz/85 g coarsely chopped pitted black olives

1 large cucumber, peeled, seeded, and chopped

2½ oz/71 g minced red onion

2 hard-boiled eggs, chopped

1½ oz/43 g capers

4 tsp/12 g minced garlic

Salt, as needed

Ground black pepper, as needed

1. Purée the vinegar, basil, parsley, anchovies, and jalapeño in a blender. With the motor running, slowly pour in the oil to emulsify.

2. Cut the rolls in half lengthwise and scoop out the insides, leaving a shell ½ in/1 cm thick.

3. Crumble the removed bread and combine it with the tuna, tomatoes, roasted peppers, olives, cucumber, onion, eggs, capers, and garlic. Add enough dressing to moisten and bind the filling. Season to taste with salt and pepper.

4. **Sandwich Assembly:** For each sandwich, brush a roll with some of the remaining dressing. Fill the roll with 5 oz/142 g filling, and firmly press the sandwich closed. Wrap each sandwich tightly with deli paper and let rest at room temperature at least 1 hour before serving.

Roast Beef on a Roll

YIELD: 10 SANDWICHES

10 sandwich rolls, 5 to 6 in/13 to 15 cm diameter

5 oz/142 g Aïoli (page 36)

1 lb 4 oz/567 g watercress, cleaned and trimmed

2 lb 4 oz/1.02 kg roast beef, rare, sliced thin

10 oz/283 g Pickled Red Onions (page 485), drained

1. Split each roll in half and spread ½ oz/14 g horseradish sauce inside.

2. Place 2 oz/57 g watercress on each roll.

3. Layer 1¾ oz/50 g roast beef on top of the watercress, place 1 oz/28 g pickled onions over the beef, and top onion with another 1¾ oz/50 g beef. Top the final layer of beef with another 2 oz/57 g watercress and top with the other half of the roll. It is best if these sandwiches are made right before serving. Wrap them gently in parchment paper rather than plastic wrap.

Roasted Chicken and Peppers on Olive Bread

YIELD: 10 SANDWICHES

2 lb 8 oz/1.13 kg roasted chicken meat (from two 3-lb/1.36-kg chickens)

1 lb 4 oz/567 g Marinated Peppers and Mushrooms (page 94)

1 lb 1⅓ oz/491 g Whole-Milk Ricotta Cheese (page 347)

2 oz/57 g Mascarpone (page 346)

1 oz/28 g grated Parmesan cheese

Ground white pepper, as needed

20 slices olive bread

2⅔ fl oz/80 mL Basic Herb Oil (page 490), made with rosemary

1. Shred the chicken to approximately batonnet size. Stir it into the peppers and mushrooms. Adjust seasoning as needed.

2. Mix together the ricotta, mascarpone, and Parmesan. Season with white pepper.

3. **Sandwich Assembly:** For each sandwich, brush 2 slices of bread with rosemary olive oil and grill on both sides until toasted. Spread about 1 oz/28 g cheese mixture on one slice of bread. Mound 5 oz/142 g chicken salad over the cheese spread and top with the second slice of bread. Cut the sandwich diagonally and serve immediately.

PRESENTATION IDEA: Accompany with a salad of tossed baby greens, fresh mozzarella cubes, diced tomato, and Basic Red Wine Vinaigrette (page 27).

Roast Chicken with Salsa Verde on Focaccia

YIELD: 10 SANDWICHES

10 Focaccia pieces (page 540), cut into 5-in/13-cm squares

5 fl oz/150 mL Basic Mayonnaise (page 35)

5 fl oz/150 mL Salsa Verde (page 42)

5 oz/142 g romaine or watercress, trimmed and torn into pieces

2 lb 8 oz/1.13 kg chicken breast, boneless and skinless, roasted

5 pequilla peppers, seeded, halved, and roasted

Salt, as needed

Pepper, as needed

1. Slice the chicken as thinly as possible without shredding, with an electric slicer or by hand.

2. For each serving, split a focaccia square horizontally. Spread each piece with ½ fl oz/15 mL lemon mayonnaise, ½ fl oz/15 mL salsa verde, and top with ½ oz/14 g romaine.

3. Arrange 4 oz/113 g sliced chicken on one piece and top with one pequilla pepper half; spread the pepper open so it covers as much of the chicken as possible. Season and close the sandwich, secure with picks, and slice.

OPTIONAL: Wrap sandwiches in butcher or deli paper for counter service.

Garlic-Roasted Leg of Lamb Sandwich

YIELD: 10 SANDWICHES

3 lb/1.36 kg boneless leg of lamb (half a leg)

2 fl oz/60 mL olive oil

1¼ oz/35 g slivered garlic (8 cloves)

1 tbsp/3 g chopped fresh rosemary

1½ tsp/7.50 g salt

¾ tsp/1.50 g coarse-ground black pepper

10 Focaccia pieces (page 540), cut into 4-in/10-cm squares

5 fl oz/150 mL Basic Mayonnaise (page 35) made with olive oil

1. Trim the lamb and lay flat. Combine 1 fl oz/30 mL of the oil with the garlic, rosemary, salt, and pepper. Spread this mixture evenly over the roast, roll, and tie.

2. Rub the roast with the remaining olive oil and marinate under refrigeration overnight.

3. Preheat a charcoal grill and the oven to 375°F/191°C. Remove the roast from the refrigerator and let it warm slightly at room temperature for 25 to 30 minutes.

4. Sear the roast on a charcoal grill. Roast it in the oven to an internal temperature of 130°F/54°C.

5. Rest the roast for 20 minutes in a warm place, then slice thinly.

6. **Sandwich Assembly:** For each sandwich, split a piece of focaccia horizontally and spread it with ½ fl oz/15 mL mayonnaise. Mound about 4 oz/113 g sliced meat on one piece of the focaccia. Close the sandwich and serve.

PRESENTATION IDEA: Hearts of Artichoke Salad (page 95) makes a great accompaniment for this sandwich, as do Mediterranean Potato Salad (page 104) and Artichoke Chips (page 486).

Salmon B.L.T.

YIELD: 10 SANDWICHES

9 fl oz/270 mL Basic Mayonnaise (page 35)

1 oz/14 g chopped capers

Salt, as needed

Ground black pepper, as needed

2 fl oz/60 mL olive oil

10 salmon fillets (4 oz/113 g each)

30 slices Basic Bacon (page 210), cooked

20 slices bread

20 leaves green leaf lettuce

30 slices tomato (5 tomatoes)

1. Stir together the mayonnaise and capers. Season with salt and pepper.

2. Season the oil generously with salt and pepper.

3. **Sandwich Assembly:** For each sandwich, brush 1 salmon piece with the seasoned oil. Grill the salmon until cooked through, about 2 minutes on each side. Crisp 3 slices bacon over medium heat, about 2 minutes. Drain briefly.

4. Toast 2 slices of bread and spread with caper mayonnaise. Place 1 lettuce leaf and the grilled salmon on 1 slice of toast. Layer it with a second lettuce leaf, bacon, and tomato. Top with the remaining slice of toast. Secure the sandwich with long toothpicks and cut in half.

OPEN-FACED SALMON B.L.T. WITH AÏOLI: Spread a toasted slice of whole-grain bread with 1 fl oz/30 mL Aïoli (page 36). Assemble the sandwich by layering the lettuce leaf, tomato, bacon, and salmon over the aïoli. Serve open-faced.

Grilled Chicken Sandwich with Pancetta, Arugula, and Aïoli

YIELD: 10 SANDWICHES

2½ fl oz/75 mL olive oil

2½ oz/71 g garlic, sliced

1 tbsp/3 g fresh thyme

1 oz/28 g lemon zest

Pinch salt

Pinch ground black pepper

10 boneless and skinless chicken breasts (4 oz/113 g each)

30 slices Pancetta (page 212), ⅛ in/3 mm thick

20 slices sourdough bread

10 fl oz/300 mL Aïoli (page 36)

6 oz/170 g arugula, washed and dried

1. Combine the oil, garlic, thyme, lemon zest, salt, and pepper.

2. Pound the chicken breasts to an even thickness and marinate, refrigerated, in the oil mixture overnight.

3. Preheat the grill and the oven to 350°F/177°C. Lay the pancetta on a sheet pan and place in the oven until crisp.

4. **Sandwich Assembly:** For each sandwich, lightly brush 2 slices of bread with the olive oil mixture and grill over medium heat until golden and crispy on the outside but soft on the inside. Reserve. Grill a chicken breast until cooked through.

5. Spread 1 fl oz/30 mL aïoli on the grilled bread. Place a few leaves of arugula, 3 slices of crispy pancetta, and the chicken breast on one side of the bread. Top with the other half of bread and slice diagonally.

PRESENTATION IDEAS: In the summer, serve with Marinated Tomatoes (page 93), and in the winter with Celeriac and Tart Apple Salad (page 101).

Horseradish-Marinated Grilled Chicken Wrap

YIELD: 10 SERVINGS

2 lb/907 g chicken breast, boneless, skinless

2 oz/57 g horseradish, grated

2 oz/57 g Vidalia or other sweet onion, grated

2 fl oz/60 mL balsamic vinegar

1 fl oz/30 mL olive oil

2 garlic cloves, minced

½ tsp/0.50 g crushed juniper berries

1 tsp/1 g chopped rosemary

Olive oil, as needed

Salt, as needed

Pepper, as needed

10 flour tortillas, 10 in/25 cm diameter

1 lb 8 oz/680 g mixed greens

8 fl oz/240 mL Creamy Black Pepper Dressing (page 39)

1. Trim all visible fat from the chicken breasts. Cut each breast in half lengthwise and place in a shallow dish.

2. Purée the horseradish, onion, vinegar, oil, garlic, juniper berries, and rosemary in a food processor. Pour the puréed mixture over the chicken and turn each piece to coat. Cover and refrigerate for 4 hours, turning once.

3. Preheat the grill to high. Remove the breasts from the marinade, scraping off any excess. Blot the chicken dry with absorbent paper toweling. Brush with oil and season with salt and pepper.

4. Grill the chicken about 3 to 4 minutes on each side, or until cooked through and firm to the touch. Thinly slice the chicken breast and reserve.

5. Warm a tortilla in a hot skillet for about 15 seconds on each side.

6. Toss the salad greens with the dressing. For each tortilla, place 1 cup/240 mL salad and 3¼ oz/92 g sliced chicken breast on the warmed tortilla. Wrap tightly and secure with a toothpick. Serve immediately.

Vegetable Burger

YIELD: 10 SANDWICHES

1 lb 8 oz/680 g carrots

4 oz/113 g celery

4 oz/113 g onion

½ red pepper

½ green pepper

8 oz/227 g white mushrooms, chopped

4 oz/113 g walnuts, ground

4 oz/113 g green onions, finely chopped

2 eggs

Sesame oil, as needed

Soy sauce, as needed

Tabasco sauce, as needed

Ground ginger, as needed

Salt, as needed

Ground black pepper, as needed

1 oz/28 g matzo meal, or as needed

5 oz/142 g cornflake crumbs, or as needed

Oil for frying, as needed

10 soft hamburger rolls

5 fl oz/150 mL yogurt sauce (see Chef's Note)

3½ oz/99 g alfalfa sprouts

1. Preheat the oven to 350°F/177°C. Grind the carrots, celery, onion, and peppers through a medium die. Press out any excess liquid. Add the mushrooms, walnuts, green onions, eggs, sesame oil, soy sauce, Tabasco sauce, ginger, salt, and pepper. Mix well.

2. Add enough matzo meal to firm up and bind the mixture.

3. Form a small test patty, coat in cornflake crumbs, and pan-fry. Adjust seasoning as necessary.

4. Form the remaining mixture into 10 patties of equal size. Roll in cornflakes to coat.

5. **Sandwich Assembly:** For each sandwich, pan-fry both sides of 1 vegetable burger in oil and finish in the oven until cooked thoroughly. Split and toast a roll; spread with yogurt sauce. Place the vegetable burger and alfalfa sprouts on one half of the roll. Top with the other half and serve immediately.

CHEF'S NOTE: To make the yogurt sauce, add the juice of 2 lemons and 2 tsp/6 g finely minced garlic to 32 fl oz/960 mL plain yogurt. Season with salt and pepper.

Turkey Club Sandwich

YIELD: 10 SANDWICHES

30 slices white Pullman bread

10 oz/283 g Basic Mayonnaise (page 35)

20 leaves green leaf lettuce, washed and dried

1 lb 4 oz/567 g roast turkey breast, sliced thin

1 lb 4 oz/567 g Smoked Ham (page 214), sliced thin

20 slices tomatoes, sliced thin

15 strips Basic Bacon (page 210), cut in half, cooked

1. **Sandwich Assembly:** For each sandwich, toast 3 pieces of bread and spread with mayonnaise. Top one piece of toast with a lettuce leaf and 2 oz/57 g each turkey and ham. Cover with a second piece of toast.

2. Top with 1 lettuce leaf, 2 tomato slices, and 3 half strips of bacon. Top with the remaining toast, secure with 4 club frill picks, and cut into four triangles.

Smoked Turkey on Focaccia

YIELD: 10 SANDWICHES

2 lb 8 oz/1.13 kg Smoked Turkey Breast (page 202), skinless, boneless breast

10 Focaccia pieces (page 540), cut into 4-in/10-cm squares

1 oz/28 g butter, softened

15 oz/425 g Apple Chutney (page 478)

5 oz/142 g watercress sprigs, trimmed, rinsed, and dried

Salt, as needed

Ground black pepper, as needed

1. Slice the turkey breast as thinly as possible, without shredding, with a slicer or by hand.

2. **Sandwich Assembly:** For each serving, split a focaccia square horizontally and spread ½ tsp/2 g butter on each half. Spread ¾ oz/21 g apple chutney on each half and top with ½ oz/14 g watercress.

3. Arrange 4 oz/113 g sliced turkey on one piece. Season with salt and pepper and close the sandwich, secure with picks, and slice.

OPTIONAL: Wrap sandwiches in butcher or deli paper for counter service.

Duck Confit with Apples and Brie on a Baguette

YIELD: 10 SANDWICHES

6 oz/170 g duck fat (from confit)

12 oz/340 g onions, cut into julienne

1 lb/454 g Granny Smith apples, peeled, cut into small dice (about 3 each)

Salt, as needed

Ground black pepper, as needed

½ oz/14 g Dijon mustard

1½ fl oz/45 mL white wine vinegar

3 fl oz/90 mL olive oil

2 lb/907 g Duck Confit (page 219), shredded meat

10 oz/283 g frisée lettuce, cleaned

2 baguettes, 20 in/51 cm each, cut into 4-in/10-cm lengths and split

1 lb 14 oz/850 g Brie, sliced into 1-oz/28-g slices

1. Heat 2 tbsp (about 1 oz/28 g) of the duck fat in a large skillet over high heat. Add the onions and apples and sauté, stirring frequently, until pale golden, about 10 minutes. Season to taste with salt and pepper. Cool and reserve.

2. Whisk together the mustard and vinegar. Slowly drizzle in the olive oil, whisking constantly. Season with salt and pepper. Set aside. (Before using, whisk to recombine.)

3. **Sandwich Assembly:** Heat 1 tbsp (about ½ oz/14 g) duck fat in a medium sauté pan. Add 3½ oz/99 g duck meat and 2 oz/57 g onion mixture. Toss to coat in the fat and heat through, about 1 minute.

4. Remove the pan from the heat and add ½ fl oz/15 mL vinaigrette and 1 oz/28 g frisée. Toss to combine ingredients in the pan and immediately spoon onto a split baguette.

5. Top the mixture with three 1-oz/28-g slices brie. Place the sandwich in a 450°F/232°C oven to crisp the bread and melt the cheese, about 2 minutes. Serve immediately.

Smoked Salmon on Challah

YIELD: 10 SANDWICHES

1 lb 14 oz/851 g Smoked Salmon (page 196)

20 slices challah

5 oz/142 g Aïoli (page 36)

5 oz/142 g watercress, trimmed, rinsed, and dried

10 oz/283 g seedless cucumber, peeled and thinly sliced

Salt, as needed

Ground black pepper, as needed

1. Slice the salmon, by hand, as thinly as possible without shredding.

2. For each sandwich, spread 2 slices of challah with ½ oz/14 g aïoli per slice. Top each piece of challah with ½ oz/14 g watercress. Top one slice with 3 oz/85 g sliced smoked salmon and place 1 oz/28 g sliced cucumber on top of the salmon. Season with salt and pepper and close the sandwich, secure with picks, and slice.

OPTIONAL: Wrap sandwiches in butcher or deli paper for counter service.

New England Lobster Roll

YIELD: 10 SANDWICHES

Lobster rolls are synonymous with summertime throughout New England and Long Island. The opening of roadside stands selling these luscious sandwiches is a seasonal highlight. It may seem incongruous to pair lobster with frankfurter rolls, but the combination is wonderful. Any other bread, no matter how wonderful, changes the entire character of the sandwich.

3 Maine lobsters (1 lb 8 oz/680 g each), cooked (page 547)

6 oz/170 g celery (3 to 4 stalks), cut into small dice

10 oz/283 g Basic Mayonnaise (page 35)

½ oz/14 g Dijon mustard

2 tsp/10 mL lemon juice

Pinch salt

Pinch ground white pepper

10 frankfurter rolls

1. Remove the lobster meat from the shells and cut into ½-in/1-cm dice.

2. Combine the lobster meat with the celery, mayonnaise, mustard, lemon juice, salt, and pepper in a mixing bowl. Adjust seasoning.

3. **Sandwich Assembly:** For each sandwich, open a roll and toast it on a griddle until golden brown. Fill immediately with some of the lobster salad and serve.

Soft-Shell Crab Sandwich with Rémoulade Sauce

The crabs may be pan-fried to order, or they may be prepared in batches if necessary.

8 oz/227 g all-purpose flour

½ oz/14 g Old Bay seasoning

1 tbsp/6 g ground mustard

2 tsp/10 g salt

¼ tsp/0.50 g cayenne

32 fl oz/960 mL peanut oil, or as needed

10 jumbo soft-shell crabs, cleaned
(page 550)

16 fl oz/480 mL milk

10 soft sandwich rolls, split

5 fl oz/150 mL Rémoulade Sauce
(page 36)

20 lettuce leaves, shredded

2 lemons, cut into wedges

1. Combine the flour, Old Bay, mustard, salt, and cayenne.

2. Heat 1 in/3 cm peanut oil in a rondeau to 375°F/191°C.

3. **Sandwich Assembly:** For each sandwich, dip a crab into the milk and dredge it in the seasoned flour. Pan-fry the crab in the hot peanut oil until golden on both sides, 4 to 5 minutes total. Drain on absorbent paper towels.

4. Toast a roll and spread with ½ to 1 fl oz/15 to 30 mL rémoulade sauce. Add a layer of lettuce. Top with the crab and close the sandwich with the top of the bun. Serve with lemon wedges.

Eggplant Wrap

YIELD: 10 SANDWICHES

4 fl oz/120 mL olive oil

3 garlic cloves, crushed

2 tsp/4 g ground cumin, toasted

½ oz/14 g salt

2 tsp/4 g ground black pepper

1 lb 9 oz/709 g eggplant, peeled and cut into medium dice

13 oz/369 g tomatoes, peeled, seeded, and chopped

2½ tbsp/7.50 g chopped cilantro

1 fl oz/30 mL lemon juice

⅛ tsp/0.25 g cayenne

1¼ tsp/6.25 mL red wine vinegar

10 flour tortillas, 10 in/25 cm diameter

11 oz/312 g mesclun greens, chopped romaine, or other greens

1. Heat 2 fl oz/60 mL olive oil with the garlic cloves, ½ tsp cumin, and 1 tsp/5 g salt until aromatic. Remove from the heat, allow to infuse for 30 minutes to 1 hour, strain, and reserve.

2. Sauté the eggplant in a large sauté pan with the remaining olive oil over medium-high heat until tender and golden brown, about 15 minutes. Season with the remaining salt and the pepper.

3. Combine the tomatoes with the eggplant, cilantro, lemon juice, cayenne, vinegar, and remaining cumin. Cool and reserve.

4. Warm each of the tortillas on a dry pan heated over high heat. Stack and cover with a clean towel until ready to prepare the wraps.

5. Spread the tortillas on a table. Using a pastry brush, lightly paint the inside of the tortillas with the infused oil.

6. For each wrap, place 4 oz/113 g mesclun greens on one-quarter of a tortilla.

7. Spoon 3 oz/85 g eggplant mixture next to the greens. Fold the tortilla edges in toward the center and roll it up. This wrap may be made several hours ahead, wrapped, and served as needed.

Eggplant and Prosciutto Panini

8⅔ oz/246 g whole-milk Ricotta Cheese (page 347)

2 tsp/2 g chopped fresh basil

1 tsp/2 g coarse-ground black pepper

1 tsp/1 g chopped oregano

1 tsp/1 g chopped flat-leaf parsley

½ tsp/2.50 g salt

10 Italian hard rolls

5 fl oz/150 mL oil from marinated eggplant

1 lb 4 oz/567 g Marinated Eggplant Filling (recipe follows)

1 lb 4 oz/567 g prosciutto, sliced thin

1. In a bowl combine the ricotta cheese, basil, pepper, oregano, parsley, and salt and mix well. Cover and refrigerate overnight.

2. **Sandwich Assembly:** For each sandwich, split a roll lengthwise and brush the inside with oil from the marinated eggplant. Spread 1 oz/28 g herbed ricotta mixture on half of the roll and top with 2 oz/57 g each eggplant filling and prosciutto. Top with the other half of the roll.

Marinated Eggplant Filling

1 lb/454 g Italian eggplant

½ oz/14 g salt

16 fl oz/480 mL olive oil

3 garlic cloves, crushed

1½ fl oz/45 mL red wine vinegar

2 tbsp/12 g dried oregano

1 tbsp/6 g dried basil

1 tbsp/6 g coarse-ground black pepper

Pinch crushed red pepper flakes

1. Slice the eggplant into ⅛-in/3-mm slices. Layer the slices in a colander, salting each layer liberally. Let sit 1 hour.

2. Rinse off the bitter liquid and blot the slices dry with absorbent paper towels.

3. Combine the remaining ingredients to make a marinade.

4. Toss the eggplant slices in marinade; cover and refrigerate for 3 to 4 days. Stir every day.

CHEF'S NOTE: The eggplant is ready when the flesh is relatively translucent and no longer tastes raw.

Falafel in Pita Pockets

YIELD: 10 SERVINGS

1 lb/454 g dried chickpeas

8½ oz/241 g onion, coarsely chopped

1 tbsp/9 g garlic, minced

½ bunch cilantro, large stems removed

1 tbsp/6 g ground coriander

4 tsp/8 g ground cumin

½ tsp/1 g cayenne

½ oz/14 g salt

16 fl oz/480 mL pure olive oil

5 pitas, halved

6 oz/170 g shredded lettuce

20 fl oz/600 mL Tahini Sauce (page 42)

1. Sort the dried chickpeas and remove any stones. Rinse and drain. Cover with fresh cold water and soak overnight or up to 24 hours. Drain. Rinse with fresh water and drain again thoroughly.

2. Place the chickpeas in a food processor fitted with a blade attachment and process until finely ground. Process in batches as necessary. Remove and place in a large bowl.

3. Place the onion, garlic, cilantro, coriander, cumin, cayenne, and salt in the food processor and pulse until the onion, cilantro, and garlic are evenly minced and well blended with the spices. Combine with the ground chickpeas.

4. Form 30 small patties, approximately 1¼ oz/35 g each and about 1½ in/4 cm in diameter.

5. Heat half of the olive oil in a large frying pan until very hot but not smoking. Gently lay half of the patties in the hot oil. Fry, browning the first side, about 5 minutes. Reduce the heat to medium-low, flip the patties, and cook slowly so the raw chickpea mixture is cooked all the way through. Remove to a rack or sheet pan lined with absorbent paper towels. Drain. Serve warm. Cook the second half of the mixture in fresh oil.

6. Heat a pita half and make a pocket in it. Put lettuce in the pita, add 3 falafel patties, and top with tahini sauce. Repeat for each sandwich.

Shrimp Open-Faced Sandwich

YIELD: 30 OPEN-FACED SANDWICHES

30 shrimp (26/30 count), cooked, peeled, and deveined

5 fl oz/150 mL Green Mayonnaise (page 35)

30 slices French bread, cut ¼ in/6 mm thick on the bias

30 mâche sprigs

10 radishes, sliced

1. Slice the shrimp in half lengthwise.

2. **Sandwich Assembly:** Spread 1 tsp/5 mL green mayonnaise on each bread slice. Top with 1 shrimp, halved. Garnish with a sprig of mâche, 2 radish slices, and a small dollop of green mayonnaise.

Tuna Salad Open-Faced Sandwich

YIELD: 30 OPEN-FACED SANDWICHES

12 oz/340 g Italian oil-packed tuna, drained

2⅔ fl oz/80 mL extra-virgin olive oil

1½ fl oz/45 mL balsamic vinegar

2 oz/57 g small-dice onion

3 oz/85 g small-dice celery

Salt, as needed

Ground black pepper, as needed

Baby red leaf lettuce, as needed

Baby romaine lettuce, as needed

30 whole wheat bread triangles

5 Kalamata olives, slivered

15 green olives, halved

1. Flake the tuna and combine with the oil, vinegar, onion, and celery. Toss lightly. Season with salt and pepper; set aside and keep cool.

2. **Sandwich Assembly:** Place a small piece of red leaf lettuce and a small piece of romaine on each bread triangle. Top with ½ oz/14 g tuna salad, 2 slivers of Kalamata olive, and 1 green olive half.

Curried Chicken Salad Open-Faced Sandwich

YIELD: 30 OPEN-FACED SANDWICHES

1 lb/454 g cooked chicken meat, cut into small dice

4 oz/113 g small-dice celery

12 fl oz/360 mL Basic Mayonnaise (page 35)

½ oz/14 g curry powder

Salt, as needed

Ground white pepper, as needed

1 head Bibb or Boston lettuce, washed and dried

4 oz/113 g butter, whipped

30 slices French bread, cut ¼ in/6 mm thick on the bias

8 oz/227 g cashews, roasted

2 Red Delicious apples, peeled and sliced thin

1. Combine the chicken, celery, mayonnaise, and curry powder; mix well. Season to taste with salt and pepper.

2. Cut the lettuce leaves to fit the bread slices.

3. **Sandwich Assembly:** Spread butter on the bread slices. Top with a piece of lettuce and 1½ oz/43 g chicken salad. Garnish with 1 cashew and 2 apple slices.

Muffuletta

YIELD: 12 SANDWICHES

6 oz/170 g picholine olives, pitted and chopped

8 oz/227 g Kalamata olives, pitted

4 fl oz/120 mL extra-virgin olive oil

3 oz/85 g flat-leaf parsley, chopped

5 oz/142 g pequilla peppers, roasted and chopped

2 anchovy fillets

½ fl oz/15 mL red wine vinegar

½ fl oz/15 mL lemon juice

1 tsp/2 g dried oregano

2 Focaccia (page 540), 1 lb 8 oz/680 g each

20 leaves romaine lettuce, trimmed, cleaned, and left whole (about 10 oz/283 g)

12 oz/340 g mortadella, sliced thin

12 oz/340 g provolone cheese, sliced thin

12 oz/340 g soppressata, sliced thin

1. Combine the olives, oil, parsley, peppers, anchovies, vinegar, lemon juice, and oregano in the bowl of a food processor fitted with a blade attachment. Pulse until combined and homogeneous. Allow to marinate for several hours, covered and refrigerated, before using.

2. **Sandwich Assembly:** Cut the focaccia in half lengthwise. Hollow out the top and bottom of each loaf slightly to make room for the filling. Spread olive mixture evenly over both sides of each romaine leaf. Line the hollows with romaine leaves.

3. Place mortadella over the olive spread, cheese over the Mortadella, and soppressata over the cheese. Top with the other half of the bread, which is already lined with lettuce and olive spread. Cut each loaf into 6 wedges and serve each wedge as one serving.

Mediterranean Salad Sandwich

YIELD: 10 SANDWICHES

10 pitas, 6 in/15 cm diameter

10 oz/283 g mesclun mix, chopped

4 oz/113 g red onion, sliced thin

10 oz/283 g European cucumber, diced

10 oz/283 g tomato, diced

2 fl oz/60 mL extra-virgin olive oil

1 fl oz/30 mL lemon juice

½ tsp/2.50 g sea salt

¼ tsp/0.50 g ground black pepper

10 oz/283 g feta cheese, crumbled

5 oz/142 g Kalamata olives, whole, pitted

15 oz/425 g Hummus (page 51)

1. Warm the pitas slightly in a 300°F/149°C oven for 10 minutes or individually in a dry pan over medium heat for 3 to 4 minutes. Hold under a clean dampened linen towel so they stay moist and pliable.

2. Place the mesclun, onion, cucumber, and tomato in a large bowl. Season with the olive oil, lemon juice, salt, and pepper. Toss gently. Add the feta cheese and olives and toss to combine.

3. **Sandwich Assembly:** Cut off the top quarter of a pita to create a large pocket. Spread 1½ oz/43 g hummus inside on one side of the pita. Place about 1 cup/240 mL seasoned salad inside of the pita. Repeat for each sandwich.

Bruschetta with Oven-Roasted Tomatoes and Fontina

YIELD: 10 SANDWICHES

¼ baguette (5 in/13 cm)

Olive oil, as needed

5 plum tomatoes

¾ tsp/3.75 g salt

¼ tsp/0.50 g ground black pepper

1½ fl oz/45 mL olive oil

½ fl oz/15 mL balsamic vinegar

¾ tsp/0.75 g chopped marjoram

5 oz/142 g Fontina, grated

1. Cut the baguette on the bias into slices ¼ in/6 mm thick. Brush the sliced bread with oil and toast in a 375°F/191°C oven for about 10 minutes, or until crisp and lightly golden along the edges.

2. Blanch and peel the tomatoes. Slice them in half lengthwise and scoop out the seeds. Place the tomatoes cut side up on a wire rack and place the rack on a parchment-lined sheet pan.

3. Season the tomatoes with salt and pepper, drizzle with oil and vinegar, and finish by sprinkling with the marjoram. Turn the tomatoes cut side down on the rack. Season the opposite side with salt, pepper, and a small drizzle of oil.

4. Roast the tomatoes in a 325°F/163°C oven until moisture in the tomatoes is reduced by half, about 1 hour.

5. Place ½ oz/14 g cheese on each of the toasts.

6. **Sandwich Assembly:** Top each toast with a tomato and heat in a 375° F/191°C oven for 7 to 10 minutes, or until the cheese has melted and begun to brown.

Mushroom Bruschetta

YIELD: 10 SANDWICHES

1 lb/454 g oyster mushrooms

3½ fl oz/105 mL olive oil

2 tsp/5 g minced garlic

1¼ tsp/1.25 g chopped thyme

1¼ tsp/1.25 g chopped oregano

1¼ tsp/1.25 g chopped marjoram

1¼ tsp/6.25 g salt

¼ tsp/0.50 g ground black pepper

¼ baguette (5 in/13 cm)

1. Trim the mushrooms and gently rub off any dirt with paper towels.

2. Heat 2½ fl oz/75 mL oil over low heat. Sauté the mushrooms in the oil until lightly caramelized. Add the garlic and continue sautéing until fragrant.

3. Add the thyme, oregano, and marjoram. Remove the pan from the heat. Season well with salt and pepper.

4. Cut the baguette into slices about ¼ in/6 mm thick, brush with the remaining oil, and toast in a 375°F/191°C oven for about 10 minutes, or until lightly golden along the edges.

5. Top the toasts with about ¾ oz/21 g sautéed mushrooms. Serve warm or at room temperature.

NOTE: Grated cheese may be sprinkled on top and the bruschetta finished under a broiler or hot oven.

Mussel Crostini

YIELD: 10 CROSTINI

½ baguette (10 in/25 cm)

2½ oz/71 g Garlic and Parsley Compound Butter (page 54), softened

2½ fl oz/75 mL white wine

2½ fl oz/75 mL water

1 tbsp/9 g minced garlic

½ bay leaf, dried

30 mussels (about 1 lb 11 oz/765 g), cleaned and debearded

1 oz/28 g minced shallots

1½ tsp/7.50 mL olive oil

2½ oz/71 g tomato concassé

Sherry vinegar, as needed

1½ tsp/1.50 g chopped flat-leaf parsley

Salt, as needed

Ground black pepper, as needed

1. Cut the baguette on the bias into 10 slices, each ¼ in/6 mm thick. Brush each slice with garlic butter and toast in a 400°F/204°C oven for 10 to 12 minutes.

2. Combine the wine, water, garlic, and bay leaf in a large pot and bring to a simmer.

3. Add the mussels, cover, and cook over high heat for 5 minutes, or just until the mussels open.

4. Remove the mussels and cool. Reduce the cuisson by three-quarters and reserve.

5. Sauté the shallots in the oil for 3 to 4 minutes, or until translucent. Add the tomatoes and reduced cuisson and cook for 3 minutes, or until the mixture simmers and the aroma of the mussels is apparent from the reduction. Allow to cool completely.

6. Remove the mussels from the shells. Just before serving, add the vinegar, parsley, and salt and pepper to taste.

7. Place 3 mussels on each crostini. Garnish each with 1 tsp/5 mL tomato mixture.

Lobster and Prosciutto Crostini

YIELD: 10 CROSTINI

¼ baguette (5 in/13 cm)

2½ oz/71 g Garlic and Parsley Compound Butter (page 54), softened

Olive oil, for frying, as needed

10 sage leaves

2½ oz/71 g goat cheese

2¾ oz/78 g lobster meat, cooked

2¾ oz/78 g prosciutto, thinly sliced

1. Cut the baguette on the bias into 10 slices, each ¼ in/6 mm thick. Brush each slice with garlic butter and toast in a 400°F/204°C oven for 10 to 12 minutes, or until slightly browned on the edges.

2. Heat 1 in/3 cm olive oil in a small sauté pan. Lay the sage leaves in the oil and lightly fry for 2 to 3 minutes. Remove and drain on absorbent paper. Hold at room temperature until needed.

3. Spread ¼ oz/7 g cheese on each of the toasted baguette slices. Place ¼ oz/7 g thinly sliced prosciutto on top of the cheese and top with ¼ oz/7 g lobster meat. Garnish each with a fried sage leaf.

NOTE: The prosciutto will not hold long at room temperature.

Cannellini Bean Purée with Prosciutto Crostini

YIELD: 30 CROSTINI

6 oz/170 g dried cannellini beans

1 smoked ham hock

1 baguette (20 in/51 cm long)

7½ oz/213 g Garlic and Parsley Compound Butter (page 54), softened

2½ oz/71 g onions, diced

1 fl oz/30 mL extra-virgin olive oil, plus to taste

3 garlic cloves, minced

½ tsp/1 g dried thyme leaves

Salt, as needed

Ground black pepper, as needed

1 oz/28 g parsley, chopped

6 oz/170 g prosciutto, thinly sliced, cut into julienne

1. Soak the cannellini beans overnight, drain, and discard the soaking water. Cover with fresh cold water, add the ham hock, and place over medium-high heat until they come to a boil. Partially cover, reduce heat, and simmer the beans for 2½ to 3 hours, or until they just begin to fall apart. Remove the hock. Drain the water from the beans and purée in a food processor or food mill, adding about 1 fl oz/30 mL cooking liquid to make a smooth purée. Reserve additional cooking liquid to adjust the final consistency of the purée. Finely dice the hock and fold into the puréed mixture.

2. Cut the baguette on the bias into 30 slices, each ¼ in/6 mm thick.

3. Brush each slice with garlic butter and toast in a 400°F/204°C oven for 10 to 12 minutes.

4. Sweat the onions in 1 fl oz/30 mL of the oil over medium heat until they begin to turn translucent. Add the garlic and thyme and cook for an additional 2 to 3 minutes without browning. Remove the mixture from the heat.

5. Add the bean purée to the onion mixture and mix well. Season to taste with salt and pepper and adjust the consistency with the reserved cooking liquid. The mixture should be smooth, but firm enough to spread. Allow the mixture to cool completely.

6. Fold in the chopped parsley and add oil to taste.

7. Spread ½ oz/14 g bean mixture on each slice of bread and top with prosciutto.

Goat Cheese and Sweet Onion Crostini

YIELD: 10 CROSTINI

¼ baguette (5 in/13 cm)

2½ oz/71 g Garlic and Parsley
Compound Butter (page 54), softened

7 oz/198 g small white onions

½ oz/14 g sun-dried tomatoes, chopped

Olive oil, for sautéing, as needed

1 tsp/3 g garlic, chopped

1½ tsp/7.50 g sugar

2 tsp/10 mL red wine vinegar

Salt, as needed

Ground black pepper, as needed

2½ oz/71 g goat cheese

1. Cut the baguette on the bias into 10 slices, each ¼ in/6 mm thick. Brush each slice with garlic butter and toast in a 400°F/204° oven for 10 to 12 minutes, or until crisp and lightly browned around the edges.

2. Roast the onions in a 350°F/177°C oven for 1½ to 2 hours, or until tender. Allow to cool, then peel and cut into medium dice and reserve.

3. To prepare the relish, sweat the sun-dried tomatoes in a little oil over medium heat for about 10 minutes, or until slightly tender. Stir the mixture with a wooden spoon to prevent breaking up the ingredients. Add the garlic and onions and continue to cook over low heat for 12 to 15 minutes, or until the ingredients are warm and the flavors are blended together.

4. Add the sugar and vinegar. Season to taste with salt and pepper.

5. Spread ¼ oz/7 g goat cheese on each slice of baguette, top with ¾ oz/21 g onion/sun-dried tomato mixture, and serve.

Watercress Tea Sandwich

YIELD: 30 TEA SANDWICHES

4¼ oz/120 g Crème Fraîche (page 351)

20 slices white Pullman bread,
¼ in/6 mm thick, crusts removed

3 bunches watercress

Sandwich Assembly: Spread a thin layer of crème fraîche on one side of the bread slices. Place sprigs of watercress over half of the bread slices. Top with the remaining bread and slice each sandwich into 3 smaller rectangular tea sandwiches.

Egg Salad Tea Sandwich

YIELD: 60 TEA SANDWICHES

20 hard-cooked eggs, chopped

4 oz/113 g chopped celery

1 oz/28 g green onions, thinly sliced

2 fl oz/60 mL cider vinegar

12 fl oz/360 mL Basic Mayonnaise (page 35)

Salt, as needed

Ground white pepper, as needed

30 slices pumpernickel bread, crusts removed

1. Combine the eggs, celery, green onions, vinegar, and mayonnaise. Add salt and pepper to taste; mix well.

2. **Sandwich Assembly:** Spread the egg salad over half of the bread slices. Top with the remaining bread and slice each sandwich into 4 smaller square tea sandwiches.

Cucumber Tea Sandwich

YIELD: 40 TEA SANDWICHES

8½ oz/241 g Crème Fraîche (page 351)

3 tbsp/9 g chopped dill

20 slices white Pullman bread, ¼ in/6 mm thick, crusts removed

4 European cucumbers, peeled, sliced ⅛ in/3 mm thick

1. Combine the crème fraîche and dill.

2. **Sandwich Assembly:** Spread one side of each bread slice with the dilled crème fraîche. Layer the cucumber slices over half of the bread slices. Top with the remaining bread and slice each sandwich into 4 smaller triangular tea sandwiches.

Deviled Ham Tea Sandwich

YIELD: 40 TEA SANDWICHES

1 lb/454 g ham, cut into medium dice

4 fl oz/120 mL Basic Mayonnaise (page 35)

½ oz/14 g prepared mustard

1 tbsp/6 g dry mustard

½ fl oz/15 mL Worcestershire sauce

½ tsp/2.50 mL Tabasco sauce

¼ tsp/0.50 g cayenne

20 slices white Pullman bread, ¼ in/6 mm thick, crusts removed

1. Combine the ham, mayonnaise, mustard, dry mustard, Worcestershire sauce, Tabasco sauce, and cayenne in a food processor and purée until very smooth. Remove, adjust seasoning, and refrigerate until ready to use.

2. **Sandwich Assembly:** Spread 10 bread slices with 2 oz/57 g deviled ham each. Top with the remaining bread slices. Cut each sandwich into 4 smaller triangular tea sandwiches.

Smoked Salmon Tea Sandwich

YIELD: 40 TEA SANDWICHES

8½ oz/241 g Crème Fraîche (page 351)

2 tbsp/6 g chopped chives

20 slices seedless rye bread, ¼ in/6 mm thick

1 lb/454 g Smoked Salmon (page 196), cut into thin slices

1. Combine the crème fraîche and chives.

2. **Sandwich Assembly:** Spread each slice of bread with the crème fraîche. Lay salmon slices over half of the bread slices and top with the remaining bread. Using a cutter 1½ in/4 cm in diameter, cut 4 rounds from each sandwich.

CURED AND SMOKED FOODS

The first preserved foods were most likely produced by accident. In fishing communities, fish were brined in seawater and left on the shore to either ferment or dry. To keep them away from scavenging animals, hunting communities and tribes hung meats near the fire, where they smoked and dried. Salted, dried, and smoked foods added much-needed proteins and minerals to a diet that could otherwise have been woefully inadequate to keep body and soul together.

five

Preserved foods differ from fresh in various ways. They are saltier, drier, and have sharper flavors. All of these attributes stem from the judicious application of key ingredients: salt, curing agents, sweeteners, and spices.

Food preservation techniques from the most ancient to the most high-tech are all intended to control the effects of a wide range of microbes, eliminating some and encouraging the growth of others. This is accomplished by controlling the food's water content, temperature, acidity levels, and exposure to oxygen.

Today's garde manger may be less responsible for ensuring a steady source of food intended to last from seasons of plenty through seasons of want, but the practical craft and science of preserving foods remains important if only because we have learned to savor and enjoy hams, bacons, gravlax, confits, and rillettes. These same techniques are used to produce sausages (Chapter 6) and cheeses (Chapter 8).

This chapter explains the ingredients, methods, and processes for these preservation techniques:

- Curing and brining

- Smoking

- Drying

- Preserving in fat

The Ingredients for Preserving Foods

Salt

The basic ingredient used by the garde manger to preserve foods is salt. This common seasoning, found in virtually every kitchen and on every table, meant the difference between life and death to our ancestors, and it is still important to us from both a physiological and a culinary point of view.

Salt changes foods by drawing out water, blood, and other impurities. In so doing it preserves them, making them less susceptible to spoilage and rot. The basic processes in which salt plays an important role are:

- Osmosis

- Dehydration

- Fermentation

- Denaturing proteins

OSMOSIS Osmosis happens without human intervention all the time, but to make use of osmosis for preserving foods, it is helpful to have a basic idea of how the process works. A simple definition is that osmosis is the movement of a solvent (typically water) through a semipermeable membrane (cell walls) in order to equalize the concentration of a solute (typically salt) on both sides of the membrane. In other words, when you apply salt to a piece of meat, the fluids inside the cell travel across the cell membrane in an effort to dilute the salt on the other side of the membrane. Once there is more fluid outside the cell than in, the fluids return to the cell's interior, taking with them the dissolved salt. Getting the salt inside the cell, where it can kill off harmful pathogens, is the essence of salt-curing foods.

DEHYDRATION The presence of "free" water is one of the indicators of a food's relative susceptibility to spoilage through microbial action. In order to keep foods safe and appealing to eat for long periods of time, it is important to remove as much excess water as possible. Applying salt to foods can dry them effectively, as the salt tends to attract the free water, making it unavailable to microbes. Exposure to air or heat for controlled periods allows the water to evaporate, reducing the overall volume and weight of the food.

FERMENTATION Substances known as *enzymes* feed on the compounds found in energy-rich foods such as meats and grains. They ferment the food by breaking down the compounds in these foods into gases and organic compounds. The gases may be trapped, producing an effervescent quality in beverages, holes in cheeses, or the light texture of yeast-raised breads, or they may simply disperse, leaving behind the organic acid, as occurs when preparing sauerkraut or other pickles.

By increasing the acid levels in foods, enzymes also help preserve them, as most harmful pathogens can thrive only when the levels of acids are within a specific range (pH). Of course, a higher acid level also means that the food's flavor is changed as well; it is sharper and more tart.

Left unchecked, the process of fermentation would completely break down a food. Salt is an important control on this process, as it affects how much water is available to the enzymes. Like bacteria and other microbes, enzymes cannot live without water. Salt "uses up" the water and thereby prevents fermentation from getting out of hand.

DENATURING PROTEINS Whenever you preserve foods, you inevitably change the structure of the proteins found in it. This change, known as *denaturing the protein,* involves the application of heat, acids, alkalis, or ultraviolet radiation. Simply put, the strands that make up the protein are encouraged to lengthen or coil, open or close, recombine or dissolve in such a way that foods that were once soft may become firm. Smooth foods may become grainy. Translucent foods may become cloudy. Firm foods may soften and even become liquid. Examples of these changes include preparing a seviche from raw fish, blooming gelatin, and cooking meats.

Curing Salts: Nitrates and Nitrites

For thousands of years, humans have been eating meats cured with unrefined salt. Those meats took on a deep reddish color. The reason for the color change was discovered at the beginning of the twentieth century, when German scientists unlocked the mystery of how nitrates and nitrites—compounds present in unrefined salts—cause cured meats to redden. Saltpeter, or potassium nitrate, the first curing agent to be identified as such, did not produce consistent results; the color of the meat did not always set properly and the amount of residual nitrates was unpredictable. Its use has been limited since 1975, when it was banned as a curing agent in commercially prepared cured meats.

Nitrates (NO₃) take longer to break down in cured foods than nitrites do. For that reason, foods that undergo lengthy curing and drying periods must include the correct level of nitrates. Nitrites (NO₂) break down faster, making them appropriate for use in any cured item that will later be fully cooked.

THE NITROSAMINE CONTROVERSY Today, we know that sodium nitrate and sodium nitrite are important elements in keeping meats safe from botulism infection. But we also know that when nitrates and nitrites break down in the presence of extreme heat (specifically, when bacon is cooked), potentially dangerous substances known as *nitrosamines* may form in the food.

The presence of nitrosamines in cured products has been a concern since 1956, when they were discovered to be carcinogenic. The amount of nitrosamine in any individual, like his or her cholesterol level, is influenced not only by the foods he or she eats but also the amount of nitrosamine produced by the salivary glands and in the intestinal tracts.

Although more than 700 substances have been tested as possible nitrate replacements, none has been identified as effective. Nitrites *do* pose some serious health threats when they form nitrosamines. There is little doubt that without nitrites, however, deaths from botulism would increase significantly and pose a more serious risk than the dangers associated with nitrosamines. The use of nitrates and nitrites is closely regulated (see Table 5-1).

TABLE 5-1 | **USDA Regulations for Recommended Nitrite/ Nitrate Levels in Various Meats**

PRODUCT	INGOING NITRITE LEVEL (PPM)*	INGOING NITRATE LEVEL (PPM)*
Bacon, pumped	120 (with 550 ppm ascorbate or erythrobate)	None
Bacon, immersion-cured	200 (2 lb/907 g to 100 gal/384 L brine)	None
Cooked sausage	156 (¼ oz/7 g to 100 lb/45.36 kg meat)	None
Dry and semidry sausage	625 (1 oz/28 g to 100 lb/45.36 kg meat dry-cured)	1719 (2¾ oz/80 g to 100 lb/45.36 kg meat)
Dry-cured meats	156 (¼ oz/7 g to 100 lb/45.36 meat)	2188 (2 lb/907 g to 100 gal/384 L brine at 10% pump)

*Parts per million.

TINTED CURE MIX, PINK CURE, AND PRAGUE POWDER I A blend of agents known simply as *TCM* combines 94 percent sodium chloride (salt) and 6 percent sodium nitrite. It is tinted pink (by adding FD&C#3) to make it easily identifiable and thus help avoid its accidental use. When used at the recommended ratio of 4 oz/113 g TCM to each 100 lb/45.36 kg meat, the meat is treated with only 6.84 g pure nitrite, or slightly less than ¼ oz.

PRAGUE POWDER II Prague Powder II contains salt, sodium nitrite, sodium nitrate, and pink coloring. It is used to make dry and dry-fermented products. The longer curing and drying periods require the presence of the nitrate in order to cure the meats safely.

CURE ACCELERATORS: SODIUM ERYTHORBATE AND ASCORBATE Both sodium erythorbate and ascorbate are cure accelerators that work together with nitrite to enhance color development and flavor retention in cured foods. They have also been shown to inhibit nitrosamine formation in cooked bacon. Since the 1950s, federal regulations have permitted a measured amount of ascorbic acid, sodium ascorbate, or sodium erythorbate to be included in commercially prepared cured meat.

These cure accelerators have some of the same reddening effects as nitrites and nitrates, though the effect is temporary. More importantly, they cannot be used as substitutes for nitrites or nitrates when those ingredients are called for to preserve or cure foods properly.

Seasoning and Flavoring Ingredients

Salt-cured foods have a harsh flavor unless additional ingredients are included with the cure. Sugar and other sweeteners, spices, aromatics, and wines have all been used over time to create regional adaptations of hams, bacons, and preserved fish and poultry.

SUGAR (SWEETENER) Sweeteners—including dextrose, sugar, corn syrup, honey, and maple syrup—can be used interchangeably in most recipes. Some sweeteners have distinct flavors, so be certain the one you choose will add the taste you intend. Dextrose is often called for in cures because it mellows the harsh salt and increases moisture without adding an extremely sweet flavor of its own. Sweeteners can:

- Help overcome the harshness of the salt in the cure.
- Balance the overall flavor palette.
- Counteract bitterness in liver products.
- Help stabilize color in cured meats.
- Increase water retention (moisture) in finished products.
- Provide a good nutrient source for fermentation.

SPICES AND HERBS A variety of spices and herbs are used in curing and brining processes to enhance a product's flavor and give it a particular character. Traditionally, many of the sweet spices, such as cinnamon, allspice, nutmeg, mace, and cardamom, have been used. These spices, individually and in blends, are still used in many classic recipes.

In addition, ingredients such as dry and fresh chiles, infusions and essences, wines, fruit juices, and vinegars can be incorporated to give a contemporary appeal to cured meats, fish, and poultry. When you change a classic seasoning mix, make several tests to determine the best combinations and levels of intensity before putting anything new on your menu.

Cures and Brines

Cure is the generic term used for brines, pickling or corning solutions, and dry cures. When salt, in the form of a dry cure or brine, is applied to a food, the food is referred to as *cured, brined, pickled,* or *corned.* The term *corned,* less familiar now, derives from the fact that the grains of salt used to cure meats and other foods were likened to cereal grains, or corn, because of their size and shape. Salt brines may also be known as *pickles;* this is true whether or not vinegar is added to the brine.

Although unrefined salt and seawater were most likely the original cures or brines, we have learned over time about how the individual components of cures and brines work. Refined and purified salts, sugar, and curing ingredients (nitrates and nitrites) have made it possible to regulate the process more predictably. This means we can now produce high-quality, wholesome products with the best texture and taste.

Dry Cures

A dry cure can be as simple as salt alone, but more often it is a mixture of salt, a sweetener of some sort, flavorings, and, if indicated or desired, a commercially or individually prepared curing blend. (Brand names of commercially prepared curing mixes include tinted curing mix (TCM) and Prague Powders I and II. This mixture is then packed or rubbed over the surface of the food (Figure 5-1).

Keeping the foods in direct contact with the cure helps ensure an evenly preserved product. Some foods are wrapped in cheesecloth or food-grade paper; others are packed in bins or curing tubs with layers of cure scattered around them and between layers. Foods should be turned or rotated periodically as they cure. This process is known as *overhauling.* Larger items such as hams may be rubbed repeatedly with additional cure mixture over a period of days. (See Table 5-2 for a chart of dry-cure times.) If there is an exposed bone in the item, it is important to rub the cure around and over the exposed area to cure it properly.

5-1. Spreading cure on a bacon slab.

TABLE 5-2 | **Dry-Cure Time for Meats**

ITEM TO BE CURED	APPROXIMATE CURING TIME
¼ in/6 mm thick, approximate	1–2 hours
1 in/3 cm thick, approximate (lean meat)	3–8 hours
1½ in/4 cm thick pork belly	7–10 days
Ham, bone-in (15–18 lb/6.80–8.16 kg)	40–45 days

When a dry cure is dissolved in water, it is known as a *wet cure,* or a *brine.* As you make the brine, you may opt to use hot water or even to bring it to a simmer to infuse it with spices or other aromatics. However, the brine must be thoroughly chilled before you use it to cure foods.

The brine may be applied in two ways, depending on the size and composition of the food you are brining. For small items such as quail, chicken breasts, and ham hocks, it is usually enough to submerge the food in the brine, a process sometimes referred to as *brine-soaking.* These foods are placed in enough brine to completely cover them, topped with a weight to keep them submerged as they cure, and allowed to rest in the solution for the required number of days (consult specific recipes for information).

Larger items such as turkeys and hams are injected with brine to ensure that it penetrates completely and evenly in a shorter period of time. (See Figure 5-2A for a diagram showing points of injection.) An amount of brine equivalent to 10 percent of the item's weight is injected into the meat. A turkey breast weighing

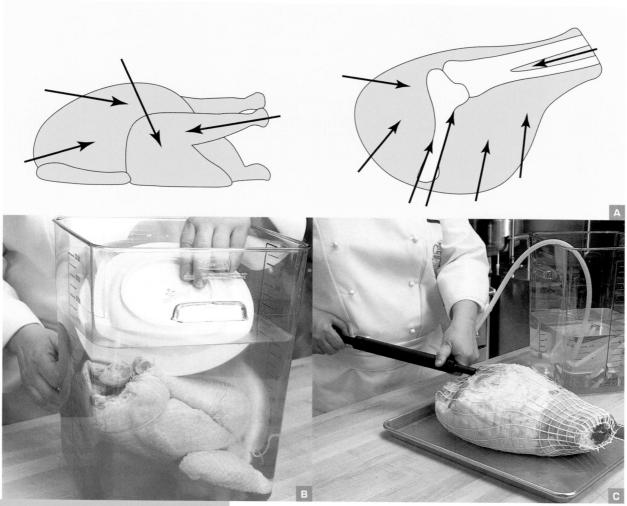

5-2. Brine Application. **A.** Points of brine injection.   **B.** Submerging a whole turkey in brine.   **C.** Using a continuous-feed pump to brine a ham.

12 lb/5.44 kg, for example, requires 1 lb 3 oz/539 g brine. Once the brine is injected, the product is generally submerged in a brine bath throughout the curing period. Figure 5-2B shows a turkey pumped with brine being submerged in a brine bath. (Table 5-3 gives the brining times for various meats.)

In addition to curing meats, brining also helps with flavor development and boosting moisture content. A number of tools are used to inject brine. Syringe and continuous-feed pumps are the most popular tools for small operations. (Figure 5-2C shows a continuous-feed pump being used to brine a ham; a diagram of the pump is shown in Figure 5-3.)

Commercial operations use a variety of high-production systems. In some, vacuum pressure is used to force brine into the meat. Another process, known as *artery pumping*, was first introduced by a New Zealand undertaker named Kramlich in 1973. In this method, brine is injected through the arterial system. Stitch pumps inject brine via a single needle inserted into the meat at specific points. Multiple needle pumps rapidly inject meats through a large number of evenly spaced offset needles.

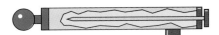

Brine pump with needle properly stored

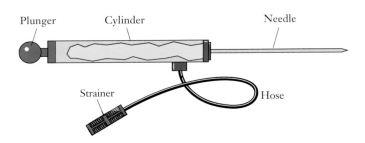

5-3. Diagram showing cutaway side views of a continuous-feed brine pump.

TABLE 5-3 | **Brining Time for Meats**

ITEM	NOT PUMPED	PUMPED (10% OF WEIGHT)
Chicken or duck breast	24–36 hours	Not recommended
Chicken, whole	24–36 hours	12–16 hours
Pork butt or loin (boneless)	5–6 days	2½–3 days
Turkey, whole, 10–12 lb/4.54–5.44 kg	5–6 days	3 days
Corned brisket	7–8 days	3–5 days
Ham, boneless	6 days	4 days
Ham, bone-in	20–24 days	6–7 days

Smoke

Smoke has been intentionally applied to foods since it was first recognized that holding meats and other provisions off the ground near the smoky fires did more than dry them quickly or prevent animals from getting to them: The hanging foods, treated to a smokebath, took on new and enticing flavors.

Today we enjoy smoked foods for their special flavors. By manipulating the smoking process, it is possible to create a range of products, both traditional and nontraditional. Besides such perennial favorites as smoked salmon (see Figure 5-4A), hams, bacon, and sausages, many unusual smoked products are being featured on contemporary menus: smoked chicken salad, smoked tomato broth, even smoked cheeses, fruits, and vegetables.

Several types of smokers are available. The basic features they share are a smoke source, a smokehouse where the food is exposed, circulation, and ventilation (see Figure 5-4B).

Hickory, oak, cherry, walnut, chestnut, apple, alder, mesquite, and wood from citrus trees are good choices for smoking. They produce a rich, aromatic smoke with proportionately few of the particles that make smoked foods taste sooty or bitter. Softwoods, such as pine, burn hot and fast with too much tar, making them unsuitable for smoking foods.

In addition to hardwoods, other flammable materials can be used for smoking. Teas, herb stems, whole spices, grapevine clippings, corn husks, fruit peels (such as orange and apple), and peanut shells can be added to the smoker to give a special flavor. A special smoking mixture is used to prepare Asian-Style Tea-Smoked Moulard Duck Breasts (page 204).

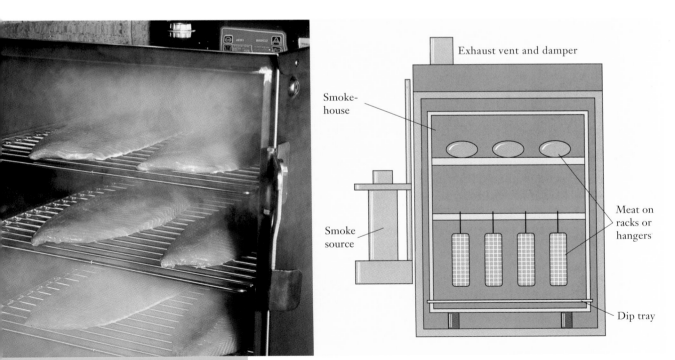

5-4. Basic Smoker. **A.** Sides of salmon in a Cookshack smoker. **B.** Smoke is generated in the smoke source chamber and travels up a pipe into the smokehouse. The smokehouse has its own heating unit, air-circulating fan, and damper control.

A. Pellicle has formed after curing whole and filleted trout. The fish is ready to be smoked.

B. Whole and filleted trout after smoking.

Wood for smoking can be purchased in chunks or chips. If you use a wood-burning oven to create smoke-roasted specialties, you can use larger pieces of wood, available for purchase by the bundle, truckload, or cord. Make the effort to purchase woods from a reputable source. You should be certain that the wood is free of contaminants such as oil and chemicals. Never use pressure-treated wood under any circumstances—it is deadly poisonous.

Pellicle Formation

Before cured foods are smoked, they should be allowed to air-dry long enough to form a tacky skin, known as a *pellicle*. The pellicle plays a key role in producing excellent smoked items. It acts as a protective barrier for the food and helps capture the smoke's flavor and color.

Most foods can be properly dried by placing them on racks or by hanging them on hooks or sticks. It is important that air be able to flow around all sides. Foods should be air-dried, uncovered, in the refrigerator or a cool room. To encourage pellicle formation, place the foods so that a fan blows air over them. The exterior of the item must be sufficiently dry if the smoke is to adhere. Figure 5-5A shows trout with the pellicle formed before smoking. Figure 5-5B shows the trout again after smoking.

Cold Smoking

Some of the basic criteria used to determine which foods are suitable for cold smoking include the type and duration of the cure and whether or not the food will be air-dried after smoking. Smithfield hams, for example, are allowed to cold smoke for one week; after that, they are air-dried for six months to a year. But cold smoking need not be reserved just for hams that will be air-dried or salmon ren-

5-6. Top: cottage butts, pork loins. Bottom: ham hocks.

dered safe by virtue of the salt cure. It can also be used to prepare foods that will be cooked by another means before they are served.

Cold smoking can be used as a flavor enhancer for items such as pork chops, beef steaks, chicken breasts, and scallops. The item can be cold-smoked for a short period, just long enough to give a touch of flavor. Such foods are ready to be finished to order by such cooking methods as grilling, sautéing, baking, and roasting, or they may be hot smoked to the appropriate doneness for an even deeper smoked flavor.

Cheeses, vegetables, and fruits can be cold smoked for extra and distinctive flavor. Typically, a very small measure of smoke is best for these foods—just enough to produce a subtle change in the food's color and flavor.

Smokehouse temperatures for cold smoking should be maintained below 100°F/38°C. (Some processors keep their smokehouses below 40°F/4°C to keep foods safely out of the danger zone.) In this temperature range, foods take on a rich, smoky flavor, develop a deep mahogany color, and tend to retain a relatively moist texture. They are not cooked as a result of the smoking process, however.

Keeping the smokehouse temperature below 100°F/38°C prevents the protein structure of meats, fish, and poultry from denaturing. At higher temperatures, proteins change and take on a more crumbly texture. The difference is easy to imagine: Think of the difference in texture between smoked and baked salmon fillets.

Hot Smoking

Hot smoking exposes foods to smoke and heat in a controlled environment. Although we often reheat or cook foods that have been hot smoked, they are typically safe to eat without any further cooking. Hams and ham hocks are fully cooked once they are properly smoked.

Hot smoking occurs within the range of 165°F/74°C to 185°F/85°C. Within this temperature range, foods are fully cooked, moist, and flavorful. If the smoker is allowed to get hotter than 185°F/85°C, the foods will shrink excessively, buckle, or even split. Smoking at high temperatures also reduces yield, as both moisture and fat are "cooked" away.

Smoke-Roasting

Smoke-roasting refers to any process that has the attributes of both roasting and smoking. This smoking method is sometimes referred to as *barbecuing* or *pit-roasting*. It may be done in a smoke-roaster, closed wood-fired oven or barbecue pit, any smoker that can reach above 250°F/121°C, or in a conventional oven (one you don't mind having smoky all the time) by placing a pan filled with hardwood chips on the floor of the oven so the chips smolder and produce a smokebath.

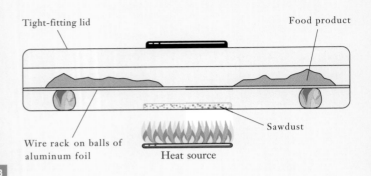

5-7. Pan-Smoker. **A.** Brook trout in a pan-smoker. **B.** Diagram of a pan-smoker setup.

Pan-Smoking

It is possible to produce smoked foods even if you don't have a smoker or smokehouse. Pan-smoking is a simple and inexpensive way to give a smoke-enhanced flavor to foods in a relatively short time. Figure 5-7A shows trout in a pan-smoker. The pan-smoking procedure requires two disposable aluminum pans, a rack, and some hardwood chips. The drawback of pan-smoking is that it is hard to control the smoke. Only through experience will you know the appropriate amount of heat and wood chips to use; too much of either, and the resulting flavor will be too intense and bitter.

Drying

In addition to drying items to form a pellicle before they are smoked, you may also need to air-dry certain items in lieu of or in addition to smoking them.

Air-drying requires a careful balance of temperature and humidity control. It is important to place foods in an area where you can monitor both, as dried hams may take weeks, months, or more to cure and dry properly. Be sure to learn and follow all the safe food-handling precautions for foods that undergo extended drying periods.

Several world-famous hams, including Serrano ham from Spain, Smithfield ham from the United States, and prosciutto crudo di Parma from Italy, are cured, cold-smoked, and then dried for an extended period, making them safe to store at room temperature and eat without further cooking. Other products, including Roman-Style Air-Dried Beef (page 216), Bresealo, and Beef Jerky (page 125), are also preserved by drying as well.

Air-dried hams and beef.

Preserving in Fat: Confits and Rillettes

Confit and rillettes are classically preserved foods. To prepare a confit of poultry or other small game animals such as rabbit and hare, the legs and other portions of the bird or animal are cured and then gently simmered in rendered fat, ideally from the animal itself. After this long cooking process is complete, the pieces are packed in crocks and completely covered with the fat. The fat acts as a seal, preventing the meat from being exposed to the air, which would turn it rancid.

Duck or goose confit is a traditional component of cassoulet and other long-simmered dishes based on beans. Today's chef has adapted this traditional dish to suit contemporary tastes. You will find confit prepared not only from ducks, geese, and rabbits but also made from tuna (see page 220) and red onions (see page 482), which are allowed to stew gently in butter or oil to a rich, jamlike consistency.

Rillettes are made by stewing boned meats in broth or fat with vegetables and aromatics. The thoroughly cooked meat is blended with fat to form a paste. This mixture is typically stored in crocks or pots, covered with a layer of fat that acts as a seal, and served with bread or as a topping or filling for canapés and profiteroles.

Gravlax

YIELD: 2 LB 12 OZ/1.25 KG; 12 TO 14 SERVINGS

Fishermen in Scandinavia once prepared this salt-cured, unsmoked salmon by packing a dry cure of salt and sugar over freshly filleted salmon. They buried the fish near the stream or river, and continued in this way upstream.

1 salmon fillet, skin on (about 3 lb/ 1.36 kg)

2 fl oz/60 mL lemon juice

1 fl oz/30 mL Akavit or gin (optional)

CURE MIX

6 oz/170 g salt

3 to 6 oz/85 to 170 g sugar (see Chef's Note)

½ oz/14 g cracked black pepper

¾ oz/21 g coarsely chopped fresh dill

1. Remove the pin bones from the salmon and center it skin side down on a large piece of cheesecloth. Brush the lemon juice (and Akavit or gin, if desired) over the salmon.

2. Mix the cure ingredients and pack evenly over the salmon as shown. (The layer should be slightly thinner where the fillet tapers to the tail.) Cover with chopped dill.

3. Wrap the salmon loosely in the cheesecloth and place it in a perforated hotel pan set in a regular hotel pan as shown. Top with a second hotel pan and press with a 2-lb/907-g weight.

4. Cure the salmon under refrigeration for 3 days. After the third day, gently scrape off the cure. The salmon is now ready to slice as shown, or it may be held under refrigeration for up to 5 days.

Gravlax. **A.** Salmon fillet being covered with cure and dill. **B.** Perforated pan enables the juices to drip away from the fish. **C.** Thinly slicing the cured salmon, holding the knife at a 30-degree angle.

Ratios of salt to sugar may range from 2 parts salt to 1 part sugar, to equal parts of each, or up to relatively sweet cures made with 1 part salt to 1½ to 2 parts sugar. Adding more sugar to any dry cure lends a moister texture and a sweeter flavor.

SOUTHWESTERN-STYLE GRAVLAX: Proceed as for Gravlax, substituting lime juice for the lemon juice and 1 oz/28 g tequila for the Akavit or gin. Replace the dill with a equal amount of chopped cilantro. This version can be served with Papaya Black Bean Salsa (page 44).

Norwegian Beet and Horseradish Cure

YIELD: 2 LB 12 OZ/1.25 KG; 12 TO 14 SERVINGS

This is a vibrant, magenta-colored, spicy version of basic smoked salmon with a sweet-hot flavor.

1 salmon fillet, skin on (about 3 lb/ 1.36 kg)

CURE MIX

12 oz/340 g finely chopped or grated raw beets

1 lb/454 g grated fresh horseradish

6 oz/170 g sugar

6 oz/170 g salt

½ oz/14 g cracked black pepper

1. Remove the pin bones from the salmon and center it skin side down on a large piece of cheesecloth or plastic wrap.

2. Mix the cure ingredients and pack evenly over the salmon. (The layer should be slightly thinner where the fillet tapers to the tail.)

3. Wrap the salmon loosely in the cheesecloth or plastic wrap and place it in a hotel pan.

4. Cure the salmon under refrigeration for 3 days. After the third day, gently scrape off the cure.

5. The salmon is ready for service now, or it may be wrapped and stored for up to 1 week.

Pastrami-Cured Salmon

YIELD: 2 LB 12 OZ/1.25 KG; 12 TO 14 SERVINGS

1 salmon fillet, skin on (about 3 lb/ 1.36 kg)

2 fl oz/60 mL lemon juice

CURE MIX

6 oz/170 g salt

3 to 6 oz/85 to 170 g granulated sugar

½ oz/14 g cracked black pepper

1 bunch coarsely chopped cilantro

1 bunch coarsely chopped parsley

4 oz/113 g minced shallots

3 fl oz/90 mL molasses

½ tsp/1 g cayenne

5 crushed bay leaves

2 tsp/4 g crushed coriander seed

2 tsp/4 g paprika

2 tsp/4 g ground black pepper

1. Remove the pin bones from the salmon and center it skin side down on a large piece of cheesecloth. Brush with lemon juice.

2. Mix the cure ingredients and pack evenly over the salmon. Combine the cilantro, parsley, and shallots; pack evenly over the salmon.

3. Wrap the salmon loosely in the cheesecloth and cure under refrigeration for 3 days. After the third day, gently scrape off the cure.

4. Bring the molasses, cayenne, and bay leaves to a simmer; remove from the heat and cool. Brush evenly over the salmon. Blend the coriander, paprika, and black pepper. Press evenly over the salmon.

5. Rest uncovered under refrigeration for at least 12 hours before serving. The salmon may be wrapped and stored for up to 1 week.

Smoked Shrimp

YIELD: 3 LB 8 OZ/1.59 KG

To prepare the shrimp for smoking, completely remove the shells, the tail section, and the veins. Even though it has been a standard practice to leave the tails on, removing them is more easily accomplished during kitchen preparation than by your guest. It is safer too, as there is no chance that someone might accidentally swallow a bit of shell.

5 lb/2.27 kg shrimp

BASIC SEAFOOD BRINE

3½ oz/99 g salt

2¼ oz/64 g sugar

½ tsp/1 g garlic powder

½ tsp/1 g onion powder

½ fl oz/15 mL lemon juice

64 fl oz/1.92 L hot water

1. Peel and devein the shrimp. Place in a plastic or stainless-steel container.

2. Stir together the salt, sugar, garlic and onion powders, and lemon juice. Add the hot water and stir until the dry ingredients are dissolved. Cool.

3. Pour enough brine over the shrimp to completely submerge them. Use a plate or plastic wrap to keep them completely below the surface. Cure at room temperature for 30 minutes.

4. Remove the shrimp from the brine; rinse and blot dry. Cold smoke below 100°F/38°C for 45 minutes to 1 hour.

5. The shrimp are ready to grill, sauté, poach, stew in a sauce, or prepare according to other needs, or they may be wrapped and stored for up to 1 week.

CHEF'S NOTES: This brine recipe can be doubled or tripled and used according to need. It can be held, covered, under refrigeration for up to 2 weeks. If preferred, the seafood may be pan-smoked to an internal temperature of 145°F/63°C for 6 to 8 minutes and served hot, warm, or cold. This brine is also suitable for mussels, oysters, and eel. Curing time for this shrimp can range from 10 to 30 minutes depending on the desired flavor profile.

PRESENTATION IDEA: These lightly smoked, sweet items can be used as a component of appetizers or composed salads. For an hors d'oeuvre they can be cut in half to garnish a canapé.

SMOKED SCALLOPS: 4 lb/1.81 kg scallops may be substituted for the shrimp. The tough muscle tab should be removed before smoking.

Smoked Salmon

Although imported smoked salmon carries a distinct cachet, there are many advantages to producing your own. With experience, you can learn to control the subtleties of smoking and create a product that is not only tailored to your guests' taste but also more profitable. Making your own can save you between 50 and 75 percent of the purchase cost of good-quality smoked salmon.

1 salmon fillet, skin on (about 3 lb/ 1.36 kg)

DRY CURE

8 oz/227 g salt

4 oz/113 g sugar

2 tsp/4 g onion powder

¾ tsp/1.50 g ground cloves

¾ tsp/1.50 g ground or crushed bay leaf

¾ tsp/1.50 g ground mace

¾ tsp/1.50 g ground allspice

⅛ tsp/0.60 g tinted curing mix (TCM) (optional)

1. Remove the pin bones from the salmon and center it skin side down on a large piece of cheesecloth.

2. Mix the cure ingredients thoroughly and pack evenly over the salmon. (The layer should be slightly thinner where the fillet tapers to the tail.)

3. Wrap the salmon loosely in the cheesecloth and place it in a hotel pan.

4. Cure the salmon under refrigeration for 12 to 24 hours. Gently rinse off the cure with cool water and blot dry.

5. Air-dry, uncovered, on a rack under refrigeration overnight to form a pellicle.

6. Cold smoke at 100°F/38°C or less for 4 to 6 hours.

7. The smoked salmon is now ready for service, or it may be wrapped and stored for up to 1 week.

PRESENTATION IDEAS: Smoked salmon is an ideal carving item for a buffet or reception and can be served on brioche or pumpernickel croutons with a dollop of Crème Fraîche (page 351). Traditional accompaniments include capers, finely chopped onions, hard-cooked eggs, and parsley. Basic Mayonnaise (page 35) and sour cream–based sauces flavored with caviar, mustard, or horseradish are often served with smoked salmon.

CHEF'S NOTES: The dry cure can be doubled or tripled, if desired. Store, tightly covered, in a cool, dry area until ready to use.

For additional flavor dimensions, brush the salmon with a liquor such as brandy, vodka, or tequila before it is air-dried.

Trim or end pieces can be used for rillettes, mousse, or cream cheese–based spreads for canapés, tea sandwiches, or bagels.

Southwest-Style Smoked Salmon

YIELD: 2 LB 12 OZ/1.25 KG; 12 TO 14 SERVINGS

1 salmon fillet, skin on (about 3 lb/ 1.36 kg)

SOUTHWEST-STYLE DRY CURE

8 oz/227 g salt

3 oz/85 g brown sugar

1 tbsp/6 g dry mustard

2 tsp/4 g ground cumin

2 tbsp/12 g dried oregano leaves

½ tsp/1 g ground allspice

½ tsp/1 g ground ginger

½ tsp/1 g ground nutmeg

⅔ oz/19 g mild red chili powder

1 tbsp/6 g paprika

2 tsp/4 g ground white pepper

1 oz/28 g chopped cilantro

2 tsp/4 g onion powder

1 tsp/2 g garlic powder

½ tsp/1 g cayenne

¼ tsp/1.25 g tinted curing mix (TCM) (optional)

2 fl oz/60 mL tequila

1. Prepare the salmon and apply the cure as in Steps 1 through 4 for Smoked Salmon (page 196).

2. Brush the salmon with tequila before air-drying and smoking (Steps 5 and 6).

PRESENTATION IDEAS: This can be used as a pizza garnish with Lime-Flavored Crème Fraîche (page 351) or tossed with pasta. As an hors d'oeuvre, it can be served on tiny corn pancakes with cilantro cream.

Swiss-Style Smoked Salmon

YIELD: 2 LB 12 OZ/1.25 KG; 12 TO 14 SERVINGS

This recipe was brought to the Institute by one of our past chefs, who learned it while working at the Palace Hotel in Gstaad, Switzerland. Although it takes a little more time and is a little more expensive to produce than the basic smoked salmon, the smooth, buttery results speak for themselves.

1 salmon fillet, skin on (about 3 lb/ 1.36 kg)

DRY CURE

8 oz/227 g salt

4 oz/113 g sugar

½ oz/14 g coarse-ground black pepper

1 bunch dill, coarsely chopped

1 lemon, cut into 5 slices

1 orange, cut into 5 slices

32 fl oz/960 mL white wine, or as needed

32 fl oz/960 mL milk, or as needed

1. Remove the pin bones from the salmon and center it skin side down on a large piece of cheesecloth.

2. Mix the cure ingredients and pack evenly over the salmon. (The layer should be slightly thinner where the fillet tapers to the tail.) Cover the salmon with a layer of chopped dill. Lay alternating slices of lemon and orange over the dill.

3. Wrap the salmon loosely in the cheesecloth and place it in a hotel pan.

4. Cure the salmon under refrigeration for 24 hours. Gently wipe off the cure and return the salmon to a clean container. Add enough cold white wine to completely cover the fillet. Marinate overnight.

5. Remove the salmon from the white wine. Add enough cold milk to completely cover the fillet. Marinate overnight.

6. Remove the salmon from the milk and air-dry, uncovered, on a rack under refrigeration for at least 8 and up to 14 hours to form a pellicle.

7. Cold smoke below 100°F/38°C for 4 to 6 hours.

8. The smoked salmon is now ready for service, or it may be wrapped and stored for up to 1 week.

PRESENTATION IDEAS: Smoked salmon should be sliced as thin as possible, as needed. This version can be used in the same manner as the basic version.

Hot-Smoked Rainbow Trout

YIELD: 30 WHOLE TROUT (6 ½ OZ/184 G EACH AFTER SMOKING)

30 rainbow trout, pan dressed
(8 oz/227 g each)

BRINE

2 gal/7.68 L water

2 lb 8 oz/1.13 g salt

4 oz/113 g dark brown sugar

1½ tsp/3 g garlic powder

1 tbsp/6 g onion powder

1½ oz/43 g pickling spice

3 oz/85 g honey

1. Place the trout in a deep plastic or stainless-steel container.

2. Combine the brine ingredients.

3. Pour enough brine over the trout to submerge them. Use a plate or plastic wrap to keep them completely below the surface. Cure the trout under refrigeration for 8 hours.

4. Rinse the trout in cool water and soak in fresh water for 10 minutes. Blot them dry with absorbent paper towels.

5. Hot smoke at 215°F/102°C to an internal temperature of 145°F/63°C, or about 2 hours.

6. Cool the trout completely before serving. Smoked trout can be held covered under refrigeration for up to 2 weeks.

PRESENTATION IDEAS: Fish should be filleted and boned and served 1 fillet per serving. Smoked trout fillets can be served whole as a cold appetizer with Swedish Mustard Sauce (page 475), or flaked into bite-sized pieces for tea sandwiches or canapés with Horseradish Butter (page 534).

Citrus-Scented Hot-Smoked Sturgeon

YIELD: 4 LB 8 OZ/2.04 KG; 24 TO 30 SERVINGS

1 sturgeon fillet, skin on (about 5 lb/ 2.27 kg)

CITRUS DRY CURE

1 lb/454 g salt

10 oz/283 g light brown sugar

1½ oz/43 g minced lime zest

1½ oz/43 g minced lemon zest

1. Remove the pin bones from the sturgeon and center it skin side down on a large piece of cheesecloth.

2. Mix the cure ingredients and pack evenly over the sturgeon. (The layer should be slightly thinner where the fillet tapers to the tail.)

3. Wrap the sturgeon loosely in the cheesecloth and place it in a hotel pan.

4. Cure the sturgeon under refrigeration overnight. Gently rinse off the cure with cool water and blot dry.

5. Air-dry, uncovered, on a rack under refrigeration overnight to form a pellicle.

6. Hot smoke at 160°F/71°C to an internal temperature of 145°F/63°C, or about 1 hour.

7. The smoked sturgeon is ready for service now, or it may be wrapped and stored for up to 1 week.

CHEF'S NOTES: This sturgeon tastes great served warm right out of the smoker or at room temperature as a component of an appetizer or hors d'oeuvre. Sturgeon can be sliced thin and served warm or cold. It can be substituted for the salmon in the Smoked Salmon with Potato Galette (page 446).

Smoked Turkey Breast

YIELD: 7 LB/3.18 KG USABLE MEAT

2 turkey breasts, bone in (12 lb/
5.44 kg each)

BASIC POULTRY BRINE

1 lb 8 oz/680 g salt

12 oz/340 g dextrose, honey, or white or
light brown sugar

1 tbsp/6 g garlic powder (optional)

1½ tbsp/9 g onion powder (optional)

7 oz/198 g tinted curing mix (TCM)

3 gal/11.52 L warm water

1. Trim any excess fat from the turkey.

2. Stir together the salt, sweetener, garlic and onion powders, if desired, and TCM. Add the water and stir until the dry ingredients are dissolved. Cool the brine completely.

3. Weigh the turkey breasts individually and pump each with 10 percent of its weight in brine evenly throughout the breast as shown in Figure 5-2A on page 185. Place in a deep plastic or stainless-steel container.

4. Pour enough brine over the turkey breasts to submerge them. Use a plate or plastic wrap to keep them completely below the surface. Brine 2 to 3 days under refrigeration.

5. Remove the turkey from the brine, rinse, and blot dry. Allow to air-dry overnight under refrigeration.

6. Hot smoke at 185°F/85°C to an internal temperature of 165°F/74°C, or about 4 hours.

CHEF'S NOTE: Instead of hot smoking, you can opt to pan-smoke the turkey breast for approximately 1 hour and finish roasting the turkey in a 275°F/135°C oven to an internal temperature of 165°F/74°C, or about 30 minutes.

PRESENTATION IDEAS: Smoked turkey makes a great presentation on a buffet, especially if it is sliced to order in front of guests. It can also be sliced and arranged on a buffet platter with Cranberry Relish (page 480). Slice it for sandwiches, or cube the meat for smoked turkey salad or Cobb Salad (page 128).

BOURBON-SMOKED TURKEY BREAST: Prepare the Smoked Turkey Breast as directed above, pan-smoking the turkey for 1 hour as directed in the Chef's Note. Bring to a simmer: 8 fl oz/240 mL bourbon, 4 fl oz/120 mL pure maple syrup, and 2 oz/57 g brown sugar. Keep warm. Brush the turkey with this glaze 2 or 3 times during the final 30 minutes of roasting.

Smoked Duck

YIELD: 6 DUCKS

6 Long Island ducks, 4 to 6 lb/1.81 to 2.72 kg each

DUCK BRINE

12 fl oz/360 mL Madeira

6 bay leaves

1½ tsp/1.50 g thyme leaves

1½ tsp/1.50 g juniper berries

1½ tsp/1.50 g chopped sage

3 gal/11.52 L Basic Poultry Brine (page 202)

1. Trim excess fat from the ducks.

2. Combine the Madeira, herbs, and spices with the basic brine.

3. Weigh the ducks individually and inject each with brine equal to 10 percent of its weight, as explained on page 185. Place in a deep plastic or stainless-steel container. Pour enough brine over the ducks to submerge them. Use a plate or plastic wrap to keep them completely below the surface. Cure the ducks under refrigeration for 12 hours.

4. Rinse the ducks in cool water and soak in fresh water for 1 hour; blot dry. Air-dry, uncovered, under refrigeration for at least 8 hours or overnight.

5. Hot smoke at 185°F/85°C to an internal temperature of 165°F/74°C, or 4½ to 5 hours.

6. Cool the ducks completely before serving. Smoked ducks can be held, covered, under refrigeration for up to 2 weeks.

PRESENTATION IDEAS: Smoked duck can be used in numerous dishes, including hors d'oeuvre, salads, and main courses. It is featured in the Smoked Duck Malfatti Salad with Roasted Shallot Vinaigrette (page 133), Smoked Duck Mousse Canapé with Raspberry (page 384), and Smoked Breast of Duck Niçoise Style (page 478). It is also used as a garnish in Chilled Clear Borscht (page 72).

Asian-Style Tea-Smoked Moulard Duck Breasts

YIELD: 6 BREASTS

Asian flavors can be incorporated into duck breasts using an alternative smoke mixture that conveys an intriguing flavor.

6 boneless, skinless Moulard duck breasts, 3 lb 8 oz/1.59 kg per double breast

1 recipe Duck Brine (page 203)

SMOKING MIXTURE

1½ oz/43 g black tea leaves

4 oz/113 g light brown sugar

1¾ oz/50 g dry jasmine rice

1 tbsp/6 g Szechwan peppercorns

2 whole cinnamon sticks, crushed

Zest of ½ orange

1. Submerge the duck breasts in the brine and cure for 12 hours. Rinse and dry the breasts.

2. Combine the smoking mixture in the bottom of a disposable roasting pan. Set a rack over the smoking mixture, place the cured breasts on the rack, and cover the pan tightly with a second roasting pan (see page 190). Smoke for 8 minutes.

3. Roast in a 275°F/135°C oven to an internal temperature of 165°F/74°C, or about 30 to 40 minutes.

PRESENTATION IDEAS: This style of duck can be served as part of an Asian-style appetizer platter or with Soba Noodle Salad (page 114) or Asian Vegetable Slaw (page 100).

CHEF'S NOTES: The skin can be slowly rendered in a sauté pan with a few drops of water to help give a crisper finished product. For a lower-fat version, remove the skin completely and reserve. Lay the reserved skin over the top during the final roasting to keep the duck from drying out.

Smoked Honey-Cured Quail

YIELD: 24 QUAIL

These quail are flavored with a hint of honey, although they are not distinctly sweet. The quail are cold smoked, so it is important to fully cook them by roasting, sautéing, or grilling before service.

24 quail (3½ oz/99 g each), glove boned (see Chef's Note)

24 sage leaves

24 sprigs thyme

Cracked or coarse-ground black pepper, as needed

HONEY BRINE

1 gal/3.84 L water

8 oz/227 g salt

5½ oz/156 g honey

4 oz/113 g dark brown sugar

2⅓ oz/65 g tinted curing mix (TCM)

2 tsp/4 g onion powder

1 tsp/2 g garlic powder

1½ oz/43 g pickling spice

1. Put 1 leaf of sage, 1 sprig of thyme, and a pinch of pepper into the cavity of each quail. Tie the quail legs together with string to maintain shape. Place in a deep plastic or stainless-steel container.

2. Combine the brine ingredients.

3. Pour enough brine over the quail to submerge them. Use a plate or plastic wrap to keep them completely below the surface and cure under refrigeration for 8 hours or overnight. Rinse the quail and blot dry. Air-dry under refrigeration overnight to form a pellicle.

4. Cold smoke the quail at 100°F/38°C for 3 hours.

5. Grill, sauté, or roast the quail to an internal temperature of 165°F/74°C for immediate service, or wrap and store under refrigeration for 7 to 10 days.

PRESENTATION IDEAS: Honey-smoked quail can be used in salads, appetizers, and entrées. It is a featured garnish in Southwestern Quail Pâté en Croûte (page 318).

CHEF'S NOTE: Glove-boned quail have the backbone, rib cage, and keel bone removed.

Smoked Ham Hocks

YIELD: 35 LB/15.88 KG

The basic meat brine in this recipe may be used for all types of pork products, beef products, and other red meats. The recipes that follow show several uses for it.

45 lb/20.41 kg ham hocks

BASIC MEAT BRINE

3 gal/11.52 L cold water

2 lb/907 g salt

1 lb/454 g corn syrup

7 oz/198 g tinted curing mix (TCM)

1. Place the ham hocks in a deep plastic or stainless-steel container.

2. Combine the brine ingredients and mix until dissolved.

3. Pour enough brine over the ham hocks to submerge them. Use a plate or plastic wrap to keep them completely below the surface. Cure the ham hocks under refrigeration for 3 days.

4. Rinse the ham hocks in cool water and soak in fresh water for 1 hour; drain. Air-dry, uncovered, under refrigeration overnight.

5. Hot smoke at 185°F/85°C to an internal temperature of 150°F/66°C, or about 4 hours.

6. Cool the ham hocks completely before storing. Smoked ham hocks can be held, covered, under refrigeration for up to 6 weeks.

CHEF'S NOTE: Smoked ham hocks are a staple in many kitchens and are a concentrated source of flavor for stews, soups, beans, braised greens, and sauerkraut.

Smoked Pork Loin

YIELD: 16 LB/7.26 KG

3 boneless pork loins (about 7 lb/3.18 kg each)

1 recipe Basic Meat Brine (page 206)

1. Cut the roasts in half, if desired; tie or net them.

2. Weigh the pork loin roasts individually and inject each with brine equal to 10 percent of its weight. Place the roasts in a plastic or stainless-steel container.

3. Pour enough brine over the pork loin roasts to submerge them. Use a plate or plastic wrap to keep them completely below the surface. Cure the pork loin under refrigeration for 3 days.

4. Rinse the pork loin roasts in cool water and soak in fresh water for 1 hour; blot dry. Air-dry, uncovered, under refrigeration for at least 16 hours.

5. Hot smoke at 185°F/85°C to an internal temperature of 150°F/66°C, or about 4 hours.

6. The pork loins are now ready for slicing and serving. They can be held, covered, under refrigeration for up to 2 weeks.

PRESENTATION IDEAS: Carve the smoked pork loin to order at a buffet station and offer it with an assortment of chutneys and relishes. It is also excellent in sandwiches and salads. Edible trim can be added to pâtés, terrines, soups, and stews.

CANADIAN BACON: Trim the roasts down to the eye muscle. Cut the roasts in half, if desired, and tie or net them. Pump with brine; cure, submerged in brine, for 2 days. Smoke and store as for smoked pork loin.

Corned Beef

YIELD: 16 TO 18 LB/7.26 TO 8.16 KG

Corned beef is a favorite slicing meat for deli-style sandwiches. Four briskets and the brine specified below will fit comfortably into a 10-gal/38.40-L pail.

4 briskets (10 to 12 lb/4.54 to 5.44 kg each)

CORNED BEEF BRINE

3 gal/11.52 L cold water

2 lb/907 g salt

10 oz/283 g corn syrup

7 oz/198 g tinted curing mix (TCM)

6 garlic cloves, minced to a fine paste

½ oz/14 g pickling spices

1. Trim the fat cover on the briskets to ¼ in/6 mm.

2. Combine the water, salt, corn syrup, and TCM. Mix well to dissolve completely.

3. Combine 16 fl oz/480 mL of the brine mixture with the garlic and spices in a blender and process until evenly blended. Add to the remaining brine.

4. Weigh the briskets individually and inject each with brine equal to 10 percent of its weight.

5. Place the briskets in a deep plastic or stainless-steel container and add enough brine to submerge them. Cover with plastic wrap to keep them completely below the surface. Cure under refrigeration for 4 to 5 days.

6. Rinse the briskets in cool water and drain thoroughly. Allow to rest for 24 hours under refrigeration.

A Slicing meat. **A.** Slicing corned beef. **B.** Slicing pastrami across the grain.

7. Place the briskets in a deep pot. Cover them with cool water and bring the water to a simmer. Continue to cook the brisket until fork-tender, about 3 hours.

8. Remove the brisket from the cooking liquid. Trim excess fat. It is now ready to carve or slice for hot or warm service (see Chef's Note), or cool the brisket, wrap, and refrigerate for up to 2 weeks.

CHEF'S NOTE: To rewarm cold corned beef for slicing warm, steam until heated through and slice on a machine or hand carve (see photo).

PASTRAMI: Pastrami may be prepared from either the brisket or plate of beef. Trim the exterior fat to ¼ in/6 mm. Prepare a brisket as directed for the Corned Beef through Step 5, but do not split. Mix 2 oz/57 g each cracked coriander seed and black peppercorns, and coat the brisket. Cold smoke at 100°F/38°C for 2 hours, then hot smoke at 185°F/85°C for 8 hours. The pastrami can be simmered as directed in Steps 6 and 7 above, or it may be slow roasted at 300°F/149°C to an internal temperature of 150°F/66°C.

Kassler Ribchen

YIELD: 2 ROASTS

The German city of Kassel is famous for its smoked pork products. This specialty is made from the prized pork loin cut. It is one of the main components of choucroute garni, the famous dish of smoked meats and sauerkraut enjoyed throughout Germany and Alsace.

2 center-cut pork loins, with 10 to 11 rib bones (about 8 lb/3.63 kg each)

1 recipe Basic Meat Brine (page 206)

1. Weigh the pork loins individually and inject each with brine equal to 10 percent of its weight. Place the loins in a plastic or stainless-steel container.

2. Pour enough brine over the pork loins to submerge them. Use a plate or plastic wrap to keep them completely below the surface. Cure them under refrigeration for 3 to 4 days.

3. Rinse the pork loins in cool water and soak in fresh water for 1 hour; blot dry. Air-dry, uncovered, under refrigeration for 16 hours.

4. Hot smoke at 185°F/85°C to an internal temperature of 150°F/66°C, or about 5 hours.

5. The pork loins are ready now for roasting whole or slicing into individual chops for grilling, sautéing, or use in other preparations. They can be held, covered, under refrigeration for up to 2 weeks.

Basic Bacon

YIELD: 45 LB/20.41 KG

Bacon is an example of a fully cooked smoked item that first undergoes a conventional dry-curing method based on a standard ratio of 2 parts salt to 1 part sugar. For the most accurate results, weigh the fresh pork bellies and then determine how much of the cure mixture you will need. A useful ratio is 8 oz/227 g dry cure for every 10 lb/4.54 kg fresh belly.

5 fresh pork bellies, skin on (10 lb/4.54 kg each)

BASIC DRY CURE

1 lb 4 oz/567 g salt

14 oz/397 g brown or white sugar

4 oz/113 g tinted curing mix (TCM)

1. Weigh the pork bellies and adjust the basic cure as necessary, using a ratio of 8 oz/227 g cure for every 10 lb/4.54 kg pork belly.

2. Mix the cure ingredients thoroughly.

3. Rub the cure mix over the bellies, making sure to cover all areas. Stack skin side down in plastic or stainless-steel tubs.

4. Cure under refrigeration for 7 to 10 days, overhauling them every other day.

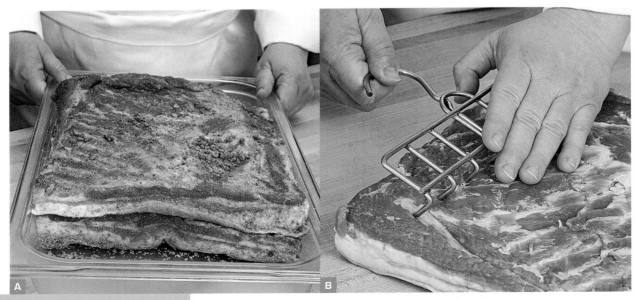

Dry curing bacon.   A. Placing slabs in a container to marinate.   B. Preparing a slab to hang dry.

5. Rinse the bellies and pat dry. Hang them on hooks and air-dry for 18 hours.

6. Hot smoke at 185°F/85°C to reach an internal temperature of 150°F/66°C, or about 3½ hours; cool. Remove rind.

7. The bacon is now ready to slice or cut as required for baking, sautéing, or griddling, or for use as a flavoring in other dishes. It may be wrapped and stored under refrigeration for up to 2 weeks.

CHEF'S NOTE: A cured belly will lose 7 to 8 percent of its water volume through curing and smoking.

HONEY-CURED BACON: Substitute 16 fl oz/480 mL honey for the white sugar in the Basic Dry Cure.

MAPLE SUGAR-CURED BACON: Substitute 16 fl oz/480 mL maple syrup for the white sugar in the Basic Dry Cure.

BROWN SUGAR-CURED BACON: Substitute brown sugar for the white sugar in the Basic Dry Cure and adjust the salt-to-sugar ratio to 10 parts salt to 8 parts sugar.

Pancetta

YIELD: 45 LB/20.41 KG

Pancetta can be prepared in a natural shape, known as *stresa*, or it may be rolled into a cylinder and tied before air-drying, referred to as *arrotola*.

5 fresh pork bellies, skin on (10 lb/4.54 kg each)

PANCETTA DRY CURE

2 lb 8 oz/1.13 kg salt

10 oz/283 g brown sugar

10 oz/283 g cracked black pepper

5 oz/142 g juniper berries, crushed

20 bay leaves, crushed

5 tsp/11 g grated nutmeg

½ oz/14 g thyme leaves

20 garlic cloves, mashed

2½ oz/71 g tinted curing mix (TCM)

1. Weigh the pork bellies and adjust the basic cure as necessary, using a ratio of 8 oz/227 g cure for every 10 lb/4.54 kg pork belly.

2. Combine the cure ingredients in a bowl and mix well.

3. Cure the bellies as for Basic Bacon (page 210) through Step 4.

4. Rinse the bellies in cool water. Remove the skin.

5. Roll up into a cylinder and tie tightly, if desired. Hang the pancetta and allow to air-dry for 2 to 3 weeks in a dry, cool area.

6. The pancetta is now ready to slice as desired for sautéing or other preparations. It may be stored, well wrapped, under refrigeration for 2 to 3 weeks.

Preparing Pancetta.   **A.** Rolling the pancetta.   **B.** Tying the pancetta.   **C.** Pan-frying sliced pancetta.

Tasso (Cajun-Style Smoked Pork)

YIELD: ABOUT 4 LB 8 OZ/2.04 KG

Tasso is a spicy cured and smoked pork butt used primarily as a flavoring ingredient in Cajun dishes such as gumbo and jambalaya. It also makes a zesty addition to pasta, rice, and forcemeats. It is featured as a flavorful garnish in the recipe for Southwestern Quail Pâté en Croûte (page 318).

1 pork butt (about 5 lb/2.27 kg)

4 oz/113 g Basic Dry Cure (page 199)

SEASONING MIX

½ oz/14 g ground white pepper

1½ tbsp/9 g cayenne

½ oz/14 g ground marjoram

½ oz/14 g ground allspice

1. Cut the pork across the grain into slices 1 in/3 cm thick.

2. Press the pork slices into the dry cure; cure for 3 hours at room temperature.

3. Rinse off the cure in cool water, drain the meat well, and blot dry.

4. Combine the ingredients for the seasoning mix, dredge the meat in it on all sides, and air-dry, uncovered, under refrigeration overnight.

5. Hot smoke at 185°F/85°C to an internal temperature of 150°F/66°C, or about 2¼ hours.

6. The tasso is now ready to use, or it may be wrapped and stored under refrigeration for up to 2 weeks.

Smoked Whole Ham

YIELD: 1 SMOKED HAM

1 fresh ham (pork leg roast, bone in, about 20 lb/9.07 kg)

1 recipe Basic Meat Brine (page 206)

1. Trim the ham, leaving 6 inches of skin around the shank. Remove the aitchbone and weigh the ham; inject with brine equal to 10 percent of its weight at the injection points illustrated in Figure 5.2A on page 185. Place the ham in a plastic or stainless-steel container.

2. Pour enough brine over the ham to submerge it. Use a plate or plastic wrap to keep it completely below the surface. Cure the ham under refrigeration for 7 days.

3. Rinse the ham in cool water and soak in fresh water for 1 hour; blot dry. Air-dry, uncovered, under refrigeration for 16 hours.

4. Hot smoke at 185°F/85°C to an internal temperature of 150°F/66°C, or about 12 hours.

5. The ham is now ready to be sliced for cold preparations, or reheated, sliced, and served hot. Ham can be held, covered, under refrigeration for up to 2 weeks.

PRESENTATION IDEAS: Smoked hams can be used in any number of ways. They can be carved hot on buffet lines or wrapped in a brioche dough and baked for a more elegant presentation. Use smoked ham in any pâté or terrine recipe that calls for ham, either as a liner or an internal garnish. The trim can be used in a variety of sandwiches and salads and used to flavor pasta dishes and soups.

Beef Jerky

YIELD: 12 OZ/340 G

Although once a necessary provision for people who needed lightweight, nutritious road food, beef jerky is now enjoyed primarily for its intense, robust flavor. It makes a great snack food and is wonderful pub or bar food. This version of beef jerky is tender enough to cut into a garnish or flavoring ingredient for sauces, pasta dishes, and salads.

3 lb/1.36 kg top round beef

JERKY CURE

½ oz/14 g salt

1 tsp/2.75 g tinted curing mix (TCM)

1 tsp/2 g onion powder

1 tsp/2 g garlic powder

1 tsp/2 g ground black pepper

2 fl oz/60 mL dark soy sauce

2 fl oz/60 mL Worcestershire sauce

1. Cut the beef across the grain into thin strips, ¼ by 2 by 8 in/6 mm by 5 cm by 40 cm.

2. Combine with the cure ingredients and cure 24 hours under refrigeration.

3. Place the meat on lightly oiled racks and cold smoke for 2 hours at 100°F/38°C; continue to dry at 80°F/27°C for 24 hours.

CHEF'S NOTE: Buffalo, venison, and other red game meat can be used instead of the beef. Most lean cuts, such as leg cuts, are appropriate.

Roman-Style Air-Dried Beef

YIELD: 4 LB/1.81 KG

This mild cured beef is a specialty of Rome. It is less dry than the more traditional bresaola of northern Italy.

5 lb 8 oz/2.49 kg beef eye round or top round	1 tsp/2 g red pepper flakes
	2 bay leaves
MARINADE	1 sprig rosemary
96 fl oz/2.88 L dry red wine, or as needed	1 oz/28 g Prague Powder II
4 oz/113 g salt	7 garlic cloves, mashed to a paste
1 tbsp/6 g cracked black pepper	

1. Trim the beef and place it in a deep hotel pan or other suitable container.

2. Combine the marinade ingredients.

3. Pour enough marinade over the beef to submerge it. Use a plate or plastic wrap to keep it completely below the surface. Cure the beef under refrigeration for 8 days. Turn the beef at least once a day as it marinates.

4. Remove the beef from the marinade, blot dry, wrap in clean cheesecloth, and hang to dry in a cool, dry area for 4 to 5 days.

5. The beef is now ready to slice thinly and serve, or it may be properly wrapped and refrigerated until ready to use. (Consult local health authorities if you have any concern about food safety and the service of this item to your guests.)

PRESENTATION IDEAS: This air-dried beef makes a great antipasto component, or it can be served alone with crusty bread and good olive oil.

Smoke-Roasted Sirloin of Beef

YIELD: 3 LB/1.36 KG

3 lb 4 oz/1.47 kg strip loin roast, oven-ready, tail removed

HERB MIXTURE

3 garlic cloves, minced

1 tbsp/3 g chopped rosemary

1 tbsp/3 g chopped thyme

2 tsp/10 g salt

1 tbsp/6 g ground black pepper

1. Trim the roast's fat cover to ⅛ in/3 mm; remove backstrap. Tie the roast to give a uniform shape.

2. Combine the ingredients for the herb mixture and spread evenly over the beef. Let the beef rest, uncovered, under refrigeration overnight.

3. Smoke-roast at 185°F/85°C to a final internal temperature of 140°F/60°C, or 3½ to 4 hours.

PRESENTATION IDEAS: Smoke-roasting enhances the flavor of the meat and gives it chargrilled flavor. It can be served as an entrée, or it can be cooled and sliced as a buffet item.

CHEF'S NOTES: This dish can be pan-smoked, if desired. Review the information about a pan-smoking setup on page 190. Pan-smoke the beef for 20 to 30 minutes. Remove from the pan-smoker and finish roasting at 275°F/135°C and remove at an internal temperature of 130°F/54°C to reach a final temperature of 140°F/60°C. Because this preparation does not actually cure the meat, it should not be held for more than 3 to 4 days.

Carolina Barbecued Pork Butt

YIELD: 8 TO 9 LB/3.63 TO 4.08 KG PULLED MEAT

The barbecue rub given here can be used for other cuts of pork, including spareribs, loin roasts, and cottage butts.

2 pork butts (5 to 6 lb/2.27 to 2.72 kg each)	1 oz/28 g sugar
	1 tbsp/6 g dry mustard
BARBECUE DRY RUB	2 tsp/4 g black pepper
2 oz/57 g sweet paprika	2 tbsp/12 g dried thyme
1 oz/28 g chili powder	2 tbsp/12 g dried oregano
1¼ oz/35 g salt	1 tsp/2 g cayenne
1 tbsp/6 g ground cumin	

1. Trim the pork butts of excess fat, leaving approximately ¹⁄₁₆ in/1.5 mm. Score the fat in a criss cross pattern to allow spices to penetrate.

2. Combine the dry rub ingredients and rub well over all surfaces of the pork. Allow to rest overnight under refrigeration. Place on roasting racks.

3. Hot smoke at 185°F/85°C to an internal temperature of 150°F/66°C.

4. Pull the meat off the pork bone and shred it by hand. Remove any excess fat.

5. The pork is now ready to use in other dishes, or it may be cooled, wrapped, and stored under refrigeration for up to 7 days.

Duck Confit

YIELD: 3 LB/1.36 KG

5 to 6 lb/2.27 to 2.72 kg duck legs (Moulard)

CONFIT CURE MIX

2 to 3 oz/57 to 85 g kosher salt

2 oz/57 g light brown sugar

1 tbsp/3 g quatre épices

1 tsp/2 g ground thyme

2 garlic cloves, minced

10 peppercorns

½ tsp/1.50 g tinted curing mix (TCM) (optional)

64 fl oz/1.92 L duck fat

16 fl oz/480 mL water

1. Disjoint the duck; reserve any trim for stock or a similar use.

2. Combine the cure mix ingredients; rub the duck pieces well with the cure mixture.

3. Place the duck in a stainless-steel pan, cover, and press with a weight. Let the duck cure under refrigeration for 2 to 3 days.

4. Rinse any remaining cure from the duck pieces and blot dry.

5. Bring the duck fat and water to a simmer; add the duck pieces and simmer for 3 hours, or until very tender.

6. Allow the duck confit to cool to room temperature in the duck fat. Hold the confit in the fat under refrigeration. Remove it from the fat as needed and use as directed in other recipes.

CHEF'S NOTES: The duck fat for this recipe can be the fat reserved from ducks, including the fatty skin, or you can purchase duck fat. Be sure to properly strain the duck fat so it can be reused to make a second batch of confit.

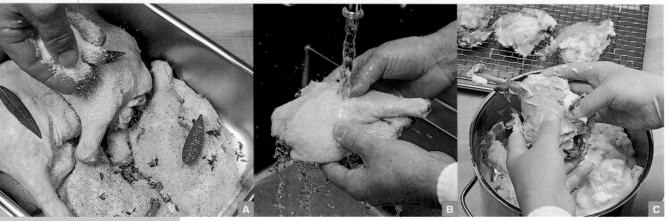

Curing Duck. A. Curing the duck with salt and spices. B. Rinsing off the cure. C. The duck confit is cooled in the fat. The excess fat is later wiped off.

Tuna Confit

YIELD: 1 LB/454 G

1¼ oz/35 g salt

1 lb 8 oz/680 g tuna (steak, belly strip, or good-sized trimmings)

HERBED OIL

4 oz/113 g sliced yellow onion

4 garlic cloves, quartered lengthwise

1 fennel bulb, sliced thin

1 serrano, split lengthwise, seeded (optional)

4 basil stems, bruised

4 thyme sprigs, bruised

4 bay leaves, crushed

1 tsp/2 g black peppercorns

24 to 32 fl oz/720 to 960 mL mild olive oil

1. Salt the fish liberally so there is a visible coating of salt on the surface. Small pieces should rest for 1 hour; large pieces should rest under refrigeration overnight.

2. Place the onion, garlic, fennel, chile, basil, thyme, bay leaves, peppercorns, and olive oil into a 64-fl-oz/1.92-mL saucepan and bring to 180°F/82°C for 20 to 30 minutes.

3. Add the salted fish and gently poach it in the oil. Watch the fish carefully; when it is barely pink in the center, remove it from the oil. Adjust seasoning.

4. Cool the oil, strain if desired, and pour over the fish. Serve immediately or hold under refrigeration.

PRESENTATION IDEAS: Use tuna confit on antipasto plates and in composed salads. It may also be eaten cold as a spread on toasted bread or crackers, or as canapés.

CHEF'S NOTES: This is best if served immediately. It may be held under refrigeration for several days, but the delicate texture will be affected. The herbed oil mixture can be kept refrigerated for up to a week and used to flavor salads, for cooking, or to prepare more tuna confit.

Chile-Rubbed Tenderloin

YIELD: 3 LB 8 OZ/1.59 KG

CHILE PASTE

2 oz/57 g dried ancho chiles

1½ tbsp/9 g ground cumin, toasted

1½ tsp/4.50 g garlic, minced

½ tsp/1 g chili powder

Pinch cayenne

Salt, as needed

4 lb/1.81 kg beef tenderloin, trimmed

Oil, as needed

1. To prepare the chile paste: Remove the seeds and stems from the chiles and place them in a bowl. Pour enough hot water over them to barely cover. Soak until the chiles are soft, about 30 minutes. Alternatively, toast the chiles on a flattop until soft. Using a slotted spoon, transfer the chiles to a blender or food processor. Add the cumin, garlic, chili powder, cayenne, and salt. Purée to a smooth paste, adding some of the soaking liquid from the chiles if necessary to adjust the consistency; it should spread over the beef evenly.

2. Trim the tenderloin and tie to even the shape of the meat. Rub the chile paste evenly over all surfaces of the beef. Let marinate for at least 4 and up to 24 hours.

3. Prepare a smoker and set the beef on a rack in it. Cold smoke at 80°F/26°C until flavored, no more than 2 hours. Any more time in the smoker might cause botulism to occur.

4. Remove the beef from the smoker. Sear the tenderloin in very hot oil over high heat until browned, turning to color all sides. Transfer to a rack in a roasting pan and roast at 350°F/177°C to an internal temperature of 130°F/54°C for medium rare, about 40 minutes.

5. Let the tenderloin rest for at least 10 minutes before untying and slicing. The meat will slice more easily (for use on platters, canapés, and similar cold presentations) if it is refrigerated at least 4 and up to 24 hours before slicing and serving.

NOTE: For use with canapés, bruschetta, sandwiches, and composed salads, portion as appropriate. Also appropriate for use at a carving/action station on a buffet line.

Roast Beef for Sandwiches

3 lb/1.36 kg beef top loin

1 oz/28 g salt

¾ oz/21 g pepper

1. Allow the roast to stand at room temperature for 1 hour. Season with salt and pepper. Place on a rack in a half sheet pan and set in a 500°F/260°C oven on the top shelf.

2. Check the roast after 25 minutes; it should be seared and developing a brown crust.

3. Lower the oven temperature to 350°F/177°C degrees and continue to cook for 50 minutes ,or until the roast has an internal temperature of 125°F/52°C.

4. Remove the roast from the oven and allow it to rest at room temperature for 30 minutes. The roast is ready to use at this point, or it may be wrapped and held under refrigeration.

Glazed Corned Beef

10 lb/4.54 kg Corned Beef (page 208)

8 oz/227 g apricot preserves or jam

8 oz/227 g currant jelly

4 fl oz/120 mL dry sherry

1½ tsp/4.50 g minced garlic

4 oz/113 g Dijon-style mustard

2 oz/57 g light or dark brown sugar

1 oz/28 g horseradish, prepared and brined

1. Trim the corned beef and simmer as directed on page 209.

2. To prepare the glaze, combine the apricot preserves, currant jelly, sherry, garlic, mustard, brown sugar, and horseradish in a saucepan. Bring to a simmer over low heat and simmer until smooth and lightly thickened, 2 to 3 minutes. Keep warm.

3. Place the corned beef on a rack in a roasting pan. Roast at 300°F/149°C, brushing with the glaze at 10- to 12-minute intervals, until very tender and well browned, 60 to 80 minutes. Remove the corned beef from the oven and let rest 20 minutes before carving or slicing, or cool the corned beef, wrap well, and chill thoroughly before slicing.

NOTE: One corned beef brisket weighs about 10 to 12 lb/4.54 to 5.44 kg and has an approximate yield of 78 percent.

Dilled Salmon Rillettes

YIELD: 2 LB/907 G

8 oz/227 g butter

1 lb/454 g salmon, cut into 1-in/3-cm pieces

6 fl oz/180 mL white wine

3 oz/85 g minced shallots

1¼ oz/35 g salt

¼ tsp/0.50 g ground white pepper

3 dill sprigs, minced

1 tsp/3 g lemon zest, finely chopped

1. Melt the butter in a saucepan over low heat.

2. Add the salmon, wine, shallots, salt, pepper, dill, and lemon zest; simmer slowly over very low heat for 15 to 20 minutes.

3. Remove the pan from the heat and cool until the butter begins to firm.

4. Transfer the mixture to a chilled mixer bowl. Mix on medium speed with a paddle attachment until a smooth paste is formed.

5. Test for appropriate seasoning and consistency. Make any adjustments before placing in molds.

6. Fill desired mold(s) and store, covered, under refrigeration until needed.

SMOKED SALMON RILLETTES: Half the salmon can be replaced with smoked salmon for a lightly smoke-flavored rillette.

Pork Rillettes

YIELD: ABOUT 5 LB/2.27 KG

5 lb/2.27 kg pork butt, very fatty, cubed

1 lb/454 g Mirepoix (page 522), cut into large dice

1 Standard Sachet d'Épices (page 523)

96 fl oz/2.88 L White Beef Stock (page 529), as needed

1¼ oz/35 g salt, or as needed

2 tsp/4 g ground black pepper, or as needed

1. Place the pork, mirepoix, and sachet in a heavy saucepan. Add stock almost to cover.

2. Simmer, covered, very slowly on the stove, or braise in a 350°F/177°C oven until the meat is cooked and very tender, at least 2 hours.

3. Lift out the pork, reserving the stock and rendered fat. Discard the mirepoix and sachet. Let the meat cool slightly.

4. Transfer the meat to a chilled mixer bowl. Add the salt and pepper. Mix on low speed until the meat breaks into pieces. Test for appropriate seasoning and consistency. Adjust consistency by adding back some of the fat and stock (consistency should be spreadable, not runny or dry). Make any adjustments before filling the mold. (Refer to seasoning and texture adjustment information on page 191.)

5. Divide the rillettes among earthenware molds no larger than 32 fl oz/960 mL. Ladle some reserved fat over them, and allow to cool before serving. (The fat is scored for a decorative effect) Rillettes can be held under refrigeration for 2 to 3 weeks.

SMOKED CHICKEN RILLETTES: Substitute 3 lb/1.36 kg cured, cold-smoked chicken leg meat and 2 lb/907 g pork butt for the pork.

SMOKED HAM RILLETTES: Substitute cured, cold-smoked pork butt for the fresh pork. Add mustard and cayenne to the seasoning.

DUCK RILLETTES: Substitute duck meat for the pork and add a small sprig of rosemary to the sachet.

SAUSAGE

The word sausage comes from the Latin word *salsus,* meaning "salted," and it was in ancient Rome and Greece that some of the earliest sausages were created—from just about everything available, from nuts to dormice. In the ninth century B.C.E., Homer wrote about his famous hero Odysseus consuming sausages during his historic journey, and the Egyptians were producing their own form of sausage by 641 C.E.

six

Lucanica sausages, produced in a part of Italy known today as Basilicata, traveled with the conquering Romans into ancient France and whetted the Gauls' appetites for this versatile and useful food. These same long, nonsegmented, spicy smoked sausages are still eaten today and have found a place in other cuisines as well. They are known in Portugal and Brazil as *linguica,* and in Spain as *longaniza.*

By the Middle Ages, distinct regional forms of sausage had begun to evolve all over Europe. Spices and herbs varied from region to region, as did the choice to smoke or dry the sausage, or leave it fresh. Grains and potatoes were often added to extend expensive or scarce meat supplies, and some devout Christians made sausage from fish to enjoy on meatless fasting days. Even the variety of wood used to smoke sausages and other foods changed from area to area, yielding subtle flavor characteristics.

The influence of nearby cultures gave further diversity to this important foodstuff. French- and German-influenced cuisines feature blood sausages, the addition of apples to flavor the sausage, and traditional sweet spices such as mace, allspice, and coriander. The sausages of the Mediterranean are more likely to be made from either pork or lamb and are flavored with fennel, rosemary, and oregano.

Sausage Ingredients

Sausages are made by grinding raw meats along with salt and spices. This mixture is then stuffed into natural or synthetic casings. The original containers were formed from intestines, stomachs, and other animal parts. In fact, the Italian word for sausages, *insacatta,* literally means "encased."

Main ingredient

The sausages in this chapter are made with pork, veal, beef, lamb, venison, pheasant, chicken, and turkey. Traditionally, sausages have been made from the tougher cuts of meat from the leg or shoulder. The more exercised the muscle, the more highly developed the flavor. Any tendency toward toughness is eliminated by grinding the meat.

Meats for sausages should be trimmed, if necessary, and cut into dice or strips. When pork liver is called for in a sausage recipe, cut it into cubes before grinding. The seasonings or cure mix are tossed together with the meat before grinding.

CERTIFIED PORK Pork sausages that undergo lengthy smoking or drying procedures but aren't cooked must be made with certified pork. This means that the pork has been treated in a way that destroys the pathogens responsible for trichinosis. You can purchase certified pork, or prepare it yourself by observing the appropriate freezing times and temperatures listed below:

MINIMUM TEMPERATURE	MINIMUM FREEZING AND HOLDING TIME
5°F/ –15°C	20 days
–10°F/ –23°C	12 days
–20°F/ –29°C	6 days

Pack pork in containers to a depth of 6 in/15 cm.

Fat

Fat is an integral part of any delicious sausage. Today we are accustomed to foods with a reduced percentage of fat; this is true of our hamburgers and chops as well as our pâtés and sausages. While the percentage of fat considered appropriate for a forcemeat might have been as high as 50 percent in earlier formulations, today an average of 25 to 30 percent is generally preferred.

Reducing the amount of fat in a formula even further requires additional understanding of the role each ingredient plays in a forcemeat as well as a careful analysis of the reduced-fat version to be sure it will fulfill your expectations as well as those of your guests.

Although all types of animal fat have been used at one time or another to produce a specialty product, you will find that most contemporary forcemeat recipes call for pork fat (jowl fat or fatback) or heavy cream.

Seasonings and cure mixes

The sausages in this chapter can be successfully prepared using ordinary table salt, but you can substitute other salts, such as kosher or sea salt. Be sure to weigh salt, as different salts have differing volume-to-weight relationships.

Sausages that are dried or cold smoked must include either nitrate or a nitrite-nitrate combination in order to fully and safely cure the sausage. One such curing blend is available for purchase under the brand name of Prague Powder II. Hot-smoked sausages and fresh sausages do not require nitrite.

Sugar, dextrose, honey, and various syrups are added to the curing mixture to mellow the sausage's flavor and make the finished product moister. For more information about the role of sweeteners and curing agents, see page 183.

Spices

Spices are added to sausages as whole toasted seeds, ground, or in special blends such as quatre épices and pâté spice. To get the most from your spices, purchase them whole whenever reasonable. Toast them in a dry pan or in the oven and grind them just before you are ready to use them. Or, if you prefer, make larger batches of spice blends and store them in airtight cans or jars away from heat, light, and moisture.

Spice blend recipes can be found in Chapter 12.

Herbs

Sausage formulas often call for dried herbs. These should be handled in the same way as dried spices. When fresh herbs are necessary, be sure to rinse and dry them well before chopping. You may substitute fresh herbs for dried herbs, but the taste will be different, and you must taste the sample carefully. As a general rule, you will need about two to three times more fresh herbs compared to dried herbs.

Many types of aromatic ingredients are included in sausage recipes, including vegetables (especially the onion family, mushrooms, and celery), wines, and citrus zests. Vegetables, though they may be left raw for some special formulas, are most often cooked. The cooking method and the degree of cooking has an impact on the finished flavor of the dish. Onions are generally cooked, but those cooked just until translucent and limp have a decidedly different flavor than onions that have been slowly caramelized to a deep mahogany color. Be sure to allow any cooked ingredient to cool completely before incorporating it into the sausage.

Additional aromatic flavorings and seasonings added to sausages include prepared sauces (such as Tabasco and Worcestershire), powdered onions and garlic, and stock. Highly acidic ingredients such as wines or vinegars should be added with care; too much can give the finished sausage a grainy texture.

Equipment Selection, Care, and Use

Electric meat grinders, food processors, choppers, mixers, and sausage stuffers have all but replaced the hand tools once used to make sausages and other forcemeats. These tools are certainly great for saving time and labor, but even more important, they produce sausages of superior quality to those made by the laborious process the original charcuterie and garde manger chefs knew.

Use the following guidelines:

1. **MAKE SURE THE EQUIPMENT IS IN EXCELLENT CONDITION.** Evaluate any machinery you use in the kitchen and consider its functionality and safety as part of a standard checklist. Are the blades sharp? Are all the safety features fully functional? Are the cords and plugs in good repair?

6-1, 6.2.   **Left:** Chilling grinder parts in ice water.   **Right:** Placing the blade onto the grinder with the flat part facing the die.

2. **MAKE SURE THE EQUIPMENT IS SCRUPULOUSLY CLEAN BEFORE SETTING TO WORK.** Every part of the equipment must be thoroughly cleaned and sanitized between uses. Cross contamination is a serious problem, especially for foods as highly processed and handled as sausages.

3. **CHILL ANY PART OF THE MACHINE THAT COMES INTO DIRECT CONTACT WITH THE SAUSAGE INGREDIENTS.** Place parts in the freezer or refrigerator, or chill equipment rapidly by placing it in a sink or container of ice water (see Figure 6-1). Remember that if your sausage mixture becomes warm during production, you may need to cool both the mixture and the equipment before continuing.

4. **CHOOSE THE RIGHT TOOL FOR THE JOB.** Do not overload your equipment. If you do not have equipment large enough to handle bulk recipes, then break the formula down into batches that your equipment can handle without straining.

5. **ASSEMBLE THE GRINDER CORRECTLY.** Novices often make the mistake of improperly setting up the blade and die assembly. Be certain that the blade is sitting flush against the die (see Figure 6-2). This cuts the food neatly, rather than tearing or shredding it. Make sure the power is disconnected before assembling or disassembling the grinder.

Basic Grind Sausages

Sausages produced using the basic grind method have a medium to coarse texture. When left loose, they are referred to as *bulk sausages*. Each of the following sausage types is made with the basic grind method:

- **FRESH SAUSAGES** are raw sausages that are typically pan-fried, broiled, grilled, baked, or braised before serving.

- **COOKED SAUSAGES** are poached or steamed after they are shaped; they may be sliced and served cold or prepared by grilling, baking, or pan-frying.

6-3. Meat-grinding dies. **A.** Coarse die. **B.** Medium die. **C.** Fine die.

- **SMOKED AND DRIED SAUSAGES** are cold or hot smoked, then allowed to air-dry in a curing room to the desired texture; they may be prepared for service in the same way as cooked sausages. Sausages that are not fully cooked during smoking or are not fully dried must be fully cooked before serving.

1. **GRIND CHILLED AND DICED MEATS, AS WELL AS OTHER INGREDIENTS AS REQUIRED BY RECIPE, TO THE DESIRED TEXTURE.** Meat or other foods should be cut into a size and shape that fits the feed tube (see Figure 6-3). You should not have to force foods through the tube with a tamper. When foods are correctly cut, the worm will pull them evenly along without requiring you to exert undue pressure. If you have cut your food properly and it is still sticking to the sides of the feed tube, you may need to coax the pieces along.

If you discover that the products are not flowing smoothly through the grinder, stop immediately. This is a sign that the meat is being squeezed and torn rather than cut cleanly. Disassemble the grinder unit, remove any obstructions, and reassemble the grinder properly.

2. **MIX THE GROUND SAUSAGE MEAT(S) UNTIL IT BECOMES HOMOGENEOUS.** Once the sausage is properly ground, it should be mixed long enough to distribute evenly the fat and lean components as well as the spices and other seasonings. The process of mixing also continues to draw out the proteins responsible for the finished texture of the sausage.

Mixing may be done by hand with a wooden spoon. An ice bath under the mixing bowl helps keep the sausage properly chilled as you work. Add any liquids gradually, making sure they are very cold when added.

If you are using an electric mixer, be certain that the parts that come in contact with the sausage are properly chilled. Do not overload the bowl; it is more efficient in both the short and the long run to work in smaller batches. Overloading the machine could cause an uneven mix as well as unnecessary friction that will overheat the sausage. Depending on the quantity of forcemeat being mixed, total mixing time should be about one to three minutes. The sausage is properly mixed when the ingredients become homogeneous. Look for a tacky appearance and a slightly sticky texture.

3. **THE SAUSAGE MIXTURE IS NOW READY TO TEST, GARNISH, AND SHAPE** (see pages 235–239).

Emulsion Sausages

Emulsion sausages such as frankfurters and mortadella are made from a basic mixture referred to as *5-4-3 forcemeat,* a name that reflects the ratio of ingredients: 5 parts trimmed raw meat to 4 parts fat (pork jowl fat) to 3 parts water (in the form of ice) by weight. Many emulsion sausages are poached before smoking. If your production needs demand it, you can freeze uncooked emulsion sausages very successfully. Once finished, the sausages should be properly packaged, wrapped, and stored under refrigeration.

1. **CURE THE MEAT, THEN GRIND THROUGH THE FINE DIE.** Meats should be trimmed of gristle, sinew, and connective tissue. Add the cure mix (see Figure 6-4A), tossing to coat the meat evenly. The cured meat is ground through the fine plate of the meat grinder and must be kept very cold while grinding the fat. The meat and the fat should be kept separate at this point.

2. **GRIND THE CHILLED FATBACK THROUGH THE FINE GRINDER DIE.** The fat (jowl fat is typical) may be partially frozen after it is cubed. Grind it through a fine grinder plate and keep it well chilled until required.

3. **CHOP TOGETHER THE GROUND MEAT AND CRUSHED ICE AND PROCESS UNTIL THE TEMPERATURE DROPS BELOW 30°F/−1°C.** Place the meat in the bowl of a high-speed chopper or processor. Place the ice on top of the meat and start to process the mixture (see Figure 6-4B). Process until the temperature first drops below 30°F/−1°C and then begins to climb up.

6-4. Emulsion sausage. **A.** Tinted curing mixture (TCM) is essential to maintain a pink color in cured products. **B.** Ice is added. **C.** Temperature is carefully monitored. **D.** Ground fat is added when the ground meat is 40°F/4°C. **E.** The edges are scraped down to ensure a homogeneous mixture.

4. **ADD THE GROUND FAT TO THE MEAT WHEN THE TEMPERATURE REACHES 40°F/4°C.** Check the temperature frequently to be sure the mixture is within the desired temperature range (see Figure 6-4C). Add the ground fat when the temperature reaches 40°F/4°C (see Figure 6-4D). Continue processing until the temperature is between 45° and 50°F/7° and 10°C. The fat is added just at this point to form a good emulsion with the lean meat. The mechanical mixing action, as well as the friction created by the coarse ice and the effect of the salt, produces a light, almost spongy texture.

5. **ADD THE NONFAT DRY MILK (AND ANY REMAINING SEASONINGS) WHEN THE TEMPERATURE REACHES 50°F/10°C.** Once the temperature nears 50°F/10°C, add the powdered nonfat dry milk. Continue to process the force-meat until it reaches 58°F/14°C. This process requires the sausage to reach a higher temperature than other sausages and forcemeats; the goal is for the fat to liquefy enough to blend evenly with the lean meat. The texture of an emulsion sausage must be very even. To ensure the best results, scrape down the bowl as the sausage is mixed (see Figure 6-4E).

Make a test and evaluate the forcemeat before garnishing, shaping, and finishing the sausage.

Garnishing

Some sausage recipes call for a garnish. Usually, the garnish item is diced and added to the forcemeat after it has been tested and adjusted. Cheeses, vegetables, cured or smoked meats, nuts, and dried fruits are all examples of garnishes that can be added to sausages. Add the garnish by folding it into the base mixture in the electric mixer, if desired, or working by hand over an ice bath.

6-5, 6.6. **Left:** Sausage shaping. Rolling loose sausage into a cylinder with plastic wrap. **Right:** Assortment of synthetic casings.

6-7. Natural casings. **A.** Left: hank of hog casings; right: hank of sheep casings. **B.** Top left: set of beef middles; top right: hank of beef rounds; bottom: beef bung.

Sausage Shaping

Sausage meat may be used either in bulk (loose) form, made into patties, or stuffed into natural or synthetic casings and then formed into links, loops, spirals, or other special shapes.

Loose or bulk sausages

To shape bulk sausage into a roll, place about 1 lb/454 g sausage on a square of plastic wrap. Roll it up and twist the ends to form a solid log (see Figure 6-5). Once rolled, the sausage can be sliced into patties. Bulk sausage can also be shaped into patties and wrapped in caul fat, if desired.

Sausages in casings

Various types of casings, both natural and synthetic, are available today. Natural casings are made from the intestines and stomach of sheep, hogs, and cattle. Synthetic casings are made from a variety of food-grade materials, some edible and some not. They may be colored, lined with herbs, or netted (see Figure 6-6).

Hog and sheep casings are shown in Figure 6-7A. Beef casings are made from various parts of the intestines: middle, round, and bung (see Figure 6-7B). The diameter of each type of casing varies. Individual links are typically made from lamb, sheep, or hog casings. Larger sausages are made with beef middles or bungs. (See Figure 6-8 on page 236 for casing charts.)

ITEMS	SIZE	LENGTH	CAPACITY	COMMENTS/USES
Sheep casing	18 mm and less	100 yd/hank	38–41 lb	Cocktail franks
Sheep casing	24–26 mm (4 ft/lb)	100 yd/hank	60–64 lb	Pork sausage, frankfurters, andouille
Sheep casing	28 mm and up	100 yd/hank	65–70 lb	

Hog Casings

ITEMS	SIZE	LENGTH	CAPACITY	COMMENTS/USES
Hog casing (small intestine)	32–35 mm (2 ft/lb)	100 yd/hank	105–115 lb	Country-style and pork sausage, large frankfurters, pepperoni
Hog middles (middle of intestine)	4 in	13 ft (27 ft/set)		
Hog bung (end)	2 in and up	4 ft long		
Sewed hog bungs	4 in wide	36 in long	8½–9½ lb	Salami, liverwurst casings

Beef Casings

ITEMS	SIZE	LENGTH	CAPACITY	COMMENTS/USES
Beef round (tight curl)	43–46 mm	100 ft/set	75–80 lb (15 in/lb)	Ring liver, ring bologna, sausage kielbasa, blood and mettwurst holsteiner
Beef middle (large intestine)	60–65 mm	57 ft/set	70–80 lb (9 in/lb)	Lyoner-style sausages and other types of bologna, dry and semidry cervelats, dry and cooked salami, kishka (stuffed derma), and veal sausage
Beef bung cap (appendix)	120 mm	23–27 in	17–20 lb	Capicolla, large bologna, lebanon, and cooked salami

1. Rewind the casings and store covered in salt. Lay out the casings and remove any knots. Form into bundles of the required length (see Figure 6-8A). If you will be holding the casings for a few days, store them covered with salt (see Figure 6-8B).

2. Before using the casings, rinse them thoroughly in tepid water, forcing the water through the casing to flush out the salt (see Figure 6-8C). Repeat this step as often as necessary to remove all traces of salt and any other impurities.

3. Cut the casing into lengths, if necessary (consult specific recipes), and tie a bubble knot in one end of the casing (see Figures 6-8D and 6-8E).

Piece of casing caught between knot 1 and 2

Bubble knot

Loop for hanging sausage

6-8. Preparing natural casings. **A.** Rewinding casings into smaller units. **B.** Storing casings in salt. **C.** Pushing water through the casing. The ends of each strand are hung over the edge of the bowl to help prevent tangling. **D.** Casings are measured and cut into lengths; a bubble knot is tied. **E.** Tying a bubble knot.

A. Casings are fitted on the end of the stuffer tube and gently drawn forward as they fill with sausage.   **B.** Pinching the links.   **C.** Tying links for smoked sausage.

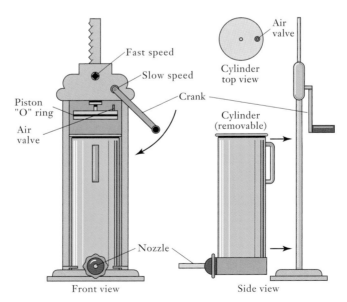

Diagram of a sausage stuffer.

6-10. More tying. **A.** Tying the end of kielbasa. **B.** Tying the end of a summer sausage. **C.** Four types of sausages, clockwise from top right: beef middle for kielbasa, beef bung for summer sausage, sheep casings for Italian sausage, hog casings for bratwurst. **D.** Poking air holes with a teasing needle.

STUFFING THE CASING The following method describes the procedure for filling sausage casings using a sausage-stuffing machine (see the diagram on page 238).

1. Assemble and fill the sausage stuffer properly. Keep the nozzle of your stuffer as well as the work surface lubricated with a bit of water as you work to prevent the casing from sticking and tearing. Be sure that all parts of the sausage stuffer that will come in contact with the forcemeat are clean and chilled. Fill the stuffer with the sausage meat, tamping it down well to remove air pockets.

2. Press the sausage into the prepared casing. Gather the open end of the casing over the nozzle of the sausage stuffer. Press the sausage into the casing (if you are using a hand stuffer or piping the sausage into the casing, slide the open end over the nozzle of the hand stuffer or over the tip of the pastry bag). Support the casing as the forcemeat is expressed through the nozzle and into the casing (see Figure 6-9A).

3. Twist or tie the sausage into the appropriate shape. If the sausage is to be made into links, use either of the following methods: Press the casing into links at the desired intervals (see Figure 6-9B) and then twist the link in alternating directions for each link, or tie the casing with twine at the desired intervals (see Figure 6-9C).

Other typical sausage shaping methods are shown in Figures 6-10A to 6-10C. Larger sausages should be secured with a second bubble knot to allow the sausage to expand as it cooks.

After the sausage has been formed into links, loops, or other shapes, pierce the casing with a teasing needle, sausage maker's knife, or similar tool (see Figure 6-10D) to allow the air bubbles to escape.

Mexican Chorizo

YIELD: 11 LB/4.99 KG BULK; 88 LINKS

Mexican chorizo is often left loose and used as an ingredient in soups and bean dishes and as a filling for omelets and soft tortillas.

10 lb/4.54 kg boneless pork butt (70% lean, 30% fat), cubed

SEASONINGS

3¼ oz/92 g salt

5½ oz/156 g ground dried chiles

1 oz/28 g Spanish paprika

1¾ oz/50 g minced garlic, sautéed and cooled

5 tsp/10 g ground cinnamon

5 tsp/10 g ground oregano

5 tsp/10 g ground thyme

5 tsp/10 g ground cumin

5 tsp/10 g ground black pepper

2½ tsp/5 g ground cloves

2½ tsp/5 g ground ginger

2½ tsp/5 g ground nutmeg

2½ tsp/5 g ground coriander

2½ tsp/5 g ground bay leaf

6 fl oz/180 mL red wine vinegar

42 ft/12.80 m sheep casings, rinsed (optional)

1. Toss the pork butt with the combined seasonings. Chill well.

2. Grind through the medium plate (¼ in/6 mm) of a meat grinder into a mixing bowl over an ice bath.

3. Mix on low speed for 1 minute, adding the vinegar a little at a time.

4. Mix on medium speed for 15 to 20 seconds, or until the sausage mixture is sticky to the touch.

5. Make a test. Adjust seasoning and consistency before shaping into patties or filling casings and shaping into individual 5-in/13-cm links.

6. Prepare the sausage for immediate service by pan-frying, baking, grilling, or broiling to an internal temperature of 150°F/65°C, or refrigerate for up to 3 days.

Breakfast Sausage

YIELD: 11 LB/4.99 KG BULK; 88 LINKS

Breakfast sausage is a basic fresh sausage, commonly shaped into bulk, 2-oz/57-g patties, or links. Sheep casings are the most common choice for links, but larger sausages can be made in hog casings.

10 lb/4.54 kg boneless pork butt (70% lean, 30% fat), cubed

SEASONINGS

3½ oz/99 g salt

⅔ oz/19 g ground white pepper

½ oz/14 g poultry seasoning

16 fl oz/480 mL ice-cold water

42 ft/12.80 m sheep casings, rinsed (optional)

1. Toss the pork butt with the combined seasonings. Chill well.

2. Grind through the medium plate (¼ in/6 mm) of a meat grinder into a mixing bowl over an ice bath.

3. Mix on low speed for 1 minute, gradually adding water.

4. Mix on medium speed for 15 to 20 seconds, or until the sausage mixture is sticky to the touch.

5. Make a test. Adjust seasoning and consistency before shaping into patties, cylinders, or filling casings and shaping into individual 5-in/13-cm links.

6. Prepare the sausage for immediate service by pan-frying, baking, grilling, or broiling to an internal temperature of 150°F/66°C, or refrigerate for up to 3 days.

SMOKED BREAKFAST SAUSAGE: Add ⅓ oz/9 g tinted curing mix (TCM) to the seasoning mixture. Stuff into sausage casings; pin and twist into 5-in/13-cm links. Dry overnight under refrigeration and cold smoke for 1 hour. Prepare for service as directed above.

Green Chile Sausage

YIELD: 11 LB 8 OZ/5.22 KG BULK; 46 LINKS OR PATTIES

10 lb/4.54 kg boneless pork butt (70% lean, 30% fat), cubed

SEASONINGS

3½ oz/99 g salt

1½ oz/43 g chili powder

5 tsp/10 g ground cumin

5 tsp/10 g sweet Spanish paprika

5 tsp/10 g oregano

5 tsp/10 g basil

1½ tsp/3 g onion powder

6 garlic cloves, minced

2½ fl oz/75 mL Tabasco sauce

12 oz/340 g poblano chiles, roasted, seeded, peeled, and cut into ⅛-in/3-mm dice

3 jalapeños, seeded and minced

12 fl oz/360 mL ice-cold water

21 ft/6.40 m hog casings, rinsed

1. Toss the pork butt with the combined seasonings. Chill well.

2. Grind through the fine plate (⅛ in/3 mm) of a meat grinder into a mixing bowl over an ice bath.

3. Mix on low speed for 1 minute, gradually adding poblanos, jalapeños, and ice water. Mix on medium speed for 15 to 20 seconds, or until the sausage mixture is sticky to the touch. Make a test. Adjust seasoning and consistency before filling the prepared casings and shaping into 4-in/10-cm links.

4. Prepare the sausage for immediate service by pan-frying, baking, grilling, or broiling to an internal temperature of 150°F/66°C, or refrigerate for up to 3 days.

SMOKED GREEN CHILE SAUSAGE: Add ½ oz/14 g tinted curing mix (TCM) to the seasonings. Cold smoke at 80°F/27°C for 2 hours and then cut into separate links.

Venison Sausage

YIELD: 9 LB/4.08 KG BULK; 70 LINKS

Venison sausage makes excellent use of less tender cuts and trim from the shoulder or leg. These sausages can be used to add another dimension to a main course featuring prime cuts such as loin or chops. This not only allows you to be more creative but lowers costs at the same time.

4 lb/1.81 kg boneless venison shoulder, cubed

2 lb/907 g boneless pork butt, cubed

2 lb/907 g fatback, cubed

SEASONINGS

3 oz/85 g salt

1¼ oz/35 g dextrose

3¾ oz/106 g onion powder

2¾ tsp/5.50 g ground black pepper

2 tsp/3 g crushed juniper berries

½ tsp/1 g garlic powder

2 tbsp/6 g minced sage

12 fl oz/360 mL Venison Stock (page 528), cold

32 ft/9.75 m sheep casings, rinsed

1. Toss the venison, pork butt, and fatback with the combined seasonings. Chill well.

2. Grind through the fine plate (⅛ in/3 mm) of a meat grinder into a mixing bowl over an ice bath.

3. Mix on low speed for 1 minute, gradually adding the cold venison stock a little at a time. Mix on medium speed for 15 to 20 seconds, or until the sausage mixture is sticky to the touch. Make a test. Adjust seasoning and consistency before filling prepared casings and shaping into 5-in/13-cm links.

4. Prepare the sausage for immediate service by pan-frying, baking, grilling, or broiling to an internal temperature of 150°F/66°C, or refrigerate for up to 3 days.

SMOKED VENISON SAUSAGE: Add 1½ tbsp/9 g tinted curing mix (TCM) to the seasoning mixture. Stuff into sausage casings and shape into 5-in/13-cm links. Twist them and cut into individual links. Dry overnight under refrigeration and cold smoke for 1 hour. Prepare for service as directed above.

Sweet Italian Sausage

YIELD: 11 LB/4.99 KG BULK; 44 LINKS

10 lb/4.54 kg boneless pork butt (70% lean, 30% fat), cubed

SEASONINGS

3½ oz/99 g salt

1 oz/28 g dextrose

1 oz/28 g coarse-ground black pepper

1 oz/28 g fennel seeds

1 oz/28 g sweet Spanish paprika

16 fl oz/480 mL ice-cold water

23 ft/7.01 m hog casings, rinsed

1. Toss the pork butt with the combined seasonings. Chill well.

2. Grind through the coarse plate (⅜ in/9.5 mm) of a meat grinder into a mixing bowl over an ice bath.

3. Mix on low speed for 1 minute, gradually adding the water.

4. Mix on medium speed for 15 to 20 seconds, or until the sausage mixture is sticky to the touch. Make a test. Adjust seasoning and consistency before shaping.

5. Stuff into prepared casings and twist into 5-in/13-cm links. Cut into individual links.

6. Prepare the sausage for immediate service by pan-frying, baking, grilling, or broiling to an internal temperature of 150°F/66°C, or refrigerate for up to 3 days.

HOT ITALIAN SAUSAGE: Replace the fennel seeds and sweet paprika with 2½ oz/71 g Hot Italian Spice Blend (page 527).

ITALIAN SAUSAGE WITH CHEESE: Grind 2 lb/907 g cubed provolone cheese, 1 lb/454 g cubed Parmesan cheese, and 1 oz/28 g chopped parsley along with the pork in Step 2. This recipe makes approximately 50 links weighing 4½ oz/128 g each. Or cut the casings into 15-in/38-cm lengths and coil into a spiral as shown on page 239. Secure the spiral with a 6-in/15-cm skewer and bake or broil before serving.

LOW-FAT ITALIAN SAUSAGE: Trim all the exterior fat from the pork butt. Grind 2 lb/907 g well-cooked rice pilaf along with the pork in Step 2. Season as desired with sweet or hot spice blends.

SMOKED ITALIAN SAUSAGE: Add 1½ tsp/9 g tinted curing mixture (TCM) to the cubed pork before grinding. Cold smoke the sausages at 80°F/27°C for 2 hours. Because the sausages are cold smoked, they must be fully cooked before service, as directed above.

Greek Sausage (Loukanika)

Traditionally made with lamb and scented with orange peel, this makes a wonderful grilled or roasted sausage. Pork can be substituted for lamb, if desired.

10 lb/4.54 kg fatty lamb shoulder, cubed

SEASONINGS

3½ oz/99 g salt

4 oz/113 g minced orange peel

1 tbsp/6 g ground black pepper

1 tsp/2 g ground bay leaves

1 tsp/2 g ground allspice

1 tsp/2 g crushed red pepper

1 tsp/2 g cayenne

3 tbsp/9 g chopped flat-leaf parsley

1 tbsp/3 g chopped oregano

1½ tsp/1.50 g chopped thyme

1 lb 4 oz/567 g minced onion, sautéed and cooled

1½ tsp/4.50 g minced garlic, sautéed and cooled

10 fl oz/300 mL ice-cold water

2 lb 8 oz/1.13 kg caul fat (optional)

48 flat-leaf parsley pluches

1. Toss the lamb with the combined seasonings; chill well. Grind through the fine plate (⅛ in/ 3 mm) of a meat grinder into a mixing bowl over an ice bath.

2. Mix on low speed for 1 minute, gradually adding the water. Mix on medium speed for 15 to 20 seconds, or until the sausage mixture is sticky to the touch. Make a test. Adjust seasoning and consistency before shaping.

3. Portion the sausage meat into patties of about 3 oz/85 g each. Optional: Wrap each patty in a piece of caul fat, placing pluches of parsley below the patty, and fold the edges over the sausage.

4. Prepare the sausage for immediate service by pan-frying, baking, grilling, or broiling to an internal temperature of 150°F/66°C, or refrigerate for up to 3 days.

Merguez

YIELD: 10 LB/4.54 KG BULK; 27 LINKS

7 lb/3.18 kg lean lamb trim, cubed

SEASONINGS

12 fl oz/360 mL red wine

2 tsp/5.50 g tinted curing mix (TCM)

3½ oz/99 g salt

2 tbsp/10 g sugar

2 lb/907 g beef fat, cubed

1 lb/454 g red peppers, roasted, skinned

1 tbsp/4.50 g crushed chiles

2½ oz/71 g harissa paste

1½ tsp/3 g Quatre Épices (page 524)

1½ oz/42 g garlic, minced

38 ft/11.58 m sheep casings, rinsed

1. Combine lamb trim, red wine, TCM, salt, and sugar and marinate for at least 1 hour.

2. Add the remaining ingredients and mix thoroughly.

3. Grind through a medium (¼ in/6 mm) plate.

4. Mix until sticky.

5. Make a test. Adjust seasoning and consistency before shaping.

6. Stuff into prepared sheep casings and twist into 15-in/38-cm links. Cut into individual links. Make a spiral with each link and secure with a 6-in/15-cm skewer.

7. Prepare the sausage for immediate service by pan-frying, baking, grilling, or broiling to an internal temperature of 150°F/66°C, or refrigerate for up to 7 days.

German Bratwurst

YIELD: 11 LB/4.99 KG BULK; 44 LINKS

10 lb/4.54 kg boneless pork butt (70% lean, 30% fat), cubed

SEASONINGS

4 oz/113 g salt

½ oz/14 g rubbed sage

¾ oz/21 g ground white pepper

½ tsp/1 g ground celery seed

½ tsp/1 g ground mace

16 fl oz/480 mL ice-cold water

22 ft/6.71 m hog casings, rinsed and tied at one end

1. Toss the pork with the combined seasonings. Chill well.

2. Grind the pork through the fine plate (⅛ in/3 mm) of a meat grinder into a mixing bowl over an ice bath.

3. Mix on low speed for 1 minute, gradually adding the water. Mix on medium speed for 15 to 20 seconds, or until the sausage mixture is sticky to the touch. Make a test. Adjust seasoning and consistency before shaping.

4. Stuff into prepared casings and twist into 5-in/13-cm links.

5. Poach the sausages in simmering water (165°F/74°C) for 15 to 18 minutes to an internal temperature of 150°F/66°C, then shock in an ice water bath to an internal temperature of 60°F/16°C.

6. Prepare the sausage for immediate service by sautéing, grilling, broiling, or baking just until hot, or wrap and refrigerate for up to 7 days.

CHEF'S NOTE: Smaller bratwurst may be made using sheep casings and twisting the sausages into 4-in/10-cm lengths.

SMOKED BRATWURST: Add ½ oz/14 g tinted curing mix (TCM) to the seasonings. Do not separate the sausages into links until after cold smoking at 80°F/27°C for 2 hours. Cook the sausage as directed above before serving.

Bavarian Bratwurst

YIELD: 10 LB/4.53 KG BULK; 40 LINKS

See Chapter 5, page 182, for the USDA regulations for dry curing sausages.

10 lb/4.54 kg boneless pork butt (70% lean, 30% fat), cubed

SEASONINGS

3½ oz/99 g salt

1½ tbsp/9 g ground black pepper

1 tsp/2 g ground mace

2 oz/57 g sugar

¼ tsp/0.75 g lemon zest

1½ tbsp/9 g ground marjoram

8 oz/227 g ice

22 ft/6.71 m hog casings, rinsed and tied at one end

1. Toss the pork with the combined seasonings.

2. Grind the pork butt through a medium plate; grind fatback through a fine plate.

3. Add the ice and mix until sticky.

4. Stuff into hog casings and form links by tying every 6 in/15 cm.

5. Poach to an internal temperature of 145°F/63°C.

6. Prepare the sausage for immediate service by sautéing, grilling, broiling, or baking just until hot, or wrap and refrigerate for up to 3 days.

Szechwan-Style Sausage

YIELD: 8 LB/3.63 KG BULK; 46 LINKS

See Chapter 5, page 182, for the USDA regulations for dry curing sausages.

11 lb/4.99 kg boneless pork butt (70% lean, 30% fat), cubed

SEASONINGS

2 oz/57 g salt

1 tbsp/21 g Prague Powder II

4 oz/113 g sugar

2 oz/57 g chili powder

1 tsp/2 g ground white pepper

½ oz/14 g Chinese Five-Spice Powder (page 523)

½ oz/14 g Szechwan peppercorn powder

4 fl oz/120 mL soy sauce

2½ fl oz/75 mL white liquor or vodka

23 ft/7.01 m hog casings, rinsed and tied at one end

1. Toss the pork butt with the combined seasonings, soy sauce, and liquor. Chill well.

2. Grind through the medium plate (¼ in/6 mm) of a meat grinder into a mixing bowl over an ice bath.

3. Mix on low speed for 1 minute, then mix on medium speed for 15 to 20 seconds, or until the sausage mixture is sticky to the touch. Make a test. Adjust seasoning and consistency before shaping.

4. Stuff into prepared casings and twist into 8-in/20-cm links. Dry for 3 days.

5. Poke small holes in the casing. Steam to an internal temperature of 150°F/66°C, about 15 minutes. Prepare the sausage for immediate service by sautéing, grilling, broiling, or baking just until hot, or wrap and refrigerate for up to 7 days.

Cajun-Style Sausage

YIELD: 11 LB/4.99 KG BULK; 88 LINKS

10 lb/4.54 kg boneless pork butt (70% lean, 30% fat), cubed

SEASONINGS

4 oz/113 g salt

1 tbsp/8.25 g tinted curing mix (TCM)

½ oz/14 g onion powder

½ oz/14 g hot Hungarian paprika

2 tbsp/6 g dried oregano

4 tsp/8 g coarse-ground black pepper

4 tsp/8 g ground white pepper

4 tsp/8 g garlic powder

2 tsp/4 g cayenne

16 fl oz/480 mL ice-cold water

44 ft/13.41 m sheep casings, rinsed

1. Toss the pork butt with the combined seasonings. Chill well.

2. Grind through the coarse plate (⅜ in/9.5 mm) of a meat grinder, then the fine plate (⅛ in/ 3 mm), into a mixing bowl over an ice bath.

3. Mix on low speed for 1 minute, gradually adding the water.

4. Mix on medium speed for 15 to 20 seconds, or until the sausage mixture is sticky to the touch. Make a test. Adjust seasoning and consistency before shaping.

5. Stuff into prepared casings and twist into 6-in/15-cm links.

6. Hang the sausages under refrigeration overnight to form a pellicle.

7. Cold smoke at 80°F/27°C for 4 to 5 hours.

8. Prepare the sausage for immediate service by pan-frying, baking, grilling, braising, or broiling to an internal temperature of 150°F/66°C, or refrigerate for up to 7 days.

Kassler Liverwurst

YIELD: 16 SAUSAGES (1 LB/454 G EACH)

5 lb/2.27 kg boneless pork butt, cubed

4 lb/1.81 kg pork liver

3 lb/1.36 kg jowl fat, cubed, or skinless pork bellies

SEASONINGS

5½ oz/156 g salt

½ oz/14 g tinted curing mix (TCM)

2 tsp/4 g ground white pepper

2 tsp/4 g Pâté Spice (page 526)

4 oz/113 g onions, minced

12 oz/340 g potato starch

8 fl oz/240 mL dry white wine

12 eggs

1 lb/454 g boiled ham, cut into small dice

4½ oz/128 g pistachio nuts, blanched, peeled, and halved

16 pieces beef middle casings, rinsed, cut into 12-in/30-cm lengths, and tied at one end

1. Combine the pork, liver, and jowl fat with seasonings.

2. Grind through a fine plate (⅛ in/3 mm).

3. Blend the meat mixture with the onions and potato starch in a mixer on low speed, about 1 minute.

4. Add the wine and eggs and mix on low speed for 1 minute, or until relatively homogeneous. Mix on medium speed for 15 to 20 seconds, or until the sausage mixture is sticky to the touch. Make a test. Adjust seasoning and consistency before garnishing and shaping.

5. Fold the ham and pistachio nuts into the forcemeat by hand over an ice bath.

6. Stuff into the prepared casings and tie the ends with bubble knots.

7. Poach at 165°F/74°C to an internal temperature of 155°F/68°C, then shock and blot dry.

8. Cold smoke at 80°F/27°C for 2 to 4 hours, or until desired color.

Smoked Pheasant Sausage

YIELD: 11 LB/4.99 KG BULK; 85 LINKS

7 lb/3.18 kg boneless pheasant meat

3 lb/1.36 kg fatback, cubed

SEASONINGS

4 oz/113 g salt

1 tbsp/8.25 g tinted curing mix (TCM)

1 oz/28 g sugar

½ oz/14 g ground white pepper

½ oz/14 g poultry seasoning

1 tbsp/6 g onion powder

12 fl oz/360 mL ice-cold water or stock

44 ft/13.41 m sheep casings, rinsed

1. Toss the pheasant meat with the fatback and the combined seasonings. Chill well.

2. Grind through the medium plate (¼ in/6 mm) of a meat grinder into a mixing bowl over an ice bath.

3. Mix on low speed for 1 minute, gradually adding the water. Mix on medium speed for 15 to 20 seconds, or until the mixture is sticky to the touch. Make a test. Adjust seasoning and consistency before shaping.

4. Stuff into prepared casings and twist into 5-in/13-cm links. Hang overnight under refrigeration to form a pellicle.

5. Cold smoke at 80°F/27°C for 1 to 2 hours.

6. Prepare the sausage for immediate service by poaching, sautéing, baking, or grilling to an internal temperature of 165°F/74°C, or wrap and refrigerate for up to 3 days.

PHEASANT SAUSAGE WITH WILD RICE: Reduce the amount of fatback to 2 lb 8 oz/1.13 kg. Add 8 oz/227 g cooked wild rice to the meat after it has been ground and before the second mixing in Step 3.

Andouille Sausage

YIELD: 8 LB/3.63 KG BULK; 25 LINKS

6 lb 4 oz/2.83 kg boneless pork butt (70% lean, 30% fat), cubed

SEASONINGS

2¾ oz/78 g salt

1 tsp/7 g tinted curing mix (TCM)

½ oz/14 g dextrose

½ oz/14 g cayenne

1 tsp/2 g ground mace

1 tsp/2 g ground allspice

1 tsp/2 g ground marjoram

¾ tsp/1.50 g ground thyme

¼ tsp/0.50 g ground cloves

1 lb 4 oz/567 g onions, coarsely chopped

1¼ oz/35 g minced garlic

4 oz/113 g nonfat dry milk powder

32 ft/9.75 m sheep casings, rinsed

1. Toss the pork butt with the combined seasonings, onions, and garlic. Chill well.

2. Grind through the fine plate (⅛ in/3 mm) of a meat grinder into a mixing bowl over an ice bath.

3. Add the dry milk powder.

4. Mix on low speed for 1 minute or until the sausage mixture is sticky to the touch. Make a test. Adjust seasoning and consistency before shaping.

5. Stuff into prepared casings and tie into 10-in/25-cm links. Do not cut. Hang overnight under refrigeration to form a pellicle.

6. Cold smoke at 80°F/27°C for 12 to 14 hours. Allow the sausages to dry in a cool, dry area or curing room for an additional 12 to 24 hours.

7. Prepare the sausage for immediate service by poaching, sautéing, grilling, or baking just until hot to an internal temperature of 155°F/68°C, or wrap and refrigerate for up to 2 weeks.

Summer Sausage

YIELD: 7 LB/3.18 KG BULK; 6 LINKS

3 lb 8 oz/1.59 kg boneless beef shoulder clod (70% lean, 30% fat), cubed

3 lb/1.36 kg boneless pork butt (70% lean, 30% fat), cubed

SEASONINGS

2½ oz/71 g salt

2 tsp/5.50 g tinted curing mix (TCM)

1¼ oz/35 g dextrose

1 tbsp/6 g ground black pepper

1 tbsp/6 g ground coriander

1 tbsp/6 g ground mustard

1 tsp/2 g garlic powder

3 oz/85 g nonfat dry milk powder

6 beef middle casings, rinsed, cut into 10-in/25-cm lengths and tied at one end

1. Grind the beef through the medium plate (¼ in/6 mm) of a meat grinder. Chill if necessary.

2. Toss the beef and pork with the combined seasonings and mix thoroughly. Transfer to a container, cover with plastic wrap, and cure in a 38° to 40°F/3° to 4°C refrigerator for 2 to 3 days.

3. Grind the meat through the fine plate (⅛ in/3 mm) of a meat grinder into a bowl over an ice bath. Add the dry milk powder. Mix on low speed for 1 minute. Mix on medium speed for 15 to 20 seconds, or until the sausage mixture is sticky to the touch. Make a test. Adjust seasoning and consistency before shaping.

4. Stuff into casings, tying with bubble knots. Hang under refrigeration overnight to form a pellicle.

5. Cold smoke at 80°F/27°C for 12 to 14 hours. Hot smoke at 160°F/71°C to an internal temperature of 155°F/68°C. Dry 1 to 2 hours in a smoker.

6. Refrigerate for up to 2 weeks.

Landjäger

YIELD: 7 LB 5⅓ OZ/3.33 KG BULK; 25 LINKS

See Chapter 5, page 182, for the USDA regulations for dry curing sausages.

7 lb 8 oz/3.40 kg beef, bottom round

5 lb/2.27 kg certified pork butt, trimmed (see Chef's Notes)

SEASONINGS

4½ oz/128 g salt

½ oz/14 g Prague Powder II

2 tsp/4 g ground caraway seeds

1 oz/28 g dextrose

¾ oz/21 g ground black pepper

1½ tsp/3 g garlic powder

3 oz/85 g nonfat dry milk powder

5 fl oz/150 mL ice-cold water

40 ft/12.19 m hog casings, rinsed and tied at one end

1. Toss the beef and certified pork with the combined seasonings. Chill well.

2. Grind through the fine plate (⅛ in/3 mm) of a meat grinder into a mixing bowl over an ice bath.

3. Add the dry milk powder. Mix on low speed for 1 minute, gradually adding the water, until the sausage mixture is sticky to the touch. Make a test. Adjust seasoning and consistency before shaping.

4. Stuff into prepared hog casings and twist into 6-in/15-cm links. Cut at every other twist to separate into pairs of links.

5. Press in a landjäger press (see Chef's Notes).

6. Place on a plastic sheet pan, cover with another plastic sheet pan, press with two cutting boards, and refrigerate for 2 to 4 days.

7. Cold smoke at 80°F/27°C for 12 to 24 hours, then dry until desired firmness, 3 to 4 days.

CHEF'S NOTES: This is a dry-type sausage and is not cooked, so the pork used must be certified to prevent trichinosis. Certified pork may be purchased, or you can certify it yourself by freezing the pork at the appropriate temperature for a prescribed period (see page 228).

A landjäger press is used to shape the sausage. The press is typically made of a hard wood and is about 18 to 20 in/46 to 51 cm long. There is a rectangular well in the center of the mold, about 1 in/3 cm wide and ¾ in/2 cm deep. Once the sausage is stuffed into the casing, the links are laid into the mold and then covered with plastic wrap. Weight the sausages by setting two wooden cutting boards on top of the press. This creates the typical rectangular shape of landjäger sausages.

Frankfurter

YIELD: 12 LB 8 OZ/5.67 KG BULK; 80 LINKS

"The noblest of all dogs is the hot-dog: it feeds the hand that bites it."—Laurence J. Peter

5 lb/2.27 kg lean boneless beef shoulder clod, cubed

CURE MIX

4⅓ oz/123 g salt

½ oz/14 g tinted curing mix (TCM)

1 oz/28 g dextrose

4 lb/1.81 kg jowl fat, cubed, partially frozen

3 lb/1.36 kg crushed ice

SPICE BLEND

½ oz/14 g onion powder

1 tbsp/6 g ground white pepper

1 tbsp/6 g ground coriander

1 tbsp/6 g ground nutmeg

½ tsp/14 g garlic powder

7½ oz/213 g nonfat dry milk powder

50 ft/15.24 m sheep casings, rinsed

1. Toss the beef with the cure mix; chill well. Grind through the fine plate (⅛ in/3 mm) of a meat grinder onto a plastic wrap–lined sheet pan and place in the freezer until semifrozen.

2. Grind the jowl fat through the fine plate; reserve.

3. Transfer the ground beef to a chilled chopper bowl. Place the ice and the spice blend on top of the ground beef. Process the ingredients until the mixture drops to a temperature of 30°F/–1°C. Continue running the machine until the mixture's temperature rises to 40°F/4°C.

4. Add the jowl fat and process until the mixture reaches 45°F/7°C. Add the dry milk powder and continue processing until the mixture reaches 58°F/14°C. Make a test. Adjust seasoning and consistency before shaping.

5. Stuff into the prepared casings, twist, and tie into 6-in/15-cm links. Hang overnight under refrigeration to form a pellicle.

6. Hot smoke at 160°F/71°C until the desired color is achieved, about 45 minutes. Poach in water at 165°F/74°C to an internal temperature of 155°F/68°C, 10 to 20 minutes, then shock in ice water to an internal temperature of 60°F/15°C. Blot dry.

7. Prepare the sausage for immediate service by sautéing, grilling, broiling, or baking just until hot, or wrap and refrigerate for up to 7 days.

REDUCED-FAT FRANKFURTERS: For lower-fat frankfurters, increase the amount of meat by 2 lb/907 g and decrease the amount of fat by 2 lb/907 g. If desired, other combinations of pork, veal, and beef may be used.

Bologna

YIELD: 12 LB 8 OZ/5.67 KG BULK; 16 LINKS

5 lb/2.27 g boneless beef shoulder clod, cubed

CURE MIX

4⅓ oz/123 g salt

½ oz/14 g tinted curing mix (TCM)

1 oz/28 g dextrose

4 lb/1.81 kg jowl fat, cubed, partially frozen

3 lb/1.36 kg crushed ice

SPICE BLEND

1½ oz/43 g onion powder

½ oz/14 g ground white pepper

2 tsp/4 g ground caraway seeds

2 tsp/4 g ground nutmeg

7½ oz/213 g nonfat dry milk powder

1 beef bung or 8 beef middle casings, cut into 6-in/15-cm lengths, tied at one end with a bubble knot

1. Toss the beef with the cure mix. Chill well and grind through the fine plate (⅛ in/3 mm) of a meat grinder. Place in the freezer until semifrozen.

2. Grind the jowl fat through the fine plate; reserve.

3. Transfer the ground beef to a chilled chopper bowl. Add the ice and the spice blend on top of the ground beef. Process the ingredients until the mixture drops to a temperature of 30°F/−1°C. Continue running the machine until the mixture's temperature rises to 40°F/4°C.

4. Add the jowl fat and process until the mixture reaches 45°F/7°C. Add the dry milk powder and continue processing until the mixture reaches 58°F/14°C. Make a test. Adjust seasoning and consistency before shaping.

5. Stuff into the prepared casings and tie each end with a bubble knot. Hang under refrigeration overnight to form a pellicle.

6. Hot smoke at 160°F/71°C until desired color is achieved, 1 to 2 hours. Poach in water at 165°F/74°C to an internal temperature of 155°F/68°C (10 to 30 minutes for beef round, 1 to 3 hours for beef bung), then shock in ice water to an internal temperature of 60°F/16°C. Blot dry.

7. Refrigerate for up to 2 weeks.

VARIATIONS: To each fully prepared basic bologna recipe, fold in the following garnish ingredients before shaping. Each variation produces 11 sausages at 14 in/36 cm each using beef casing (casings should be precut 16 in/41 cm and tied) or one 16 lb 8 oz/7.48 kg sausage using beef bung.

HAM BOLOGNA: 4 lb/1.81 kg cured pork, cut into cubes ¾ to 1 in/2 to 3 cm.

AMISH BOLOGNA: 4 lb/1.81 kg cured, cooked, diced pig head meat, cut into ¾-in/2-cm cubes.

TONGUE BOLOGNA: 4 lb/1.81 kg cured, cooked beef tongue, cut into cubes ¾ to 1 in/2 to 3 cm.

French Garlic Sausage

YIELD: 25 LB/11.34 KG BULK; 16 LINKS

12 lb/5.44 kg boneless pork butt, cut into dice of ¼ to ½ in/6 mm to 1 cm

CURE MIX

8½ oz/241 g salt

1 oz/28 g tinted curing mix (TCM)

2 oz/57 g dextrose

5 lb/2.27 kg lean beef shoulder clod, cubed

SPICE BLEND

1¼ oz/35 g chopped garlic

1 oz/28 g ground white pepper

½ oz/14 g dry mustard

4 lb/1.81 kg jowl fat, cubed and partially frozen

3 lb/1.36 kg crushed ice

7½ oz/213 g nonfat dry milk powder

19 ft/5.79 m beef middle casings, rinsed, cut into 14-in/36-cm lengths and tied at one end

1. Toss the pork with half the cure mix. Chill well and reserve for garnish.

2. Toss the beef with the remaining cure mix and the spice blend. Chill well and grind through the fine plate (⅛ in/3 mm) of a meat grinder. Place in the freezer until semifrozen.

3. Grind the jowl fat through the fine plate; reserve.

4. Transfer the ground beef to a chilled chopper bowl. Add the ice to the ground beef. Process the ingredients until the mixture drops to a temperature of 30°F/−1°C. Continue running the machine until the mixture's temperature rises to 40°F/4°C.

5. Add the jowl fat and process until the mixture reaches 45°F/7°C . Add the dry milk powder and continue processing until the mixture reaches 58°F/14°C. Make a test. Adjust seasoning and consistency before shaping.

6. Fold the pork garnish into the sausage in a mixer or by hand over an ice bath. Stuff into prepared casings and tie each end with a bubble knot. Refrigerate, uncovered, overnight on paper towel–lined trays to form a pellicle.

7. Poach in water at 165°F/74°C to an internal temperature of 150°F/66°C, then shock in ice water to an internal temperature of 60°F/16°C. Blot dry. Slice the sausage for immediate service, or wrap and refrigerate for up to 7 days.

CHEF'S NOTE: For more smoke color, cold smoke at 80°F/27°C for up to 12 hours, then finish cooking by poaching, as described in Step 7 above.

DUCK SAUSAGE: Substitute duck meat for all meats; instead of beef casings, substitute hog casings, cut into 5-in/13-cm lengths; follow the same method as above.

Kielbasa

9 lb/4.08 kg boneless pork butt

5 lb/2.27 kg lean boneless beef top or bottom round

4 lb/1.81 kg jowl fat

3 lb/1.36 kg crushed ice

CURE MIX

7½ oz/213 g salt

1½ oz/43 g tinted curing mix (TCM)

1½ oz/43 g dextrose

SPICE BLEND

1 oz/28 g ground white pepper

½ oz/14 g dry mustard

½ tsp/1 g garlic powder

7½ oz/213 g nonfat dry milk powder

21 beef round casings, rinsed, cut into 15-in/38-cm lengths and tied at one end with a bubble knot

1. Trim the pork and cube; reserve. Cube the beef; reserve. Cube the jowl fat; freeze until needed. Scale the ice; keep frozen until needed.

2. Toss the pork with half of the cure mix. Chill well. Grind through the coarse plate (⅜ in/9 mm) of a meat grinder and reserve for garnish.

3. Toss the beef with the remaining cure mix and the spice blend. Chill well and grind through the fine plate (⅛ in/3 mm) of a meat grinder. Place in freezer until semifrozen.

4. Grind the jowl fat through the fine plate; reserve.

5. Transfer the ground beef to a chilled chopper bowl. Add the ice on top of the ground beef. Process the ingredients until the mixture drops to a temperature of 30°F/−1°C. Continue running the machine until the mixture's temperature rises to 40°F/4°C.

6. Add the jowl fat and process until the mixture reaches 45°F/7°C. Add the dry milk powder and continue processing until the mixture reaches 58°F/14°C. Make a test. Adjust seasoning and consistency before shaping.

7. Fold the ground pork garnish into the sausage in a mixer or by hand over an ice bath. Stuff into the prepared casings and tie the open ends with a bubble knot. Hang overnight under refrigeration to form a pellicle.

8. Hot smoke at 160°F/71°C until desired color is achieved, 1½ to 2 hours.

9. Poach in water at 165°F/74°C to an internal temperature of 150°F/66°C, then shock in ice water to an internal temperature of 60°F/16°C. Blot dry.

10. Prepare the sausage for immediate service by sautéing, grilling, broiling, or baking just until hot, or wrap and refrigerate for up to 7 days.

Kielbasa is a smoked sausage originally made in Poland.

Fine Swiss Bratwurst

YIELD: 15 LB/6.80 KG BULK; 115 LINKS

5 lb/2.27 kg boneless veal top or bottom round, cubed

CURE MIX

5 oz/142 g salt

1 oz/28 g dextrose

5 lb/2.27 kg jowl fat, cubed and partially frozen

4 lb/1.81 kg crushed ice

SPICE BLEND

½ oz/14 g ground white pepper

½ oz/14 g dry mustard

1 tbsp/6 g ground mace

1½ tsp/3 g ground ginger

9 oz/255 g nonfat dry milk powder

60 ft/18.29 m sheep casings, rinsed

1. Toss the veal with the cure mix. Chill well and grind through the fine plate (⅛ in/3 mm) of a meat grinder. Grind the jowl fat through the fine plate; reserve separately. Place in the freezer until semifrozen.

2. Transfer the ground veal to a chilled chopper bowl. Add the crushed ice and the spice blend on top of the ground veal.

3. Run the machine and process the ingredients until the mixture reaches a temperature of 30°F/−1°C. Continue running the machine until the mixture's temperature rises to 40°F/4°C.

4. Add the fat and process until the mixture reaches 45°F/7°C. Add the dry milk powder and continue processing until the mixture reaches 58°F/14°C. Make a test. Adjust seasoning and consistency before shaping.

5. Stuff into prepared casings, twist, and tie into 5-in/13-cm links.

6. Poach in water at 165°F/74°C to an internal temperature of 150°F/66°C, 10 to 20 minutes, then shock in ice water to an internal temperature of 60°F/16°C. Blot dry.

7. Prepare the sausage for immediate service by sautéing, grilling, broiling, or baking just until hot, or wrap and refrigerate for up to 7 days.

TURKEY BRATWURST: Replace the veal with turkey thigh meat.

CHIPOLATA: Prepare as directed above, stuffing the sausage into sheep casings and shaping into 3-in/8-cm links.

SMOKED BRATWURST: Add ½ oz/14 g tinted curing mix (TCM) to the cure mix. Stuff into casings and shape into 5-in/13-cm links. Twist and cut into individual links. Dry overnight under refrigeration and cold smoke for 1 hour.

WEISSWURST: Omit the ginger and mustard. Add finely chopped lemon zest as needed.

Mortadella

YIELD: 14 LB/6.35 KG BULK; 14 LINKS

5 lb/2.27 kg boneless pork butt, cubed

CURE MIX

4½ oz/128 g salt

1 oz/28 g dextrose

½ oz/14 g tinted curing mix (TCM)

3½ fl oz/105 mL dry white wine

4 lb/1.81 kg jowl fat, cubed

3 lb/1.36 kg crushed ice

SPICE BLEND

½ oz/14 g ground white pepper

1 tbsp/6 g ground mace

1 tbsp/6 g sweet Spanish paprika

1 tbsp/6 g ground nutmeg

1 tbsp/6 g ground coriander

1 tsp/2 g ground cloves

1 tsp/2 g ground bay leaves

½ tsp/1 g garlic powder

7½ oz/213 g nonfat dry milk powder

14 beef middles, rinsed, cut into 10-in/ 25-cm lengths and tied at one end

GARNISH

1 lb/454 g pork fat, diced, blanched, and cooled

7 oz/198 g pistachios, blanched and peeled

1. Toss the pork with the cure mix. Chill well and grind through the fine plate (⅛ in/3 mm) of a meat grinder. Place in the freezer until semifrozen.

2. Grind the jowl fat through the fine plate; reserve.

3. Transfer the ground pork to a chilled chopper bowl. Add the crushed ice and spice blend on top of the ground pork. Run the machine and process the ingredients until the mixture reaches a temperature of 30°F/–1°C. Continue running the machine until the mixture's temperature rises to 40°F/4°C.

4. Add the jowl fat and process until the mixture reaches 45°F/7°C. Add the dry milk powder and continue processing until the mixture reaches 58°F/14°C. Make a test. Adjust seasoning and consistency before shaping.

5. Working over an ice bath, stir in the garnish ingredients. Stuff into the prepared casings and tie with a bubble knot. Cure overnight under refrigeration.

6. Poach at 165°F/74°C to an internal temperature of 150°F/66°C, 2½ to 3 hours, then shock in ice water to an internal temperature of 60°F/16°C. Blot dry.

7. Hang under refrigeration overnight to form a pellicle.

8. If desired, cold smoke at 80°F/27°C for 1 to 2 hours. Refrigerate for up to 7 days.

PRESENTATION IDEAS: For a nontraditional garnish, add 1 lb/454 g pork fat, cut into ¼-in/6-mm dice, blanched and cooled, and 1¾ oz/50 g whole black peppercorns, soaked in hot water and drained.

Chicken and Vegetable Sausage

YIELD: 16 LB/7.26 KG BULK; 95 LINKS

7 lb/3.18 kg chicken thigh meat, diced

CURE MIX

6¼ oz/177 g salt

1½ oz/43 g dextrose

2 lb/907 g jowl fat, diced

GARNISH

8 oz/227 g carrots, cut into small dice

8 oz/227 g celery, cut into small dice

1 lb/454 g onions, cut into small dice

1 oz/28 g vegetable oil

2 lb/907 g mushrooms, cut into small dice

8 fl oz/240 mL dry white wine

2 tbsp/6 g chopped flat-leaf parsley

3 lb/1.36 kg crushed ice

SPICE BLEND

¾ oz/21 g ground white pepper

1 tbsp/6 g poultry seasoning

1 tsp/2 g powdered thyme

7½ oz/213 g nonfat dry milk powder

50 ft/15.24 m sheep casings, rinsed and tied at one end

1. Toss the chicken with the cure mix and grind through the fine plate (⅛ in/3 mm) of a meat grinder. Place in the freezer until semifrozen. Grind the jowl fat and reserve separately under refrigeration.

2. Sauté the carrots, celery, and onions in oil, until cooked; add the mushrooms. Sauté until the mushrooms release water, then add the wine and parsley and reduce until almost dry. Chill.

3. Transfer the ground chicken to a chilled chopper bowl. Add the crushed ice and the spice blend on top of the ground chicken. Run the machine and process the ingredients until the mixture reaches a temperature of 30°F/−1°C. Continue running the machine until the mixture's temperature rises to 40°F/4°C.

4. Add the jowl fat and process until the mixture reaches 45°F/7°C. Add the dry milk powder and continue processing until the mixture reaches 58°F/14°C. Transfer to a bowl. Stir in the garnish, working over an ice bath. Make a test. Adjust seasoning and consistency before shaping.

5. Stuff into the prepared casings and tie off into 5-in/13-cm links. Poach in water at 170°F/77°C to an internal temperature of 165°F/74°C, then shock in ice water to an internal temperature of 60°F/16°C and blot dry.

6. Prepare the sausage for immediate service by sautéing, grilling, or broiling just until hot, or wrap and refrigerate for up to 3 days.

Braunschweiger

YIELD: 12 LB/5.44 KG BULK; 12 SAUSAGES

5 lb/2.27 kg pork liver, cubed

2 lb/907 g boneless pork butt, cubed

CURE MIX

3½ oz/99 g salt

½ oz/14 g tinted curing mix (TCM)

1 oz/28 g dextrose

3 lb/1.36 kg slab bacon, cubed

1 lb 2 oz/510 g crushed ice

SPICE BLEND

½ oz/14 g onion powder

1 tbsp/6 g ground white pepper

½ tsp/1 g ground allspice

½ tsp/1 g ground cloves

½ tsp/1 g rubbed sage

½ tsp/1 g ground marjoram

½ tsp/1 g ground nutmeg

½ tsp/1 g ground ginger

8 oz/227 g nonfat dry milk powder

12 ft/3.66 m beef middles, rinsed, cut into 10-in/25-cm lengths and tied at one end

1. Toss the liver and pork butt with the cure mix. Chill well and grind through the fine plate (⅛ in/3 mm) of a meat grinder. Place in the freezer until semifrozen.

2. Grind the slab bacon through the fine plate; reserve separately.

3. Transfer the ground liver and pork to a chilled chopper bowl. Add the crushed ice and the spice blend on top of the ground pork. Process the ingredients until the mixture drops to a temperature of 30°F/−1°C. Continue running the machine until the mixture's temperature rises to 40°F/4°C.

4. Add the slab bacon and process until the mixture reaches 45°F/7°C. Add the dry milk powder and continue processing until the mixture reaches 58°F/14°C. Make a test. Adjust seasoning and consistency before shaping.

5. Stuff into the prepared casings and tie closed with bubble knots. Hang overnight under refrigeration to form a pellicle.

6. Hot smoke at 160°F/71°C until desired color is achieved, 1½ to 2 hours.

7. Poach in water at 165°F/74°C to an internal temperature of 150°F/66°C, then shock in ice water to an internal temperature of 60°F/16°C. Blot dry.

8. Refrigerate for up to 2 weeks.

Seafood Sausage

YIELD: 10 LB/4.54 KG BULK; 68 LINKS

This mild seafood sausage can be served with sautéed Napa cabbage as an appetizer or it can be used as part of a seafood medley in a number of dishes. If you wish, fold in up to 2 oz/57 g chopped black truffles, as shown here.

MOUSSELINE

3 lb/1.36 kg sole fillet, diced

3 lb/1.36 kg sea scallops, muscle tabs removed

1½ oz/43 g salt

½ oz/14 g Old Bay seasoning

3¼ oz/92 g fresh white bread crumbs

40 fl oz/1.20 L heavy cream, cold

10 egg whites

GARNISH

1 lb/454 g shrimp, peeled and deveined, cut into ¼-in/6-mm dice

1 lb/454 g crab or lobster meat, diced (from three blanched lobsters, 1 lb 4 oz/567 g each)

1 lb/454 g salmon meat, cut into ¼-in/6-mm dice

1 lb/454 g bay scallops, muscle tabs removed

2 tbsp/6 g chopped parsley

36 ft/10.97 m sheep casings, rinsed, or 18 ft/5.49 m hog casings, rinsed

1. Combine the sole, scallops, salt, and Old Bay seasoning. Grind through the fine plate (⅛ in/3 mm) of a meat grinder. Chill in the freezer for 15 minutes.

2. Soak the bread crumbs in half of the heavy cream to make a panada.

3. Pureé the seafood in a food processor until as smooth as possible. Add the egg whites and panada. Pulse in the remaining cream. Make a test. Adjust seasoning and consistency before shaping.

4. Fold in the garnish ingredients to coat evenly; refrigerate.

5. Stuff into the prepared casings and twist into 5-in/13-cm links. Cut into individual links.

6. Poach in water at 165°F/74°C to an internal temperature of 145°F/63°C. Shock in ice water to an internal temperature of 60°F/16°C. Blot dry.

7. Prepare the sausage for immediate service by removing the strings and either sautéing the sausage in clarified butter until golden brown or reheating in a 350°F/177°C oven for 10 to 12 minutes. To store, wrap and hold under refrigeration for up to 3 days.

Smoked Foie Gras Sausage

YIELD: 6 LINKS (1 LB/454 G EACH)

3 lb/1.36 kg foie gras, cleaned and cut into large dice

1 oz/28 g salt

4 fl oz/120 mL Armagnac

1 tsp/2 g ground white pepper

1 tbsp/3 g chopped chives

1 tbsp/3 g chopped chervil

1 lb 4 oz/567 g duck meat

CURE MIX

⅔ oz/19 g salt

½ tsp/1.33 g tinted curing mix (TCM)

1½ tsp/7.50 g dextrose

1 lb/454 g jowl fat

12 oz/340 g crushed ice

SPICE BLEND

½ tsp/1 g dry mustard

1 oz/28 g shallots, sautéed and cooled

2 tsp/4 g Pâté Spice (page 526)

1½ oz/43 g nonfat powdered milk

8 ft/2.44 m beef round casings, cut into 15-in/38-cm lengths and tied at one end

1. Combine the foie gras with the salt, Armagnac, pepper, chives, and chervil. Marinate 24 hours.

2. Combine the duck with the cure mix and chill well.

3. Grind the duck and the jowl fat separately through the fine plate (⅛ in/3 mm) of a meat grinder. Keep separate.

4. Transfer the ground duck to a chilled chopper bowl. Add the crushed ice and the spice blend on top of the ground duck.

5. Run the machine and process the ingredients until the mixture reaches a temperature of 30°F/−1°C. Continue running the machine until the mixture's temperature rises to 40°F/4°C. Add the fat and process until the mixture reaches 45°F/7°C. Add the dry milk powder and continue processing until the mixture reaches 58°F/14°C.

6. Transfer the sausage mixture to a bowl over an ice bath. Make a test and adjust if necessary. Fold in the foie gras, making sure individual pieces are evenly coated in the forcemeat. Stuff into the casings and tie. Refrigerate, uncovered, overnight to dry.

7. Cold smoke at 80°F/27°C for 1 hour. Hot smoke at 160°F/71°C for 1 hour.

8. Poach the sausages in water (170°F/77°C) to an internal temperature of 165°F/74°C. Remove from the water and shock in an ice water bath to an internal temperature of 60°F/16°C. Wrap and hold under refrigeration for up to 3 days.

Blood Sausage with Apples

YIELD: 6 LB/2.72 KG BULK; 44 LINKS

Unlike other sausages, the blood sausage mixture is loose enough to pour through a funnel into the prepared casings.

1½ oz/43 g fresh white bread crumbs

12 fl oz/360 mL heavy cream

48 fl oz/1.44 L beef blood

⅔ oz/19 g salt

½ tsp/1 g Quatre Épices (page 524)

½ oz/14 g brown sugar

2 lb/907 g fatback, cut into small dice

1 lb 8 oz/680 g finely diced onions

1 lb 4 oz/567 g cored and peeled apples, sautéed and puréed

24 ft/7.32 m hog casings, cut into 24-in/61-cm lengths and tied at one end

1. Soak the bread crumbs in the heavy cream to make a panada. Knead gently to moisten evenly.

2. Mix the blood with the salt, quatre épices, and brown sugar.

3. Render 8 oz/227 g of the fatback in a heavy sautoir. Add the onions and sweat until translucent.

4. Mix in the rest of the diced fatback, the apples, panada, and seasoned blood, while stirring. Gently heat while stirring until the mixture reaches 100°F/38°C. Remove from the heat.

5. Stuff into the prepared casings, making sure all the components are distributed evenly. Take care not to overstuff the casings to prevent them from bursting when cooking.

6. Poach the sausages in 165°F/74°C water and cook for 20 minutes, then prick with a teasing needle. If brown liquid comes out, they are done; if blood comes out, let them cook a few more minutes and check again.

7. When ready, shock the sausages in ice water for 5 minutes, drain them, dry them with paper towels, lay them on a pan, and brush with melted lard or duck fat. Place them in the refrigerator to finish cooling.

PRESENTATION IDEAS: To serve, cut the sausages into lengths, prick them all over with a fork, and sauté or grill them. Traditional accompaniments are mashed or home-fried potatoes, fried apple rings, and sauerkraut.

Southwest Dry Sausage

YIELD: 6 LB/2.72 KG: 18 LINKS

3 lb 4 oz/1.47 kg diced bottom round of beef, chilled

2 lb 4 oz/1.02 kg diced certified pork (see page 182), chilled

1½ tsp/3 g garlic powder

2½ fl oz/75 mL cold water

2 tsp/4 g chili powder

1 tsp/2 g onion powder

1 tsp/2 g ground cumin

4 tsp/8 g coarse-ground black pepper

½ tsp/2.50 mL Tabasco

1 tbsp/6 g Prague Powder II

4 oz/113 g dextrose

2 oz/57 g salt

1½ oz/43 g nonfat dry milk powder

14 feet/4.27 m hog casings

1. Grind the beef and pork together through the fine plate (⅛ in/3 mm) of a meat grinder into a mixing bowl over an ice bath.

2. Add the remaining ingredients to the ground meats; mix on low speed until the sausage mixture feels sticky to the touch, 15 to 20 seconds. Make a test. Adjust seasoning and consistency before shaping.

3. Place the sausage meat into the stuffer and tamp down to remove air pockets. Stuff into the prepared hog casings and tie into 9-in/23-cm links.

4. Arrange on drying sticks and cure for 4 days. (See Chapter 5, page 182, for the USDA regulations for dry curing sausages.)

5. Cold smoke at 80°F/27°C for 24 to 36 hours to the desired color. Allow the sausages to continue to dry until they have the desired firmness.

TERRINES, PÂTÉS, GALANTINES, AND ROULADES

The French are famous for their contributions to the world of terrines, pâtés, and other forcemeat specialties. From the rustic appeal of a peasant-style pâté grand-mère to a luxurious foie gras and truffle pâté, these dishes are part of the worldwide tradition of classic cold dishes.

seven

In this chapter, we look at the methods for preparing four basic forcemeat styles (straight, country, gratin, and mousseline) and the shaping methods to produce items from forcemeats (terrines, pâtés en croûte, galantines, and roulades), as well as a special commodity featured in the cold kitchen (foie gras). In addition, we give several examples of nontraditional terrines made without forcemeats.

Forcemeats

One of the basic components of charcuterie and garde manger items is a preparation known as a *forcemeat*. A forcemeat is a lean meat and fat emulsion that is established when the ingredients are processed together by grinding, sieving, or puréeing. Depending on the grinding and emulsifying methods and the intended use, the forcemeat may have a smooth consistency or may be heavily textured and coarse. The result must not be just a mixture but an emulsion, so that it will hold together properly when sliced. Forcemeats should have a rich and pleasant taste and feel in the mouth.

Forcemeats may be used for quenelles, sausages, pâtés, terrines, roulades, and galantines, as well as to prepare stuffings for other items (a salmon forcemeat may be used to fill a paupiette of sole, for example). Each forcemeat style has a particular texture.

- **STRAIGHT FORCEMEATS** combine pork and pork fat with a dominant meat in equal parts through a process of progressive grinding and emulsification. The meats and fat are cut into cubes, seasoned, cured, rested, ground, and then processed.

- **COUNTRY-STYLE FORCEMEATS** are rather coarse in texture. They are traditionally made from pork and pork fat, often with a percentage of liver and other garnish ingredients.

- **IN GRATIN FORCEMEATS,** some portion of the dominant meat is sautéed and cooled before it is ground. The term *gratin* means "browned."

- **MOUSSELINE, A VERY LIGHT FORCEMEAT** is based on tender, lean white meats (veal or poultry), shellfish, or fish. The inclusion of cream and eggs gives mousselines their characteristic light texture and consistency.

Main ingredients

Forcemeats, like sausages, are made from raw products, with the exception of gratin forcemeat. Some classic choices for forcemeats include pork; fish such as pike, trout, and salmon; seafood such as shrimp and scallops; game meats such as venison, boar, and rabbit; poultry and game birds; and poultry, game, veal, and pork livers. When selecting cuts of red and white meat, opt for well-exercised cuts, which have a richer flavor than very tender cuts, such as the tenderloin or loin. However, meats to be used as garnishes can easily be the more delicate portions: tenderloin of lamb, rabbit, or pork, or poultry breasts, for example. Often, recipes for shrimp or scallop mousseline call for a quantity of pike to ensure a good primary bind.

An adequate amount of fat is also important. Fatback is considered to have a neutral flavor and can be paired with most meats. Mousselines made from delicate white meats, fish, or shellfish generally call for heavy cream.

To prepare the meat and fatback for a forcemeat, they should first be trimmed of gristle, sinew, and skin. The meat is then cut into dice so it can drop easily through the feed tube of a grinder or be quickly processed to a paste in a food processor.

Salt and seasonings

Salt plays a vital role in producing good forcemeats. It acts to draw out the proteins in the meat (these proteins are the primary source of the forcemeat's "bind"), and it adds its own unique flavor. Classic recipes often call for ground spices such as quatre épices, which is a combination of pepper, nutmeg, allspice, and cinnamon. Seasoning or marinating meat prior to grinding will further enhance the flavor.

Herbs, aromatic vegetables such as onions and mushrooms, wines, cognacs, grain-based spirits, or vinegars may also be added. In some cases, a reduction of garlic or shallots, herbs, wines, glace de viande or volaille, and other flavoring ingredients may be made. This reduction should be thoroughly chilled before adding it to the meats.

It is always important to follow basic formulas carefully as you are learning to make forcemeats and to properly test and taste forcemeats each time you make them.

Secondary binders

The proteins in meats and fish are the basic source of the forcemeat's structure, texture, and bind. In some special cases, however, you may need to add a secondary binder, which is generally required for country-style and gratin forcemeats. There are three basic types of secondary binders: eggs, nonfat dry milk powder, and panadas. Panadas are made from starchy (farinaceous) items—well-cooked rice or potatoes, bread soaked in milk, pâte à choux (a cooked dough made from flour, water, butter, and eggs), or plain flour.

Garnish ingredients

Garnishes give the chef an opportunity to add color, flavor, and texture to a basic formula. Traditional garnishes include the poultry breast, pork, beef, veal, or lamb tenderloin portions, nuts (especially pistachios and pine nuts), mushrooms, truffles, and diced foie gras. The quantity of garnish added to a forcemeat can range from a few chopped nuts scattered through a pâté to a terrine in which a predominant garnish is bound together with a small amount of forcemeat (see, for example, St. Andrew's Terrine, page 305).

You can add garnishes to a forcemeat in two ways. They can be simply folded into the forcemeat; in that case, they are known as *internal* or *random garnishes*. The second means of introducing the garnish is to place it in the forcemeat as you are filling the mold or laying it out for a roulade or galantine. These garnishes are known as *inlays*, though you may also hear them called *centered garnishes*. Care should be taken to shape and place the garnish so each slice will have a uniform, consistent appearance, whether the slice comes from the end or center of the pâté. Both styles of garnishing are illustrated in Figure 7-1.

If you are preparing forcemeat items for display or competition, you may want to dust garnish them very lightly with a bit of powdered gelatin or albumen (dried and powdered egg whites), or a combination of these two items, to glue them into place. This will improve the adherence of the forcemeat to the garnish, making it less likely that they will separate when the item is cut into slices.

7-1. Garnishes. **A.** Slicing a terrine with random garnish. **B.** Adding a placed garnish (duck breast shown here) to a pâté en croûte.

Making forcemeats

CHILL INGREDIENTS, CHILL EQUIPMENT Maintaining both the ingredients and equipment used to prepare a forcemeat below 30°F/-1°C keeps the food out of the danger zone, reducing the risk of food-borne illness. Temperature control is also the key to achieving the best results. When forcemeats are kept well chilled throughout processing, mixing, and cooking, they require less fat, yet still have a smooth texture and an appealing mouthfeel. The flavor of the forcemeat itself is generally better, as well.

PROGRESSIVE GRINDING The most common piece of equipment for grinding the meats for straight, country, and gratin forcemeats is a meat grinder. Review all the cautions and instructions found in Chapter 6.

Some forcemeat formulas call for some or all of the meats and fat to be ground through a succession of increasingly smaller grinder plates. This is known as *progressive grinding*. Figure 7-2 shows how the texture of the meat changes as it undergoes progressive grinding. Review the recipe to determine if you will need one or more grinding plates. Grind the meat directly into a well-chilled mixing bowl set over ice.

Mousseline forcemeats are typically made from start to finish in a food processor, although some chefs prefer to grind the meat or fish before placing it in the bowl of the food processor. After fully processing the appareil is typically passed through a tamis. If you make a significant quantity of forcemeats using a food processor, it is a good idea to dedicate one very sharp blade to that purpose only.

MIXING AND PROCESSING Once ground, the forcemeat is mixed in order to blend any seasonings, panadas, or other ingredients thoroughly and evenly. More importantly, an adequate mixing period is crucial to the development of the correct texture.

Mixing can be done by beating the forcemeat with a rubber spatula or wooden spoon over an ice bath, in a mixer, or in a food processor. Care should be taken not to overmix or to heat up the product, especially when you use a machine. Be careful not to overload the bowl. Depending on the amount of product, 1 to 3 minutes

A. Chunks of meat are ground using the coarse die first. Meat, containers, and equipment must be kept cold at all times. **B.** Meat is ground through a medium-coarse die. **C.** In the last step of a progressive grind, meat is passed through a small die.

at the lowest speed should be sufficient. The forcemeat's color and texture will change slightly when it is properly mixed.

Mixing in a food processor is very fast and provides a smoother texture. Most food processors handle relatively small batches. It is critical to keep an eye on the forcemeat as it processes. Your forcemeat can go from properly processed to overworked in a matter of seconds. This can cause pockets or bubbles to form in the item you are preparing, a distraction on a plated item presented to a guest and grounds for losing points in competition work.

Testing a forcemeat

Forcemeats are poached directly in a liquid (as for galantines, roulades, or quenelles) or in a waterbath (terrines), or baked in a crust (pâté en croûte). You can only be sure of the quality of the forcemeat after it is cooked, and the method below for testing a forcemeat will give you an opportunity to evaluate the quality, seasoning, and texture.

This important step takes some time to do properly, but it can save you time and money. To make a test, wrap a 1-ounce portion of the forcemeat in plastic

Testing a forcemeat.

wrap as shown in Figure 7-3 and poach it to the appropriate internal temperature (145°F/63°C for fish, 150°F/66°C for pork, beef, veal, lamb, and game, and 165°F/74°C for any item including poultry and poultry liver). Cool the forcemeat to the correct service temperature before you taste it. You will be checking for flavor, seasoning, and consistency.

The test portion itself will not taste or feel exactly the same as the finished product, since it is a general practice to allow forcemeat items to rest two or three days before they are served. However, with experience, you can train your palate to recognize the evidence of quality in a forcemeat, or to detect a flaw. This is the same "taste memory," built up through experience and practice, that

7-4. Straight forcemeat. **A.** Adding cream. **B.** Keeping the mixture cold. **C.** Filling a fatback-lined mold with forcemeat.

permits a cellar master to foretell with some accuracy the qualities a wine will have when it is mature, even when the wine is far too young to actually drink.

If the texture is poor, evaluate just what kind of problem you have. Rubbery forcemeats can be improved by adding more fat or cream. Loose forcemeats, on the other hand, may be improved by adding egg whites or a bit of panada. Take into account whether or not the item will be pressed or coated with aspic before you make a dramatic change however.

Straight forcemeat

This basic forcemeat is used to prepare pâtés, terrines, and galantines. It is generally made by grinding the meat and fat through a medium plate, then further processing it in a mixer or food processor.

Process the ground meat with any additional ingredients. An egg may be added to the forcemeat to give a better bind. A quantity of heavy cream may also be included in some recipes to give the forcemeat a smooth texture and a richer flavor, if desired (see Figure 7-4A).

Once the forcemeat is tested and any adjustments to seasoning or consistency are made, you may add garnish ingredients. This may be done in the mixer or by hand, working over an ice bath to keep the forcemeat properly chilled (see Figure 7-4B).

Straight forcemeats may be used to fill a pâté en croûte (see Figure 7-4C) and to prepare terrines and galantines. For more information on preparing a pâté en croûte, terrines, and galantines, see pages 277–288.

Country-style forcemeat

Country-style forcemeats are less refined in texture and heartier in flavor than others and are traditionally made from pork and pork liver.

The texture of this forcemeat is achieved by grinding the pork through a coarse die, then reserving most of this coarse grind. If desired, a portion of the

Mixing garnish into forcemeat.

ground meat may be ground again through a medium die before the forcemeat is blended with its panada and processed as for a straight forcemeat. The coarsely ground meat as well as the processed forcemeat is then combined, as shown in Figure 7-5. Because at least part of the forcemeat is left as a coarse grind, a panada is almost always included to help the finished product hold together after cooking.

Gratin forcemeat

A gratin forcemeat is similar to a straight forcemeat, with the exception of the way in which the main meat is handled. The meat is very quickly seared—just enough to enhance the flavor and color, but not enough to cook it through. The meat is changed enough by the searing that a panada is required to help produce the desired texture.

The first step is to sear the meat. Get the pan or grill very hot, sear the meat on all sides as quickly as possible, and just as quickly cool it down. The best way to accomplish this is to work in small batches, to avoid crowding the meat in the pan, as shown in Figure 7-6A. Remove the meat to a sheet pan, and cool it quickly in the refrigerator or freezer. An optional step is shown in Figure 7-6B, preparing an aromatic reduction to flavor the forcemeat.

Follow the same procedure for grinding as for a straight forcemeat, and process it with a panada and any additional ingredients as suggested or required by the recipe (see Figure 7-6C). The texture of a properly processed gratin forcemeat is shown in Figure 7-6D. Be sure to test the forcemeat properly before continuing on to add the garnish ingredients.

Gratin forcemeats can be used in the same general applications as straight forcemeats.

7-6. Gratin forcemeat. **A.** Searing the meat. **B.** The garnish may also be seared. Sherry is added to deglaze the pan. **C.** The puréed ground meat is puréed with a panada (shown here, milk-soaked bread and an egg). **D.** The gratin forcemeat is puréed to a homogeneous mixture.

Mousseline forcemeat

Although individual recipes differ, the formula shown here works as an excellent starting point. The amount of cream indicated produces a good texture for terrines and other forcemeat items that will be sliced. If the mousseline will be used to prepare a timbale or other similar applications, the quantity of cream can be increased by nearly double the amount indicated below:

Meat or fish—1 lb/454 g

Salt—1 tsp/5 g

Egg (or egg white)—1

Cream—8 fl oz/240 mL

When preparing a mousseline forcemeat, you may simply dice the main ingredients and proceed to grind them in the food processor, as shown on page 278, or you may wish to grind the main ingredient through a coarse or medium plate before processing it with an egg white (see Figure 7-7A).

7-7. Mousseline. **A.** Adding egg whites to previously ground salmon. **B.** The cream is fully incorporated. **C.** A mousseline should be sieved through a tamis to ensure complete smoothness. Mousseline forcemeats are very light in texture and are typically made from either white meat, fish, or shellfish with the addition of heavy cream as the fat component of the forcemeat. **D.** Cream worked in by hand.

7-8. Mousseline applications. **A.** Quenelles of mousseline are poached and used as a garnish in consommé. **B.** Mousseline may have a chunky garnish added, as in this filling for tortelloni. **C.** Salmon stays moist in a poached mousseline roulade. **D.** Salmon and scallop mousselines are layered in a leek-lined terrine mold.

Process the meat and salt just long enough to develop a paste with an even texture. Add the egg white, followed by the cream. In order to blend the mousseline properly, it is important to scrape down the bowl. Continue processing only until the forcemeat is smooth and homogeneous, generally about 30 seconds (see Figure 7-7B).

Fine forcemeats may be passed through a drum sieve (tamis) to be sure that a very delicate texture is achieved (Figure 7-7C). Be sure the forcemeat is very cold as you work, and work in small batches to prevent the forcemeat from heating as you proceed.

Optional: For a very light mousseline, you may prefer to work the cream in by hand (see Figure 7-7D). This is more time-consuming and exacting than using a food processor, but the results are worth the extra effort. Both the base mixture and the cream must be very cold in order to add the cream in higher proportions than those suggested in the basic formula above. Work over an ice bath for the best results.

Mousseline forcemeats are often featured as appetizers, fillings, and stuffings, and are used to coat or wrap poached fish or poultry suprêmes (see Figures 7-8A to 7-8C). Another interesting way to use this forcemeat is to layer mousselines of different colors to create a special effect in a terrine (see Figure 7-8D).

Terrines

The terrine, the shortened name of a dish known classically as *pâté en terrine,* is traditionally understood to be a forcemeat mixture baked in an earthenware mold with a tight-fitting lid. The preparation gets its name from its association with the material used to make the mold, once exclusively earthenware of unglazed clay, or terra-cotta. Today, terrine molds are produced from materials such as stainless steel, aluminum, ceramic, enameled cast iron, ovenproof plastic, and glazed earthenware. These materials are more durable and more sanitary than the unglazed earthenware once favored by charcutières.

Some classic pâtés en terrine are still referred to simply as *pâtés*. Pâté de campagne and pâté grand-mère are two examples. More often today, we tend to abbreviate the term to *terrine*. This may cause some initial confusion, so it is worth remembering that the word *pâté* does not, all by itself, automatically imply *en croûte*.

Traditionally, terrines were served directly from the mold. Now it is more common to present terrines in slices. This improves the chef's ability to control both the presentation and the portioning of the dish. This is clearly in the best interest of both the guest and the chef. In some special cases, however, terrines are still served in their molds. A terrine of foie gras, for instance, may be presented in a small decorative mold, accompanied by toasted brioche. Guests use a special service spoon or knife to serve themselves.

Today, some nontraditional terrines are also made by binding items such as roasted meats or poultry, roasted or grilled vegetables, poached salmon, or seared lamb loins with a little aspic, making them similar to a head cheese. Examples from among the recipes in this chapter include Seared Lamb, Artichoke, Mushroom Terrine (page 308) and Terrine of Scallop and Salmon (page 304). Terrines made from layered vegetables can be bound with a custard or cheese. Roasted Vegetable Terrine with Goat's Milk Cheese (page 316) and Mozzarella, Prosciutto, and Roasted Tomato Terrine (page 317) are two examples.

7-9. Terrines.   **A.** The terrine is lined with plastic wrap and prosciutto.   **B.** The terrine is in a water bath, ready to go into the oven.   **C.** A terrine being weighted as it cools.   **D.** Aspic being added to the terrine.

Making forcemeat terrines

1. **PREPARE THE TERRINE MOLD BY LINING IT.** Terrine molds were traditionally lined with fatback, then filled with a forcemeat and any garnish called for by the recipe. This liner, also referred to as a chemise or jacket, is still used today, but fatback may be replaced today with proscuitto, bacon, caul fat, crêpes, leeks, spinach, or even seaweed. A liner is not always required, and may be replaced with plastic wrap; this makes it easy to remove the terrine neatly from the mold. Figure 7-9A shows a terrine mold lined with plastic wrap and prosciutto.

2. **FILL THE PREPARED MOLD WITH FORCEMEAT AND ANY GARNISH REQUIRED.** Use a spatula to spread the forcemeat into all corners, working to remove air pockets. Then the liner is folded over the forcemeat to completely encase it, and a lid or foil covers the terrine. Firmly tap the assembled terrine on the countertop to further eliminate air pockets.

3. **COOK THE TERRINE GENTLY IN A WATER BATH (BAIN-MARIE).** Terrines must be properly cooked at a carefully regulated temperature. A water bath acts to insulate the terrine from temperature extremes. Set the filled, covered terrine mold in a baking pan on a clean side towel or several layers of paper towels. Add enough simmering water to come about two-thirds to three-quarters of the way up the mold's sides. Monitor the water bath's temperature (see Figure 7-9B); it should be at a constant 170°F/77°C. An oven temperature of approximately 300°F/149°C should keep the water bath's temperature where it belongs, but if necessary, it should be adjusted.

4. **COOK TO THE CORRECT INTERNAL TEMPERATURE.** Check for doneness by measuring the terrine's internal temperature with an instant-read thermometer. Remember to allow for carryover cooking when deciding whether the terrine is ready. The amount of carryover cooking will vary depending on the material used to make the mold, the forcemeat, and the overall shape and size of the mold.

5. **COOL, PRESS, AND STORE THE TERRINE UNTIL READY TO SERVE.** Remove the fully cooked terrine from the water bath and allow it to rest at room temperature until the internal temperature drops to 90°F/32°C.

   Set a press plate on the terrine. You can create a press plate by cutting Styrofoam, Plexiglas, or wood to the inside dimensions of the mold. Wrap the press plate in plastic wrap or foil before use.

   Place a 2-lb/907-g weight on top of the press plate (see Figure 7-9C). Set this assembly in a hotel pan and let the terrine rest under refrigeration for at least 2 to 3 days to mellow and mature the flavor. If desired, coat the terrine with melted aspic (see Figure 7-9D). Techniques and ratios for aspic gelée can be found on page 23.

Aspic-bound terrines

To produce high-quality aspic-bound terrines, you should, of course, season and prepare the main ingredients with care; they are the foundation of the terrine. The aspic, though an important part of the dish, should be added only as needed to

Adding warm aspic to the main ingredients.

bind the major flavoring ingredients properly. Still, it is important to take the time to select a rich, full-flavored base liquid. Clear stocks, broths, consommés, juices, and wines can be used singly or in combination to prepare an aspic of slicing strength.

An alternative to an aspic is a reduced stock, glace de viande, or essence. The action of cooking the stock down drives off the water but leaves the gelatinous proteins in place.

The aspic can be prepared in advance and stored under refrigeration. To use it, warm the aspic over a hot water bath just enough to melt it. It should be incorporated while still warm so it will blend properly with the ingredients (see Figure 7-10).

Pâté en Croûte

Making pâté en croûte

Today, pâtés en croûte are often made in rectangular molds. The advantage to these molds is that they have regular dimensions and straight sides. This encourages even baking and helps reduce the chances of undercooking the dough. Another reason to choose a rectangular mold is that it allows the chef to make uniform slices. However, an oval pâté en croûte may yield a more dramatic presentation if it is being served whole on a buffet or being displaying uncut, as a retail item for sale. (Various shapes for pâté and terrine molds are shown in Figure 7-11A.)

1. **LINE THE PÂTÉ MOLD WITH DOUGH.** First, roll out sheets of dough to approximately ⅛ to ¼ in/3 to 6 mm thick. It is important to roll the dough evenly and to handle it gently to avoid tearing or stretching it as you line the mold (see Figure 7-11B).

Now, mark the dough by pressing all sides of the mold very lightly into the dough. This will produce the appropriate pattern for the interior of the mold. To line a straight-edged terrine mold, allow an overhang of ½ in/1 cm on one side piece as well as enough to fold over the mold's opening, plus ½ in/1 cm to secure it into the sides (see Figure 7-11C). Allow an overhang of about 1 to 1½ in/3 to 4 cm for oval or round molds.

The excess dough in the corners should be cut out before the dough is transferred to the mold. Reserve the excess dough to make the reinforcements for the vent holes you will cut in the top of the pâté and for any decorations you may wish to apply.

Set the dough in the mold so the overhang on one side of the mold is enough to completely cover the top of the mold and extend down into the mold on the opposite side at least ½ in/1 cm. The overhang on the other side will be about ½ in/1 cm. Use egg wash to glue the pastry together in the corners and pinch the seams.

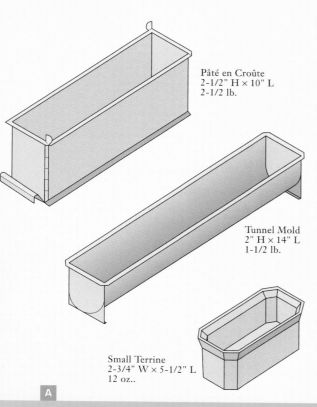

A. Molds for pâté en croûte terrines. **B.** The dough is cut into the proper shape for lining the mold. **C.** Pinching the seams at the corners. **D.** Lining the dough with ham. **E.** Tucking in the top.

Pâté en Croûte
2-1/2" H × 10" L
2-1/2 lb.

Tunnel Mold
2" H × 14" L
1-1/2 lb.

Small Terrine
2-3/4" W × 5-1/2" L
12 oz..

If you wish, you may add a second liner at this time. Fatback is commonly used, but prosciutto and other thinly sliced cooked meats can be used to add flavor and create a special effect (see Figure 7-11D).

At this point, fill the mold with the forcemeat and any inlay garnish. Fold the liner and then the dough over the top of the forcemeat. The dough should overlap itself along one side of the mold. Stretch the dough and push it down into the mold using a metal spatula (see Figure 7-11E).

A top crust, or cap, is the traditional way to finish enclosing the forcemeat in pastry. Straight-sided pâtés can be prepared without a separate cap piece as follows: Remove the pins of the mold, place the bottom of the mold on the top of the pâté, reinsert the pins, and invert the entire assembly. This will give a smooth, neat top piece without any extra layers of dough. It also allows the weight of the pâté and mold to hold the seams along the edges of the mold, preventing them from blowing out as the pâté bakes.

Ovals and other shapes should have a separate cap piece. Cut a piece of dough large enough to completely cover the mold. Trim away any excess and tuck the edges down into the mold.

2. **BAKE THE PÂTÉ, ADDING THE CHIMNEY AND ANY ADDITIONAL DOUGH GAR-NISHES AS DESIRED.** The top crust of the pâté should be vented to permit steam to escape during baking. If the vents are not cut, the pressure will cause the dough to burst. Be sure the cut extends completely through every layer of dough and liner. Reinforce the vent's opening by gluing a ring of dough into

place with some egg wash. Insert a tube of rolled aluminum foil, known as a *chimney,* to keep the hole from closing as the pâté bakes.

Any decorations made from dough scraps can be added now. (For more information about creating decorations with dough, refer to page 537.) You can complete these tasks before baking the pâté. Egg wash should be brushed over the entire surface for color and sheen as well as to secure the reinforcing ring of dough and any decorations to the top crust.

An alternative method is to cover the pâté with foil and partially bake at 450°F/232°C for 15 minutes, or until the dough has a dry and light-brown appearance. Remove the foil and use round cutters to make one or two holes in the top piece; brush with egg wash.

Secure any additional decorative pieces to the cap piece, gluing them in place with egg wash. Finally, egg wash the entire top of the pâté. Return the uncovered pâté to the oven and finish baking at 350°F/177°C to the appropriate internal temperature.

3. **COOL THE PÂTÉ EN CROÛTE AND FINISH WITH ASPIC.** Let the pâté cool for 1 or 2 hours. Insert a funnel into the foil chimney and ladle in melted warm aspic. Let the pâté rest under refrigeration at least 24 hours and up to 3 days before slicing and serving. Once a pâté en croûte is shaped, baked, and finished with aspic, it may be held for approximately 5 to 7 days.

Galantines and Roulades

Galantines, as we know them, have been popular since the French Revolution (1789–1799). The chef of the house of the Marquis de Brancas, a M. Prévost, began producing a savory cold dish made from boned poultry that was sewn back into the bird's skin, poached in a rich stock, and preserved in the natural jelly. The origin of the dish itself appears relatively straightforward. The origins of the word, however, are less obvious.

According to *Larousse Gastronomique,* the term derives primarily from an old French word for chicken: *géline* or *galine.* According to this source, the association with chicken is so specific, in fact, that all by itself, the term *galantine* indicates chicken, unless otherwise specified in the title. Other experts have promoted the idea that *galantine* more likely comes from the word *gelatin,* with the current spelling gradually superseding earlier forms of the word, such as *galentyne, galyntyne, galandyne,* and *galendine.*

Two additional terms, *ballotine* and *dodine,* are occasionally used in the same way as *galantine.* Ballotines may be served hot or cold. Dodines, also normally made from poultry, especially duck and goose, are quite similar to galantines except that they are roasted rather than poached, and they are always served hot.

Roulades differ from galantines in that they are rolled in cheesecloth or plastic wrap, not in the natural skin casing featured in galantines. Another distinction between the two items is that, while galantines are firmly associated with poultry, roulades have no such identity. Instead, they are made from a wide range of base products, including foie gras and mousseline forcemeats made of fish or poultry.

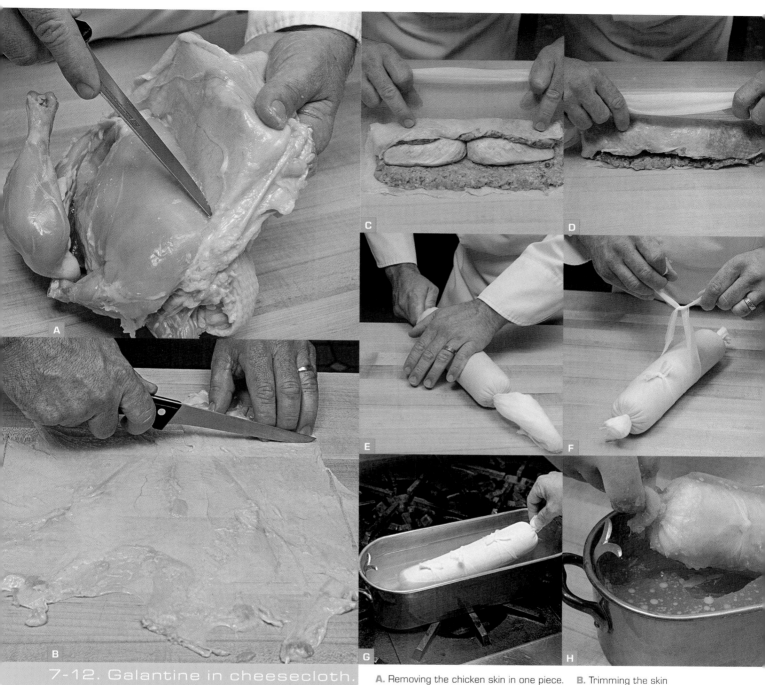

7-12. Galantine in cheesecloth. **A.** Removing the chicken skin in one piece. **B.** Trimming the skin into a square. **C.** Forcemeat is spread evenly over the skin. Seared chicken breast is placed in the middle. **D.** Cheesecloth is used to roll up the galantine. **E.** The galantine is rolled and tightly tied. **F.** If using cheesecloth, two extra bands are tied to support the shape. **G.** The galantine is poached in chicken stock. **H.** The galantine has cooled in the stock.

1. **CAREFULLY REMOVE THE SKIN AND BONE THE BIRD FOR A GALANTINE.** The first step in preparing a galantine is to carefully remove the skin from the bird. Make an incision along the backbone and carefully pull and cut away the skin from the meat (see Figure 7-12A). Keep the skin in a single piece and trim it to an even rectangle (see Figure 7-12B).

You may wish to save the breast portion or tenderloin to use as a garnish. These choice parts can be seared or cured, if desired. They may be placed as a center garnish (see Figure 7-12C) or flattened to form the exterior of the galantine (see Figure 7-13A).

2. **FILL AND ROLL THE GALANTINE OR ROULADE.** Lay out plastic wrap and/or cheesecloth, which should be several inches larger than the skin's dimensions. If you are using cheesecloth, remember to rinse it well and wring it until it is damp but not dripping wet.

Lay out the skin on the cheesecloth or plastic wrap and fill it with the force-meat and any garnish. Roll the galantine or roulade carefully around the forcemeat. The skin should just overlap itself by about ½ inch, forming a seam (see Figure 7-12D). A roulade can be rolled like a jelly roll to create a spiral effect, or as you would for a galantine to keep a centered garnish in place. Secure the galantine or roulade by crimping each end and smoothing the forcemeat away from the ends (see Figure 7-12E). You may need a pair of extra hands to maintain a compact shape while you tie the ends. Use butcher's twine to tie several knots to keep the roulade from unraveling as it poaches. Tie two cheesecloth bands or a paper sheath around the galantine (see Figures 7-12F and 7-13B).

7-13. Galantine rolled in plastic. **A.** Alternatively, pounded chicken breast is laid on the skin while the forcemeat is mounded in the center. **B.** For a galantine rolled in plastic wrap, parchment paper is used to stabilize and support the shape.

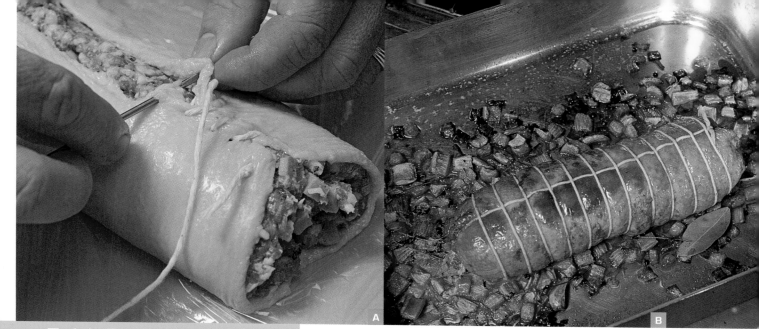

A. If a galantine is to be roasted, the skin must be sewn. Stitches should be small and tight without ripping the skin. **B.** The sewn galantine is tied with string, as is a roast. The galantine is seared and then roasted with mirepoix.

In an alternative method for a roasted galantine or dodine, the skin is sewn together at the seam and then the entire galantine is tied as for a roast (see Figure 7-14A).

3. **PREPARE THE GALANTINE OR ROULADE BY POACHING OR ROASTING.**
Galantines and roulades are commonly poached (see Figure 7-12G). Lower the galantine or roulade into a simmering pot of stock (water is fine if the roulade is wrapped in plastic wrap rather than cheesecloth). To keep the galantine submerged, weight it down with small plates. This helps cook the galantine evenly. A roasted galantine (see Figure 7-14B) is placed on a bed of mirepoix and cooked, uncovered, to the appropriate internal temperature.

Once properly cooked (check the internal temperature for accurate results), the galantine should be completely cooled. Galantines may be cooled directly in the cooking liquid (see Figure 7-12H); roulades are generally removed from the poaching liquid and cooled. Both should be tightly rewrapped after cooling and allowed to rest under refrigeration (see specific recipes for resting times) to produce an even, appealing texture.

Foie Gras

Foie gras is one of the world's great luxury items. The earliest records of foie gras date back to 2500 B.C.E. The tombs dedicated to Ti, an Egyptian counselor to the Pharaoh, show scenes of Egyptians hand-feeding figs to geese.

The first published recipe for pâté de foie gras appeared in *Le Cuisiner Gascon*, a cookbook published in 1747. Jean-Pierre Clause developed another classic preparation in Strasbourg. He took a foie gras and truffles, wrapped them in a pastry case, and baked the dish. Escoffier included a version of this same dish, Pâté Strausbourgiose, in *Le Guide Culinaire*.

Today, foie gras is produced from both geese and ducks. Fresh foie gras is finally available to chefs in the United States. Izzy Yanay, an Israeli who moved to the United States in 1981, is currently producing domestic foie gras from the Moulard, a hybrid breed resulting from cross breeding Muscovy (or Barbary) and Pekin ducks.

Working with foie gras

GRADES Foie gras may receive an A, B, or C grade (see Figure 7-15A) based on the size, appearance, and texture of the liver. To receive a grade of A, the liver must weigh at least 1 lb 8 oz/680 g. It should be round and firm, with no blemishes. These livers are used for terrines and pâtés.

B-grade foie gras weighs between 1 lb and 1 lb 3 oz/454 and 539 g. It should have a good texture but is not necessarily as round in shape as foie gras graded A. These livers are good for roasting or sautéing.

Foie gras that weighs less than 1 lb/454 g, is slightly flattened, and has some visual imperfections will receive a grade of C. These livers may have some soft spots. They are used primarily for mousses.

UPON ARRIVAL

1. INSPECT THE FOIE GRAS. This is an expensive product, whatever grade you buy, so take the time to be certain you are getting the quality you are paying for. First, look to be certain the packaging is still intact. Any rips or punctures may have damaged the foie gras. Weigh the foie gras yourself and inspect it carefully for imperfections.

2. PREPARE THE FOIE GRAS FOR REFRIGERATED STORAGE. Set the foie gras on a bed of crushed ice in a perforated hotel pan set inside a standard hotel pan. Pack more ice around the liver and keep this assembly in the refrigerator until you are ready to prepare the foie gras.

3. TEMPER THE FOIE GRAS BEFORE CLEANING. Soak the foie gras in salted water at room temperature for at least 2 hours. This will temper the foie gras, making it easier to manipulate as you remove the veins. Inspect the surface and remove visible bruises or blemishes or traces of green bile with a sharp paring knife.

4. SEPARATE THE FOIE GRAS INTO LOBES AND REMOVE THE VEINS. Holding the liver in both hands, gently pull the two lobes apart at their natural seam. Cut about one-third of the way into a lobe. Using a combination of pulling and loosening, expose the vein network (see Figure 7-15B). Starting from the top of the lobe, where the veins are thickest, pull out the veins, using tweezers, the tip of a knife, and/or your fingertips (see Figure 7-15C). Try to remove as much of the vein network in one piece as possible. Once the small vessels break, they are very hard to grip. Work carefully but quickly to avoid overhandling the foie gras. You want to keep the lobes as intact as possible.

This procedure takes practice, but, once mastered, it should take only a few minutes to complete. If you are not ready to proceed with a recipe, be sure to store the cleaned foie gras, well wrapped in plastic, at approximately 34°F/1°C. It is important to keep the foie gras as cold as possible, both to keep it safe and wholesome and to keep it firm enough to slice or dice neatly.

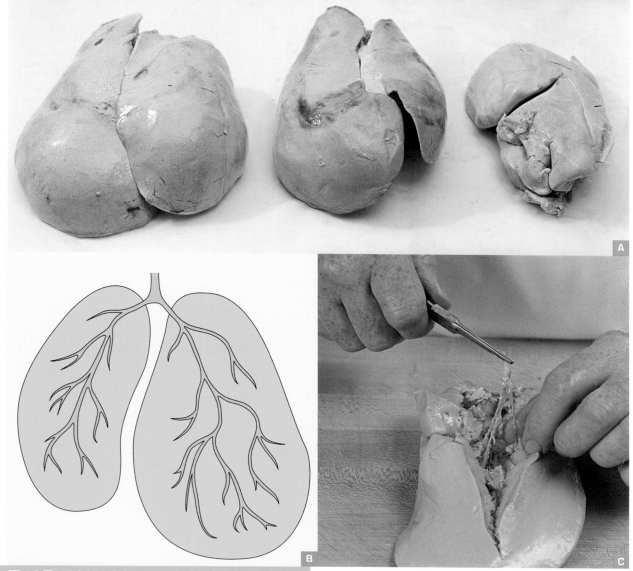

7-15. Working with foie gras. **A.** (From left to right) Grades A, B, C. **B.** Veins of the foie gras.
C. Carefully pull the main vein from the liver.

MARINATING FOIE GRAS Foie gras terrines, pâtés, and roulades typically call for marinated foie gras. Place the cleaned foie gras in a suitable container and add seasonings as indicated by the recipe. Sauternes, port, Cognac, and Armagnac are among the classic marinade ingredients. You may also wish to incorporate additional flavorings such as quatre épices, cinnamon, or allspice to give the finished dish a special flavor. Turn the foie gras to coat it evenly with the marinade and let it rest, covered, under refrigeration for at least 12 and up to 24 hours.

Pâtés, roulades, and terrines of foie gras are still made according to time-honored methods (recipes for these items appear on pages 292, 302, and 328). Today, they may be presented to the guest still in their ceramic crock, cut into slices, or shaped into quenelles. A classic presentation, made famous by Fernand Point, features foie gras baked in brioche. Foie gras mousse is another popular item; it has been used with great effect to make special canapés and appetizers (see page 327 for a mousse recipe).

Pâté Grand-Mère

YIELD: 3 LB/1.36 KG TERRINE; 18 TO 20 SERVINGS

1 lb 4 oz/567 g chicken livers, sinew removed

½ fl oz/15 mL vegetable oil, or as needed

1 oz/28 g shallots, minced

1 fl oz/30 mL brandy

SEASONINGS

1½ oz/43 g salt

1 tsp/2 g coarse-ground black pepper, plus more as needed for liner

¼ tsp/0.50 g ground bay leaf

½ tsp/1 g ground thyme

1 tsp/2.75 g tinted curing mixture (TCM)

1 lb 1 oz/482 g pork butt, cubed

1 tbsp/3 g chopped flat-leaf parsley

PANADA

2½ oz/71 g crustless white bread, cut into small dice

5 fl oz/150 mL milk

2 eggs

3 fl oz/90 mL heavy cream

¼ tsp/0.50 g ground white pepper

Pinch freshly ground nutmeg

8 thin slices fatback (⅟₁₆ in/1.5 mm), or as needed for liner

6 to 8 fl oz/180 to 240 mL Aspic Gelée (page 23), melted

1. Sear the livers briefly in hot oil; remove them from the pan and chill. Sauté the shallots in the same pan; deglaze with the brandy and add to the livers. Mix in the combined seasonings. Chill thoroughly.

2. Grind the pork butt, liver and shallot mixture, and parsley through the fine plate (⅛ in/3 mm) of a meat grinder into a bowl.

3. Combine the bread and milk; let soak to form a panada. Add the eggs, heavy cream, pepper, and nutmeg. Mix with the ground meats on medium speed for 1 minute, until homogeneous. Test the forcemeat and adjust seasoning if necessary before proceeding.

4. Line a terrine mold with plastic wrap and then the fatback slices, leaving an overhang. Sprinkle the fatback with ground pepper, pack the forcemeat into the mold, and fold over the liners. Cure overnight under refrigeration. Cover the terrine and poach in a 170°F/77°C water bath in a 300°F/149°C oven to an internal temperature of 165°F/74°C, 60 to 75 minutes.

5. Remove the terrine from the water bath and allow it to cool to an internal temperature of 90° to 100°F/32° to 38°C. Pour off the juices from the terrine, add enough aspic to coat and cover the terrine, and let it rest under refrigeration for 2 days. The terrine is now ready to slice and serve, or wrap and refrigerate for up to 10 days.

Pâté de Campagne (Country-Style Terrine)

YIELD: 3 LB/1.36 KG TERRINE; 18 TO 20 SERVINGS

2 lb 8 oz/1.13 kg pork butt, cubed

8 oz/227 g pork liver, cleaned and trimmed

SEASONINGS

2 garlic cloves, minced, sautéed, and cooled

4 oz/113 g onion, finely chopped

5 parsley sprigs, finely chopped

1½ oz/43 g salt

¾ tsp/2 g tinted curing mix (TCM)

½ tsp/1 g Pâté Spice (page 526)

½ tsp/1 g ground white pepper, plus more as needed for liner

PANADA

4 fl oz/120 mL heavy cream

2 eggs

2½ oz/71 g flour

1 fl oz/30 mL brandy

8 thin slices fatback (1⁄16 in/1.5 mm), or as needed for liner

6 to 8 oz/180 to 240 mL Aspic Gelée (page 23), melted

1. Grind the pork through the coarse plate (3⁄8 in/9.5 mm) of a meat grinder. Reserve 1 lb 8 oz/680 g, then grind the remainder with the liver and the combined seasonings through the fine plate (1⁄8 in/3 mm) of a meat grinder into a bowl.

2. Combine the panada ingredients in a bowl. Whisk together until smooth; add to the ground meats. Mix on low speed for 1 minute, until homogeneous. Then mix on medium speed until the mixture feels sticky to the touch.

3. Test the forcemeat and adjust seasoning if necessary before proceeding.

4. Line a terrine mold with plastic wrap and then the fatback slices, leaving an overhang. Sprinkle the fatback with pepper, pack the forcemeat into the mold and fold over the liners. Cure overnight in the refrigerator. Cover the terrine and poach in a 170°F/77°C water bath in a 300°F/149°C oven to an internal temperature of 150°F/66°C, 60 to 75 minutes.

5. Remove the terrine from the water bath and allow it to cool to an internal temperature of 90° to 100°F/32° to 38°C. Pour off the juices from the terrine, add enough aspic to coat and cover the terrine, and let it rest under refrigeration for 2 days. The terrine is now ready to slice and serve, or wrap and refrigerate for up to 10 days.

PÂTÉ MAISON: Use 3 lb/1.36 kg pork butt and eliminate the liver, if desired.

Duck and Smoked Foie Gras Terrine

YIELD: 2 LB 8 OZ/1.13 KG TERRINE; 16 TO 18 SERVINGS

1 lb/454 g duck leg and thigh meat, skinned and boned

8 oz/227 g fatback

GARNISH

1 oz/28 g butter

8 oz/227 g smoked foie gras, cut into ½-in/1-cm dice (see Chef's Note)

1 skinless duck breast, cut into ½-in/1-cm dice

4 oz/113 g smoked ham, cut into ½-in/1-cm dice

1 oz/28 g minced shallots

1 tsp/3 g minced garlic

2 fl oz/60 mL port wine

1 tbsp/6.50 g flour

¼ tsp/0.50 g tinted curing mix (TCM)

¾ oz/21 g salt

1 egg

4 fl oz/120 mL heavy cream

1 tsp/2 g coarse-ground black pepper

½ tsp/1 g poultry seasoning

1. Cut the leg and thigh meat and the fatback into ½-in/1-cm dice. Reserve.

2. Prepare the garnish: Melt the butter in a sauté pan. Lightly and quickly sear the smoked foie gras; remove and chill quickly. In the same pan, brown the duck breast and ham; remove, chill, and add to the foie gras. Sweat the shallots and garlic. Add the port wine and reduce to a thick syrup; chill well. Combine with the duck leg meat and fatback; marinate 2 hours under refrigeration.

3. Combine the leg meat mixture with the flour, TCM, and salt, toss to coat evenly, and grind through the fine plate (⅛ in/3 mm) of a meat grinder.

4. Transfer the ground meats to a chilled mixing bowl. Add the egg and heavy cream. Mix on medium speed for 1 minute, until homogeneous. Add the pepper and poultry seasoning; mix to incorporate. Test the forcemeat and adjust seasoning if necessary before proceeding.

5. Fold the garnish mixture into the forcemeat by hand over an ice bath.

6. Line a terrine mold with plastic wrap, leaving an overhang. Pack the forcemeat into the mold and fold over the liner. Cover the terrine and poach in a 170°F/77°C water bath in a 300°F/149°C oven to an internal temperature of 165°F/74°C, 60 to 75 minutes.

7. Remove the terrine from the water bath and allow it to cool to an internal temperature of 90° to 100°F/32° to 38°C. Pour off the juices from the terrine and let it rest under refrigeration overnight. The terrine is now ready to slice and serve, or wrap and refrigerate for up to 5 days.

CHEF'S NOTE: To prepare smoked foie gras, soak and clean the liver as directed on page 289. Cold smoke at 80°F/27°C for about 20 minutes. The intention is simply to give a little smoke flavor to the foie gras; it should not be cooked through.

Southwest Chile-Chicken Terrine

YIELD: 3 LB/1.36 KG TERRINE; 18 TO 20 SERVINGS

1 chicken (about 3 lb/1.36 kg)

2 chicken legs

8 oz/227 g fatback, cubed

SEASONINGS

2 oz/57 g minced shallots, sautéed and cooled

1 tbsp/6 g mild chili powder

2 tsp/6 g minced jalapeño

2 tsp/6 g minced garlic, sautéed and cooled

2 tsp/10 g salt

1 tbsp/3 g chopped oregano

½ tsp/1 g ground white pepper

1 tsp/5 mL Tabasco sauce

2 fl oz/60 mL heavy cream

GARNISH

1 oz/28 g ham, cut into fine dice, sautéed, and cooled

6 oz/170 g cooked pinto beans

3½ oz/99 g green chiles, roasted and diced

Aspic, as needed

1. Debone the chicken and chicken legs. Dice the leg and thigh meat (you should have 1 lb/454 g). Cut the breast into 1-in/3-cm cubes (you should have 12 oz/340 g). Reserve separately.

2. Toss the leg meat and fatback with the seasonings. Grind through the fine plate (⅛ in/ 3 mm) of a meat grinder into a chilled mixing bowl. Add the heavy cream and mix on medium speed for 1 minute, until homogeneous. Chill. Test the forcemeat and adjust seasoning if necessary before proceeding.

3. Fold the garnish ingredients mixture into the forcemeat by hand over an ice bath.

4. Line a terrine mold with plastic wrap, pack the forcemeat into the mold, and fold over the liner. Cover the terrine and poach in a 170°F/77°C water bath in a 300°F/149°C oven to an internal temperature of 165°F/74°C, 60 to 75 minutes.

5. Remove the terrine from the water bath and allow it to cool to an internal temperature of 90° to 100°F/32° to 38°C. Add enough aspic to coat and cover the terrine.

6. Let the terrine rest under refrigeration, covered with a 2-lb/907-g press plate, if desired, for at least 24 hours and up to 2 days. The terrine is now ready to slice and serve, or wrap and refrigerate for up to 7 days.

Venison Terrine

YIELD: 3 LB/1.36 KG TERRINE; 18 TO 20 SERVINGS

2 lb/907 g venison shoulder, boneless or leg meat

1 lb/454 g fatback

SEASONINGS

2 fl oz/30 mL red wine

½ tsp/1 g ground cloves

1 tbsp/6 g crushed black peppercorns

1 tsp/2.75 g tinted curing mix (TCM)

1 oz/28 g minced onions, sautéed and cooled

1 oz/28 g salt

2 tsp/4 g ground black pepper

1 oz/28 g dried cèpes or morels, ground to powder

3 eggs

6 fl oz/180 mL heavy cream

1 tbsp/3 g chopped tarragon

1 tbsp/3 g chopped flat-leaf parsley

GARNISH

2 oz/57 g golden raisins, plumped in 4 fl oz/120 mL brandy

4 oz/113 g mushrooms, diced, sautéed, and cooled

8 thin slices ham (⅟₁₆ in/1.5 mm), or as needed for liner

1. Dice the venison and fatback into 1-in/3-cm cubes. Marinate them with the combined seasonings and refrigerate overnight.

2. Prepare a straight forcemeat by grinding the marinated venison and fatback into a chilled mixing bowl. Mix in the eggs, heavy cream, tarragon, and parsley on medium speed for 1 minute, or until homogeneous. Fold in the garnish ingredients.

3. Line a terrine mold with plastic wrap and the ham, leaving an overhang. Pack the forcemeat into the terrine mold and fold over the ham and plastic. Cover the terrine.

4. Poach the forcemeat in a 170°F/77°C water bath in a 300°F/149°C oven to an internal temperature of 150°F/66°C, 60 to 70 minutes.

5. Remove the terrine from the water bath and allow it to cool to an internal temperature of 90° to 100°F/32° to 38°C. Let the terrine rest under refrigeration overnight. The terrine is now ready to slice and serve, or wrap and refrigerate for up to 10 days.

Duck Terrine with Pistachios and Dried Cherries

YIELD: 3 LB/1.36 KG TERRINE; 18 TO 20 SERVINGS

1 lb 12 oz/794 g duck meat, trimmed and cubed (from a 4- to 5-lb/1.81- to 2.26-kg bird)

8 oz/227 g fatback

SEASONINGS

⅔ oz/19 g salt

2 tbsp/6 g chopped sage

1 tsp/2 g white pepper

1 tbsp/3 g chopped flat-leaf parsley

¼ tsp/0.75 g tinted curing mix (TCM)

GARNISH

4 oz/113 g ham, cut into small dice

3 oz/85 g roasted and peeled pistachios

2½ oz/71 g dried cherries

8 thin slices ham (¹⁄₁₆ in/1.5 mm), or as needed for liner

1. Combine 1 lb/454 g of the duck meat, the fatback, and the seasonings and grind through the medium plate (¼ in/6 mm) and then the fine plate (⅛ in/3 mm) of a meat grinder.

2. Sear the remaining duck meat and the diced ham; let cool. Test the forcemeat and adjust seasoning before adding garnish.

3. Fold in the duck, ham, pistachios, and cherries, working over an ice bath.

4. Line a terrine mold with plastic wrap and ham slices, leaving an overhang, then pack with the forcemeat. Fold the liners over the terrine and cover the mold. Poach in a 170°F/77°C water bath in a 300°F/149°C oven to an internal temperature of 165°F/74°C, 50 to 60 minutes.

5. Let the terrine rest for 1 hour. Weight it with a 2-lb/907-g press overnight and up to 3 days under refrigeration. The terrine is now ready to slice and serve, or wrap and refrigerate for up to 7 days.

Terrine of Wild Boar

YIELD: 3 LB/1.36 KG TERRINE; 18 TO 20 SERVINGS

1 lb 8 oz/680 g boar meat (butt or leg), cubed

1 lb/454 g fatback

4 oz/113 g pork liver

MARINADE

2 oz/57 g leek, white and light green parts, thinly sliced

1 oz/28 g white mushrooms, thinly sliced

3 fl oz/90 mL gin

¼ tsp/0.75 g tinted curing mix (TCM)

4 juniper berries, pulverized

1 oz/28 g salt

½ tsp/1 g ground black pepper

4 oz/113 g cooked long-grain rice, cooled

2 eggs

4 fl oz/120 mL heavy cream

½ tsp/1 g ground coriander

1 bunch savory, chopped

4 oz/113 g cèpes, sautéed and cooled

8 thin slices prosciutto (⅟₁₆ in/1.5 mm), or as needed for liner

1. Combine the boar meat, fatback, liver, and marinade ingredients. Marinate under refrigeration overnight. Drain and dry the meat.

2. Sear the boar meat and liver on both sides and allow to cool. Return the seared meats to the marinating fatback.

3. Grind the marinated meat and fatback, leeks, and mushrooms through the medium plate (¼ in/6 mm) of a meat grinder.

4. Combine the ground meats and the rice; grind once more through the fine plate (⅛ in/ 3 mm) into a chilled mixing bowl.

5. Mix in the eggs, cream, coriander, and savory. Fold in the cèpes. Test the forcemeat and adjust seasoning if necessary.

6. Line a terrine mold with plastic wrap and the prosciutto, leaving an overhang. Pack with the forcemeat, fold over the liners, and cover the terrine. Poach in a 170°F/77°C water bath at 300°F/149°C to an internal temperature of 150°F/66°C, about 55 minutes.

7. Remove the terrine from the water bath and allow it to cool to an internal temperature of 90° to 100°F/32° to 38°C. Let the terrine rest under refrigeration overnight. The terrine is now ready to slice and serve, or wrap and refrigerate for up to 10 days.

Pork Tenderloin Roulade

YIELD: 2 LB 8 OZ/1.13 KG ROULADE; 16 TO 18 SERVINGS

1 pork tenderloin (about 1 lb 8 oz/680 g)

BRINE

16 fl oz/480 mL Basic Meat Brine
(page 206)

3 star anise pods

2 oz/57 g ginger, coarsely chopped

2 tsp/4 g Szechwan peppercorns

MOUSSELINE

1 lb/454 g ground chicken breast

2 tsp/10 g salt

2 egg whites

8 fl oz/240 mL heavy cream

2 tsp/6 g minced garlic

2 tsp/6 g minced ginger

8 oz/227 g fresh shiitake mushrooms, cut
into medium dice, sautéed, and chilled

1 tsp/5 mL dark soy sauce

1 tsp/5 mL sherry

3 green onions, minced

½ tsp/1 g ground black pepper

1 fl oz/30 mL Glace de Volaille or
Viande (page 531), warm

1. Trim the pork tenderloin, removing all fat and silverskin; you should have 10 to 12 oz/283 to 340 g after trimming.

2. Cover the pork with the brine ingredients; use small plates or plastic wrap to keep it completely submerged. Cure under refrigeration for 12 hours. Rinse the tenderloin and dry well.

3. Prepare the chicken mousseline: Place the ground chicken and salt in the bowl of a food processor. Process to a relatively smooth paste. Add the egg whites. With the machine running, add the cream and process just to incorporate. Pass the forcemeat through a drum sieve and fold in the remaining ingredients. Test the forcemeat and adjust the seasoning if necessary before proceeding.

4. On a sheet of plastic wrap, spread half of the mousseline. Place the tenderloin in the middle and spread the other half of the mousseline evenly over the tenderloin. Roll tightly into a cylinder and secure the ends with twine. Poach in a 170°F/77°C water bath in a 300°F/149°C oven to an internal temperature of 165°F/74°C, 50 to 60 minutes. Remove the roulade from the water bath and allow it to cool. Rewrap the roulade tightly.

5. Let the roulade rest under refrigeration for at least 24 hours and up to 2 days. The roulade is now ready to slice and serve, or wrap and refrigerate for up to 7 days.

CHEF'S NOTE: If desired, line the plastic wrap with mustard seeds and chopped parsley before spreading the mousseline and rolling the roulade to achieve the effect shown here.

Lobster Terrine with Summer Vegetables

YIELD: 2 LB/907 G TERRINE; 10 TO 12 SERVINGS

4 oz/113 g diced scallops

4 oz/113 g diced shrimp

SEASONINGS

½ fl oz/15 mL Pernod

1 tsp/5 mL lemon juice

1 tsp/5 g salt

½ tsp/1 g ground white pepper

½ tsp/1.50 g grated lemon zest

Pinch cayenne

1 egg white

5 fl oz/150 mL heavy cream, chilled

GARNISH

10 oz/283 g assorted vegetables, cut into ¼-in/6-mm dice, cooked, cooled, and drained (see Chef's Note)

10 oz/283 g lobster meat, poached and cut into medium dice

1. Make a mousseline forcemeat by grinding the scallops, shrimp, and seasonings in the bowl of a food processor. Process to a relatively smooth paste. Add the egg white. With the motor running, add the cream and process just to incorporate. Pass the forcemeat through a drum sieve, if desired. Test the forcemeat and adjust seasoning if necessary before proceeding.

2. Fold in the garnish by hand, working over an ice bath.

3. Oil a terrine mold and line it with plastic wrap, leaving an overhang. Pack the forcemeat into the lined mold, making sure to remove any air pockets. Fold the liner over the forcemeat to completely encase the terrine; cover.

4. Poach the terrine in a 170°F/77°C water bath in a 300°F/149°C oven to an internal temperature of 145°F/63°C, 60 to 75 minutes. Remove the terrine from the water bath and allow it to cool slightly.

5. Let the terrine rest at least overnight, weighted with a 2-lb/907-g press plate. The terrine is now ready to slice and serve, or wrap and refrigerate for up to 5 days.

PRESENTATION IDEAS: Serve with Basic Mayonnaise (see page 35) flavored with chopped basil; garnish with tomato concassé.

CHEF'S NOTE: For a vegetable garnish, choose from broccoli, carrots, zucchini, squash, and shiitake or other mushrooms.

Chicken and Crayfish Terrine

YIELD: 2 LB/907 G TERRINE; 10 TO 12 SERVINGS

MOUSSELINE

1 lb/454 g finely ground chicken breast

2 egg whites

2 tsp/10 g salt

½ tsp/1 g ground black pepper

6 fl oz/180 mL Shellfish Essence (recipe follows), chilled

2 fl oz/60 mL heavy cream, chilled

GARNISH

8 oz/227 g cooked crayfish tails, shelled and deveined

1 chipotle in adobo sauce, minced

6 fresh shiitake mushrooms, cut into medium dice, sautéed, and chilled

2 tbsp/6 g chopped cilantro

1 tbsp/3 g chopped dill

1. Prepare a mousseline-style forcemeat by processing the ground chicken, egg whites, salt, and pepper until smooth. Add the shellfish essence and cream with the motor running, and process just to incorporate. Pass the forcemeat through a drum sieve, if desired. Test the forcemeat and adjust the seasoning if necessary before proceeding.

2. Fold in the crayfish tails, chipotles, mushrooms, cilantro, and dill, working over an ice bath.

3. Oil a terrine mold and line it with plastic wrap, leaving an overhang. Pack the forcemeat into the lined mold, making sure to remove any air pockets. Fold the liner over the forcemeat to completely encase the terrine; cover.

4. Poach the terrine in a 170°F/77°C water bath in a 300°F/149°C oven to an internal temperature of 165°F/74°C, 60 to 75 minutes. Remove the terrine from the water bath and allow it to cool slightly.

5. Let the terrine rest at least overnight, weighted with a 2-lb/907-g press plate. The terrine is now ready to slice and serve, or wrap and refrigerate for up to 5 days.

CHEF'S NOTE: The shellfish essence can be prepared using the shells reserved from this recipe or from other uses. Be sure to freeze the shells if they cannot be used within 12 hours.

Shellfish Essence

YIELD: 6 FL OZ/180 ML

1 lb/454 g crayfish, shrimp, or lobster shells

½ fl oz/15 mL vegetable oil

2 shallots, minced

2 garlic cloves, minced

12 fl oz/360 mL heavy cream

3 bay leaves

2 tsp/4 g poultry seasoning

1 tbsp/6 g chili powder

1 fl oz/30 mL Glace de Volaille or Viande (page 531)

1. Sauté the shells in the vegetable oil until red. Add the shallots and garlic; sauté until aromatic.

2. Add the heavy cream, bay leaves, poultry seasoning, and chili powder; reduce to half the original volume. Add the glace and squeeze through a cheesecloth (final volume should be 6 fl oz/180 mL); chill to below 40°F/4°C.

Sweetbread and Foie Gras Terrine

YIELD: 2 LB 12 OZ/1.25 KG TERRINE; 14 TO 16 SERVINGS

1 lb/454 g veal sweetbreads	8 fl oz/240 mL heavy cream
8 fl oz/240 mL milk	⅔ oz/19 g salt
64 fl oz/1.44 L Court Bouillon (page 531)	½ tsp/1 g ground white pepper
12 oz/340 g foie gras, grade B	
½ oz/14 g albumen powder or powdered gelatin (optional)	1 tbsp/3 g chopped chervil
	1 tbsp/3 g chopped chives
MOUSSELINE	8 thin slices cooked smoked tongue (¹⁄₁₆ in/1.5 mm), or as needed
1 lb/454 g lean veal	
1 egg white	

1. Soak the sweetbreads in the milk overnight. Drain and poach in the court bouillon at 170°F/77°C until just done and still pink inside. Cool and remove membranes. Break the sweetbreads into pieces approximately 1-in/3-cm square.

2. Cut the foie gras into 1-in/3-cm cubes. Dust with the albumen powder, if using.

3. Prepare a mousseline-style forcemeat by processing the veal, egg white, cream, salt, and pepper until smooth. Test the forcemeat and adjust if necessary before proceeding.

4. Fold the sweetbreads, foie gras, and herbs into the forcemeat.

5. Line a terrine mold with plastic wrap and the sliced tongue, leaving an overhang. Fill the mold with the forcemeat and smooth with a palette knife. Fold over the tongue and plastic wrap. Poach in a 170°F/77°C water bath in a 300°F/149°C oven to an internal temperature of 138°F/58°C, 60 to 70 minutes.

6. Remove the terrine from the water bath and allow it to cool to an internal temperature of 90° to 100°F/32° to 38°C. Press with a weight of about 6 lb/2.72 kg. Let the terrine rest under refrigeration overnight.

7. The terrine is now ready to slice and serve, or wrap and refrigerate for up to 3 days.

Mediterranean Seafood Terrine

YIELD: 3 LB/1.36 KG TERRINE; 18 TO 20 SERVINGS

This recipe was developed by Chef Mark Erickson to meet the special requirements of the Institute's nutritional cuisine restaurant. The vegetable and seafood garnish takes center stage, making this a dish that appeals to those concerned with nutrition as well as those who focus on the flavor and taste of a dish.

MOUSSELINE

4 oz/113 g shrimp, peeled, deveined, and diced

10 oz/283 g scallops, diced

2 tsp/10 g salt

½ tsp/1 g ground white pepper

2 egg whites

5 fl oz/150 mL heavy cream, infused with saffron and chilled (see Chef's Note)

GARNISH

½ lb/227 g shrimp (16/20 count), split and cut into eighths

8 oz/227 g sea scallops, quartered

1 tbsp/3 g chopped flat-leaf parsley

2 tsp/2 g chopped basil

1. Prepare a mousseline-style forcemeat by processing the shrimp, scallops, salt, pepper, egg whites, and saffron cream until smooth. Test the forcemeat and adjust if necessary before proceeding.

2. Fold the garnish ingredients into the forcemeat, working over an ice bath.

3. Line a terrine mold with plastic wrap, leaving an overhang, and fill it with the forcemeat. Fold over the plastic and cover the terrine.

4. Poach the terrine in a 170°F/77°C water bath in a 300°F/149°C oven to an internal temperature of 145°F/63°C, 20 to 25 minutes. Remove the terrine from the water bath and allow it to cool to an internal temperature of 90° to 100°F/32° to 38°C. Let the terrine rest under refrigeration overnight.

5. The terrine is now ready to slice and serve, or wrap and refrigerate for up to 3 days.

PRESENTATION IDEA: This terrine can be served with Red Pepper Coulis (page 54).

CHEF'S NOTE: To make saffron-infused cream, heat 5 fl oz/150 mL heavy cream to 160°F/71°C. Add a pinch of crushed saffron and allow the saffron to steep in the cream, away from the heat, until the cream turns a brilliant yellow-gold color. Chill the cream well before using in the mousseline.

Terrine of Scallop and Salmon

12 oz/340 g salmon fillet

MOUSSELINE

1 lb 14 oz/850 g bay scallops, cleaned

1¼ oz/35 g salt

4 egg whites

16 fl oz/480 mL heavy cream

2 fl oz/60 mL lemon juice

¼ tsp/0.50 g ground white pepper

2 oz/57 g truffle peelings

2 oz/57 g chives, minced

1. Cut the salmon fillet into 3 strips the length of the mold and about ½ in/1 cm square. Reserve.

2. Prepare a mousseline-style forcemeat by processing the scallops, salt, egg whites, cream, and lemon juice until smooth. Do not overmix. Season with pepper. Test the forcemeat and adjust seasoning if necessary before proceeding.

3. Fold in the truffle peelings and chives, working over an ice bath.

4. Oil a terrine mold and line it with plastic wrap, leaving an overhang.

5. Pack half the forcemeat into the lined mold, making sure to remove any air pockets. Lay the salmon strips on the forcemeat for the inlay garnish. Cover with the remaining forcemeat and smooth the surface.

6. Poach in a 160°F/71°C water bath in a 300°F/149°C oven to an internal temperature of 145°F/63°C, 60 to 70 minutes.

7. Cool the terrine for 1 hour. Let it rest under refrigeration, covered with a 2-lb/907-g press plate, if desired, at least 24 hours.

8. The terrine is now ready to slice and serve, or wrap and refrigerate for up to 4 days.

Saint Andrew's Vegetable Terrine

Saint Andrew's Vegetable Terrine, shown with Duck and Smoked Foie Gras Terrine (page 293).

12 oz/340 g raw chicken breast, cubed

1 egg white

6 fl oz/180 mL heavy cream

2 tsp/10 g salt, or as needed

Ground white pepper, as needed

6 oz/170 g spinach, sautéed and coarsely chopped

1 roasted red pepper, cut into medium dice

8 oz/227 g summer squash and/or zucchini, finely diced, blanched

8 oz/227 g carrots, finely diced, fully cooked

2 oz/57 g yellow turnip, finely diced, fully cooked

½ oz/14 g powdered gelatin

½ oz/14 g minced fresh herbs, such as marjoram, dill, and/or chives

Pinch grated nutmeg

½ tsp/1 g ground cardamom, roasted

1. Make a mousseline-style forcemeat by processing the chicken, egg white, cream, salt, and pepper until smooth. Test the forcemeat and adjust seasoning, if necessary, before proceeding.

2. Toss the vegetables in a mixing bowl with salt and ground pepper. Add the gelatin powder and toss to coat evenly. Fold the vegetables with the herbs, nutmeg, and cardamom into the forcemeat, working over an ice bath.

3. Oil a terrine mold and line it with plastic wrap, leaving an overhang. Pack the forcemeat into the lined mold, making sure to remove any air pockets. Fold over the liners.

4. Poach the terrine in a 170°F/77°C water bath in a 300°F/149°C oven to an internal temperature of 165°F/74°C, 60 to 75 minutes. Let the terrine rest under refrigeration, weighted with a 1-lb/454-g press plate, if desired, for at least 12 hours.

5. The terrine is now ready to slice and serve, or wrap and refrigerate for up to 4 days.

Roasted Pepper and Eggplant Terrine

YIELD: 3 LB/1.36 KG TERRINE; 18 TO 20 SERVINGS

1 lb/454 g eggplant, peeled and sliced lengthwise ¼ in/6 mm thick

3 lb/1.36 kg red peppers (about 6)

3 lb/1.36 kg yellow peppers (about 6)

3 lb/1.36 kg green peppers (about 6)

2 tsp/10 g salt

½ tsp/1 g ground black pepper

1 oz/28 g powdered gelatin

12 fl oz/360 mL Basic Red Wine Vinaigrette (page 27)

1. Salt the eggplant for 30 minutes and let it drain on toweling before grilling. Grill the eggplant and peppers on a hot grill. Peel and seed the peppers; cool. Trim to fit a terrine mold. Season with salt and pepper.

2. Line the mold with plastic wrap, leaving an overhang (or see Presentation Idea).

3. Dissolve the gelatin in the vinaigrette. Layer the peppers and eggplant alternately with the vinaigrette to fill the mold. Fold the liner over the top of the terrine.

4. Cover the terrine with plastic and weigh down with a 2-lb/907-g weight for 2 days under refrigeration. The terrine is now ready to slice and serve, or wrap and refrigerate for up to 7 days.

PRESENTATION IDEA: Line the terrine mold with sliced, fully cooked carrots for the presentation shown in the photo.

Carolina Barbecue Terrine with Apricot Barbecue Sauce

YIELD: 3 LB/1.36 KG TERRINE; 18 TO 20 SERVINGS

1 pork butt

DRY RUB

1 oz/28 g sweet Spanish paprika

1 oz/28 g salt

1 oz/28 g sugar

1 oz/28 g dark brown sugar

2 tbsp/12 g cumin

2 tbsp/12 g chili powder

1 tbsp/6 g finely ground black pepper

1 tbsp/6 g cayenne

SPICED VINEGAR

2 fl oz/60 mL cider vinegar

1 tbsp/15 g sugar

1 tbsp/6 g crushed red pepper flakes

1 tsp/5 g salt

½ tsp/1 g finely ground black pepper

1 lb/454 g collard greens, cleaned, blanched, and coarsely chopped

4 fl oz/120 mL Chicken or Turkey Stock (page 529)

4 fl oz/120 mL Glace de Volaille, warmed (page 531)

2 pork tenderloins, brined overnight in Basic Meat Brine (page 206) and hot smoked

1. Trim the pork butt of excess fat, leaving approximately ¼ in/6 mm fat cover. Score the fat in a crisscross pattern.

2. Combine the dry rub ingredients and rub into the pork butt. Allow it to sit overnight under refrigeration.

3. Combine the spiced vinegar ingredients in a saucepan. Heat and allow to steep for 30 minutes.

4. Smoke-roast the pork butt at 225°F/107°C for 4 to 6 hours to an internal temperature of 150°F/66°C, or until tender, basting with the spiced vinegar. Remove from the oven and allow it to rest until cool enough to handle. Dissolve the gelatin in the stock.

5. Pull the meat from the bones, discarding any fat and gristle. Shred the meat into small pieces and combine with the dissolved gelatin, collards, stock, and glace.

6. Oil a terrine mold and line with plastic wrap, leaving an overhang. Pack the meat into the mold. Place the fully cooked pork tenderloins as center garnishes. Fold the liner over the top of the terrine.

7. Let the terrine rest under refrigeration for 2 to 3 days, weighted with a 4-lb/1.81-kg press plate, if desired. The terrine is now ready to slice and serve, or wrap and refrigerate for up to 7 days.

Seared Lamb, Artichoke, and Mushroom Terrine

YIELD: 2 LB/907 G TERRINE; 10 TO 12 SERVINGS

1 whole lamb loin, bone in

SPICES

1½ tsp/3 g curry powder

1½ tsp/3 g celery seed

1½ tbsp/9 g whole coriander seed

1 tbsp/6 g ground zaatar (see Chef's Notes)

1 tbsp/6 g fennel seed

1 oz/28 g salt, or as needed

2 tbsp/12 g cumin seed

1 tsp/2 g anise seed

1½ fl oz/45 mL olive oil

3 oz/85 g cèpes, quartered

Salt, as needed

Ground white pepper, as needed

ASPIC

1 oz/28 g tomato paste

8 oz/227 g Mirepoix (page 522)

16 fl oz/480 mL Chicken Stock (page 529)

¾ oz/21 g powdered gelatin

3 artichoke bottoms, cooked and quartered

2 tbsp/6 g chopped tarragon

2 tbsp/6 g chopped flat-leaf parsley

1. Bone the loin, reserving the loins and tenderloins separately. Reserve the bones to prepare a stock.

2. Cut the lamb loins lengthwise into 2 pieces, making 4 loin strips plus 2 tenderloin pieces.

3. Toast the spices; grind and rub over the lamb. Marinate for 4 hours.

4. Sear the lamb to medium rare in a very hot sauté pan in 1 fl oz/30 mL of the olive oil. Cool and reserve.

5. Sauté the cèpes in the remaining ½ fl oz/15 mL olive oil, season with salt and pepper, and cook through. Cool and reserve.

6. Brown the lamb bones in the oven. Add the tomato paste and mirepoix; brown. Transfer the bones and mirepoix to a saucepan; add the chicken stock. Bring to a simmer and reduce by one-third.

7. Strain through cheesecloth and cool. When cool, add the gelatin; bloom and heat to clear. Heat the aspic to 120°F/49°C.

8. Oil a terrine mold and line it with plastic wrap, leaving an overhang. Mix the lamb, artichokes, cèpes, and herbs. Mix in all but 4 fl oz/120 mL of the aspic thoroughly and pack into the terrine mold. Pour the remaining aspic on top, spreading it over the entire length of the terrine. Use more stock, if necessary.

9. Fold over the liner and press with a 2-lb/907-g press plate. Chill the terrine for at least 24 hours before slicing and serving, or wrap and refrigerate for up to 10 days.

Mushroom Terrine

YIELD: 2 LB/907 G TERRINE; 10 TO 12 SERVINGS

1 lb 8 oz/680 g assorted mushrooms, sliced

2 shallots, minced, sautéed, and cooled

3 garlic cloves, minced, sautéed, and cooled

1 fl oz/30 mL vegetable oil

4 fl oz/120 mL Madeira

2 fl oz/60 mL brandy

2 tbsp/6 g minced tarragon

2 tbsp/6 g minced chives

2 tbsp/6 g minced flat-leaf parsley

1 fl oz/30 mL Glace de Volaille (page 531), melted

2 tsp/10 g salt

½ tsp/1 g ground white pepper

12 oz/340 g raw chicken breast, diced

1 egg

8 fl oz/240 mL heavy cream

1. Sauté the mushrooms, shallots, and garlic in the vegetable oil. Add the Madeira and brandy and reduce until ½ fl oz/15 mL liquid remains. Transfer to a bowl and add the tarragon, chives, parsley, glace, and half the salt and pepper. Chill.

2. Make a mousseline-style forcemeat by processing the chicken, the remaining salt and pepper, the egg, and the cream until smooth. Test the forcemeat and adjust seasoning if necessary before proceeding.

3. Fold in the mushroom and herb mixture, working over an ice bath.

4. Oil a terrine mold and line it with plastic wrap, leaving an overhang. Pack the forcemeat into the lined mold, making sure to remove any air pockets. Fold the liner over the forcemeat to completely encase the terrine; cover.

5. Poach the terrine in a 170°F/77°C water bath in a 300°F/149°C oven to an internal temperature of 165°F/74°C, 60 to 75 minutes. Remove the terrine from the water bath and allow it to cool to an internal temperature of 90° to 100°F/32° to 38°C. Press with a 2-lb/907-g weight and let it rest under refrigeration overnight.

6. The terrine is now ready to slice and serve, or wrap and refrigerate for up to 3 days.

CHEF'S NOTE: Scallops or salmon fillet can be substituted for the chicken.

Bouillabaisse en Terrine

VEGETABLE GARNISH

8 oz/227 g fennel, cut into medium dice

8 oz/227 g onions, cut into medium dice

8 oz/227 g celery, cut into medium dice

8 oz/227 g carrots, cut into medium dice

3 tbsp/27 g minced garlic

2 fl oz/60 mL olive oil

64 fl oz/1.92 L Fish Stock (page 530)

1 tbsp/6 g ground fennel seeds

1 tsp/2 g ground anise seeds

6 parsley stems

1 tsp/1 g chopped thyme

2 bay leaves

Zest of 1 lemon, chopped

1 tbsp/2 g saffron

1 fl oz/30 mL Pernod

4 oz/113 g tomato paste

10 fl oz/300 mL dry white wine

¼ tsp/0.50 g cayenne

2 tsp/10 g salt

SEAFOOD GARNISH

1 lb/454 g raw lobster meat, cut into medium dice

8 oz/227 g shrimp, peeled and deveined, cut into medium dice

8 oz/227 g scallops, cut into medium dice

8 oz/227 g salmon fillet, skinless, cut into medium dice

1 lb/454 g monkfish fillet, cleaned, cut into medium dice

ASPIC GELÉE

5 egg whites, whipped to soft peaks

1 lb 4 oz/567 g tomato concassé

Juice of 1 lemon

2 tbsp/6 g chopped flat-leaf parsley

1 tbsp/3 g chopped tarragon

8 oz/227 g monkfish trim, ground

15 saffron threads

2¼ oz/64 g powdered gelatin, softened in 3 fl oz/90 mL cold water

1. Sweat the fennel, onions, celery, carrots, and 1 tbsp/9 g garlic in the olive oil over low heat until they are very tender; do not let them color. As the vegetables cook, occasionally add a small amount of fish stock to moisten. Remove and cool.

2. In a stockpot, place the fennel and anise seeds, parsley stems, thyme, bay leaves, lemon zest, saffron, Pernod, tomato paste, the remaining 2 tbsp/18 g garlic, 8 oz/240 mL of the wine, the cayenne, salt, and the remaining fish stock and bring to a boil. Simmer for 45 minutes, then strain.

3. Poach the seafood and fish at 170°F/77°C in the strained stock until just done, 5 to 6 minutes. They must be cooked through but not overcooked. Remove from the stock and refrigerate.

4. Strain the stock through a fine-mesh strainer into a soup pot and cool to 100°F/38°C.

5. Add the egg whites, tomato concassé, lemon juice, parsley, tarragon, monkfish trim, and the remaining wine to the strained stock. Stir well.

6. Gradually bring to a simmer to form a raft over medium-high heat; simmer for 30 minutes without stirring.

7. Strain the clarified stock into a bowl containing the saffron and adjust seasoning. Add the softened gelatin and stir to combine thoroughly. Test for gelatin strength (see page 57) and add more gelatin if necessary. Cool this aspic.

8. Line a terrine mold with plastic wrap, leaving an overhang. Arrange the fish, seafood, and vegetables randomly in the mold, pour in enough aspic to cover, and refrigerate overnight. The terrine is now ready to slice and serve, or wrap and refrigerate for up to 4 days.

PRESENTATION IDEAS: Bouillabaisse en Terrine is classically served with Rouille (page 36). Alternatively, serve it with French bread toast topped with Tapenade (page 52) and Vinaigrette Gourmande (page 30).

CHEF'S NOTES: Blanched spinach or savoy cabbage may be used as a liner, if desired. If preferred, replace the salmon fillet with mullet, rouget, bass, or snapper.

Terrine of Roasted Pheasant

YIELD: 2 LB 8 OZ/1.13 KG TERRINE; 14 TO 16 SERVINGS

1 pheasant, about 3 lb/1.36 kg

64 fl oz/1.92 L Basic Poultry Brine (page 202), chilled

ASPIC

32 fl oz/960 mL Chicken Stock (page 529)

½ bunch parsley stems

4 thyme sprigs

2 tsp/3 g crushed juniper berries

4 fl oz/120 mL Madeira

½ oz/14 g black peppercorns

4 oz/113 g baby braising greens, blanched and coarsely chopped

2 tbsp/6 g chopped flat-leaf parsley

2 tsp/10 g salt

½ tsp/1 g coarse-ground black pepper

1 tsp/2 g Old Bay seasoning

1. Cover the pheasant with the brine and weigh it down with a plate to be sure it is completely submerged. Cure overnight. Remove the pheasant and rinse thoroughly.

2. Roast the pheasant to an internal temperature of 165°F/74°C, 35 to 45 minutes. Remove the pheasant from the oven and allow it to cool.

3. Pull the meat from the bones. Reserve the bones and discard the skin. Shred the meat coarsely, cover, and keep under refrigeration until ready to assemble the terrine.

4. Place the bones in a large pot and cover with the chicken stock. Bring to a slow, even simmer. Add the parsley stems, thyme, juniper berries, Madeira, and peppercorns; continue to simmer for at least 2 hours, or until the stock has a good flavor.

5. Strain the stock through a fine-mesh strainer, return it to the stove, and reduce it to 8 fl oz/ 240 mL. Keep warm.

6. Line a terrine mold with plastic wrap, leaving an overhang. Combine the pheasant with the aspic, braising greens, parsley, salt, pepper, and Old Bay. Pack into the mold. Fold over the liner.

7. Let the terrine rest under refrigeration for at least 24 hours and up to 2 days. The terrine is now ready to slice and serve, or wrap and refrigerate for up to 7 days.

CHEF'S NOTES: Do not use red beet greens or red Swiss chard; they will discolor the terrine. A julienne of vegetables can also be added.

Poached Chicken Terrine

YIELD: 2 LB/907 G TERRINE; 10 TO 12 SERVINGS

2 lb/907 g chicken breast, boneless

1 gal/3.84 L Chicken Stock (page 529)

1 Standard Sachet d'Épices (page 523)

1 tsp/5 g salt

½ tsp/1 g ground white pepper

1 oz/28 g gelatin powder

8 oz/227 g zucchini

8 oz/227 g yellow squash

1 lb 4 oz/567 g spinach, cleaned, seasoned, and blanched

8 oz/227 g carrots, cut into small dice, fully cooked

1 oz/28 g Fines Herbes (page 526)

1. Simmer the chicken in the chicken stock with the sachet d'épices until it is tender.

2. Shred the chicken meat into thick strips (about ¼ by 3 in/6 mm by 8 cm).

3. Degrease and strain the stock; return to the heat and reduce to about 24 fl oz/720 mL. Season with the salt and pepper. Cool. Sprinkle the gelatin on top of the stock. Let bloom 10 minutes. Melt over a double boiler until clear.

4. Remove the seeds from the zucchini and yellow squash. Cut into small dice and blanch. Lay the spinach leaves out on an piece of plastic wrap 8 by 12 in/20 by 30 cm so that each leaf slightly overlaps the previous one. Cover with another piece of plastic wrap and roll with a rolling pin to flatten.

5. Lay the spinach in the plastic wrap in the mold. Remove the top piece of plastic and paint the spinach leaves with a small amount of reduced stock. Sprinkle a thin layer of fines herbes over the painted spinach.

6. Mix the chicken, zucchini, yellow squash, carrots, and the fines herbes. Place this mixture into the mold. Pour in the stock. Fold over the liner.

7. Cover the terrine with plastic wrap and store overnight under refrigeration. The terrine is now ready to slice and serve, or wrap and refrigerate for up to 7 days.

PRESENTATION IDEAS: Serve 2 thin slices of the terrine with 2 oz/57 g Papaya and Black Bean Salsa or Mango-Lime Salsa (page 44).

CHEF'S NOTE: The vegetables should be blanched separately to ensure even coloring and to prevent color transfer.

Poached Salmon and Lemon Terrine

YIELD: 3 LB/1.36 KG TERRINE; 18 TO 20 SERVINGS

This terrine is very flavorful and attractive, but it requires particular attention when preparing and assembling.

2 lb/907 g salmon fillet

64 fl oz/1.92 L Court Bouillon (page 531), or as needed

Salt, as needed

GARNISH

3 egg whites, poached, cut into small dice

4 lemons, sectioned and seeded

Zest of 2 lemons, blanched and finely chopped

6 oz/170 g roasted red pepper, peeled, seeded, and cut into small dice

2 tbsp/6 g coarsely chopped flat-leaf parsley

1 tbsp/3 g coarsely chopped tarragon

1 oz/28 g finely diced shallots, blanched

½ tsp/1 g white pepper

24 fl oz/720 mL Aspic Gelée (page 57), made with Fish Stock (page 530)

1. Cut the salmon fillet into 5 strips the length of the terrine mold and about ¾ in/2 cm square. Poach in the court bouillon until barely cooked, about 10 minutes. Drain and chill well.

2. Season the gelée with salt. Line a terrine with plastic wrap, leaving an overhang, then brush the sides and bottom with a thin layer of the gelée.

3. Working over an ice bath, fit the salmon and the combined garnish ingredients into the mold, covering each layer with fish aspic gelée. Make sure the garnish is evenly distributed from end to end.

4. Fold over the plastic wrap, cover, and let rest at least 24 hours, weighted with a 2-lb/907-g press plate, if desired. The terrine is now ready to slice and serve, or wrap and refrigerate for up to 4 days.

Roasted Vegetable Terrine with Goat's Milk Cheese

YIELD: 3 LB/1.36 KG TERRINE; 18 TO 20 SERVINGS

2 lb/907 g zucchini (about 3)

2 lb/907 g yellow squash (about 3)

1 lb 4 oz/567 g eggplant (about 1 large)

2 lb/907 g tomatoes (about 4)

2 portobello mushrooms

MARINADE

1 fl oz/30 mL olive oil

½ oz/14 g Dijon mustard

1 tbsp/3 g chopped flat-leaf parsley

1 tbsp/3 g chopped chives

2 garlic cloves, minced, sautéed, and cooled

2 tsp/2 g chopped rosemary

2 tsp/10 g anchovy paste (about 4 fillets)

½ oz/14 g honey

2 tsp/10 g salt

½ tsp/1 g ground white pepper

8 oz/227 g fresh goat's milk cheese

1 egg

1. Cut all the vegetables lengthwise into slices ⅛ in/3 mm thick.

2. Combine the marinade ingredients and add to the vegetables.

3. Line sheet pans with oiled parchment paper and lay out the vegetables in a single layer.

4. Dry in a 200°F/93°C oven for 1 hour, or until dry but not brittle. Remove from the oven and cool.

5. Mix the goat's milk cheese with the egg to make the custard.

6. Line a terrine mold with plastic wrap, leaving an overhang, and assemble the terrine by alternating layers of vegetables and the cheese mixture until the terrine is filled. Fold over the liner.

7. Cover the terrine and poach in a 170°F/77°C water bath in a 300°F/149°C oven to an internal temperature of 145°F/63°C, about 1 hour. Remove the terrine from the water bath and allow it to cool slightly.

8. Let the terrine rest at least overnight and up to 3 days under refrigeration, weighted with a 2-lb/907-g press plate, if desired. The terrine is now ready to slice and serve, or wrap and refrigerate for up to 7 days.

CHEF'S NOTES: Using a piping bag for the goat's milk cheese custard makes it easier to distribute evenly within the terrine. The vegetables can be marinated and grilled instead of dried.

Mozzarella, Prosciutto, and Roasted Tomato Terrine

YIELD: 2 LB 8 OZ/1.13 KG TERRINE; 14 TO 16 SERVINGS

8 oz/227 g Spinach Pasta (page 539)

12 oz/340 g Mozzarella Cheese (page 352)

3 lb/1.36 kg ripe tomatoes

½ oz/14 g basil chiffonade

2 fl oz/60 mL olive oil

2 tsp/10 g salt

2 tsp/4 g ground black pepper

8 oz/227 g thin slices prosciutto (1⁄16 in/1.5 mm)

1. Prepare the spinach pasta as directed on page 539. Roll the pasta into thin sheets and trim as necessary to match the dimensions of your terrine mold. Cook the sheets until tender in simmering salted water. Drain, refresh in cold water, and drain again. Reserve.

2. Prepare the mozzarella through Step 4 as directed on page 352. Roll and stretch the mozzarella into thin sheets (⅛ in/3 mm thick) and trim as necessary to match the dimensions of your terrine mold. If using purchased mozzarella, cut it into thin slices to layer the terrine.

3. Slice the tomatoes ¼ in/6 mm thick and season with the basil, oil, salt, and pepper. Lay them on a roasting rack and dry in a 200°F/93°C oven for 2 to 3 hours. Cool and reserve.

4. Cut the cooked pasta into 5 sheets to fit the inside dimensions of the terrine mold. Line the terrine mold with plastic wrap, leaving an overhang.

5. Assemble the terrine by layering the pasta sheets, prosciutto, mozzarella, and roasted tomatoes, creating layers that cover the entire surface of the mold. Repeat the process until the ingredients are used up and the mold is filled. Finish with a layer of pasta. Fold the plastic wrap over and smooth over the top. Cover with a lid and place in a water bath in a 250°F/121°C oven for 30 minutes.

6. Cover with a 2-lb/907-g weight and let rest under refrigeration overnight. The terrine is now ready to slice and serve, or refrigerate for up to 3 days.

7. To serve, cut into ⅜-in/9.5-mm slices, with the plastic wrap still on. Remove the plastic wrap after the slices are plated.

PRESENTATION IDEAS: This terrine may be served with a vinaigrette, such as a tomato or balsamic, and a green salad. Grissini (page 540) or French bread slices topped with Tapenade (page 52) are also good accompaniments.

Southwestern Quail Pâté en Croûte with Tomato-Cilantro Crust

YIELD: 2 LB 8 OZ/1.13 KG MOLD; 14 TO 16 SERVINGS

8 quail (3 to 4 oz/85 to 113 g each)

16 fl oz/480 mL Honey Brine (page 205)

2 garlic cloves, minced

2 shallots, minced

½ fl oz/15 mL vegetable oil

3 fl oz/90 mL tequila

6 oz/170 g pork butt, ground

6 oz/170 g fatback, ground

¼ tsp/0.75 g tinted curing mix (TCM)

2 tsp/10 g salt

Ground black pepper, as needed

2 tsp/2 g chopped thyme

1 tsp/1 g chopped oregano

4 green onions, minced

4 oz/113 g Tasso (page 213), cut into small dice

1 lb 8 oz/680 g Tomato-Cilantro Pâté Dough (page 536)

8 thin slices ham (¹⁄₁₆ in/1.5 mm), or as needed

1 egg

½ fl oz/15 mL milk

8 oz/227 g Aspic Gelée (page 57), melted, or as needed to coat the mold

1. Remove the leg and thigh meat from the quail and reserve. Submerge the bone-in breasts in the brine and cure for 4 hours. Dice the leg and thigh meat; reserve. Debone the breasts; reserve.

2. Sweat the garlic and shallots in the oil; add the tequila and reduce by three-quarters. Cool.

3. Combine the quail leg and thigh meat, pork, fatback, TCM, salt, pepper, thyme, oregano, green onions, and garlic mixture in a chilled food processor bowl. Process until homogeneous. Test the forcemeat and adjust seasoning if necessary before proceeding. Fold the tasso into the forcemeat, working over an ice bath.

4. Roll out the pâté dough and line a hinged mold with it. Line the dough with the sliced ham, leaving an overhang.

5. Pack one-third of the forcemeat into the lined mold, making sure to remove any air pockets. Place 8 quail breasts on top, overlapping slightly. Add one-third more forcemeat and the remaining 8 quail breasts. Spread the remaining third of the forcemeat on top. Tap the terrine to settle the forcemeat.

6. Fold the ham and the dough over the forcemeat, cutting away any excess. Add a cap piece. Cut and reinforce vent holes. Beat the egg and milk together for an egg wash. Brush the surface with the egg wash.

7. Bake at 450°F/232°C for 15 to 20 minutes; reduce heat to 350°F/177°C and finish baking to an internal temperature of 165°F/74°C, about 50 minutes.

8. Remove the pâté from the oven and allow it to cool to 90° to 100°F/32° to 38°C. Ladle the aspic through a funnel into the pâté. Chill for at least 24 hours. The pâté is now ready to slice and serve, or wrap and refrigerate for up to 3 days.

Salmon Pâté en Croûte

YIELD: 2 LB 8 OZ/1.13 KG MOLD; 14 TO 16 SERVINGS

1 lb/454 g shrimp (16/20 count), peeled, deveined, and cut into medium dice

12 oz/340 g salmon, diced

1 oz/28 g salt

1 tbsp/6 g ground black pepper

2 egg whites

18 fl oz/540 mL heavy cream

2 tbsp/12 g Old Bay seasoning

8 drops Tabasco sauce

6 oz/170 g crayfish tails, cleaned

2 tbsp/6 g snipped chives

3 tbsp/9 g chopped basil

1 truffle, cut into small dice (optional)

1 lb 8 oz/680 g Saffron Pâté Dough (page 536)

3 pieces salmon fillet, cut into strips 1 in/3 cm wide and the length of the mold

1 egg

½ fl oz/15 mL milk

6 to 8 fl oz/180 to 240 mL Aspic Gelée (page 57), melted, or as needed to coat the mold

1. Grind 12 oz/340 g of the shrimp, the diced salmon, salt, and pepper through the medium plate (¼ in/6 mm) of a meat grinder.

2. Make a mousseline-style forcemeat by processing the ground seafood, egg whites, cream, Old Bay, and Tabasco sauce until smooth. Test the forcemeat and adjust if necessary before proceeding.

3. Fold the remaining shrimp and the crayfish, chives, basil, and truffle into the forcemeat, working over an ice bath.

4. Roll out the pâté dough and line a hinged mold, leaving an overhang. Pack half the forcemeat into the lined mold. Place the salmon strips down the center; cover with the remaining forcemeat.

5. Fold the dough over the forcemeat, cutting away any excess. Add a cap piece (see Chef's Note). Cut and reinforce vent holes. Beat the egg and milk together for an egg wash. Brush the surface with the egg wash.

6. Bake at 450°F/232°C for 15 to 20 minutes; reduce the heat to 350°F/177°C and finish baking to an internal temperature of 145°F/63°C, about 50 minutes.

7. Remove the pâté from the oven and allow it to cool to 90° to 100°F/32° to 38°C. Ladle the aspic through a funnel into the pâté. Chill for at least 24 hours. The pâté is now ready to slice and serve, or wrap and refrigerate for up to 3 days.

PRESENTATION IDEA: Serve with Red Pepper Coulis (page 54).

CHEF'S NOTE: Instead of making a separate cap piece, you may invert the pâté before cutting vent holes, as described on page 282.

Turkey Pâté en Croûte

12 oz/340 g turkey leg and thigh meat, cleaned and cubed

6 oz/170 g pork butt, cubed

6 oz/170 g fatback, cubed

¼ tsp/0.75 g tinted curing mix (TCM)

2 tsp/10 g salt

2 shallots, minced

2 garlic cloves, minced

½ fl oz/15 mL vegetable oil

3 fl oz/90 mL brandy

6 juniper berries, crushed

1 oz/28 g Dijon mustard

1 tbsp/3 g chopped sage

1 tbsp/3 g chopped thyme

Pinch ground nutmeg

½ tsp/1 g ground black pepper

1 fl oz/30 mL Glace de Viande or Volaille, melted (page 531)

1 egg

GARNISH

1 oz/28 g dried cherries, plumped in 8 fl oz/240 mL Triple Sec

1 oz/28 g dried apricots, quartered, plumped in 8 fl oz/240 mL Triple Sec

1 lb 8 oz/680 g Sweet Potato Pâté Dough (page 537)

8 thin slices ham (¹⁄₁₆ in/1.5 mm), or as needed for liner

3 pieces turkey breast, cut into strips 1 in/3 cm wide and length of the mold

1 egg

½ fl oz/15 mL milk

6 to 8 fl oz/180 to 240 mL Aspic Gelée (page 57), melted

1. Combine the turkey meat, pork butt, fatback, TCM, and salt. Grind through the fine plate (⅛ in/3 mm) of a meat grinder.

2. Sweat the shallots and garlic in the oil; deglaze with the brandy. Cool.

3. Combine the ground meats, shallot mixture, juniper berries, mustard, sage, thyme, nutmeg, pepper, and glace; marinate 1 hour.

4. Transfer the ground meats to a chilled food processor bowl and add the egg. Process for 1 minute, or until smooth. Test the forcemeat and adjust seasoning if necessary before proceeding.

5. Drain the garnish ingredients and fold them into the forcemeat, working over an ice bath.

6. Roll out the dough and line a hinged mold. Line the dough with the sliced ham, leaving an overhang. Pack half the forcemeat into the lined mold. Lay the turkey breast on top; cover with the remaining forcemeat.

7. Fold the ham and the dough over the forcemeat, cutting away any excess. Add a cap piece (see Chef's Note). Cut and reinforce vent holes. Beat the egg and milk together for an egg wash. Brush the surface with the egg wash.

8. Bake at 450°F/232°C for 15 to 20 minutes; reduce the heat to 350°F/177°C and finish baking to an internal temperature of 165°F/74°C, about 50 minutes.

9. Remove the pâté from the oven and allow it to cool to 90° to 100°F/32° to 38°C. Ladle the aspic through a funnel into the pâté. Chill the pâté for at least 24 hours. The pâté is now ready to slice and serve, or wrap and refrigerate for up to 5 days.

CHEF'S NOTE: Instead of making a separate cap piece, you may invert the pâté before cutting the vent holes, as described on page 282.

Rabbit Pie in Parmesan Prosciutto Crust

YIELD: ONE 10-IN/25-CM TART; 16 SERVINGS

1 lb/454 g lean rabbit meat (from a 3-lb/1.36-kg rabbit)

8 oz/227 g fatback

2 oz/57 g minced shallots

1 garlic clove, minced

1 oz/28 g butter

½ tsp/1.50 g tinted curing mix (TCM)

2 tsp/10 g salt

1 fl oz/30 mL sherry

1 egg

4 fl oz/120 mL heavy cream

1 tbsp/3 g chopped flat-leaf parsley

1 tsp/2 g poultry seasoning

½ tsp/1 g ground white pepper

1 recipe Parmesan-Prosciutto Crust (recipe follows)

1. Cut the rabbit meat and fatback into medium dice.

2. Sweat the shallots and garlic in the butter until soft. Cool.

3. Combine the shallot mixture with the rabbit meat, fatback, TCM, salt, and sherry; marinate 6 hours.

4. Grind through the medium plate (¼ in/6 mm) of a meat grinder. Chill, if necessary, before grinding through the fine plate (⅛ in/3 mm).

5. Transfer the ground meat to a chilled mixing bowl. Add the egg and cream and mix on medium speed for 1 minute, until homogeneous. Add the parsley, poultry seasoning, and pepper. Mix well. Test the forcemeat and adjust seasoning if necessary before proceeding.

6. Place the forcemeat in the crust. Bake at 300°F/149°C to an internal temperature of 165°F/74°C, about 40 minutes. Chill 24 hours. Slice and serve, or wrap and refrigerate for up to 5 days.

PRESENTATION IDEA: Serve the pie garnished with quartered Seckel pears that have been poached in sweet wine and Orange-Jalapeño Sauce (page 49).

Parmesan-Prosciutto Crust

YIELD: CRUST FOR ONE 10-IN/25-CM TART

4 oz/113 g fresh white bread crumbs

½ oz/14 g flour

2 tsp/4 g coarse-ground black pepper

1 tsp/1 g dried oregano

1 tsp/1 g dried basil

1 tsp/1 g dried thyme

2 oz/57 g butter, melted

2 egg yolks

1 oz/28 g grated Parmesan cheese

2 oz/57 g finely diced prosciutto

1. Combine the bread crumbs, flour, pepper, oregano, basil, and thyme. Add the butter and egg yolks; mix well with a kitchen fork. Mix in the cheese and prosciutto.

2. Press into a buttered 10-in/25-cm tart pan. Bake at 350°F/177°C until slightly brown, about 10 minutes. Cool. Fill and bake as directed.

Pheasant Galantine

YIELD: 1 GALANTINE (2 BY 14 IN/5 BY 36 CM); 10 TO 12 SERVINGS

1 pheasant (about 3 lb/1.36 kg)

1 fl oz/30 mL vegetable oil

8 oz/227 g Mirepoix (page 522)

8 fl oz/240 mL Madeira

96 fl oz/2.88 L Chicken Stock (page 529)

10 black peppercorns

3 bay leaves, crushed

4 oz/113 g pork butt, trimmed of visible fat, diced

4 oz/113 g fatback, diced

¼ tsp/1.25 g tinted curing mix (TCM)

2 tsp/10 g salt

1½ tsp/2 g chopped rosemary

1½ tsp/2 g chopped sage

2 tsp/2 g chopped flat-leaf parsley

2 tsp/2 g chopped thyme

3 juniper berries, crushed

1 egg

GARNISH

¾ oz/21 g dried currants, plumped in Madeira

¾ oz/21 g dried cherries, plumped in Madeira

¾ oz/21 g dried apricots, quartered, plumped in Madeira

1 tsp/2 g pink peppercorns

1. Debone the pheasant and remove the skin, keeping it intact. Dice the meat. Chop the carcass. Reserve the skin.

2. Brown the carcass in the oil; add the mirepoix and brown. Add the Madeira, 16 fl oz/480 mL of the chicken stock, the peppercorns, and the bay leaves. Simmer for 3 hours. Strain, return to the heat, and reduce to 2 fl oz/60 mL. Chill.

3. Combine the pheasant meat, pork, and fatback. Add the reduced pheasant stock, TCM, salt, rosemary, sage, parsley, thyme, and juniper berries. Mix well and marinate overnight under refrigeration.

4. Grind the meat through the medium plate (¼ in/6 mm) of a meat grinder. Chill, if necessary, before grinding through the fine plate (⅛ in/3 mm).

5. Transfer the ground meats to a chilled food processor bowl. Process on medium speed for 1 minute, until homogeneous. Add the egg and process until smooth.

6. Test and adjust the forcemeat if necessary before proceeding.

7. Drain the plumped fruit. Stir the garnish ingredients into the forcemeat, working over an ice bath.

8. Place a damp cheesecloth on a work surface and lay the pheasant skin on top. Spread the forcemeat over the skin in an even layer. Use the cheesecloth to help roll the galantine. Carefully lap the skin over itself at the seam. Tie.

9. Heat the remaining chicken stock in a pot to 170°F/77°C. Place the galantine in the chicken stock and poach to an internal temperature of 165°F/74°C, 45 to 50 minutes. Remove the pot from the heat and place over an ice bath. Let the galantine cool in the chicken stock. Refrigerate overnight. Rewrap the galantine and refrigerate at least 12 hours. Slice and serve, or refrigerate for up to 5 days.

PRESENTATION IDEAS: Serve with a classic Cumberland Sauce (page 48) or Cranberry Relish (page 480). Apricot-Cherry Chutney (page 477) or Dried Apricot Relish (page 482) would also be a good accompaniment.

CHEF'S NOTE: Replace the garnish ingredients with equal parts dried cherries and whole pistachios.

Chicken Galantine

PANADA

2 eggs

1½ fl oz/45 mL brandy

1 tsp/2 g Pâté Spice (page 526)

3 oz/85 g flour

⅔ oz/19 g salt

¼ tsp/0.50 g ground white pepper

8 fl oz/240 mL heavy cream, heated

1 chicken (about 3 lb/1.36 kg), boned, wing tips removed, skin removed intact

1 lb/454 g pork butt, cut into 1-in/3-cm cubes and chilled

6 fl oz/180 mL Madeira

4 oz/113 g fresh ham or cooked tongue, cut into ¼-in/6-mm cubes

3 tbsp/16 g black truffles, chopped

4 oz/113 g pistachio halves, blanched

Chicken Stock (page 529), as needed

1. Prepare the panada: Mix the eggs, brandy, pâté spice, flour, salt, and pepper.

2. Temper the egg mixture with the hot cream. Add the cream to the egg mixture and cook over low heat until thickened.

3. Weigh the leg and thigh meat from the chicken. Add an equal amount of pork butt, or enough for approximately 2 lb/907 g meat. Grind the chicken leg and thigh meat and pork twice, using the fine plate (⅛ in/3 mm) of a meat grinder. Keep the breast of the chicken in large pieces as you bone out the bird. Butterfly or slice the breast meat.

4. Pound the chicken breast to a thickness of ⅛ in/3 mm, place it on a sheet pan lined with plastic wrap, cover with plastic wrap, and reserve under refrigeration.

5. Cut the chicken tenderloin into ½- to ¾-in/1- to 2-cm cubes. Season to taste. Marinate the breast meat in the Madeira under refrigeration for at least 3 hours.

6. Drain the chicken breast, reserving the Madeira. Add the Madeira and panada to the ground meat mixture. Blend well.

7. Fold in the ham, truffles, and pistachios. Mix well.

8. Lay out the reserved skin on plastic wrap and place the pounded chicken breast on top. Add the forcemeat and roll the galantine securely.

9. Poach the galantine in enough stock to cover at 170°F/77°C to an internal temperature of 165°F/74°C, 60 to 70 minutes.

10. Transfer the galantine and the poaching liquid to a storage container. Let it cool at room temperature. Remove the galantine from the stock and wrap it in new cheesecloth to firm its texture; chill at least 12 hours. To serve the galantine, unwrap and slice it.

Roasted Asian Duck Galantine

YIELD: 2 LB/907 G GALANTINE; 10 TO 12 SERVINGS

1 duck (4 to 5 lb/1.81 to 2.27 kg)

16 fl oz/480 mL Basic Poultry Brine (page 202)

MARINADE

2 shallots, minced, sautéed, and cooled

3 garlic cloves, minced

2 tsp/6 g minced ginger

½ fl oz/15 mL vegetable oil

6 oz/170 g lean pork butt, cubed

6 oz/170 g fatback, cubed

½ fl oz/15 mL oyster sauce

½ fl oz/15 mL soy sauce

2 tsp/10 mL sesame oil

1 tbsp/3 g minced thyme

1 tbsp/3 g minced cilantro

1 jalapeño, stemmed, seeded, and finely chopped

½ tsp/1 g Chinese Five-Spice Powder (page 523)

1 oz/28 g honey

¼ tsp/0.75 g tinted curing mix (TCM)

6 shiitake mushrooms, stems removed, finely diced

4 oz/113 g finely diced carrots, fully cooked

3 green onions, minced

2 tsp/9.50 g powdered gelatin

1. Remove the skin from the duck in one piece, starting from the back. Debone the duck; reserve legs for forcemeat and breast for garnish. Square off the ends of the breasts and add the pieces of trim to the forcemeat.

2. Cover the duck breasts with the brine; cure under refrigeration for 4 hours.

3. Lay the skin out on a sheet pan lined with plastic wrap and freeze. When the skin is frozen, remove all the excess fat using a chef's knife in a scraping motion.

4. Sweat the shallots, garlic, and ginger in the vegetable oil and cool. Combine this mixture with the duck leg and thigh meat, the trim from the breasts, and the pork, fatback, oyster sauce, soy sauce, sesame oil, thyme, cilantro, jalapeño, five-spice powder, honey, and TCM; marinate for 1 hour.

5. Grind the meat through the medium plate (¼ in/6 mm) of a meat grinder. Chill, if necessary, before grinding through the fine plate (⅛ in/3 mm).

6. Transfer the ground meats to a chilled mixing bowl. Mix on medium speed for 1 minute, until homogeneous. Test and adjust the forcemeat if necessary before proceeding.

7. Toss the mushrooms, carrots, and green onions with the gelatin. Fold the vegetables into the forcemeat, working over an ice bath.

8. Place the duck skin on a large piece of aluminum foil. Pipe the forcemeat onto the skin and smooth with a palette knife. Place the breasts in the middle and roll into a galantine. Wrap the galantine in foil, forming a roulade.

9. Place the galantine on a sheet pan and roast in a 300°F/149°C oven to an internal temperature of 165°F/74°C, 50 to 60 minutes. To serve the galantine, unwrap and slice.

Foie Gras Mousse

1 lb 8 oz/680 g quality foie gras, cleaned and veins removed

2 tsp/10 g salt

½ tsp/0.50 g ground white pepper

2 fl oz/60 mL Sauternes

2 oz/57 g minced shallots

1 garlic clove, minced

4 oz/113 g butter

6 fl oz/180 mL heavy cream, whipped to medium peaks

1. Marinate the foie gras in the salt, pepper, and Sauternes overnight.

2. Drain the foie gras and cut it into 1-in/3-cm chunks.

3. Sauté the shallots and garlic in the butter until soft; do not brown. Add the foie gras and cook over high heat, stirring continuously, until the foie gras is cooked through, 4 to 5 minutes.

4. Cool the mixture to 90°F/32°C and purée in a food processor. Pass this mixture through a drum sieve into a 32-fl-oz/1.92-L bowl set over an ice bath. Stir the mixture continuously until it begins to thicken. Fold the whipped cream into the mixture and adjust seasoning.

5. Line a 2-lb/907-g terrine mold with plastic wrap, leaving an overhang. Fill with the foie gras mousse and smooth the top. Chill overnight before serving. Wrap and refrigerate for up to 3 days.

PRESENTATION IDEAS: Foie gras mousse is best enjoyed on simple toasted croutons, but it can be used to embellish other hors d'oeuvre—for example, to fill prunes soaked in Armangac.

Foie Gras Terrine

YIELD: 2 LB/907 G TERRINE; 10 TO 12 SERVINGS

Foie gras terrines are traditionally served directly in the mold used to prepare them. A layer of fat is allowed to remain in place, acting as a protective barrier to slow down the deterioration that occurs when the terrine is exposed to air, moisture, and flavor transfers from strongly flavored foods such as cheeses, certain fruits, or vegetables. Alternative presentation methods can, of course, be used.

2 lb 12 oz/1.25 kg foie gras, grade A

1¼ oz/35 g salt, or as needed

2 tsp/4 g ground white pepper, or as needed

1 tbsp/15 g sugar

¼ tsp/0.75 g tinted curing mix (TCM)

16 fl oz/480 mL white port

Assembling a terrine. **A.** Pack the foie gras into the plastic wrap–lined terrine mold. **B.** The excess fat is poured off. **C.** The terrine will be ready to unmold after 24 to 48 hours. **D.** Pull the plastic wrap off the unmolded terrine. **E.** Leave the plastic wrap on to help keep slices as neat as possible.

1. Clean the livers, remove all veins, and dry well. Combine 1 oz/28 g of the salt, 1 tsp/2 g of the pepper, the sugar, TCM, and port and marinate the livers in the mixture overnight under refrigeration.

2. Line a 2-lb/907-g terrine mold with plastic wrap.

3. Remove the marinated foie gras from the refrigerator, place it on a cutting board, and slice it into large pieces that will fit snugly into the mold. Place them in the mold so that their smooth sides form the exterior of the terrine; season as needed with the remaining salt and pepper. Fill the mold up to the inner lip and press the pieces down tightly to remove any air pockets. Cover the terrine mold.

4. Poach the terrine in a hot water bath, maintaining it at a constant 160°F/71°C, for 45 to 50 minutes. The oven temperature may need to be adjusted to keep the water at a constant temperature. If it gets too hot, add cold water immediately to lower the temperature. Foie gras has the best texture and flavor when cooked to an internal temperature of 118°F. (Be sure to check with your local and state health authorities, however.)

5. Remove the terrine from the water bath and rest for 2 hours at room temperature, then pour off the fat. Cover the terrine with a press plate and top with a 1- to 2-lb/454- to 907-g weight. Let the terrine rest under refrigeration for at least 24 hours and up to 48 hours to mellow and mature.

6. Remove the plastic wrap and carefully remove the congealed fat. Tightly rewrap in fresh plastic wrap. Refrigerate the terrine until ready to slice and serve, up to 3 days.

PRESENTATION IDEAS: Foie gras terrines may be sliced for plated presentations, shaped into quenelles, or served directly in the terrine.

Take the time to select the most appropriate accompaniments. You may want to consult with your sommelier or make suggestions yourself to the dining room staff so they can help guests choose the most appropriate wine or other beverage with which to enjoy the terrine.

When you are ready to serve the terrine, remove the weight and carefully pull off the press plate. To neaten its appearance, smooth the top with a small knife and clean the edges of the terrine with a towel. You may wish to score the top of the terrine in a cross-hatch pattern if it is to be served directly in the terrine.

CHEF'S NOTES: To determine the amount of foie gras needed to fill any size mold, simply measure the volume of water the terrine can hold. The number of ounces in volume will equal the number of ounces in weight of foie gras necessary to fill the mold.

For easier service, slice the terrine with the plastic wrap intact. Remove the plastic after the slices are plated. A warm, beveled knife works best. Save any fat removed in Step 5 to use to sauté vegetables or potatoes.

FOIE GRAS ROULADE: Prepare the foie gras as directed for the terrine. Arrange the marinated foie gras on a large sheet of plastic wrap; wrap tightly around the foie gras to form a roulade. If desired, insert whole truffles into the foie gras lobes before rolling the roulade. Poach in a 160°F/71°C water bath to an internal temperature of 118°F/48°C. Remove from the water, cool, and rewrap. Let the roulade rest under refrigeration for at least 24 hours before slicing. This roulade may also be baked in brioche (see page 542) and served as an appetizer.

Chicken Liver Pâté

YIELD: 2 LB/907 G TERRINE; 18 TO 20 SERVINGS

1 lb 8 oz/680 g chicken livers, cleaned, sinew removed

16 fl oz/480 mL milk, or as needed for soaking

¼ tsp/0.75 g tinted curing mix (TCM)

1 oz/28 g salt

2 oz/57 g minced shallots

2 garlic cloves, minced

8 oz/227 g fresh fatback, cut into medium dice

1 tsp/2 g ground white pepper

½ tsp/1 g ground allspice

½ tsp/1 g dry mustard

1⅓ oz/37 g fresh white bread crumbs

1 fl oz/30 mL sherry

3 oz/85 g bread flour, unsifted

2 tsp/9.50 g powdered gelatin

3 eggs

6 fl oz/180 mL heavy cream

1. Soak the chicken livers in the milk with 1½ tsp/7.50 g of the salt and the TCM for 12 to 24 hours. When ready to use, drain well and pat dry with paper towels.

2. Place the livers, the remaining salt, the shallots, garlic, fatback, pepper, allspice, mustard, bread crumbs, sherry, flour, gelatin, and eggs in a blender. Purée to a smooth, loose paste.

3. Pass the purée through a fine-mesh strainer into a stainless-steel bowl. Stir in the cream. Let the mixture rest under refrigeration for 2 hours.

4. Pour the mixture into a terrine mold lined with plastic wrap, cover, and poach in a 170°F/77°C water bath in a 300°F/149°C oven to an internal temperature of 165°F/74°C, 45 minutes to 1 hour. Remove from the oven and let the terrine cool at room temperature for 30 minutes.

5. Press with a 1-lb/454-g weight and refrigerate overnight before unmolding and slicing.

SMOKED CHICKEN LIVER PÂTÉ: Cut 8 oz/227 g of the livers into medium dice and pan-smoke (see page 190) for a flavorful contrasting garnish. For even more flavor, line the terrine with sliced ham.

Duck Liver Terrine

YIELD: 2 LB/907 G TERRINE; 18 TO 20 SERVINGS

The next best thing to foie gras! This recipe combines the richness of butter with the flavor of duck livers in proportions that create a wonderful, smooth, rich terrine.

1 lb 4 oz/567 g duck livers, cleaned, soaked in milk overnight, and dried

2 fl oz/60 mL Madeira

1½ oz/43 g minced shallots, sautéed and cooled

1 tsp/5 g salt

¼ tsp/0.50 g ground white pepper

⅛ tsp/0.33 g tinted curing mix (TCM)

10 fl oz/300 mL heavy cream

BEURRE MANIÉ

1 lb/454 g butter, softened

1 oz/28 g flour, sifted

2 eggs, beaten

1. Combine the livers, Madeira, shallots, salt, pepper, and TCM. Grind through the fine plate (⅛ in/3 mm) of a meat grinder into a chilled bowl.

2. Reduce the cream by half and keep warm.

3. Knead the butter and flour together to make a beurre manié.

4. Transfer the liver mixture to a food processor and process until smooth. Add the eggs and blend to incorporate.

5. With the motor running, carefully add the beurre manié to the liver mixture, a little at a time, until completely incorporated. Scrape down the sides of the processor.

6. Add the warm cream to the liver mixture and combine until homogeneous. (It will look very grainy.) Pass the forcemeat through a fine drum sieve. Test and adjust the forcemeat if necessary before proceeding.

7. Oil a 2-lb/907-g terrine mold and line it with plastic wrap. Pour the forcemeat into the lined mold and tap the mold on a table to remove any air pockets. Fold the liner over the forcemeat to completely encase the terrine; cover.

8. Poach the terrine in a 170°F/77°C water bath in a 300°F/149°C oven to an internal temperature of 165°F/74°C, 60 to 75 minutes.

9. Remove the terrine from the water bath and allow it to chill at least overnight or up to 3 days under refrigeration, weighted with a 2-lb/907-g press plate, if desired. Slice and serve immediately, or wrap and refrigerate for up to 7 days.

CHEF'S NOTES: If desired, line the mold with fatback, prosciutto, or ham before filling with forcemeat. An internal garnish of diced truffles or truffle peelings may be folded into the forcemeat before baking.

CHEESE

Wines, sausages, dried foods, and cheeses are all the fruits of preservation practices known to ancient humankind, then refined, recorded, and evolved over time. We know that cheeses were enjoyed by the ancient Sumerians, whose writings about many aspects of daily life are believed to date from 3000 B.C.E. Early records of cheese have been found on earthenware vessels from Egyptian tombs dating as far back as 2300 B.C.E. The Bible includes numerous references to cheese, beginning with Genesis. Later in the Bible, David is said to have carried ten cheeses to the troops just before slaying the giant Goliath.

eight

The Romans were the first to mass-produce cheese to be carried on long journeys and used by their armies as a convenient form of concentrated nutrition. They carried their formulas into conquered lands as their empire expanded, marrying them with indigenous cheeses. During the period of European history known as the Dark Ages, the traditions of cheese making were preserved and refined by religious houses and monasteries, as were the traditions of wine and spirit making. Some religious orders are still creating handmade cheeses using the same original formulas and methods.

Until the early to mid-1800s, cheese production was continued on an individual home or cottage level by families who were fortunate enough to own sheep, goats, and cows. As farms grew in size and were able to supply communities with agricultural products, so the cheese business grew as well, although the cheese-making process continued to be both painstaking and time-consuming.

This chapter explores the basic cheese-making process in order to provide a better understanding of the special characteristics of cheeses and why some are so highly prized. It also discusses the basic cheese categories—fresh, rind-ripened, semisoft, blue, pasta filata, hard, and very hard—and the basic principles used to select cheeses for a cheese course offered on the menu, a cheese platter or tray for buffets, or a cheese cart for the dining room.

Fresh cheeses can be produced with relatively little in the way of special equipment. These can easily become a signature piece in an appetizer, salad, sandwich, entrée, or dessert item. Mozzarella, mascarpone, ricotta, and other cultured dairy items such as crème fraîche and yogurt are among the recipes and techniques included in this chapter.

Cheese Making

The techniques used today to produce cheese have changed little since the times of the Romans and the medieval monasteries, but scientific discoveries have led to better control of the natural processes involved in cheese making: acidification and coagulation of the milk, salting, cutting and draining the curds, shaping the cheese, and, finally, ripening.

In the nineteenth century, scientists were able to identify the many bacteria present in the milk, the air, and the caves used for ripening. Bacteria that interfered with the process could be eliminated, and the strains that contribute to the desirable character of individual cheeses could be cultivated and standardized. By the turn of the century, "pure cultures" were made available and allowed for more uniform results from cheese maker to cheese maker when producing cheese within a single variety.

In 1851, the first real cheese factory in America was established in Rome, New York, by Jesse Williams. It was obvious that the market for cheese was ready, because within the next fifteen years five hundred more of these operations were established in New York alone. In 1990, over eight billion pounds of cheese and cheese-related products were produced in the United States, and today, the United States is the largest producer of cheese as well as the largest importer.

Increasing renown is being accorded to today's high-quality handcrafted cheeses. These artisanal cheeses are being produced all over the country, on the same small scale and with the same high standards of years ago. Familiar varieties as well as brand-new cheeses are becoming available on the local level, making the opportunity for the garde manger to feature excellent and unusual cheeses constant.

What is cheese?

Cheese is defined as a food product made from the pressed curd of milk. Like wine, cheese is thought of as a living food because of the "friendly" living bacteria that are continually changing it. You may hear cheeses referred to as "natural" to distinguish them from highly processed cheeses that are not expected to ripen.

It is believed that sheep's and goat's milk were first used to make cheese, as these were probably the first domesticated animals appropriate for milking. Today, cow's milk is the base for many cheeses, followed by goat's and then sheep's milk. The milk of water buffalo, yak, camel, llama, and mare are also used to create the special cheeses of the societies where these animals were domesticated.

The Cheese-Making Process

For the most part, the only changes in cheese making since the early days have been in understanding how to control the complicated interaction of the biological agents and processes involved. The basic stages in the modern production are:

- THE PRETREATMENT OF MILK, homogenizing, pasteurizing, or heating

- THE ACIDIFICATION OF MILK, to change its pH level

- SALTING THE CURDS

- COAGULATING (CURDLING) THE MILK to create curds

- SEPARATING THE CURDS AND WHEY

- SHAPING, CUTTING, OR MOLDING THE CURDS into their appropriate shapes

- RIPENING

Considering how few ingredients are needed to make cheese, there is astonishing variety in the types that can be produced. Hundreds of distinct cheeses can be made by introducing only slight modifications: Choosing sheep's milk instead of cow's milk, using a different starter culture, draining the cheese a little more or less, cutting the curds very fine or leaving them whole or in slabs, rubbing the cheese with salt at a different point in the process, and shaping it into a disk, a wheel, or a round will produce different cheeses, with unique textures, flavors, and aromas.

Different steps applied during the ripening process can play a critical role as well; the rind may be washed with a brine or coated with wax, additional molds or cultures can be introduced directly to the cheese or applied to the surface, and so forth.

Milk

The type of milk the cheese maker chooses is critical to the development of the cheese. Not only are there milks of different animals, there are also various ways to collect, combine, and treat them. One famous cheese, Parmigiano-Reggiano, for instance, traditionally is made by combining the richer milk collected in the evening with the leaner milk of the next day's first milking.

In large-scale cheese production, milk is routinely handled as follows: It is tested for quality, pasteurized, and homogenized, and the milkfat content is standardized. Although cheeses aged more than sixty days may be made from raw milk, the majority of cheeses in the United States are produced from pasteurized milk.

Pasteurization is the process by which a liquid, in this case milk, is heated to a particular temperature and held there for a specific period to destroy naturally occurring bacteria. This landmark discovery in food safety came at a price for cheese makers. The down side is twofold. First, the process destroys not only pathogens but also the "friendly" bacteria, which are not only safe but also play an important role in producing cheeses. Second, heating the milk gives it a cooked flavor.

The importance of food safety outranks the changes to the flavor and quality of the cheese, however, and cheese makers have worked to compensate for the loss of naturally present bacteria and changes in flavor.

Acidification

The serious business of cheese making gets underway when the milk is acidified, or soured. The milk is heated to a specific temperature, and a starter is added that contains either an acid or an organism that produces lactic acid.

To produce many of the soft fresh cheeses featured in this chapter, lemon juice, vinegar, or citric or tartaric acid—the acid starters—can be used. Mozzarella and provolone (of the pasta filata type) as well as most ripened cheeses are produced by souring the milk with a culture composed of a lactic acid–producing organism—the enzyme starters. Acid development is critical to controlling the growth of undesirable organisms and the rate of coagulation.

The starter is added at a ratio that will produce the appropriate level of acid. If there is too much acid, the curd may take several days to release the whey. If there is too little, a seemingly dry cheese may begin to leak whey several weeks after it has been shaped and pressed.

Salting

Salt may be added at various points in the cheese-making process. It may be stirred into the milk along with the starter or shortly afterward. Coarse salt may be spread over the surface of the curd, or the cut and drained curd may be submerged in or rubbed with a salt brine.

Salt is important to cheese making in a number of ways. In addition to adding its own flavor, salt affects the cheese's flavor because of its role in controlling fermentation. The quantity of carbon dioxide and alcohol released as a by-product of this bacterial activity gives each cheese its unique flavor. Salt limits spoilage by creating an inhospitable environment for the organisms that cause it. Salt also affects the finished texture of the cheese by acting to dry it. The drier the cheese, the longer its useful life. Very dry grating cheeses, such as Pecorino Romano, are so salty they can be used as a substitute for some of the salt in a dish.

Coagulating (curdling) the milk

Acid starters will change the milk rapidly, souring the milk as well as forming curds. The effect of any acid on a protein is to tighten it. This is the basic action in curdling milk. Enzyme starters, including rennet, result in a sweeter curd. The action of the so-called friendly bacteria (either in the milk or in the starter) produces lactic acid, resulting in a sweeter-tasting curd, as less overall acid is required.

Rennet was originally obtained from the fourth stomach of young ruminant animals such as cows, sheep, and goats. It can also be derived from certain plants. Today both animal- and plant-based forms are available, as well as a genetically engineered substitute called *chymosin*.

Separating the curds and whey

8-1. Fresh Lemon Cheese (page 348).

When the milk coagulates, it generally forms a soft mass of curd that must be broken up to allow the noncoagulated portion of the milk, known as the *whey*, to drain off. Figure 8-1 shows fresh lemon cheese being hung to drain. If the curd is cut only a little, you can create soft, creamy cheeses. When the curd is cut quite small, more of the whey drains away, and the cheese will have a drier texture. For some very dry cheeses, the curds and whey are even cooked to further shrink the curds and allow even more moisture to escape.

Shaping

There are a number of methods for draining and shaping cheeses, each specified both by tradition and by the role it plays in producing the desired flavor and texture in the finished cheese. After the curds are drained of the freed whey, some are placed in cheesecloth bags, baskets, or molds and set on racks or hung and allowed to drain and dry for the prescribed time. For fresh and soft cheeses, draining and shaping is accomplished simultaneously. Some cheeses—notably Cheddars—are shaped into thick slabs and then stacked so that the weight of the cheese itself presses out the whey.

Ripening

The last stage of cheese making is ripening, also known as *aging* or *curing*. This is where the magic of flavor development takes place. The ripening process may take anywhere from thirty days to several years, depending on the cheese being made. During that time, the cheese undergoes changes that affect its flavor, body, texture, and, occasionally, its color. What began as rubbery fresh cheese curd is transformed into smooth and mellow ripened cheese.

Originally, cheeses were aged in caves, where conditions were perfect for ripening. Today, most cheeses are aged in temperature- and humidity-controlled environments that simulate caves.

Cheeses may be ripened in leaves, ashes, wax rinds, or with no rind at all. Some are rubbed or washed, and some are simply left to cure naturally. In some cases, holes are made in the cheeses to allow gases produced by bacteria to escape; in others, the gases are confined deliberately to form holes ranging in size from tiny to the size of a quarter, as in Swiss cheese. Special additional bacteria cultures or molds are introduced in many cheeses by injecting, spraying, or washing them. Once these steps are done, the rest of the work is left to nature.

Cheese Classifications

The many cheeses available today can be categorized in several ways. Milk type, country of origin, region, handling, aging, and texture are some of the classification strategies that are used. Although most experts agree that none of these classifications is completely adequate, so far no one has been able to come up with one that really covers all the variables. Even when two experts agree on which method to use, they do not necessarily agree on which cheeses fall into which categories.

For the sake of discussion, this section presents several broad groups of cheese that have been loosely categorized according to texture.

Soft fresh cheeses

Soft fresh cheeses are those that are unripened and generally have a fresh, clean, creamy flavor. These cheeses are typically the most perishable and are sometimes held in brines. Examples of soft fresh cheeses are cottage cheese, pot cheese, queso blanco, and cream cheese.

Ricotta cheese, made by recooking whey, actually began in Italy as a by-product of the cheese-making industry. (The name literally means "recook.") When whey is heated, the proteins fuse together and create a new curd that, when drained, becomes a snowy white ricotta high in moisture and naturally low in fat. It is commonly used in Italian cooking as a filling for pastas or as a base for cheese-cakes. Today, some ricottas are made with added part-skim or whole milk for a richer flavor.

Mascarpone is a fresh cheese made by curdling heavy cream with citric acid. The process releases excess moisture and yields a rich, creamy cheese that is mildly acidic and adapts to both sweet and savory preparations. One of the most famous uses of mascarpone is in the dessert tiramisù, in which the rich cheese is layered with sponge cake or ladyfingers that have been dipped in espresso and Marsala wine. Savory mascarpone dishes such as dips and spreads may also include herbs and spices.

In the United States, fresh goat's milk cheeses have become popular of late and are being produced in many parts of the country. They can be found in a variety of shapes and may be coated in herbs or edible ash.

Soft ripened cheeses

Soft ripened cheeses are those that typically have been sprayed or dusted with a mold and allowed to ripen. The two most popular varieties are probably Brie and Camembert. Neither name is protected by law, so both have been counterfeited in many places, with vast differences in quality.

8-2. Cheese Classifications.

A. Soft ripened cheeses, from left to right: Brie, Camembert, Pyramids.
B. Semisoft cheeses, from left to right: Edam, Fontina, Port-Salut. **C. Blue-veined cheeses,** from left to right: Maytag blue, Roquefort, Stilton, Gorgonzola. **D. Pasta filata:** Shaping mozzarella curd into balls. **E. Hard cheeses,** from left to right: Cheddar, Emmentaler, Manchego. **F. Very hard cheeses,** from left to right: Romano, Parmigiano, dry Jack, aged goat's milk cheese logs.

Soft ripened cheeses (see Figure 8-2A) are available in varying degrees of richness. For example, single, double, and triple cream cheeses have 50, 60, and 70 percent butterfat, respectively.

Soft ripened cheeses should be eaten only when properly ripened. An underripe cheese is firm and chalky, an overripe cheese runs when cut, and a cheese ready for eating will bulge when cut and barely hold its shape. Soft ripened cheeses will ripen only until they are cut into. After that they begin to dry and deteriorate. To check for ripeness before cutting, press firmly but gently in the middle of the cheese. It should have some feel of softness to the center. An overripe cheese can be identified by an ammonia odor.

Soft ripened cheeses can be served at room temperature as a dessert cheese or as an appetizer. For those who are not purists, they can also be served warm by baking them in a crust of flaky dough or toasted almonds. It still remains a matter of taste as to whether soft ripened cheeses should be eaten with the rind. Even the experts don't agree on that age-old discussion, so the choice should be left to the individual.

Semisoft cheeses

Semisoft cheeses include a wide variety ranging from mild and buttery to pungent and aromatic (see Figure 8-2B). They are allowed to ripen in several ways.

RIND-RIPENED CHEESES Wash-rind cheeses are periodically washed with brine, beer, cider, wine, brandy, or oils during the ripening period. This remoistening encourages bacterial growth, sometimes known as a *smear,* which allows the cheese to be ripened from the outside in. Popular examples of this type include Limburger and its famous American counterpart, Liederkranz, both of which are intensely pungent, as well as Muenster, Saint Paulin, and Port-Salut.

DRY-RIND CHEESES Dry-rind cheeses are those that are allowed to form a natural rind during ripening. Bel Paese ("beautiful country") is a cheese of Italian origin that has become quite popular since it was first made in 1929. Its soft texture and very mild flavor contribute to its popularity. Havarti, another popular dry-rind cheese, has a buttery flavor that is often enhanced with herbs or spices such as dill, caraway, and basil.

WAXED-RIND CHEESES Gouda and Edam are semisoft cheeses that are sealed in wax prior to aging. These cheeses, which get their names from two towns in Holland, have been made for eight hundred years. Gouda is made from whole milk and tends to be softer and richer than Edam, which is made from part-skim milk and is firmer in texture. These cheeses may be either flavored or smoked, and are available in mild and aged varieties.

Blue-veined cheeses

Blue or blue-veined cheeses are thought to have been among some of the first cheeses produced. Although no specific research has proved the theory, it is believed that the mold was first introduced to cheese from moldy bread that had come in contact with it.

In the modern production of blue cheeses, needles are used to form holes that allow gases to escape and oxygen to enter to support mold growth within the cheese. The cheese is then salted or brined and allowed to ripen in caves or under cavelike conditions. Some of the most famous blue cheeses are the French Roquefort, Italian Gorgonzola, English Stilton, and American Maytag blue (see Figure 8-2C).

Roquefort, made strictly from raw sheep's milk, has been made since ancient times in the Rouergue area of southern France. The Roquefort Association, Inc., ensures that quality standards and name integrity are protected. Today the cheeses are still ripened in the caves of Cambalou for three months to develop their unique character. They may be eaten after the initial ripening but are more typically stored for an additional three to twelve months, as the market allows.

One of the factors that makes Roquefort unique is that the mold is not grown in a laboratory, as are molds for many other blue cheeses. Instead, Roquefort mold is developed naturally from rye bread. Roquefort should therefore be highlighted for what it is, and when used in dips or dressings should be clearly identified on the menu.

Gorgonzola is another special blue cheese. Unlike Roquefort, Gorgonzola is made from cow's milk, and its mold is from a completely different strain, which is now commercially produced. Gorgonzola is made with evening milk and the following day's morning milk. Two varieties are available: sweet, which is aged three months, and naturale, which is aged longer and has a fuller, more robust flavor.

Pasta filata cheeses

Pasta filata literally means "spun curds" or "spun paste." During manufacture, the curds are dipped into hot water and then stretched or spun until the proper consistency and texture is achieved. They are then kneaded and molded into the desired shapes. Pasta filata cheeses are related by the process used in their manufacture rather than by their textures. In fact, the textures of pasta filata cheeses run the gamut from soft to hard, depending on how they are aged, if at all.

The most common cheese in this category is mozzarella. In 1990, more than 1.5 billion pounds of mozzarella were produced in the United States alone. Today, two types of mozzarella are available: the traditional fresh style, which is available in a variety of shapes and sizes, and the newer American invention of low-moisture mozzarella, which has a longer shelf life than the fresh style. Both whole milk and part-skim varieties are available. The recipe for fresh mozzarella appears on page 352 (see Figure 8-2D).

Provolone is another popular pasta filata cheese that is similarly handled, but it is made with a different culture. Once the curd is stretched and kneaded, it is rubbed with brine and tied into shape. It is then hung and left to dry in pieces ranging from 8¾ oz to 200 lb/248 g to 90.72 kg. Provolone is often smoked and/or aged for additional character and firmer texture.

Hard cheeses

Hard cheeses are produced throughout the world (see Figure 8-2E). Cheddars and Swiss-style cheeses are among the best known.

Originating in England, Cheddar has become the most popular hard cheese in the United States. The Pilgrims brought Cheddar formulas to the United States, and by 1790 it was produced in such quantities that it was exported back to England. Cheddar derives its name from the process used in its manufacture. The cheddaring process involves turning and stacking the slabs of young cheese to extract more whey and give the cheese its characteristic texture. The yellow color of some Cheddars is achieved through the addition of annatto seed paste and has nothing to do with the flavor.

Once the cheddaring process is complete, the cheeses are wrapped in cheese-cloth dipped in wax and allowed to ripen. Cheddars are categorized by age. Current Cheddar is aged for thirty days, mild for one to three months, medium for three to six months, sharp for six to nine months, and extra-sharp for nine months to five years.

Many cheeses that originated in the United States are produced using the cheddaring method. American cheese is said to have gotten its name after the American Revolution, when the proud producers of Cheddar in the United States did not want their cheeses to be mistaken for anything that might have originated in England and aptly labeled them *American cheese.*

Colby, another truly American cheese, was invented in the town of Colby, Wisconsin, in 1874. When Colby slabs are cut in half, they are popularly known as *longhorns.*

Monterey Jack is also an American original produced in the style of Cheddar. It was first made by David Jacks in Monterey, California, in 1849, and it remains popular to this day. Aged Monterey Jack cheese, known as *dry Jack,* makes an excellent grating cheese.

The family of cheeses generically referred to as *Swiss* are also hard cheeses. These are characterized by holes, sometimes called *eyes,* that range in size from tiny to the size of a quarter. Swiss cheeses are often mellow in flavor and have excellent melting properties. Some of the better known varieties of Swiss cheese are Gruyère, Emmentaler, Beaufort, and Jarlsberg.

Very hard cheeses

In Italy, these cheeses are known as the *granas,* or grainy cheeses, because of their granular texture (clearly visible in the cheeses shown in Figure 8-2F). The most popular are Parmesan and Romano; these are both now produced in the United States and South America, but in versions different from their Italian predecessors. Very hard cheeses are most often grated or shaved, but they are also traditionally eaten in chunks broken off with a special knife.

True Parmigiano-Reggiano is often called the king of cheeses. It is believed that the formula for this cheese has not changed in more than seven hundred years, and its origins date back even further. This legendary cheese is made slowly and carefully, following strict guidelines that require it to be aged a minimum of fourteen months, although most are aged for twenty-four months. Stravecchio, or extra-aged, is ripened for as much as three years.

The flavor of Parmigiano-Reggiano is complex and unique. Steven Jenkins, author of *The Cheese Primer,* describes it as "spicy like cinnamon or nutmeg; salty like liquor accompanying an oyster; sweet like ginger cookies; and nutty like black walnuts—all at the same time."

Romano cheeses—named for the city of Rome—come in several varieties. Pecorino Romano, which is made with sheep's milk, is probably the best known. Caprino Romano is a very sharp goat's milk version, and Vacchino Romano is a mild version made from cow's milk.

Cheese Service

Selecting the cheese

A variety of approaches may be taken when developing a cheese board. Cheeses should be selected based on color, shape, texture, richness, and intensity. A modest selection might simply include a single cheese of the best quality from the soft, blue, and hard categories. More extensive selections build their offerings by expanding selections within categories and developing a special selection to feature local or regional favorites.

Cheese plates, boards, or carts often contain a variety of cheeses, but sometimes it is interesting to compose a board that features only one type of milk, sometimes referred to as a *flight of cheeses,* in the same way that a flight of Chardonnays or Pinot Noirs might be offered. A sheep's milk cheese board, for instance, gives the guest a chance to taste and compare a variety of cheeses made from the same main ingredient. This is an opportunity many people have never had but would probably be interested in taking.

Presenting the cheese

Cheeses should be allowed to come to room temperature before they are served. This process, known as *aromatization,* brings out the fullest flavor of the cheese, so all its nuances can be enjoyed.

STYLES OF PRESENTATION Cheeses may be served as a course in and of themselves, often preceding, or in place of dessert. In à la carte service, some restaurants present their customers with a cheese cart from which they may sample a variety of cheeses. The customer chooses which he or she would like to try, and the server then prepares a plate tableside consisting of the desired cheeses, bread or crackers, and, occasionally, some fruit.

On a buffet, cheese boards are eye-catching items that have always been popular. The board itself can be as simple as a piece of wood, reserved strictly for cheese board service, that has been decoratively lined with clean, nontoxic leaves. More common, however, are service platters, mirrors, and marble.

PARTNERS AND ACCOMPANIMENTS FOR CHEESE Three types of foods have a natural affinity for cheese: wine or beer, bread and crackers, and fruit. Bread is probably the original accompaniment. The combination provided portable sustenance for the traveler and a convenient meal for others.

Wine, particularly tannic wine, offers a perfect contrast to the richness of cheese. The wine's acidity cuts through the cheese's butterfat. Beer, on the other hand, works well to contrast the salt component of cheese, making it an ideal accompaniment.

The sweet juiciness of many fruits also pairs well with the earthy richness of cheeses. Classic examples include apples with Cheddar and pear with blue cheese.

Because cheese is a living food with active biological attributes, it is critical to maintain the highest standards in sanitation during handling. Cheese may be a potentially hazardous food, if handled improperly.

When handling cheese that is not going to be cooked, it is important to either use utensils or wear food-service gloves to prevent the contamination of the cheese with bacteria from your hands and the formation of unsightly fingerprints on the cheese. All food contact areas should be cleaned and sanitized properly with hot, soapy water and sanitizing solution to prevent cross contamination. All cheese-cutting equipment should be similarly sanitized.

If cheeses become unnaturally moldy, they may be trimmed by cutting ½ to 1 in/1 to 3 cm past the mold. Care should be taken not to transfer the mold from the bad spot to the good portion.

Cheeses should never be allowed to sit out at room temperature for periods beyond the time required to aromatize the cheeses. Always keep cheeses and cheese preparations properly covered and refrigerated.

Making Cheese in the Kitchen

Cheese making, especially for the fresh cheeses in the following recipes, is a practical and reasonable way to expand the range of handcrafted specialty items you can offer your guests. The raw ingredients can be obtained easily, and most of the necessary equipment is already part of a standard kitchen setup. Because cheese making involves acid, the equipment should be made of or lined with nonreactive materials such as stainless steel, enamel, or food-grade plastic. All equipment should be thoroughly sterilized before use.

- Whole milk, heavy cream, and half-and-half are used to prepare the fresh cheeses here. You can often substitute (in whole or in part) lower-fat milk for whole milk or heavy cream for half-and-half, or substitute milk from sheep or goats. The milk should be pasteurized and homogenized to help yield consistent results.

- Fresh cheeses are most often curdled with an acid. Our recipes use cider vinegar, citric acid, tartaric acid, and lemon juice. Each acid has a particular effect on the finished cheese, and you may wish to experiment with different starters to find one that gives you the flavor you want.

- The curd for mozzarella is prepared with a rennet or other enzymatic starter. The curd can be purchased and used to prepare fresh mozzarella.

- Two of the recipes in this section call for direct-set cultures. These cultures start curdling the milk almost instantly, without requiring an extended incubation period.

Mascarpone

YIELD: 32 FL OZ/960 ML

This is a delicious, rich cheese with a very high fat content. It can be used as a base for sauces by sweetening or adding fruit purées, or it can be served as is to accompany fresh or poached fruits.

64 fl oz/1.92 L heavy cream   ½ tsp/2.50 mL tartaric acid

1. Heat the cream to 180°F/82°C, stirring often to prevent scorching. Remove from the heat. Add the tartaric acid and let the cream coagulate into a curd.

2. Drain the curd for at least 24 hours under refrigeration in a strainer lined with a coffee filter. The mascarpone is now ready to use. Alternatively, transfer to a storage container and hold, covered, under refrigeration for up to 1 week.

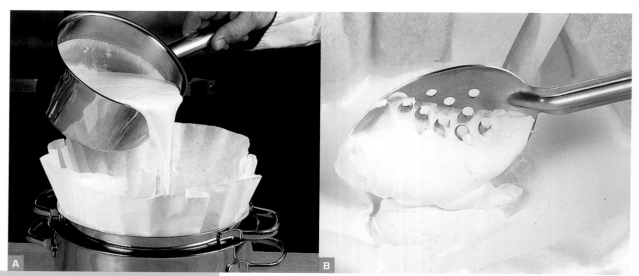

Making mascarpone. **A.** Drain the curdled cream in a lined colander. **B.** The finished consistency of fresh mascarpone.

Whole-Milk Ricotta Cheese

YIELD: 8 OZ/227 G

Although ricotta cheese is traditionally made by recooking the whey, it can also be made by substituting milk for some or all of the whey. This version calls for whole milk. If you prefer a lower-fat cheese, use skim milk for all or part of the whole milk.

1 tsp/5 mL citric acid

2 fl oz/60 mL water

1 gal/3.84 L whole milk

2 tsp/10 g salt

1. Dissolve the citric acid in the water.

2. Heat the milk, citric acid solution, and salt to 185°F/85°C, stirring often to prevent scorching. Skim away the scum as it rises to the surface.

3. When the milk reaches 185°F/85°C, remove from the heat and allow it to set for 10 minutes.

4. Drain the curd for at least 1 and up to 3 hours under refrigeration in a cheesecloth-lined colander or a cheesecloth or muslin bag set over a bowl.

5. The cheese is now ready to use. Alternatively, transfer to a storage container and hold, covered, under refrigeration for up to 1 week.

CHEF'S NOTES: If desired, substitute ½ fl oz/15 mL diluted liquid citric acid for the citric acid. If a creamier product is desired, add 2 fl oz/60 mL heavy cream to the curd.

Making ricotta. A. Skimming. B. Curd forming.

Lemon Cheese

YIELD: 3 LB/1.36 KG

This cheese has a pronounced lemon flavor. The texture is a bit drier and coarser than mascarpone, the result of using a slightly lower-fat dairy product, as well as the additional draining and pressing this cheese undergoes.

96 fl oz/2.88 L milk

32 fl oz/960 mL heavy cream

10 fl oz/300 mL lemon juice, strained and chilled

2 tsp/10 g salt

½ tsp/1.50 g grated lemon zest

1. Heat the milk and cream over simmering water to exactly 100°F/38°C (not higher).

2. Remove from the heat and add the lemon juice. Stir very gently and briefly until the mixture starts to curdle or thicken. Rest at room temperature for 3 to 4 hours.

3. Drain the curd for 8 to 12 hours under refrigeration in a cheesecloth-lined colander or a cheesecloth or muslin bag set over a bowl.

4. Transfer the cheese to a bowl and work in the salt and lemon zest with wooden spoons. Be careful not to overwork the cheese.

5. Press the cheese into a mold, top with a weight, and allow to rest overnight under refrigeration. The cheese is now ready to unmold and serve, or wrap and hold it under refrigeration for up to 4 days.

Making lemon cheese. **A.** Drape rinsed cheesecloth over a bowl and add the curdled milk and cream mixture. **B.** Tie cheesecloth into a bag; suspend cheese and allow to drain. **C.** Work in the salt. **D.** Pack the cheese into a mold.

PEPPERED LEMON CHEESE: Add ½ oz/14 g coarse-ground black pepper with the lemon zest in Step 4.

DRIED FRUIT AND HAZELNUT CHEESE: Replace the lemon zest with 3 oz/ 85 g each toasted hazelnuts and dried fruit.

Queso Blanco

YIELD: 4 LB/1.81 KG

Queso blanco is a white, slightly salty, fresh cheese featured in Mexican and other Latin American cuisines. Its texture is somewhat firm and crumbly, similar to that of farmer's cheese.

1 gal/3.84 L whole milk	2½ oz/71 g kosher salt
2 fl oz/60 mL cider vinegar	

1. Heat the milk to 185°F/85°C, stirring often to prevent scorching.

2. Add the vinegar and salt gradually, stirring constantly. Remove from the heat when the milk has solidified into a curd.

3. Drain the curd for at least 1 and up to 3 hours under refrigeration in a cheesecloth-lined colander or a cheesecloth or muslin bag set over a bowl.

4. The cheese is now ready to use, or transfer it to a storage container and hold, covered, under refrigeration for up to 1 week.

Herbed Yogurt Cheese

YIELD: 32 FL OZ/960 ML

Yogurt cheese can be made from low-fat or nonfat yogurt with good results. It can be used as a dip or a spread.

64 fl oz/1.92 L plain yogurt

⅔ oz/19 g salt

2½ tsp/5 g coarse-ground black pepper

1 tbsp/3 g chopped oregano

2 tsp/2 g chopped thyme

2 small chiles, split

2 bay leaves

16 fl oz/480 mL extra-virgin olive oil

1. Mix the yogurt, salt, and pepper and drain for 3 days under refrigeration in a cheesecloth-lined colander or a cheesecloth or muslin bag set over a bowl.

2. Divide the cheese into 2-oz/57-g portions and place them on parchment-lined trays. Allow to drain and dry overnight under refrigeration.

3. Combine the remaining ingredients for a marinade. Add the cheese and marinate 24 hours before serving. The cheese can be held in the marinade under refrigeration for up to 4 weeks.

Fromage Blanc

YIELD: 96 FL OZ/2.88 L

Fromage blanc (French for "white cheese") has the texture of cream cheese without the calories. It can be used to make dips and spreads for sandwiches and hors d'oeuvre. Fresh herbs, spices, and dried and fresh fruits and vegetables can be added to this cheese to give it additional flavor and texture.

1 gal/3.84 L whole milk

2 packets direct-set Fromage Blanc Starter Culture

1. Warm the milk to 72°F/22°C. Stir in the starter culture. Cover and allow to set (incubate) for 24 hours, or until a solid white curd forms.

2. Drain the curd for at least 3 and up to 6 hours under refrigeration in a cheesecloth-lined colander or a cheesecloth or muslin bag set over a bowl.

3. The cheese is now ready to use, or transfer it to a storage container and hold, covered, under refrigeration for up to 1 week.

CHEF'S NOTE: A shorter draining gives a spreadable consistency; longer draining yields a cream cheese consistency.

Crème Fraîche

YIELD: 24 to 32 FL OZ/720 TO 960 ML

Crème fraîche is made by fermenting heavy cream—with a butterfat content as high as 60 percent—with a lactic acid and the appropriate bacteria cultures. The flavor of newly prepared crème fraîche is sweet, and it has a loose, almost pourable texture. As it ages, the flavor becomes more pronounced and tart, and it thickens to the point to which it can nearly hold a spoon upright. It is important to the garde manger as a base or spread for canapés, in salad dressings, and served with fresh fruit.

32 fl oz/960 mL half-and-half	1 packet direct-set Crème Fraîche Starter Culture

1. Warm the half-and-half to 72°F/22°C. Stir in the starter culture. Cover and allow to set (incubate) for 24 hours, until a very thick curd forms.

2. The crème fraîche is now ready to use, or transfer it to a storage container and hold, covered, under refrigeration for up to 1 week.

LIME-FLAVORED CRÈME FRAÎCHE: Add fresh lime juice to taste.

CHEF'S NOTE: Créme Fraîche may also be made by combining 32 fl oz/960 mL heavy cream with 8 fl oz/240 mL buttermilk and allowing the mixture to set, covered, at room temperature (75°F/24°C) for 24 hours.

Mozzarella Cheese

YIELD: 2 LB/907 G

Mozzarella belongs to a category of cheese known as *pasta filata*, or spun curd. The procedure for turning fresh curds into mozzarella is demonstrated in the accompanying photographs.

6 oz/170 g salt

1 gal/3.84 L water

2 lb/907 g cheese curd, cut into ½-in/ 1-cm cubes

1. Add the salt to the water and bring to 160°F/71°C. Remove the pot from the heat.

2. Lower the cheese curd in a colander into the hot water; the curds must be completely submerged.

3. Work the curd with wooden spoons, stretching it until it becomes a smooth but stringy mass. Maintain the water temperature at a constant 160°F/71°C during this process.

4. Remove the cheese from the water and continue stretching until the curd is smooth, being careful not to overwork or the cheese will become tough.

5. Working in ice water, shape the cheese into 4-oz/113-g balls and store in plastic wrap or brine. The cheese may be held, covered, under refrigeration for up to 5 days.

Making mozzarella. **A.** Submerge the curd in 160°F/71°C water. **B.** Gently stir and stretch the curd until all the lumps are gone. **C.** Working in ice water, shape the mozzarella into balls.

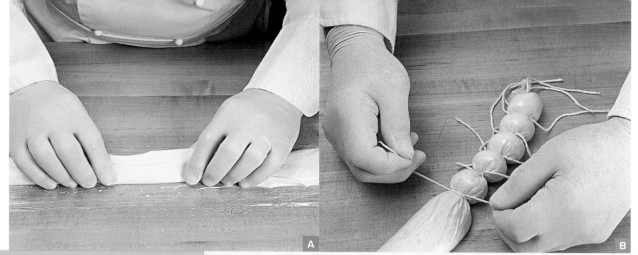

Making bocconcini. **A.** Shape the mozzarella into a log. **B.** Tie off into 1-in/3-cm balls.

MARINATED BOCCONCINI: Prepare the mozzarella as directed through Step 4. On plastic wrap, form the cheese into a long tube, about 1 in/3 cm in diameter, and roll up. Tie at 1-in/3-cm intervals to form balls. Hold at least 8 hours under refrigeration. Cut into individual balls and remove the plastic wrap. Add 1½ fl oz/45 mL olive oil, ½ fl oz/15 mL sherry vinegar, ½ oz/14 g basil chiffonade, and ½ tsp/2.50 mL red pepper flakes. Marinate overnight. This recipe makes about 60 pieces. If desired, accompany the marinated bocconcini with roasted peppers.

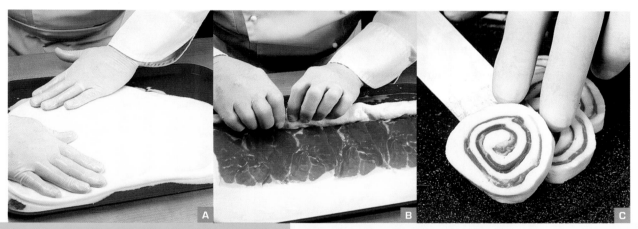

Making mozzarella roulade. **A.** Spread the mozzarella into a sheet. **B.** Roll the filled roulade. **C.** Place the roulade on a platter.

MOZZARELLA ROULADE WITH PROSCIUTTO: Prepare the mozzarella through Step 4. Working on a plastic tray or plastic wrap, stretch the curd into a rectangle. It should be about ¼ in/6 mm thick and 12 by 14 in/30 by 36 cm. While the cheese is still warm, lay 10 paper-thin slices of prosciutto over the mozzarella in an even layer. Roll into a roulade with plastic wrap and secure the ends tightly with string. Return to the hot water for 2 to 3 minutes to lock in the garnish. Remove from the water and retie the ends to secure. Chill the roulade overnight in a water bath before slicing. The wrapped roulade can be held under refrigeration for up to 7 days. This recipe makes about thirty 1-oz/28-g portions.

Marinated Sheep's Milk Cheese with Herbes de Provence

YIELD: 10 SERVINGS (4 OZ/113 G EACH)

2 lb 8 oz/1.13 kg fresh sheep's milk cheese

2 oz/57 g Herbes de Provence (page 527)

1½ tsp/7.50 g salt

¾ tsp/1.50 g ground black pepper

10 grape leaves, rinsed

10 fl oz/300 mL olive oil

20 slices peasant-style bread

1. Divide the cheese logs into 4 equal portions.

2. Mix together the herbs, salt, and pepper and press gently into cheese, shaping the cheese portions into even disks about 3 in/8 cm in diameter.

3. Wrap the disks in the grape leaves and place in a container. Pour the oil over the wrapped cheeses and marinate under refrigeration overnight. The cheese is now ready to use, or hold under refrigeration for up to 3 days.

GRILLED MARINATED SHEEP'S MILK CHEESE WITH COUNTRY BREAD: Brush slices of country-style bread with olive oil. Grill the bread and the drained wrapped cheese over hot coals until marked on both sides. The cheese should be soft and runny. Serve the cheese on a bed of greens, if desired, with the toasted bread, or arrange it on a platter for buffet-style service.

MARINATED GOAT'S MILK CHEESE: Substitute buttons or logs of fresh goat's milk cheese for the sheep's milk cheese.

Hudson Valley Camembert Crisps

YIELD: 12 SERVINGS (2 OZ/57 G EACH)

2 eggs

½ fl oz/15 mL milk

6 sheep's milk Camembert (4 oz/113 g each)

12 phyllo dough sheets

6 oz/170 g butter, melted, or as needed

Vegetable oil for pan-frying, as needed

1. Beat together the eggs and milk to make an egg wash. Set aside.

2. Cut the square Camembert from corner to corner, forming 2 equal triangles.

3. Layer 3 sheets of phyllo, brushing each layer with the melted butter. Repeat with the remaining sheets for a total of 4 stacks.

4. Cut each layered phyllo stack lengthwise into 3 equal strips. Wrap one strip around a triangle of cheese. Secure the seam by brushing with a bit of egg wash. Repeat the procedure until all the cheese is wrapped in phyllo. Cheese can be held under refrigeration for up to 24 hours before preparing further.

5. Pan-fry the wrapped Camembert over high heat in the oil until well browned on both sides and quite crisp. Drain briefly and serve hot or at room temperature.

PRESENTATION IDEA: This can be served warm with a fruit chutney, peasant-style bread, air-dried venison, and a tossed salad.

Blue Cheese Tart

YIELD: FIVE 4-IN/10-CM TARTS

1 lb/454 g Pâté Dough (page 535)

8 oz/227 g cream cheese

8 oz/227 g blue cheese

4 oz/113 g pasteurized eggs (or 2 whole eggs)

3 fl oz/90 mL sour cream

4 fl oz/120 mL heavy cream

1 tbsp/3 g minced chives

1 tbsp/3 g minced flat-leaf parsley

2 tsp/2 g minced thyme

1 tsp/3 g minced shallots, sautéed

½ tsp/2.50 g salt

¼ tsp/0.50 g ground white pepper

1. Roll out the dough and use it to line five 4-in/10-cm tart molds; bake blind at 350°F/177°C for 15 to 20 minutes.

2. Cream the cheeses in a mixer until smooth. Add the eggs gradually, scraping down the sides often. Add the sour cream, heavy cream, herbs, shallots, salt, and pepper.

3. Pour the mixture into the prepared crusts and bake at 300°F/149°C, or until a knife comes out clean when inserted in the center of the tart, about 20 minutes.

4. Let the tarts rest at least 10 to 15 minutes before slicing. They may be served warm or at room temperature.

CHEF'S NOTE: For canapés, pour the custard into 50 prepared barquettes and bake as directed above. Garnish with chopped toasted walnuts or pistachios.

BLUE CHEESE FLAN: Omit the crust and prepare the custard mixture in lightly oiled 1- or 2-oz/28- or 57-g molds. Bake in a 160°F/71°C water bath in a 300°F/149°C oven until lightly set. Serve warm or at room temperature.

Savory Roquefort Cheesecake

YIELD: ONE 9-IN/23-CM CAKE (24 SERVINGS)

This recipe makes an excellent element of any buffet or reception offering. Serve a wedge of the cheesecake as an intermezzo salad on a bed of dressed greens, with a cheese course, or as an accompaniment to a wine tasting.

CRUST

2 oz/57 g dry bread crumbs

1 oz/28 g butter

2¼ oz/64 g chopped walnuts, toasted

12 oz/340 g Roquefort cheese

1 lb 4 oz/567 g cream cheese

½ oz/14 g flour

3 shallots, minced, sautéed, and cooled

4 eggs

2 fl oz/60 mL heavy cream

2 tbsp/6 g chopped dill

1. Brown the bread crumbs in the butter; add the toasted walnuts. Cool. Press the mixture into a 9-in/23-cm springform pan.

2. Line the pan with a paper collar about 3 in/8 cm high.

3. In a food processor, blend the cheeses until smooth. Add the flour, shallots, eggs, and cream. Blend in the dill and pour into the prepared pan.

4. Bake in a 160°F/71°C water bath in a 300°F/149°C oven until set, 30 to 40 minutes.

5. Allow to cool overnight. Cut into 24 equal slices.

APPETIZERS AND HORS D'OEUVRE

The distinctions between appetizers and hors d'oeuvre have more to do with how and when they are served than the actual foods being served. The term *hors d'oeuvre*—which translates from French as "outside the meal"—is universally recognized; we have not developed an exact equivalent in English capable of conveying as much information as this short French phrase. Typically served as a prelude to a meal, hors d'oeuvre are some of the most intriguing and demanding items produced by the garde manger. Appetizers are served as the first course of a meal.

nine

The usual admonition to build a menu from one course to the next calls for some logical connection between the appetizer and all the courses that follow. For every rule you read about what types of foods should or shouldn't constitute an appetizer, you will find at least one good exception. What most appetizers have in common is careful attention to portioning and proper technical execution and plating. Typically, appetizers are small portions of very flavorful items, meant just to take enough edge off the appetite to permit thorough enjoyment of an entrée.

Most cuisines have a well-established form of preparing and presenting hors d'oeuvre. The zakuski table, served before banquets in Russia, features smoked and pickled fish, blinis with caviar, and a host of special salads. In Spain, tapas are traditionally served as bar food and derive their name from the piece of bread once used to cover up a glass of sherry. "Little dishes" known as *mezzes* are popular throughout the Mediterranean regions; they feature olives, nuts, dips, spreads, and highly seasoned items such as grilled kebabs of meat or fish. In the Scandinavian countries, a smorgasbord showcases the special dishes, hot and cold, of that region, including herring, cheeses, and pickled foods.

Hors d'oeuvre also have a place on a menu, where they may be featured as antipasti or hors d'oeuvre variées. You may be familiar with the chef's tasting or amuse-gueule—a small portion of something exotic, unusual, or otherwise special that is served when the guests are seated.

Even though hors d'oeuvre are small bite-sized items, today it is increasingly common for clients to request an entire menu made up of hors d'oeuvre to serve at a reception or cocktail party. These "standing meals" can be quite extensive, running the gamut from small portions of cold soups, meats, fish, cheeses, vegetable dishes, and pastas to desserts and confections. In a break with the traditional notion that hors d'oeuvre should be small enough to eat in one bite and never require a knife and fork, some items at these special receptions may be plated. For such events to run smoothly, it is important to have adequate service staff on hand to continually relieve guests of used plates and cups, picks, and napkins, rather than forcing them to resort to using ashtrays and potted palms for disposal.

The items you choose to serve as hors d'oeuvre may be very simple, requiring little if any preparation on the part of the garde manger beyond slicing and presenting. Nuts, plain or marinated olives, and hard-cooked eggs are all traditional offerings. Dips and spreads are often served with crudité (raw or chilled lightly blanched vegetables), crackers, or chips. Sausages, pâtés, terrines, and cheeses are also served as reception or buffet items, as are thinly sliced or hand-carved smoked fish and meats. Freshly shucked clams with Salsa Verde and Oysters with Mignonette are classics. One simple but elegant food, caviar, is also featured on its own as an hors d'oeuvre.

There are a few precepts to remember in general hors d'oeuvre preparation:

- When selecting hors d'oeuvre, keep in mind the nature of the event as well as the menu to follow.

- Ice carvings and ice beds are often used to keep seafood and caviar very cold, as well as for their dramatic appeal. Be certain that the ice can drain properly and that heavy or large ice carvings are stable.

- Hors d'oeuvre served on platters or passed on trays butler-style should be thoughtfully presented so that the last person to take one is not rummaging among jumbled garnishes.

Composed Hors d'Oeuvre

Composed hors d'oeuvre are built from two or more components. Many of these components can be prepared in advance, but often the final assembly and garnish must be done at nearly the last moment. These special items—including canapés, profiteroles, tartlets, and barquettes—add greatly to the variety of offerings. Cured and smoked foods, pâtés, foie gras, salads, and vegetables are all appropriate as elements in any composed hors d'oeuvre. One special item, mousse, can be featured as a spread, piped into molds or edible containers, rolled into a roulade and sliced, or shaped into quenelles.

Barquettes and tartlets

Pâté dough (see page 535) can be used to line a pâté en croûte as well as to create small edible containers, known as *barquettes* or *tartlets*. These may be filled with a cold mousse or other savory fillings.

9-1. Barquettes. **A.** Cutting the dough to fit a barquette mold. **B.** Pressing the dough into a tartlet mold. **C.** Pressing the dough into a barquette mold. **D.** Baking the assembly upside down. **E.** Finished barquettes and tartlets.

The dough should be rolled out in a thin sheet using a pasta machine or by hand. Cut the dough to fit the mold (see Figure 9-1A). Set the dough in the mold and top with a second mold to press it into shape (see Figures 9-1B and 9-1C). Set this assembly upside down on a baking sheet (see Figure 9-1D). Bake until golden brown (see Figure 9-1E), unmold, and store in an airtight container until needed.

These shells can be filled and garnished as for canapés, though it is generally not necessary to add a separate spread. Select the filling carefully. Very moist fillings can quickly make the pastry shell soggy. These hors d'oeuvre are best when assembled as close as possible to service time.

Other pastry or bread cases can be used to prepare hors d'oeuvre. Some classics from cuisines around the world include bouchées, empanadas, beurrecks and tiropettes, dim sum, and spring rolls.

Canapés

Canapés are small open-faced sandwiches. The base for a canapé is a small piece of bread, cut to shape and toasted. A spread of some sort—a plain or flavored butter, spreadable cheese, or mayonnaise—is applied to the bread to act as a moisture barrier.

The filling or topping is added next. It should be cut neatly so that nothing hangs over the edge of the base. A garnish gives a fresh and appealing look to the canapé, but take the time to select something appropriate and attractive. It is important to take into account the timing and size of the event.

Appetizers on the à la Carte Menu

It is important to provide enough appropriate options that work with the main course offerings. In an à la carte situation, the garde manger may have relatively little control over what a guest might choose. Furthermore, there is no guarantee that the guests will order an appetizer just as a first course. This has led to some interesting and challenging new approaches to featuring appetizers on the menu. Grazing menus or degustation menus are produced by selecting a series of appetizer-size portioned items served in a logical sequence.

Guests today may look for appetizers that can be shared or that can be ordered in a larger size to enjoy as a main course. In some restaurants, wait staff may suggest an appetizer for the table to share and enjoy while their entrées are being prepared, both as a way to expose guests to something new or unusual as well as to sell up the menu.

Appetizers for a Banquet

Banquet menus frequently call for one or more appetizers. In this case, the chef does have the ability to build a menu, progressing from one flavor and texture experience to the next, so in this instance, thoughtful consideration of how each element of the menu relates to what precedes it and follows is the key to success. Taking a cue from the principles used by sommeliers to build from one wine to another, going from the understated to the robust, it is a common practice for the meal to progress from subtle to more assertive flavors.

It is important to consider the entire experience when designing appetizers in a banquet menu. They should be served in sensible portions, perhaps smaller than you might offer on an à la carte menu, so guests can sample several and still enjoy their main course and dessert.

Selecting and Preparing Appetizers

Classic hors d'oeuvre can be served as appetizers if you increase the portion size slightly. Perfectly fresh clams and oysters, for example, shucked as close to service time as possible and served with sauces designed to enhance their naturally briny savor, or a classic shrimp cocktail, served with a cocktail sauce, salsa, or other pungent sauce, are perennial favorites in any appetizer category.

Smoked fish, meats, and poultry; sausages, pâtés, terrines, and galantines; air-dried hams and beef sliced paper thin—all of these items can be used to create appetizer plates, on their own with a few accompaniments or garnishes or as a sampler plate. Refer to Chapters 6, 7, and 8 for specific recipes and presentation ideas.

Salads are also served as appetizers. Several salads in Chapter 3 can fit this category quite well. You may prefer to change the portion size, substitute a different sauce or garnish for a special look, vary it from season to season, or showcase a range of flavors and textures from other cuisines.

Warm and hot appetizers may include small portions of pastas, such as ravioli or tortellini, served on their own or in a sauce or broth. Puff pastry shells can be cut into vols-au-vent or made into turnovers, filled with savory ragoûts or foie gras. Broiled or grilled fish, shellfish, or poultry may be featured. Crêpes, blinis, and other similar dishes are popular in many cuisines. Meatballs and other highly seasoned ground meat appetizers are also found on today's menu. Swedish meatballs share space in the garde manger's repertoire with kefta (spicy kebabs made from ground lamb).

Vegetables are more important than ever as an appetizer. They may be presented simply; for example, steamed artichokes may be served with a dipping sauce such as a flavored mayonnaise or vinaigrette, chilled asparagus may be served drizzled with a flavored oil, or a plate of grilled vegetables may be accompanied by a vinaigrette sauce.

Principles for Presenting Appetizers

The recipes in this chapter include such traditional favorites as carpaccio, melon and prosciutto, foie gras in brioche, and vitello tonnato. Keep in mind the following basic principles as you select, prepare, and plate appetizers (see Figure 9-2).

- SERVE ALL APPETIZERS AT THE PROPER TEMPERATURE. Remember to chill or warm plates.

- SEASON ALL APPETIZER ITEMS WITH METICULOUS CARE. Appetizers are meant to stimulate the appetite, so seasoning is of the utmost importance.

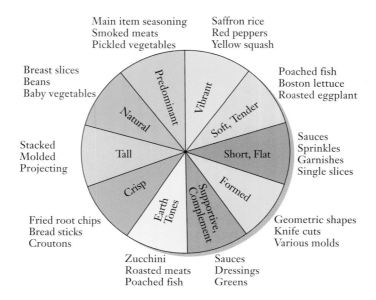

9-2. Plated appetizer composition balance wheel.

- SLICE, SHAPE, AND PORTION APPETIZERS PROPERLY. There should be just enough of any given item to make the appetizer interesting and appealing from start to finish, but not so much on the plate that the guest is over-whelmed.

- NEATNESS ALWAYS COUNTS, BUT ESPECIALLY WITH APPETIZERS. Your guests will most likely judge their entire meal based on the impression the appetizer gives.

- WHEN OFFERING SHARED APPETIZERS, CONSIDER HOW THEY WILL LOOK WHEN THEY COME TO THE TABLE. It may be more effective to split a shared plate in the kitchen rather than expect the guests to divide it up themselves.

- COLOR, SHAPE, AND WHITE SPACE ALL PLAY A ROLE IN THE OVERALL COM-POSITION OF YOUR PLATE. Take the time to choose serving pieces of the right size and shape and to provide the guest with all the items necessary for the appetizer, including cups for dipping sauces, special utensils, and, if necessary, finger bowls.

COLD SAVORY MOUSSES: The French word *mousse* literally means "foam" or "froth." For the garde manger, the term indicates a cold item prepared by combining three basic elements: a base, a binder, and an aerator. Mousses are often featured as an hors d'oeu-vre, piped decoratively on a canapé base or into a barquette or tartlet mold; used to fill a cucumber cup or endive leaf; or shaped in a special mold as either a single portion, perhaps topped with a layer of crystal-clear aspic gelée, or as loaves or roulades to be sliced.

A cold mousse, as the term is understood today, is one that is not cooked after being as-sembled. It is never served hot, as subjecting the gelatin or fat binder in the mousse to heat would melt and deflate it. A hot mousse indicates a small portion of a mousseline forcemeat that has been molded in a fashion similar to a cold mousse before being cooked and served hot.

THE BASE: Mousse prepared by the garde manger is produced from savory items such as cooked or smoked meats and fish, cheeses, or prepared vegetables. This base is then puréed until very smooth. In some cases it may be necessary to add a liquid or moist product such as velouté, béchamel, unwhipped cream, or mayonnaise to adjust the consistency. The intent is to have the base at a consistency similar to that of pastry cream before adding the binder, if it is required, and the aerator.

For the best possible texture, sieve the puréed base (see Figure 9-3A). This removes any last bits of sinew or fiber and gives a very delicate finished product.

THE BINDER: Gelatin, either powdered or in sheets, is added in a proportion similar to that called for when preparing an aspic gelée. Soften (bloom) the gelatin in a cool liquid. Warm it to 90° to 110°F/32° to 43°C to dissolve the granules or melt the sheets. Stir the dissolved gelatin into the base. It is important to blend the gelatin evenly throughout the entire base (see Figure 9-3B).

In some cases, the base product has enough body and bind to hold the mousse together without an additional binder. Cheese is a good example.

The key is to obtain the proper balance of binder and base so the mousse will keep a distinct shape when chilled, without melting or sagging. The amount of binder in a product should be adjusted depending on the final use of the product. For example, if a mousse must be sliced and lined up on a buffet platter that will be sitting out for any length of time, it will need more binder (gelatin) than a single serving of mousse that is taken directly from the refrigerator immediately before it is served.

THE AERATOR: Beaten egg whites and/or whipped cream give the mousse its frothy texture. Beat the whites or cream to soft peaks for the best results. If the aerator is overbeaten, it could begin to collapse or give the mousse a grainy appearance and texture.

Fold the aerator into the base carefully. It is a good idea to add about one-third the total amount of aerator first to make it easier to fold in the remaining two-thirds. This technique keeps the maximum volume in the finished mousse (see Figure 9-3C).

9-3. **A.** The base is pushed through a sieve. **B.** The gelatin solution is added. **C.** The whipped cream is folded in.

Basic Formula for a Mousse

Although each base ingredient may call for an adjustment in the amount of binder and aerator, this basic formula is a good reference. It can and should be altered depending on the type of mousse being made and the intended use of the final product.

Base	2 lb/907 g
Binder (if required by recipe)	1 oz/28 g gelatin
Liquid (to bloom the gelatin)	1 cup/240 mL
Aerator	2 cups/480 mL

9-4. Piping salmon mousse into barquettes.

Once the mousse is prepared, it should be shaped in the desired way. Transfer immediately to a pastry bag and pipe out without delay into the desired container (see Figure 9-4), or apply it as a topping or filling for tea sandwiches and canapés. A mousse can also be rolled in the same way as a roulade, carefully secured, and chilled before slicing. Terrine molds may be used to shape a mousse into a loaf; be sure to oil the mold and line it with plastic wrap to make it easy to remove the mousse once it is properly chilled.

Caviar

Caviar, a delicacy made from the roe of sturgeon, was described by Aristotle in the fourth century B.C.E. During the Roman Empire, trumpets heralded the arrival of caviar to the table; it was presented with garlands of flowers.

Today caviar remains among the most expensive and exclusive of all preserved foods, partly because of overfishing and pollution and partly because caviar is labor-intensive to produce and extremely perishable. Caviar will probably never again be given away with glasses of beer "to encourage libation," as it once was in this country. Efforts at farm-raising sturgeon and developing techniques to remove the roe without killing the fish have not yet shown signs of making caviar less expensive.

From roe to caviar

The roe sac must be harvested from the sturgeon while it is still alive (when the fish dies, the membranes surrounding the individual eggs deteriorate and rupture). The roe sacs are carefully rubbed over a sieve; the eggs (or berries) are caught in a container, washed in fresh water, drained, and then graded.

The master grader looks for consistency of grain, size, color, fragrance, flavor, gleam, firmness, and vulnerability of the roe skin. The bigger and lighter in color

(Clockwise from top): Wasabi tobikko, beluga, pressed, salmon, sevruga, orange tobikko, golden osetra.

the eggs, the more rare and expensive the finished caviar.

Eggs of the highest quality are prepared by a method called *molossal* or "little salt," indicating that salt is added at a rate of less than 5 percent of the egg's weight. Lower-quality caviar is processed with greater amounts of salt. Salt both preserves the caviar and gives it its texture and flavor. However, even though caviar is a salted food, it remains quite perishable; it must be carefully refrigerated throughout processing and storage.

Types of caviar

In both France and the United States, only the processed roe of sturgeon can be called *caviar;* France still strictly enforces this rule. In the United States, however, the law has been interpreted more leniently, and as long as the type of fish is identified on the label, various kinds of fish roe may be sold as caviar (see Figure 9-5).

TRUE CAVIAR The major sturgeon species used to produce true caviar today are beluga, osetra, and sevruga. Sterlet, which is nearly extinct, was the source of the fabled "golden caviar of the Czars." One of the reasons caviar is so expensive is directly related to the age and size a sturgeon must reach before developing the valuable roe.

The individual eggs, or berries, are graded for color, with 000 indicating the lightest-colored caviar and 0 the darkest. Color alone, however, does not indicate quality. The eggs are also sized. Beluga caviar has the largest eggs, graded large or coarse; osetra eggs are slightly smaller than beluga; sevruga is the smallest of all.

- BELUGA CAVIAR ranges in color from light steel gray to dark gray. The beluga sturgeon takes as long as twenty years to achieve maturity, when it may weigh up to a ton. This long growth cycle means that beluga caviar is the most expensive and least readily available. It is always sold in blue jars or tins.

- OSETRA CAVIAR is a brownish color with a golden tinge and can be distinguished from other caviar by its strong nutty flavor. This sturgeon reaches a size of ten feet and five hundred pounds and grows to maturity in twelve to fourteen years. It is always sold in yellow jars or tins.

- SEVRUGA CAVIAR berries are dark brown, the smallest of the true caviars, with a strong flavor. Sevruga can grow to seven feet and about 150 pounds in eight to ten years. Sevruga caviar is less expensive than beluga and osetra. It is always sold in red jars or tins.

Pressed caviar (known in Russian as *pajusnay*) is made from mature, broken, or overripe eggs. The salted eggs are put into a linen sack and pressed (using a grape press) until all of the fatty liquid is released. The result is a marmalade-like substance, doted on by the Russians, who spread it on black bread and enjoy it with chilled vodka. The flavor of pressed caviar is more intense than other caviars, and the eating experience is quite different. Pressed caviar is also used to prepare special dishes and cold sauces.

OTHER TYPES OF CAVIAR Other fish roes can be processed in the same manner as sturgeon. The United States and other countries produce caviar from the roe of salmon, paddlefish, whitefish, lumpfish, and cod. These caviars are available pasteurized or fresh. Each type is different in size, texture, and taste.

Salmon caviar is either golden or pink in color. The eggs are large, flavorful, and attractive.

Whitefish from the Great Lakes and Canada produces a roe with a natural golden color, crunchy texture, and a mild, fresh taste.

The processed roe of cod and carp are quite small and are often salted, pressed, and sold as *tarama*. The gray mullet is also the source of the Mediterranean delicacy known as *poutargue* or *boutargue* in France and *botarga* in Italy. In Greece, tarama caviar is made from the roe of the gray mullet. To further confuse the issue, in the United States, tarama, which is imported, is made not from mullet but from the roe of tuna.

The roe of crab, flying fish (tobikko), cod (tarako), and sea urchin (uni) are also processed in a similar fashion and are staples of sushi bars in Japan. They are sometimes flavored with wasabi or other ingredients to produce special flavors and colors.

9-6. Caviar service.

Lumpfish roe, though widely available and inexpensive, is not a good substitute for true caviar. Because lumpfish roe has an unappetizing off-gray color, it is typically dyed red, gold, or black using vegetable-based dyes or cuttlefish ink.

Buying and storing caviar

Fresh sturgeon caviar should be plump and moist, with each individual egg shiny, smooth, separate, and intact. When you taste caviar, the eggs should release a savory flavor, faintly nutty with a hint of the sea. It should be surrounded by its own thick natural oils but never appear to be swimming in oil.

Caviar should always be properly stored under refrigeration at 28° to 32°F/−2° to 0°C. True caviar can be held unopened under refrigeration for four weeks and opened for two to thee days. Pressed caviar will keep at 40°F/4°C for ten days to two weeks; once opened, it should be eaten within five days. One of the primary reasons caviar goes bad after opening is cross contamination. Be sure to use a clean spoon each time you dip some caviar from its container.

Pasteurized "caviars" and those processed with greater amounts of salt will keep in the refrigerator unopened for several weeks or even months, but once opened, they too should be consumed within two to three days.

Caviar can be purchased in jars weighing from 1 to 2½ oz/28 to 71 g. Larger quantities are generally packed in tins and are available in various weights from 4 oz to 2.2 lb/113 to 998 g.

Serving caviar

The best caviar needs no special accompaniments. It is often served in special iced containers (see Figure 9-6), with mother-of-pearl, bone, horn, or glass spoons to avoid the flavor changes that may occur with metal spoons. Toast points, brioche, or blinis are often served as a base for a caviar canapé, perhaps with a few dollops of crème fraîche.

This precious item is also used as a garnish for other hors d'oeuvre and appetizers. Lower-quality caviar may be appropriate for garnishing some items. Remember that caviar should never be added to foods while they are cooking.

Profiteroles

YIELD: 40 PIECES

Pâte à choux, the batter used to make profiteroles can also be piped into miniature éclair shapes and filled with a wide variety of fillings.

8 fl oz/240 mL water	4 eggs
4 oz/113 g butter	1 tsp/5 g salt
4½ oz/128 g all-purpose flour, sifted	

1. Combine the water, butter, and salt and bring to a boil.

2. Add the flour all at once and stir in well; cook until the mass comes away from the pot.

3. Transfer to a mixer and mix on medium speed for about 1 minute. Add the eggs one at a time, mixing well after each addition, to achieve a stiff but pliable texture.

4. Transfer the dough to a pastry bag with a No. 5 plain tip and pipe the desired shape onto parchment-lined sheet pans. One-in/3-cm balls produce profiteroles; other shapes such as éclairs may also be prepared.

5. Bake at 400°F/204°C until golden brown, then reduce the temperature to 325°F/163°C to cook through, 12 to 15 minutes.

6. When ready to fill, slice off the tops with a sharp knife. Add the filling and replace the top.

Working with pâte à choux. **A.** Pâte à choux should be stiff but still pliable. **B.** Pâte à choux is baked at high and then low temperatures to produce a hollow middle.

Gougères (Gruyère Cheese Puffs)

YIELD: 40 PIECES

These puffs make a great snack item or casual reception food with cocktails. They are best when served warm from the oven, but they can be cooled, held in airtight containers, and served at room temperature if necessary.

8 fl oz/240 mL water	1 egg white
4 oz/113 g butter	4 eggs
1 tsp/5 g salt	3 oz/85 g grated Gruyère cheese
4½ oz/128 g all-purpose flour, sifted	1 tbsp/5 g grated Parmesan cheese

1. Combine the water, butter, and salt and bring to a boil.

2. Add the flour all at once and stir in well; cook, stirring constantly, until the mass comes away from the sides of the pot.

3. Transfer to a mixer and mix on medium speed for about 1 minute. Add the egg white and eggs one at a time, mixing well after each addition, to achieve a stiff but pliable texture.

4. Add the grated Gruyère and Parmesan and continue mixing for 1 minute.

5. Transfer the dough to a pastry bag with a No. 5 plain tip and pipe the desired shape onto parchment-lined sheet pans.

6. Bake at 400°F/204°C until golden brown, then reduce the temperature to 325°F/163°C to cook through, 12 to 15 minutes. Serve warm or store in an airtight container, as for crackers.

Palmiers with Prosciutto

YIELD: 40 TO 45 PIECES

This is a savory variation of the classic French pastry. The "palm leaves" are lined with prosciutto, and a dusting of Parmesan replaces the granulated sugar. The name reflects the fact that the dough puffs into a palm-leaf shape as it bakes.

8 oz/227 g Blitz Puff Pastry sheets (page 538)

2 oz/57 g tomato paste

12 slices prosciutto

¾ oz/21 g finely grated Parmesan cheese

1. Lay out the puff pastry sheets and brush each with a small amount of tomato paste.

2. Lay thin slices of prosciutto over the puff pastry and dust with cheese. Roll the long sides in so they meet toward the center. Slice ¼ in/6 mm thick and bake on parchment-lined sheet pans at 400°F/204°C until golden brown, about 10 minutes.

CHEF'S NOTE: These can be made up in batches and frozen, then baked as needed and served warm.

Clockwise from top left: Cheese Sticks, Palmiers with Prosciutto, and Gougères

Cheese Sticks (Paillettes)

YIELD: 30 PIECES

Cheese sticks are a quick and simple way to add a signature look and flavor to a reception table, dining table, or bar. The sticks may be twisted, curled, or shaped as desired before baking. Fanciful shapes presented in tall glasses or jars serve as eye-catching edible decorations.

1 egg yolk

½ fl oz/15 mL whole milk

1 Blitz Puff Pastry sheet (page 538)

1½ oz/43 g grated Parmesan cheese

Sweet Spanish paprika, as needed

1. Whisk together the egg yolk and milk to make an egg wash. Brush the puff pastry sheet with the egg wash.

2. Sprinkle the cheese and paprika evenly over the puff pastry sheet. Cut the sheet lengthwise into ¼-in/6-mm strips.

3. Bake on parchment-lined sheet pans at 400°F/204°C until golden brown, about 10 minutes.

CHEF'S NOTE: Cajun Spice Blend (page 525), cayenne, poppy seeds, or sesame seeds may be used as alternative garnishes.

Crabmeat and Avocado Profiteroles

YIELD: 30 PIECES

4 oz/113 g crabmeat, cleaned

½ ripe avocado, cut into small dice

Juice of 1 lime (2 fl oz/60 mL)

½ fl oz/15 mL buttermilk

2 tsp/2 g finely cut chives

1 tbsp/3 g chopped cilantro

Salt, as needed

Cayenne, as needed

30 Profiteroles (page 372)

1. Combine the crabmeat, avocado, lime juice, and buttermilk. Fold in the chives and cilantro and season with salt and cayenne.

2. Split the puffs and fill with the crabmeat mixture.

Southwest Chicken Salad in Profiteroles

YIELD: 30 PIECES

2 chicken legs, cooked and cut into small dice

2 oz/57 g tomato concassé

1 lime, sectioned into suprêmes and cut into small dice

½ oz/14 g roasted pepper, cut into small dice

1 tsp/5 mL minced jalapeño

1 oz/28 g minced shallots

1 garlic clove, minced

2 tbsp/6 g chopped cilantro

2 tsp/2 g chopped marjoram

2 tsp/2 g minced chives

Salt, as needed

Ground black pepper, as needed

30 Profiteroles (page 372)

1. Combine the chicken, tomato, lime, roasted pepper, jalapeño, shallots, garlic, and herbs. Season with salt and pepper. Marinate for 2 hours under refrigeration.

2. Split the puffs and fill with the chicken salad.

Duck Rillettes in Profiteroles

YIELD: 30 PIECES

4 oz/113 g Duck Rillettes (page 224)

1 fl oz/30 mL heavy cream

1 oz/28 g Dijon mustard

Few drops Tabasco sauce

30 Profiteroles (page 372), split

1 oz/28 g green peppercorns, crushed
(1 per profiterole)

1. In a mixing bowl on low speed, work the rillettes until softened.

2. Whip the cream to soft peaks. Fold the whipped cream, mustard, and Tabasco gently but thoroughly into the rillettes.

3. Pipe the rillette mixture into the profiteroles. Garnish each with a green peppercorn. Replace the cover.

Smoked Whiskey Shrimp

YIELD: 30 PIECES

30 shrimp (21/25 count)

1½ fl oz/45 mL whiskey or bourbon

Juice of 2 limes

½ fl oz/15 mL balsamic vinegar

1 oz/28 g honey

1 shallot, minced

2 garlic cloves, minced

1½ fl oz/45 mL olive oil

1½ fl oz/45 mL vegetable oil

1 tbsp/3 g minced cilantro

4½ oz/128 g tomato concassé

Tabasco sauce, as needed

Salt, as needed

Ground black pepper, as needed

1. Remove the shells from the shrimp and devein.

2. Combine the whiskey, lime juice, vinegar, honey, shallot, and garlic. Whisk in the oils. Add the cilantro and tomatoes and adjust seasoning with Tabasco, salt, and pepper. Marinate the shrimp in the mixture for at least 2 hours and up to overnight.

3. Drain the shrimp and hot smoke at 185°F/85°C for 10 to 12 minutes, or until cooked through. Cool.

PRESENTATION IDEAS: Serve the shrimp on a canapé base with a chive cream cheese spread and cucumber rings. Garnish with a few curls of fine-julienne red pepper and chives.

Smoked Salmon Mousse Barquettes

YIELD: 30 SMALL PIECES

5 oz/142 g Smoked Salmon (page 196), diced

6 fl oz/180 mL Fish Velouté (page 532)

1 fl oz/30 mL Aspic Gelée (page 57), softened

4 fl oz/120 mL heavy cream

¼ tsp/1.25 mL Tabasco sauce

2 tsp/10 g kosher salt

Ground black pepper, as needed

30 barquettes made from Pâté Dough (pages 363, 535), prebaked

2 oz/57 g salmon roe

30 dill sprigs

1. Make the mousse by puréeing the smoked salmon and velouté in a food processor until very smooth. Add the warm aspic gelée while the processor is running. Once fully incorporated, transfer to a bowl.

2. Whip the cream to soft peaks and fold gently but thoroughly into the salmon mixture. Season with the Tabasco, salt, and pepper.

3. **Barquette Assembly:** Pipe about ½ oz/14 g salmon mousse into each barquette, garnish with a little salmon roe and a dill sprig and chill until firm. The barquettes are now ready to serve, or they can be refrigerated for up to 1 hour.

Creamed Wild Mushroom Tartlets

YIELD: 30 PIECES

1 lb/454 g assorted wild mushrooms (shiitake, porcini, oyster, etc.), cut into small dice

2 shallots, minced

2 oz/57 g butter

½ fl oz/15 mL brandy

½ fl oz/15 mL sherry

2 fl oz/60 mL heavy cream

30 tartlet shells made from Pâté Dough (page 363, 535), baked blind

GARNISH

2 oz/57 g dry Jack cheese, finely grated

1 oz/28 g chopped flat-leaf parsley

2 tsp/4 g ground black pepper

1. Sauté the mushrooms and shallots in the butter; add the brandy, sherry, and cream to finish the duxelles.

2. Combine the garnish ingredients and reserve.

3. **Tartlet Assembly:** Fill each tartlet with ½ oz/14 g duxelles and top with a sprinkle of the garnish mixture. Serve warm.

Sun-Dried Tomato and Goat Cheese Tartlets

YIELD: 30 PIECES

1 lb/454 g Blitz Puff Pastry (page 538)

1 tbsp/9 g minced garlic

1 tsp/2 g ground white pepper

3 tbsp/9 g basil, chopped

6 fl oz/180 mL whole milk

2 fl oz/60 mL dry sherry

3 large eggs

1 tbsp/7 g all-purpose flour

4 oz/113 g fresh goat cheese, crumbled

1 oz/28 g green onions, minced

3½ oz/99 g sun-dried tomatoes, minced

1. Roll the puff pastry dough to ⅛ in/3 mm thick. Dock the dough.

2. Cut 30 rounds from the puff pastry using a cutter 2 in/5 cm in diameter and press gently into the 1¾-in/4-cm diameter tart molds.

3. Cover the dough in the molds with a small piece of foil and fill with uncooked dried beans or pastry weights. Bake in a 425°F/218°C oven for 5 minutes. Allow it to cool completely. Remove the foil and beans or weights.

4. Combine the garlic, pepper, basil, milk, and sherry in a food processor. Add the eggs and flour and process until just blended.

5. Toss together the goat cheese, green onions, and sun-dried tomatoes.

6. Place 2½ tsp/12.50 mL of the goat's milk cheese mixture into each tartlet.

7. Fill each tartlet two-thirds full with the egg mixture.

8. Bake in a 350°F/177°C oven for about 15 minutes, or until set.

Goat's Milk Cheese Canapés with Sweet Peppers

YIELD: 30 PIECES

½ jalapeño, seeded and minced

15 oz/425 g Roasted Pepper Salad (page 94)

8 oz/227 g soft fresh goat's milk cheese or sour cream

8½ oz/241 g clabbered cream or sour cream

30 whole wheat bread canapé bases, toasted

30 cilantro leaves

1. Add the jalapeño to the pepper salad and allow to marinate.

2. Blend the goat's milk cheese and clabbered cream until smooth and pipeable.

3. **Canapé Assembly:** Pipe the goat's milk cheese mixture in a ring around the canapé bases. Mound about ½ oz/14 g pepper salad in the center and top with a cilantro leaf.

Steak Tartare Canapés

YIELD: 30 PIECES

Steak tartare is traditionally made by mincing beef tenderloin very fine. It should be made as close as possible to service time for the best flavor and texture.

1 lb/454 g beef tenderloin, cleaned

1 oz/28 g pasteurized egg yolks

1 oz/28 g onions, minced

1 oz/28 g capers, chopped

Salt, as needed

Ground black pepper, as needed

Worcestershire sauce, as needed

30 rye bread canapé bases, toasted

5 oz/142 g Anchovy Butter (page 533), softened

2 oz/57 g hard-cooked egg, chopped, or as needed

2 oz/57 g minced onion, or as needed

2 oz/57 g minced parsley, or as needed

1. Chop the tenderloin fine. At service time, combine the beef, egg yolks, onions, and capers to prepare the tartare. Add salt, pepper, and Worcestershire to taste.

2. **Canapé Assembly:** Spread the canapé bases with 1 tsp/5 g anchovy butter and ½ oz/14 g tartare mixture. Top with the chopped eggs, onion, and parsley.

Smoked Trout Canapés

YIELD: 30 PIECES

15 oz/425 g Hot Smoked Rainbow Trout (page 200)

30 rye bread canapé bases, toasted

5 oz/142 g Horseradish Butter (page 534), softened

10 pimiento-stuffed olives, sliced

1. Flake the trout, following natural seams, into pieces ¾ to 1 in/2 to 3 cm wide.

2. **Canapé Assembly:** Spread each canapé base with 1 tsp/5 g horseradish butter; top with a piece of trout. Garnish with a slice of olive.

Smoked Shrimp Canapés

YIELD: 30 PIECES

15 Smoked Shrimp (21/25 count) (page 195)

30 whole wheat bread canapé bases, toasted

5 oz/142 g Pimiento Butter (page 533), softened

Small watercress pluches, as needed

1. Split the shrimp in half lengthwise.

2. **Canapé Assembly:** Spread the canapé bases with 1 tsp/5 g pimiento butter and top with 1 piece smoked shrimp and a small sprig of watercress.

Smoked Duck Mousse Canapés with Raspberry Butter

YIELD: 30 PIECES

4 oz/113 g Smoked Duck (page 203), diced

2 tsp/6 g powdered gelatin

1 fl oz/30 mL water

2 fl oz/60 mL heavy cream, whipped

1 fl oz/30 mL puréed raspberries, strained (see Chef's Note)

4 oz/113 g butter, softened

30 whole wheat canapé bases, toasted

30 thin slices Smoked Duck breast (cut to dimension of canapé base)

30 fresh raspberries

1. Purée the diced duck until smooth.

2. Soften the gelatin in the water. Warm gently until dissolved. Add the gelatin to the duck and fold in the cream.

3. Blend the raspberry purée and butter together until smooth.

4. **Canapé Assembly:** Spread the raspberry butter on each base. Pipe the mousse onto each; garnish with a slice of duck and a raspberry.

CHEF'S NOTES: To prepare a raspberry purée, purée berries in a blender or food processor. Strain through a fine sieve. Taste and adjust seasoning as required with sugar and a few drops of balsamic vinegar.

The mousse is best if prepared as close as possible to service time. When preparing these canapés, prepare the raspberry purée first and have all other mise en place ready before beginning the mousse.

Salt Cod Canapés with Piperada

YIELD: 30 PIECES

1 lb 4 oz/567 g salt cod fillets (about 3)

6½ oz/184 g olive oil

8 oz/227 g onions, cut into julienne

1 tsp/5 g sugar

Salt, as needed

Ground black pepper, as needed

2 oz/57 g red pepper, cut into small dice

2 oz/57 g green pepper, cut into small dice

30 slices baguette, ¼ in/6 mm thick

1. Soak the salt cod in cold water for 24 hours, changing the water several times. Remove from the water and pat dry. Remove the blood line. Shred the fish and set aside.

2. Heat 1½ fl oz/45 mL of the oil in a large sauté pan over medium heat. Add the onions and sweat, stirring often, until softened but not browned, about 15 minutes.

3. Increase the heat to medium high and add the cod and sugar. Sauté until heated through and well combined, 3 to 4 minutes. Season to taste with salt and pepper.

4. To make the piperada, heat ½ fl oz/15 mL of the oil in a small sauté pan over medium-high heat. Add the peppers and cook, stirring often, until softened, about 5 minutes. Remove from the heat and set aside.

5. Brush the slices of bread with the remaining oil and toast lightly in a 350°F/177°C oven.

6. Top each bread slice with a tablespoon (about ½ oz/14 g) cod mixture. Garnish with the piperada and serve warm.

Prosciutto and Melon Canapés

YIELD: 30 PIECES

8 slices prosciutto, sliced very thin (about 5 oz/142 g)

30 white bread canapé bases, toasted

5 oz/142 g Mascarpone Cheese Spread (see Chef's Note)

30 pieces honeydew melon, scooped into small balls

30 pieces cantaloupe, cut into small dice or petit pois shape

30 mint leaves, cut into fine chiffonade

1. Cut the prosciutto to fit canapé bases.

2. **Canapé Assembly:** Spread the canapé bases with mascarpone spread and top with a piece of prosciutto. Pipe a small mound of mascarpone in the center of each canapé. Top with melon balls, diced cantaloupe, and mint.

CHEF'S NOTE: To prepare Mascarpone Cheese Spread, add Tabasco, Dijon mustard, salt, and pepper as needed to 5 oz/142 g Mascarpone (page 346). Mix well.

Deviled Quail Egg Canapés

YIELD: 30 PIECES

15 quail eggs (see Chef's Note)

Dijon mustard, as needed

Basic Mayonnaise (page 35), as needed

Worcestershire sauce, as needed

Salt, as needed

Ground white pepper, as needed

30 pumpernickel bread canapé bases, toasted and lightly buttered

1 oz/28 g caviar

¼ bunch fresh dill

1. Simmer the quail eggs for 6½ minutes; shock and peel as quickly as possible under cold water.

2. Cut the eggs in half lengthwise, remove the yolks, and reserve the whites.

3. Push the yolks through a sieve into a mixing bowl. Add just enough mustard and mayonnaise to make the mixture easy to pipe. Season with Worcestershire sauce, salt, and pepper.

4. **Canapé Assembly:** Pipe a small rosette of the deviled yolk mixture onto the pumpernickel bread. Place the egg white on top at a slight angle tilting upward. Pipe enough yolk mixture into the cavity of the egg white just to fill it. Garnish with a small dollop of caviar and a very small sprig of dill.

CHEF'S NOTE: You may wish to add 1 or 2 hard-cooked yolks (from chicken eggs) to supplement the quail egg yolks in this recipe.

VARIATION: Substitute sliced truffles for the caviar and use chervil instead of dill sprigs.

Red Pepper Mousse in Endive

YIELD: 30 PIECES

3 oz/85 g minced onions

1 garlic clove, finely minced

1 fl oz/30 mL vegetable oil

3 red peppers, cut into small dice
(1 lb 4 oz/567 g)

8 fl oz/240 mL Chicken Stock (page 529)

Pinch saffron threads, crushed

1 oz/28 g tomato paste

Salt, as needed

Ground white pepper, as needed

1 tbsp/9 g powdered gelatin

2 fl oz/60 mL white wine

6 fl oz/180 mL heavy cream, whipped

30 endive spears

GARNISH

Red pepper, slivered, as needed

1. Sauté the onions and garlic in the oil until golden. Add the diced peppers, stock, saffron, tomato paste, salt, and pepper. Simmer until all ingredients are tender and the liquid is reduced by half.

2. Bloom the gelatin in the wine.

3. Purée the red pepper mixture in a blender. Add the bloomed gelatin while the red pepper mixture is still hot and blend to combine all ingredients well.

4. Cool the mixture over an ice bath until it mounds when dropped from a spoon. Fold the whipped cream into the mixture.

5. **Hors d'Oeuvre Assembly:** Pipe the mousse into the endive spears and garnish with a sliver of red pepper.

Blue Cheese Mousse

YIELD: 2 LB/907 G

1 lb 4 oz/567 g blue cheese

12 oz/340 g cream cheese

1 tbsp/15 g kosher salt

½ tsp/1 g ground black pepper

4 fl oz/120 mL heavy cream, whipped to soft peaks

1. Purée the blue and cream cheeses in a food processor fitted with a metal blade attachment until very smooth. Add the salt and pepper.

2. Fold the whipped cream into the mousse until well blended. There should be no lumps.

3. The mousse is now ready to use to prepare canapés or as a filling or dip.

GOAT'S MILK CHEESE MOUSSE: Substitute fresh goat's milk cheese for the blue cheese.

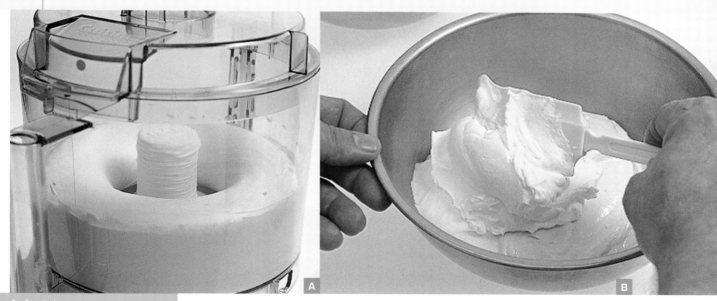

Making mousse. **A.** Puréed base. **B.** Adding whipped cream to the base.

Smoked Trout Mousse

YIELD: 1 LB 8 OZ/680 G

1 lb/454 g Hot Smoked Rainbow Trout (page 200) fillets, boneless

8 fl oz/240 mL Aspic Gelée (page 57) made from Fish Stock (page 530), warmed

4 fl oz/120 mL Basic Mayonnaise (page 35)

1 tsp/5 mL Worcestershire sauce

¼ tsp/1.25 mL Tabasco sauce

½ fl oz/15 mL dry white wine

½ oz/14 g prepared horseradish

1 tsp/5 mL lemon juice

6 fl oz/180 mL heavy cream, whipped to soft peaks

1. Place the trout, aspic, mayonnaise, Worcestershire sauce, Tabasco, wine, horseradish, and lemon juice in a food processor and process until very fine.

2. Fold the whipped cream into the trout mixture.

3. The mousse is now ready to use to prepare canapés, profiteroles, and other applications.

Barbecued Shrimp and Bacon

YIELD: 30 PIECES

30 shrimp (16/20 count), peeled and deveined

15 strips Basic Bacon (page 210), partially cooked and cut in half

8 fl oz/240 mL Apricot-Ancho Barbecue Sauce (page 55)

30 bamboo skewers

1. Soak 30 bamboo skewers in water for 30 minutes to prevent burning. Wrap each shrimp with a bacon strip. Thread each shrimp on a small bamboo skewer.

2. Place the skewers on a wire rack set into a foil-lined sheet pan.

3. Broil the shrimp 1 to 2 minutes on the first side. Turn and broil another 1 to 2 minutes, or until the bacon gets crispy and the shrimp are just cooked through. Remove from the broiler and baste with the barbecue sauce.

CHEF'S NOTE: Soak the skewers in water before using to prevent them from catching fire when the shrimp are cooking.

SERRANO-WRAPPED SHRIMP: Replace the bacon with thin slices of Serrano ham. Baste lightly with oil before grilling or broiling as directed above.

Stuffed Grape Leaves

YIELD: 36 PIECES

6 oz/170 g onions, minced

1½ tsp/4.50 g garlic, minced

2 oz/57 g green onion, cut into fine dice

½ oz/14 g chopped parsley

2 oz/57 g olive oil

1 tbsp/3 g chopped dill

1 tbsp/3 g chopped mint

1½ tsp/1 g chopped oregano

1½ tsp/3 g ground turmeric

1½ tsp/3 g ground cumin

1½ tsp/3 g ground coriander

1½ tsp/3 g fennel seed

½ tsp/1 g ground cinnamon

1½ oz/43 g ginger, minced

3 oz/85 g pine nuts, toasted

3 large eggs, beaten

6 oz/170 g rice, cooked and drained

1 lb 8 oz/680 g lamb, ground

Salt, as needed

Ground black pepper, as needed

36 grape leaves, soaked in water

24 fl oz/720 mL Chicken Stock (page 529), hot

BRUSHING SAUCE

2 fl oz/60 mL olive oil

1 tbsp/3 g chopped mint

1½ tsp/1 g chopped oregano

1½ oz/43 g lemon juice

1. Sauté the onions, garlic, green onion, and parsley in the oil and cool.

2. Combine the herbs, spices, pine nuts, eggs, rice, lamb, salt, and pepper and mix well.

3. Place 1½ oz/43 g of the filling in a grape leaf, fold in the ends of the leaf over the filling, and roll up. Repeat with the remaining filling and grape leaves.

4. Place the finished grape leaves in a pan, seam side down. Add enough hot stock to just cover the leaves. Cover with a lid and bake in a 350°F/177° oven for 1 hour, or until the filling is tender.

5. Combine all ingredients for the sauce and brush it over the finished grape leaves.

Beef Negimaki

YIELD: 30 PIECES

1 lb 12 oz/794 g beef strip loin

6 fl oz/180 mL water

5 fl oz/150 mL soy sauce

3 oz/85 g honey

1 oz/28 g ginger, grated

½ fl oz/15 mL dark sesame oil

3 garlic, cloves minced to a paste

6 oz/170 g green onions, green tops only, left whole

1¼ tsp/3.75 g cornstarch

¾ oz/21 g sesame seeds

2 tbsp/6 g chives, chopped

1. Remove the silverskin and fat from the beef, leaving only the muscle. Wrap well and freeze just until very firm but not frozen solid, about 3 hours.

2. Combine the water, soy sauce, honey, ginger, sesame oil, and garlic in a saucepan. Simmer over low heat until flavorful, about 5 minutes. Strain the marinade, cool, and reserve under refrigeration.

3. Using an electric slicer, slice the semifrozen beef into thin slices, about 1 oz/28 g each. Lay them out, overlapping, in groups of 8 on a parchment-lined sheet pan.

4. Arrange the green onions lengthwise on the beef and roll the beef tightly around them. Transfer the rolls to a hotel pan and pour three-quarters of the marinade over the beef. Cover and marinate under refrigeration for at least 4 and up to 12 hours.

5. To prepare the glaze, make a cornstarch slurry by stirring ½ fl oz/15 mL cool water into the cornstarch. Bring the remaining marinade to a simmer in a saucepan. Add the cornstarch slurry to the simmering marinade while stirring or whisking constantly. When the mixture has a coating consistency, remove it from the heat.

6. Squeeze the beef rolls to remove the excess marinade and arrange seam side down on a greased sheet pan.

7. Broil the rolls under high heat until the beef is browned and cooked through, about 5 minutes. Remove them from the broiler or salamander, brush lightly with the glaze, and sprinkle with sesame seeds and chives.

8. Use skewers or picks to secure the roll and mark into portions. Cut into bite-size pieces and serve at once.

Beef Saté

YIELD: 30 PIECES

1 lb 14 oz/851 g tenderloin tips or sirloin tips

4 tsp/12 g garlic, minced

2 tsp/6 g ginger, minced

1 small chile, crushed

2 tsp/4 g curry powder

2 tbsp/6 g cilantro, chopped

2 fl oz/60 mL soy sauce

1 fl oz/30 mL sesame oil

1 tbsp/3 g lemongrass, minced (optional)

8 fl oz/240 mL Peanut Sauce (page 50)

1. Slice the meat lengthwise into equal 1-oz/28-g portions.

2. Combine the garlic, ginger, chile, curry, cilantro, soy sauce, sesame oil, and lemongrass, if desired. Add the meat to the mixture and turn to coat. Cover and refrigerate for at least 1 hour and up to 2 hours.

3. Soak 30 bamboo skewers, 6 in/15 cm long, in water for 30 minutes to prevent burning.

4. Remove the meat from the marinade, scraping off any excess. Weave each slice of meat onto a skewer.

5. Sear on a hot griddle, or broil until medium rare, about 1 minute per side.

6. Serve with warm peanut dipping sauce.

NOTE: Lamb may be substituted for the beef.

Beef Saté with Peanut Sauce

Lamb Brochettes with Mint Pesto

YIELD: 30 PIECES

2 lb 8 oz/1.13 kg leg of lamb, boned and trimmed of connective tissue

1 fl oz/30 mL lemon juice (about ½ lemon)

3 large garlic cloves, crushed

1 tsp/5 g salt

½ tsp/1 g ground black pepper

2 oz/57 g extra-virgin olive oil

2 tbsp/6 g mint, chopped

8 oz/227 g pancetta, thinly sliced, or bacon (about 15 slices)

16 fl oz/480 mL Mint Pesto Sauce (page 46)

1. Cut the lamb into ¾-in/2-cm cubes. Combine the lemon juice, garlic, salt, and pepper, whisk until blended, and add the oil and mint.

2. Toss the lamb in the mixture to coat well, cover, and marinate under refrigeration, tossing occasionally, for a minimum of 4 hours.

3. Soak 30 bamboo skewers, 6 in/15 cm long, in water for 30 minutes to prevent burning.

4. Thread 2 pieces of lamb and ½ slice of pancetta on each skewer and arrange on a sheet pan.

5. Roast in a 450°F/232°C oven for 8 to 12 minutes, or until the lamb is nicely browned outside yet still pink and juicy inside.

6. Serve with mint pesto sauce for dipping.

NOTE: If using bacon, blanch it in a large saucepan of slowly simmering water for 5 minutes. The bacon will become opaque and firm. Drain and pat dry before using.

Pork Piccadillo Empanadas

YIELD: 30 EMPANADAS

PORK FILLING

2 tsp/10 mL olive or vegetable oil

12 oz/340 g pork butt, coarsely ground

½ oz/14 g jalapeño, minced

2 tsp/4 g chili powder

1 tsp/2 g ground cumin

1 tsp/2 g ground cinnamon

¼ tsp/0.50 g ground allspice

2 oz/57 g golden raisins, plumped in warm water

1¾ oz/50 g blanched almonds, toasted and chopped

1½ fl oz/45 mL lime juice

Salt, as needed

Ground black pepper, as needed

1 oz/28 g sour cream, or as needed

EMPANADA DOUGH

6¾ oz/191 g all-purpose flour

4 oz/113 g masa harina

3½ tsp/10.50 g baking powder

1 tsp/5 g salt

4 oz/113 g lard, melted and cooled

6 fl oz/180 mL water, or as needed

2 eggs

Oil for frying, as needed

8 fl oz/240 mL Salsa Verde (page 42), Salsa Fresco (page 43), or Chipotle Pico de Gallo (page 45)

1. Heat the oil in a sauté pan over medium heat. Add the pork and sauté, breaking up the meat, until it is no longer pink, about 10 minutes. Stir in the jalapeño, chili powder, cumin, cinnamon, and allspice. Continue to sauté until most of the liquid evaporates, 5 to 6 minutes more. Transfer to a bowl and fold in the raisins and almonds. Season with lime juice, salt, and pepper. Fold in the sour cream, adding just enough to gently bind the filling. Cool the filling, cover, and hold under refrigeration until ready to assemble the empanadas, up to 2 days.

2. To prepare the dough, blend the flour, masa harina, baking powder, and salt in a mixing bowl. Add the lard and mix by hand or on low speed in a mixer until evenly moistened. Blend 4 fl oz/120 mL water and 1 egg and add the mixture gradually to the dough, stirring or blending with a dough hook as you work. Knead the dough until it is pliable, about 3 minutes.

3. Whisk together the remaining egg and 2 fl oz/60 mL water to make an egg wash.

4. To assemble the empanadas, roll out the dough very thin (¹⁄₁₆ in/1.5 mm) and cut into circles (3 in/8 cm) to make at least 30 circles. Place ½ oz/14 g filling on each circle. Brush the edges with egg wash, fold in half, and seal the seams. Transfer to parchment-lined sheet pans, cover, and keep refrigerated until ready to fry. They may be held for up to 24 hours, or frozen for up to 3 weeks.

5. Heat the oil in a deep fryer (or to a depth of 2 in/5 cm in a rondeau) to 350°F/177°C. Add the empanadas to the hot oil and fry, turning if necessary to brown both sides evenly, until golden brown and crisp, 4 to 5 minutes. Drain and blot briefly. Serve while very hot with the salsa or pico de gallo.

Chinese Skewered Bites

YIELD: 30 SERVINGS (½ OZ/14 G EACH)

32 fl oz/960 mL dry red wine

14 oz/397 g green onions, minced

8 fl oz/240 mL light soy sauce

6 fl oz/180 mL plum sauce

4 fl oz/120 mL dark sesame oil

2 oz/57 g sesame seeds, toasted

½ oz/14 g garlic, finely minced

1 tsp/1 g dried thyme leaves

1 lb/454 g pork loin, cut into bite-size pieces

1. Combine the wine, green onions, soy sauce, plum sauce, sesame oil, sesame seeds, garlic, and thyme in a small saucepan and boil for 5 minutes. Allow the mixture to cool to room temperature. Pour the marinade over the pork and refrigerate, covered, for at least 1 hour.

2. Soak 30 bamboo skewers, 2 in/5 cm long, in water for 30 minutes.

3. Remove the pork from the marinade and place on the skewers.

4. Simmer the marinade for 10 minutes, or until thick.

5. While the marinade is simmering, broil or grill the meat for 5 to 7 minutes, or until done.

6. Strain the marinade and use it for a dipping sauce.

VARIATION: Substitute beef or chicken for the pork.

Fried Wontons

YIELD: 75 PIECES

1 lb 4 oz/567 g pork, ground (from shoulder)

10 oz/283 g savoy cabbage, shredded very fine

6 oz/170 g red pepper, minced very fine

6 oz/170 g shiitake mushrooms, minced very fine

2¾ oz/78 g green onions, sliced

1 tbsp/9 g garlic, minced to a paste

1 tbsp/9 g ginger, minced very fine or grated

½ fl oz/15 mL oyster sauce

½ fl oz/15 mL soy sauce

½ fl oz/15 mL dark sesame oil

1 tbsp/3 g cilantro, coarsely chopped

¾ tsp/3.75 g salt, or as needed

1 tsp/2 g ground black pepper, or as needed

1 egg

2 fl oz/60 mL water

75 wonton wrappers

1. Sauté the pork in a wok or skillet over high heat until it is cooked through, about 6 minutes. Drain the pork in a colander to remove excess fat.

2. Return the pan to high heat and add the cabbage, red pepper, and shiitake mushrooms. Sauté, stirring the vegetables as necessary, until they are almost tender, about 10 minutes. Add the green onions, garlic, and ginger and cook until aromatic, 2 to 3 minutes. Add the pork to the vegetable mixture.

3. Remove the pork and cabbage mixture from the heat and stir in the oyster sauce, soy sauce, sesame oil, cilantro, salt, and pepper. Allow the mixture to rest for 20 minutes to blend the flavors.

4. Whisk together the egg and water to make an egg wash.

5. To fill the wontons, place about ½ oz/14 g filling into a wrapper and brush the edges with egg wash. Pull the wrapper over the top of the filling and seal the edges. Pull the tips back toward each other and pin together (see Steamed Wontons on page 402 for shaping photos).

6. Fry the wontons in 350°F/177°C oil, turning as necessary, until evenly brown and crispy, 3 to 4 minutes.

NOTE: If preparing this filling mixture in advance, cool it rapidly and store under refrigeration. Make a sample wonton and check seasoning. Make any necessary adjustments before filling all the wrappers.

Steamed Wontons with Shrimp

YIELD: 25 PIECES

12 oz/340 g shrimp, peeled and deveined	Salt, as needed
½ fl oz/15 mL sesame oil	Ground black pepper, as needed
2¼ tsp/11.25 g sugar	4 oz/113 g cooked brown rice
1 tsp/3 g ginger, minced very fine	25 wonton wrappers
1 tsp/3 g garlic, minced very fine	⅔ oz/19 g green onions, thinly sliced on the bias
1 tsp/1 g flat-leaf parsley, minced	1½ tbsp/9 g sesame seeds, toasted

1. Make the filling in a food processor by puréeing the shrimp, sesame oil, sugar, ginger, garlic, parsley, salt, and pepper into a coarse paste, pulsing the machine on and off in short blasts. Transfer the shrimp mixture to a bowl. Purée the rice in the food processor very briefly, just enough to break up the grains. Fold the rice into the shrimp mixture until evenly blended, making sure to scrape the bowl while folding. If making in advance, cover, label, and store under refrigeration for up to 24 hours. Make a sample wonton and check seasoning. Make any necessary adjustments before filling all the wrappers.

2. To assemble the wontons, transfer the shrimp and rice filling to a pastry bag with no tip. Fill each wrapper with 1 tsp/4 g filling. Brush the edges of each wrapper with water. Fold the wonton in half to make a triangle. Press to seal the edges securely. Bring the two corners along the base of the triangle in toward each other, overlap them, and press to seal securely. Transfer to a parchment-lined sheet pan and refrigerate until ready for service. The wontons can be stored for up to 24 hours under refrigeration or frozen for up to 3 weeks.

3. For each serving, arrange 3 or 4 wontons in a small bamboo steamer and steam over boiling water until the wrappers are tender and translucent and the filling is completely cooked, 10 to 12 minutes. Transfer the steamer to a plate; garnish with sliced green onions and sesame seeds. Serve with a container of dipping sauce (1½ fl oz/45 mL per serving) in the center of a basket with chopsticks.

Making wontons. **A.** Filling the wonton using a pastry bag. **B.** Brushing the edge of the wonton wrapper with water. **C.** Folding the wonton over. **D.** Bringing the edges of the filled wonton together.

Shrimp Tempura

YIELD: 30 PIECES

12 oz/340 g all-purpose flour

½ tsp/2.50 g salt

¾ oz/21 g baking powder

24 fl oz/720 mL water, cold

2 fl oz/60 mL sesame oil

30 shrimp (26/30 count), peeled and deveined

1 oz/28 g salt

½ tsp/1 g ground black pepper

32 fl oz/960 mL vegetable oil, for pan-frying

1. Whisk together the flour, the ½ tsp/2.50 g salt, and the baking powder. Stream in the water and sesame oil all at once and gently whisk until combined. The batter should be very smooth and about the thickness of pancake batter. Keep the batter chilled until ready to prepare the tempura.

2. Blot the shrimp dry, season with salt and pepper, and dip in the batter; hold the shrimp over the bowl, allowing excess batter to drip off.

3. Deep-fry in 350°F/177°C oil for 4 to 5 minutes, or until the shrimp tails turn a light pink color and the batter is puffed and light golden brown. Drain on absorbent paper.

4. Serve at once with dipping sauce.

VEGETABLE TEMPURA: Substitute 2 lb 12 oz/1.25 kg assorted vegetables (e.g., broccoli, zucchini, mushrooms) for the shrimp. Blot the vegetables dry before seasoning and frying them.

Mussels Stuffed with Vegetables

YIELD: 30 PIECES

30 mussels (about 1 lb 5 oz/595 g)

2 fl oz/60 mL white wine

1 oz/28 g butter

2 oz/57 g onion, minced

1 garlic clove, minced

2 oz/57 g carrot, cut into brunoise

1 oz/28 g leek, white part only, minced (about a 2-in/5-cm section)

1 oz/28 g flour

8 fl oz/240 mL milk

1 egg yolk

Salt, as needed

Pepper, as needed

5 oz/142 g bread crumbs

1½ fl oz/45 mL olive oil

1. Clean the mussels and remove the beards. Combine the mussels and wine in a large pot over high heat and bring to a boil. Cover and steam the mussels until just opened, 3 to 5 minutes. Discard any unopened mussels.

2. Remove the meat from the shells and chop. Reserve the steaming liquid. Separate the shells and discard half of them. Rinse and dry the remaining shells and set aside.

3. Heat the butter in a saucepan over medium heat. Add the onions, garlic, carrot, and leek and sweat for 3 minutes. Add the flour and cook, stirring constantly, until the flour begins to turn a golden brown.

4. Whisk in the milk and 2 fl oz/60 mL of the reserved steaming liquid. Simmer the mixture, stirring occasionally, for 12 to 15 minutes, or until the sauce is thickened.

5. Temper the egg yolk into the thickened sauce. Add the mussel meat. Stir for 1 minute, or until the meat is heated through. Season with salt and pepper.

6. Fill each of the shells with ½ oz/14 g filling and refrigerate until cool.

7. Combine the bread crumbs with the olive oil and sprinkle evenly over the filled shells. Broil until golden brown and heated through, about 2 minutes.

8. Serve hot as individual passed hors d'oeuvre, or 3 each for an appetizer serving.

Crab Cakes with Creole Honey-Mustard Sauce

YIELD: 30 PIECES

1 lb/454 g lump crabmeat, picked clean

2 strips bacon, cooked crisp and crumbled

4¼ oz/120 g fresh white bread crumbs

1 oz/28 g celery, cut into small dice

2 green onions, minced

2 garlic cloves, minced

2 tsp/10 g Dijon mustard

2 tsp/4 g dry mustard

Salt, as needed

Cayenne, as needed

Basic Mayonnaise (page 35), as needed

Juice of ½ lemon

5½ oz/156 g Asian-style bread crumbs (panko)

8 fl oz/240 mL vegetable oil

8 fl oz/240 mL Creole Honey-Mustard Sauce (page 39)

1. Combine the crabmeat, bacon, white bread crumbs, celery, green onions, garlic, Dijon mustard, dry mustard, salt, cayenne, and mayonnaise; use just enough mayonnaise to hold the mixture together. Adjust seasoning.

2. Portion the crab cakes into ½-oz/14-g balls, flatten slightly, and bread with the Asian-style bread crumbs. At this point, the cakes may be refrigerated or frozen for later use.

3. Heat the oil to 350°F/177°C. Pan-fry the crab cakes in oil until golden. Drain briefly on paper towels. Serve immediately with the honey-mustard sauce.

Petite Cod Cakes with Black Olive Butter Sauce

YIELD: 30 PIECES

COD CAKES

1 lb/454 g potatoes, steamed or boiled and puréed

1 lb/454 g cod fillet, poached

1 fl oz/30 mL olive oil

1 tsp/3 g minced garlic

Pinch cayenne

½ tsp/2.50 g salt

Olive oil for sautéing, as needed

1 recipe Black Olive Butter Sauce (recipe follows), warm

GARNISH

5 oz/142 g tomatoes, peeled, seeded, and cut into allumettes

1½ oz/43 g Niçoise olive slivers

½ oz/14 g basil chiffonade

1. Combine the potatoes, cod, oil, garlic, cayenne, and salt, making sure first to dry both the cod and the potatoes thoroughly. Shape into 30 cylinders, each 1 in/3 cm in diameter and 2 in/5 cm long.

2. **Hors d'Oeuvre Assembly:** For each serving, heat oil and sauté 3 cakes, browning only on the top and bottom. Finish in a 400°F/204°C oven for about 5 minutes.

3. Spoon ½ oz/14 g butter sauce on a warm plate and place 3 cakes on top. Toss ½ oz/14 g tomatoes, a generous teaspoon of olives, and a pinch of basil quickly in a hot sauté pan and mound next to cod cakes.

Black Olive Butter Sauce

YIELD: 5 OZ/142 G

2 fl oz/60 mL red wine

1 tbsp/12 g minced shallots

1 sprig thyme

½ bay leaf

1 oz/28 g chopped Niçoise olives

1 fl oz/30 mL heavy cream

5 oz/142 g butter

2 tsp/10 mL soy sauce

Salt, as needed

Ground black pepper, as needed

1. Simmer the wine, shallots, thyme, bay leaf, and olives until reduced to a syrupy consistency.

2. Add the cream and reduce to a coating consistency. Finish by whisking or swirling in the butter.

3. Season with the soy sauce, salt, and pepper; strain through a sieve.

Chicken Croustade

YIELD: 30 PIECES

1 loaf soft white bread, sliced

6 fl oz/180 mL heavy cream

8 oz/227 g raw chicken breast meat, cut into small dice

½ fl oz/15 mL olive oil

4 oz/113 g prosciutto ham, cut into small dice

Ground black pepper, as needed

1 egg yolk

¾ oz/21 g grated Parmesan cheese, plus as needed for topping

1 tbsp/3 g chopped basil

1 tbsp/3 g chopped flat-leaf parsley

Salt, as needed

1. With a rolling pin, roll out each bread slice until thin. Cut out bread with a plain round cutter 1½ in/4 cm in diameter and flatten again with a rolling pin. Oil small muffin tins and place the bread rounds inside. Bake in a 325°F/163°C oven until golden. Store the croustade shells, covered, in a dry area.

2. Reduce the cream by half and reserve until needed.

3. Sauté the chicken in the oil until half done. Add the prosciutto and continue to cook until the prosciutto is thoroughly heated and the chicken is thoroughly cooked.

4. Add the cream and pepper; bring to a simmer. Temper the egg yolk and add to the mixture, being careful not to boil.

5. Add the Parmesan, basil, and parsley. Season with salt.

6. Fill the croustade shells; sprinkle with a little additional grated Parmesan, and brown lightly under a broiler or salamander. Serve warm.

Risotto Croquettes with Fontina

YIELD: 30 PIECES

1 oz/28 g finely diced onion

2 oz/57 g butter

1 lb/454 g Arborio rice

8 fl oz/240 mL white wine

48 fl oz/1.44 L Chicken Stock (page 529), hot

4 oz/113 g Parmesan cheese

Salt, as needed

15 oz/425 g Fontina cheese, cut into thirty ¼-in/6-mm cubes

4½ oz/128 g flour

2 eggs

1 fl oz/30 mL water or milk

3½ oz/99 g bread crumbs

Vegetable oil for frying, as needed

30 slices plum tomatoes (about 8 oz/ 227 g), roasted

Olive oil, as needed

Herbs (thyme, basil, marjoram), as needed

1. Sauté the onions in the butter. Add the rice and coat with butter; cook until parched.

2. Add the wine; simmer until absorbed, then add the stock in 3 parts. Cook over low heat, stirring frequently, until the rice is done, about 18 minutes. Add the Parmesan.

3. Transfer the risotto to a sheet pan and spread in an even layer. Allow the rice to cool completely. Season with salt, if necessary.

4. Form the chilled risotto into 30 small balls wrapped around a cube each of Fontina.

5. Coat the balls using the standard breading procedure (see page 548).

6. Deep-fry the croquettes at 350°F/177°C until golden brown. Garnish with an oven-roasted tomato slice, olive oil, and fresh herbs.

CHEF'S NOTES: This recipe works best when the risotto is prepared a day in advance. Other fillings can be used in place of Fontina, such as cooked sausage, seafood, vegetables, or Toasted Almonds (page 546).

Risotto and Pancetta Cakes with Sun-Dried Tomato Pesto

YIELD: 30 PIECES

8 oz/227 g pancetta, thinly sliced

1 oz/28 g butter

1 oz/28 g onion, minced

7 oz/198 g Arborio rice

28 fl oz/840 mL Chicken Stock (page 529), hot

2 tbsp/6 g parsley, minced

1 fl oz/30 mL dry white wine

4 oz/113 g Parmesan cheese, grated

Salt, as needed

Ground black pepper, as needed

14 oz/397 g panko bread crumbs

3 eggs

4 fl oz/120 mL milk

8 oz/227 g all-purpose flour, or as needed

8 fl oz/240 mL vegetable oil for frying, or as needed

12 oz/340 g Sun-Dried Tomato Pesto (page 47)

1. Bake the pancetta slices in a single layer on parchment-lined sheet pans in a 350°F/177°C oven until crisp, 10 to 12 minutes. Let cool, roughly chop, and set aside.

2. Heat the butter in a saucepan over medium-high heat. Add the onion and sweat until softened and translucent, 6 to 8 minutes. Increase the heat to high and add the rice. Cook, stirring constantly, for 1 minute.

3. Add one-third of the stock to the rice and cook, stirring every 3 to 5 minutes, until the rice absorbs it. Repeat using half of the remaining stock. Add the remaining stock and stir the risotto until the rice is tender and most of the liquid is absorbed. Remove from the heat and stir in the parsley, wine, pancetta, and 2 oz/57 g of the cheese. Season with salt and pepper.

4. Evenly spread the risotto onto a quarter sheet pan lined with lightly oiled parchment paper. Cover and refrigerate until firm and cool. Cut the chilled risotto into 30 pieces, about 1½ in/4 cm square.

5. For the breading, combine the bread crumbs and remaining cheese. Whisk together the eggs and milk. Dip a risotto cake into the flour and tap off excess. Dip in the egg mixture and then in the bread crumb mixture, turning to coat thoroughly each time. Repeat with the remaining cakes.

6. Heat the oil in a large skillet over medium-high heat. Pan-fry the risotto cakes until golden brown and crisp, 1 to 2 minutes on each side.

7. Serve hot, garnished with a dollop of sun-dried tomato pesto.

NOTE: For appetizer-size pieces, cut the chilled risotto into 10 equal pieces, about 1¾ by 3½ in/4 by 9 cm.

Spanikopita

YIELD: 12 PIECES

½ oz/14 g butter

1 oz/28 g shallots, minced

1 tbsp/9 g garlic, minced

6 oz/170 g spinach, cleaned and stems removed

½ tsp/1 g grated nutmeg

1½ tsp/1.50 g dill, chopped

3 oz/85 g feta cheese, crumbled

1 oz/28 g mozzarella cheese, grated

½ tsp/2.50 g salt

Pinch of ground black pepper

6 phyllo dough sheets

4 oz/113 g butter, melted

1. Melt the butter in a sauté pan over medium heat until it starts to bubble. Add the shallots and garlic and sweat until translucent.

2. Add the spinach, nutmeg, and dill and sauté gently until the spinach is wilted, 1 to 2 minutes. Transfer the spinach mixture to a stainless-steel bowl and allow it to cool to room temperature. Add the cheeses and season with salt and pepper. Keep the filling refrigerated until needed.

3. Lay 1 sheet of phyllo dough on a cutting board. Brush it lightly with melted butter. Place another sheet of phyllo dough directly onto the buttered sheet and brush it lightly with butter. Repeat for a third time.

4. Cut the phyllo dough lengthwise into 6 even strips. Place 1 oz/28 g spinach filling onto the bottom right corner of each strip. Fold the bottom right corner of a strip diagonally to the left side of the strip to create a triangle of dough encasing the filling. Fold the bottom left point of the dough up along the left side of the dough to seal in the filling.

5. Fold the bottom left corner of the dough diagonally to the right side of the dough to form a triangle. Fold the bottom right point up along the right edge of the dough. Repeat until the end of the strip is reached and you have a triangle of layered phyllo dough with the filling wrapped inside. Repeat with each strip.

6. Place the phyllo triangles on a parchment-lined sheet pan and brush each with melted butter.

7. Bake in a 400°F/204°C oven until golden brown, 15 to 20 minutes. Serve immediately.

Crispy Herbed Mushrooms

YIELD: 30 PIECES

30 medium white mushrooms	12 fl oz/360 mL beer
6¼ oz/177 g all-purpose flour	12 oz/340 g bread crumbs
1 oz/28 g baking powder	1½ tbsp/4.50 g parsley, chopped
½ tsp/2.50 g salt	1½ tbsp/4.50 g chives, chopped
¼ tsp/0.50 g ground white pepper	2¼ tsp/2.25 g marjoram, chopped
½ oz/14 g sugar	48 fl oz/1.44 L vegetable oil, for frying

1. Wash and trim the mushrooms. Toss in 1¼ oz/35 g of the flour.

2. Combine the remaining flour with the baking powder, salt, pepper, sugar, and beer. Mix the bread crumbs with the herbs. Heat the oil to 325°F/163°C.

3. Dip the mushrooms in the batter and roll them in the bread crumb mixture. Deep-fry the mushrooms in the oil until golden brown. Serve immediately.

Wrapped Shrimp with Asian Barbecue Sauce

YIELD: 30 PIECES

1 lb/454 g pineapple, cleaned and trimmed

1 lb/454 g medium shrimp, peeled and deveined

Salt, as needed

Pepper, as needed

15 pieces bacon, parbaked and halved

½ fl oz/15 mL olive oil or vegetable oil

2¼ oz/64 g onions, diced

1½ oz/43 g celery, diced

1 garlic clove, chopped

1 fl oz/30 mL rice vinegar

4 oz/113 g ketchup

4 oz/113 g chili sauce

1 fl oz/30 mL soy sauce

2¼ fl oz/68 mL plum sauce

2 tsp/10 mL Worcestershire sauce

2⅓ oz/66 g green onions, thinly sliced

3 oz/85 g toasted coconut

1. Cut thirty ½-in/1-cm chunks of pineapple and finely chop the rest.

2. Season the shrimp with salt and pepper. Place a chunk of pineapple on each shrimp and wrap with a piece of bacon.

3. Place a 6-in/15-cm skewer through each shrimp unit and reserve. (Do not hold for too long, as the pineapple will denature the shrimp.)

4. Heat the oil in a large skillet over medium heat and sweat the onions, celery, and garlic until softened but not brown, 3 to 4 minutes.

5. Add the reserved pineapple, vinegar, ketchup, chili sauce, soy sauce, plum sauce, and Worcestershire sauce to the onion mixture. Bring to a simmer and cook for 15 minutes, or until the sauce is glossy and thickened. Adjust the consistency with water, if necessary, and season with salt and pepper. Keep the sauce warm.

6. To cook the shrimp, spoon or brush a small amount of sauce (about 1 tsp/5 mL each) over each skewer and place in a 400°F/204°C oven until the meat just turns white, about 10 minutes.

7. Remove from the oven and neatly arrange on serving platters. Garnish with the green onions and coconut. Serve immediately, with the remaining sauce on the side for dipping.

Potato Crêpes with Crème Fraîche and Caviar

YIELD: 30 PIECES

12 oz/340 g puréed cooked potatoes

1 oz/28 g flour

2 eggs

3 egg whites

2 fl oz/60 mL heavy cream, or as needed

Salt, as needed

Ground white pepper, as needed

Pinch grated nutmeg

Vegetable oil, as needed

4 fl oz/120 mL Crème Fraîche (page 351)

1 oz/28 g caviar

Dill sprigs, as needed

6 oz/170 g smoked salmon slices (optional)

1. Combine the potatoes and flour in a mixer. Add the eggs one at a time, then the whites. Adjust the consistency with the cream to that of a pancake batter; season with salt, pepper, and nutmeg.

2. **Hors d'Oeuvre Assembly:** Coat a nonstick griddle or sauté pan lightly with oil. Pour the batter as for pancakes into silver dollar–size portions. Cook until golden brown; turn and finish on the second side, about 2 minutes total cooking time.

3. Serve the crêpes warm with small dollops of crème fraîche and caviar, a small dill sprig, and a smoked salmon slice, if desired.

CHEF'S NOTE: For dill crêpes, chop some of the dill and add it to the heavy cream, lightly heated. Cool before preparing the crêpe batter.

New Potatoes with Snails and Brie

YIELD: 30 PIECES

1 bunch basil

2 garlic cloves, minced

½ oz/14 g pine nuts, toasted

1 oz/28 g grated Parmesan cheese

3 fl oz/90 mL olive oil

24 fl oz/720 mL water

8 fl oz/240 mL white wine

8 oz/227 g Mirepoix (page 522)

2 bay leaves

2 tsp/4 g dried thyme

2 tsp/10 g salt, plus more as needed

1 tbsp/6 g cracked black pepper, plus more as needed

30 fresh snails, cleaned and rinsed

4 lb/1.81 kg new red potatoes (30 B size; see Chef's Note)

Vegetable oil for deep-frying, as needed

15 oz/425 g Brie, cut into ½-oz/14-g pieces

1. Purée the basil, garlic, pine nuts, and cheese in a food processor fitted with a metal blade attachment. Slowly add 2 fl oz/60 mL of the oil. Reserve.

2. Combine the water, wine, mirepoix, bay leaves, thyme, salt, and pepper; simmer 5 minutes. Add the snails; simmer 5 to 7 minutes. Remove the snails from their shells. Cool the snails in the liquid.

3. Scoop out a hole in the center of the potatoes and square off the bottoms. Blanch the potatoes in salted boiling water until they are almost cooked through but still firm. Remove and dry.

4. Deep-fry the potatoes until golden, drain on paper towels, and keep warm.

5. Remove the snails from the cooking liquid and sauté them in the remaining olive oil. Remove from the heat and add the basil sauce to the pan. Mix well and adjust seasoning if necessary.

6. Place a snail in each of the potatoes with a little of the basil sauce. Top with a slice of Brie, melt in a hot oven, and serve very warm.

CHEF'S NOTE: If small new potatoes are not available, use 15 larger ones. Cut the potatoes in half lengthwise and square off the bottoms. Scoop out a hole in the center of each half.

Bluepoint Oyster Martini with Beluga Caviar

YIELD: 30 PIECES

MIGNONETTE

1¼ oz/35 g minced shallots

2 oz/57 g chopped chives

2⅔ fl oz/80 mL Champagne vinegar

1½ oz/43 g cracked black pepper

30 oysters

1 oz/28 g beluga caviar

1. To prepare the mignonette, combine the shallots, chives, vinegar, and pepper and reserve.

2. Shuck the oysters, loosen the muscle from the bottom shell, and then remove with the top shell.

3. **Hors d'Oeuvre Assembly:** Place the shells on a bed of crushed ice. Place an oyster inside each shell. Top each with mignonette sauce and a dollop of caviar.

Carpaccio-Wrapped Watercress with Blue Cheese Dip

YIELD: 30 PIECES

10 oz/283 g beef tenderloin

3 bunches watercress, washed and dried

6 fl oz/180 mL Roquefort Dressing (page 40)

1. Slice the tenderloin paper thin (see Beef Carpaccio, page 428, for more detailed instructions).
2. Trim the watercress to approximately 2½ in/6 cm long and make into 30 small bundles.
3. Wrap each bundle with a thin slice of carpaccio.
4. Serve with the dressing on the side.

PROSCIUTTO ROLL FILLED WITH ARUGULA: Sauté blanched arugula in a little olive oil and garlic. Season with salt and pepper. Chill thoroughly. Roll in thinly sliced prosciutto as in Step 3.

Dates Stuffed with Boursin Cheese

YIELD: 30 PIECES

3 oz/85 g Boursin au Poivre cheese

3 oz/85 g cream cheese

30 pistachios, shelled

15 fresh dates, pitted and split

1. Combine the cheeses; mix until well blended and soft.
2. Split the pistachios following the natural seam of the nut.
3. Pipe the cheese mixture into the cavity of each date using a No. 3 plain tip.
4. Garnish with 2 pistachio halves per date.

Grapes Rolled in Blue de Bresse

YIELD: 50 PIECES

4 oz/113 g Blue de Bresse (or other blue cheese)

4 oz/113 g cream cheese

50 seedless green grapes

4 oz/113 g shelled pistachios

1. Combine the cheeses in a mixer fitted with a paddle attachment and mix well; there should be very few lumps. Refrigerate for 1 hour.

2. Wrap a small amount of cheese around each grape by rolling in the palms of your hands. Store on a sheet pan lined with parchment paper. Chill under refrigeration at least 1 hour and up to overnight.

3. Pulse the pistachios in a food processor; force them through a drum sieve.

4. Roll the grapes in the nut powder and shape with the palms of your hands. This can be done up to 1 hour before service. Do not refrigerate the grapes once they have been rolled in the nut powder.

PRESENTATION IDEA: The grapes can be arranged on a platter in the shape of a natural bunch of grapes.

Scallop Seviche in Cucumber Cups

YIELD: 30 PIECES

6 oz/170 g sea scallops, cut into brunoise

1 tomato, peeled, seeded, and cut into brunoise

1 tsp/1 g minced chives

1 tbsp/3 g chopped cilantro

½ jalapeño, minced

¼ green pepper, cut into brunoise

½ fl oz/15 mL olive oil

5 drops Tabasco sauce

Juice of 1 or 2 limes

1 tsp/5 g kosher salt

Ground black pepper, as needed

3 cucumbers, sliced ½ in/1 cm thick (30 slices total)

Sour cream, as needed (optional)

2 tsp/2 g cilantro leaves (optional)

1. To make the seviche, combine the scallops, tomato, herbs, jalapeño, pepper, oil, and Tabasco. Add enough lime juice to cover the scallops. Season with salt and pepper. Marinate at least 8 hours, stirring occasionally.

2. Trim the cucumber slices with a round cutter to remove the rind. Scoop a pocket out of the middle of the cucumber slices. Do not cut all the way through the slice.

3. Fill the cucumber cups with the seviche. Garnish each seviche cup with a small dot of sour cream and a cilantro leaf, if desired.

Pickled Shrimp

YIELD: 60 PIECES

8 fl oz/240 mL white vinegar

16 fl oz/480 mL water

½ oz/14 g salt

2 garlic cloves, crushed

1 tbsp/6 g mustard seed

1 tbsp/6 g celery seed

1 tsp/2 g ground cumin

2 cloves

12 allspice berries

1 oz/28 g light brown sugar

3 jalapeños, minced

4 bay leaves

60 shrimp (21/25 count), cooked and deveined

1. Combine the vinegar, water, salt, garlic, mustard seed, celery seed, cumin, cloves, allspice berries, sugar, jalapeños, and bay leaves and bring to a boil. Cool.

2. Pour the cold pickling mixture over the shrimp and marinate overnight.

PRESENTATION IDEA: Roll out and cut Pâté Dough (page 537) to make netting for an attractive buffet presentation.

Scallop Seviche in Cucumber Cups

Sushi

YIELD: 24 PIECES

4 oz/113 g short-grain rice	3 sheets nori
1 fl oz/30 mL rice vinegar, or as needed	1½ oz/43 g avocado, cut into julienne
2¼ tsp/11.25 g sugar	1½ oz/43 g cucumber, cut into julienne
Salt, as needed	1½ oz/43 g crabmeat

1. Wash the rice 3 times or until the water runs clear. Add water so it comes to 1 in/3 cm over the rice and cook, simmering, for 20 minutes, or until tender.

2. Warm the vinegar with the sugar and salt, but do not boil.

3. Fold the warm vinegar mixture into the hot rice. Allow the rice to cool completely.

4. Place a bamboo mat on a cutting board and lay 1 sheet of nori on top. Evenly spread 4 oz/113 g rice over the nori sheet, leaving a ½-in/1-cm band along one of the long sides of the nori sheet exposed.

5. Place ½ oz/14 g each of the avocado, cucumber, and crabmeat on the rice across the long edge of the nori sheet. Roll up carefully, brush the exposed strip of nori with rice vinegar, and press to seal.

6. Cut each roll into 8 equal pieces. Serve with pickled ginger and wasabi paste mixed with soy sauce.

CUCUMBER ROLL: Follow the recipe as stated above, but sprinkle 1 tsp/2 g unhulled sesame seeds on the spread rice and replace the filling ingredients with 1 oz/28 g julienned cucumber per roll.

AVOCADO ROLL: Follow the recipe as stated above, but sprinkle 1 tsp/2 g unhulled sesame seeds on the spread rice and replace the filling ingredients with 1 oz/28 g julienned avocado per roll.

A. Spreading rice on a nori sheet.   **B.** Placing the garnish ingredients on the rice.   **C.** Rolling a sushi roll, using a bamboo mat.   **D.** Slicing the roll into pieces.

Spiced Mixed Nuts

YIELD: 1 LB/454 G

1½ oz/43 g butter

½ fl oz/15 mL Worcestershire sauce

1 lb/454 g unsalted raw whole mixed nuts

½ tsp/1 g celery seed

½ tsp/1 g garlic powder

½ tsp/1 g chili powder

¼ tsp/0.50 g ground cumin

Pinch cayenne

½ tsp/2.50 g salt

1. Melt the butter over medium heat. Add the Worcestershire sauce and bring to a simmer. Add the nuts and toss well to coat evenly.

2. Sprinkle the combined spices and salt over the nuts and toss well to coat evenly.

3. Place the nuts on a nonstick or well-greased sheet pan and bake in a 375°F/191°C oven, stirring occasionally, for 10 to 12 minutes, or until evenly browned. Cool completely before serving.

4. Store in an airtight container for up to 2 weeks.

CHEF'S NOTE: If saltier nuts are desired, sprinkle with kosher salt while still warm.

Chili-Roasted Peanuts with Dried Cherries

YIELD: 1 LB/454 G

1 oz/28 g unsalted butter

1 lb/454 g raw peanuts

1 tbsp/6 g mild chili powder

2 tsp/4 g ground cumin

2 tsp/4 g ground white pepper

½ oz/14 g salt

½ tsp/1 g dried oregano

½ tsp/1 g cayenne

8 oz/227 g dried cherries or raisins

1. Melt the butter in a small saucepan. Coat the peanuts with the melted butter.

2. Mix together the chili powder, cumin, pepper, salt, oregano, and cayenne; reserve.

3. Place the peanuts on a large sheet pan and lightly toast in a 300° to 325°F/149° to 163°C oven for about 10 minutes, shaking the pan occasionally. Transfer the peanuts to a large bowl and coat with the dry ingredients. Mix in the cherries until uniformly blended.

4. Store in an airtight container for up to 2 weeks.

Chile-Roasted Peanuts
with Dried Cherries

Candied Pecans

YIELD: 1 LB/454 G

2 egg whites

1 fl oz/30 mL water

1 lb/454 g pecan halves

4½ oz/128 g superfine sugar

2 tsp/10 g salt

1 tbsp/6 g ground cinnamon

2 tsp/4 g ground ginger

2 tsp/4 g ground cardamom

1½ tsp/3 g ground allspice

1 tsp/2 g ground coriander

Pinch cayenne

1. Beat together the egg whites and water. Stir the nuts into the egg white mixture until completely coated. Drain well in a colander.

2. Combine the sugar, salt, and spices and toss the nuts in this mixture until evenly coated.

3. Turn the nuts onto a sheet pan and spread in a single layer. Bake in a 250°F/121°C oven for about 10 minutes, then lower the temperature to 225°F/107°C and bake, stirring occasionally, for another 10 minutes, or until the nuts are dark golden brown. Cool completely before serving.

4. Store in an airtight container for up to 2 weeks.

CHEF'S NOTE: These nuts are used to garnish the Smoked Duck Tart (page 449).

Toasted Almonds

YIELD: 1 LB/454 G

1 lb/454 g whole almonds

1 fl oz/30 mL pure olive oil

Kosher salt, as needed

1. Place the almonds on a sheet pan and roast in a 400°F/204°C oven. As the almonds toast, stir them periodically, so they roast evenly. Check for doneness after 10 minutes. Cut an almond open. It should be the color of a wooden cutting board.

2. When the almonds are done, put them in a bowl and toss them with the olive oil and salt. Let cool before serving.

3. Store in an airtight container for up to 2 weeks.

SMOKED TOASTED ALMONDS: Cold smoke almonds on a cooling rack before roasting.

Spicy Curried Cashews

YIELD: 1 LB/454 G

1 lb/454 g whole raw cashews

1 oz/28 g unsalted butter, melted

½ tsp/2.50 g salt

1 tbsp/6 g curry powder

¼ tsp/0.50 g garlic powder

¼ tsp/0.50 g onion powder

Pinch cayenne

1. Toss the cashews and melted butter together until evenly coated. Combine the salt and spices; reserve.

2. Place the cashews on a sheet pan and bake in a 350°F/177°C oven until golden brown. Remove the cashews from the oven and toss with the combined spices while still warm. Allow to cool before serving.

3. Store in an airtight container for up to 10 days.

Beef Carpaccio

YIELD: 10 SERVINGS

Carpaccio was first served at Harry's Bar in Venice, Italy. Mr. Cipriani was inspired by an exhibition of art by the famed Italian artist Carpaccio; the deep red color of the beef is typical of Carpaccio's color palette. In this presentation, the greens are nestled in a cucumber ring.

1 lb 8 oz/680 g beef sirloin or tenderloin, trimmed of all fat and silverskin

1 fl oz/30 mL pure olive oil

1 tbsp/3 g chopped rosemary

1 tbsp/3 g chopped sage

1 tbsp/3 g chopped thyme

½ fl oz/15 mL balsamic vinegar

2 tsp/10 g kosher salt

½ oz/14 g mignonette pepper

GARNISH

10 oz/283 g mixed greens, washed and dried

5 fl oz/150 mL Lemon Vinaigrette (page 29)

2 fl oz/60 mL olive oil

3 oz/85 g Parmesan cheese, shaved into curls

2 tbsp/6 g chopped flat-leaf parsley

2 oz/57 g capers, rinsed, dried, and fried in hot oil (optional)

1. Optional: Tie the beef to give it a uniform shape. Heat the oil over high heat and sear the beef on all sides. Remove it from the heat and cool.

2. Combine the herbs, vinegar, salt, and pepper and coat the beef evenly with this mixture. Wrap tightly in plastic wrap and freeze just until solid to be able to slice thinly.

3. **Appetizer Assembly:** For each serving, cut 6 or 7 very thin slices of beef by hand or with an electric slicer. Arrange on a chilled plate. Toss 1 oz/28 g greens with ½ fl oz/15 mL vinaigrette and arrange on the plate. Drizzle the meat with a few drops of extra-virgin olive oil and sprinkle with Parmesan curls, parsley, and fried capers, if desired.

Tuna Carpaccio with Shiitake Salad

YIELD: 10 SERVINGS

Tuna makes a beautiful carpaccio, without the fat and cholesterol of beef. The tuna for this dish must be of the highest quality and impeccably fresh.

1 lb 9 oz/709 g trimmed tuna fillet

SALAD

8 oz/227 g shiitake mushrooms, stemmed and cut into julienne

3 oz/85 g carrot, cut into julienne

3 oz/85 g red onion, cut into julienne

2 oz/57 g bok choy, cut into chiffonade

4 fl oz/120 mL rice wine vinegar

2 fl oz/60 mL sake

1 fl oz/30 mL reduced-sodium soy sauce

WASABI SAUCE

2 oz/57 g low-fat sour cream

Wasabi powder, as needed

Reduced-sodium soy sauce, as needed

1. Slice the tuna very thin and flatten it between layers of plastic wrap to the dimensions of the plating area of your appetizer plate.

2. Combine the salad ingredients and reserve. (The salad may be prepared up to 3 hours before serving.) Combine the wasabi sauce ingredients; keep refrigerated until ready to assemble the appetizer.

3. **Appetizer Assembly:** For each serving, lay 2½ oz/71 g sliced tuna on a chilled plate and mound 1 oz/28 g shiitake salad in the center of the tuna. Pipe or drizzle the wasabi sauce over the plate.

CHEF'S NOTE: The tuna can be flattened ahead of time and held between sheets of plastic wrap for up to 3 hours.

Salsa Cruda di Tonno

YIELD: 10 SERVINGS

1 lb 9 oz/709 g tuna fillet, very cold

SALSA CRUDA

8 fl oz/240 mL olive oil

5 oz/142 g picholine olives, pitted and finely chopped

4 oz/113 g celery hearts (stalks and leaves reserved separately), thinly sliced

2 oz/57 g red onion, cut into brunoise

2 oz/57 g jalapeño, cut into brunoise

1 oz/28 g salted capers, soaked twice for 20 minutes each time

1 oz/28 g flat-leaf parsley, cut into chiffonade

1 tsp/3 g garlic, minced to a paste

1 oz/28 g lemon zest, blanched, cut into brunoise

Sea salt, as needed

Ground black pepper, as needed

4 oz/113 g frisée lettuce, white leaves only

4 oz/113 g arugula, picked over and cleaned

4 oz/113 g radish, cut into julienne

4 oz/113 g fennel fronds

½ oz/14 g celery leaves

3½ oz/99 g Lemon-Parsley Vinaigrette (page 30)

10 oz/283 g Croutons (page 549), brunoise size

1. Slice the tuna very thin and flatten it between layers of plastic wrap, using a mallet, to the dimensions of your appetizer plate. Cover and keep chilled until ready to assemble the appetizer.

2. Combine the oil, olives, celery, onion, jalapeño, capers, parsley, garlic, and lemon zest. Taste and season with salt and pepper. Cover and marinate under refrigeration for at least 24 hours.

3. Toss together the frisée, arugula, radish, fennel fronds, and celery leaves. Reserve until ready to assemble the appetizer.

4. **Appetizer Assembly:** For each serving, lay 2 oz/57 g sliced tuna on a chilled plate and mound about 1 oz/28 g salsa cruda in the center of the tuna. Toss about 1 oz/28 g mixed greens and radishes with 2 tsp/10 mL lemon-parsley vinaigrette and mound on the plate. Scatter croutons over the plate and serve.

Escabèche of Tuna

YIELD: 10 SERVINGS

Escabèche, originally an Arabic form of preserving cooked fish in an acid, gets its name from the Spanish word meaning "headless," since the fish were beheaded before preparing them as an escabèche. Today, many foods are prepared throughout South America in this fashion, including cooked poultry, game, vegetables, and even eggs.

30 oz/851 g tuna steak

Salt, as needed

Ground black pepper, as needed

2 fl oz/60 mL olive oil

1½ fl oz/45 mL lime juice

3 oz/85 g small-dice tomato concassé

½ oz/14 g small-dice red onion

½ serrano chile, minced

1 green onion, thinly sliced on the bias

½ tsp/1.50 g minced garlic

1 tsp/1 g chopped cilantro

1. Cut the tuna into 1-in/3-cm cubes or 3-oz/85-g steaks. Season with salt and pepper, rub with 1 fl oz/30 mL of the oil, and sear in a hot, well-seasoned pan. (It should be cooked "black and blue"—colored on the exterior but still extremely rare.) Remove the tuna and chill thoroughly.

2. To make the marinade, mix the remaining olive oil with the lime juice, tomato, onion, chile, green onion, garlic, and cilantro. Pour the marinade over the tuna and turn or gently toss to coat evenly. Marinate at least 12 hours or overnight before serving.

PRESENTATION IDEAS: This dish can be served with a small salad as an appetizer, used to fill cucumber cups as an hors d'oeuvre, or served as part of an antipasto offering.

Vitello Tonnato
(Cold Veal with Tuna Sauce)

The traditional recipe for this northern Italian dish calls for the veal to be gently stewed or braised in a mixture of water, wine, and seasonings. Here, however, we have opted to roast the veal for a deep, intense flavor. Remember to deglaze the roasting pan and add the drippings to the tonnato sauce. The veal must chill at least 12 hours before slicing and serving.

1 lb 8 oz/680 g veal bottom round, tied and seasoned

TONNATO SAUCE

2 oz/57 g onion, cut into small dice

1 oz/28 g carrot, cut into small dice

1 oz/28 g celeriac, cut into small dice

1 fl oz/30 mL olive oil

½ oz/14 g tomato paste

½ tsp/1.50 g minced garlic

½ oz/14 g drained capers

4 anchovy fillets

2 fl oz/60 mL lemon juice

4 fl oz/120 mL white wine

8 fl oz/240 mL Brown Veal Stock (page 528)

1 sachet d'épices made of bay leaf, cracked pepper, thyme sprig, and rosemary sprig

2 oz/57 g canned imported tuna or Tuna Confit (page 220)

4 fl oz/120 mL Basic Mayonnaise (page 35)

Salt, as needed

Ground white pepper, as needed

GARNISH

1 red onion, sliced paper thin

1¾ oz/50 g capers, drained and rinsed

10 anchovy fillets

1. Roast the veal to an internal temperature of 145°F/63°C. Chill for 12 hours or up to 3 days.

2. Sauté the onion, carrot, and celeriac in the oil until browned; add the tomato paste and garlic and sauté another minute. Add the capers, anchovies, lemon juice, wine, stock (as well as the fond from the roasting pan, if available), and sachet d'épices; simmer for 30 minutes and strain. Return the strained sauce to the heat and reduce to 6 fl oz/180 mL. Let cool.

3. Purée the tuna with the reduced sauce until smooth. Finish the sauce with the mayonnaise and season with salt and pepper.

4. **Appetizer Assembly:** For each serving, slice the cold veal about ⅛ in/3 mm thick and arrange 2 to 3 slices (about 2 oz/57 g) on a pool of 1½ fl oz/45 mL tonnato sauce. Garnish each portion with red onion, 1 tsp/5 g capers, and an anchovy fillet.

Herb-Marinated and Grilled Skirt Steak Fajitas

YIELD: 10 SERVING

2 fl oz/60 mL lime juice

1½ oz/43 g coarsely chopped jalapeño

½ oz/14 g garlic, minced

½ tsp/1 g cracked black pepper

1 bunch cilantro, chopped

2 tbsp/12 g cumin seeds, toasted

1 tsp/1 g dried oregano

1 tsp/5 g salt

1 lb 8 oz/680 g skirt steak

2 flour tortillas, 10 in/25 cm in diameter

5 oz/142 g Tomatillo Salsa (page 45)

1. Combine the lime juice, jalapeño, garlic, pepper, cilantro, cumin seeds, oregano, and salt in a bowl. Remove the outer membrane from both sides of the skirt steak and cut into pieces 6 in/15 cm long. Marinate the steaks in the lime juice mixture for 2 to 3 hours under refrigeration.

2. Preheat the grill to its highest setting for at least 30 minutes. Twenty minutes before grilling, remove the steaks from the marinade and scrape off any excess herb mixture. Cover and let them sit at room temperature for 15 to 20 minutes.

3. Grill the steaks on the first side until marked. Turn the steaks once and continue to grill on the second side to the desired degree of doneness. Generally it will take 5 minutes per side to cook a steak of this size medium to medium-well. Slice the steaks using a sharp slicing knife into strips about ¼ in/6 mm wide.

4. Cut eight 3-in/8-cm rounds from each of the tortillas. Grill the tortillas for 15 seconds on each side. Do not allow them to become crisp. Hold them in a basket lined with a warm towel.

5. **Hors d'Oeuvre Assembly:** For each serving, spread ½ oz/14 g salsa on an open tortilla to within ½ in/1 cm of the edge. Fan or lay 2¼ oz/64 g meat on the salsa, fold each of the sides in, and secure with toothpicks.

Barbecued Lamb Tamales

10 corn husks

2 fl oz/60 mL Chicken Stock (page 529), hot

1½ tsp/7.50 g salt

7 oz/198 g masa harina

4 oz/113 g lard

1 lb 8 oz/680 g Braised Lamb Filling for Tamales (recipe follows)

10 oz/283 g Barbecue Sauce (page 56)

1. Weigh down and submerge the corn husks in warm water to soak. Tear enough strips to tie 10 tamales closed.

2. Stir the hot stock and the salt into the masa. Mix by hand until a stiff, smooth paste forms.

3. Blend the lard in a mixer fitted with a paddle attachment on medium speed until it is light and fluffy, about 3 minutes. Add the masa a handful at a time until all of it is incorporated and the dough is smooth. The dough may be used now or covered and kept under refrigeration for up to 24 hours before assembling the tamales. If made ahead of time, the dough will need to be whipped again until fluffy before use.

4. To assemble each large tamale, spread 2 oz/57 g tamale dough on each husk and top with 2¼ oz/64 g braised lamb. Fold the tamale closed and secure by tying with a strip of corn husk. The tamales may be steamed now, or wrapped and held under refrigeration for a day or frozen immediately.

5. Arrange the tamales on a steamer insert. Steam over rapidly boiling water until very hot and the tamale dough is completely cooked, about 45 minutes.

6. Reheat the barbecue sauce, if necessary. Serve the tamales with the sauce.

Braised Filling for Lamb Tamales

YIELD: 2 LB 12 OZ/1.25 KG

1 oz/28 g ancho chile powder

2 tbsp/12 g ground cumin

2 tbsp/12 g ground coriander

2 tsp/10 g salt, or as needed

2 tsp/4 g ground black pepper

3 lb/1.36 kg lamb shoulder, boneless

1 fl oz/30 mL vegetable oil

12 fl oz/360 mL Barbecue Sauce (page 56)

12 fl oz/360 mL Chicken Stock (page 529)

2 oz/57 g cilantro chiffonade

1. To prepare the seasoning rub, combine the chile powder, cumin, coriander, salt, and pepper. Reserve.

2. Trim the lamb and cut it into pieces weighing about 4 oz/113 g each. Season the lamb with the seasoning rub on all surfaces and let rest under refrigeration for at least 1 and up to 12 hours.

3. Heat the oil in a braising pan over high heat. Add the lamb pieces and sear until lightly browned, turning to brown all surfaces.

4. Add the barbecue sauce and stock and bring to a gentle simmer over low heat. Cover and simmer until the meat is tender enough to shred easily, 2½ to 3 hours. You can braise the meat in the oven at 300°F/149°C to ensure a gentle simmer.

5. When the lamb is cool enough to handle, use gloves to pull the meat into fine shreds. Add the cilantro and enough of the braising liquid to moisten and bind the lamb. (Reserve the remaining braising liquid for sauce.) Cool properly, wrap, and refrigerate for at least 12 and up to 24 hours to permit the flavors to develop before using to fill tamales.

NOTE: The rub can be prepared in bulk and stored in a closed container in a cool, dark area.

Fennel and Chorizo Strudel

YIELD: 10 SERVINGS

5 oz/142 g butter, melted

2 shallots, minced

4 oz/113 g chorizo, sliced thin, skin removed

10 to 12 oz/283 to 340 g fennel bulb, diced

1½ tbsp/4.50 g minced tarragon leaves

1½ tsp/1.50 g minced chives

1 egg

7 oz/198 g dry bread crumbs

1 tsp/5 g salt

¼ tsp/0.50 g ground black pepper

6 phyllo dough sheets, thawed

1. Heat about 1 oz/28 g of the butter in a sauté pan over medium heat. Add the shallots and sauté them until they are translucent. Add the chorizo and allow some of the fat to render. Add the fennel and gently cook it until tender. It may be necessary to reduce the heat slightly so the mixture does not burn. Allow the mixture to cool to room temperature.

2. Process the mixture to a coarse paste in a food processor. Add the tarragon leaves, chives, egg, and enough bread crumbs (about 1¾ oz/50 g) to lightly bind the mixture. Season to taste with the salt and pepper.

3. Brush each sheet of phyllo dough with melted butter and sprinkle it evenly with 1 to 1½ tsp/2 to 3 g bread crumbs. Top this with another sheet of phyllo dough and repeat the process.

4. When three sheets are stacked, place half of the chorizo-fennel mixture down the left side of the dough and roll the sheets over the chorizo-fennel mixture. Brush the top with butter. Repeat with the remaining dough and filling.

5. Chill the strudel for about 30 minutes. Score the top on the diagonal to divide each strudel into 10 sections.

6. Bake the strudels at 400°F/204°C for 10 to 15 minutes, or until they are browned. Slice and serve immediately.

Herbed Goat Cheese in Phyllo Dough

YIELD: 10 SERVINGS

4½ oz/128 g goat cheese

1½ tbsp/4.50 g chopped basil

1½ tbsp/4.50 g chopped chervil

1½ tbsp/4.50 g chopped tarragon

1½ tbsp/4.50 g chopped chives

6 fl oz/180 mL heavy cream

½ tsp/2.50 g salt

½ tsp/1 g ground black pepper

9 phyllo dough sheets (14 by 18 in/36 by 46 cm), thawed

6 oz/170 g clarified butter, melted

1. Combine the goat cheese, basil, chervil, tarragon, chives, and heavy cream. Season with the salt and pepper. Reserve under refrigeration until needed.

2. Brush a sheet of phyllo dough with melted butter. Lay another sheet of dough on top and brush it with butter. Repeat this process once more so three layers of phyllo dough are stacked. Cut the dough lengthwise into 2-in/5-cm strips.

3. Place ½ oz/14 g filling at the base of each strip and fold into triangles (see the Spanikopita recipe on page 410). Brush the triangles with additional melted butter and place on a sheet pan. Repeat with the additional phyllo dough and filling until all is used.

4. Bake the triangles at 400°F/204°C for 10 to 12 minutes, or until browned. Serve immediately.

Baked Camembert with Rhubarb Compote

YIELD: 10 APPETIZERS

1 lb 2 oz/510 g Camembert cheese

1 lb/454 g Brioche Dough (page 542)

2 oz/57 g clarified butter, or as needed

5 oz/142 g baby greens (arugula or spinach), cleaned and dried

2½ fl oz/75 mL Port Vinaigrette (page 34)

12 fl oz/360 mL Rhubarb Compote (page 480)

1. Cut the Camembert into wedges or triangles, 1¾ oz/50 g each.

2. Roll the brioche dough into a thin rectangle, about ⅛ in/3 mm thick. Brush the dough liberally with the clarified butter. Cut into rectangles 3 by 4 in/8 by 10 cm, and wrap around the cheese triangles or wedges. Hold under refrigeration until ready to bake.

3. Bake the brioche-wrapped cheese in a 500°F/260°C oven until golden brown on both sides, turning once during baking if needed, 5 to 6 minutes. Bake the cheese as close to service as possible.

4. **Appetizer Assembly:** For each serving, toss ½ oz/14 g greens with ½ tbsp/7.50 mL vinaigrette. Spoon 1 oz/28 g rhubarb compote onto a plate. Mold the dressed greens on top of the rhubarb compote. Place the baked Camembert on top of the greens.

Roasted Vegetables Provençale Style

YIELD: 30 SERVINGS

This dish can be baked and served in a decorative shallow baking dish or casserole, if desired. It may be served warm, at room temperature, or chilled.

4 fl oz/120 mL olive oil

1 tbsp/3 g chopped thyme

1 tbsp/3 g chopped savory

1 oz/28 g roasted garlic purée

1 oz/28 g salt

2 tsp/4 g ground black pepper

2 lb/907 g eggplant, sliced into rounds ¼ in/6 mm thick

1 lb/454 g yellow squash, sliced on the bias into ovals ¼ in/6 mm thick

1 lb/454 g zucchini, sliced on the bias into ovals ¼ in/6 mm thick

1 lb/454 g Spanish onion, sliced into rounds ⅛ in/3 mm thick

1 lb/454 g ripe red tomatoes, sliced into rounds ¼ in/6 mm thick

2 tbsp/6 g basil chiffonade

1. Combine the oil with the thyme, savory, roasted garlic, salt, and pepper. Brush some of this mixture on a sheet pan and layer the sliced vegetables on the pan. Drizzle the vegetables with a little of the olive oil mixture.

2. Bake, uncovered, in a 200°F/93°C oven for 4 to 5 hours, or until the vegetables are tender and wilted. Drizzle them with a little more of the oil mixture every hour as they roast.

3. Arrange the vegetables on a serving platter and garnish with the basil chiffonade. The vegetables can be served warm, cold, or at room temperature.

NOTE: Optional: Prepare as individual servings or larger batches in a ceramic or earthenware casserole; shingle the vegetables, alternating colors. Serve from the baking dish.

Grilled Vegetable Appetizer with Balsamic Vinaigrette

YIELD: 10 SERVINGS

4 fl oz/120 mL olive oil

½ bunch thyme, leaves only

Salt, as needed

Ground black pepper, as needed

1 lb/454 g eggplant, sliced into rounds ½ in/1 cm thick

1 lb/454 g zucchini, sliced on the bias into ovals ½ in/1 cm thick

1 lb/454 g yellow squash, sliced on the bias into ovals ½ in/1 cm thick

1 lb 8 oz/680 g red peppers, cut into eighths

12 oz/340 g yellow peppers, cut into eighths

1 lb/454 g portobello mushrooms, stems removed

5 plum tomatoes, cored and halved

10 green onions, trimmed

15 fl oz/450 mL Balsamic Vinaigrette (page 27)

1. Combine the oil with the thyme, salt, and pepper. Brush the vegetables with this mixture. Grill the eggplant until very soft and cooked through. Grill or broil the remaining vegetables to mark on all sides; they should be tender and very hot. Slice the portobellos as necessary to make 10 servings.

2. **Appetizer Assembly:** For each serving, arrange 2 or 3 slices each of eggplant, zucchini, and yellow squash on a plate. Add 2 strips red pepper and 1 strip yellow pepper, a grilled tomato half, and a green onion. Drizzle with vinaigrette and serve warm or at room temperature.

CHEF'S NOTE: Use a variety of tomatoes, if available, for extra color in this dish. If preferred, the tomatoes may be lightly broiled just until hot. They should retain their shape.

Marinated Tomatoes with Mozzarella

YIELD: 10 SERVINGS

Select a variety of tomatoes—red and yellow slicing tomatoes; cherry, pear, or currant tomatoes—whenever they are in season. Rub a slice of sturdy peasant-style bread with garlic and olive oil and grill it lightly to accompany this simple seasonal favorite.

2 lb/907 g Mozzarella Cheese (page 352)

1 red tomato

1 yellow tomato

2 lb 8 oz/1.13 kg Marinated Tomatoes (page 93)

3 tbsp/9 g basil chiffonade

1. Slice the mozzarella ¼ in/6 mm thick and reserve.

2. Slice the tomatoes ¼ in/6 mm thick, and halve or quarter the slices. Reserve.

3. **Appetizer Assembly:** For each serving, mound 4 oz/113 g tomato salad on a chilled plate. Arrange 3 oz/85 g sliced mozzarella and several slices of red and yellow tomatoes around the tomato salad. Scatter a little basil chiffonade over the appetizer. Serve chilled or at room temperature.

PRESENTATION IDEAS: For buffet presentation, mound the tomato salad on a chilled platter and arrange sliced tomatoes and mozzarella around the salad. You may wish to add a small bed of a mixed green salad, lightly dressed with a Basic Red Wine or Balsamic Vinaigrette (page 27), for individual servings.

Prosciutto and Summer Melon Salad

YIELD: 10 SERVINGS

This classic presentation pairs the silky-smooth texture of the best prosciutto ham with sweet, cool melon, drizzled with authentic balsamic vinegar. The combination of aromas and textures is exquisite. Prepare this dish with fresh figs when they are in season.

1 lb 4 oz/567 g prosciutto di Parma

1 lb 14 oz/851 g sliced or diced mixed melons (cantaloupe, honeydew, casaba, etc.)

1 fl oz/30 mL aged balsamic vinegar (optional)

Cracked black pepper, as needed

20 Grissini (page 540)

1. Slice the prosciutto as thin as possible, laying it out on butcher's paper for easy handling. This should be done as close to service time as possible.

2. **Appetizer Assembly:** For each serving, arrange the melon on a plate and add the prosciutto (drape it over melon slices or arrange it next to diced melon). If desired, drizzle a few drops of excellent aged balsamic vinegar on the melon just before serving. Scatter a little pepper on the plate and serve with 2 grissini.

CHEF'S NOTES: This simple appetizer can be prepared as a plattered item for buffet service. Alternatively, individual cubes or spears of melon may be wrapped with a bit of prosciutto and skewered for service as an hors d'oeuvre.

If you have a prosciutto slicing stand in the dining room, this appetizer can be prepared by slicing the prosciutto to order in front of the guest, as long as the melon mise en place has been properly assembled by the kitchen staff.

Tofu with Red Curry Paste, Peas, Green Onions, and Cilantro

YIELD: 10 SERVINGS

Grapeseed oil, as needed

1 lb/454 g tofu, drained, cut into 1-in/3-cm cubes

1 fl oz/30 mL lime juice

3½ oz/99 g onion, cut into small dice

⅔ oz/19 g garlic, minced

8 fl oz/240 mL coconut milk

2 oz/57 g red curry paste

1 tbsp/6 g ground turmeric

Salt, as needed

Ground black pepper, as needed

7 oz/198 g peas, blanched

6 oz/170 g grape tomatoes, cut in half

⅓ bunch cilantro, chopped

½ bunch green onions, minced

1 lb 2 oz/510 g brown rice, cooked

10 oz/283 g baby greens

6 oz/170 g black sesame seeds

1. Heat a small amount of the oil in a medium nonstick sauté pan. Add the tofu and cook until the moisture is evaporated and the tofu is a light golden brown. Remove the tofu from the pan and sprinkle with the lime juice.

2. Heat more oil in the pan, add the onion, and cook until translucent. Add the garlic and cook for an additional 2 minutes.

3. Add the coconut milk, curry paste, and turmeric. Season with salt and pepper. Reduce the heat and simmer until the sauce is slightly thickened.

4. Add the peas, tomatoes, and tofu to the mixture and simmer just to combine. Adjust seasoning if necessary. Toss the mixture with 1 tbsp/6 g each of the cilantro and green onions.

5. Place a molded 2½-fl-oz/75-mL cylinder of rice in the center of a small bowl. Pour the tofu mixture in front of the rice. Rest baby greens against the rice. Sprinkle black sesame seeds on top of the rice.

Smoked Salmon with Potato Galettes

YIELD: 10 SERVINGS

GALETTE

2 lb 8 oz/1.13 kg Yukon gold potatoes, peeled

Salt, as needed

Ground white pepper, as needed

4 oz/113 g butter

16 fl oz/480 mL Crème Fraîche (page 351)

2½ oz/71 g minced shallots

2 tbsp/12 g chopped Fines Herbes (page 526)

1 lb 9 oz/709 g Smoked Salmon (page 196), sliced thin

5 bunches mâche

5 fl oz/150 mL Chive Oil (page 490)

1 bunch chives, minced

1 oz/28 g sevruga caviar

1. Grate the potatoes on a mandoline or box grater into fine julienne. Season with salt and pepper.

2. Heat the butter in a griswold or rondeau. Drop spoonfuls of the potatoes into the butter to make galettes (they should be about 4 in/10 cm in diameter and ¼ in/6 mm thick—30 galettes in all). Sauté until golden brown on both sides; remove from the pan and keep warm until ready to assemble the appetizer.

3. Fold the crème fraîche together with the shallots and fines herbes and season with salt and pepper.

4. **Appetizer Assembly:** For each serving, place a small dollop of seasoned crème fraîche on a plate. Top with 1 galette and about 1½ oz/43 g sliced smoked salmon. Drizzle the salmon with a little more crème fraîche; top with a second galette. Roll another slice of smoked salmon into a rosette and place on top of the galette. Garnish the salmon with ½ bunch mâche. Drizzle chive oil on the plate and garnish with the chives and caviar. Top with another galette and then more salmon. Place dressed mâche sprigs inside the salmon so they appear to flower up.

Air-Dried Ham with Lentil Salad

YIELD: 10 SERVINGS

8 oz/227 g air-dried ham (Serrano or prosciutto)

20 cherry tomatoes, halved

6 fl oz/180 mL Basic Red Wine Vinaigrette (page 27), made with sherry wine vinegar

1 lb 4 oz/567 g Lentil and Walnut Salad (page 109)

10 oz/283 g mixed baby greens

2 tbsp/6 g chopped flat-leaf parsley

1. Slice the ham as thin as possible and lay it out on food-service paper. Cover and hold under refrigeration.

2. Toss the cherry tomatoes in 1 fl oz/30 mL of the vinaigrette and roast in a 275°F/135°C oven until dry, about 2 hours. Reserve.

3. **Appetizer Assembly:** For each serving, place 2 oz/57 g lentil salad on the plate and drape with 2 to 3 slices of ham (about ¾ oz/21 g). Toss 1 oz/28 g greens with ½ fl oz/15 mL vinaigrette and arrange on the plate. Add 4 roasted cherry tomato halves. Garnish with parsley.

Grilled Smoked Honey-Cured Quail with Mango-Lime Salsa

YIELD: 10 SERVINGS

10 Grilled Smoked Honey-Cured Quail (page 205)

1 lb 9 oz/709 g Mixed Bean and Grain Salad (page 109)

20 fl oz/600 mL Mango-Lime Salsa (page 44)

3 oz/85 g mixed baby greens

1½ fl oz/45 mL Basic Red Wine Vinaigrette (page 27)

1. Grill the quail until heated through and marked.

2. **Appetizer Assembly:** For each serving, arrange 2½ oz/71 g bean and grain salad on the plate. Place 2 oz/57 g of the salsa and top with the grilled quail. Arrange a few leaves of the dressed baby greens on the plate.

Smoked Breast of Duck Niçoise Style

YIELD: 10 SERVINGS

1 lb 4 oz/567 g Smoked Duck Breast (page 203)

8 oz/227 g haricots verts

1 lb 9 oz/709 g Mediterranean Potato Salad (page 104)

5 tomatoes, blanched, peeled, seeded, and cut into strips

2 fl oz/60 mL Basic Red Wine Vinaigrette (page 27)

2½ fl oz/75 mL Tapenade (page 52)

1. Slice the duck breast thin and reserve until ready to assemble the appetizer.

2. Blanch the haricots verts and refresh.

3. **Appetizer Assembly:** For each serving, arrange 2½ oz/71 g potato salad on the plate. Fan 2 oz/57 g sliced duck on the plate. Toss ¾ oz/21 g haricots verts and several strips of tomato in the vinaigrette and arrange on the plate. Garnish with 1½ tsp/7.50 mL tapenade.

Duck Confit with Frisée and Roasted Shallot Vinaigrette

YIELD: 10 SERVINGS

10 pieces Duck Confit, legs only (page 219)

5 Idaho potatoes, peeled and sliced into rounds measuring 1½ by ⅛ in/4 cm by 3 mm

32 fl oz/960 mL duck fat, for frying

Salt, as needed

Coarse-ground black pepper, as needed

2 lb/907 g frisée lettuce, washed and dried

15 fl oz/450 mL Roasted Shallot Vinaigrette (page 33)

1. Scrape excess fat from the duck legs, reserving it for frying potatoes. Roast the duck legs in a 450°F/232°C oven until warm and crisp, about 15 minutes. Keep warm.

2. Fry the potatoes in duck fat heated to 350°F/177°C until browned and crisp, about 8 minutes. Drain on absorbent paper, season with salt and pepper, and keep warm.

3. **Appetizer Assembly:** For each serving, toss 3 oz/85 g frisée in 1½ fl oz/45 mL vinaigrette and mound on a chilled plate. Top with a duck leg, 2 oz/57 g fried potatoes, and a few roasted shallots from the dressing. Serve at once.

CHEF'S NOTE: Serve this as an appetizer, composed salad, or light meal.

Smoked Duck Tart

YIELD: ONE 10-IN TART; 12 SERVINGS

8 oz/227 g Pâté Dough (page 535)

1 Smoked Duck (page 203)

¼ oz/7 g powdered or sheet gelatin

1 fl oz/30 mL brandy

4 fl oz/120 mL heavy cream, whipped

36 Candied Pecan halves (page 426)

10 fl oz/300 mL Cumberland Sauce (page 48)

1. Roll out the dough to a thickness of about ³⁄₁₆ in/5 mm. Line a tart pan with a removable bottom with the dough, trimming the edges. Bake blind at 350°F/177°C for 8 minutes, until golden brown and fully baked. Reserve until the mousse is prepared.

2. Remove the bones and skin from the duck. Trim the breast portions and slice very thin for garnish; reserve. Dice the leg and thigh meat, removing all sinew and gristle.

3. Make a mousse as described on page 368: Grind leg, thigh, and any additional usable trim through the medium plate (¼ in/6 mm) of a meat grinder. Purée the ground duck to a fine paste. Bloom the gelatin in the brandy, warm to dissolve the gelatin, and fold into the duck mixture. Fold in the cream.

4. Fill the prepared tart shell with mousse and top with thin-sliced duck breast arranged symmetrically in a spiral pattern covering the surface of the tart. Garnish the rim of the tart with candied pecans. Chill at least 4 hours before slicing and serving.

5. Slice the tart into 12 servings. Serve on chilled plates with 1 fl oz/30 mL Cumberland sauce per serving.

Jerked Pork Spareribs

YIELD: 10 APPETIZER SERVINGS

8 oz/227 g green onions

4 fl oz/120 mL orange juice

2 fl oz/60 mL lime juice

1 oz/28 g Scotch bonnet or habanero chiles, stems removed (about 3)

2 oz/57 g thyme leaves

2 fl oz/60 mL vegetable oil

1 oz/28 g garlic, minced

1 oz/28 g ginger, minced

½ oz/14 g salt

2 tsp/4 g ground allspice

1 tsp/2 g ground black pepper

1 tsp/2 g ground cinnamon

½ tsp/1 g grated nutmeg

4 lb/1.81 kg pork spareribs, baby back or St. Louis style

1. Combine the green onions, orange juice, lime juice, chiles, thyme, oil, garlic, ginger, salt, allspice, pepper, cinnamon, and nutmeg in a blender or food processor. Process to form a paste.

2. Trim the pork ribs and rub them evenly with the jerk rub. Cover tightly and marinate under refrigeration for at least 8 and up to 12 hours.

3. Remove the spareribs from the jerk mixture. Reserve any mixture remaining to baste the ribs as they grill. Place the ribs on sheet pans and cook at 250° to 300°F/121° to 149°C for 2 hours, or until tender.

4. Grill the spareribs over a moderately hot fire (coals should be covered with a layer of white ash), turning frequently and basting as necessary, until the meat is hot. Remove the ribs from the grill. Let them rest briefly before cutting into servings.

Shrimp and Avocado Quesadillas

YIELD: 10 SERVINGS

2 lb/907 g Smoked Shrimp (21/25 count) (page 195)

8 oz/227 g tomatillos, charred, husks removed (about 9)

2 avocados, pitted, peeled, and diced

1 onion, diced, sautéed until golden

¼ bunch cilantro, chopped

1 tbsp/6 g toasted cumin seeds

Salt, as needed

Ground black pepper, as needed

20 flour tortillas (4 in/10 cm in diameter)

8 oz/227 g Monterey Jack cheese, shredded

1 fl oz/30 mL olive oil

2 bunches watercress, washed and dried

7 fl oz/210 mL Orange Vinaigrette (page 29)

1. Peel and devein the shrimp; reserve.

2. Chop the tomatillos fine. Combine with the avocado and onion and work with a wooden spoon or a fork to form a coarse paste. Stir in the cilantro and cumin and season with salt and pepper. Spread this mixture on a tortilla, top with ¾ oz/21 g cheese, and close with a second tortilla. Continue until 10 quesadillas are filled. This may be done up to 1 hour in advance.

3. **Appetizer Assembly:** When ready to serve, lightly oil both sides of a quesadilla and cook over low heat in a well-seasoned or nonstick pan until golden brown on both sides. Place the quesadilla on a plate; top with 4 shrimp. Dress ¾ oz/21 g watercress with 2 tsps/10 mL vinaigrette and arrange on the plate. Drizzle the perimeter of the plate with another 2 tsp/10 mL vinaigrette.

Small Seared Lobster and Vegetable Quesadillas

YIELD: 10 SERVINGS

3 lb 8 oz/1.59 kg lobster (2)

½ tsp/1 g cumin, toasted and ground

¼ tsp/0.50 g chili powder

Pinch cayenne

Olive oil, as needed

4 oz/113 g onion, cut into ¼-in/6-mm dice

1½ tsp/4.50 g garlic, chopped

7 oz/198 g poblano peppers, roasted and cut into ¼-in/6-mm dice

3 oz/85 g red pepper, roasted and cut into ¼-in/6-mm dice

Pinch salt

3 oz/85 g queso blanco, grated

8 flour tortillas, 8 in/20 cm in diameter

1. Cook the lobsters in simmering salted water for 6 minutes, shell, and coat the meat with the cumin, chili powder, and cayenne.

2. Heat the oil in a sauté pan over high heat and pan-sear the lobster. Cut the lobster into ¼-in/6-mm dice.

3. Heat additional oil in a sauté pan over medium heat and sauté the onion and chopped garlic. Mix the onion and peppers together and season with salt. Mix the lobster with the vegetable mixture and the queso blanco.

4. Using a 2½-in/6-cm ring mold, cut 20 rounds from the tortillas for appetizer-size quesadillas.

5. Heat some oil in a sauté pan and lightly sauté both sides of the tortilla rounds over medium-high heat. Place ½ oz/14 g filling on 10 of the tortilla rounds and top with the remaining rounds.

6. Arrange the assembled quesadillas on a sheet pan. Place a half sheet of parchment paper on top of the quesadillas. Weigh down the quesadillas with a half sheet pan to flatten.

7. Bake in a 400°F/204°C oven for 8 to 10 minutes, until the cheese is melted, or brown the quesadillas in a cast-iron pan. Serve immediately.

NOTE: Smoked chicken works well as a substitution for the lobster.

Marinated Sweet and Sour Fish

YIELD: 10 SERVINGS

3 lb/1.36 kg sardines or mackerel

All-purpose flour, as needed

Vegetable oil, as needed

Salt, as needed

6 fl oz/180 mL pure olive oil

1 lb 8 oz/680 g onions, sliced thin

2 bay leaves

16 fl oz/480 mL red wine vinegar

Pinch ground cinnamon

Salt, as needed

Ground black pepper, as needed

2 oz/57 g pine nuts, toasted

2 oz/57 g golden raisins, plumped in wine and drained

Parsley, as needed for garnish

1. Clean the fish and remove the heads. Open the fish flat and rinse them; pat dry with paper towels. Dredge the fish in flour, shaking off the excess.

2. Heat the vegetable oil to 375°F/191°C. Add the fish carefully, working in batches, and deep-fry until crisp, 1 to 3 minutes. Drain on a paper towel–lined sheet pan. Season with salt.

3. Heat the olive oil in a nonreactive saucepan set over medium heat. Cook the onions and bay leaves, stirring often, until the onion is translucent. Add the vinegar and season with cinnamon, salt, and pepper. Boil for 2 minutes, then remove the pan from the heat. Remove and discard the bay leaves.

4. Arrange the fish in layers in a large, shallow bowl. Scatter the pine nuts and the drained raisins between layers. Slowly add the onion mixture. Marinate, covered, under refrigeration for at least 24 hours. Garnish with parsley.

NOTE: Thinly sliced yellow and red peppers may be included; sweat them with the onions.

Crabmeat Rolls with Infused Pepper Oils, Fried Ginger, and Tamari-Glazed Mushrooms

YIELD: 10 SERVINGS

Traditional Asian ingredients are combined in a modern presentation for this exciting appetizer. This dish can easily be adapted for hors d'oeuvre by cutting the colorful rolls into bite-sized pieces and standing them on end.

1 lb 8 oz/680 g lump crabmeat

4 oz/113 g carrot, cut into fine julienne

1 oz/28 g red pepper, cut into brunoise

1 oz/28 g yellow pepper, cut into brunoise

1 oz/28 g green pepper, cut into brunoise

½ oz/14 g minced chives

1 tbsp/6 g black sesame seeds

1½ fl oz/45 mL rice wine vinegar

Salt, as needed

Ground white pepper, as needed

10 rice paper wrappers (8 in/20 cm in diameter)

10 oz/283 g Tamari-Glazed Mushrooms (see Chef's Note)

2 fl/60 mL Red Pepper Oil (page 492)

2 fl/60 mL Green Pepper Oil (page 492)

2 fl/60 mL Yellow Pepper Oil (page 492)

2 ginger pieces (2 in/5 cm long), peeled, sliced thin, and fried for garnish

1. Clean the crabmeat, removing any shell or cartilage. Combine with the carrot, peppers, chives, sesame seeds, and vinegar. Season with salt and pepper.

2. Moisten the rice paper wrappers and fill each with about 3 oz/85 g crabmeat mixture. Roll the wrapper to completely encase the filling; it should be about 1 in/3 cm in diameter. Keep covered with a lightly dampened cloth under refrigeration until ready to serve.

3. **Appetizer Assembly:** For each serving, cut 1 crab roll on the bias and arrange on a chilled plate. Add 1 oz/28 g tamari-glazed mushrooms, 1 tsp/5 mL each of the pepper-flavored oils, and a few pieces of fried ginger.

CHEF'S NOTE: To make Tamari-Glazed Mushrooms, sauté 1 lb/454 g sliced shiitake mushrooms in 1 fl oz/30 mL olive oil until very hot. Add 1 fl oz/30 mL tamari sauce to deglaze the pan. Season to taste with sugar, dark sesame oil, salt, and pepper.

Seared Sea Scallops with Artichokes and Peperonato

YIELD: 10 APPETIZER SERVINGS

2 lb/907 g sea scallops

2 lb/907 g Peperonato (recipe follows)

Hearts of Artichoke Salad (page 95)

Salt, as needed

Ground black pepper, as needed

5 fl oz/150 mL olive oil

5 fl oz/150 mL Red or Yellow Pepper Oil (page 492)

1. Remove and discard the muscle tab from the scallops.

2. For each serving, heat 3 oz/85 g peperonato and 4 pieces of artichoke heart from the salad. Season with salt and pepper. Keep warm.

3. Heat 1 oz/28 g olive oil in a sauté pan over medium-high heat. Add 3 oz/85 g scallops and sear on both sides until golden brown but still translucent in the center, 1 to 2 minutes per side.

4. Mound the peperonato on a heated plate and arrange the artichoke salad and scallops on the plate. Drizzle with red or yellow pepper oil and serve at once.

Peperonato

YIELD: 10 SERVINGS

2 fl oz/60 mL olive oil

5 oz/142 g onions, thinly sliced

½ oz/14 g garlic cloves, thinly sliced

½ tsp/0.50 g dried Italian oregano

½ tsp/1 g red pepper flakes

1 lb/454 g red peppers, cut into julienne

1 lb/454 g yellow peppers, cut into julienne

1 lb/454 g green peppers, cut into julienne

½ oz/14 g flat-leaf parsley, chopped

1 tbsp/3 g thyme leaves

Salt, as needed

Ground black pepper, as needed

1. Heat the olive oil in a sauté pan over medium heat. Add the onions and sauté, stirring occasionally, until tender and translucent with no color, about 8 minutes. Add the garlic, oregano, and red pepper flakes; sauté until aromatic, about 1 minute. Add the peppers and continue to cook, stirring from time to time, until the peppers are soft and tender, 5 to 6 minutes more.

2. Add the parsley and thyme. Taste and season with salt and pepper. Simmer over low heat until flavorful, stirring as necessary to avoid browning the mixture, about 15 minutes.

3. The peperonato is ready to serve now, or it may be properly cooled and stored for up to 5 days.

Lobster Rillettes

YIELD: 10 SERVINGS

5 lobsters (1 lb 8 oz/680 g each), steamed or boiled

6 fl oz/180 mL Basic Mayonnaise (page 35)

4 oz/113 g butter, softened

1½ oz/43 g Glacé de Viande (page 351)

1 fl oz/30 mL lemon juice

4 oz/113 g celeriac, blanched, cut into fine dice

1 tsp/5 g salt

¼ tsp/0.50 g ground black pepper

2 oz/57 g avocado, cut into small dice

2 tbsp/6 g chives, minced

10 oz/283 g salad greens, rinsed and dried

2 fl oz/60 mL Tarragon Oil (page 490)

5 fl oz/150 mL Grapefruit Emulsion (page 28)

1. Remove the meat from the lobsters. Reserve the claw and knuckle meat to garnish the plate. Dice the remaining lobster meat for the rillettes.

2. Blend the mayonnaise, butter, glacé de viande, and lemon juice until smooth and light. Stir in the celeriac. Taste and season with salt and pepper.

3. Fold in the diced lobster and the avocado and chives. Press into a mold or ramekin. Cover and chill for at least 3 and up to 12 hours.

4. For each serving, make a small bed of salad greens. Unmold the lobster rillettes onto the plate. Drizzle with tarragon oil and grapefruit emulsion. Garnish with the reserved claw meat.

Shrimp Cakes with Spicy Rémoulade Sauce

YIELD: 10 SERVINGS

½ oz/14 g butter, unsalted

1 oz/28 g celery stalk, peeled, finely diced

1 oz/28 g green onions, finely sliced

1 oz/28 g Asian-style bread crumbs

2 dashes Tabasco

1 oz/28 g eggs, well beaten

1 fl oz/30 mL Basic Mayonnaise (page 35)

½ oz/14 g chives, finely snipped

1 lb/454 g shrimp, cleaned, deveined, and cut into ¼-in/6-mm dice

¼ tsp/1.25 g salt

Pinch ground black pepper

6 oz/170 g fresh white bread crumbs

Clarified butter, as needed

1. Melt the butter in a sauté pan over medium heat. Sweat the celery in the butter until slightly translucent. Add the green onions and continue cooking over medium heat until soft. This will happen quickly. Transfer the mixture to a bowl and allow to cool to room temperature.

2. Add the Asian-style bread crumbs, Tabasco, eggs, mayonnaise, chives, and shrimp. Season with salt and pepper.

3. Divide the mixture into 2-oz/57-g portions. Shape each into a small cake, 2 in/5 cm in diameter. Dip both sides of each shrimp cake in the fresh white bread crumbs.

4. Heat the clarified butter in a sauté pan over medium-high heat and cook the shrimp cakes for 4 to 5 minutes on each side, or until the shrimp is fully cooked and the cakes are golden brown.

Shrimp Mousse with Dill Gelée

YIELD: 10 SERVINGS

32 fl oz/960 mL Court Bouillon (page 531)

½ bunch dill, separated into leaves and stems

1 lb/454 g shrimp (in the shell)

¼ oz/7 g powdered or sheet gelatin

1 fl oz/30 mL cool water

4 egg whites, whipped to soft peaks

8 fl oz/240 mL heavy cream, whipped to soft peaks

Salt, as needed

Ground white pepper, as needed

Lemon juice, as needed

Pinch cayenne

GARNISH

½ oz/14 g caviar

2 seedless cucumbers, sliced thin

2 fl oz/60 mL Lemon Vinaigrette (page 29)

1. To cook the shrimp and prepare the aspic: Bring the court bouillon and dill stems to a simmer. Add the shrimp and poach just until cooked through, about 5 minutes. Remove the shrimp. Strain the court bouillon and reserve 7 fl oz/210 mL; keep warm (90°F/32°C). Bloom the gelatin in the water and add to 4 fl oz/120 mL warm court bouillon. Stir until the gelatin is completely dissolved. Reserve.

2. To prepare the mousse: Shell and devein the shrimp. Split 5 shrimp in half lengthwise. Dice the remaining shrimp and purée with 3 fl oz/90 mL of the court bouillon to form a smooth paste. Transfer to a mixing bowl and fold in the egg whites and cream. Season with salt, pepper, lemon juice, and cayenne.

3. Pipe the mousse into 2-in/5-cm PVC pipe molds (or other molds, as desired). Top each mousse with a shrimp half and ½ oz/14 g aspic. Chill for at least 3 hours before unmolding. Garnish with caviar, dill, and cucumbers dressed in vinaigrette.

Lobster and Truffle Salad

YIELD: 10 SERVINGS

Although it is called a salad, this elegant dish works well as an appetizer or even a light luncheon main dish.

5 whole lobsters (1 lb/454 g each)

8 oz/227 g haricots verts

5 bunches mâche

VINAIGRETTE

Juice of 3 oranges

2 fl oz/60 mL Champagne vinegar

1½ oz/43 g Fines Herbes (page 526)

Salt, as needed

Ground white pepper, as needed

4 fl oz/120 mL extra-virgin olive oil

GARNISH

1 tomato, peeled, seeded, and cut into diamond shapes

½ oz/14 g chervil pluches

1 oz/28 g truffles

1. Cook the lobsters in simmering salted water until fully cooked, 9 to 10 minutes. Remove and cool under refrigeration. When cold, remove the tail and claw meat. Slice each tail in half to make 10 equal servings; hold the lobster under refrigeration until ready to assemble the appetizer.

2. Blanch the haricots verts in boiling salted water until bright green; refresh, drain, and hold under refrigeration until ready to assemble the appetizer.

3. Rinse the mâche carefully and divide each bunch in half. Dry thoroughly and hold under refrigeration until ready to assembly the appetizer.

4. To prepare the vinaigrette, combine the orange juice, vinegar, fines herbes, salt, and pepper. Gradually add the oil, whisking constantly. Adjust seasoning and reserve.

5. **Appetizer Assembly:** For each serving, slice 1 portion of lobster tail meat into medallions. Dress ¾ oz/21 g haricots verts and ½ bunch mâche with ½ fl oz/15 mL vinaigrette and arrange on chilled plates. Add the lobster tail medallions and a claw portion. Garnish with tomato diamonds and a chervil pluche. Shave a few pieces of truffle over the salad and serve at once.

Lobster Tabbouleh with Mango Sauce

YIELD: 10 SERVINGS

5 whole lobsters

MANGO SAUCE

2 mangos, flesh only

2 fl oz/60 mL extra-virgin olive oil

2 fl oz/60 mL orange juice

½ fl oz/15 mL lemon juice

Salt, as needed

Ground white pepper, as needed

Cayenne, as needed

1 lb 4 oz/567 g Tabbouleh Salad (page 107)

1 lb 4 oz/567 g mixed baby greens

5 fl oz/150 mL Lemon Vinaigrette (page 29)

10 basil leaves, cut into fine chiffonade

1. Cook the lobster in simmering salted water until fully cooked, 9 to 10 minutes. Remove and cool under refrigeration. When cold, remove the tail and claw meat. Slice each tail in half to make 10 equal servings; hold the lobster under refrigeration until ready to assemble the appetizer. Optional: Reserve the roe and roast in a 200°F/93°C oven until dry and a brilliant red color. Cool, then push through a fine-mesh sieve. Reserve for garnish.

2. Using a small melon baller (petit pois size), scoop 5 oz/142 g mango balls and reserve for garnish. To prepare the mango sauce, purée the remaining mango with the oil and orange and lemon juices in a blender until very smooth. Add the salt, pepper, and cayenne. Hold under refrigeration until ready to assemble the appetizer.

3. **Appetizer Assembly:** For each serving, mold 2 oz/57 g tabbouleh in a 2½-in/6-cm ring mold in the center of a chilled plate. Slice ½ lobster tail into medallions and lay over the salad. Add 1 claw portion. Dress 2 oz/57 g mixed greens with ½ fl oz/15 mL vinaigrette and arrange on the plate. Finish with a generous tablespoon of mango sauce. Garnish with mango balls, sieved lobster roe (if desired), and basil.

Foie Gras Roulade with Roasted Beet Salad and Smoked Duck Breast

YIELD: 10 SERVINGS

1 lb/454 g Foie Gras Roulade (page 329) or Terrine (page 329)

15 oz/425 g Smoked Duck (page 203) breasts

1 lb 4 oz/567 g Roasted Beet Salad (page 93), made with gold and red beets

20 pieces Parsnip Chips (page 486)

1 lb 4 oz/567 g baby beet greens

5 fl oz/150 mL Beet Vinaigrette (page 34)

1. Slice the foie gras roulade into 10 servings, each weighing about 1½ oz/43 g. If done in advance, hold the slices, covered, under refrigeration until ready to assemble the appetizer.

2. Slice the duck breasts thin and portion at 4 slices per appetizer.

3. **Appetizer Assembly:** For each serving, place 1 slice foie gras on the plate and serve with 2 oz/57 g beet salad, 4 slices duck breast, 2 parsnip chips, and 2 oz/57 g baby beet greens dressed with ½ fl oz/15 mL vinaigrette.

CHEF'S NOTE: Fresh figs can also be used to garnish this dish.

Foie Gras in Brioche

YIELD: 10 SERVINGS

This traditional presentation for foie gras is one of the great legacies of Fernand Point, chef of La Pyramide, Vienne, France.

2 lb 8 oz/1.13 kg Brioche Dough (page 542)

½ recipe Foie Gras Roulade (page 329), well chilled

1 lb 4 oz/567 g Port Wine Gelée (page 57)

20 red grapes, sliced very thin

1. Roll or press the brioche dough into a rectangle as long as a Pullman loaf pan and twice its width.

2. Unwrap the foie gras roulade and center it on the dough. Roll the dough around the roulade, pressing to seal the seams. Set in a well-greased Pullman loaf pan, seam side down. Place the lid on the Pullman pan. Allow the brioche dough to rise for 30 minutes. Bake at 350°F/177°C for about 40 minutes, or until the brioche is thoroughly baked. Let cool before unmolding and cutting into 10 equal slices.

3. **Appetizer Assembly:** Pool 2 oz/57 g aspic on each plate, decorate with sliced grapes, and allow to firm under refrigeration. At service, top with a slice of foie gras in brioche.

CONDIMENTS, CRACKERS, AND PICKLES

Condiments, crackers, and pickles are those little extras that can elevate a dish from the ordinary to the sublime. Although most of these foods are available commercially, they are not difficult to produce, and they are always more interesting when made by hand.

ten

Condiments

Condiments are assertive, saucelike creations, typically served on the side and added to dishes at the diner's discretion. However, condiments can also be found as spreads or dips, adding a little extra to sandwiches, dressings, and salads.

Mustard

Plain and flavored mustards have a wonderful aroma and a complex flavor that pairs beautifully with meats, cheeses, and poultry; mustard can even be served as a dip. It is frequently added to vinaigrettes and other dressings and used to glaze meats as they roast. Special mustards from around the world each have their own unique qualities. Some are very hot, others are mild; some are very smooth, others are grainy.

Ketchup

Lancelot Sturgeon, a British author, wrote that ketchup was invented by the French in the seventeenth century. However, early French cookbooks claim that the British formulated the condiment. Still others trace its origins to East Asia. Early English recipes for ketchup called for such ingredients as kidney beans, mushrooms, anchovies, liver, and walnuts. Now predominantly tomato-based, the product is also spelled *catsup* or even *catchup*.

Chutney

Chutneys are sweet-and-sour condiments, often fruit-based (though vegetable-based versions exist as well) and generally highly spiced, favored in Indian cuisines. Chutneys may be cooked, similar to a pickle or relish, or they may be raw, making them similar to cold raw sauces such as salsa.

Mango chutney is probably most familiar worldwide, but tomatoes, eggplant, melons, apples, and pineapples are also commonly used to prepare chutneys.

Relish

A relish may be as simple as a mound of sliced cucumbers or radishes, or as complex as a curried onion relish, cooked in a pickle or brine, highly seasoned and garnished with dried fruits.

Compote

Compotes are often made by cooking fruits in a syrup. For the garde manger, savory compotes can be used to accompany galantines or pâtés in much the same way that a Cumberland sauce is used.

Flavored Oils and Vinegars

Good-quality oils and vinegars can be infused with spices, aromatics, herbs, and fruits or vegetables to produce products with many applications. They work well as condiments, added in a drizzle or as droplets to lend a bit of intense flavor and

Beer Mustard with
Caraway Seeds

color to a plated dish. They also are excellent to use as a dressing for vegetables, pastas, grains, or fruits. And, of course, they are well suited to use in vinaigrettes and other dressings for a special effect.

To infuse oils and vinegars, use one of the following methods:

- **METHOD 1: A WARM INFUSION** Heat the oil or vinegar very gently over low heat with flavoring ingredients such as citrus zest, just until the aroma is apparent. Let the oil or vinegar steep off the heat with the flavoring ingredients until cool, then pour it into storage bottles or containers. You may opt to strain the vinegar or oil for a clearer final product, or leave the flavoring ingredients in for a more intense flavor.

- **METHOD 2: STEEPING** Place the herbs or other aromatics in a glass or plastic bottle. Heat the oil or vinegar briefly, just until warm. Pour the warm oil or vinegar over the aromatics. Let the vinegar rest until the desired flavor is achieved. You may wish to add fresh aromatics after the oil or vinegar has steeped for several days to give an even more intense flavor (see Figure 10-1A).

- **METHOD 3: PURÉES** Purée raw, blanched, or fully cooked vegetables, herbs, or fruits and bring the purée to a simmer, reducing if necessary to concentrate the flavors. Add the oil or vinegar and transfer to a storage container. You may leave the oil and vinegar as is and use it as you would a purée, or you may strain it to remove the fiber and pulp (Figure 10-1B).

- **METHOD 4: COLD INFUSION** Combine room-temperature oil or vinegar with ground spices and transfer to a storage container. Let the mixture settle until the vinegar or oil is clear and the spices are settled in the bottom of the container. Carefully decant the vinegar or oil once the desired flavor is reached.

Note: When you introduce fresh or raw ingredients to an oil or vinegar, you run the risk of food-borne illness if the finished products are not carefully stored. Although commercially prepared versions of flavored oils and vinegars are shelf-

10-1. Infusion methods. **A. Steeping:** Making flavored vinegar with garlic, rosemary, basil, and peppercorns. **B. Straining:** Wringing yellow pepper oil through cheesecloth.

stable, you should keep yours stored under refrigeration, especially if you use raw garlic or shallots. Use them within a few days to be sure they have the best flavor and color.

Pickles

The term *pickle* encompasses any food that has been brined. Pickles can be made from vegetables, fruit, or eggs. The brine often contains vinegar, though a salt brine can also be used. Pickles may be extremely tart, like cornichons, or sweet, like the sweet pickle chips on page 483.

Chips and Crisps

Crackers and other breads may be eaten alone or as a support item that adds flavor and a textural counterpoint. They are served to accompany dips and spreads, or with a salad or appetizer to add a bit of crunch to the plate.

10-2. Fried and baked chips. **A.** Slicing artichokes on an electric slicer. **B.** Basket of deep-fried artichoke chips. **C. Fruit Chips.** Oven-dried pear chips.

Fried and baked chips

We are all familiar with potato chips, made by slicing potatoes very thin and frying them in oil until crisp. Other vegetables can also be made into chips: sweet potatoes, beets, and artichokes are all excellent choices (Figures 10-2A and 10-2B).

Baked chips are wonderful additions to salads and composed appetizers, or on their own as snack food. Pears, apples, bananas, and other fruits can be sliced thin and then baked until they are dry and crisp (Figures 10-2C). If they are sliced a little thicker and baked at a lower temperature, they take on an appealing chewy texture.

Crackers

Crackers can be produced in a number of ways. Icebox-style crackers are made in much the same way as cookies. A savory dough is prepared, rolled into a log, chilled, and then sliced and baked. Cheese and nuts are often used to season and flavor these crackers.

Still other crackers are made from a batter that is baked. These delicate crackers can be shaped before baking by spreading them on a greased sheet pan or silicone baking pad. They can be shaped when they are still warm from the oven by draping them over rolling pins or pressing them into cups or other molds (Figures 10-3).

10-3. Packing potato, polenta, parsnip, and risotto crackers for storage.

Harissa

YIELD: 16 FL OZ/480 ML

This intense sauce can be used as a condiment or to flavor dips and spreads.

10 jalapeños, roasted, peeled, and seeded

3 or 4 red peppers, roasted, peeled, and seeded

1 tbsp/6 g whole cumin seeds, toasted and ground

1 tbsp/10 g garlic paste

¾ oz/21 g hot Hungarian paprika

1½ tsp/3 g cayenne

6 fl oz/180 mL olive oil

1½/45 mL lemon juice

Salt, as needed

1. Combine the jalapeños, peppers, cumin, garlic paste, paprika, and cayenne in a blender. Grind to a paste.

2. Remove the paste to a bowl. Slowly whisk in the oil to create a smooth sauce. Add the lemon juice and salt to taste.

3. Transfer the sauce to a clean storage container. Hold, covered, under refrigeration for up to 2 weeks.

Heywood's Mustard

YIELD: 32 FL OZ/960 ML

4¼ oz/120 g dry mustard

1 oz/28 sugar

2 tsp/10 g salt

12 oz/340 g pasteurized eggs

16 fl oz/480 mL malt vinegar

¼ tsp/1.25 mL Tabasco sauce

4 oz/113 g honey

1. Combine the mustard, sugar, and salt. Add the eggs and mix until smooth. Whip in the vinegar, Tabasco, and honey. Let rest under refrigeration for 1 to 2 hours.

2. Beat the mixture over a double boiler until thick and creamy. Chill.

3. Transfer the mustard to a clean storage container. Hold, covered, under refrigeration for up to 2 weeks.

Southwestern Spicy Green Chile Mustard

YIELD: 32 FL OZ/960 ML

3 oz/85 g dry mustard

6 fl oz/180 mL dark Mexican beer

6 fl oz/180 mL sherry wine vinegar

12 egg yolks

½ fl oz/15 mL soy sauce

1 cup/170 g green chiles, diced

1 jalapeño, minced

¾ oz/21 g cumin seeds, toasted

2 tbsp/12 g dried Mexican oregano

4 oz/113 g honey

1½ tsp/7.50 g salt

1. Combine the mustard, beer, vinegar, egg yolks, and soy sauce in a stainless-steel bowl. Let rest under refrigeration for 1 hour.

2. Beat the mixture over a double boiler until thick and creamy. Add the green chiles, jalapeño, cumin, oregano, honey, and salt. Mix well.

3. Transfer the mustard to a clean storage container. Hold, covered, under refrigeration for up to 2 weeks.

Dried Cranberry Mustard

YIELD: 32 FL OZ/960 ML

3 oz/85 g dry mustard

6 eggs

8 fl oz/240 mL cranberry juice

3 fl oz/90 mL white vinegar

½ tsp/2.50 g salt

½ fl oz/15 mL Worcestershire sauce

2 oz/57 g packed brown sugar

2½ oz/71 g chopped dried cranberries

1. Combine the mustard, eggs, cranberry juice, vinegar, salt, Worcestershire sauce, and sugar in a stainless-steel bowl.

2. Cook over a boiling water bath, stirring constantly until thick and smooth. Add the cranberries and mix well.

3. Hold, covered, under refrigeration for 48 hours before using. Store, covered, under refrigeration for up to 2 weeks.

Beer Mustard with Caraway Seeds

YIELD: 32 FL OZ/960 ML

12 fl oz/360 mL dark beer

6 eggs

4⅔ oz/132 g dry mustard

2 tsp/10 g salt

1 tsp/5 mL Worcestershire sauce

2 oz/57 g packed brown sugar

2 fl oz/60 mL white vinegar

½ oz/14 g caraway seeds, toasted

1. Combine the beer, eggs, mustard, salt, Worcestershire sauce, sugar, and vinegar and mix well. Let the mixture rest for 1 hour.

2. Cook the mixture over a double boiler until thick and smooth. Add the caraway seeds and mix well.

3. Transfer the mustard to a clean storage container. Hold, covered, under refrigeration for up to 2 weeks.

Swedish Mustard Sauce

YIELD: 32 FL OZ/960 ML

5⅓ fl oz/160 mL prepared mustard

2⅓ oz/66 g minced fresh horseradish

16 fl oz/480 mL Basic Mayonnaise (page 35)

1 tsp/5 g salt

2 tsp/10 mL Worcestershire sauce

8 fl oz/240 mL heavy cream, whipped

1. Purée the mustard, horseradish, mayonnaise, salt, and Worcestershire sauce in a food processor fitted with a metal blade. Fold in the cream; chill.

2. Transfer the sauce to a clean storage container. Hold, covered, under refrigeration for up to 12 hours.

Tomato Ketchup

YIELD: 32 FL OZ/960 ML

3½ oz/99 g sugar

3 oz/85 g minced onion

1 tbsp/9 g minced garlic

96 fl oz/2.88 L crushed tomatoes

2 roasted red peppers, chopped

8 fl oz/240 mL red wine vinegar

4 fl oz/120 mL balsamic vinegar

Cayenne, as needed

1. Cook the sugar in a heavy-bottomed saucepan over medium heat until it turns an amber color. Add the onion and garlic. Add the tomatoes and roasted peppers; cook 5 to 10 minutes over medium heat.

2. Add the vinegars and reduce until thickened, about 20 minutes. Season with cayenne to taste; the heat should be fairly mild.

3. Strain the mixture through a fine sieve. Transfer the ketchup to a clean storage container. Hold, covered, under refrigeration for up to 2 weeks.

Yellow Pepper Ketchup

YIELD: 32 FL OZ/960 ML

2 lb/907 g yellow peppers, seeded and coarsely chopped (about 8)

3 oz/85 g jalapeños, seeded and chopped (about 4)

12 oz/340 g onions, coarsely chopped (about 2)

⅔ oz/19 g chopped garlic

Vegetable oil, as needed

6 fl oz/180 mL red wine vinegar

5⅓ oz/151 g sugar

Salt, as needed

Ground white pepper, as needed

1. Sauté the peppers, jalapeños, onions, and garlic in oil until tender but not browned, about 12 minutes. Add the vinegar and sugar; simmer 30 to 45 minutes.

2. Purée in a food processor fitted with the metal blade until smooth. Season with salt and pepper.

3. Cool the ketchup and transfer it to a clean storage container. Hold, covered, under refrigeration for up to 2 weeks.

Spicy Mango Chutney

YIELD: 32 FL OZ/960 ML

3 mangos, peeled and chopped

3½ oz/99 g raisins

1 jalapeño, minced

4 garlic cloves, minced

½ oz/14 g minced ginger

7¾ oz/220 g packed dark brown sugar

8 fl oz/240 mL white wine vinegar

½ tsp/2.50 g salt

1 tsp/2 g turmeric

1. Combine the mangos, raisins, jalapeño, garlic, ginger, and sugar. Let the mixture rest under refrigeration for 24 hours.

2. Add the vinegar; bring to a boil and simmer 15 minutes. Add the salt; simmer 10 minutes. Add the turmeric; simmer 5 minutes.

3. Cool the chutney and transfer to a clean storage container. Hold, covered, under refrigeration for up to 2 weeks.

Apricot-Cherry Chutney

YIELD: 32 FL OZ/960 ML

4 oz/113 g onion, sliced thin

1 oz/28 g minced ginger

½ fl oz/15 mL peanut oil

4 fl oz/120 mL cider vinegar

4 oz/113 g honey

8 fl oz/240 mL orange juice

16 fl oz/480 mL water

Juice of 1 lemon

½ tsp/1 g ground coriander

¼ tsp/0.50 g ground cardamom

½ tsp/1 g curry powder

¼ tsp/0.50 g red pepper flakes

8 oz/227 g dried apricots, halved

8 oz/227 g dried cherries

1. Sauté the onion and ginger in the peanut oil until limp but not browned. Add the remaining ingredients and simmer for 20 minutes. Add more water if the chutney is too thick.

2. Cool the chutney and transfer it to a clean storage container. Hold, covered, under refrigeration for up to 2 weeks.

Beet Chutney

YIELD: 32 FL OZ/960 ML

6 beets

Water, as needed

1 tsp/5 g kosher salt

½ oz/14 g finely chopped ginger

2 fl oz/60 mL vegetable oil

2 tsp/10 g salt

1 fl oz/30 mL red wine vinegar

½ fl oz/15 mL lime juice

¼ tsp/0.50 g cayenne

1 tsp/6 g finely chopped jalapeño

1 tbsp/3 g finely chopped cilantro

1. Wash the beets well. Leave 1 in/3 cm of stem attached to the beets. Put the beets in a 2-in/5-cm hotel pan, in a single layer, and add water just to cover the bottom of the pan. Season with the kosher salt. Cover the pan with aluminum foil and roast the beets in a 375°F/191°C oven until fork tender, about 1 hour, depending on size. Shake the pan every 20 minutes so the beets do not stick or burn.

2. When the beets are done but still warm, remove the skin. Cut the beets into small dice and combine with the remaining ingredients. (*Note:* If preferred, add the jalapeño and cilantro on the day of service.) This chutney should be very spicy.

3. Cool the chutney and transfer it to a clean storage container. Hold, covered, under refrigeration for up to 2 weeks.

Apple Chutney

YIELD: 3 LB/1.36 KG

6 oz/170 g light brown sugar

5 oz/142 g onion, cut into fine dice

4 oz/113 g golden raisins

2 oz/57 g walnuts, toasted and chopped

2 fl oz/60 mL cider vinegar

1 fl oz/30 mL lemon juice

½ oz/14 g ginger, grated

½ oz/14 g hot chile, chopped

2 tsp/6 g lemon zest, minced or finely grated

1 tsp/3 g garlic, minced to a paste

½ tsp/1 g ground mace

½ tsp/1 g ground cloves

2 lb 4 oz/1.02 kg Granny Smith apples, peeled, cored, and cut into medium dice

1. Combine the sugar, onion, raisins, walnuts, vinegar, lemon juice, ginger, chile, lemon zest, garlic, mace, and cloves in a saucepan and simmer, covered, over low heat for 10 minutes.

2. Add the apples and simmer until they are very tender and the juices are reduced and slightly thickened, 10 to 15 minutes. Cool properly, cover, and hold under refrigeration until service.

Papaya Chutney

YIELD: 32 FL OZ/960 ML

4 fl oz/120 mL vegetable oil

5 oz/142 g onion, cut into small dice

8 oz/227 g red pepper, cut into small dice

6 oz/170 g green pepper, cut into
small dice

4 garlic cloves, minced

2 tsp/4 g ground allspice

2 tsp/4 g curry powder

2 tsp/4 g cumin powder

1 lb/454 g papaya, ripe, peeled, seeded,
cut into small dice

4 fl oz/120 mL white vinegar

8 fl oz/240 mL pineapple juice

1½ oz/43 g molasses

2 fl oz/60 mL lemon juice

1 tsp/5 g salt

½ tsp/1 g ground black pepper

1. In a large sauté pan, heat the vegetable oil over medium heat until hot but not smoking. Add the onion and sauté 5 to 7 minutes, stirring frequently, until they are lightly caramelized.

2. Add the peppers and cook an additional 2 minutes, or until they just begin to soften, stirring frequently. Add the garlic, allspice, curry, and cumin and cook an additional 2 minutes, stirring constantly. The mixture will be quite dry at this point.

3. Add the papaya, vinegar, pineapple juice, and molasses, stir well, and bring to a boil. Reduce the heat to low and cook until the mixture coats the back of a spoon.

4. Add the lemon juice, salt, and pepper to taste. Cool properly, cover, and hold under refrigeration until service.

Rhubarb Compote

YIELD: 32 FL OZ/960 ML

2 lb/907 g rhubarb, trimmed and diced

8 oz/227 g sugar

8 fl oz/240 mL water

8 fl oz/240 mL red wine vinegar

2 oz/57 g dried Zante currants

½ oz/14 g finely minced garlic

¾ oz/21 g finely minced ginger

½ oz/14 g finely grated lemon zest

1. Combine the rhubarb, sugar, water, vinegar, currants, garlic, ginger, and lemon zest. Bring to a boil, then reduce the heat and simmer until the compote thickens and has a good flavor, about 20 minutes. Skim the surface as necessary while simmering.

2. Transfer the compote to a clean container and cool completely before storing under refrigeration for up to 3 weeks.

Cranberry Relish

YIELD: 32 FL OZ/960 ML

12 oz/340 g cranberries

3 fl oz/90 mL orange juice

3 fl oz/90 mL triple sec (optional)

3 oz/85 g sugar

Zest and segments, with membranes removed, of 2 oranges

1. Combine the cranberries, orange juice, triple sec (if desired), sugar, and zest in a saucepan and stir to combine. Cover and let simmer 15 to 20 minutes, stirring occasionally.

2. Cook until all the berries burst and the liquid starts to thicken. Remove from the heat and add the orange segments. Adjust sweetness with sugar.

3. Transfer the relish to a clean storage container. Hold, covered, under refrigeration for up to 2 weeks.

Curried Onion Relish

YIELD: 16 FL OZ/480 ML

1 lb/454 g onions, cut into ¼-in/6-mm dice

1 garlic clove, minced

8 fl oz/240 mL white vinegar

7 oz/198 g sugar

½ tsp/2.50 g salt

¾ oz/21 g pickling spice, tied into a sachet

1 tbsp/6 g curry powder

1. Combine all ingredients; mix well.

2. Simmer, covered, in a small nonreactive saucepan until the onions are tender and the liquid is mostly evaporated. Stir often, being careful not to scorch. Chill.

3. Transfer the relish to a clean storage container. Hold, covered, under refrigeration for up to 2 weeks.

Red Onion Confiture

YIELD: 32 FL OZ/960 ML

1 fl oz/30 mL vegetable oil

1 lb 8 oz/680 g red onions, cut into julienne

4 oz/113 g honey (see Chef's Note)

4 fl oz/120 mL red wine vinegar

6 fl oz/180 mL red wine

Salt, as needed

Ground white pepper, as needed

1. Heat the oil in a sauté pan over high heat. Sweat the onions. Stir in the honey; cook the mixture until the onions are lightly caramelized. Add the vinegar and wine; reduce until the liquid is cooked away. Season with salt and pepper.

2. Cool the confiture and transfer it to a clean storage container. Hold, covered, under refrigeration for up to 2 weeks.

CHEF'S NOTE: Grenadine substituted for the honey adds sweetness and enhances the color as well.

Dried Apricot Relish

YIELD: 32 FL OZ/960 ML

1 lb/454 g dried apricots, cut into medium dice

½ tsp/1.50 g minced garlic

2 drops Tabasco sauce

Juice and zest of 1 lemon

8 oz/227 g honey

1 fl oz/30 mL soy sauce

16 fl oz/480 mL ginger ale

4 oz/113 g sliced almonds, toasted

1. Combine the apricots, garlic, Tabasco, lemon juice and zest, honey, soy sauce, and ginger ale. Simmer for 20 minutes. Cool. Stir in the almonds.

2. Transfer the relish to a clean storage container. Hold, covered, under refrigeration for up to 2 weeks.

Sweet Pickle Chips

YIELD: 4 LB/1.81 KG

4 lb/1.81 kg cucumbers

1 lb/454 g onions

24 fl oz/720 mL cider vinegar

⅔ oz/19 g salt

1 tsp/2 g mustard seeds

1 lb 12½ oz/808 g sugar

64 fl oz/1.92 L water

20 fl oz/600 mL white vinegar

½ oz/14 g celery seed

1 tbsp/6 g whole allspice, crushed

2 tsp/4 g turmeric

1. Wash the cucumbers and slice ¼ in/6 mm thick. Slice the onions ¼ in/6 mm thick.

2. Combine the cucumbers and onions with the cider vinegar, salt, mustard seeds, 1 oz/28 g of the sugar, and the water. Simmer for 10 minutes and drain. Discard the liquid.

3. Bring the white vinegar, celery seed, allspice, turmeric, and the remaining sugar to a boil. Pour this mixture over the cucumbers and onions and let rest under refrigeration for 3 to 4 days before serving.

4. Hold under refrigeration for up to 1 week.

Dill Pickles

YIELD: 10 LB/4.54 KG

10 lb/4.54 kg pickling cucumbers

6 gal 64 fl oz/24.96 L water

2 lb 4 oz/1.02 kg salt

64 fl oz/1.92 L white or cider vinegar

1½ tbsp/9 g dill seed

2 oz/43 g pickling spice

1 tbsp/6 g ground turmeric

4 oz/113 g sugar

4 dried hot chiles

1 bunch dill sprigs

5 garlic cloves, smashed

1. Soak the cucumbers overnight or up to 48 hours in 6 gal/23.04 L of the water combined with 2 lb/907 g of the salt. Drain.

2. Combine the remaining water and salt and the vinegar, dill seed, pickling spice, turmeric, and sugar and bring to a boil; simmer for 10 minutes.

3. Pack the cucumbers in a large plastic bucket with the chiles, dill sprigs, and garlic. Pour the pickling liquid over the cucumbers; weigh them down with plates and cover with cheese-cloth. Let cool for 30 minutes to 1 hour, then refrigerate.

4. The pickles may be used after 1½ weeks. Hold under refrigeration for up to 4 weeks.

Half-Sour Pickles

YIELD: 3 LB/1.36 KG

½ oz/14 g dill sprigs

3 garlic cloves, smashed

2 bay leaves

4 lb/1.81 kg pickling cucumbers, cut into spears

64 fl oz/1.92 L water

6 oz/170 g salt

8 fl oz/240 mL white vinegar

1. Place the dill, garlic, and bay leaves in a noncorrosive container. Pack the cucumber spears on top.

2. Bring the water, salt, and vinegar to a boil, pour over the pickles, and allow to cool.

3. Hold under refrigeration at least 3 days and up to 4 weeks.

CHEF'S NOTE: The pickles will change in texture from half-raw/half-cured to fully cured as they sit in the refrigerator.

Pickled Vegetables

YIELD: 6 LB/2.72 KG

32 fl oz/960 mL water

8 fl oz/240 mL malt vinegar

5 oz/142 g salt

7 oz/198 g sugar

1 oz/28 g pickling spices

6 lb/2.72 kg assorted vegetables: baby golden, red, or Chioggia beets; pearl onions; okra; baby carrots; broccoli, trimmed and cut into small pieces

⅔ oz/19 g minced garlic

2 dill sprigs

1. Bring the water, vinegar, salt, sugar, and pickling spices to a boil to make a brine.

2. Pack the vegetables, garlic, and dill in a plastic container. Pour the brine over the vegetables. Let cool and then cover.

3. Allow to marinate for at least 24 hours before serving. The pickles' holding ability will depend on the vegetables used.

Pickled Grapes or Cherries

YIELD: 64 FL OZ/1.92 L

3 lb 9 oz/1.62 kg sugar

44 fl oz/1.32 L white wine vinegar

3 cinnamon sticks

1 tsp/5 g salt

5 lb/2.27 kg seedless grapes, stemmed, or sweet cherries, pitted

1. Combine the sugar, vinegar, cinnamon sticks, and salt. Simmer for 5 minutes.

2. Pour the liquid over the grapes or cherries, allow to cool, and refrigerate.

3. The grapes or cherries are ready to serve now, or hold, covered, under refrigeration overnight.

Pickled Red Onions

YIELD: 32 FL OZ/960 ML

12 fl oz/360 mL red wine vinegar

3 oz/85 g sugar

6 fl oz/180 mL water

1½ tsp/7.50 g salt

½ tsp/1 g cracked black pepper

1 lb 2 oz/510 g red onions, sliced in thin rings

1. Combine the vinegar, sugar, water, salt, and pepper in a small nonreactive saucepan and bring to a boil. Remove from the heat, but keep hot.

2. Bring a large pot of water to a boil. Add enough salt to flavor the water. Add the onions and boil for 1 minute, or until tender. Drain immediately.

3. Pour the hot vinegar mixture over the blanched onions. Cool the onions in the vinegar solution to room temperature and chill for 6 to 8 hours or overnight.

4. Transfer the onions and liquid to a clean storage container. Hold, covered, under refrigeration for up to 2 weeks.

Assorted Vegetable Chips

YIELD: 30 SERVINGS

8 oz/227 g taro root	8 oz/227 g beets
8 oz/227 g sweet potatoes	8 oz/227 g plantains
8 oz/227 g parsnips	Vegetable oil, as needed
8 oz/227 g carrots	Salt, as needed
8 oz/227 g baking potatoes (such as Idaho or russet)	

1. Peel all the vegetables. Slice all very thin (1/16 in/1.5 mm). Hold the taro and potato slices separately in cold water; all other vegetables may be held dry. Keep them separate, as they all require different cooking times.

2. Heat a fryer with clean oil to 275°F/135°C. Fry each vegetable separately until crisp, drain on paper towels, and season with salt.

3. Serve immediately or hold in an airtight container, as you would crackers, for later service. Serve within 24 hours for best quality.

ARTICHOKE CHIPS: Remove the choke and some of the stem. Slice trimmed artichokes very thin on a slicer and fry in 350°F/177°C oil until crisp. Drain and salt to taste.

FENNEL CHIPS: Remove the stem ends from fennel, trim the root ends, and halve or quarter (depending on the size of the fennel bulb). Slice very thin using a knife, electric slicer, or mandoline. Fry in 350°F/177°C vegetable oil in a deep fryer or over medium heat until crisp. Drain and salt to taste.

GARLIC CHIPS: Use large garlic (elephant garlic) and slice peeled cloves very thin using a knife or a garlic slicer. Fry in olive oil over medium heat until lightly browned. Reserve the flavored oil for another use, if desired.

APPLE OR PEAR CHIPS: Remove the core from rinsed apples or pears, slice thin, and bake on a silicone baking pad or a lightly oiled sheet pan in a 375°F/191°C oven for 20 to 30 minutes, or until crisp.

Pepper Jack and Oregano Crackers

YIELD: 100 CRACKERS

9 oz/255 g all-purpose flour

8 oz/227 g shredded pepper Jack cheese

2 tsp/4 g dried oregano, or 1 tbsp/3 g fresh oregano

½ tsp/2.50 g salt

½ tsp/1 g ground black pepper

4 fl oz/120 mL vegetable oil

4 to 5 fl oz/120 to 150 mL water

SPICE MIXTURE

¼ tsp/0.50 g cayenne

1 tsp/5 g sugar

1 tsp/5 g kosher salt

1. Combine the flour, cheese, oregano, salt, and pepper in a food processor or by hand. Add the oil and mix just until a coarse meal consistency is achieved. Add the water gradually until the dough forms a cohesive ball that pulls away from the sides of the bowl.

2. Divide the dough into two equal portions, wrap, and refrigerate. Combine the spice mixture ingredients; reserve.

3. Roll the dough through a pasta machine to ⅛ in/3 mm thick. Cut the dough using a pizza cutter, knife, or shaped cutters into the desired cracker shapes and place on a doubled sheet pan. Sprinkle with the spice mixture.

4. Bake at 325°F/163°C until lightly golden; turn and bake until medium golden brown, 15 to 20 minutes. Allow to cool completely on a rack and store in an airtight container.

CHEF'S NOTE: Chill the dough if it becomes soft during rolling or cutting.

Cheddar and Walnut Crisps

YIELD: ABOUT 100 SMALL CRISPS

4 oz/113 g butter

8 oz/227 g aged Cheddar cheese, grated

6½ oz/184 g flour

1 tsp/5 g salt

2 oz/57 g finely chopped walnuts

1. Cream the butter, add the cheese, and mix well.

2. Add the flour and salt and mix well. Blend in the walnuts.

3. Roll out into 3 logs, about 1½ in/4 cm in diameter. Chill at least 1 hour.

4. Cut into ⅛-in/3-mm slices and place them on a parchment-lined sheet pan. Bake in a 350°F/177°C oven until crisp. Cool on a wire rack. Store in an airtight container. Serve within 3 days.

BLUE CHEESE AND PECAN CRISPS: Substitute an equal amount of blue cheese for the Cheddar and pecans for the walnuts.

Potato Crisps

YIELD: 50 CRISPS

1 lb/454 g russet potatoes

2 fl oz/60 mL egg whites

Milk, as needed

1. Bake the potatoes until done, about 1 hour.

2. Scoop out the pulp and pass through a food mill. Cool.

3. Mix in the egg whites; add milk and mix to the consistency of crêpe batter.

4. Lay out a thin layer of the mixture on a silicone baking pad or nonstick sheet pan and bake in a convection oven at 300°F/149°C for 3 to 4 minutes. Score into crisps of the size and shape desired; finish baking until golden, 2 to 3 minutes. Cool on a wire rack and store in an airtight container. Serve within 3 days.

PARSNIP CRISPS: Replace potatoes with parsnips.

CELERIAC CRISPS: Replace potatoes with peeled celeriac (celery root).

Cheddar and Walnut Crisps

Basil Oil (Basic Herb Oil)

YIELD: 16 FL OZ/480 ML

3 oz/85 g basil leaves

16 fl oz/480 mL pure olive oil

1 oz/28 g flat-leaf parsley leaves

1. Blanch the basil and parsley leaves in salted water for 20 seconds. Shock and drain on paper towels.

2. Combine the blanched herbs with half the oil in a blender and purée very fine. Add this purée to the remaining oil. Strain the oil through cheesecloth, if desired.

3. Transfer the oil to a storage container or squirt bottle. Keep chilled. Use within 3 to 4 days.

CHEF'S NOTE: This recipe works well with most green herbs, including chives, tarragon, chervil, and parsley.

CHIVE OIL: Replace the basil leaves with chives. Blanching is not necessary.

Cinnamon Oil (Basic Spice Oil)

YIELD: 16 FL OZ/480 ML

19 fl oz/570 mL sunflower oil

12 cinnamon sticks, crushed

1 nutmeg, quartered

1. Heat the oil in a small saucepan with the cinnamon and nutmeg until approximately 150°F/66°C. Remove from the heat and allow to cool.

2. Strain the oil into a bottle or other clean container. Allow to cool and recap.

3. Store in a cool, dark area. Use within 3 to 4 days.

CURRY OIL: Replace the cinnamon and nutmeg with 2 oz/57 g Curry Powder (page 525).

Orange Oil (Basic Citrus Oil)

YIELD: 24 FL OZ/720 ML

12 fl oz/360 mL pure olive oil

12 fl oz/360 mL extra-virgin olive oil

3 oranges, zest only, cut into strips measuring 1 by 3 in/3 by 8 cm

1. Combine the oils and heat to 140°F/60°C. Do not leave oil unattended—it warms very quickly.

2. Add the orange zest. Transfer the mixture to a storage container and infuse overnight under refrigeration.

3. The next day, taste and strain out the zest if the flavor is good, or allow to infuse longer.

4. Keep chilled. Use within 3 to 4 days.

Red Pepper Oil

YIELD: 20 FL OZ/600 ML

8 red peppers	20 fl oz/600 mL olive oil
2 oz/57 g mustard	Salt, as needed

1. Wash the peppers, remove the stems and seeds, and cut roughly into small dice.

2. Purée the peppers very fine in a blender. Place the purée in a stainless-steel saucepan and reduce to one-quarter the original volume. Strain through a fine-mesh strainer and cool.

3. Add the mustard to the cooled purée. Add the olive oil. Season with salt.

4. Transfer to a storage container or squirt bottle. Keep chilled. Use within 2 to 3 days.

CHEF'S NOTES: Yellow or green peppers can be substituted with excellent results. For a spicy variation, use chiles and omit the mustard.

Raspberry and Thyme Vinegar (Basic Flavored Vinegar)

YIELD: 16 FL OZ/480 ML

16 fl oz/480 mL red wine vinegar	25 raspberries
8 to 10 thyme sprigs	

1. Heat the vinegar until slightly warm, about 120°F/49°C.

2. Place the thyme sprigs and raspberries in a glass jar or other storage container.

3. Pour the vinegar into the bottle over the thyme and berries. Allow to cool and recap.

4. Keep chilled. Use within 5 to 6 days.

CHEF'S NOTE: Champagne vinegar can be substituted for the red wine vinegar.

Rosemary-Garlic Vinegar

YIELD: 16 FL OZ/480 ML

16 fl oz/480 mL white wine vinegar

4 garlic cloves

6 to 8 rosemary sprigs

1 opal basil sprig (optional)

1 tbsp/6 g whole black peppercorns

1. Heat the vinegar until slightly warm, about 120°F/49°C.

2. Thread the garlic on a skewer. Place it in a glass or plastic bottle with the rosemary, basil (if desired), and peppercorns.

3. Pour the vinegar over the herbs and garlic. Allow to cool and recap.

4. Keep chilled. Use within 5 to 6 days.

THE MODERN BUFFET

Buffets are one of the garde manger's most exciting professional challenges. They demand a unique blend of culinary and management skills. The practical aspects of a buffet make them advantageous to virtually any type of operation. The creative challenges and opportunities they open up to the garde manger make them a meaningful way to advance and develop a career.

eleven

The work of the garde manger as banquet chef can be divided into four distinct phases. In the first phase, the concept or theme is identified so planning can begin. In the second phase, the menu and theme are worked out together, culminating in a production plan that makes good culinary and business sense from the menu to the plans for food presentation and service. In the third stage, the chef prepares plans for the layout and setup of the buffet lines, tables, and platters; the goal is to make the buffet attractive and welcoming to the guest as well as efficient and practical for the service staff to replenish. The final stage, the actual production and display of the food, flows directly from the planning and preparation in the preceding stages.

Flexible enough to incorporate new trends—both the foods you serve and the style of service you offer—buffets are an important aspect of many food-service operations, no matter what their size or menu. All facets of the food-service industry have found effective uses for buffets, from fast food outlets through supermarkets and delis to family or multi-unit restaurants, fine dining establishments, and corporate and institutional dining.

Concepts and Themes

A buffet may center on a particular meal period, special occasion, or holiday. The event's theme is typically the starting point for developing a plan for the buffet itself. Another fundamental decision is the menu.

Buffets may be designed to attract guests to the restaurant. Examples include Sunday brunches, pasta or seafood buffets, as well as "quick-service" breakfast or lunch menus.

Buffets are also integral to many special events. The event could be a personal or family celebration—a wedding, birthday, anniversary, christening, or bar mitzvah. It may be a seasonal or holiday celebration, such as New Year's Eve, Mother's Day, or Thanksgiving.

Buffets can be part of a fund-raiser, a gala, or an opening reception for a new business, product, or gallery showing. They are a part of many meetings, conferences, conventions, and similar corporate events.

The season, the weather, and the guests' comfort and expectations hold together the theme. These elements have a direct impact on the selection of specific dishes for the buffet as well as the ways they are presented. When a buffet is part of a special event or celebration, the food should set the mood and enhance the occasion without overshadowing the occasion itself.

When the concept or theme is maintained throughout the buffet presentation, guests can easily recognize it. At each stage of buffet work, from the development of the menu through replenishing the platters during the event, the theme or concept guides you to the best choice for a particular situation.

The Menu

Because they can maintain a focus on the guest, banquet chefs have an enviable opportunity to create a unique dining experience. The menu selections and their presentation convey an integrated message to the guest. Buffet-style service offers guests variety, the freedom to choose, and unlimited portions.

In most operations, buffets also serve as a creative and profitable outlet for a wide range of foods, if priced properly. Whenever you can sell more of the food you bought, you lower overall food costs for the entire business. Banquets are a good way to attract new market segments or keep your current clientele coming back regularly. They allow you to showcase additions to the menu.

Throughout the menu development and planning process, the banquet chef needs to keep abreast of current trends and the competition to be sure the new menu is one that meets customers' expectations and reflects to advantage the skills and abilities of the facilities and the staff.

The food is generally the focal point for the guest. Food supplies the majority of the drama, excitement, and interaction of a buffet, and it falls to the garde manger to produce food that is flavorful and attractive. The successful banquet chef generates and executes menus that please guests whether they are looking for a global flair or traditional elegance.

Price Range

Establish the price range for any buffet at the outset of planning. Consider a variety of factors, including the competition's price for a comparable buffet, your guest's expectations or special requests, and any special conditions or limitations on the menu or the service.

The price range determines, to some extent, the number of options that can be offered as well as the specific ingredients or dishes you choose. Food cost can be difficult to estimate if you cannot predict the exact number of guests—but even if you can, there is no certainty that guests will eat the foods you predict in the amounts you estimated.

Food cost is an important piece of information. Use standard costing procedures to arrive at a cost per piece or portion. (For more information about food costing, see *Culinary Math* by Hill and Blocker.) This step identifies costly ingredients or those that may have a limited shelf life. This does not mean that these items must be dropped from the menu, though you may wish to revise the portion, presentation, or preparation method to help control costs.

In addition to the cost of the food for a buffet, the banquet chef considers other items as well. The cost to produce a specific item (labor cost) can be calculated and used as part of the overall evaluation of any item. High labor costs on one item may be offset by low costs for others. However, any item that has markedly higher labor costs than the other items on the menu should be reviewed to determine where those costs could be cut.

You may be able to use different purchasing strategies to reduce labor and/or service costs. Precut, prewashed, preportioned items that meet your quality standards may be one way to reduce labor, for instance. Organizing the workload differently—for instance, grouping mise en place more efficiently—may reduce costs as well.

Foods must be at the height of quality when presented, but many buffet foods must be prepared well in advance and then held. They, along with foods that are prepared just before they are served, must also maintain their quality while they are on the buffet line.

Review each proposed item to determine how well it will hold before and during the meal period. Consider how the food will taste and look, the safety of the guests, and any restrictions imposed by the pace of service, budget, equipment, and the skills of the buffet attendants.

Some foods lend themselves readily to banquet service, including carved or sliced meats, salads, some pasta dishes, and canapés. Foods that must be prepared and served immediately may require special handling during preparation or presentation; this may increase the cost of serving the food. Whenever possible, weed out items that may require special handling not only to make service more efficient but also to reduce the cost of service items like chafing dishes, heat lamps, and portable cooking devices.

Although not all dishes are equally suitable, there are often techniques and strategies you can employ if a dish is particularly important to the guest or the theme. These strategies may affect both labor cost and food cost. One such strategy is to present these foods at an action station, especially foods such as pasta or omelets that are made or finished to order. Another is preplating.

Menu Development for Buffets

Menu development is a process aimed at crafting a menu that satisfies the guest or client while making a profit for the operator. It is the responsibility of the banquet chef to consider all aspects of the banquet, including the overall theme, the price range, and the guest's expectations.

First, review the concept or theme and establish the appropriate menu selections for the buffet. The number of options within those categories and the exact dishes to be prepared are areas in which the chef can make adjustments.

When you select a potential menu, highlight any special requests, seasonal or holiday items, and the like. These items will require special consideration as you refine the list.

Although the food may be presented all at the same time, guests expect to see options for the soup course, main course, side dishes, salads, and dessert on a dinner buffet.

Some menu items may be drawn from previous events. The advantage in working with familiar recipes and presentations is that you already know what they cost to produce and serve. Others may be new to your repertoire of buffet recipes. The advantages in offering new items are the ability to reflect popular trends, to customize a menu for a special event, and to introduce a new concept or theme.

Continue to list more items that work within the theme you've established. Assign them to menu categories and work toward establishing a list that appropriately covers all the courses your menu should include.

Meeting and Exceeding Expectations

As you develop the menu for a specific event, list the items guests expect. If it is a special occasion, this may include dishes specifically requested by the client. If the buffet has a regional theme, representative dishes should be featured. For a dinner brunch, the guests in your area may expect a certain number of courses to be represented.

Authenticity is the key to the success of an ethnic or regional buffet. Customs, methods, and foods should be studied carefully. Researching the items for your menu may mean reading about a special cuisine or reviewing notes from previous banquets. Learning about the menus and prices for other buffets in your area is another important research tactic.

It is safest to have more items on your development list than you intend to actually serve. As you go through the process of evaluating each item, some will be dropped and others may be modified. Keep in mind that, from the guests' point of view, two of the main advantages of buffets are the variety of choices and the amount of food offered.

A careful review process for every menu item identifies areas you can improve, modify, or adapt to meet all of your objectives—great food, great service, a great experience, and, when the day is done, a profit.

The successful banquet chef uses specific strategies to deliver uncompromisingly high quality in all areas to the guest, coupled with a wide range of strategies to control costs.

If your buffet plans include action stations, select foods for those stations carefully. They should add something more than simply another menu item. Guests enjoy these stations because they see them as a custom experience; foods are made, sliced, or presented to their order as they watch. Highlight the special talents of your staff as they make crêpes and fill them or carve a steamship round of beef. Action stations are also a good way to introduce interaction between the guests and the staff. For example, a cheese display staffed by a knowledgeable attendant is effective not only with respect to serving the guests but it also increases the chances the guest will return.

Before making a final menu selection for dishes to feature at an interactive station, consider the specific skills necessary to successfully staff a station as well as the needs the attendant will have during service, especially space and equipment availability.

RAW BAR: A raw bar setup is a sure way to impress your guests. It is very popular and will make any event look and feel extravagant.

Oysters, clams, mussels, shrimp, and crab are the seafood typically used for service at a raw bar. When serving raw seafood it is important to be aware of the associated hazards. All raw shellfish must come with a tag stating the point of origin, the date of harvest, and the wholesale grower and seller. These stipulations, set by the National Shellfish Sanitation Program, guarantee that shellfish may be traced in the case of a disease outbreak. The warning on the tag reads:

RETAILERS INFORM YOUR CUSTOMERS *Thoroughly cooking foods of an animal origin such as shellfish reduces the risk of foodborne illness. Individuals with certain health conditions such as liver disease, chronic alcohol abuse, diabetes, cancer, stomach, blood, or immune disorders, may be at higher risk if these foods are consumed raw or undercooked. Consult your physician or public health official for further information.*

With this risk in mind, it is important to use only the freshest and highest quality shellfish for raw bar service.

Oysters

Throughout the world, oysters are commonly eaten raw. Four species of oyster typically cultivated for consumption include the Atlantic oyster (*Crassostrea virginica,* also known as the Eastern or American oyster), the Pacific oyster (*Crassostrea gigas,* also known as the Japanese oyster), the European flat oyster (*Ostrea edulis*), and finally, the Kumamoto oyster (*Crassostrea sikamea*). Each species of oyster has one of two distinct flavor profiles, a result of the water in which they were cultivated. Warm-water oysters are mild, with a buttery flavor and a creamy texture. Cold-water varieties, on the other hand, are characteristically briny, with a metallic flavor and a firm, crisp texture. When served raw, the delicate and subtle flavor differences among oyster varieties becomes apparent.

Checking oysters for freshness

Oysters do not open and close as readily as clams and mussels do, making it difficult to determine freshness from their outside appearance. Good indicators of an oyster's freshness are shellfish that do not open easily, meat that is moist and plump, and a fresh smell.

When preparing oysters for service in a raw bar, it is important to shuck them carefully. This prevents damage to the oyster's flesh and ensures that the bottom shell remains intact.

11-1. Clams with Salsa Verde (page 42) and Oysters Mignonette (page 417).

Clams

Clams served raw on the half-shell, while popular in select regions throughout the world, are much less common than oysters. Only varieties of hard-shell clams (*Mercenaria mercenaria*) are served raw, Littlenecks and Topnecks being the most popular variety, as they are the smallest and most tender. Cherrystones are medium-sized clams that are slightly tougher than Littlenecks and Topnecks; nevertheless, they are commonly served raw.

Checking clams for freshness

Fresh clams should have a tightly closed shell, moist, plump flesh, and a sweet smell. Shucking for service on the half-shell, as with oysters, must be done carefully to prevent damaging the clam's flesh.

Steamed Mussels

The remaining seafood popularly served on a raw bar—mussels, shrimp, and crab—are not served raw but rather they are steamed. The majority of the mussels purchased today are cultivated; therefore, they are free of barnacles. Typically, a cultivated mussel has a better meat-to-shell ratio than does a wild mussel. Cultivated mussels are more uniform in size, cleaner, and less frequently have broken shells.

Checking mussels for freshness

Fresh mussels, like clams, have a tightly closed shell, moist, plump flesh, and a sweet smell. Mussels must be cleaned before steaming: Remove and discard any mussels with cracked or broken shells, and debeard as close to service as possible.

A basic method for steaming mussels

Flavor the steaming liquid with shallots, white wine, cracked black pepper, and garlic. Bring the mixture to a boil, add the mussels, cover, and steam until just open. Steam mussels as close to service as feasible.

Shrimp

Varieties of shrimp are too numerous to mention; however, for culinary purposes, shrimp are available as small, large, or jumbo, and are sold in a variety of forms: PUD (peeled undeveined), PND (peeled and deveined), and IQF (individually quick frozen). Head-on shrimp may also be purchased to provide a dramatic display—although, unless purchased very fresh, they are generally of lower quality.

Checking shrimp for freshness

Fresh shrimp are free of ammonia odor, slimy feel, and residue, and they are sweet smelling.

Prepare a court bouillon or other flavorful liquid and simmer for a short time to develop the flavors. Place the shrimp in the liquid, turn off the stove, and allow the shrimp to cook via the residual heat until firm and opaque. Drain the shrimp and allow them to cool at room temperature before refrigerating. For this method, the shrimp must be fully defrosted before they are cooked. Also, they must be completely submerged and "swimming" in the cooking liquid. Overcrowding the shrimp in the liquid prevents even cooking. To preserve flavor, shrimp that will be served cold should be peeled after cooking.

Crabs

Steamed crabs, available in many varieties, are a pleasant addition to any raw bar. Claws are generally the only part of the crab that is served; however, the legs of some varieties are eaten as well. Crab claws are most often purchased cooked, either in or out of the shell. The most common crabs served on a raw bar include King, Snow, Jonah, and Stone crabs.

The Red King Crab is of higher quality than most of the other varieties. For this reason, it is a popular choice for raw bar use. The claws and legs of the crab are served. The Snow Crab and the Jonah Crab, of lower quality than the King Crab, are also known as Cocktail Claws. A rather expensive crab from the Gulf Coast Region and Florida is the Stone Crab. Though it is purchased cooked, the Stone Crab must be cracked prior to service.

Raw Bar Safety

In order to ensure the safety of a raw bar, purchase depurated oysters, clams, and mussels. Depuration is a system that purges the shellfish of impurities and sand. The process occurs when the shellfish are placed in tanks and fresh water is pumped throughout.

To further decrease the risks associated with raw bar, it is advisable to purchase cultivated oysters, clams, and mussels. Cultivated shellfish are raised in a controlled environment and therefore are generally cleaner and safer.

Sauces, Condiments, and Accompaniments

Popular accompaniments to a raw bar include but are not limited to:

LEMONS

COCKTAIL SAUCE

HOT SAUCE (TABASCO)

VINEGARS (MALT)

SALSAS

MIGNONETTE SAUCE

Equipment

Equipment essential for a safe, functional, and attractive raw bar includes:

ICE

KNIVES for shucking

GLOVES (The New York State glove law calls for protection while shucking.)

SELF-DRAINING DISPLAYS (available in a variety of shapes and materials)

Service Instructions

Prior to service, all shellfish should be scrubbed and held on ice between 35° and 40°F/2° and 4°C, for no more than two to three days. Shellfish should be served with accompaniments, on a tray filled with ice, and replenished as consumed.

Controlling Costs

Well-planned menus leave no detail to chance. They take advantage of every opportunity to meet and exceed customers' expectations in terms not only of the food but also its presentation and display. Equally important in all these considerations is the development of a menu that is profitable for the operation. Your goal is to create a balance between cost control and the guests' freedom of choice.

Mise en Place and Production for Buffets

Menu selection and development leads to the next phase of planning. At this point, information about the number or count to be prepared and portioning is finalized. The chef analyzes the menu to determine the best scheduling for mise en place and production work. By maintaining a direct concentration on the important aspects of the buffet—the theme, the anticipated number of guests, customer expectations, and the pace of service—it is possible to improve quality and efficiency.

Chefs use a variety of means to arrive at the number of portions or pieces to make for each menu item. You cannot simply make enough for everyone to have a specific number of each item. Guests may ignore one item altogether but devour another. The problem is magnified if there is no firm guest count, as there might be at a luncheon or dinner buffet. Chefs rely on information from previous buffets to make an educated guess; throughout the course of each buffet, they have another opportunity to collect more information. Keeping track of not only actual production but also actual consumption is an important activity during the buffet itself. It is also important to improving the quality and profitability of future buffets.

Portions for buffets are typically smaller than for à la carte service. Smaller portions are an advantage to guests facing a full buffet. They can take small portions of many items, or take as much of a single item as they wish. At the same time that this approach increases freedom of choice for guests, it also reduces the amount of food that is wasted. Large portions that are only partially consumed are of no use to the guest. It becomes a more difficult task to get accurate information about customer preferences to use in the future.

The banquet chef organizes food production to maximize the quality of the food, lower the overall labor cost, and to cut down on food loss. Writing a logical, simple, but detailed plan is vital to good organization. In some operations, this plan is known as a *buffet production order*. These instructions set out the flow of food throughout preparation and service. Assign a specific individual (or individuals) to be responsible for the food, making sure that safe food-handling practices are observed, that foods are properly prepared and portioned, and that exact counts are taken and recorded.

Tasks can be organized to prevent a last-minute scramble. Some foods can be prepared, either up to the point of service or to some intermediate point, well in advance, as long as adequate and appropriate storage space is available.

An interesting and challenging aspect of cooking for a buffet is that you must make large quantities of food and then portion it into many small pieces. Excellent cutting skills and precise work is mandatory. The banquet chef's knives and cutters must be perfectly sharp. Clean cuts, straight edges, and precise angles do more to naturally enhance the foods you serve than any garnish. They show off the foods' color, texture, and shape.

Cleanliness and order are critical to a successful food presentation, regardless of the overall design. These two aspects of presentation assure the guest that foods have been properly and professionally handled.

As you place foods on a platter, pay attention to the spacing between pieces and between other lines. All spacing should be as regular as possible. Individual pieces like canapés and crab cakes should be regularly shaped and evenly sized.

Arranging Foods

Arranging the food for service is the banquet chef's responsibility as well as his or her opportunity to improve the quality of the guest's experience. Food is necessarily handled as it is transferred to platters and other service pieces. From a food-safety standpoint, it is critical to avoid contaminating the food as you work. Gloves, tongs, and other tools keep you from touching the food with your bare hands and prevent cross contamination. They also cut down on the number of smudges or fingerprints that might mar the food or the platter.

Slicing and sequencing

Slicing and sequencing foods that have tapered shapes, such as turkey breasts, or that have an internal garnish, such as a terrine, make it possible to create strong lines from foods that are not perfectly regular in shape and size.

Set up a complete station mise en place to be sure you have all the tools you need to slice and hold the food—knives, a steel, a holding tray, and plastic wrap or dampened toweling to keep foods from discoloring or toughening as you work.

You may choose to include an element on your platter or tray known as a *grosse pièce,* which is simply a large piece of the sliced item you are displaying. If your platter calls for a gross pièce, determine which portion of the item to keep whole and how large the piece should be before you start to slice. Working from the opposite end, make even slices. As each piece is carved, transfer it to a work tray and keep it in numerical sequence. Work in a logical and consistent order to avoid mistakes in sequencing later as you arrange the slices on the platter. Keep the same side of each slice facing up, especially if the item you are slicing has an internal garnish. This prevents you from reversing the slices as you arrange them. Transfer the slices from the holding tray to the platter in reverse numerical order—that is, position the last slice you cut on the platter first. The first slice you made is the last slice you place on the platter.

Buffet Design

Once the theme for an event is determined and you have made your best estimate of the head count, you can diagram the layout for tables, buffet lines, and stations. In addition, you can choose the serving pieces and centerpieces for the buffet. As you work through the tasks involved in preparing the buffet's design, evaluate your decisions to see if they help reinforce the theme, improve service, and control costs.

Number and placement of lines and stations

One of the ways in which buffets differ from à la carte service is that the food is on display as it is being served to the guest. In an à la carte setting, the chef controls how foods are arranged on the plate. During a buffet, the chef's challenge is to create an attractive, thematic, logical, and functional display of food. This stage of buffet planning may send you right back into an earlier stage, such as menu development, in order to overcome a specific problem of service or presentation. Even a long-established buffet can often be improved by a careful analysis of its design.

The number of guests you anticipate directly affects how many lines or stations you need for a given buffet. Thus it also changes how crowded the room may be once it is full of guests. Practical considerations must always be kept in mind. Place buffet lines with an adequate amount of room around them for walking.

The buffet should make it easy for guests to access the food as well as for attendants to serve guests or replenish the line. Being as close as possible to the kitchen means that waiters can deliver food more quickly, so it tastes and looks fresher.

Buffet tables should not block entrances, emergency exits, or other doors used by either the servers or the guests. If electricity is required on a line, it makes sense to try to locate the line or station close to the electrical source.

In some cases, you may have to adapt your buffet design to a specific style of seating. For instance, at a wedding buffet, a dance floor may take up some of the floor space. At a lecture, there may be theater or classroom-style seating to contend with.

Guest tables, dance floors, and presentation areas take up floor space. (However, they can be turned to advantage, as utensils, glassware, and napkins, as well as condiments and other items, can be removed to them from the buffet line.)

If the guests are expected to serve themselves from a buffet and then sit down to eat, try to place lines and stations so they can get from the buffet line to their table in the fewest possible steps.

Account for structural elements in the room, such as pillars and columns, to avoid placing a line or station too close to these immovable objects.

All of these possibilities should be evaluated to determine the best combination of numbers of lines and stations as well as their placement in the room.

LINES A buffet line permits the guest to select from a variety of dishes. The more lines you have, the more quickly all the guests are served. Depending on the overall configuration of the room, it may be possible to establish two or more zones to reduce the time guests spend standing in line.

STATIONS Smaller stations, sometimes referred to as *satellite* or *action stations*, break up the traditional line for a more contemporary service style. With stations, you can showcase special items or cooking demonstrations, encourage interaction between the guests and the attendants, and make traffic flow more smoothly through the room.

One of the drawbacks of a traditional buffet line is that it results in long lines that tend to build up during the initial stages of buffet service. In some settings, tradition single- or double-sided buffet lines are reconfigured as a number of smaller stations. These stations may be self-service, attended, or interactive. Stations make it easier for the guest to home in on the dishes they find most appealing—without a long wait.

Setting up and staffing several stations puts additional demands on the kitchen and service staff. For some buffets, especially a featured concept buffet that offers speedy service, stations are kept to a minimum or not used at all.

Table configuration and setup

The configuration and setup of the tables for a buffet plays an important role in how the guest perceives the event. They can improve access to food, make replenishing unobtrusive and efficient, control the flow of traffic by speeding or slowing it, and maintain the appearance of a bountiful, varied display throughout the meal.

You can adapt a configuration to control consumption, which may be a concern in an unlimited, all-you-can-eat setting with an extended service period, by using a one-sided display and limiting the number of satellite stations. It is even possible to eliminate a traditional line in favor of more demonstration or action stations. This configuration encourages a more leisurely pace of service. Certain configurations lend themselves to large displays and centerpieces. Others accommodate many dishes and stations in a relatively small amount of floor space.

The size and shape of the tables and their configuration adds to the mood of the meal. The simplest layout is a long, straight line, arranged to serve foods from one or both sides of the table. A serpentine line, made by combining a series of horseshoe tables, has a more fluid, contemporary look, and it can hold more food than a straight line.

You can also create other configurations by combining round, square, rectangular, and serpentine tabletop shapes. The ability to create a number of configurations in the dining room permits you to adapt the buffet table and the amount of access guests have (from one side, two sides, or all around), as in the case of large rounds, squares, and T- and L-shaped arrangements.

Rectangles, squares, zigzags, and H-, T-, V-, and L-shapes are made by combining rectangular and/or square tables. These configurations are conducive to multiple lines and zones. They can be single-sided or double-sided. If there are multiple zones, each zone must be completely set up with food and service items. Round, half-round, and serpentine table shapes joined together create circles or ovals, alone or in combination with squares and rectangles. Less common table shapes are sometimes available, including octagons, triangles, and ovals.

Tables can be joined in such a way that they are left open in the center as well as at one end. If the configuration is a single-sided display, the open center of a circle, square, or U-shape can be used to hold very large or tall display pieces. If possible, arrange the tables so that access to the center of the configuration is positioned as close as possible to the kitchen or other food-holding area to make replenishing easy and unobtrusive.

LINENS We can thank the Roman Empire for the tablecloth. At Roman feasts, tablecloths reached from the table to the floor and served as napkins, while the napkins the guests brought with them were reserved as doggie bags. Today, linens, including tablecloths, napkins, and skirting, are made in a wide range of colors, materials, textures, and weights. Prints, stripes, bold or subtle colors, and geometric shapes are a great way to spice up the look and feel of a buffet. Use dramatic and innovative draping techniques for special effects with skirting. Try out various napkin folds to add color, height, and texture to a tabletop. Alternatively, use a popular tactic seen in Japanese banquet halls: Strip the table bare to let gleaming wood show through.

CHINA, FLATWARE, GLASSWARE The china and flatware settings are important to the look and feel of the buffet. Plates are located on the line for guests to serve themselves. The location of flatware and glassware may be either preset on tables or located on the line itself, generally at the end.

When tabletops are preset, you can introduce special elements, including centerpieces, candles, and place cards. Plain white china works with almost any style of food or service, but for a more individual look, you can often find china with an unusual shape, color, or pattern that works with the food and the overall theme.

SERVICE PIECES Match the size of the serving piece to the number of pieces or servings. Leave enough room between pieces or lines to permit foods to be easily arranged in the kitchen and served in the dining room.

Platters, steam tables, chafing dishes, and bowls are the most common service pieces used in buffet service.

Use steam tables and chafing dishes to keep foods hot. They are usually best for soft, spoonable, or pourable items like soups and vegetable dishes. Standard-size chafing dishes have inserts in a wide range of sizes. This allows the chef to choose the best size for the pace of service, the quality of the food, and the size of the staff.

Platters of many shapes and sizes can be used to present both hot and cold food, but they will not, unless specifically adapted to that purpose, keep them hot or cold for very long. Oval, round, square, and rectangular platters are widely available, some with handles to make service and replenishing easier.

The color, texture, and shape of your serving pieces can bolster the theme. Instead of bowls or platters, for instance, you might use copper cookware or slabs of stone or marble. Mirrors add elegance as well as dimension. Specially made presentation pieces add interest and functionality to the buffet line. Hollowed vegetables and other natural containers promote a feeling that the buffet is fresh and natural.

Whether the buffet is formal or informal, you may be able to introduce whimsy or fun by using items we do not normally think of as serving pieces to display foods. Children's beach toys, toy boats, paper or lacquered boxes and trays, sporting paraphernalia, and fashion accessories can join ranks with your steam tables and platters for an unusual display.

SERVING TOOLS Spoons, ladles, tongs, and other serving pieces not only make it possible for the food to get from the service piece onto the guest's plate, they also have a direct impact on how the food looks and how certain foods are portioned.

Generally speaking, kitchen tools are not the best choice for buffet service. Not only do they look inappropriate in the dining room, they are often too large. As you consider a serving piece's use, try to anticipate how big a portion the tool can lift or hold as well as how easily the food will release from the serving tool onto the plate. Long-handled ladles can be awkward. Foods may stick and build up on serving pieces. Assign a specific tool for each menu item during menu development to be sure these tools are on hand for the buffet.

Planning for waste

Some foods generate waste—shrimp shells, skewers, or strawberry stems, for instance. Guests may take a clean plate to try new items, leaving a dirty plate behind. The ability to clear away this waste makes the difference between cleanliness and chaos.

You may need or want to include receptacles for waste as part of the buffet line's design. This may mean positioning containers and either labeling them or "seeding" them with a skewer or shell to make their purpose clear to the guest. Attentive service can also regulate the amount of waste. Removing debris from the line throughout service should be a high priority for anyone involved with staffing the buffet.

Preplating

Foods that are difficult to present and serve as individual portions from larger platters or chafing dishes may be preplated. For the guest, preplating adds elegance and ease to a self-service line or station. For the chef, it means better control over portioning and far less waste.

As a further advantage to preplating, the chef can use this strategy to create a focal point or a permanent display. For instance, if slices of cake are preplated and arranged around a whole, fully decorated cake, the cake becomes part of the display and won't be cut into.

On the other hand, preplating does increase labor and service costs. It takes more skill and time to make up a large number of uniformly presented plates. Those plates, too, take up more valuable space on the line than a platter. Finally, the wait staff must work harder to replenish such a display.

Garnishes

To be successful and to create the best and most integrated theme, consider the type of garnish you might add to a dish. This may mean garnishing individual portions or plates as well as larger platters or trays containing multiple portions.

When foods are purchased and prepared with quality in mind, they develop the best possible flavor, texture, and colors. A garnish cannot make up for poor or marginal quality.

Garnishes can be used to add visual, textural, or flavor appeal to a dish or a platter. Rather than a last-minute decision based on whatever is closest at hand, garnish selection as part of overall menu development and review is a sensible part of planning. You will be better equipped not only when it is time to order but also during scheduling and food production.

Garnishes are often applied to individual plates or portions. They are selected using the same criteria you would use to select an individual item as part of an overall menu. The garnish should make sense in terms of the rest of the dish. Fresh herbs are a common garnish; these make the most sense if they either echo or complement the flavors and herbs already in the dish. They make sense because they function as an aromatic or flavoring as well as a visual element.

When the only purpose for a garnish is to add a shape or a color, find a better option. Sprigs of parsley or watercress added to a platter simply for a bit of green color are nonfunctional garnishes—but if the watercress is actually a bed for a marinated salad or other item and its flavor and texture become a significant element in the dish, it is a functional garnish.

The selection of a garnish for individual items may be governed by tradition, but it is often the development of an original garnish that creates the impression of a new item, something that is modern, trendy, and fashionable.

Enhancing Food Presentation

The banquet chef can take advantage of many opportunities to enhance the foods' presentation and, at the same time, enhance the guests' experience. Food presentation is the banquet chef's chance to emphasize the theme and showcase the talents of the garde manger staff.

Practical considerations in food presentation: function and meaning

A good design serves a function. The function of a buffet is to serve the guest. Therefore, a properly devised buffet design places foods logically. Guests should be able to tell what they are eating. They should be able to reach the food easily and to find all the appropriate service tools, including plates and silverware, positioned where they are easy to see and easy to reach. If there is a chance that a food might cause an allergic reaction, guests should be warned, either through placards or a printed menu or by positioning knowledgeable wait staff on the line. The design and layout should account for keeping foods properly heated or chilled and safe from cross contamination. These elements of the overall design must be accounted for first.

Guests typically expect that a buffet will provide both a wide array of choices as well as the option to take as much as they like of any offering. The design of a buffet should support this expectation. At this stage of banquet planning, menu items have already been scrutinized for their costs, appropriateness to the theme, and customer acceptance. The banquet chef next begins to apply design principles and elements. The result is a composition that is echoed throughout every part of the buffet, from a single, tiny garnish on an individual canapé to ice carvings and display buffets.

The role of design

When we like the way many elements are combined in a single display, we use a variety of words to describe the effect: simple, elegant, balanced, integrated, unified, organic, even synergistic. The banquet chef's task is to exploit the full sensory potential of every dish to create a presentation that is practical, functional, and appealing to all the senses. Planning a design that enhances food presentation is an important way to highlight the work of the garde manger and to benefit from the special skills that go into planning and producing a unified, thematic, and successful buffet.

Pâté and terrine platter

Seafood display on
a marble slab

Judgments about what is fashionable or beautiful are subjective. They change over time, sometimes quite rapidly. However, the basic principles behind good design and presentation remain constant, even if the specific expressions of those principles keep evolving into new styles and trends.

Among the primary purposes of food presentation are functionality and practicality. Enhanced food presentations integrate all aspects of the buffet, including the theme, the menu, the style of service, and your clients' expectations. The goal is never to simply meet those expectations and standards but always to exceed them. A well-thought-out and well-executed plan is a distinct advantage in any successful buffet. It is important to remember and always think of these techniques as enhancements to the foods' appeal; the real importance and focus of the food should always lie, ultimately, in its flavor and texture.

Balance, as it relates to the work of the banquet chef, is achieved by combining the physical aspects of food in the context of specific design principles. Food supplies the important visual elements: colors, textures, and shapes. Additionally, the foods you serve also supply two important, but nonvisual, elements: aroma and flavor. The design principles at the chef's disposal include symmetrical or asymmetrical compositions, contrasting or complementary arrangements, and the use of lines to create patterns or indicate motion. In creating a balanced presentation, also be sure to take into consideration the accessibility of each item to be placed on the platter. Place larger items in the rear and lower items in front. Items

such as sauceboats should be kept in an area that does not disturb the design but allows the guest easy access.

A certain amount of regularity and repetition is comfortable and appealing, but too much of anything becomes monotonous, whether it is an ingredient, a color, a shape, a flavor, or a texture. Introducing contrasting elements adds energy and motion to an arrangement. However, when every element seems to stand on its own, the effect can be chaotic.

Throughout menu development and buffet design, record information about each menu item. Include not only estimates of amounts to prepare and portioning information but also colors, textures, and other important characteristics. You can use this information as you plan the layout for individual platters or other displays.

A food's natural color is one important tool in platter presentation. The color of a food can be used as an element in design. We associate with colors in specific ways. Greens give the impression of freshness and vitality. Browns, golds, and maroons are warming, comforting, and rich. Orange and red are intense, powerful colors. Colors that harmonize are those that touch each other on the color wheel (for example, green, blue, and violet are complementary colors, while blue and orange are contrasting). Clashing colors are rarely a problem. A more common concern is the overuse of one color on a single display.

Texture is important to the way the food looks as well as the way it feels in our mouths. Food surfaces tend to either reflect light or absorb it, making some foods appear glossy and others matte. Some foods have highly textured exteriors, while others are very smooth. The way the food feels when you bite into it is another aspect of texture that the chef must include in a plan. Too much of the same texture is monotonous.

Antipasto display

Cooking technique is vital to great presentation because no matter how artful the display, the way the food tastes is the most important element. In addition to assuring that foods are flavorful and at the right temperature, the process of cooking gives the chef a chance to enhance the food in other significant ways. "Visual flavor" is an important concept to the garde manger chef creating a cold food display. Unlike hot foods, with their abundant aromas to entice the guest, the aromas of cold foods are less apparent, making it necessary for guests to "see" the flavors. Some techniques deepen or darken the food's exterior; grilling, roasting, and smoking are a few examples. With these cooking methods it is also relevant for the guests to be able to see the seasonings used on the food—that is, specks of seasonings and herbs or the shine of oil from a dressing. Other techniques introduce new elements, such as coatings or wrappers; pan-frying and deep-frying are two such techniques. For an interesting selection throughout the menu, introduce a number of techniques for a variety of flavors, colors, and textures.

The shape and height of the food is an important part of buffet presentation. Food has three dimensions. Cubes, cylinders, spheres, and pyramids are just some of the shapes food can assume. Alternating or repeating shapes in a design is one way to add visual interest to food arrangements. You can alter the natural shape of a food by cutting or slicing it. To give height to foods that are naturally flat, you can roll or fold them, arrange them in piles or pyramids, or use serving pieces such as pedestals, columns, and baskets to raise foods.

A focal point serves an important function on a platter. It introduces a large shape into a field of smaller shapes. It adds height. The focal point can make the arrangement logical and sensible to the guest; a common focal point, the *grosse pièce*, is simply a portion of a larger item, such as a roast leg of lamb or a terrine, left intact and arranged on the platter. The guest can instantly identify the food on the platter. Sometimes, in place of a *gross pièce,* there may be one or more significant garnish elements. Such garnishes function in the same way as a *gross pièce;* they too are most effective and attractive when they offer information about the food instead of simply adding a spot of color.

Strong, clean lines arrange the food neatly and logically. Lines can be straight, curved, or angled. When two lines meet, they create a shape. When you repeat a line, you create a pattern. The more evenly spaced the lines, the more obvious the pattern. The wider the spaces, the more obvious they are as discrete lines. In order to have a line, you need a starting and ending point; the focal point in an arrangement is that reference point. Lines can move away from or toward this point and thereby introduce a sense of flow or motion into the arrangement.

The platter's layout can be symmetrical or asymmetrical. The position of the focal point on a platter or plate determines how the food is arranged. A focal point positioned off center means that one side of the arrangement appears to have more weight than the other. The lines extending away from the focal point are of different lengths. When the focal point is positioned in the center, it gives the impression that both sides of the arrangement are in equilibrium. The lines radiating from the focal point are the same length. Asymmetrical arrangements tend to look natural, while symmetrical arrangements look formal.

Arrangement of items on a line

Because a buffet line contains more than one offering or dish, give some thought to the sequence and arrangement of those dishes. Arrange dishes on the buffet line so they are easy to see, easy to reach, and easy to serve.

What follows is a collection of general guidelines you can use to determine the best display sequence. Not every one will be useful for every type of buffet, though all of them have a practical purpose. Some of the most popular and creative solutions used in buffets today were arrived at only by creatively disregarding a widely accepted rule.

Place plates where they are easy to see at the start of a line and at each independent station where they are easy to reach. They should also be easy for the wait staff to monitor and replenish. Utensils and napkins are best placed at the end of the line, so guests won't have to juggle them as they make their selections.

Keep foods that might drip or spill closest to the guests.

Use pedestals and similar devices to lift some platters higher. This is especially effective when you need to save space or when you would like to control the service of expensive items.

Keep hot foods near one another, likewise group chilled foods in their own area.

Place sauces and condiments directly with the foods they accompany so guests understand how to use them. Each one should have its own underliner and serving tool, if required.

Replenishing

Exchanging full serving pieces for empty ones is an important part of service for any buffet. Obviously, no empty platter or chafing dish should be left sitting on the line for any appreciable amount of time. Each operation may have a different standard concerning exactly when to pull a platter and replace it with a fresh one. It depends somewhat on the item being served and the size of the serving piece itself. However, the decision should be made ahead of time, then clearly communicated to the entire staff. The kitchen should be prepared to supply full platters promptly. The dining room staff should remove platters and chafing dishes as appropriate and immediately replace each item to avoid disrupting service.

Large mirrors or silver platters provide a dramatic backdrop for the food displays that are the hallmark of a buffet. They demand considerable space on the buffet and considerable time to set up and dismantle, however. They are also a challenge to replenish. Moving big pieces around during service invariably inconveniences the guest and slows service. It can be awkward or dangerous to attempt moving marble slabs or big mirrors with guests in proximity to the buffet table.

If the buffet is meant to accommodate guests over a long period—for instance, throughout a two-hour reception—it can be difficult to keep the display attractive. As the guests help themselves from the display, the arrangement begins to look messy and, eventually, skimpy.

The modern buffet often features a more contemporary approach to food display in order to make the buffet as attractive, fresh, and appealing as possible as well as to make it easier to replenish the buffet.

Instead of using one large piece, the garde manger is more likely to arrange foods on smaller serving pieces, then arrange these individual serving pieces into a larger overall composition. That arrangement can be used to reinforce or to enhance the concept or theme as well as the arrangement of individual platters.

Another distinct advantage of more frequent replenishment of smaller platters or chafing dishes is that it permits you to adapt quickly to the guests' behavior.

Smaller platters make
replenishing simple. They are
easy to remove and replace
with an entire new platter of
the same design.

Creative solutions, such as the use of plastic inserts, can also ease the task of replenishing.

During planning for food production, you estimate how many platters containing a certain number of items to prepare. If your prediction is off, you can more easily adapt to prevent shortages or to cut losses on items that are not in significant demand. This information can help you keep the customer satisfied and control costs by limiting wasted food.

Smaller serving pieces generally eliminate the temptation to combine fresh items with those that have already been on display. Uneaten portions should be counted and recorded on the appropriate form and then dealt with according to safe food-handling policy.

There should be a clear-cut policy on how to handle foods that are returned unused to the kitchen. Foods still safe for use in other applications should be carefully processed to keep them safe and wholesome.

Centerpieces and Displays

Truly successful garnishes and focal points add excitement and interest to a presentation. But they can do more than simply that. They also improve the quality of the entire experience. They reinforce or magnify the buffet's theme or concept. They provide important visual elements that help the guest decipher the function or meaning of any presentation.

When you turn your attention to the presentation of the entire line or even the entire room, you can see that centerpieces and displays can and should serve the same functions as focal points or garnishes. They too should fit in with the featured concept or theme. It isn't enough that they match the other elements of the design, however. Just as you should develop a garnish to have a purpose and a meaning, you can also develop a similar plan for the buffet's centerpieces and displays.

These important design elements may be composed of edible or nonedible materials. Some traditional examples include ice, salt, or tallow sculptures, floral arrangements and displays of fruits, vegetables, breads, or even wines.

Take care of practical considerations as you incorporate these elements into your overall design. Tall centerpieces and very large displays must be carefully located. They should not block the guests' view or make it difficult to reach the food. Position any display pieces that might drip or shed well away from the food. Stabilize tall or top-heavy pieces during the buffet setup to be certain they do not wobble or fall over.

ICE CARVING Ice is a challenging medium for the sculptor and makes special demands. Unlike marble, stone, or clay, ice carvings eventually melt. The costs of acquiring and storing the ice, the skills to carve it into an attractive three-dimensional sculpture or display piece, transport it, and set it up are significant. Yet ice carvings remain a powerful tool for setting the tone at any event. The fleeting life span of an ice carving, coupled with its high demands in terms of skill and artistry, sends out a vivid message to guests, offering them entertainment, excitement, and a good dose of the highly desirable "wow" factor.

The recent resurgence of this historic art form at catered events, buffets, banquets, and receptions brings it out of the eighteenth century and into the twenty-first. Large and small ice carvings are used for both display and individual service. Carvers today sculpt mirror images into the ice, pack it with snow, and create a white-on-clear display that looks almost like a holograph. Less demanding displays are easy to make from a split block of ice that sandwiches a logo. Numerals and letters are also relatively easy to carve into the face of the ice as a bas-relief. Simple bowls or cups of ice can be made using molds and then set on the table filled with individual appetizers, such as shrimp cocktail. By carving channels or depressions, ice carvings can be used to dispense drinks. Some ice carvings are intended to hold food. Others can be finished with fresh flowers, fruits, vegetables, and other decorations to complement a theme.

Ice blocks weigh 300 lb/136 kg and measure 11 by 22 by 42 in/28 by 56 by 107 cm. The ice should be free of rough edges, clean, free from impurities, and should not have a cloudy core, sometimes referred to as feathered ice. If the water is kept in circulation as it freezes, the ice remains clear. Ice houses are equipped to freeze ice so it has no core, but it is difficult for an individual operator to still-freeze ice without some feathered ice in the finished piece.

The quality of molds for both large and small ice display pieces has improved and the costs have dropped, making them more affordable for smaller operations. Some clients still prefer something original made just for them. The chef need not be a world-class artist, but certain skills make the job easier.

First, you need a design. You can sketch from life or find appropriate images in magazines, books, or from the Internet. Examine the design and try to break it down into one or more of the following basic shapes: cube, cone, cylinder, or sphere. Leave a base for the carved portion of the sculpture to sit on. The base is normally the full size of the end of the block and about 5 in/13 cm tall, but you may prefer to have an oversized base that raises small carvings up higher for better show.

As ice carvings melt, their shape stays the same because melting happens evenly for all parts. Thinner portions of the carving melt faster than thicker portions, so if your panther ice carving is resting on four legs, be sure those legs start out big enough to last throughout the service without giving way under the weight of the panther's body.

Transfer the sketch to graph paper and then use a predetermined scale to enlarge the design. Trace this design onto cardboard or a similar material. Cut out the design using a sharp blade and then transfer the design to the ice block. Secure the template in position and use an ice pick to mark the ice. After that, use saws, chisels, scoops, shavers, and scrapers to remove the excess ice. The colder the ice is when you carve it, the easier carving is. The ideal temperature range for carving is between 10° and 28°F/−12° and −2°C; the warmer the air where you are working, the more quickly you must work to compensate for faster melting. Keep the ice and your tools as clean as possible to avoid contaminating the ice, especially if the ice carving will hold foods to be served to the guests.

Large ice carvings must be set up carefully. Display them on very sturdy and level tables or stands. To capture the melting water that runs off the carving, set the carving directly in a pan fitted with a valve or drain that connects to a hose. The water is siphoned away from the carving and into a collection bucket or tub. Alternatively, set the sculpture on wooden blocks in a pan large and deep enough to hold water. Drape the pan setup with cloths or camouflage it with flowers, ferns, or other display items. Be sure any lights used in or near the display are properly installed. Spotlights should be located far enough away so their heat does not melt the ice carving. Lights can be placed directly beneath or behind the carving for a dramatic look, but great care must be taken to be certain that water will not drip on the lights or wiring. Check that any wiring, cords, or drainage items are discreetly positioned and cannot trip unwary guests or servers.

Use great care when transporting ice carvings; they break as easily as glass. You can "weld" pieces back onto a carving to replace or repair them. Use the same technique to attach appendages to carvings that are bigger than a single block (wings, tusks, and tails, for example). Gouge an indentation in the carving at the appropriate location, insert the piece, pack it with wet snow, and freeze for one or two days. Scrape away any excess snow before displaying the sculpture.

If an ice carving has a small break, you can usually repair it by sprinkling both surfaces of the break with ice, then holding the pieces together until they fuse again. Another option is to hold a piece of dry ice along a fissure to refreeze the ice. (Never hold dry ice with bare hands. Always wear gloves to protect your hands.)

SURFACE EFFECTS The surface of an ice carving can be very smooth for a glassy effect, or it can be scored to give it texture and a three-dimensional quality. Usually, allowing the ice carving to rest at room temperature for at least 1 hour before the event is enough time to make the carving glisten. If time is short, you can rub the carving with hot towels or pour water over the surface.

BASIC RECIPES

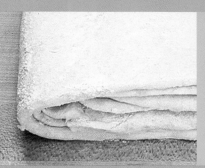

twelve

Mirepoix

YIELD: 1 LB/454 G

8 oz/227 g onions, peeled and chopped

4 oz/113 g carrots, trimmed and chopped

4 oz/113 g celery, trimmed and chopped

Cut the vegetables into an appropriate size based on the cooking time of the dish.

WHITE MIREPOIX: For 1 lb/454 g: Reduce the onions to 4 oz/113 g. Replace the carrots with 4 oz/113 g each chopped leeks (white parts only) and parsnips. If desired, add 2 to 3 oz/57 to 85 g mushroom trimmings.

Standard Bouquet Garni

YIELD: 1 BOUQUET, ENOUGH TO FLAVOR 1 GAL/3.84 L STOCK

4 oz/113 g whole celery stalk, trimmed

3 or 4 parsley stems

1 thyme sprig

1 bay leaf

2 or 3 leek leaves

1. Halve the celery stalk crosswise. Sandwich the herbs between the celery pieces and fold the leek leaves around the herbs and celery.

2. Tie the bundle securely with butcher's twine, leaving a long tail of string to tie the bouquet to the stockpot handle.

CHEF'S NOTE: Savory, sage, rosemary, and other fresh herbs may be used in addition to or in place of the ingredients called for above, depending on the recipe and desired result.

Standard Sachet d'Épices

YIELD: 1 SACHET, ENOUGH TO FLAVOR 1 GAL/3.84 L STOCK

3 or 4 parsley stems

½ tsp/0.50 g thyme leaves

1 bay leaf

½ tsp/1 g cracked peppercorns

1 garlic clove, crushed (optional)

Place all ingredients on a piece of cheesecloth approximately 4 in/10 cm square. Gather up the edges and tie with butcher's twine, leaving a long tail of string to tie to the stockpot handle.

CHEF'S NOTE: Cloves, dill, tarragon stems, juniper berries, star anise, allspice, and other herbs and spices may be included, depending on the recipe and desired result.

Chinese Five-Spice Powder

YIELD: ABOUT 8 OZ/227 G

2 oz/57 g star anise

3 tbsp/0.50 g cloves

3 tbsp/18 g Szechwan pepper

¾ oz/21 g fennel seeds

¾ oz/21 g ground cinnamon (or cassia)

Grind the spices in a spice mill or with a mortar and pestle. Store any unused powder in an airtight container in a cool, dry place. The powder keeps well for several weeks.

Quatre Épices

YIELD: ABOUT 8 OZ/227 G

2½ oz/71 g black peppercorns

½ oz/14 g ground nutmeg

½ oz/14 g ground cinnamon

2 tbsp/12 g whole cloves

½ oz/14 g ground ginger (optional)

Grind together the spices in a spice mill or with a mortar and pestle. Store any unused spice blend in an airtight container in a cool, dry place.

Barbecue Spice Mix

YIELD: ABOUT 8 OZ/227 G

1 oz/28 g hot Hungarian paprika

2 tbsp/12 g chili powder

1¼ oz/35 g salt

4 tsp/8 g ground cumin

½ oz/14 g sugar

1 tbsp/6 g dried thyme

2 tsp/4 g dry mustard

2 tsp/4 g ground black pepper

2 tsp/4 g dried oregano

2 tsp/4 g curry powder

1 tsp/2 g cayenne

Combine all ingredients thoroughly. Store any unused spice blend in an airtight container in a cool, dry place.

Cajun Spice Blend

YIELD: ABOUT 8 OZ/227 G

1½ oz/43 g hot Hungarian paprika

½ oz/14 g kosher salt

2 tbsp/12 g onion powder

2 tbsp/12 g garlic powder

2 tbsp/12 g cayenne

1 tbsp/6 g ground white pepper

1 tbsp/6 g ground black pepper

1 tbsp/6 g dried thyme

1 tbsp/6 g dried oregano

Combine all ingredients thoroughly. Store any unused spice blend in an airtight container in a cool, dry place.

Curry Powder

YIELD: ABOUT 8 OZ/227 G

3 tbsp/18 g cumin seeds

3 tbsp/15 g coriander seeds

2 tsp/8 g whole mustard seeds

8 dried red chiles, or as needed

½ oz/14 g ground cinnamon

2 tbsp/12 g ground turmeric

½ oz/14 g ground ginger

1. Combine all the seeds and chiles. Roast them in a 350°F/177°C oven for 5 minutes. Remove and cool slightly. Split the chiles and remove and discard the seeds.

2. Grind the whole seeds, ground spices, and chiles in a spice mill or with a mortar and pestle until evenly blended. Store any unused powder in an airtight container in a cool, dry place.

CHEF'S NOTE: Add hot Hungarian paprika, cloves, or fresh curry leaves to the blend.

Fines Herbes

YIELD: 2 OZ/57 G

½ oz/14 g chervil leaves

½ oz/14 g chives

½ oz/14 g parsley leaves

½ oz/14 g tarragon leaves

Rinse and dry all the herbs. Combine them and chop or mince them to the desired fineness. Use at once.

Pâté Spice

YIELD: 14 OZ/397 G

1½ oz/43 g white peppercorns

3 oz/85 g coriander seeds

1¾ oz/50 g dried thyme

1¾ oz/50 g dried basil

3 oz/85 g whole cloves

1½ oz/43 g grated nutmeg

½ oz/14 g bay leaves

¾ oz/21 g mace

1 oz/28 g dried cèpes (optional)

Combine all ingredients and grind them using a mortar and pestle or a spice mill. Store any unused spice blend in an airtight container in a cool, dry place.

Hot Italian Sausage Blend

YIELD: ABOUT 8 OZ/227 G

½ oz/14 g fennel seeds

2 tbsp/12 g ground coriander

½ oz/14 g sugar

½ oz/14 g sweet Spanish paprika

½ oz/14 g hot Hungarian paprika

1½ tsp/3 g cayenne

⅔ oz/19 g crushed red pepper

1 tbsp/6 g coarse-ground black pepper

Combine all ingredients. Store any unused spice blend in an airtight container in a cool, dry place.

Herbes de Provence

YIELD: ABOUT 8 OZ/227 G

½ oz/14 g dried thyme

1 oz/28 g dried marjoram

½ oz/14 g dried savory

1 tbsp/6 g dried rosemary

1 tsp/2 g dried sage

1 tsp/2 g dried mint

1 tsp/2 g dried fennel seeds

1 tsp/5 mL dried lavender flowers

Combine all ingredients. Store any unused spice blend in an airtight container in a cool, dry place. The herbs may be crushed fine with a mortar and pestle before use if desired.

CHEF'S NOTES: Crushed bay leaves are sometimes included in this blend. As with other spice blends in this chapter, the amounts of individual herbs may be adjusted according to personal taste.

Brown Veal Stock

YIELD: 1 GAL/3.84 L

8 lb/3.63 kg veal bones, including knuckles and trim

1 gal 64 fl oz/5.76 L cold water

1 lb/454 g Mirepoix (page 522)

6 oz/170 g tomato paste

1 Standard Sachet d'Épices (page 523)

1. Rinse the bones and dry them well. Preheat an oiled roasting pan in a 450°F/232°C oven. Brown the bones in the roasting pan in the oven.

2. Combine the bones and water in a stockpot. Bring the stock to a boil over low heat. Simmer for about 6 hours, skimming the surface as necessary.

3. Brown the mirepoix and tomato paste; add to the stock in the last hour of simmering. Deglaze the drippings in the roasting pan with water and add to the stock. Add the sachet d'épices.

4. Simmer an additional hour. Strain the stock. Cool and store under refrigeration.

VENISON STOCK: Replace the veal bones with an equal weight of venison bones and lean trim. Include fennel seeds and/or juniper berries in the sachet d'épices, if desired.

Chicken Stock

YIELD: 1 GAL/3.84 L

8 lb/3.63 kg chicken bones, cut into 3-in/8-cm lengths

1 gal 64 fl oz/5.76 L cold water

1 lb/454 g Mirepoix (page 522)

1 Standard Sachet d'Épices (page 523)

1. Rinse the bones in cool water. Combine the bones and water in a stockpot.

2. Bring the stock to a boil over low heat. Skim the surface, as necessary. Simmer 4 to 5 hours.

3. Add the mirepoix and the sachet d'épices in the last hour of simmering. Strain the stock. Cool and store under refrigeration.

WHITE DUCK STOCK: Substitute an equal amount of duck bones for the chicken bones.

TURKEY STOCK: Substitute an equal amount of turkey bones for the chicken bones.

WHITE BEEF STOCK: Substitute an equal amount of beef bones for the chicken bones. Increase the simmering time in Step 2 to 6 to 7 hours.

Shellfish Stock

YIELD: 1 GAL/3.84 L

10 lb/4.54 kg shellfish shells (lobster, shrimp, or crab)

2 fl oz/60 mL vegetable oil

1 lb/454 g Mirepoix (page 522)

3 to 4 oz/85 to 113 g tomato paste

1 gal 32 fl oz/4.80 L cold water

1 Standard Sachet d'Épices (page 523)

8 fl oz/240 mL white wine

1. Sauté the shellfish shells in the oil until deep red. Add the mirepoix and continue to sauté another 10 to 15 minutes. Add the tomato paste and sauté briefly.

2. Add the water, sachet, and wine and simmer 30 minutes. Strain the stock. Cool and store under refrigeration.

FISH STOCK: Substitute an equal amount of bones and trim from lean white-fleshed fish for the shellfish shells. In Step 1, sauté the bones in oil over low heat until they become white. Use White Mirepoix (page 522). Omit the tomato paste.

Vegetable Stock

YIELD: 1 GAL/3.84 L

2 fl oz/60 mL vegetable oil

4 oz/113 g onions, sliced

4 oz/113 g leeks, green and white parts, chopped

2 oz/57 g celery, chopped

2 oz/57 g green cabbage, chopped

2 oz/57 g carrots, chopped

2 oz/57 g turnips, chopped

2 oz/57 g tomatoes, chopped

3 garlic cloves, crushed

1 tsp/2 g fennel seeds

3 cloves

1 Standard Sachet d'Épices (page 523)

1 gal 16 fl oz/4.32 L cold water

1. Heat the oil. Add the vegetables and garlic and sweat for about 5 minutes.

2. Place the fennel seeds and cloves in the sachet d'épices.

3. Add the water and sachet d'épices to the vegetables and simmer for 30 to 40 minutes. Strain the stock. Cool and store under refrigeration.

Glace de Viande

YIELD: 4 TO 8 OZ/113 TO 227 G (SEE CHEF'S NOTE)

32 fl oz/960 mL Brown Veal Stock (page 528)

1. Place the stock in a heavy-bottomed pot over medium heat. Bring to a simmer and cook until volume is reduced by one-half, then transfer to a smaller pot.

2. Continue to reduce, transferring to successively smaller pots, until the liquid is very thick and syrupy.

CHEF'S NOTE: The yield will vary depending on cooking time and desired consistency.

GLACE DE VOLAILLE: Substitute Chicken Stock (page 529) for the brown veal stock.

Court Bouillon

YIELD: 1 GAL/3.84 L

80 fl oz/2.40 L cold water

80 fl oz/2.40 L white wine

2 tsp/10 g salt (optional)

12 oz/340 g carrots, sliced

1 lb/454 g onions, sliced

Pinch dried thyme leaves

3 bay leaves

1 bunch parsley stems

½ oz/14 g black peppercorns

1. Combine the water, wine, salt (if desired), carrots, onions, thyme, bay leaves, and parsley stems. Simmer for 50 minutes.

2. Add the peppercorns and simmer for an additional 10 minutes. Strain the bouillon before using.

VINEGAR COURT BOUILLON: Double the amount of water. Replace the white wine with 8 fl oz/240 mL vinegar.

Chicken Consommé

YIELD: 1 GAL/3.84 L

1 lb/454 g Mirepoix (page 522)

3 lb/1.36 kg lean chicken, ground

10 egg whites, beaten

12 oz/340 g tomato concassé

1 gal 32 fl oz/4.80 L Chicken Stock (page 529), cold

1 clove

2 allspice berries

1 Standard Sachet d'Épices (page 523)

1 tsp/5 g kosher salt

½ tsp/1 g ground white pepper

1. Mix the ingredients for the clarification and blend with the stock. Mix well.

2. Bring the mixture to a slow simmer, stirring frequently until a raft forms.

3. Place the clove and allspice berries in the sachet d'épices. Add the sachet to the stock and simmer for 45 minutes, or until the appropriate flavor and clarity are achieved. Baste the raft occasionally.

4. Strain the consommé; season with salt and pepper.

Velouté

YIELD: 64 FL OZ/1.92 L

80 fl oz/2.40 L Chicken Stock (page 529)

4 to 8 oz/113 to 227 g white blonde roux, or as needed

½ tsp/2.50 g salt

¼ tsp/0.50 g ground black pepper

1. Bring the stock to a boil. Whip the roux into the stock; work out all the lumps. Simmer for 30 to 40 minutes, skimming the surface as necessary.

2. Season with salt and pepper to taste and then strain the sauce.

FISH VELOUTÉ: Use Fish Stock (page 530) instead of chicken stock.

SHELLFISH VELOUTÉ: Use Shellfish Stock (page 536) instead of chicken stock.

VEGETABLE VELOUTÉ: Use Vegetable Stock (page 530) instead of chicken stock.

Pimiento Butter

YIELD: 1 LB/454 G

12 oz/340 g butter, softened

3½ oz/99 g pimientos, minced

¼ tsp/0.75 g minced garlic

½ fl oz/15 mL lemon juice

Salt, as needed

Pepper, as needed

Purée all the ingredients in a food processor fitted with a metal blade and mix well. Wrap tightly and refrigerate until needed. Soften, if necessary, for spreading.

Anchovy Butter

YIELD: 1 LB/454 G

1 lb/454 g butter, softened

1 to 1½ fl oz/30 to 45 mL lemon juice

1 to 2 oz/28 to 57 g anchovy paste

Salt, as needed

Ground black pepper, as needed

½ oz/14 g chopped drained capers

Combine all ingredients and mix well. Wrap tightly and refrigerate until needed. Soften, if necessary, for spreading.

Horseradish Butter

YIELD: 1 LB 4 OZ/567 G

3 oz/85 g prepared horseradish

1 lb/454 g butter, softened

½ oz/14 g prepared mustard

2 tsp/10 mL Worcestershire sauce

1 tbsp/15 g sugar

1 tsp/5 mL lemon juice

Squeeze excess liquid out of the horseradish. Combine all ingredients and mix well. Wrap tightly and refrigerate until needed. Soften, if necessary, for spreading.

Mayonnaise Collée

YIELD: 24 FL OZ/720 ML

16 fl oz/480 mL Basic Mayonnaise (page 35)

8 fl oz/240 mL Aspic Gelée (page 57), firm gel strength, warmed to 110°F/43°C

2 tsp/10 g kosher salt

1¼ oz/35 g ground white pepper

Tabasco sauce, as needed

Combine the mayonnaise with the aspic. Strain. Add seasonings.

Pâté Dough

YIELD: 1 LB 8 OZ/680 G

1 lb/454 g bread flour	4 oz/113 g butter, cold, cut into cubes
2 tsp/6 g baking powder	1 egg
½ oz/14 g salt	2 tsp/10 mL cider vinegar
1 tsp/5 g sugar	8 fl oz/240 mL whole milk

1. Combine the dry ingredients and mix well.

2. With two knives or a pastry cutter, cut the butter into the dry ingredients. Work the dough until it becomes crumbly.

3. Mix the wet ingredients into the dough until fully incorporated. Knead the dough until smooth and not sticky.

4. Shape the dough into a 10-in/25-cm disk. Wrap and refrigerate for at least 1 hour or overnight.

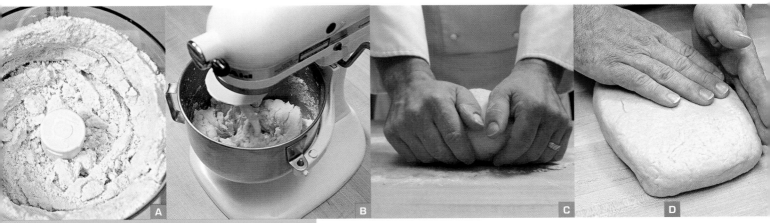

Working with pâté dough. **A.** Cutting together flour and butter in a food processor. **B.** Mixing pâté dough in a mixer fitted with a dough hook. **C.** Kneading the dough on a lightly floured board. **D.** Blocking the dough.

Tomato-Cilantro Pâté Dough

YIELD: 1 LB 8 OZ/680 G

1 recipe Pâté Dough (page 535)

2 tsp/4 g ground coriander

2 tsp/4 g ground cumin

1½ oz/43 g tomato paste

2 tbsp/6 g chopped cilantro

Prepare the pâté dough according to the basic recipe, adding the coriander and cumin in Step 1 and the tomato paste and cilantro in Step 3.

Saffron Pâté Dough

YIELD: 1 LB 8 OZ/680 G

Large pinch saffron

5 fl oz/150 mL warm water

1 recipe Pâté Dough (page 535)

2 tbsp/6 g chopped dill (optional)

2 tbsp/6 g chopped chives (optional)

Infuse the saffron in the water. Replace 5 oz/150 mL of the milk with the saffron water in the basic pâté dough recipe. Add the chopped herbs, if desired, in Step 3.

Sweet Potato Pâté Dough

YIELD: 1 LB 8 OZ/680 G

1 recipe Pâté Dough (page 535)

½ tsp/1 g ground cinnamon

½ tsp/1 g ground cardamom

½ tsp/1 g ground mace

5 oz/142 g sweet potato, baked, boiled, or steamed, and puréed

Prepare the pâté dough according to the basic recipe, adding the ground spices in Step 1 and the sweet potato in Step 3. You may need to reduce the amount of milk called for in the recipe.

CHEF'S NOTES: To make decorative display pieces with the pâté dough, roll it into thin sheets using a pasta machine. Here, pâté dough is cut to give the effect of fish netting. Score the dough with a lattice cutter. Gently pull apart the dough, lay it on crumbled foil, and paint it with egg wash. The crumbled foil gives additional height and texture to the pâté dough netting. Bake at 325°F/163°C for 8 to 10 minutes, until dried and cooked through.

Pâté dough. **A.** Rolling the dough in a pasta machine. **B.** Cutting netting. **C.** Baking netting.

Making decorations for pâté en croûte. **A.** Cutting out leaf shapes. **B.** Making veins. **C.** Grape clusters with leaves and tendrils.

Blitz Puff Pastry

YIELD: 2 LB 8 OZ/1.13 KG

8 oz/227 g cake flour

8 oz/227 g bread flour

1 lb/454 g butter, cubed and chilled

9 fl oz/270 mL cold water

1½ tsp/7.50 g salt

1. Combine the cake and bread flour in the bowl of a stand mixer. Add the butter and toss with your fingertips until the butter is coated with flour. Combine the water and salt; add all at once. Mix on low speed with the dough hook until the dough forms a shaggy mass.

2. Tightly cover the mixture with plastic wrap and allow to rest under refrigeration, until the butter is firm but not brittle, about 20 minutes.

3. Place the shaggy mass on a lightly floured work surface and roll out into a rectangle about 12 by 30 in/30 by 76 cm and ½ in/1 cm thick.

4. Administer a book-fold, roll out the dough to the same dimensions, and administer a second book-fold. Tightly wrap the dough in plastic wrap and allow to rest under refrigeration for 30 minutes.

5. Repeat this process twice more for a total of 4 book-folds, refrigerating and turning the dough 90 degrees each time before rolling. After completing the final fold, wrap the dough in plastic wrap and allow it to firm under refrigeration for at least 1 hour. (The dough can be held under refrigeration or frozen.)

CHEF'S NOTE: More folds will yield finer and more even layers with less height. Fewer folds yield a lighter product, with irregular layers and more height.

Making puff pastry. **A.** Combine ingredients for the dough. **B.** A loose, shaggy mass is formed. **C.** Roll the dough into a rectangle. **D.** First stage of a book-fold. **E.** Completed book-fold.

Pasta Dough

YIELD: 1 LB 8 OZ/680 G

1 lb/454 g all-purpose or bread flour

6 eggs

2 tsp/10 g salt

2 fl oz/60 mL water, or as needed

1. Combine all ingredients in a large bowl and knead the mixture until it is smooth and elastic.

2. Cover the dough and allow it to rest for 1 hour before rolling and shaping.

SPINACH PASTA: Add 6 oz/170 g puréed raw spinach. Add extra flour if necessary.

MALFATTI PASTA: Run the basic pasta dough through a pasta machine to create thin sheets. Cut the pasta into rectangles 1½ by 2½ in/4 by 6 cm.

Simple Syrup

YIELD: 32 FL OZ/960 ML

32 fl oz/960 mL water	Juice of 3 lemons
8 oz/227 g sugar	Juice of 3 oranges

1. Bring the water and sugar to a boil. Stir until the sugar dissolves; cool.

2. Flavor with the lemon and orange juice and refrigerate until needed.

Focaccia

YIELD: 3 LB/1.36 KG

Cornmeal, as needed

18 fl oz/540 mL water

½ oz/14 g compressed yeast

2 fl oz/60 mL extra-virgin olive oil

1 lb 12 oz/794 g hard wheat flour

½ oz/14 g salt

GARNISH OPTIONS

Crumbled goat's milk cheese, as needed

Olives, pitted and sliced, as needed

Pine nuts, as needed

Sun-dried tomatoes, as needed

Chopped herbs such as basil and oregano, as needed

1. Line 3 sheet pans with parchment paper. Dust with cornmeal.

2. Combine the water, yeast, and oil until the yeast is dissolved. Add the flour and salt. Mix the dough until smooth and elastic. Cover the bowl and allow the dough to ferment for 1 hour and 15 minutes.

3. Punch down and scale the dough at 10 oz/283 g per focaccia. Round off the dough. Place the dough on the prepared sheet pans and proof for 1 hour.

4. Press the balls of dough flat and stretch slightly. Brush with olive oil and add the garnish items desired. Pan-proof an additional 30 minutes.

5. Bake in a 425°F/218°C oven for about 30 minutes.

GRISSINI: Prepare the dough through Step 2. Punch down and scale at 1½ oz/43 g. Round off the dough. Place on a sheet pan and proof for 1 hour. Roll the balls into long, thin sticks. Brush with olive oil or egg wash and top with desired seasoning: kosher salt, sesame seeds, or fresh herbs. Pan-proof an additional 15 minutes. Bake in 425°F/218°C oven for 10 to 12 minutes.

Whole Wheat Pita Bread

YIELD: 15 PITAS

2¼ tsp/9 g active dry yeast	1 lb/454 g whole wheat flour
20 fl oz/600 mL warm water (100°F/38°C)	½ oz/14 g salt
1 lb/454 g bread flour	¾ fl oz/23 mL olive oil

1. Combine the yeast with the warm water and mix well.

2. Add the remaining ingredients and mix the dough on the lowest speed of an electric mixer until it is quite elastic, 3 to 4 minutes.

3. Place the dough in a large bowl. Brush it with olive oil, cover, and allow to double in size at room temperature, 1 to 2 hours. Punch down the dough.

4. Scale the dough into 4 oz/113 g balls and line the balls 3 by 5 on an oiled sheet pan. Cover with plastic wrap. Allow the scaled pita breads to double in size before rolling.

5. Dust the work surface with flour. Roll the pita dough out to about 7 in/18 cm in diameter. Rest, covered, at room temperature until the dough is well relaxed, 15 minutes.

6. Load the pitas directly onto the deck of a 500°F/260°C oven, or onto a baking stone, or onto a preheated sheet pan and bake until puffed but not browned, 3 to 4 minutes. Stack the pitas five high and wrap each stack in a cloth. Cool before serving.

Brioche Dough

YIELD: 3 LB/1.36 KG

1 lb 8 oz/680 g bread flour	2 oz/57 g sugar
2½ tsp/10 g instant dry yeast	2 tsp/10 g salt
8 oz/227 g eggs, 40°F/4°C (4 large)	12 oz/340 g butter, cut into cubes, softened but still pliable (60° to 65°F/ 16° to 18°C)
4 fl oz/120 mL whole milk	

1. Combine the flour and yeast in the bowl of a 5-qt mixer. Add the eggs, milk, sugar, and salt; mix with a dough hook attachment on low speed until evenly blended, scraping down the bowl as needed, 4 minutes.

2. Gradually add the butter with the mixer running on low speed, scraping down the bowl as necessary, 2 minutes. After the butter is fully incorporated, increase to medium speed and mix until the dough begins to pull away from the sides of the bowl and is quite elastic, 15 minutes.

3. Remove the dough from the bowl, shape into a brick, wrap well, and refrigerate at least 12 hours before using. Brioche dough can be frozen for up to 2 months.

Roasting Garlic

The flavor of garlic and shallots becomes rich, sweet, and smoky after roasting. Roasted garlic can be found as a component of marinades, glazes, and vinaigrettes, as well as a spread for grilled breads and focaccia.

1. Place an unpeeled head of garlic (or shallot bulbs) in a small pan. Some chefs like to place it on a bed of salt, which holds the heat, roasting the garlic quickly and producing a drier texture in the finished product.

2. Roast at a medium temperature until the garlic or shallots are quite soft and any juices that run from the garlic or shallots are brown. The aroma should be sweet and pleasing, with no hints of harshness or sulfur.

Tomato Concassé

Make only enough tomato concassé to last through a single service period. Once peeled and chopped, tomatoes begin to lose some of their flavor and texture.

1. Cut away the core ends of the tomatoes and score the skin using a paring knife.

2. Bring a pot of water to a rolling boil. Drop the tomatoes into the water. After 10 to 35 seconds (depending on the tomatoes' age and ripeness), remove them with a slotted spoon, skimmer, or spider. Immediately plunge them into very cold or ice water. Pull away the skin.

3. Halve each tomato crosswise at its widest point and gently squeeze out the seeds. (Plum tomatoes are more easily seeded by cutting lengthwise.)

4. Cut the flesh into dice or julienne, as desired.

Roasting Tomatoes

Roasted tomatoes can be made by either halving or slicing ripe tomatoes. While the flavor of roasted tomatoes is deeper and more intense than that of fresh or canned unroasted tomatoes, it is not so intense as that of sun-dried tomatoes.

1. Core the tomatoes and cut them into halves or slices.

2. Coat lightly with oil and add seasonings and aromatics as desired. Salt, pepper, fresh or dried herbs, plain or infused oils, chopped garlic, and shallots are all good choices.

3. Roast the tomatoes in a 350°F/177°C oven until they are browned and have a rich roasted aroma.

Roasting Peppers

To roast and peel small quantities, roast the peppers over a flame:

1. Hold the pepper over the flame of a gas burner with tongs or a kitchen fork, or place it on a grill. Turn the pepper and roast it until the surface is evenly charred.

2. Place the pepper in a plastic or paper bag or under an inverted bowl to steam the skin loose.

3. When the pepper is cool enough to handle, remove the charred skin, using a paring knife, if necessary.

For larger quantities, oven-roast the peppers:

1. Halve the peppers and remove the stems and seeds. Place cut side down on an oiled sheet pan.

2. Place in a 475°F/246°C oven or under a broiler. Roast or broil until evenly charred.

3. Remove from the oven or broiler and cover immediately, using an inverted sheet pan. This will steam the peppers, making the skin easier to remove.

4. Peel, using a paring knife, if necessary.

Roasting Corn

1. To roast corn, dampen the husk and place in a hot oven (475° to 500°F/246° to 260°C) or over hot coals. Roast or grill for 15 to 20 minutes. The husks should become a deep brown. The corn should be tender (to check for doneness, pull back some of the husk and pierce a kernel).

2. When the corn is cool enough to handle, pull away the corn and the silk. Cut the corn away from the cob with a sharp paring knife.

Plumping Dried Fruits and Vegetables

1. Check the dried ingredient and remove any obvious debris or seriously blemished or moldy specimens.

2. Place the ingredient in a bowl or other container and add enough boiling or very hot liquid (water, wine, fruit juices, or broth can all be used) to cover.

3. Let the dried ingredient steep in the hot water for several minutes, until softened and plumped.

4. Pour off the liquid, reserving it, if desired, for use in another preparation. If necessary, the liquid can be strained through a coffee filter or cheesecloth to remove debris.

Toasting Nuts, Seeds, and Spices

Toasting nuts, seeds, and spices improves their flavor, as long as they are not allowed to scorch. To toast small quantities, use a dry skillet (cast iron is an excellent choice, but other materials also work well).

1. Heat the skillet over direct heat and add the nuts, seeds, or spices.

2. Toss or stir frequently, stopping just as a good color and aroma are achieved.

3. Pour the nuts, seeds, or spices into a cool container and spread into a thin layer to stop any further browning.

Large quantities can be toasted in a medium oven (350°F/177°C).

1. Spread out the nuts, seeds, or spices on a dry sheet pan and toast just until a pleasant aroma is apparent. The oils in nuts, seeds, and spices can scorch quickly, so be sure to check frequently. Stir often to encourage even browning.

2. Be sure to transfer nuts and spices toasted in the oven to a cool container so they don't become scorched from residual heat in the pan.

TOASTING DRIED CHILES: Dried chiles may be toasted in the same manner, in a dry skillet or in the oven. They may also be passed repeatedly through a flame until toasted and softened. The pulp and seeds are then scraped from the skin, or the whole chile may be used, according to individual recipes.

Rendering Fats

Occasionally the fat from ducks, geese, or pork may be required for such dishes as confit and rillettes.

1. Cube the fat, if necessary.

2. Place the fat in a sauté pan. Add about ½ in/1 cm water to the uncooked fats if no drippings are present.

3. Cook over low heat until the water evaporates and the fat is released. This is the actual clarifying process.

4. Remove the cracklings, if any, with a slotted spoon. They may be reserved for garnish.

5. Store the rendered fat under refrigeration for up to several weeks.

Cooked Lobster

To remove the meat from the shell, pull away the tail. Split the shell on the underside with kitchen shears and pull out the tail meat in one piece. To remove the meat from the claw, crack the claw in half with the spine of a knife. Pull out the meat carefully in order to keep the meat intact. Cut the knuckles from end to end and remove nuggets of meat.

Parmesan Crisp

1. To prepare a Parmesan crisp, shred Parmesan cheese. Preheat oven to 350°F/177°C and line a sheet pan with parchment paper. If desired, trace a circle or other shape on the paper. Allow room in the tracing to permit some spread (about ½ in/1 cm). Scatter the cheese in an even layer (enough to cover the paper, but not too thick).

2. Bake the cheese for 10 minutes, or until it is melted and bubbly and looks like lace. Remove the sheet pan from the oven and allow the cheese to cool for a few minutes. The cheese crisp can be rolled or draped inside bowls or over dowels or cups to create containers or fans, as desired. This must be done while the cheese is very warm.

3. Cheese crisps will keep for several days, stored in a parchment-lined airtight container.

Bread Crumbs

Bread crumbs may be "dry" or "fresh." Fresh bread crumbs (mie de pain) are prepared by grating or processing a finely textured bread, such as hard rolls that are a day or two old. Dry bread crumbs can be prepared from slightly stale bread that has been additionally dried or toasted in a warm oven.

Standard Breading Procedure

For the best possible results, breading needs a little time to firm up before it is pan-fried. If you bread an item and then immediately put it into hot oil, there is a good chance it will fall away. Not only will this have a negative impact on the dish's finished texture, it will also make the cooking oil break down quickly, and subsequent batches cooked in the same oil will blacken without cooking properly.

1. Dry the main item well, then hold it in one hand (left hand if you are right-handed, and right hand if you are left-handed) and dip it in the flour. Shake off any excess flour and transfer the food to the container of egg wash.

2. Switch hands, pick up the food, and turn it if necessary to coat it on all sides. Transfer it to the container of bread crumbs. Use your dry hand to pack bread crumbs evenly around the food. Shake off any excess, then transfer the food to a holding tray.

3. Let the food rest under refrigeration for about 1 hour or longer before continuing with pan-frying.

4. Discard any unused flour, egg wash, and bread crumbs.

Croutons

YIELD: 1 LB/454 G

1 lb/454 g white bread

4 oz/113 g butter, melted, or olive oil

1 tsp/5 g salt, or as needed

½ tsp/1 g pepper (optional), or as needed

1. Remove the crust from the bread, if desired. Slice and cube the bread to the desired size (from small cubes to garnish soups served in cups to large cubes to garnish salads). If the bread is very fresh, let the bread cubes dry in the oven for 5 minutes before continuing.

2. Toss the bread, butter or oil, and seasonings together on a baking sheet or in a hotel pan.

3. Bake for 8 to 10 minutes, or until lightly golden.

CHEF'S NOTES: Croutons can be prepared in advance and stored in an airtight container for several days. For smaller batches, the croutons can be cooked on top of the stove in a skillet or sauté pan, although quicker, deep-fat frying is not recomended for croutons. They absorb too much oil and become greasy.

GARLIC-FLAVORED CROUTONS: Add 2 tsp/6 g very finely minced garlic (garlic paste) to the oil or butter before tossing with the bread cubes.

CHEESE CROUTONS: After the bread cubes have been tossed with the butter, toss them generously with grated Parmesan, Romano, or other hard grating cheese to taste.

HERB-FLAVORED CROUTONS: Add chopped fresh or dried herbs (such as oregano or rosemary) to the bread cubes along with the butter.

Robialo Cheese Croutons

YIELD: 20 CROUTONS

½ baguette (10 in/25 cm)

8 oz/227 g Robialo or Tellagio cheese

1 fl oz/30 mL extra-virgin olive oil

Salt, as needed

Ground black pepper, as needed

1. Slice the baguette ¼ in/6 mm thick on the bias (about 20 slices).

2. Cut the cheese into 20 slices.

3. Lightly brush olive oil on both sides of each bread slice. Bake at 450°F/232°C until lightly crisp, about 4 minutes. Remove from the oven.

4. Flip each crouton over. Put 1 slice of cheese on each crouton and season with salt and pepper. Return to the oven for 30 seconds, or until cheese is just melted. Serve 2 croutons with each portion of salad.

Cleaning a Soft-Shelled Crab

1. Peel back the pointed shell and scrape away the gill filament on each side.

2. Cut off the head and carefully squeeze out the green bubble behind the eyes.

3. Bend back the apron and twist to remove it and the intestinal vein at the same time.

Glossary

A

Acid: A substance having a sour or sharp flavor. A substance's degree of acidity is measured on the pH scale; acids have a pH of less than 7. Most foods are somewhat acidic. Foods generally referred to as acids include citrus juice, vinegar, and wine. See *alkali.*

Aerobic bacteria: Bacteria that require the presence of oxygen to function.

Aïoli (Fr.): Garlic mayonnaise, often based on olive oils (Italian, *allioli;* Spanish, *aliolio).*

Air-drying: Exposing meats and sausages to proper temperature and humidity conditions to change both flavor and texture for consumption or further processing. Times and temperatures vary depending on the type of meat or sausage.

Albumen: The white of an egg; also the major protein in egg whites (also spelled albumin); used in dry form in some cold food preparations.

Alkali: A substance that tests higher than 7 on the pH scale. Alkalis are sometimes described as having a slightly soapy flavor. Olives and baking soda are some of the few alkaline foods. See *acid.*

Allumette (Fr.): Vegetables, potatoes, or other items cut into pieces the size and shape of matchsticks; ⅛ by ⅛ by 1 to 2 in/3 by 3 mm by 3 to 5 cm is the standard.

Anaerobic bacteria: Bacteria that do not require oxygen to function.

Andouille: A spicy pork sausage that is French in origin but is now more often associated with Cajun cooking. There are hundreds of variations of this regional specialty.

Antipasto (It.): Italian for "before the pasta." Typically a platter of cold hors d'oeuvre that includes meats, olives, cheese, and vegetables.

AP/As-purchased weight: The weight of an item before trimming or other preparation (as opposed to edible portion weight, or EP).

Appareil (Fr.): A prepared mixture of ingredients used alone or as an ingredient in another base preparation, such as duchesse potatoes or duxelles.

Appetizer: One or more of the initial courses in a meal. These may be hot or cold, plated, or served as finger food. They should stimulate the appetite and go well with the rest of the meal.

Aromatics: Plant ingredients, such as herbs and spices, used to enhance the flavor and fragrance of food.

Arrowroot: A powdered starch made from cassava, a tropical root. Used primarily as a thickener. Remains clear when cooked.

Aspic: A clear jelly made from clarified stock (or occasionally from fruit or vegetable juices) thickened with gelatin. Used to coat foods, or cubed and used as a garnish.

B

Bacteria: Microscopic organisms. Some have beneficial properties; others can cause foodborne illnesses when contaminated foods are ingested.

Bain-marie (Fr.): A water bath used to cook foods gently by surrounding the cooking vessel with simmering water. Also, a set of nesting pots with single long handles used as a double boiler. Also, a round steam table insert.

Barbecue: A variation of a roasting method involving grilling or slowly smoke-roasting food over a wood or charcoal fire. Usually a rub, marinade, or sauce is brushed on the item during cooking.

Bard: To cover an item with thin slices or sheets or strips of fat, such as bacon or fatback, to baste it during roasting. The fat is usually tied on with butcher's twine.

Barquette (Fr.): A boat-shaped tart or tartlet, which may have a sweet or savory filling.

Baste: To moisten food during cooking with pan drippings, sauce, or other liquid. Basting prevents food from drying out, improves color, and adds flavor.

Baton/Batonnet (Fr.): Literally, "stick" or "small stick." Items cut into pieces somewhat larger than allumette or julienne; ¼ by ¼ by 2 to 2½ in/6 by 6 mm by 5 to 6 cm is the standard.

Béchamel (Fr.): A white sauce made of milk thickened with white or pale roux and flavored with onion. It is one of the grand sauces.

Binder: An ingredient or appareil used to thicken a sauce or hold together a mixture of ingredients.

Blanch: To cook an item briefly in boiling water or hot fat before finishing or storing it. This sets the color and can make the skin easier to remove.

Blood sausage: Also called *black pudding* or *blood pudding*, a sausage where the main ingredient is liquid blood.

Bloom: To soften gelatin in lukewarm liquid before use. Also, to allow casing on smoked sausage to darken at room temperature after smoking.

Boil: A cooking method in which items are immersed in liquid at or above the boiling point of water (212°F/100°C).

Botulism: A food-borne illness caused by toxins produced by the anaerobic bacterium *Clostridium botulinum.*

Bouchée (Fr.): A small puff pastry shell that may be filled with meats, cheese, seafood, or even fruit. Served as an hors d'oeuvre or as a garnish on a larger entrée.

Boucher (Fr.): Butcher.

Bouillon (Fr.): Broth.

Bouquet garni (Fr.): A small bundle of herbs tied with string, used to flavor stocks, braises, and other preparations. Usually contains bay leaf, parsley, thyme, and possibly other aromatics, such as leek and celery stalk.

Braise: A cooking method in which the main item, usually a tough cut of meat, is seared in fat, then simmered in stock or another liquid in a covered vessel, slowly tenderizing it by breaking down collagen.

Brine: A solution of salt, water, and seasonings used to flavor and preserve foods.

Brisket: A cut of beef from the lower forequarter, best suited for long-cooking preparations like braising. Corned beef is cured beef brisket.

Broil: A cooking method in which items are cooked by a radiant heat source placed above the food.

Brunoise (Fr.): Small dice; ⅛ in/3 mm square is the standard. For a brunoise cut, items are first cut in julienne, then cut crosswise. For a fine brunoise, 1/16 in/1.5 mm square, cut items first into fine julienne.

Bubble knot: Also called a *triple knot,* used to tie beef round, middle, and bung casings. A piece of casing is caught between the two first knots, and a third knot is used to lock the previous knots in place. A length of string is often left at the end for hanging.

Buffet: Historically, a traditional Swedish mode of dining where people serve themselves from a table or sideboard. Buffet foods commonly include cold meat and cheese platters, pickled fish, salads, sandwiches, and desserts.

Bulk sausage: Sausage that is not contained in a casing. Sausages commonly found in bulk include breakfast sausage and Italian sausages meant to be used in pizzas or other dishes. Generally, only fresh sausage is packaged in bulk.

(Beef) Bung cap: Beef appendix, typically used for larger sausages such as bologna and mortadella. Generally 2 to 2½ ft/61 to 76 cm long with a diameter of 4 to 6 in/10 to 15 cm, a beef bung can hold from 10 to 20 pounds of sausage.

Butcher: A chef or purveyor responsible for butchering meats, poultry, and, occasionally, fish. In the brigade system, the butcher may also be responsible for breading meat and fish items and other mise en place operations involving meat.

Butterfly: To cut an item (usually meat or seafood) and open out the edges like a book or the wings of a butterfly to promote attractive appearance and even cooking.

C

Canapé (Fr.): An hors d'oeuvre consisting of a small piece of bread or toast, often cut in a decorative shape, garnished with a savory spread or topping.

Caramelization: The process of browning sugar in the presence of heat. The temperature range in which sugar begins to caramelize is approximately 320° to 360°F/160° to 182°C.

Carryover cooking: Heat retained in cooked foods that allows them to continue cooking even after removal from the cooking medium; especially important to roasted foods. The internal temperature rises, a function of cooling as the meat or item seeks equilibrium of temperature.

Casing: A synthetic or natural membrane (usually pig, beef, or sheep intestines) used to enclose sausage forcemeat.

Cassoulet (Fr.): A stew of beans baked with pork or other meats, duck or goose confit, and seasonings.

Caul fat: A fatty membrane from a pig or sheep that lines the stomach and resembles fine netting; used to bard roasts and pâtés and to encase sausage forcemeat.

Cellulose: A complex carbohydrate; the main structural component of plant cells.

Charcuterie (Fr.): The preparation of pork and other meat items, such as hams, terrines, sausages, pâtés, and other forcemeats, that are usually preserved in some manner, such as smoking, brining, and curing.

Chaud-froid (Fr.): Literally, "hot-cold." A sauce that is prepared hot but served cold as part of a buffet display, usually as a decorative coating for meats, poultry, or seafood; classically made from béchamel, cream, or aspic.

Cheesecloth: A light, fine-mesh gauze cloth used for straining liquids and making sachets and in many other kitchen operations, including cheese making.

Chiffonade (Fr.): Leafy vegetables or herbs cut into fine shreds; often used as a garnish.

Chile: The fruit of certain types of capsicum peppers (not related to black pepper), used fresh or dry as a seasoning. Chiles come in many types (for example, jalapeño, serrano, poblano) and varying degrees of spiciness and heat, measured in Scoville units.

Chili powder: Dried, ground, or crushed chiles, often including other ground spices and herbs.

Chinoise (Fr.): A conical sieve made from fine metal mesh screen, used for straining and puréeing foods.

Chipolata: A small, spicy sausage, usually made from pork or veal and stuffed into a sheep casing.

Chitterlings: Hog middle intestines.

Chop: To cut into pieces of roughly the same size. Also, a small cut of meat including part of the rib.

Choucroute (Fr.): Sauerkraut; preserved cabbage with a sour flavor. *Choucroute garni* is sauerkraut garnished with various meats such as cured meats and sausages.

Clarification: The process of removing solid impurities from a liquid (such as butter or stock). Also, a mixture of ground meat, egg whites, mirepoix, tomato purée, herbs, and spices used to clarify stock for consommé.

Clarified butter: Butter from which the milk solids and water have been removed, leaving pure butterfat. Has a higher smoking point than whole butter, but less butter flavor. Also known as *ghee*.

Coagulation: The curdling or clumping of protein, usually due to the application of heat or acid.

Coarse chop: To cut into pieces of roughly the same size; used for items such as mirepoix, where appearance is not important.

Cold smoking: A procedure used to give smoked flavor to products without cooking them.

Collagen: A fibrous protein found in the connective tissue of animals, which is used to make sausage casings as well as glue and gelatin. Breaks down into gelatin when cooked in a moist environment for an extended period.

Collagen casings: Casings made from collagen that is usually obtained from animal hides. Collagen casings are easy to use and store and have the advantage of being uniform and consistent.

Compote (Fr.): A dish of fruit—fresh or dried—cooked in syrup flavored with spices or liqueur.

Compound butter: Whole butter combined with herbs or other seasonings and usually used to sauce grilled or broiled items, vegetables, and pastas, or as a spread for sandwiches and canapés.

Concassé/concasser (Fr.): To pound or chop coarsely. Usually refers to tomatoes that have been peeled, seeded, and chopped.

Condiment (Fr.): An aromatic mixture, such as pickles, chutney, and some sauces and relishes, that accompanies food (usually kept on the table throughout service).

Confit (Fr.): Preserved meat (usually goose, duck, or pork) cooked and preserved in its own fat.

Confiture (Fr.): Referring to jam or preserves.

Corned beef: Beef brisket preserved with salt and spices. The term *corned* refers to the appearance of the chunks of salt spread over the brisket during the corning process.

Cornichon (Fr.): A small, sour pickled cucumber.

Cornstarch: A fine, white powder milled from dried corn; used primarily as a thickener for sauce and occasionally as an ingredient in batters. Viscous when hot; gelatinous when cold.

Coulis (Fr.): A thick purée, usually of vegetables or fruit. (Traditionally, meat, fish, or shellfish purée; meat jus; or certain thick soups.)

Country style: A forcemeat that is coarse in texture, usually made from pork, pork fat, liver, and various garnishes.

Court bouillon (Fr.): Literally, "short broth." An aromatic vegetable broth that usually includes an acidic ingredient, such as wine or vinegar; most commonly used for poaching fish.

Crème fraîche (Fr.): Heavy cream cultured to give it a thick consistency and a slightly tangy flavor; used in hot preparations, as it is less likely to curdle when heated than sour cream or yogurt.

Cross contamination: The transference of disease-causing elements from one source to another through physical contact.

Croustade (Fr.): A small baked or fried edible container for meat, chicken, or other mixtures; usually made of pastry but sometimes of potatoes or pasta.

Crouton (Fr.): A bread or pastry garnish, usually toasted or sautéed until crisp.

Crudité (Fr.): Usually raw vegetables but sometimes fruit, served as an appetizer or hors d'oeuvre. Some vegetables may be blanched to improve taste and appearance.

Cuisson (Fr.): Poaching liquid—stock, fumet, court bouillon, or other liquid—that may be reduced and used as a base for the poached item's sauce.

Cure: To preserve a food by salting. Also, the ingredients used to cure an item.

Curing salt: A mixture of 94 percent table salt (sodium chloride) and 6 percent sodium nitrite used to preserve meats. Also known as *tinted curing mixture,* or TCM. Curing salt is distinguished by its pink color.

Curry: A mixture of spices used primarily in Indian cuisine; may include turmeric, coriander, cumin, cayenne or other chiles, cardamom, cinnamon, clove, fennel, fenugreek, ginger, and garlic. Also, a dish seasoned with curry.

D

Deglaze/Déglacer (Fr.): To use a liquid, such as wine, water, or stock, to dissolve food particles and/or caramelized drippings left in a pan after roasting or sautéing.

Degrease/Dégraisser (Fr.): To skim the fat off the surface of a liquid, such as a stock or sauce, or to pour off excess fat from a sauté pan before deglazing.

Demi-glace (Fr.): Literally, "half-glaze." A mixture of equal proportions of brown stock and brown sauce that has been reduced by half. One of the grand sauces.

Dice: To cut ingredients into small cubes (⅛ in/3 mm for small or fine, ¼ in/6 mm for medium, and 3/4 in/2 cm for large is standard).

Drawn: A whole fish that has been scaled and gutted but still has its head, fins, and tail.

Dressed: Prepared for cooking or service. A dressed fish is gutted and scaled, and its head, tail, and fins are removed (same as pan-dressed). Dressed poultry is plucked, drawn, singed, trimmed, and trussed. Also, coated with dressing, as in a salad.

Drum sieve: A sieve consisting of a screen stretched across a shallow cylinder of wood or aluminum. Also known as a *tamis.*

Dry cure: A combination of salts and spices used usually before smoking to process meats and forcemeats.

Dumpling: Any of a number of small soft dough or batter items that are steamed, poached, or simmered (possibly on top of a stew); may be filled or plain.

Duxelles (Fr.): An appareil of finely chopped mushrooms and shallots sautéed gently in butter.

E

Egg wash: A mixture of beaten eggs (whole eggs, yolks, or whites) and a liquid, usually milk or water, used to coat baked goods before or during baking to give them a sheen or to enhance browning.

Emincer (Fr.): To cut an item, usually meat, into very thin slices.

Emulsion: A mixture of two or more liquids, one of which is a fat or oil and the other of which is water-based, so that tiny globules of one are suspended in the other. This may involve the use of stabilizers, such as egg and mustard. Emulsions may be temporary, permanent, or semipermanent.

En croûte (Fr.): Encased in a bread or pastry crust.

EP/Edible portion: The weight of an item after trimming and preparation (as opposed to the purchased weight, or AP).

F

Facultative bacteria: Bacteria that can survive both with and without oxygen.

Farce (Fr.): Forcemeat or stuffing (*farci* means "stuffed").

Fat: One of the basic nutrients used by the body to provide energy. Fats also provide flavor in food and give a feeling of fullness.

Fatback: Pork fat from the back of the pig, used primarily for barding.

Fermentation: The breakdown of carbohydrates into carbon dioxide gas and alcohol, usually through the action of yeast on sugar.

Fermento: A commonly used brand of dairy-based fermentation product for semidry fermented sausages, used to lower pH and give a tangy flavor.

Fillet/Filet (Fr.): A boneless cut of meat, fish, or poultry.

Fines herbes (Fr.): A mixture of fresh herbs, usually parsley, chervil, tarragon, and chives.

Foie gras (Fr.): The fattened liver of a force-fed duck or goose.

Food-borne illness: An illness in humans caused by the consumption of an adulterated food product. In order for a food-borne illness outbreak to be considered official, it must involve two or more people who have eaten the same food, and it must be confirmed by health officials.

Food mill: A type of strainer with a crank-operated, curved blade; used to purée soft foods.

Food processor: A machine with interchangeable blades and disks and a removable bowl and lid separate from the motor housing. It can be used for a variety of tasks, including chopping, grinding, puréeing, emulsifying, kneading, slicing, shredding, and cutting julienne.

Forcemeat: A mixture of chopped or ground meat or seafood and other ingredients used for pâté, sausages, and other preparations.

Fumet (Fr.): A type of stock in which the main flavoring ingredient is smothered with wine and aromatics; fish fumet is the most common type.

G

Galantine (Fr.): Boned meat (usually poultry) that is stuffed into its own skin, rolled, poached, and served cold, usually in aspic.

Garde manger (Fr.): Cold kitchen chef or station; the position responsible for cold food preparations, including salads, cold appetizers, and pâtés.

Garnish: An edible decoration or accompaniment to a dish.

Gelatin: A protein-based substance found in animal bones and connective tissue. When dissolved in hot liquid and then cooled, it can be used as a thickener and stabilizer.

Gelatinization: A phase in the process of thickening a liquid with starch in which starch molecules swell to form a network that traps water molecules.

Gherkin: A small pickled cucumber.

Giblets: Organs and other trim from poultry, including the liver, heart, gizzard, and neck.

Glace (Fr.): Reduced stock; ice cream; icing.

Glaze: To give an item a shiny surface by brushing it with sauce, aspic, icing, or another appareil. For meat, to coat with sauce and then brown in an oven or salamander.

Gratiné (Fr.): Browned in an oven or under a salamander (*au gratin, gratin de*). *Gratin* can also refer to a forcemeat in which some portion of the dominant meat is seared and cooled before grinding.

Gravlax: Raw salmon cured with salt, sugar, and fresh dill. A regional dish of Scandinavian origin.

Grill: A technique in which foods are cooked by a radiant heat source placed below the food. Also, the piece of equipment on which grilling is done. Grills may be fueled by gas, electricity, charcoal, or wood.

Grill pan: An iron skillet with ridges that is used on the stovetop to simulate grilling.

Grinder: A machine used to grind meat, ranging from small hand-operated models to large-capacity motor-driven models. Meat or other foods are fed through a hopper into the grinder, where the worm or auger pushes them into a blade. The blade cuts and forces the item through different-size grinder plates. Care should be taken to keep the machine as clean as possible to lessen the chances of cross contamination.

Grinder plates: Used to determine the texture of the ground meat, plates come in varying sizes, from as small as ⅛ in/3 mm for fine-textured ground meat to as large as ¾ in/ 2 cm, used mostly to create garnishes for emulsion sausages.

Griswold: Brand name for a pot, similar to a rondeau, made of cast iron; may have a single short handle rather than the usual loop handles.

Grosse pièce (Fr.): Literally, "large piece." The main part of a pâté or terrine that is left unsliced and serves as a focal point for a platter or other display.

Gumbo: A Creole soup-stew thickened with filé or okra.

H

Haricot (Fr.): Bean. *Haricots verts* are thin green beans.

Head cheese: A jellied meat product typically made from diced boiled pork head meat held together by the natural gelatin contained in the reduced stock left over from boiling the head. Garnished with pickles, pimientos, and parsley and flavored with vinegar.

Hock: The lowest part of an animal's leg, could be considered the ankle. The most familiar example is ham hock.

Hog casings: Casings made from the small and middle hog intestine. Used for countless sausages, hog casings range in diameter from 1¼ to 1⅓ in/32 to 35 mm (used for bratwurst and Italian sausage) to slightly larger (1½ to 1⅔ in/38 to 42 mm; used for Polish sausage and pepperoni). The type of hog casing used depends on the intended application.

Hors d'oeuvre (Fr.): Literally, "outside the work." An appetizer.

Hot smoking: A technique used when a fully cooked smoked item is desired. Both cured and uncured items can be hot smoked. Smoking temperature and time depend on the product.

Hygiene: Conditions and practices followed to maintain health, including sanitation and personal cleanliness.

I

Infusion: Steeping an aromatic or other item in liquid to extract its flavor. Also, the liquid resulting from this process.

Instant-read thermometer: A thermometer used to measure the internal temperature of foods. The stem is inserted in the food, producing an instant temperature readout.

J

Julienne (Fr.): Vegetables, potatoes, or other items cut into thin strips; ⅛ by ⅛ by 1 to 2 in/3 by 3 mm by 3 to 5 cm is standard. Fine julienne is 1⁄16 by 1⁄16 by 1 to 2 in/1.5 by 1.5 mm by 3 to 5 cm.

Jus (Fr.): Juice. *Jus de viande* is meat juice. Meat served *au jus* is served with its own juice.

Jus lié (Fr.): Meat juice thickened lightly with arrowroot or cornstarch.

K

Kosher: Prepared in accordance with Jewish dietary laws.

Kosher salt: Pure, refined rock salt, often preferred for pickling because it does not contain magnesium carbonate and thus it does not cloud brine solutions. Also used to kosher items. Also known as *coarse salt* and *pickling salt*.

L

Lard: Rendered pork fat used for pastry and frying. Also, the process of inserting strips of fat or seasonings into meat before roasting or braising to add flavor and succulence.

Lardon (Fr.): A strip of pork fat used for larding; may be seasoned.

Liaison (Fr.): A mixture of egg yolks and cream used to thicken and enrich sauces. Also, loosely applied to any appareil used as a thickener.

Links: Segments of sausage created when a filled casing is twisted or tied off at intervals.

Liquid smoke: Distilled and bottled smoke that can be used in place of actual smoking to provide a smoked flavor.

Looped sausage: Also known as *ring-tied sausage*; kielbasa is an example of these longer sausages. Also refers to sausage made in beef round casings.

M

Maillard reaction: A complex browning reaction that results in the distinctive flavor and color of foods that do not contain much sugar, including roasted meats. The reaction, which involves carbohydrates and amino acids, is named after the French scientist who discovered it. There are low-temperature and high-temperature Maillard reactions; high temperature starts at 310°F/154°F.

Mandoline (Fr.): A slicing device of stainless steel with carbon-steel blades. The blades may be adjusted to cut items into various cuts and thicknesses.

Marbling: The intramuscular fat found in meat that makes it tender and juicy when cooked.

Marinade (Fr.): An appareil used before cooking to flavor and moisten foods; may be liquid or dry. Liquid marinades are usually based on an acidic ingredient, such as wine or vinegar; dry marinades are usually salt- or spice-based.

Mayonnaise: A cold emulsion sauce made of oil, egg yolks, vinegar, mustard, and seasonings.

Medallion (Fr.): A small, round scallop-shaped cut of meat.

Mesophilic: A term used to describe bacteria that thrive within the middle-range temperatures—between 60° and 100°F (16° and 38°C).

Mie de pain (Fr.): The soft part of bread (not the crust) used to make fresh white bread crumbs.

Mince: To chop into very small pieces.

Mirepoix (Fr.): A combination of chopped aromatic vegetables—usually 2 parts onion, 1 part carrot, and 1 part celery—used to flavor stocks, soups, braises, and stews.

Mise en place (Fr.): Literally, "put in place." The preparation and assembly of ingredients, pans, utensils, and plates or serving pieces needed for a particular dish or service period.

Molasses: A dark brown, sweet syrup that is a by-product of sugarcane refining.

Mousse (Fr.): A dish made with beaten egg whites and/or whipped cream folded into a flavored base appareil; may be sweet or savory, and should be foamy or frothy. Can be made with cooked items, bound with gelatin, and served cold.

Mousseline (Fr.): A very light forcemeat based on white meats or seafood lightened with cream and eggs.

N

Napper/Nappé (Fr.): To coat with sauce. Also, thickened.

New potato: A small, waxy potato that is usually prepared by boiling or steaming and is often eaten with its skin. Refers to "new" harvest; not always small, but with very thin skin.

O

Offal: Variety meats, including organs (brains, heart, kidneys, lights or lungs, sweetbreads, tripe, tongue), head meat, tail, and feet.

Oignon piqué (Fr.): Literally, "pricked onion." A whole, peeled onion to which a bay leaf is attached, using a whole clove as a tack; used to flavor béchamel sauce and some soups.

Organ meat: Meat from an organ rather than the muscle tissue of an animal.

P

Panada (It.): An appareil based on starch (such as flour or crumbs) moistened with a liquid; used as a binder.

Parchment: Heat-resistant paper used to line baking pans, cook items en papillote, construct pastry cones, and cover items during shallow poaching.

Parcook: To partially cook an item before storing or finishing by another method; may be the same as blanching.

Pâte (Fr.): Pastry or noodle dough.

Pâté (Fr.): A rich forcemeat of meat, game, poultry, seafood, and/or vegetables, baked in pastry or in a mold or dish.

Pâte à choux (Fr.): Cream puff paste, made by boiling a mixture of water, butter, and flour, then beating in whole eggs. Also known as *choux paste*.

Pâte brisée (Fr.): Short (rich) pastry for pie crusts.

Pâté de campagne (Fr.): Country-style pâté, with a coarse texture.

Pâte en croûte (Fr.): Pâté baked in a pastry crust.

Paysanne/fermier cut (Fr.): A knife cut in which ingredients are cut into flat, square pieces; ½ by ½ by ⅛ in/1 by 1 cm by 3 mm is standard.

Pellicle: A sticky "skin" that forms on the outside of produce, salmon, sausage, or meats through air-drying and helps smoke particles adhere to the food, resulting in better, more evenly smoked product.

Pesto (It.): A thick, puréed mixture of an herb, traditionally basil, and oil used as a sauce for pasta and other foods and as a garnish for soup. Pesto may also contain grated cheese, nuts or seeds, and other seasonings.

pH scale: A scale with values from 0 to 14 representing degrees of acidity. A measurement of 7 is neutral, 0 is most acidic, and 14 is most alkaline. Chemically, pH measures the concentration/activity of the element hydrogen.

Phyllo dough: Flour-and-water dough rolled into very thin sheets; it is layered with butter and/or crumbs to make pastries. Also known as *filo*.

Pickling spice: A mixture of herbs and spices used to season pickles; often includes dill seed, coriander seed, cinnamon stick, peppercorns, and bay leaves.

Pilaf: A technique for cooking grains in which the grain is sautéed briefly in butter, then simmered in stock or water with various seasonings. (Also known as *pilau, pilaw, pullao*, and *pilav*.)

Pincé (Fr.): To caramelize an item by sautéing; usually refers to a tomato product.

Poach: A method in which items are cooked gently in liquid at 160° to 180°F/71° to 82°C.

Prosciutto: A dry-cured ham. True prosciutto comes from Parma, Italy, although variations can be found throughout the world.

Purée (Fr.): To process food (by mashing, straining, or chopping very fine) in order to make it into a smooth paste. Also, a product made using this technique.

Q

Quenelle (Fr.): A light poached dumpling based on a forcemeat (usually chicken, veal, seafood, or game) bound with eggs, typically shaped into an oval.

R

Ramekin: A small, ovenproof dish, usually ceramic. Also, in French, *ramequin*.

Reduce: To decrease the volume of a liquid by simmering or boiling; used to provide a thicker consistency and/or concentrated flavors and color.

Reduction: The product that results when a liquid is reduced.

Refresh: To plunge an item into, or run under, cold water after blanching to prevent further cooking. Also referred to as *shocking, boiling*, and *parcooking*.

Render: To melt fat and clarify the drippings for use in sautéing or pan-frying.

Rennet: An enzyme used in cheese making to turn milk into cheese; usually taken from the stomach lining of a calf or reproduced chemically in a laboratory.

Roast: A dry-heat cooking method in which items are cooked in an oven or on a spit over a fire.

Roe: Fish or shellfish eggs.

Roulade (Fr.): A slice of meat or fish rolled around a stuffing. Also, filled and rolled sponge cake.

S

Sachet d'épices (Fr.): Literally, "bag of spices." Aromatic ingredients, encased in cheesecloth, that are used to flavor stocks and other liquids. A standard sachet contains parsley stems, cracked peppercorns, dried thyme, and a bay leaf.

Salé (Fr.): Salted or pickled.

Salt cod: Cod that has been salted and dried to preserve it. Also referred to as *baccalà*.

Saltpeter: Potassium nitrate. Formerly used to preserve meat (it is a component of curing salt); it gives certain cured meats their characteristic pink color. Not used commercially since 1975 because its residual amounts are not consistent.

Sanitation: The practice of preparation and distribution of food in a clean environment by healthy food workers.

Sanitize: To kill pathogenic organisms by chemicals and/or moist heat.

Sauté (Fr.): A cooking method in which naturally tender items are cooked quickly in a small amount of fat in a pan on the range top.

Sauteuse (Fr.): A shallow skillet with sloping sides and a single long handle; used for sautéing. Often referred to as a *sauté pan.*

Savory: Not sweet. Also, the name of a course (savory) served after dessert and before port in traditional British meals. Also, a family of herbs (including summer and winter savory).

Scald: To heat a liquid, usually milk or cream, to just below the boiling point. May also refer to blanching fruits and vegetables.

Score: To cut the surface of an item at regular intervals to allow it to cook or cure evenly.

Sear: To brown the surface of food in fat over high heat before finishing by another method (for example, braising) to add flavor and color.

Sea salt: Salt produced by evaporating sea water. Available refined or unrefined, crystallized or ground. Also, *sel gris,* French for "gray salt."

Shallow poach: A method in which items are cooked gently in a shallow covered pan of simmering liquid. The liquid can then be reduced and used as the basis of a sauce.

Sieve: A container made of a perforated material, such as wire mesh, used to drain, rice, or purée foods. Also known as a *tamis.*

Silverskin: The tough connective tissue that surrounds certain muscles.

Simmer: To maintain the temperature of a liquid just below boiling. Also, a cooking method in which items are cooked in simmering liquid.

Slurry: Starch (flour, cornstarch, or arrowroot) dispersed in cold liquid to prevent it from forming lumps when added to hot liquid as a thickener.

Smearing: A fault in sausages; if sausage is processed at too high a temperature, fat will soften and become smeared throughout the sausage. Smeared fat has a tendency to leak out of the sausage and leave it dry.

Smoke-roasting: Roasting over wood or chips in an oven to add a smoky flavor. A method for roasting foods in which items are placed on a rack in a pan containing wood chips that smolder and emit smoke when the pan is placed on the range top or in the oven.

Smoking: Any of several methods for preserving and flavoring foods by exposing them to smoke. Methods include cold smoking (in which smoked items are not fully cooked), hot smoking (in which the items are cooked), and smoke-roasting.

Smoking point: The temperature at which a fat begins to smoke when heated.

Smorgasbord: A classic Swedish manner of dining, where guests serve themselves from a table laden with food; one of the earliest forms of buffets.

Sodium: An alkaline metal element necessary in small quantities for human nutrition; one of the components of most salts used in cooking.

Sodium nitrate: Used in curing meat products that are not going to be heated by cooking, smoking, or canning.

Sodium nitrite: Used in curing meat products that are going to be heated by cooking, smoking, or canning.

Stabilizer: An ingredient (usually a protein or plant product) added to an emulsion to prevent it from separating (for example, egg yolk, cream, or mustard). Also, an ingredient, such as gelatin, used in desserts to prevent them from separating (for example, Bavarian creams).

Standard breading procedure: The procedure in which items are dredged in flour, dipped in beaten egg, then coated with crumbs before being pan-fried (or deep-fried).

Stock: A flavorful liquid prepared by simmering bones and/or vegetables in water with aromatics until their flavor is extracted. It is used as a base for soups, sauces, and other preparations.

Straight forcemeat: A forcemeat combining pork and pork fat with another meat, made by grinding the mixture together.

Sweetbreads: The thymus glands of young animals, usually calves but sometimes lambs. Usually sold in pairs of lobes.

Table salt: Refined, granulated rock salt. May be fortified with iodine and treated with magnesium carbonate to prevent clumping.

Tart: A shallow pie without a top crust; may be sweet or savory.

Tartlet: A small, single-serving tart.

TCM/tinted curing mix: See *curing salt*.

Temper: To heat gently and gradually. May refer to the process of incorporating hot liquid into a liaison to gradually raise its temperature. May also refer to the proper method for melting chocolate.

Tenderloin: A cut of tender expensive meat, usually beef or pork, from the loin or hindquarter.

Terrine (Fr.): A loaf of forcemeat, similar to a pâté but cooked in a covered mold in a bain-marie. Also, the mold used to cook such items, usually a loaf shape made of ceramic.

Thermophilic: Heat-loving; describes bacteria that thrive within the temperature range of 110° to 171°F/43° to 77°C.

Timbale (Fr.): A small, pail-shaped mold used to shape rice, custards, mousselines, and other items. Also, a preparation made in such a mold.

Tomalley: Lobster liver, which is olive green in color and turns red when cooked or heated.

Total utilization: The principle advocating the use of as much of a product as possible in order to reduce waste and increase profits.

Trichinella spiralis: A spiral-shaped parasitic worm that invades the intestines and muscle tissue; transmitted primarily through infected pork that has not been cooked sufficiently.

Trichinosis: The disease transmitted by *Trichinella spiralis*.

Tripe: The edible stomach lining of a cow or other ruminant. Honeycomb tripe comes from the second stomach and has a honeycomb texture.

Truss: To tie up meat or poultry with string before cooking it in order to give it a compact shape for more even cooking and better appearance.

Variety meat: Meat from a part of an animal other than the muscle; for example, organs.

Velouté (Fr.): A sauce of white stock (chicken, veal, or seafood) thickened with blond (or pale) roux; one of the grand sauces. Also, a cream soup made with a velouté sauce base and flavorings (usually puréed) usually finished with a liaison.

Venison: Originally, meat from large game animals; now specifically refers to deer meat.

Vertical chopping machine (VCM): A machine, similar to a blender, that has rotating blades used to grind, whip, emulsify, or blend foods.

Vinaigrette (Fr.): A cold sauce of oil and vinegar, usually with flavorings; it is a temporary emulsion sauce. The standard proportion is 3 parts oil to 1 part vinegar.

Whip: To beat an item, such as cream or egg whites, to incorporate air. Also, a special tool (a whisk for whipping made of looped wire attached to a handle).

White mirepoix: Mirepoix that does not include carrots and may include chopped mushrooms or mushroom trimmings and parsnips; used for pale or white sauces and stocks.

White stock: A light-colored stock made with bones and/or vegetables that have not been browned.

Yeast: Microscopic fungus whose metabolic processes are responsible for fermentation; used for leavening bread and in making cheese, beer, and wine.

Yogurt: Milk cultured with bacteria to give it a slightly thick consistency and sour flavor.

Z

Zest: The thin, brightly colored outer part of citrus rind. It contains volatile oils, making it ideal for use as a flavoring.

Amendola, Joseph. *Ice Carving Made Easy.* 1st rev. ed. Chicago: National Restaurant Association, 1969.

Aylward, Larry. "The Absolute Wurst." *Meat Marketing and Technology.* February 1996.

Batterberry, Ariane. "High Livers." *Food Arts.* July–August 1993, pp. 58–60.

Beard, James. *American Cookery.* Boston: Little, Brown, 1972.

Beard, James. *Beard on Bread.* New York: Knopf, 1973.

Black, Maggie. *The Medieval Cookbook.* New York: Thames and Hudson, 1996.

Blomquist, Torsten, and Werner Voëli. *A Gastronomic Tour of the Scandinavian Arctic.* Stockholm: Timbro, 1987.

Braudel, Ferdinand. *The Structures of Everyday Life: The Limits of the Possible.* Berkeley, Calif.: 1992.

Brown, Dale. *The Cooking of Scandinavia.* New York: Time-Life Books, 1968.

Cerveny, John G. "Effects of Changes in the Production and Marketing of Cured Meats on the Risk of Botulism." *Food Technology,* May 1980, pp. 240–253.

Cetre, F. O. *Practical Larder Work.* London: Sir Isaac Pitman and Sons, 1954.

Church, Ruth Ellen. *Mary Meade's Sausage Cook Book.* Chicago: Rand McNally, 1967.

Clayton, Bernard. *The Breads of France.* Indianapolis: Bobbs-Merrill, 1978.

Costner, Susan. *Great Sandwiches.* New York: Crown, 1990.

Coxe, Antony Himmisley. *The Great Book of Sausages.* Woodstock, N.Y.: Overlook Press, 1992.

Culinary Institute of America. *The New Professional Chef,* 5th and 6th eds. Linda Glick Conway, ed. New York: John Wiley & Sons, 1991.

———. *Techniques of Healthy Cooking.* New York: John Wiley & Sons, 1993.

Dahl, J. O. *Kitchen Management: Construction, Planning, Administration.* New York: Harper and Brothers, 1928.

De Gouy, Louis Pullig. *Sandwich Manual for Professionals.* Stamford, Conn.: The Dahls, 1939.

Desaulniers, Marcel. *Burger Meisters.* New York: Simon and Schuster, 1993.

Diggs, Lawrence, J. *Vinegar.* San Francisco: Quiet Storm Trading, 1989.

Dornenburg, Andrew, and Karen Page. "Tall Food Tales." *National Culinary Review.* January 1997, pp. 12–15.

Ehlert, Friedrich W., Edouard Longue, Michael Raffael, and Frank Wesel. *Pâtés and Terrines.* New York: Hearst Books, 1984.

Escoffier, Auguste. *The Complete Guide to the Art of Modern Cookery.* London: Heinemann, 1986.

———. *The Escoffier Cookbook: A Guide to the Fine Art of Cookery.* American ed. New York: Crown, 1976. (Translation of *Le Guide Culinaire,* 4th ed.)

Flower, Barbara, and Elisabeth Rosenbaum, eds. *The Roman Cookery Book, by Apicius.* London: Harrap, 1961.

"The Foie Gras Story." *Wine Spectator.* November 1993, pp. 71–72.

Freeland-Graves, Jeanne Himich, and Gladys C. Peckham. *Foundations of Food Preparation.* 6th ed. New York: Prentice Hall, 1996.

Gerard, C. "Let Them Eat Foie Gras." *Art Culinaire* 26 (Fall 1992).

Giascosa, Ilaria Gozzini. *A Taste of Ancient Rome.* London: University of Chicago Press, 1992.

Gingrass, David. "Hand-Crafted Salamis: An Experienced Sausagemaker Shares His Method." *Fine Cooking.* February–March 1995, pp. 56–59.

Guy, Christian. *An Illustrated History of French Cuisine.* New York: Bramhall House, 1962.

Harlow, Jay. *The Art of the Sandwich.* San Francisco: Chronicle Books, 1990.

Hazan, Giuliano, and Marcella Hazan. *The Classic Pasta Cookbook.* London and New York: Dorling Kindersley, 1993.

Hodgson, W. C. *The Herring and Its Fishery.* London: Routledge and Kegan Paul, 1957.

Igoe, Robert S. *Dictionary of Food Ingredients.* New York: John Wiley & Sons, 1989.

Janericco, Terrence. *The Book of Great Hors d'Oeuvre.* New York: John Wiley & Sons, 1990.

Jensen, Albert C. *The Cod.* New York: Thomas Y. Crowell, 1972.

Jordan, Michele Anna. *The Good Cook's Book of Oil and Vinegar.* Reading, Mass.: Perseus, 1992.

Kaufman, William. *The Hot Dog Cookbook.* Garden City, N.Y.: Doubleday, 1966.

Killeen, Johanne, and George Germon. *Cucina Simpatica: Robust Trattoria Cooking.* New York: Harper, 1991.

Klein, Maggie Blyth. *The Feast of the Olive.* San Francisco: Chronicle, 1994.

Lang, Jenifer Harvey, ed. *Larousse Gastronomique.* New York: Crown, 1984.

Lawrie, R. A. *Meat Science.* New York: Pergamon Press, 1991.

Leader, Daniel, Judith Blahnik, and Patricia Wells. *Bread Alone: Bold Fresh Loaves from Your Own Hands.* New York: William Morrow, 1993.

Leto, M. T., and W. K. H. Bode. *The Larder Chef.* London: Heinemann, 1969.

Martin, Richard. "Foie Gras: Richly Diverse." *Nation's Restaurant News.* February 8, 1993, pp. 27, 33.

Martini, Anna. *Pasta and Pizza.* New York: St. Martin's Press, 1977.

McGee, Harold. *The Curious Cook: More Kitchen Science and Lore.* San Francisco: North Point Press, 1990.

————. *On Food and Cooking.* New York: Collier, 1988.

McHenry, ed. *The New Encyclopedia Britannica.* Chicago: Encyclopedia Britannica, 1992.

McNeill, F. Marian. *The Scots Kitchen: Its Traditions and Lore, with Old-Time Recipes.* London: Blackie and Son, 1971.

Mengelatte, Pierre, Walter Bickel, and Albin Abelanet. *Buffets and Receptions.* English language ed. Surrey, England: Couldson, Virtue, 1988.

Metz, Ferdinand E., and the United States Culinary Olympic Team. "The 1984 Culinary Olympics Cookbook: U.S. Team Recipes from the Sixteenth International Culinary Competition (International Kochkunst Ausstellung), Frankfurt, West Germany." Des Plaines, Ill.: *Restaurants & Institutions,* Cahners, 1985.

Metz, Ferdinand E., and L. Timothy Ryan. "Taste of Gold, the 1988 U.S. Culinary Team Cookbook: The Road to the World Championship." Des Plaines, Ill.: *Restaurants & Institutions,* Cahners, 1989.

Meyer, Danny, and Michael Romano. *The Union Square Cafe Cookbook.* New York: Harper, 1994.

Midgley, John. *The Goodness of Vinegars.* New York: Random House, 1994.

Murray, Joan. "Is Free-Range Better?" *Washingtonian,* October 1994.

Nicolas, Jean F. *Elegant and Easy: Decorative Ideas for Food Presentations.* Boston: CBI Publishing, 1983.

Nish, Wayne. "Understanding Foie Gras." December 1994–January 1995.

"Nitrate, Nitrite, and Nitroso Compounds in Foods." *Food Technology.* April 1997, pp. 127–36.

"Non Meat Ingredients." *Meat Industry,* 1986.

O'Neill, Molly. "Can Foie Gras Help the Heart?" *New York Times,* November 17, 1991.

Pearson, A. M., and F. W. Tauber. *Processed Meats.* New York: John Wiley & Sons, 1984.

Pellaprat, Henri-Paul, and John Fuller, eds. *Modern French Culinary Art: The Pellaprat of the 20th Century.* London: Virtue, 1978.

Perdue, Charles L., ed. *Pig's Foot Jelly and Persimmon Beer: Foodways from the Virginia Writers' Project.* Santa Fe: Ancient City Press, 1992.

Peterson, Sarah T. *Acquired Taste: The French Origins of Modern Cooking.* Ithaca, N.Y.: Cornell University Press, 1994.

Phalon, Richard. "Diversifying into Pâté de Foie Gras." *Forbes,* November 21, 1994.

Price, James F., and Bernard S. Schweigert, eds. *The Science of Meat and Meat Products.* Westport, Conn.: Food & Nutrition Press, 1987.

Regenstein, Joe M., and Carrie E. Regenstein. *Introduction to Fish Technology.* New York: John Wiley & Sons, 1991.

Revel, Jean François. *Culture and Cuisine.* New York: Doubleday, 1982.

Rey, Alain. *Dictionnaire historique de la langue française.* Paris: Dictionnaires le Robert, 1995.

Romans, John. *The Meat We Eat.* Danville, Ill.: Insterstate Printers & Publishers, 1985.

Root, Waverly, and Richard de Rochemont. *Eating in America: A History.* New York: Ecco Press, 1981.

Rosengarten, David. "Bringing Home the Game." *Wine Spectator,* November 30, 1993, pp. 67–70.

Schmidt, Arno. *Chefs' Book of Formulas, Yields, and Sizes.* New York: John Wiley & Sons, 1990.

Shaw, Timothy. *The World of Escoffier.* New York: St. Martin's Press, 1995.

Sonnenschmidt, Frederic H., and Jean Nicolas. *The Professional Chef's Art of Garde Manger.* Boston: Institutions/*Volume Feeding* Magazine, 1973.

————. *The Professional Chef's Art of Garde Manger.* 4th ed. New York: John Wiley & Sons, 1988.

Soyer, Alexis. *The Pantropheon: Or a History of Food and Its Preparation in Ancient Times.* New York: Paddington Press, 1977.

Strayer, Joseph R., ed. *Dictionary of the Middle Ages,* vol. 13. New York: Charles Scribner's Sons, 1983.

Time-Life Books, eds. "Terrines, Pâtés & Galantines." *The Good Cook: Techniques and Recipes.* Alexandria, Va.: Time-Life Books, 1982.

Tobias, Doris. "Gascon Commissary: Game and Foie Gras from the Wilds of Jersey City." *Wine and Spirits.* October 1993, pp. 43–45.

Toussaint-Samat, Maguelonne. *A History of Food.* Cambridge, Mass.: Blackwell Reference, 1992.

Veale, Wency. *Step by Step Garnishing.* London: Quintet Publishing, 1989.

Verroust, Jacques Winker, Michel Pastoureau, and Raymond Buren. *Le Cochon.* Paris: Sang de la Terre, 1987.

Vongerichten, Jean George. *Simple Cooking.* New York: Prentice Hall Press, 1990.

Wheaton, Barbara Ketcham. *Savoring the Past: The French Kitchen and Table from 1300 to 1789.* New York: Touchstone Books, 1996.

Whelan, Jack. *Smoking Salmon and Trout: Plus Pickling, Salting, Sausaging, and Care.* Bowser, B.C.: Aerie Publishing, 1982.

Wilson, C. Anne. *Food and Drink in Britain: From Stone Age to Recent Times.* London: Constable and Company, 1973.

Winkler, Mac, and Claire Winkler. *Ice Sculpture: The Art of Ice Carving in Twelve Systematic Steps.* Memphis, Tenn.: Duende, 1989.

A

Aïoli, 36
  Chicken Sandwich, Grilled,
    with Pancetta, Arugula
    and, 154
  in Roast Beef on a Roll,
    150
  Saffron, 36
  Salmon B.L.T.,
    Open-Faced, with, 153
Air-Dried Beef, Roman-Style,
  216
Air-Dried Pancetta, 212
Almonds
  Smoked Toasted, 427
  Toasted, 427
  Toasted, Goat's Milk
    Cheese, Baked, with
    Garden Lettuces,
    Roasted Figs, Pears
    and, 124
Ambrosia Salad, 119
Amish Bologna, 259
Ancho-Apricot Barbecue
  Sauce, 55
Anchovy(ies)
  Butter, 533
  in Caesar Salad, 92
  in Green Goddess
    Dressing, 38
  in Mediterranean Salad
    with Tuna Confit, 132
  in Pan Bagnat, 148
  in Salsa Verde, 42
  in Tapenade, 52
  in Tonnato Sauce, 432
Andalusia Gazpacho, 59
Andouille Sausage, 254
Appetizers. *See* Hors
  d'Oeuvre
Apple(s)
  Blood Sausage with, 268
  Celeriac and Tart Apple
    Salad, 101
  Chips, 486
  Chutney, 478
  Duck Confit with Brie and,
    on a Baguette, 158
  Frisée with Walnuts,
    Grapes, Blue Cheese
    and, 87
  in Waldorf Salad, 118
Apple Cider Vinaigrette, 31
Apricot(s)
  Barbecue Sauce, Carolina
    Barbecue Terrine with,
    307
  Barbecue Sauce, -Ancho,
    55

Chutney, -Cherry, 477
  Glazed Corned Beef, 222
  Relish, Dried, 482
Artichoke(s)
  Chips, 486
  and Fennel Salad, 98
  Lamb, Seared, and
    Mushroom Terrine,
    308–309
  Salad, Hearts of, 95
  Scallops, Seared Sea, with
    Peperonato and, 457
Arugula
  Chicken Sandwich, Grilled,
    with Pancetta, Aïoli
    and, 154
  in Herb Salad, Spring, 87
  Prosciutto Roll Filled with,
    418
  Salad with Hot Italian
    Sausage, Cannellini
    Beans, and Roasted
    Peppers, 135
Asian(-Style)
  Barbecue Sauce, Wrapped
    Shrimp with, 412
  Buckwheat Noodles, 112
  Dipping Sauce, 48
  Duck Galantine, Roasted,
    326–327
  Moulard Duck Breasts,
    Tea-Smoked, 204
  Vegetable Slaw, 100
Asparagus, in Couscous Salad
  with Curried
  Vegetables, 113
Aspic
  Gelée, 57, 310
  Gelée, Port Wine, 57
  in Lamb, Seared,
    Artichoke, and
    Mushroom Terrine,
    308
  in Mayonnaise Collée, 534
  in Pheasant, Terrine of
    Roasted, 312
Avocado
  in Cobb Salad, 128
  and Crab, Salad of, 123
  and Crabmeat Profiteroles,
    377
  Guacamole, 50
  and Shrimp Quesadillas,
    451
  Sushi Roll, 422
  Tomato, and Corn Salad
    with Aged Cheddar
    and Chipotle-Sherry
    Vinaigrette, 126

B

Baba Ghanoush (Roasted
  Eggplant Dip with
  Mint), 51
Bacon. *See also* Pancetta
  Basic Dry Cure, 210–211
  B.L.T., Salmon, 153
  B.L.T., Salmon,
    Open-Faced, with
    Aïoli, 153
  Brown Sugar–Cured, 211
  Canadian, 207
  in Cobb Salad, 128
  in German Potato Salad,
    106
  Honey-Cured, 211
  Maple Sugar–Cured, 211
  and Shrimp, Barbecued, 392
  Shrimp, Wrapped, with
    Asian Barbecue Sauce,
    412
  in Turkey Club Sandwich,
    157
Baguette. *See also* Bruschetta;
  Crostini
  Duck Confit with Apples
    and Brie on a, 158
  Oyster and Shrimp Po'boy,
    145
Balsamic Vinaigrette, 27
  Grilled Vegetable
    Appetizer with, 440
Bananas, in Ambrosia Salad,
  119
Barbecue(d)
  Dry Rub, 218, 307
  Lamb Tamales, 434
  Pork Butt, Carolina, 218
  Pork, Pulled, Sandwich,
    146
  Shrimp and Bacon, 392
  Spice Mix, 524
  Terrine with Apricot
    Barbecue Sauce,
    Carolina, 307
Barbecue Sauce, 146
  Apricot-Ancho, 55
  Apricot, Carolina Barbecue
    Terrine with, 307
  Asian, Wrapped Shrimp
    with, 412
  for Lamb Tamales, 56
Barquettes, Smoked Salmon
  Mousse, 379
Basil
  Corona Bean Salad with,
    117
  Oil, 490
  in Pâté Spice, 526

  in Pesto, 46
  and Tomato Soup, Cold
    Roasted, 62
Bavarian Bratwurst, 249
Bay
  in Bouquet Garni,
    Standard, 522
  in Sachet d'Épices,
    Standard, 523
Bean(s). *See also* Bean Salad;
  Chickpeas; Lentil(s)
  Arugula Salad with Hot
    Italian Sausage,
    Cannellini Beans, and
    Roasted Peppers, 135
  Papaya and Black Bean
    Salsa, 44
  Purée, Cannellini, and
    Prosciutto Crostini,
    173
Bean Salad
  Black, 116
  Corona, with Basil, 117
  Corona, with Grilled Baby
    Octopus, 131
  and Grain, Mixed, 109
  Haricots Verts with
    Prosciutto and
    Gruyère, 97
  Haricots Verts with Walnut
    and Red Wine
    Vinaigrette, 97
  Red Borlotti, with
    Rosemary, 117
  Shrimp and, 129
Beef
  Air-Dried, Roman-Style,
    216
  in Aspic Gelée, 57
  Bologna, 259
  Carpaccio, 428
  Carpaccio-Wrapped
    Watercress with Blue
    Cheese Dip, 418
  Corned, 208–209
  Corned, Glazed, 222
  Corned, in Reuben
    Sandwich, 147
  Fajitas, Skirt Steak,
    Herb-Marinated and
    Grilled, 433
  Frankfurter, 258
  Jerky, 215
  Landjäger, 257
  Negimaki, 394
  Pastrami, 209
  Roast, on a Roll, 150
  Roast, for Sandwiches, 222
  Saté, 396

Sausage, Southwest Dry, 269
Smoke-Roasted Sirloin of,
217
Steak Tartare Canapés, 382
Summer Sausage, 256
Tenderloin, Chile-Rubbed,
221
Beer Mustard with Caraway
Seeds, 475
Beet(s)
Borscht, Chilled Clear, 72
Chips, Assorted Vegetable,
386
Chutney, 478
and Horseradish Cure,
Norwegian, for
Salmon, 193
Salad, Roasted, 93
Salad, Roasted, Foie Gras
Roulade with Smoked
Duck Breast and, 463
Vinaigrette, 34
Bell Pepper(s). See Pepper(s)
Beurre Manié, 331
Black Bean
and Papaya Salsa, 44
Salad, 116
Blitz Puff Pastry, 538
Blood Sausage with Apples,
268
B.L.T., Salmon, 153
Open-Faced, with Aïoli, 153
Blue Cheese
in Cobb Salad, 128
Dip, Carpaccio-Wrapped
Watercress with, 418
Dressing, Maytag
(Reduced-Fat), 41
Flan, 357
Frisée with Walnuts,
Apples, Grapes and, 87
Grapes Rolled in Blue de
Bresse, 419
Mousse, 391
and Pecan Crisps, 488
Tart, 357
Boar, Terrine of Wild, 197
Bocconcini, Marinated, 353
Bologna, 259
Amish, 259
Ham, 259
Tongue, 259
Borlotti Bean, Red, Salad
with Rosemary, 117
Borscht, Chilled Clear, 72
Bouillabaisse en Terrine,
310–311
Bouquet Garni, Standard, 522
Bourbon-Smoked Turkey
Breast, 202
Boursin Cheese, Dates
Stuffed with, 418

Bratwurst
Bavarian, 249
Chipolata, 262
German, 248
Smoked, 248, 262
Swiss, Fine, 262
Turkey, 262
Weisswurst, 262
Braunschweiger, 265
Bread(s). See also Croutons
Brioche Dough, 542
Crackers, Pepper Jack and
Oregano, 487
Focaccia, 540
Grissini, 540
Pita, Whole Wheat, 542
Bread Crumbs
Breading Procedure, 548
Oreganata, 129
Bread Salad
Eastern Mediterranean
(Fattoush), 110
Tuscan Style (Panzanella),
111
Breakfast Sausage, 242
Smoked, 242
Brie
Duck Confit with Apples
and, on a Baguette, 158
New Potatoes with Snails
and, 416
Brine
Corned Beef, 208
Duck, 203
Honey, for Quail, 205
Meat, Basic, 206
in Pork Tenderloin
Roulade, 298
Poultry, Basic, 202
Rainbow Trout, 200
Seafood, Basic, 195
Brioche
Dough, 542
Dough, in Camembert,
Baked, with Rhubarb
Chutney, 438
Foie Gras in, 464
Broccoli, in Orzo Salad, 114
Brochettes
Beef Saté, 396
Chinese Skewered Bites, 400
Lamb, with Mint Pesto, 397
Shrimp and Bacon,
Barbecued, 392
Broth
Court Bouillon, 531
Tomato, and Vegetables,
Infusion of, 73
Brown Sugar–Cured Bacon,
211
Bruschetta
Mushroom, 170

with Tomatoes,
Oven-Roasted, and
Fontina, 169
Buckwheat Noodles,
Asian-Style, 112
Buffalo Chicken Salad, 127
Bulgur
in Bean and Grain Salad,
Mixed, 109
in Tabbouleh Salad, 107
Burger(s)
Chicken, 143
Vegetable, 156
Butter
Anchovy, 533
Beurre Manié, 331
Black Olive, Sauce, 406
Garlic and Parsley
Compound, 54
Horseradish, 534
Pimiento, 533

Cabbage
Coleslaw, 99
in Israeli Couscous and
Heirloom Grains, 107
Slaw, Asian Vegetable, 100
in Wontons, Fried, 401
Caesar Salad, 92
Cajun(-Style)
Sausage, 251
Smoked Pork (Tasso), 213
Spice Blend, 525
Camembert
Baked, with Rhubarb
Compote, 438
Crisps, Hudson Valley, 356
Canadian Bacon, 207
Canapés
Cod, Salt, with Piperada,
385
Duck Mousse, Smoked,
with Raspberry, 384
Goat Cheese, with Sweet
Peppers, 382
Prosciutto and Melon, 386
Quail Egg, Deviled, 388
Shrimp, Smoked, 383
Shrimp, Smoked Whiskey,
378
Steak Tartare, 382
Trout, Smoked, 383
Candied Pecans, 426
Cannellini Bean(s)
Arugula Salad with Hot
Italian Sausage, Roasted
Peppers and, 135
Purée and Prosciutto
Crostini, 173
Cantaloupe Soup with Lime
Granité, 62

Caper(s)
Mayonnaise, in Salmon
B.L.T., 153
in Rémoulade Sauce, 36
in Salsa Cruda of Tuna,
430
in Salsa Verde, 42
in Steak Tartare Canapés,
382
in Tapenade, 52
Caraway Seeds, Beer Mustard
with, 475
Caribbean Coconut and
Pineapple Soup, 70
Carolina
Barbecued Pork Butt, 218
Barbecue Terrine with
Apricot Barbecue
Sauce, 307
Carpaccio
Beef, 428
Beef, -Wrapped
Watercress, with Blue
Cheese Dip, 418
Tuna, with Shiitake Salad,
428
Carrot(s)
in Buffalo Chicken Salad,
127
in Chicken Terrine,
Poached, 313
Chips, Assorted Vegetable,
386
in Coleslaw, 99
in Mirepoix, 522
in Slaw, Asian Vegetable,
100
in Soba Noodle Salad, 114
Soup, Cold, 66
in Vegetable Burger, 156
in Vegetable Terrine, Saint
Andrew's, 305
Cashews, Spicy Curried, 427
Catfish Sandwich, Spicy, 142
Cauliflower
in Couscous Salad with
Curried Vegetables,
113
Soup with Sevruga Caviar,
Chilled, 69
Caviar
Beluga, Bluepoint Oyster
Martini with, 417
Potato Crêpes with Crème
Fraîche and, 415
Sevruga, Cauliflower Soup
with, Chilled, 69
Celeriac
and Apple, Tart, Salad, 101
Crisps, 488
in Vegetables, Infusion of,
73

Celery
  in Bouquet Garni,
    Standard, 522
  in Buffalo Chicken Salad,
    127
  Granité, 58
  in Mediterranean Salad
    with Tuna Confit, 132
  in Mirepoix, 522
  Mushroom Salad with
    Tuscan Pecorino and,
    102
  in Waldorf Salad, 118
Challah, Smoked Salmon on,
  159
Chaud-Froid Sauce, 55
Cheddar
  Aged, Avocado, Tomato,
    and Corn Salad with
    Chipotle-Sherry
    Vinaigrette and, 126
  Crisps, and Walnut, 488
  in Orzo Salad, 114
Cheese. *See also* Cheese
  Crisps; Cheese
  Making; *specific cheeses*
  Croque Monsieur, 144
  Croutons, 549
  Croutons, Robialo Cheese,
    550
  Italian Sausage with, 245
  in Muffuletta, 166–167
  Puffs, Gruyère (Gougère),
    373
  in Reuben Sandwich, 147
  Sticks (Paillettes), 376
Cheesecake, Savory
  Roquefort, 358
Cheese Crisps
  Camembert, Hudson
    Valley, 356
  Cheddar and Walnut, 488
  Parmesan, 547
Cheese Making
  Dried Fruit and Hazelnut
    Cheese, 349
  Fromage Blanc, 350
  Lemon Cheese, 348–349
  Lemon Cheese, Peppered,
    349
  Mascarpone, 346
  Mozzarella, 352
  Queso Blanco, 349
  Ricotta, Whole-Milk, 347
  Yogurt Cheese, Herbed, 350
Cherry(ies)
  Dried, -Apricot Chutney,
    477
  Dried, Duck Terrine with
    Pistachios and, 296
  Dried, Peanuts, Chili-
    Roasted, with, 424

Pickled, 485
Cherry Tomato(es)
  in Couscous Salad with
    Curried Vegetables, 113
  in Greek Salad with Feta
    Cheese and Whole
    Wheat Pita, 90
  in Southern Fried Chicken
    Salad, 134
Chervil
  in Fines Herbes, 526
  in Herb Salad, Spring, 87
  in Rémoulade Sauce, 36
Chicken
  Burger, 143
  -Chile Terrine, Southwest,
    294
  in Cobb Salad, 128
  Consommé, 532
  and Crayfish Terrine, 300
  Croque Madame, 144
  Croustade, 407
  Galantine, 324–325
  Glace de Volaille, 531
  Mousseline, in Terrines,
    298, 300, 305, 309
  Roast, with Salsa Verde on
    Focaccia, 151
  Salad
    Buffalo , 127
    in Profiteroles,
      Southwest, 377
    Sandwich, Curried
      Open-Faced, 166
    Southern Fried, 134
  Sandwich, Grilled, with
    Pancetta, Arugula, and
    Aïoli, 154
  Sandwich, Salad, Curried
    Open-Faced, 166
  Sausage, and Vegetable, 264
  Smoked, Rillettes, 224
  Stock, 529
  Terrine, Poached, 313
  Velouté, 532
  Wrap, Horseradish
    Marinated Grilled, 155
Chicken Liver Pâté, 330
  Grand-Mère, 290
  Smoked, 330
Chickpeas
  in Bean and Grain Salad,
    Mixed, 109
  in Couscous Salad with
    Curried Vegetables, 113
  in Falafel in Pita Pockets,
    164
  Hummus, 51
Chili(es)
  in Barbecue Sauce, 146
  Barbecue Sauce,
    Ancho-Apricot, 55

in Barbecue Sauce for
  Lamb Tamales, 56
-Chicken Terrine,
  Southwest, 294
Dried, Toasting, 546
in Harissa, 473
Jalapeño-Orange Sauce, 49
Mustard, Southwestern
  Spicy Green Chile, 474
Paste, Tenderloin,
  -Rubbed, 221
Peanuts, -Roasted, with
  Dried Cherries, 424
in Peanut Sauce, 50
Pico de Gallo, Chipotle, 45
in Pork Piccadillo
  Empanadas, 398
in Romesco Sauce,
  Hazelnut, 53
Sausage, Green Chile, 243
Vinaigrette,
  Chipotle-Sherry, 32
Vinaigrette,
  Chipotle-Sherry,
  Avocado, Tomato, and
  Corn Salad with Aged
  Cheddar and, 126
Chinese Five-Spice Powder,
  523
Chinese Skewered Bites, 400
Chipolata Bratwurst, 262
Chipotle
  in Barbecue Sauce for
    Lamb Tamales, 56
  Pico de Gallo, 45
  -Sherry Vinaigrette, 32
  -Sherry Vinaigrette,
    Avocado, Tomato, and
    Corn Salad with Aged
    Cheddar and, 126
Chips
  Apple, 486
  Artichoke, 486
  Fennel, 486
  Garlic, 486
  Pear, 486
  Vegetable, Assorted, 386
Chive(s)
  in Fines Herbes, 526
  in Green Goddess
    Dressing, 38
  in Herb Salad, Spring, 87
  Oil, 490
  in Rémoulade Sauce, 36
  in Salsa Verde, 42
Chorizo
  and Fennel Strudel, 436
  Mexican, 240
Chutney
  Apple, 478
  Apricot-Cherry, 477
  Beet, 478

Mango, Spicy, 477
Papaya, 479
Cilantro
  Gravlax,
    Southwestern-Style,
    193
  in Papaya and Black Bean
    Salsa, 44
  in Pico de Gallo, Chipotle,
    45
  in Salsa Fresca, 43
  in Salsa, Tomatillo, 45
  in Smoked Salmon,
    Southwest-Style, 198
  Tofu with Red Curry
    Paste, Peas, Green
    Onions and, 445
  Tomato Crust, Quail Pâté
    en Croûte with,
    Southwestern, 318
  -Tomato Pâté Dough, 536
Cinnamon
  Oil, 491
  in Quatre Épices, 524
Citrus Dry Cure, 201
Citrus Oil, Basic, 491
Cloves
  in Pâté Spice, 526
  in Quatre Épices, 524
Club Sandwich, Turkey, 157
Cobb Salad, 128
Cocktail Sauce, 47
Coconut
  in Ambrosia Salad, 119
  and Pineapple Soup,
    Caribbean, 70
Cod
  Cakes, Petite, with Black
    Olive Butter Sauce, 406
  Salt, Canapés with
    Piperada, 385
Coleslaw, 99
  Asian Vegetable, 100
Collard Greens, in Barbecue
  Terrine with Apricot
  Barbecue Sauce,
  Carolina, 307
Compote, Rhubarb, 438, 480
Concassé, Tomato, 543
Confit
  Duck, 219
  Duck, with Apples and
    Brie on a Baguette, 158
  Duck, with Frisée and
    Roasted Shallot
    Vinaigrette, 448
  Rendering Fats for, 546
  Tuna, 220
  Tuna, Mediterranean Salad
    with, 132
  Tuna, in Pan Bagnat, 148
Confiture, Red Onion, 482

Consommé, Chicken, 532
Corn
    Avocado, and Tomato
        Salad with Aged
        Cheddar and
        Chipotle-Sherry
        Vinaigrette, 126
    Roasted, and Tomato
        Salad, 100
    Roasting, 545
Corned Beef, 208–209
    Glazed, 222
    in Reuben Sandwich, 147
Corona Bean Salad
    with Basil, 117
    with Octopus, Grilled
        Baby, 131
Coulis
    Red Pepper, 54
    Red Pepper, Roasted, 54
Court Bouillon, 531
    Vinegar, 531
Couscous
    Israeli, and Heirloom
        Grains, 107
    Salad with Curried
        Vegetables, 113
Crab(meat)
    and Avocado, Salad of, 123
    and Avocado Profiteroles,
        377
    Cakes with Creole
        Honey-Mustard Sauce,
        405
    Rolls with Infused Pepper
        Oils, Fried Ginger, and
        Tamari-Glazed
        Mushrooms, 454
    Sandwich, Soft-Shell, with
        Rémoulade Sauce, 160
    with Seafood Sausage, 266
    Soft-Shelled, Cleaning a,
        550
    in Sushi, 422–423
Crackers. See also Crisps
    Pepper Jack and Oregano,
        487
Cranberry
    Mustard, Dried, 474
    Relish, 480
Crayfish and Chicken
    Terrine, 300
Cream(ed). See also Crème
    Fraîche
    Chaud-Froid Sauce, 55
    Saffron-Infused, 303
    Wild Mushroom Tartlets,
        379
Crème Fraîche, 351
    Lime-Flavored, 351
    Potato Crêpes with Caviar
        and, 415

Creole Honey-Mustard
    Sauce, 39
    Crab Cakes with, 405
Crêpes, Potato, with Crème
    Fraîche and Caviar, 415
Crisps
    Blue Cheese and Pecan, 488
    Camembert, Hudson
        Valley, 356
    Celeriac, 488
    Cheddar and Walnut, 488
    Parmesan, 547
    Parsnip, 488
    Potato, 488
Croque Madame, 144
Croque Monsieur, 144
Croquettes, Risotto, with
    Fontina, 408
Crostini
    Cannellini Bean Purée and
        Prosciutto, 173
    Goat Cheese and Sweet
        Onion, 174
    Lobster and Prosciutto, 172
    Mussel, 171
Croustade, Chicken, 407
Croutons, 549
    in Caesar Salad, 92
    Cheese, 549
    Cheese, Robialo, 550
    Garlic-Flavored, 549
    Herb-Flavored, 549
    in Peanut Salad, Georgia,
        88
Crust. See also Pâté en Croûte
    Parmesan-Prosciutto, 322
    Parmesan-Prosciutto,
        Rabbit Pie in, 321
    Roquefort Cheesecake,
        Savory, 358
Cucumber(s)
    in Bread Salad, Eastern
        Mediterranean
        (Fattoush), 110
    in Bread Salad
        Tuscan-Style
        (Panzanella), 111
    Cups, Scallop Seviche in,
        420
    in Gazpacho Andalusia, 59
    in Gazpacho, Southwest
        Style, 60
    Granité, 58
    in Greek Salad with Feta
        Cheese and Whole
        Wheat Pita, 90
    in Israeli Couscous and
        Heirloom Grains, 107
    in Mediterranean Salad
        Sandwich, 168
    in Pan Bagnat, 148
    Pickle Chips, Sweet, 483

Pickles, Dill, 483
Pickles, Half-Sour, 484
Soup with Dill, Leeks, and
    Shrimp, Chilled, 61
Sushi Roll, 422
Tea Sandwich, 176
Yogurt Sauce, 41
Cumberland Sauce, 48
Cure Mix. See also Dry Cure
    Bologna, 259
    Bratwurst, 262
    Braunschweiger, 265
    Chicken and Vegetable
        Sausage, 264
    Duck Confit, 219
    Foie Gras Sausage, 267
    Frankfurter, 258
    Garlic Sausage, French, 260
    Gravlax, 192–193
    Gravlax,
        Southwestern-Style,
        193
    Jerky, 215
    Kielbasa, 261
    Mortadella, 263
    Salmon, Beet and
        Horseradish,
        Norwegian, 193
    Salmon, Pastrami-, 194
Curry(ied)
    Cashews, Spicy, 427
    Chicken Salad Sandwich,
        Open-Faced, 166
    Oil, 491
    Onion Relish, 481
    Powder, 525
    Red Curry Paste, Tofu
        with Peas, Green
        Onions, Cilantro and,
        445
    Vegetables, Couscous Salad
        with, 113
    Vinaigrette, 31

D

Dates Stuffed with Boursin
    Cheese, 418
Deviled
    Ham Tea Sandwich, 177
    Quail Egg Canapés, 388
Dill(ed)
    Cucumber Soup with
        Leeks, Shrimp and,
        Chilled, 61
    Gelée, Shrimp Mousse
        with, 460
    Gravlax, 192
    Pickles, 483
    in Pickles, Half-Sour, 484
    Salmon Rillettes, 223
    Smoked Salmon,
        Swiss-Style, 199

Dipping Sauce
    Asian-Style, 48
    Peanut, 50
    Peanut, Beef Saté with, 396
    Tempura, 49
Dips and Spreads
    Blue Cheese,
        Carpaccio-Wrapped
        Watercress with, 418
    Blue Cheese Mousse, 391
    Eggplant, Roasted, with
        Mint (Baba
        Ghanoush), 51
    Fromage Blanc, 350
    Goat's Milk Cheese
        Mousse, 391
    Guacamole, 50
    Hummus, 51
    Mascarpone Cheese, in
        Prosciutto and Melon
        Canapés, 386
    Roquefort, 40
    Tapenade, 52
    Trout, Smoked, Mousse,
        392
    Tuna Confit, 220
    Yogurt Cheese, Herbed,
        350
Dough. See also Bread(s); Pasta
        Dough
    Empanada, 398
    Pâté, 535
        Saffron, 536
        Sweet Potato, 537
        Tomato-Cilantro, 536
    Pâte à Choux, 372
    Puff Pastry, Blitz, 538
Dressing(s). See also Salad(s);
        Vinaigrette
    Black Pepper, Creamy, 39
    Blue Cheese, Maytag
        (Reduced-Fat), 41
    Green Goddess, 38
    Ranch (Reduced-Fat), 40
    Roquefort, 40
    Russian, 38
    Thousand Island, 38
Dry Cure
    Bacon, Basic, 210
    Pancetta, 212
    Salmon, 196, 199
    Salmon, Southwest-Style,
        198
    Sturgeon, Citrus, 201
Dry Rub
    Barbecue, 218, 307
    Jerk, 450
    for Lamb Tamales, 435
Duck. See also Smoked Duck
    Confit, 219
    Confit with Apples and
        Brie on a Baguette, 158

Confit with Frisée and
     Roasted Shallot
     Vinaigrette, 448
  in Foie Gras Sausage,
     Smoked, 267
  Galantine, Roasted Asian,
     326
  Rillettes, 224
  Rillettes in Profiteroles,
     378
  Sausage, 260
  Terrine with Pistachios
     and Dried Cherries,
     296
  Terrine, and Smoked Foie
     Gras, 292
Duck Liver Terrine, 231

E

Egg(s)
  Fried, in Croque Madame,
     144
  in Mediterranean Salad
     with Tuna Confit, 132
  Monte Cristo, 144
  in Orzo Salad, 114
  in Pan Bagnat, 148
  Quail, Deviled, Canapés,
     388
  Quail, Poached, 86
  Salad Tea Sandwiches,
     176
Eggplant
  Dip, Roasted, with Mint
     (Baba Ghanoush), 51
  Filling, Marinated, 162
  in Gazpacho, Southwest
     Style, 60
  Panini, and Prosciutto, 162
  Terrine, Roasted Pepper
     and, 306
  in Vegetable Appetizer,
     Grilled, with Balsamic
     Vinaigrette, 440
  in Vegetables, Roasted,
     Provençale Style, 439
  in Vegetable Terrine,
     Roasted, with Goat's
     Milk Cheese, 316
  Wrap, 161
Empanadas, Pork Piccadillo,
     398
Endive, Red Pepper Mousse
     in, 389
Escabèche of Tuna, 431

F

Fajitas, Skirt Steak,
     Herb-Marinated and
     Grilled, 433
Falafel in Pita Pockets, 164
Fats, Rendering, 546

Fattoush (Bread Salad, Eastern
     Mediterranean), 110
Fennel
  and Artichoke Salad, 98
  Chips, 486
  and Chorizo Strudel, 436
  in Couscous Salad with
     Curried Vegetables,
     113
  Grilled, Salad, 98
  and Persimmon Salad, 98
  Shaved, and Parmesan
     Salad, 98
Feta
  Greek Salad with Whole
     Wheat Pita and, 90
  in Mediterranean Salad
     Sandwich, 168
  in Spanikopita, 410
Figs, Roasted, Baked Goat's
     Milk Cheese with
     Garden Lettuces,
     Pears, Toasted
     Almonds and, 124
Fines Herbes, 526
Fish. See also Anchovy(ies);
     Salmon; Smoked
     Salmon; Trout; Tuna
  Bouillabaisse en Terrine,
     310–311
  Brine, Basic Seafood, 195
  Catfish Sandwich, Spicy,
     142
  Cod Cakes, Petite, with
     Black Olive Butter
     Sauce, 406
  Cod, Salt, Canapés with
     Piperada, 385
  Marinated Sweet and Sour,
     453
  Sausage, Seafood, 266
  Sturgeon, Citrus-Scented
     Hot-Smoked, 201
  Velouté, 532
Five-Spice Powder, Chinese,
     523
Flan, Blue Cheese, 357
Focaccia, 540
  Chicken, Roast, with Salsa
     Verde on, 151
  Lamb Sandwich,
     Garlic-Roasted Leg of,
     152
  Muffuletta, 166–167
  Smoked Turkey on, 157
Foie Gras
  in Brioche, 464
  Mousse, 327
  Roulade, 329
  Roulade with Roasted Beet
     Salad and Smoked
     Duck Breast, 463

Sausage, Smoked, 267
  Smoked, and Duck
     Terrine, 292
  and Sweetbread Terrine,
     302
  Terrine, 328–329
Fontina
  Bruschetta with
     Oven-Roasted
     Tomatoes and, 169
  Risotto Croquettes with,
     408
Frankfurter, 258
  Reduced-Fat, 258
French Garlic Sausage, 260
Frisée
  Duck Confit with Roasted
     Shallot Vinaigrette
     and, 448
  in Garden Salad, Parson's,
     867
  with Walnuts, Apples,
     Grapes, and Blue
     Cheese, 87
Fromage Blanc, 350
Fruit. See also specific fruits
  Ambrosia Salad, 119
  Dried, and Hazelnut
     Cheese, 349
  Dried, Plumping, 545

G

Galantine
  Chicken, 324–325
  Duck, Roasted Asian, 326
  Pheasant, 322–323
Galette, Potato, Smoked
     Salmon with, 446
Garden Salad, Parson's, 86
Garlic
  Chips, 486
  Croutons, -Flavored, 549
  Lamb Sandwich, -Roasted
     Leg of, 152
  Mayonnaise. See Aïoli
  and Parsley Butter,
     Compound, 54
  Roasting, 543
  -Rosemary Vinegar, 493
  Sausage, French, 260
Gazpacho
  Andalusia, 59
  Southwest Style, 60
Gelée
  Aspic, 57, 310
  Aspic, Port Wine, 57
  Dill, Shrimp Mousse with,
     460
Georgia Peanut Salad, 88
German
  Bratwurst, 248
  Kassler Ribchen, 209

Potato Salad, 106
Ginger, Fried, Crabmeat Rolls
     with Infused Pepper
     Oils, Tamari-Glazed
     Mushrooms and, 454
Glace de Viande, 531
Glace de Volaille, 531
Glazed
  Corned Beef, 222
  Tamari-, Mushrooms, 454
Goat Cheese
  Baked, with Garden
     Lettuces, Roasted Figs,
     Pears, and Toasted
     Almonds, 124
  Canapés with Sweet
     Peppers, 382
  Crostini, and Sweet Onion,
     174
  Herbed, in Phyllo Dough,
     437
  Marinated, 354
  Mousse, 391
  Roasted Vegetable Terrine
     with, 316
  and Sun-Dried Tomato
     Tartlets, 380
Gougères (Gruyère Cheese
     Puffs), 373
Grains. See also specific grains
  Heirloom, and Israeli
     Couscous, 107
  Salad, Mixed Bean and,
     109
Granité
  Celery, 58
  Cucumber, 58
  Lime, 59
  Lime, Cantaloupe Soup
     with, 62
Grape(s)
  in Ambrosia Salad, 119
  Frisée with Walnuts,
     Apples, Blue Cheese
     and, 87
  in Peanut Salad, Georgia,
     88
  Pickled, 485
  Rolled in Blue de Bresse,
     419
Grapefruit
  Emulsion, 28
  Pineapple, Grilled, Jícama,
     and Red Onion Salad,
     120
Grape Leaves, Stuffed, 393
Gravlax, 192
  Southwestern-Style, 193
Greek Salad, Lemon-Infused,
     with Feta Cheese and
     Whole Wheat Pita,
     90

Greek Sausage (Loukanika), 246

Green Beans. *See* Haricots Verts

Green Goddess Dressing, 38

Green Mayonnaise (Sauce Vert), 35

Green Onions
in Beef Negimaki, 394
in Bread Salad, Eastern Mediterranean (Fattoush), 110
in Chinese Skewered Bites, 400
in Cobb Salad, 128
in Dipping Sauce, Asian-Style, 48
in Israeli Couscous and Heirloom Grains, 107
in Soba Noodle Salad, 114
in Tabbouleh Salad, 107
Tofu with Red Curry Paste, Peas, Cilantro and, 445

Greens. *See* Lettuce(s); *specific greens*

Grissini, 540

Gruyère
Cheese Puffs (Gougères), 373
Haricots Verts with Prosciutto and, 97

H

Half-Sour Pickles, 484

Ham. *See also* Prosciutto
Air-Dried, with Lentil Salad, 447
Bologna, 259
Croque Monsieur, 144
Deviled, Tea Sandwich, 177
in Orzo Salad, 114
Shrimp, Serrano-Wrapped, 392
Smoked Hocks, 206
Smoked, Rillettes, 224
Smoked Whole, 214–215
in Turkey Club Sandwich, 157

Haricots Verts
in Lobster and Truffle Salad, 461
with Prosciutto and Gruyère, 97
with Walnut and Red Wine Vinaigrette, 97

Harissa, 473

Hazelnut
and Dried Fruit Cheese, 349
Romesco Sauce, 53
Vinaigrette, -Oregano, 32

Herb(s), Herbed. *See also specific herbs*
Bouquet Garni, Standard, 522
Croutons, -Flavored, 549
Fines Herbes, 526
Goat's Milk Cheese in Phyllo Dough, 437
Herbes de Provence, 527
Herbes de Provence, Marinated Sheep's Milk Cheese with, 354
Mayonnaise, Green (Sauce Vert), 35
Mushrooms, Crispy, 411
Oil, 220, 490
Potato Soup with Lobster, Chilled, 67
Sachet d'Épices, Standard, 523
Salad, Spring, 87
Skirt Steak Fajitas, -Marinated and Grilled, 433
Vinaigrette, Gourmande, 30
Yogurt Cheese, 350

Herbes de Provence, 527
Marinated Sheep's Milk Cheese with, 354

Heywood's Mustard, 473

Honey
Bacon, -Cured, 211
-Mustard Sauce, Creole, 39
-Mustard Sauce, Creole, Crab Cakes with, 405
Quail, -Cured Smoked, 205

Hors d'Oeuvre. *See also* Canapés; Dips and Spreads; Profiteroles
Almonds, Smoked Toasted, 427
Almonds, Toasted, 427
Beef Carpaccio, 428
Beef Negimaki, 394
Beef Saté, 396
Bluepoint Oyster Martini with Beluga Caviar, 417
Camembert, Baked, with Rhubarb Chutney, 438
Carpaccio, Tuna, with Shiitake Salad, 428
Carpaccio-Wrapped Watercress with Blue Cheese Dip, 418
Cashews, Spicy Curried, 427
Cheese Puffs, Gruyère (Gougères), 373
Cheese Sticks (Paillettes), 376

Chicken Croustade, 407

Cod Cakes, Petite, with Black Olive Butter Sauce, 406

Crab Cakes with Creole Honey-Mustard Sauce, 405

Crabmeat Rolls with Infused Pepper Oils, Fried Ginger, and Tamari-Glazed Mushrooms, 454

Dates Stuffed with Boursin Cheese, 418

Duck Confit with Frisée and Roasted Shallot Vinaigrette, 448

Duck, Smoked Breast of, Niçoise Style, 448

Empanadas, Pork Piccadillo, 398

Fajitas, Skirt Steak, Herb-Marinated and Grilled, 433

Fish, Marinated Sweet and Sour, 453

Foie Gras in Brioche, 464

Foie Gras Roulade with Roasted Beet Salad and Smoked Duck Breast, 463

Goat's Milk Cheese, Herbed, in Phyllo Dough, 437

Grape Leaves, Stuffed, 393

Grapes Rolled in Blue de Bresse, 419

Ham, Air-Dried, with Lentil Salad, 447

Lamb Brochettes, with Mint Pesto, 397

Lobster Rillettes, 458

Lobster Tabbouleh with Mango Sauce, 462

Lobster and Truffle Salad, 461

Mushrooms, Crispy Herbed, 411

Mussels Stuffed with Vegetables, 404

Nuts, Spiced Mixed, 424

Palmiers with Prosciutto, 374

Peanuts, Chili-Roasted, with Dried Cherries, 424

Pecans, Candied, 426

Pork Spareribs, Jerked, 450

Potato Crêpes with Crème Fraîche and Caviar, 415

Potatoes, New, with Snails and Brie, 416

Prosciutto Roll Filled with Arugula, 418

Prosciutto and Summer Melon Salad, 443

Quail, Honey-Smoked, Grilled, with Mango Sauce, 447

Quesadillas, Lobster, Small Seared, and Vegetable, 452

Quesadillas, Shrimp and Avocado, 451

Red Pepper Mousse in Endive, 389

Risotto Croquettes with Fontina, 408

Risotto and Pancetta Cakes with Sun-Dried Tomato Pesto, 409

Scallop Seviche in Cucumber Cups, 420

Scallops, Seared Sea, with Artichokes and Peperonato, 457

Shrimp
and Bacon, Barbecued, 392
Cakes with Spicy Rémoulade Sauce, 459
Mousse with Dill Gelée, 460
Pickled, 420
Serrano-Wrapped, 392
Smoked Whiskey, 378
Tempura, 403
Wontons with, Steamed, 402
Wrapped, with Asian Barbecue Sauce, 412

Skewered Bites, Chinese, 400

Smoked Salmon Mousse Barquettes, 379

Smoked Salmon with Potato Galette, 446

Spanikopita, 410

Strudel, Fennel and Chorizo, 436

Sushi, 422–423
Avocado Roll, 422
Cucumber Roll, 422

Tamales, Barbecued Lamb, 434

Tart, Smoked Duck, 449

Tartlets, Sun-Dried Tomato and Goat's Milk Cheese, 380

Tartlets, Wild Mushroom, Creamed, 379

Tempura, Shrimp, 403

Tempura, Vegetable, 403
Tofu with Red Curry
 Paste, Peas, Green
 Onions, and Cilantro,
 445
Tomatoes, Marinated, with
 Mozzarella, 442
Tuna Carpaccio with
 Shiitake Salad, 428
Tuna, Escabèche of, 431
Tuna, Salsa Cruda of, 430
Veal, Cold, with Tuna
 Sauce (Vitello
 Tonnato), 432
Vegetable Appetizer,
 Grilled, with Balsamic
 Vinaigrette, 440
Vegetables, Roasted,
 Provençale Style, 439
Wontons, Fried, 401
Wontons with Shrimp,
 Steamed, 402
Horseradish
 and Beet Cure, Norwegian,
 for Salmon, 193
 Butter, 534
 Chicken Wrap, Marinated
 Grilled, 155
 Hot Sauce, in Buffalo
 Chicken Salad, 127
Hudson Valley Camembert
 Crisps, 356
Hummus, 51
 in Mediterranean Salad
 Sandwich, 168

I

Israeli Couscous and
 Heirloom Grains, 107
Italian Sausage
 with Cheese, 245
 Hot, 245
 Hot, Arugula Salad with
 Cannellini Beans,
 Roasted Peppers and,
 135
 Hot, Spice Blend, 527
 Low-Fat, 245
 Smoked, 245
 Sweet, 245

J

Jalapeño(s)
 in Harissa, 473
 -Orange Sauce, 49
 in Peanut Sauce, 50
Jerked Pork Spareribs, 450
Jerky Cure, 215
Jícama, Pineapple, Grilled,
 Red Onion, and
 Grapefruit Salad, 120

K

Kassler Liverwurst, 252
Kassler Ribchen, 209
Ketchup
 Tomato, 476
 Yellow Pepper, 476
Kielbasa, 261

L

Lamb
 Brochettes, with Mint
 Pesto, 397
 Grape Leaves, Stuffed, 393
 Greek Sausage
 (Loukanika), 247
 Merguez, 247
 Sandwich, Garlic-Roasted
 Leg of, 152
 Seared, Artichoke, and
 Mushroom Terrine,
 308–309
 Tamales
 Barbecued, 434
 Barbecue Sauce for, 56
 Braised Filling for, 435
Landjäger, 257
Leek(s)
 in Bouquet Garni,
 Standard, 522
 Cleaning Procedure, 96
 Cucumber Soup with Dill,
 Shrimp and, Chilled,
 61
 in Mirepoix, White, 522
 Poached, Salad, 96
 in Vegetables, Infusion of,
 73
 in Vichyssoise, 65
Lemon
 in Cantaloupe Soup with
 Lime Granité, 62
 Cheese, 348
 Cheese, Peppered, 349
 in Cumberland Sauce, 48
 and Salmon, Poached,
 Terrine, 314
 Vinaigrette, 29
 Vinaigrette, -Parsley, 30
Lentil(s)
 in Bean and Grain Salad,
 Mixed, 109
 in Israeli Couscous and
 Heirloom Grains, 107
 Salad, Air-Dried Ham
 with, 447
 Salad, and Walnut, 109
Lettuce(s). See also specific let-
 tuces
 B.L.T., Salmon, 153
 B.L.T., Salmon,
 Open-Faced, with
 Aïoli, 153

in Buffalo Chicken Salad,
 127
in Duck, Smoked, and
 Malfatti Salad with
 Roasted Shallot
 Vinaigrette, 133
Garden, Baked Goat's Milk
 Cheese with Roasted
 Figs, Pears, Toasted
 Almonds and, 124
Garden Salad, Parson's, 86
Herb Salad, Spring, 87
in Salsa Cruda of Tuna,
 430
in Southern Fried Chicken
 Salad, 134
Lime
 Crème Fraîche, -Flavored,
 351
 Granité, 59
 Granité, Cantaloupe Soup
 with, 62
 in Guacamole, 50
 -Mango Salsa, 44
 in Papaya and Black Bean
 Salsa, 44
 in Peanut Sauce, 50
 in Pico de Gallo, Chipotle,
 45
 in Salsa Fresca, 43
Liver. See also Chicken Liver
 Pâté; Foie Gras
 Duck, Terrine, 331
 Pâté de Campagne
 (Country-Style
 Terrine), 291
Liverwurst, Kassler, 252
Lobster
 in Bouillabaisse en Terrine,
 310–311
 Cooked, Removing from
 Shell, 547
 Crostini, and Prosciutto,
 172
 Potato Herb Soup with,
 Chilled, 67
 Rillettes, 458
 Roll, New England, 159
 with Seafood Sausage, 266
 Small Seared, and
 Vegetable Quesadillas,
 452
 Tabbouleh with Mango
 Sauce, 462
 Terrine with Summer
 Vegetables, 299
 Tomato Saffron Soup with
 Shellfish, Chilled, 71
 and Truffle Salad, 461
Loukanika (Greek Sausage),
 246
Low-Fat. See Reduced-Fat

M

Mâche, in Garden Salad,
 Parson's, 867
Malfatti
 Pasta Dough, 539
 and Smoked Duck Salad
 with Roasted Shallot
 Vinaigrette, 133
Mango
 in Barbecue Sauce, 146
 Chutney, Spicy, 477
 -Lime Salsa, 44
 Sauce, Lobster Tabbouleh
 with, 462
 Sauce, Quail, Grilled
 Honey-Smoked, with,
 447
Maple Sugar–Cured Bacon,
 211
Marinated, Marinade
 Beef, Roman-Style
 Air-Dried, 216
 Bocconcini, 353
 in Duck Galantine,
 Roasted Asian, 326
 Eggplant Filling, 162
 Escabèche of Tuna, 431
 Fish, Sweet and Sour,
 453
 Goat Cheese, 354
 in Octopus, Grilled Baby,
 Corona Bean Salad
 with, 131
 Pepper Salad, Roasted, 94
 Peppers and Mushrooms,
 94
 Peppers, Roasted, 94
 Sheep's Milk Cheese,
 Grilled, with Country
 Bread, 354
 Sheep's Milk Cheese with
 Herbes de Provence,
 354
 Skirt Steak Fajitas, Herb-,
 and Grilled, 433
 Tomatoes, 93
 Tomatoes with Mozzarella,
 442
 in Vegetable Terrine,
 Roasted, with Goat's
 Milk Cheese, 316
 in Wild Boar, Terrine of,
 297
Mascarpone, 346
 Cheese Spread, in
 Prosciutto and Melon
 Canapés, 386
Mayonnaise
 Aïoli (Garlic Mayonnaise),
 36
 Aïoli, Saffron, 36
 Basic, 35

Caper, in Salmon B.L.T., 153
Collée, 534
Green (Sauce Vert), 35
Maytag Blue Cheese Dressing (Reduced-Fat), 41
Meat Brine, Basic, 206
Mediterranean
Bread Salad (Fattoush), 110
Potato Salad, 104
Potato Salad, with Mussels, 104
Salad Sandwich, 168
Salad with Tuna Confit, 132
Seafood Terrine, 303
Melon
Cantaloupe Soup with Lime Granité, 62
and Prosciutto Canapés, 386
Watermelon and Red Onion Salad with Watercress, 89
Merguez, 247
Mexican Chorizo, 240
Mint
Eggplant Dip, Roasted, with (Baba Ghanoush), 51
Pea Purée with, Fresh Spring, 68
Pesto, Lamb Brochettes with, 397
Pesto Sauce, 46
in Tabbouleh Salad, 107
Mirepoix, 522
White, 522
Molasses, Pomegranate, in Muhammara, 52
Monte Cristo, 144
Mortadella, 263
Mousse
Blue Cheese, 391
Duck, Smoked, Canapés with Raspberry, 384
Foie Gras, 327
Goat Cheese, 391
Red Pepper, in Endive, 389
Salmon, Smoked, Barquettes, 379
Shrimp, with Dill Gelée, 460
Trout, Smoked, 392
Mousseline
Chicken, 298, 300, 305, 309
Seafood, 266, 299, 303, 304, 319
Veal, 302
Mozzarella, 352

Bocconcini, Marinated, 353
Prosciutto, and Roasted Tomato Terrine, 317
Roulade with Prosciutto, 353
Tomatoes, Marinated, with, 442
Muffuletta, 166–167
Muhammara, 52
Mushroom(s)
Bruschetta, 170
in Chicken Burger, 143
Crispy Herbed, 411
in Duck, Smoked, and Malfatti Salad with Roasted Shallot Vinaigrette, 133
in Haricots Verts with Walnut and Red Wine Vinaigrette, 97
and Peppers, Marinated, 94
Salad, 103
Salad with Celery and Tuscan Pecorino, 102
Salad, Shiitake, Tuna Carpaccio with, 428
Tamari-Glazed, Crabmeat Rolls with Infused Pepper Oils, Fried Ginger and, 454
Terrine, 309
Terrine, Seared Lamb, Artichoke and, 308–309
in Vegetable Appetizer, Grilled, with Balsamic Vinaigrette, 440
in Vegetable Burger, 156
Wild, Tartlets, Creamed, 379
in Wontons, Fried, 401
Mussel(s)
Crostini, 171
Potato Salad with, Mediterranean, 104
Stuffed with Vegetables, 404
Mustard
Beer, with Caraway Seeds, 475
Cranberry, Dried, 474
Deviled Ham Tea Sandwich, 177
Deviled Quail Egg Canapés, 388
Green Chile, Southwestern Spicy, 474
Heywood's, 473
-Honey Sauce, Creole, 39
-Honey Sauce, Creole, Crab Cakes with, 405
Sauce, Swedish, 475
Vinaigrette, -Walnut, 32

N
New England Lobster Roll, 159
Niçoise Style Duck, Smoked Breast of, 448
Noodle(s)
Buckwheat, Asian-Style, 112
Soba, Salad, 114
Norwegian Beet and Horseradish Cure, 193
Nutmeg
in Pâté Spice, 526
in Quatre Épices, 524
Nuts. *See also specific nuts*
Spiced Mixed, 424
Toasting, 546

O
Octopus, Grilled Baby, Corona Bean Salad with, 131
Oil(s)
Basil, 490
Chive, 490
Cinnamon, 491
Curry, 491
Herbed, 220, 490
Orange, 491
Pepper, Infused, Crabmeat Rolls with Fried Ginger, Tamari-Glazed Mushrooms and, 454
Olive(s)
in Artichoke Salad, Hearts of, 95
in Bread Salad Tuscan Style (Panzanilla), 111
Butter Sauce, Black Olive, 406
in Greek Salad with Feta Cheese and Whole Wheat Pita, 90
in Mediterranean Salad with Tuna Confit, 132
in Muffuletta, 166–167
in Orzo Salad, 114
in Pan Bagnat, 148
in Salsa Cruda of Tuna, 430
Tapenade, 52
Olive Bread, Roasted Chicken and Peppers on, 150
Olive Oil. *See* Oil(s)
Onion(s) *See also* Green Onions; Red Onion(s)
in Mirepoix, 522
Relish, Curried, 481
Sweet, and Goat Cheese Crostini, 174

in Vegetables, Roasted, Provençale Style, 439
Orange(s)
in Ambrosia Salad, 119
in Cantaloupe Soup with Lime Granité, 62
in Cumberland Sauce, 48
-Jalapeño Sauce, 49
Oil, 491
Vinaigrette, 29
Vinaigrette, Tangerine-Pineapple, 29
Oreganata Crumb Mixture, 129
Oregano
Crumb Mixture, Oreganata, 129
-Hazelnut Vinaigrette, 32
and Pepper Jack Crackers, 487
Orzo Salad, 114
Oyster
Martini, Bluepoint, with Beluga Caviar, 417
and Shrimp Po'boy, 145

P
Paillettes (Cheese Sticks), 376
Palmiers with Prosciutto, 374
Pan Bagnat, 148
Pancetta
Chicken Sandwich, Grilled, with Arugula, Aïoli and, 154
Dry Cure, 212
in Lamb Brochettes with Mint Pesto, 397
and Risotto Cakes with Sun-Dried Tomato Pesto, 409
Panini, Eggplant and Prosciutto, 162
Panzanella (Bread Salad Tuscan Style), 111
Papaya
and Black Bean Salsa, 44
Chutney, 479
Parmesan
Crisps, 547
in Crumb Mixture, Oreganata, 129
and Fennel Salad, Shaved, 98
in Pesto, 46
in Pesto Sauce, Mint, 46
in Pesto, Sun-Dried Tomato, 47
-Prosciutto Crust, 322

Parsley
  in Bouquet Garni,
      Standard, 522
  in Fines Herbes, 526
  and Garlic Butter,
      Compound, 54
  in Green Goddess
      Dressing, 38
  in Herb Salad, Spring, 87
  Lemon Vinaigrette, 30
  Oreganata Crumb Mixture,
      129
  in Sachet d'Épices,
      Standard, 523
  in Salsa Verde, 42
  in Tabbouleh Salad, 107
Parsnip(s)
  Chips, Assorted Vegetable,
      386
  Crisps, 488
  in Mirepoix, White, 522
Parson's Garden Salad, 86
Pasta Dough, 539
  Malfatti, 539
  Spinach, 539
Pasta Salad
  Bean and Grain, Mixed,
      109
  Buckwheat Noodles,
      Asian-Style, 112
  Malfatti and Smoked Duck,
      with Roasted Shallot
      Vinaigrette, 133
  Orzo, 114
  Soba Noodle, 114
  Tubettini, 112
Pastrami, 209
  Salmon, -Cured, 194
Pastry. See also Pâté en
      Croûte; Profiteroles;
      Tart(s); Tartlets
  Barquettes, Smoked
      Salmon Mousse, 379
  Camembert Crisps,
      Hudson Valley, 356
  Cheese Sticks (Paillettes),
      376
  Empanadas, Pork
      Piccadillo, 398
  Goat's Milk Cheese,
      Herbed, in Phyllo
      Dough, 437
  Palmiers with Prosciutto,
      374
  Spanikopita, 410
  Strudel, Fennel and
      Chorizo, 436
Pastry Dough. See Dough
Pâté. See also Pâté en Croûte
  de Campagne
      (Country-Style
      Terrine), 291

Chicken Liver, 330
Chicken Liver, Smoked,
      330
Grand-Mère, 290
Maison, 291
Pâte à Choux, for
      Profiteroles, 372
Pâté Dough, 535
  Saffron, 536
  Sweet Potato, 537
  Tomato-Cilantro, 536
Pâté en Croûte
  Quail, with
      Tomato-Cilantro
      Crust, Southwestern,
      318
  Salmon, 319
  Turkey, 320–321
Pâté Spice, 526
Pea(s)
  in Garden Salad, Parson's,
      86
  Purée with Mint, Fresh
      Spring, 68
  Tofu with Red Curry
      Paste, Green Onions,
      Cilantro and, 445
Peanut(s)
  Chili-Roasted, with Dried
      Cherries, 424
  Salad, Georgia, 88
  Sauce, 50
  Sauce, Beef Saté with,
      396
Pear(s)
  Chips, 486
  Goat Cheese, Baked, with
      Garden Lettuces,
      Roasted Figs, Toasted
      Almonds and, 124
Pecan(s)
  and Blue Cheese Crisps,
      488
  Candied, 426
Pecorino, Tuscan, Mushroom
      Salad with Celery and,
      102
Peperonato, 457
  Scallops, Seared Sea, with
      Artichokes and, 457
Pepper(corns)
  Cajun Spice Blend, 525
  Chinese Five-Spice
      Powder, 523
  Dressing, Creamy Black
      Pepper, 39
  Lemon Cheese, Peppered,
      349
  Pâté Spice, 526
  Quatre Épices, 524
  Sachet d'Épices, Standard,
      523

Pepper(s). See also Chili(es)
  in Bread Salad Tuscan
      Style (Panzanella),
      111
  and Chicken, Roasted, on
      Olive Bread, 150
  in Coleslaw, 99
  Coulis, Red Pepper, 54
  Coulis, Red Pepper,
      Roasted, 54
  in Crab and Avocado, Salad
      of, 123
  in Gazpacho Andalusia, 59
  in Gazpacho, Southwest
      Style, 60
  Goat's Milk Cheese
      Canapés with Sweet
      Peppers, 382
  in Harissa, 473
  Ketchup, Yellow Pepper,
      476
  Marinated Roasted, 94
  Marinated Roasted, in Pan
      Bagnat, 148
  Marinated Roasted, Salad,
      94
  in Mediterranean Salad
      with Tuna Confit,
      132
  Mousse, Red Pepper, in
      Endive, 389
  in Muhammara, 52
  and Mushrooms,
      Marinated, 94
  Oil, Red Pepper, 492
  Oils, Infused, Crabmeat
      Rolls with Fried
      Ginger,
      Tamari-Glazed
      Mushrooms and, 454
  in Papaya Chutney, 479
  Peperonato, 457
  Piperada, Salt Cod
      Canapés with, 385
  in Quesadillas, Small
      Seared Lobster and
      Vegetable, 452
  Roasted, Arugula Salad
      with Hot Italian
      Sausage, Cannellini
      Beans and, 135
  Roasted, and Eggplant
      Terrine, 306
  Roasting, 544
  in Romesco Sauce,
      Hazelnut, 53
  Salad, Marinated Roasted,
      94
  in Vegetable Appetizer,
      Grilled, with Balsamic
      Vinaigrette, 440
  in Wontons, Fried, 401

Pepper Jack and Oregano
      Crackers, 487
Persimmon and Fennel Salad,
      98
Pesto, 46
  Mint, Lamb Brochettes
      with, 397
  Mint Sauce, 46
  Sun-Dried Tomato, 47
  Sun-Dried Tomato, Risotto
      and Pancetta Cakes
      with, 409
Pheasant
  Galantine, 322–323
  Roasted, Terrine of, 312
  Sausage, Smoked, 253
  Sausage, with Wild Rice,
      253
Phyllo
  Camembert Crisps,
      Hudson Valley, 356
  Goat's Milk Cheese in,
      437
  Spanikopita, 410
  Strudel, Fennel and
      Chorizo, 436
Piccadillo Empanadas, Pork,
      398
Pickle(s), Pickled
  Chips, Sweet, 483
  Dill, 483
  Grapes or Cherries, 485
  Half-Sour, 484
  Red Onions, 485
  Shrimp, 420
  Vegetables, 484
Pico de Gallo, Chipotle,
      45
Pie(s). See Tart(s)
Pimiento Butter, 533
Pineapple
  in Ambrosia Salad, 119
  and Coconut Soup,
      Caribbean, 70
  Grilled, Jícama, Red
      Onion, and Grapefruit
      Salad, 120
  Shrimp, Wrapped, with
      Asian Barbecue Sauce,
      412
  -Tangerine Vinaigrette,
      29
Pine Nuts
  in Pesto, 46
  in Pesto Sauce, Mint, 46
  in Pesto, Sun-Dried
      Tomato, 47
Piperada, Cod, Salt, Canapés
      with, 385
Pistachios
  in Dates Stuffed with
      Boursin Cheese, 418

Duck Terrine with Dried
Cherries and, 296
Pita(s)
in Bread Salad, Eastern
Mediterranean
(Fattoush), 110
Falafel in Pita Pockets,
164
Mediterranean Salad
Sandwich, 168
Whole Wheat, 542
Whole Wheat, Greek Salad
with Feta Cheese and,
90
Plantains, Chips, Assorted
Vegetable, 386
Po'boy, Oyster and Shrimp,
145
Pomegranate
Molasses, in Muhammara,
52
Spinach Salad with
Tangerines and, 85
Pork. See also Bacon; Ham;
Pancetta; Prosciutto;
Sausage
Barbecued Butt, Carolina,
218
Barbecued Pulled,
Sandwich, 146
Barbecue Terrine with
Apricot Barbecue
Sauce, Carolina, 307
Kassler Ribchen, 209
Pâté de Campagne
(Country-Style
Terrine), 291
Pâté, Grand-Mère, 290
Pâté Maison, 291
Piccadillo Empanadas,
398
Rillettes, 224
Skewered Bites, Chinese,
400
Smoked Loin, 207
Spareribs, Jerked, 450
Tasso (Cajun-Style
Smoked), 213
Tenderloin Roulade, 298
in Wontons, Fried, 401
Port Wine
in Cumberland Sauce, 48
Gelée, 57
in Jalapeño-Orange Sauce,
49
Vinaigrette, 34
Potato(es)
Chips, Assorted Vegetable,
386
in Cod Cakes, Petite, with
Black Olive Butter
Sauce, 406

Crêpes with Crème
Fraîche and Caviar,
415
Crisps, 488
in Duck Confit with Frisée
and Roasted Shallot
Vinaigrette, 448
Galette, Smoked Salmon
with, 446
in Mediterranean Salad
with Tuna Confit,
132
New, with Snails and Brie,
416
Salad, German, 106
Salad, Mediterranean,
104
Salad, Mediterranean,
with Mussels, 104
Soup, Herb, with Lobster,
Chilled, 67
Vichyssoise, 65
Profiteroles, 372
Chicken Salad in,
Southwest, 377
Crabmeat and Avocado,
377
Duck Rillettes in, 378
Prosciutto
and Cannellini Bean Purée
Crostini, 173
and Eggplant Panini, 162
Haricots Verts with
Gruyère and, 97
and Lobster Crostini, 172
and Melon Canapés, 386
and Melon Salad, Summer,
443
Mozzarella, and Roasted
Tomato Terrine, 317
Mozzarella Roulade with,
353
Palmiers with, 374
-Parmesan Crust, 322
Roll Filled with Arugula,
418
Provençale-Style Vegetables,
Roasted, 439
Puff Pastry
Blitz, 538
Cheese Sticks (Paillettes),
376
Palmiers with Prosciutto,
374
Sun-Dried Tomato and
Goat's Milk Cheese
Tartlets, 380

Q
Quail
Honey-Cured Smoked,
205

Honey-Cured Smoked,
Grilled, with Mango-
Lime Salsa, 447
Pâté en Croûte with
Tomato-Cilantro
Crust, Southwestern,
318
Quail Egg(s)
Deviled, Canapés, 388
Poached, 86
Quatre Épices, 524
Quesadillas
Lobster, Small Seared,
and Vegetable, 452
Shrimp and Avocado,
451
Queso Blanco, 349

R
Rabbit Pie in
Parmesan-Prosciutto
Crust, 321
Radicchio
in Garden Salad, Parson's,
867
in Herb Salad, Spring, 87
Rainbow Trout, Hot-Smoked,
200
Ranch Dressing
(Reduced-Fat), 40
Raspberry
Smoked Duck Mousse
Canapés with, 384
Vinegar, and Thyme, 492
Red Onion(s)
Confiture, 482
Pickled, 485
Pickled, in Roast Beef on a
Roll, 150
Pineapple, Grilled, Jícama,
and Grapefruit Salad,
120
and Watermelon Salad
with Watercress, 89
Red Pepper. See also Pepper(s)
Coulis, 54
Coulis, Roasted, 54
Mousse in Endive, 389
Oil, 492
Reduced-Fat
Blue Cheese Dressing,
Maytag, 41
Frankfurter, 258
Italian Sausage, 245
Ranch Dressing, 40
Red Wine. See also Port Wine
Vinaigrette, Basic, 27
and Walnut Vinaigrette, 30
and Walnut Vinaigrette,
Haricots Verts with, 97
Relish
Apricot, Dried, 482

Cranberry, 480
Onion, Curried, 481
Rémoulade Sauce, 36
in Catfish Sandwich, Spicy,
142
Crab Sandwich, Soft-Shell,
with, 160
in Oyster and Shrimp
Po'boy, 145
Spicy, Shrimp Cakes with,
459
Rendering Fats, 546
Reuben Sandwich, 147
Rhubarb
Chutney, Baked
Camembert with, 438
Compote, 480
Rice
in Black Bean Salad, 116
Grape Leaves, Stuffed, 393
Risotto Croquettes with
Fontina, 408
Risotto and Pancetta Cakes
with Sun-Dried
Tomato Pesto, 409
in Sushi, 422–423
in Tofu with Red Curry
Paste, Peas, Green
Onions, and Cilantro,
445
in Wontons with Shrimp,
Steamed, 402
Ricotta
in Blue Cheese Dressing,
Maytag (Reduced-Fat),
41
in Chicken, Roasted, and
Peppers on Olive
Bread, 150
in Eggplant and Prosciutto
Panini, 162
in Ranch Dressing
(Reduced-Fat), 40
Whole-Milk, 347
Rillettes
Chicken, Smoked, 224
Duck, 224
Duck, in Profiteroles, 378
Lobster, 458
Pork, 224
Rendering Fats for, 546
Salmon, Dilled, 223
Smoked Salmon, 223
Risotto
Croquettes with Fontina,
408
and Pancetta Cakes with
Sun-Dried Tomato
Pesto, 409
Roast Beef on a Roll, 150
Robialo Cheese Croutons,
550

Romaine
  in Caesar Salad, 92
  in Cobb Salad, 128
  in Greek Salad with Feta
    Cheese and Whole
    Wheat Pita, 90
Roman-Style Air-Dried Beef,
  216
Romesco Sauce, Hazelnut, 53
Roquefort
  Cheesecake, Savory, 358
  Dressing, 40
Rosemary
  -Garlic Vinegar, 493
  Red Borlotti Bean Salad
    with, 117
Rouille, 36
Roulade
  Foie Gras, 329
  Foie Gras, with Roasted
    Beet Salad and
    Smoked Duck Breast,
    463
  Mozzarella, with
    Prosciutto, 353
  Pork Tenderloin, 298
Russian Dressing, 38
  in Reuben Sandwich, 147

S

Sachet d'Épices, Standard,
  523
Saffron
  Aïoli (Garlic Mayonnaise),
    36
  Cream, -Infused, 303
  Pâté Dough, 536
  Tomato Soup with
    Shellfish, Chilled, 71
Saint Andrew's Vegetable
  Terrine, 305
Salad(s). *See also* Bean Salad;
  Pasta Salad
  Ambrosia, 119
  Artichoke and Fennel, 98
  Artichoke, Hearts of, 95
  Arugula, with Hot Italian
    Sausage, Cannellini
    Beans, and Roasted
    Peppers, 135
  Avocado, Tomato, and
    Corn, with Aged
    Cheddar and
    Chipotle-Sherry
    Vinaigrette, 126
  Beet, Roasted, 93
  Beet, Roasted, Foie Gras
    Roulade with Smoked
    Duck Breast and, 463
  Bread, Eastern
    Mediterranean
    (Fattoush), 110

Bread, Tuscan Style
  (Panzanella), 111
Buckwheat Noodles,
  Asian-Style, 112
Caesar, 92
Celeriac and Tart Apple,
  101
Chicken, Buffalo, 127
Chicken, in Profiteroles,
  Southwest, 377
Chicken Sandwich,
  Curried Open-Faced,
  166
Chicken, Southern Fried,
  134
Cobb, 128
Coleslaw, 99
Corn, Roasted, and
  Tomato, 100
Couscous, with Curried
  Vegetables, 113
Couscous, Israeli, and
  Heirloom Grains, 107
of Crab and Avocado, 123
Duck, Smoked, and
  Malfatti, with Roasted
  Shallot Vinaigrette,
  133
Egg, Tea Sandwiches,
  176
Fennel, Grilled, 98
Fennel and Persimmon, 98
Fennel, Shaved, and
  Parmesan, 98
Frisée with Walnuts,
  Apples, Grapes, and
  Blue Cheese, 87
Garden, Parson's, 86
Goat's Milk Cheese, Baked,
  with Garden Lettuces,
  Roasted Figs, Pears,
  and Toasted Almonds,
  124
Grain and Bean, Mixed,
  109
Greek, with Feta Cheese
  and Whole Wheat Pita,
  90
Herb, Spring, 87
Leek, Poached, 96
Lentil, Air-Dried Ham
  with, 447
Lentil and Walnut, 109
Lobster and Truffle, 461
Mediterranean, Sandwich,
  168
Mediterranean, with Tuna
  Confit, 132
Mushroom, 103
Mushroom, with Celery
  and Tuscan Pecorino,
  102

Peanut, Georgia, 88
Pepper, Marinated Roasted,
  94
Pineapple, Grilled, Jícama,
  Red Onion, and
  Grapefruit, 120
Potato, German, 106
Potato, Mediterranean, 104
Potato, Mediterranean,
  with Mussels, 104
Prosciutto and Summer
  Melon, 443
Shiitake, Tuna Carpaccio
  with, 428
Shrimp and Bean Salad,
  129
Slaw, Asian Vegetable, 100
Spinach, with Tangerines
  and Pomegranate, 85
Tabbouleh, 107
Tomatoes, Marinated, 93
Tomatoes, Marinated, with
  Mozzarella, 442
Waldorf, 118
Watermelon and Red
  Onion, with
  Watercress, 89
Salad Dressing(s). *See*
  Dressing(s);
  Vinaigrette
Salmon. *See also* Smoked
  Salmon
  B.L.T., 153
  B.L.T., Open-Faced, with
    Aïoli, 153
  in Bouillabaisse en Terrine,
    310–311
  Gravlax, 192
  Gravlax,
    Southwestern-Style,
    193
  Pastrami-Cured, 194
  Pâté en Croûte, 319
  Poached, and Lemon
    Terrine, 314
  Rillettes, Dilled, 223
  and Scallop Terrine, 304
  with Seafood Sausage, 266
Salsa
  Cruda of Tuna, 430
  Fresca, 43
  Mango-Lime, 44
  Papaya and Black Bean, 44
  Pico de Gallo, Chipotle, 45
  Tomatillo, 45
  Verde, 42
  Verde, Chicken, Roast,
    with, on Focaccia, 151
Sandwich(es). *See also*
  Bruschetta; Crostini;
  Tea Sandwich(es)
  Catfish, Spicy, 142

Chicken
  Burger, 143
  Grilled, with Pancetta,
    Arugula, and Aïoli,
    154
  Roasted, and Peppers on
    Olive Bread, 150
  Roast, with Salsa Verde
    on Focaccia, 151
  Salad, Curried Open-
    Faced, 166
  Wrap, Horseradish
    Marinated Grilled,
    155
Club, Turkey, 157
Crab, Soft-Shell, with
  Rémoulade Sauce,
  160
Croque Madame, 144
Croque Monsieur, 144
Duck Confit with Apples
  and Brie on a Baguette,
  158
Eggplant and Prosciutto
  Panini, 162
Eggplant Wrap, 161
Falafel in Pita Pockets,
  164
Lamb, Garlic-Roasted Leg
  of, 152
Lobster Roll, New
  England, 159
Mediterranean Salad, 168
Monte Cristo, 144
Muffuletta, 166–167
Pan Bagnat, 148
Panini, Eggplant and
  Prosciutto, 162
Po'boy, Oyster and Shrimp,
  145
Pork, Barbecued Pulled,
  146
Reuben, 147
Roast Beef for, 222
Roast Beef on a Roll, 150
Salmon B.L.T., 153
Salmon B.L.T.,
  Open-Faced, with
  Aïoli, 153
Shrimp, Open-Faced, 165
Smoked Salmon on
  Challah, 159
Tuna Salad Open-Faced,
  165
Turkey Club, 157
Turkey, Smoked, on
  Focaccia, 157
Vegetable Burger, 156
Wrap, Chicken,
  Horseradish Marinated
  Grilled, 155
Wrap, Eggplant, 161

Sauce(s). *See also* Barbecue
    Sauce; Dipping Sauce;
    Dips and Spreads;
    Dressing(s);
    Mayonnaise; Pesto;
    Rémoulade Sauce;
    Salsa; Vinaigrette
Aspic Gelée, 57
Aspic Gelée, Port Wine,
    57
Brushing, 393
Butter, Black Olive, 406
Butter, Garlic and Parsley
    Compound, 54
Chaud-Froid, 55
Cocktail, 47
Cumberland, 48
Harissa, 473
Honey-Mustard, Creole,
    39
Hot, in Buffalo Chicken
    Salad, 127
Mango, Lobster Tabbouleh
    with, 462
Mango, Quail, Grilled
    Honey-Smoked, with,
    447
Muhammara, 52
Mustard, Swedish, 475
Orange-Jalapeño, 49
Red Pepper Coulis, 54
Red Pepper Coulis,
    Roasted, 54
Romesco, Hazelnut, 53
Rouille, 36
Tahini, 42
Tuna, Cold Veal with
    (Vitello Tonnato),
    432
Velouté, 532
    Fish, 532
    Shellfish, 532
    Vegetable, 532
Wasabi, 429
Yogurt Cucumber, 41
Yogurt, in Vegetable
    Burger, 156
Sauce Vert, 35
Sauerkraut
    Braised, 147
    in Reuben Sandwich, 147
Sausage. *See also* Bologna;
    Bratwurst; Italian
    Sausage; Smoked
    Sausage
Andouille, 254
Blood, with Apples, 268
Braunschweiger, 265
Breakfast, 242
Cajun-Style, 251
Chicken and Vegetable,
    264

Chorizo and Fennel
    Strudel, 436
Chorizo, Mexican, 240
Duck, 260
Frankfurter, 258
Frankfurter, Reduced-Fat,
    258
Garlic, French, 260
Greek (Loukanika), 246
Green Chile, 243
Kassler Liverwurst, 252
Landjäger, 257
Merguez, 247
Mortadella, 263
in Muffuletta, 166–167
Pheasant, with Wild Rice,
    253
Seafood, 266
Summer, 256
Szechwan-Style, 250
Venison, 244
Scallop(s)
    in Bouillabaisse en Terrine,
        310–311
    in Mousseline, 266, 299,
        303
    Sausage, Seafood, 266
    Seared Sea, with
        Artichokes and
        Peperonato, 457
    Seviche in Cucumber
        Cups, 420
    Smoked, 195
    Terrine, and Salmon, 304
    in Tomato Saffron Soup
        with Shellfish, Chilled,
        71
Seafood. *See* Fish; Shellfish
Seeds, Toasting, 546
Seviche, Scallop, in
    Cucumber Cups, 420
Shallot(s)
    Roasting, 543
    Vinaigrette, Roasted, 33
    Vinaigrette, Roasted, Duck
        Confit with Frisée and,
        448
    Vinaigrette, Roasted,
        Smoked Duck and
        Malfatti Salad with,
        133
Sheep's Milk Cheese
    Grilled Marinated, with
        Country Bread, 354
    Marinated, with Herbes de
        Provence, 354
Shellfish. *See also* Crab(meat);
    Lobster; Mussel(s);
    Oyster; Scallop(s);
    Shrimp
Bouillabaisse en Terrine,
    310–311

Brine, 195
Crayfish and Chicken
    Terrine, 300
Essence, 301
Mousseline, 299, 303, 304,
    319
Octopus, Grilled Baby,
    Corona Bean Salad
    with, 131
Sausage, Seafood, 266
Stock, 530
Terrine, Mediterranean
    Seafood, 303
Tomato Saffron Soup with,
    Chilled, 71
Velouté, 532
Shiitake Salad, Tuna
    Carpaccio with, 428
Shrimp
    and Bacon, Barbecued,
        392
    and Bean Salad, 129
    in Bouillabaisse en Terrine,
        310–311
    Cakes with Spicy
        Rémoulade Sauce,
        459
    Cucumber Soup with Dill,
        Leeks and, Chilled, 61
    Mousse with Dill Gelée,
        460
    in Mousseline, 299, 303,
        319
    Pickled, 420
    Po'boy, Oyster and, 145
    Quesadillas, and Avocado,
        451
    Sandwich, Open-Faced,
        165
    with Seafood Sausage, 266
    Serrano-Wrapped, 392
    Smoked, 195
    Smoked, Canapés, 383
    Smoked Whiskey, 376
    Tempura, 403
    Wontons with, Steamed,
        402
    Wrapped, with Asian
        Barbecue Sauce, 412
Simple Syrup, 540
Sirloin of Beef,
    Smoke-Roasted, 217
Slaw
    Asian Vegetable, 100
    Coleslaw, 99
Smoked Bacon
    Basic, 210–211
    Canadian, 207
Smoked Chicken Liver Pâté,
    330
Smoked Chicken Rillettes,
    224

Smoked Duck, 203
    Breast, Foie Gras Roulade
        with Roasted Beet
        Salad and, 463
    Breast of, Niçoise Style,
        448
    and Malfatti Salad with
        Roasted Shallot
        Vinaigrette, 133
    Mousse Canapés with
        Raspberry, 384
    Tart, 449
    Tea-, Moulard Breasts,
        Asian-Style, 204
Smoked Fish. *See also*
    Smoked Salmon;
    Smoked Trout
    Sturgeon, Citrus-Scented
    Hot-, 201
Smoked Foie Gras and Duck
    Terrine, 292
Smoked Ham
    Hocks, 206
    Rillettes, 224
    Whole, 214–215
Smoked Pork. *See also*
    Smoked Bacon;
    Smoked Ham;
    Smoked Sausage
    Barbecue Terrine with
        Apricot Barbecue
        Sauce, Carolina, 307
    Kassler Ribchen, 209
    Loin, 207
    Tasso (Cajun-Style), 213
Smoked Quail
    Honey-Cured, 205
    Honey-, Grilled, with
        Mango-Lime Salsa,
        447
Smoked Salmon, 196–197
    Beet and Horseradish
        Cure, Norwegian,
        193
    on Challah, 159
    Mousse Barquettes, 379
    with Potato Galette,
        446
    Rillettes, 223
    Southwest-Style, 198
    Swiss-Style, 199
    Tea Sandwich, 177
Smoked Sausage
    Bratwurst, 249, 262
    Breakfast, 242
    Dry, Southwest, 269
    Foie Gras, 267
    Green Chile, 243
    Italian, 245
    Kielbasa, 261
    Pheasant, 253
    Venison, 244

Smoked Shellfish. *See* Smoked
    Scallops; Smoked
    Shrimp
Smoked Shrimp, 195
    and Avocado Quesadillas,
        459
    Canapés, 383
    Whiskey, 376
Smoked Trout
    Canapés, 383
    Hot-, Rainbow, 200
    Mousse, 392
Smoked Turkey
    Breast, 202
    Breast, Bourbon-, 202
Smoke-Roasted Beef, Sirloin
    of, 217
Snails, New Potatoes with
    Brie and, 416
Soba Noodle Salad, 114
Soup(s). *See also* Broth; Stock
    Borscht, Chilled Clear, 72
    Cantaloupe, with Lime
        Granité, 62
    Carrot, Cold, 66
    Cauliflower, with Sevruga
        Caviar, Chilled, 69
    Chicken Consommé, 532
    Coconut and Pineapple,
        Caribbean, 70
    Cucumber, with Dill,
        Leeks, and Shrimp,
        Chilled, 61
    Gazpacho Andalusia, 59
    Gazpacho, Southwest
        Style, 60
    Pea Purée with Mint, Fresh
        Spring, 68
    Potato Herb, with Lobster,
        Chilled, 67
    Tomato, Roasted, and Basil,
        62
    Tomato Saffron, with
        Shellfish, Chilled, 71
    Vegetables, Infusion of, 73
    Vichyssoise, 65
Southern Fried Chicken
    Salad, 134
Southwest(ern-Style)
    Chicken Salad in
        Profiteroles, 377
    Chile-Chicken Terrine,
        294
    Gazpacho, 60
    Gravlax, 193
    Mustard, Spicy Green
        Chile, 474
    Quail Pâté en Croûte with
        Tomato Cilantro
        Crust, 318
    Sausage, Dry, 269
    Smoked Salmon, 198

Spanikopita, 410
Spareribs, Jerked Pork, 450
Spice(s). *See also* Cure Mix;
        Dry Cure; Dry Rub;
        Herb(s), Herbed
    Barbecue Mix, 524
    Cajun Blend, 525
    Cashews, Curried, 427
    Chinese Five-Spice
        Powder, 523
    in Curry Powder, 525
    Italian Sausage Blend, Hot,
        527
    Nuts, Mixed, 424
    Oil, Basic, 491
    Pâté Spice, 526
    Quatre Épices, 524
    Sachet d'Épices, Standard,
        523
    Toasting, 546
Spinach
    in Chicken Terrine,
        Poached, 313
    Mayonnaise, Green (Sauce
        Vert), 35
    Pasta, 539
    Salad with Tangerines and
        Pomegranate, 85
    in Spanikopita, 410
    in Vegetable Terrine, Saint
        Andrew's, 305
Squash. *See* Yellow Squash;
        Zucchini
Steak
    Skirt, Fajitas,
        Herb-Marinated and
        Grilled, 433
    Tartare Canapés, 382
Stock
    in Aspic Gelée, 57
    Chicken, 529
    Glace de Viande, 531
    Glace de Volaille, 531
    Shellfish, 530
    Veal, Brown, 528
    Vegetable, 530
    in Velouté, 532
    Venison, 528
Strudel, Fennel and Chorizo,
        436
Stuffed
    Dates, with Boursin
        Cheese, 418
    Grape Leaves, 393
    Mussels, with Vegetables,
        404
Sturgeon, Citrus-Scented
    Hot-Smoked, 201
Summer Sausage, 256
Sun-Dried Tomato(es)
    in Bean and Grain Salad,
        Mixed, 109

and Goat Cheese Tartlets,
        380
    Pesto, 47
    Pesto, Risotto and Pancetta
        Cakes with, 409
Sushi, 422–423
    Avocado Roll, 422
    Cucumber Roll, 422
Swedish Mustard Sauce, 475
Sweetbread and Foie Gras
    Terrine, 302
Sweet Potato(es)
    Chips, Assorted Vegetable,
        386
    Pâté Dough, 537
Sweet and Sour Fish,
    Marinated, 453
Swiss(-Style)
    Bratwurst, Fine, 262
    Smoked Salmon, 199
Syrup, Simple, 540
Szechwan-Style Sausage, 250

T

Tabbouleh
    Lobster, with Mango
        Sauce, 462
    Salad, 107
Tahini
    in Eggplant Dip, Roasted,
        with Mint (Baba
        Ghanoush), 51
    in Hummus, 51
    Sauce, 42
    Sauce, in Falafel in Pita
        Pockets, 164
Tamales. *See* Lamb, Tamales
Tamari-Glazed Mushrooms,
    Crabmeat Rolls with
    Infused Pepper Oils,
    Fried Ginger and,
    454
Tangerine(s)
    -Pineapple Vinaigrette, 29
    Spinach Salad with
        Pomegranate and, 85
Tapenade, 52
Taro Root, Chips, Assorted
    Vegetable, 386
Tarragon
    in Fines Herbes, 526
    in Green Goddess
        Dressing, 38
    in Rémoulade Sauce, 36
Tart(s)
    Blue Cheese, 357
    Duck, Smoked, 449
    Parmesan-Prosciutto Crust
        for, 321
    Rabbit Pie in
        Parmesan-Prosciutto
        Crust, 321

Tartlets
    Sun-Dried Tomato and
        Goat's Milk Cheese,
        380
    Wild Mushroom, Creamed,
        379
Tasso (Cajun-Style Smoked
        Pork), 213
Tea Sandwich(es)
    Cucumber, 176
    Egg Salad, 176
    Ham, Deviled, 177
    Smoked Salmon, 177
    Watercress, 174
Tea-Smoked Moulard Duck
    Breasts, Asian-Style,
    204
Tempura
    Dipping Sauce, 49
    Shrimp, 403
    Vegetable, 403
Terrine
    Barbecue, with Apricot
        Barbecue Sauce,
        Carolina, 307
    Bouillabaisse en, 310–311
    Chicken and Crayfish, 300
    Chicken, Poached, 313
    Chile-Chicken, Southwest,
        294
    Country-Style (Pâté de
        Campagne), 291
    Duck Liver, 331
    Duck, with Pistachios and
        Dried Cherries, 296
    Duck and Smoked Foie
        Gras, 292
    Foie Gras, 328–329
    Lamb, Seared, Artichoke,
        and Mushroom,
        308–309
    Lobster, with Summer
        Vegetables, 299
    Mozzarella, Prosciutto, and
        Roasted Tomato, 317
    Mushroom, 309
    of Pheasant, Roasted, 312
    Salmon, Poached, and
        Lemon, 314
    of Scallop and Salmon,
        304
    Seafood, Mediterranean,
        303
    Sweetbread and Foie Gras,
        302
    Vegetable, Roasted, with
        Goat's Milk Cheese,
        316
    Vegetable, Saint Andrew's,
        305
    Venison, 295
    of Wild Boar, 297

Thousand Island Dressing, 38

Thyme
  in Bouquet Garni, Standard, 522
  in Herbes de Provence, 527
  in Pâté Spice, 526
  and Raspberry Vinegar, 492
  in Sachet d'Épices, Standard, 523

Toasts. *See also* Bruschetta; Crostini
  Country Bread, Grilled Marinated Sheep's Milk Cheese with, 354

Tofu with Red Curry Paste, Peas, Green Onions, and Cilantro, 445

Tomatillo(s)
  in Gazpacho, Southwest Style, 60
  Salsa, 45

Tomato(es). *See also* Cherry Tomato(es); Sun-Dried Tomato(es)
  in Artichoke Salad, Hearts of, 95
  Avocado, and Corn Salad with Aged Cheddar and Chipotle-Sherry Vinaigrette, 126
  in Barbecue Sauce for Lamb Tamales, 56
  B.L.T., Salmon, 153
  B.L.T., Salmon, Open-Faced, with Aïoli, 153
  in Bread Salad, Eastern Mediterranean (Fattoush), 110
  in Bread Salad Tuscan-Style (Panzanella), 111
  Broth, and Vegetables, Infusion of, 73
  in Cobb Salad, 128
  Concassé, 543
  and Corn, Roasted, Salad, 100
  Crust, Cilantro, Quail Pâté en Croûte with, Southwestern, 318
  in Gazpacho Andalusia, 59
  in Gazpacho, Southwest Style, 60
  Ketchup, 476
  Marinated, 93
  Marinated, with Mozzarella, 442
  in Mediterranean Salad Sandwich, 168

  in Mediterranean Salad with Tuna Confit, 132
  Pâté Dough, -Cilantro, 536
  in Pico de Gallo, Chipotle, 45
  Provençale Style Vegetables, Roasted, 439
  Roasted, Mozzarella, and Prosciutto Terrine, 317
  Roasted, Oven-, Bruschetta with Fontina and, 169
  Roasting, 544
  in Salsa Fresca, 43
  Soup, Roasted, and Basil, Cold, 62
  Soup, Saffron, with Shellfish, Chilled, 71
  in Tabbouleh Salad, 107
  in Vegetable Terrine, Roasted, with Goat's Milk Cheese, 316
  Vinaigrette, 33

Tongue Bologna, 259

Tonnato Sauce, 432

Tortillas
  Chicken Wrap, Horseradish Marinated Grilled, 155
  Eggplant Wrap, 161
  Fajitas, Skirt Steak, Herb-Marinated and Grilled, 433
  Quesadillas, Lobster, Small Seared, and Vegetable, 452
  Quesadillas, Shrimp and Avocado, 451

Trout, Smoked
  Canapés, 383
  Hot-, Rainbow, 200
  Mousse, 392

Truffle
  and Lobster Salad, 461
  Vinaigrette, 28

Tubettini Pasta Salad, 112

Tuna
  Carpaccio with Shiitake Salad, 428
  Confit, 220
  Confit, Mediterranean Salad with, 132
  Escabèche of, 431
  in Pan Bagnat, 148
  Salad Sandwich, Open-Faced, 165
  Salsa Cruda of, 430
  Sauce, Cold Veal with (Vitello Tonnato), 432

Turkey
  Bourbon-Smoked Breast, 202

  Bratwurst, 262
  Club Sandwich, 157
  Pâté en Croûte, 320–321
  Smoked Breast, 202
  Smoked, on Focaccia, 157
  Tuscan Style Bread Salad (Panzanella), 111

V

Veal
  Bratwurst, Fine Swiss, 262
  Cold with Tuna Sauce (Vitello Tonnato), 432
  Glace de Viande, 531
  Mousseline, 302
  Stock, Brown, 528

Vegetable(s). *See also specific vegetables*
  Bouillabaisse en Terrine, 310–311
  Bread Salad, Eastern Mediterranean (Fattoush), 110
  Burger, 156
  Curried, Couscous Salad with, 113
  Dried, Plumping, 545
  Grilled Appetizer, with Balsamic Vinaigrette, 440
  Infusion of, 73
  Lobster Terrine with Summer Vegetables, 299
  Mirepoix, 522
  Mirepoix, White, 522
  Mussels Stuffed with, 404
  Pickled, 484
  Quesadillas, and Small Seared Lobster, 452
  Roasted, Provençale Style, 439
  Sausage, Chicken and, 264
  Slaw, Asian, 100
  Stock, 530
  Tempura, 403
  Terrine, Roasted, with Goat's Milk Cheese, 316
  Terrine, Saint Andrew's, 305
  Velouté, 532

Velouté, 532
  Fish, 532
  Shellfish, 532
  Vegetable, 532

Venison
  Sausage, 244
  Stock, 528
  Terrine, 295

Vichyssoise, 65

Vinaigrette
  Apple Cider, 31
  Balsamic, 27
  Balsamic, Grilled Vegetable Appetizer with, 440
  Beet, 34
  Chipotle-Sherry, 32
  Chipotle-Sherry, Avocado, Tomato, and Corn Salad with Aged Cheddar and, 126
  Curry, 31
  Gourmande, 30
  Hazelnut-Oregano, 32
  Lemon, 29
  Lemon-Parsley, 30
  in Lobster and Truffle Salad, 461
  Mustard-Walnut, 32
  Orange, 29
  Port, 34
  Red Wine, Basic, 27
  Shallot, Roasted, 33
    Duck Confit with Frisée and, 448
    Smoked Duck and Malfatti Salad with, 133
  Tangerine-Pineapple, 29
  Tomato, 33
  Truffle, 28
  Walnut and Red Wine, 30
  Walnut and Red Wine, Haricots Verts with, 97

Vinegar
  Court Bouillon, 531
  Raspberry and Thyme, 492
  Rosemary-Garlic, 493
  Spiced, 307

Vitello Tonnato (Cold Veal with Tuna Sauce), 432

W

Waldorf Salad, 118

Walnut(s)
  and Cheddar Crisps, 488
  Frisée with Apples, Grapes, Blue Cheese and, 87
  and Lentil Salad, 109
  in Pesto Sauce, Mint, 46
  in Vegetable Burger, 156
  in Waldorf Salad, 118

Walnut (Oil)
  Mustard-Vinaigrette, 32
  and Red Wine Vinaigrette, 30
  and Red Wine Vinaigrette, Haricots Verts with, 97

Wasabi Sauce, 429

Watercress
  Carpaccio-Wrapped,
    with Blue Cheese Dip,
    418
  in Garden Salad, Parson's,
    867
  Tea Sandwiches, 174
  Watermelon and Red
    Onion Salad with, 89
Watermelon and Red Onion
  Salad with Watercress,
  89
Weisswurst, 262
Whipped Cream, in Ambrosia
  Salad, 119
Wild Rice, Pheasant Sausage
  with, 253

Wontons, with Shrimp,
  Steamed, 402
Wrap(s)
  Chicken, Horseradish
    Marinated Grilled, 155
  Eggplant, 161

Y

Yellow Pepper. *See also*
  Pepper(s)
  Ketchup, 476
Yellow Squash
  in Chicken Terrine,
    Poached, 313
  in Vegetable Appetizer,
    Grilled, with Balsamic
    Vinaigrette, 440

in Vegetables, Roasted,
  Provençale Style, 439
in Vegetable Terrine, Saint
  Andrew's, 305
in Vegetable Terrine,
  Roasted, with Goat
  Cheese, 316
Yogurt
  Cheese, Herbed, 350
  Cucumber Sauce, 41
  in Ranch Dressing
    (Reduced-Fat), 40
  Sauce, in Vegetable Burger,
    156
  in Tahini Sauce, 42

Z

Zucchini
  in Chicken Terrine,
    Poached, 313
  in Vegetable Appetizer,
    Grilled, with Balsamic
    Vinaigrette, 440
  in Vegetables, Roasted,
    Provençale Style, 439
  in Vegetable Terrine, Saint
    Andrew's, 305
  in Vegetable Terrine,
    Roasted, with Goat
    Cheese, 316

A

Acidification, in cheese-
making process,
336, 345
Acid levels, food preservation
and, 181
Aerators, in mousses, 367
Aging cheeses, 337–338
Air-dried foods, 190
Amaranth, 77
American cheese, 342
Amuse-gueule, 362
Anchor Bar, 127
Appetizers. *See also* Caviar
on à la carte menu, 364
on banquet menu,
364–365
composition balance
wheel, 366
vs hors d'oeuvre, 360
mousses for, 289, 366–368
portioning of, 362, 366
presentation of, 365–366
types of, 365
Apples, preventing discol-
oration in, 101
Arnaud's Restaurant, 119
Aromatics
in oils and vinegars, 468,
470–471
in sausages, 230
Aromatization process, 343
Artichokes, preparing hearts,
95
Artisanal cheese, 334–335
Arugula, 78
Ascorbic acid, in cured meat,
183
Aspic
gelée, 23–24, 25, 57
for pâté en croûte, 283
for terrines, 281
Atlantic oyster, 500

B

Baby greens mix, 79
Bacon
dry curing, 210
nitrite/nitrate levels in, 182
Bacteria, in cheese-making
process, 334, 336, 337
Bain-marie, 281
Balance
in buffet presentation,
511–512
in vinaigrette, 17–18
Ballotines, 285
Banquets. *See also* Buffets
appetizers for, 364–365
garde manger role in, 5

Barbecuing (smoke-roasting),
189
Barquettes, 363–364, 369
Bean salads, 82–83
Beef
air-dried, 190
casings, for sausage, 236
cold smoking, 189
corned, brining time, 186
corned, slicing, 208
Beet greens, 78
Belgian endive, 78
red (treviso), 79
Bellissimo, Teressa, 127
Bel Paese cheese, 340
Beluga caviar, 369
Binders
in forcemeats, 273
in mousses, 367
Bitter greens, 78–79
Blanc, 101
Blue-veined cheeses, 340–341
Bocuse, Paul, 97
Botulism, 182
Boulanger, Monsieur, 4
Brandel, Catherine, 132
Bread
as canapé base, 364
with cheese service, 343
crackers, 471, 472
with green salad, 81
for sandwiches, 138–139
Bread cases, 364
Bread crumbs, fresh, 548
Brie, 338
Brigade system, 4
Brine
for meats, 184, 185–186
for pickles, 471
Brine pumps and syringes, 186
Brown Derby Restaurant, 128
Buffets, 494–519. *See also* Raw
bar
centerpieces and displays,
517–519
cheese boards, 343
concepts and themes for,
496
cost control in, 497–498,
503
food presentation, 5, 505,
508–515
garde manger role, 496
hors d'oeuvre, 362
layout and setup, 505–508
menu selection, 496–497,
498–499
portioning in, 503–504
production order, 504
replenishment of, 515–517

Business skills and responsi-
bilities, 10–12
Business tools, 8
Butterhead lettuce, 76

C

Camembert cheese, 338
Canapés
caviar, 371
mousse for, 289, 368
preparation of, 364
Cardini, Caesar, 92

Career opportunities in garde
manger, 6
Carp roe, 370
Casings, sausage, 235–239
Catering operations, garde
manger role in, 5
Caviar
preparation of, 368–369
presentation of, 371
storage of, 371
types of, 369–371
Centerpieces and displays,
517–519
Chafing dishes, in buffet service, 508
Charcutière, 3, 4
Chaud-froid, 23, 24
Cheddar cheese, 337, 341–342
Cheese, 332–345
artisanal, 334–335
baked, 340
for cheese boards, 343
classifications of, 338–342
cold smoking, 189
in dairy-based sauces, 21
defined, 335
as hors d'oeuvre, 362
in mousses, 367
presentation of, 343
sandwich filling, 140
sandwich spread, 139
storage and handling, 345
Cheesecloth bags, 337
Cheese making
blue-veined cheeses,
340–341
hard cheeses, 341–342
history of, 332, 334
in kitchen, 345
pasta filata cheeses, 341
semisoft cheeses, 340
soft fresh cheeses, 335
soft ripened cheeses, 338,
340
stages of, 335–338
very hard cheeses (granas),
342

Cheese Primer, The (Jenkins),
342
Cherrystone clams, 501
Chicken
brining time for, 186
cold smoking, 189
Chicory, 78
Chimney, in dough, 283
China, in buffet service, 507
Chips, fried and baked, 472
Choucroute garni, 209
Chutney, 22, 468
Chymosin, 337
Clams, for raw bar, 501
Clause, Jean-Pierre, 287
Closed sandwiches, 141
Club sandwiches, 141
Coating sauces, 23–25
Cocktail Claws, 502
Cod roe, 370
Colby cheese, 342
Cold infusion method, 470
Cold smoked foods, 188–189
Collard greens, 78
Color, in buffet presentation,
512
Composed hors d'oeuvre,
363–364
Composed salads, 83, 84
Compote, 22, 468
Condiments, 468
Confits, 191
Contests and competitions, 9
Cooking technique, in buffet
presentation, 514
Corned beef
brining time for, 186
slicing, 208
Corned foods, 184
Corn salad, 77
Corn syrup, in cured foods,
183
Cos lettuce, 77
Cost control, 10, 497–498,
503
Cottage cheese, 338
Coulis, 22
Country-style forcemeat, 272,
276
Court bouillon, 502
Cow's milk cheese, 335
Crabs, in raw bar, 502
Crackers, 471, 472
Cream
in mousseline forcemeat,
277
in mousses, 367
sauces, 21
soups, 26
Cream cheese, 338

Creamy-style dressings, 21, 81
Crisps, as salad garnish, 81
Crudités, 362
Cuisiner Gascon, Le, 287
Cuisson, preparing, 95
Culinary Math (Hill and Blocker), 497
Curdling, curds, in cheese-making process, 337, 341, 345
Cure, defined, 184
Cure accelerators, 183
Cured foods
   brines, 184, 185–186, 471
   dry-cure mixtures, 184
   dry-cure times, 184
   history of, 2
   as hors d'oeuvre, 363
   nitrates/nitrites in, 181–183, 229
   salt-cure process, 180–181
   sausages, 229
   seasonings/flavorings, 183
Curly endive, 78
Cutting skills, in buffet service, 504, 505

D

Dairy-based sauces, 21
Dandelion greens, 78
Decorations
   ice carvings, 362, 518–519
   with pâté dough, 283, 537
Degustation menus, 364
Dehydration, in food preservation, 181
Denaturing the protein, 181
Dextrose, in cured foods, 183
Diat, Loise, 65
Dipping sauces, 25
Dips and spreads
   dairy-based, 21
   hors d'oeuvre, 362
Dodines, 285
Dough. *See* Pâté dough
Dressings. *See also* Vinaigrette
   creamy, 21, 81
   for green salads, 81
   infused oils and vinegars in, 470
   mustard in, 468
   for potato salads, 82
Dried foods, 190
Dry-cured meats
   as appetizer, 365
   bacon, 210
   cure mixture, 184
   curing times, 184
   nitrite/nitrate levels in, 182
Dry Jack cheese, 342
Dry-rind cheeses, 340

Duck. *See also* Foie gras
   breasts, brining time for, 186
   confit, 191
   curing, 219
   fat, 219

E

Edam cheese, 340
Education and training for garde manger, 7–9
Egg wash, 283
Egg whites, in mousses, 367
Egg yolks, as emulsifier, 17
Employee benefits, 12
Employee training, 10–11, 12
Emulsifiers, 17
Emulsion sauces, cold, 16–21
Emulsion sausages, 232–234
Enzymes, in fermentation process, 181
Equipment and tools. *See also* Molds
   brine pumps and syringes, 186
   in buffet service, 504, 505, 508, 510
   for cheese making, 345
   for forcemeats, 274, 275
   management of, 10, 11
   meat grinders, 230–231, 275
   menu planning and, 11
   for raw bar, 503
   for sausage making, 230–231, 238, 257
   smokers, 187, 189, 190
   storage and placement of, 8, 11
Escarole, 78
Escoffier, Auguste, 4, 22, 288
European flat oyster, 500

F

Fats
   in confits and rillettes, 191
   duck, 219
   in forcemeats, 272–273
   oils, infused, 468, 470–471
   rendering, 546
   in sausage, 229
Felder, Eve, 124
Fermentation, in food preservation, 181
Finger sandwiches, 141
Fish. *See also* Shellfish
   mousseline, 272
   smoking, 188, 189
Fish roe. *See* Caviar
Flatware, in buffet service, 507
Flowers, edible, in green salad, 80

Focal point, in buffet presentation, 514
Foie gras
   cleaning and preparing, 288–289
   grades of, 288
   in hors d'oeuvre, 363
   marinated, 289
   mousse, 289
   pâté of, 287–288, 289
   terrine of, 279, 289
Food allergies, 510
Food costing, for buffets, 497–498
Food presentation. *See* Presentation
Food preservation. *See* Preserved foods
Food processor, forcemeat mixing in, 275
Food safety. *See also* Storage
   buffet, 504–505
   in cheese making, 336
   oils and vinegars, infused, 470–471
   raw bar, 499, 502
Forcemeats
   binders, 273
   5-4-3 mixture, for emulsion sausages, 232
   garnishes, 273, 274
   ingredients for, 272–273
   making, 274–278
   seasonings, 273
   styles and textures, 272
   terrines, 280–281
French country cooking, 73
French Revolution, 4
Frisée, 78
Fruits
   with cheese service, 343
   chips, 472
   chutneys, 468
   cold smoking, 189
   compotes, 468
   purées, in vinaigrette, 19
   salads, 83
   salsas, 22
   soups, 26

G

Galantines, 284–287, 365, 468
Game meats, forcemeats, 272
Garde manger
   buffets and, 496
   as businessperson, 10–12
   career development, 8–9
   career opportunities, 6
   defined, 1
   education and training for, 7–8
   history of, 2–4

   skills and responsibilities in, 4–5
Garlic
   infused oils and vinegars, 471
   roasted, 543
Garnishes
   in buffet service, 509
   for forcemeats, 273, 274
   for green salads, 81
   for sandwiches, 140
   for sausages, 234
Gelatin
   aspic gelée ratio, 23
   in coating sauces, 23–25
   in mousses, 367
   solution, 24
   in soups, 26
Glassware, in buffet service, 507
Goat's milk cheese, 335, 338
Goose. *See also* Foie gras
   confit, 191
Gorgonzola cheese, 341
Gouda cheese, 340
Grain salads, 82
Granités, as salad garnish, 81
Gratin forcemeat, 272, 276–277
Grazing menus, 364
Greens
   bitter, 78–79
   herbs and flowers, 80
   mild, 76–77
   prepared mixes, 79
   spicy, 77–78
Green salads, 76–81
Grinders, 230–231, 275
Grinding, progressive, 274, 275
Gross pièce, 505, 514
Guerard, Michel, 86
Guide Culinaire, Le (Escoffier), 22, 288
Guilds, food, 3–4

H

Hams
   air-drying, 190
   brining, 185, 186
   cold smoking, 188
   dry cure, 184
   hot smoking, 189
Hard cheeses, 341–342
Harry's Bar, Venice, 428
Havarti cheese, 340
Herbs
   in cured foods, 183
   flowers, edible, 80
   in forcemeats, 273
   in fruit salads, 83
   in green salads, 80

oils and vinegars, infused, 468, 470
in sausages, 229
in vinaigrette, 18
Hill and Blocker, 497
Hog casings, for sausage, 236
Homogenized milk, 336
Honey, in cured foods, 183
Hors d'oeuvre. *See also* Caviar
on appetizer plates, 365
vs appetizers, 360
barquettes and tartlets, 363–364, 368
canapés, 364, 368, 371
mousses for, 366–368
presentation of, 362–363
Hot smoked foods, 189

I

Ice beds, 362, 503
Iceberg lettuce, 76
Ice carving, 362, 518–519
Infused oils and vinegars, 468, 470–471

J

Jacks, David, 342
Japanese oyster, 500
Jellied clear soups, 26
Jenkins, Steven, 342
Job opportunities in garde manger, 6
Jonah Crab, 502

K

Ketchup, 468
Knives, 503, 504
Kumamoto oyster, 500

L

Labor costing, for buffets, 497
Lamb's lettuce, 77
Landjäger press, 257
Larousse Gastronomique, 285
Leaf lettuce, 76
Lecithin, 17
Leeks, cleaning and trimming, 96
Legume salads, 82–83
Lemon cheese, 337
Lettuces, 76–77. *See also* Greens
Liederkranz cheese, 340
Limburger cheese, 340
Linens, in buffet service, 507
Lucanica sausages, 228
Lumpfish roe, 370, 371

M

Mâche, 77
Mango chutney, 468
Maple syrup, in cured foods, 183

Marinade, for foie gras, 289
Mascarpone cheese, 338
Mayonnaise
breaks, correcting, 21
collée, 24
emulsion process, 16–17
flavorings and garnishes, 21, 35
making, 18–21
as sandwich spread, 139
storage of, 21
Meatballs, as appetizer, 365
Meats. *See also* specific meats
appetizers, 365
curing salts, 181–182
dry-cure time for, 184
for forcemeats, 272
grinders, 230–231, 275
nitrite/nitrate levels in, 182
progressive grinding, 274, 275
rillettes, 191
sandwich fillings, 140
for sausages, 228
Menus
appetizers on, 364–365
buffet, 496–497, 498–499
Mesclun mix, 79
Mezzes, 362
Middle Ages, food guilds in, 3–4
Mie de pain, 548
Milk, in cheese making, 335, 336, 345
Mise en place, in buffet service, 503–509
Mizuna, 78
Mold, cheese, 345
Molds
for cheese making, 337
for ice carving, 518
for mousses, 368
for pâté en croûte, 282
for tartlets, 363, 364
for terrines, 279, 280
Monterey Jack cheese, 342
Moulard duck, 288
Mousse
foie gras, 289
in hors d'oeuvre, 263
preparing, 366–368
Mousseline forcemeat, 272, 275, 277–279
Mozzarella cheese, 336, 341, 345
Mussels, steamed, for raw bar, 501
Mustard, 468
Mustard greens, 798

N

National Shellfish Sanitation Program, 499
Networking, professional, 9
Nitrates and nitrites, in cured foods, 181–183
Nitrosamines, in cured foods, 182
Nuts
as forcemeat garnish, 274
as hors d'oeuvre, 362

O

Oils, infused, 468, 470–471
Olives, as hors d'oeuvre, 362
Onions
aromatic, in sausages, 230
red onion confit, 191
Open-faced sandwiches, 141
Oriental greens mix, 79
Osetra caviar, 369
Osmosis, in food preservation, 180–181
Overhauling, in dry cure, 184
Oysters, in raw bar, 500

P

Pacific oyster, 500
Palace Hotel, Gstaad, 199
Panadas, in forcemeats, 273
Pan-smoking, 190
Parmigiano-Reggiano cheese, 336, 342
Pasta
as appetizer, 365
salads, 82
Pasta filata cheeses, 341
Pasta machine, 364, 537
Pasteurized milk, 336
Pastry bag, 368
Pastry dough. *See* Pâté dough
Pastry shells, puff pastry, 365
Pâté
on appetizer plate, 365
en croûte, 282–283, 363, 537
compotes with, 468
de foie gras, 287–288, 289
as hors d'oeuvre, 362, 363
en terrine. *See* Terrines
Pâté dough
for barquettes and tartlets, 363–364
decorations, 283, 537
vents, 283
working with, 535
Pecorino Romano, 336, 342
Pellicle formation, in smoked foods, 188
Physical assets, management of, 10
Pickled foods, 184, 471

Pink cure, 182
Pit-roasting (smoke-roasting), 189
Platters. *See* Serving pieces
Point, Fernand, 289
Pork. *See also* Bacon; Ham
brining time for, 186
cold smoking, 189
dry-cure time for, 184
forcemeats, 272
sausages, 228
Potassium nitrate, 181
Potato salad, 82
Pot cheese, 338
Poultry
in galantines, 285, 286
mousseline, 272
Prague powder, 183, 229
Preplating, in buffet service, 508–509
Presentation
appetizers, 365–366
in buffet design, 5, 505, 508–515
caviar, 371
cheese, 343
hors d'oeuvre, 362–363
sandwiches, 141
terrines, 279
Preserved foods, 178–191
air-dried, 190
brining, 184, 185–186
curing, 180–185
in fat, 191
history of, 2, 178
smoking, 187–190
Pressed caviar, 369–370
Prévost, M., 285
Price range, for buffets, 497–498
Production order, buffet, 504
Progressive grinding, 274, 275
Proteins, denaturing, 181
Provolone cheese, 341
Puff pastry shells, 365
Purchasing, 10, 497
Purées
coulis, 22
mousses, 367
in oils and vinegars, infused, 470
in vinaigrette, 19

Q

Queso blanco, 338

R

Rabbit confit, 191
Radicchio, 79
Raw bar
accompaniments to, 502–503

equipment and tools, 503
food safety in, 499, 502
service in, 503
shellfish for, 500–502
Red King Crab, 502
Red onion confit, 191
Relish, 22, 468
Rennet, 337
Replenishment, in buffet
service, 515–517
Ricotta cheese, 338
Rillettes, 191
Rind-ripened cheeses, 340
Ripening cheeses, 337–338
Rocket (roquette), 78
Romaine lettuce, 77
Romano cheese, 336, 342
Roquefort cheese, 341
Roulades, 285–287

S

Salads, 74–84. *See also*
Dressings; Vinaigrette
as appetizer, 365
bean, 82–83
composed, 83, 84
fruit, 83
garnishes, for, 81
green, 76–81
history of, 74, 76
hors d'oeuvre, 363
pasta and grain, 82
potato, 82
vegetable, 82
warm, 84
Salmon caviar, 370
Salsas, 22
Salt
in cheese-making process,
336
curing. *See* Cured foods
in forcemeats, 273
Saltpeter, 181
Sandwiches, 136–141
breads for, 138–139
canapés, 364
fillings for, 140, 368
garnishes for, 140
history of, 136
spreads for, 139
styles of, 138, 141
Sauces, 16–25. *See also*
Mayonnaise;
Vinaigrette
coating, 23–25
coulis and purées, 22
dairy-based, 21
emulsion, 16–21
for raw bar, 502–503
salsas, 22
special, 25
Sausages, 226–239

on appetizer plate, 365
basic grind method,
231–232
casings, 235–237
curing mixture, 229
emulsion, 232–234
equipment and tools,
230–231, 238, 257
garnishes for, 234
history of, 226, 228
as hors d'oeuvre, 362
ingredients for, 228–230
loose/bulk, 235
nitrites/nitrates in, 182,
229
stuffing casings, 238–239
tying, 239
Seasonings. *See also* Herbs;
Spices
for appetizers, 365
for cured foods, 183
for forcemeats, 273
for oils and vinegars, 468,
470–471
for sausages, 229–230
Semisoft cheeses, 340
Service costs, 497
Serving pieces
food presentation, 505,
514
replenishment of, 515–517
setup, 507–508
Sevruga caviar, 369
Shape of food, in buffet presentation, 514
Sheep casings, for sausage, 236
Sheep's milk cheese, 335
Shellfish. *See also* Raw bar
on appetizer plate, 365
as hors d'oeuvre, 362
mousseline, 272
Shrimp, in raw bar, 501–502
Smoked foods
on appetizer plate, 365
cold smoking, 188–189
as hors d'oeuvre, 362, 363
hot smoking, 189
in mousses, 367
pan-smoking, 190
pellicle formation, 188
sausages, 229, 232
smoke-roasting, 189
types of, 188
wood for, 187–188
Smoke-roasting, 189
Smokers, 187, 189, 190
Smorgasbord, 362
Snow Crab, 502
Sodium ascorbate, in cured
meat, 183
Sodium erythorbate, in cured
meat, 183

Soft fresh cheeses, 338
Soft ripened cheeses, 338, 340
Soups, 25–26
Spices
in cured foods, 183
in forcemeats, 273
oils and vinegars, infused,
468, 470
in sausages, 229
Zaatar, 309
Spicy greens, 77–78
Spreads, sandwich, 139
Stations, buffet, 506
Steam tables, in buffet serv-
ice, 508
Steeping infusion method, 470
Stone Crab, 502
Storage
of caviar, 371
of cheese, 345
equipment and tools, 11
of foie gras, 289
of mayonnaise, 21
of oils and vinegars,
infused, 470
of shellfish, 503
Strabo, 2
Straight forcemeat, 272, 275,
276
Sturgeon, Lancelot, 468
Sugar, in cured foods, 183
Sumac, 110
Sushi, making, 423
Sweeteners, in cured foods,
183
Swiss chard, 78
Swiss cheese, 342

T

Table setup, for buffets,
506–507
Tapas, 362
Tarama caviar, 370
Tartlets, 363–364
Tat-soi, 78
Tea sandwiches, 141
Terrines
on appetizer plate, 365
aspic-bound, 281
of foie gras, 279, 289
forcemeat, 280–281
as hors d'oeuvre, 362
presentation of, 279
Texture, in buffet presenta-
tion, 512
Time management, 10–11
Tinted cure mix (TCM), 182
Tiramisù, 338
Tools. *See* Equipment and
tools
Treviso radicchio, 79
Trout, smoked, 188

Tschirky, Oscar, 118
Tuna confit, 191
Turkey, brined, 185–186

V

Veal mousseline, 272
Vegetables
on appetizer plates, 365
aromatics, in oils and
vinegars, 468, 470–471
aromatics, in sausages, 230
chips, 472
cold smoking, 189
crudités, 362
in green salad, 81
as hors d'oeuvre, 363
in mousses, 367
purées, in vinaigrette, 19
salsas, 22
sandwich fillings, 140
soups, 26
for vegetable salads, 82
Very hard cheeses (granas),
342
Vichyssoise, 26
Vinaigrettes
basic, 17–18
emulsified, 16–17, 18–19
with green salad, 81
infused oils and vinegars
in, 470
mustard in, 468
reduced-fat, 19
as sandwich spread, 139
Vinegars, infused, 468,
470–471

W

Waldorf-Astoria Hotel, 118
Warm infusion method, 470
Waste disposal, in buffet serv-
ice, 508
Water bath (bain-marie), 281
Watercress, 78
Waxed-rind cheeses, 340
Wet cure, 185
Whey, in cheese-making
process, 337
Whitefish roe, 370
Williams, Jesse, 334
Wine, with cheese service, 343
Wood, for smoking, 187–188
Workplace
orderly, 11
safety, 12

Y

Yanay, Izzy, 288

Z

Zaatar, 309
Zakuski table, 362